The Editor

FRANCIS ABIOLA IRELE, formerly Professor of French, University of Ibadan, Nigeria, was for several years Professor of African, French, and Comparative Literature at the Ohio State University. After retiring from Ohio State in 2003, he became Visiting Professor of African and African American Studies at Harvard University. Among his many publications are *The Cambridge History of African and Caribbean Literature* (edited with Simon Gikandi) and two collections of essays, *The African Experience in Literature and Ideology* and *The African Imagination: Literature in Africa and the Black Diaspora*. He is a contributing editor to *The Norton Anthology of World Literature* and General Editor of the Cambridge Studies in African and Caribbean Literature series.

A NORTON CRITICAL EDITION

Chinua Achebe
THINGS FALL APART

AUTHORITATIVE TEXT
CONTEXTS AND CRITICISM

Edited by

FRANCIS ABIOLA IRELE
HARVARD UNIVERSITY

W • W • NORTON & COMPANY • *New York* • *London*

W. W. Norton & Company has been independent since its founding in 1923, when William Warder Norton and Mary D. Herter Norton first published lectures delivered at the People's Institute, the adult education division of New York City's Cooper Union. The firm soon expanded its program beyond the Institute, publishing books by celebrated academics from America and abroad. By mid-century, the two major pillars of Norton's publishing program—trade books and college texts—were firmly established. In the 1950s, the Norton family transferred control of the company to its employees, and today—with a staff of four hundred and a comparable number of trade, college, and professional titles published each year—W. W. Norton & Company stands as the largest and oldest publishing house owned wholly by its employees.

Copyright © 2009 by W. W. Norton & Company, Inc.
THINGS FALL APART by Chinua Achebe. Copyright © 1958 by Chinua Achebe. First published by William Heinemann Ltd., 1958. Reprinted by permission of Harcourt Education Limited.

Book design by Antonina Krass.
Composition by Binghamton Valley Composition.
Manufacturing by the Courier Companies—Westford division.
Production manager: Eric Pier-Hocking.

Library of Congress Cataloging-in-Publication Data
Achebe, Chinua.
Things fall apart : authoritative text, contexts and criticism / Chinua Achebe ; edited by Francis Abiola Irele. — 1st ed.
p. cm. — (A Norton critical edition)
Includes bibliographical references.
ISBN 978-0-393-93219-5 (pbk.)
1. Achebe, Chinua. Things fall apart.   2. Igbo (African people)—Fiction.
3. Tribes—Nigeria—Fiction.   4. Missionaries—Nigeria—Fiction.
5. British—Nigeria—Fiction.   6. Nigeria—Race relations—Fiction.
I. Irele, Abiola.   II. Title.
PR9387.9.A3T5   2008b
823'.914—dc22   2008043051

W. W. Norton & Company, Inc., 500 Fifth Avenue, New York, N.Y. 10110
wwnorton.com

W. W. Norton & Company Ltd., Castle House, 75/76 Wells Street, London
W1T 3QT

3 4 5 6 7 8 9 0

Contents

Preface

As with all the Norton Critical Editions, this one includes a selection of background and critical material. The abundance of the secondary literature on Chinua Achebe has made the choice of texts for inclusion in this edition of *Things Fall Apart* especially difficult. Among African writers, Chinua Achebe's work has generated the greatest volume of commentary and criticism. Achebe has also produced a rich variety of essays that not only bear directly on his work but also illuminate his thinking on issues of fundamental concern to Africans and of relevance to the rest of the world. It is hoped that the selection here will be appropriate for the needs of students as well as others who may be said to belong to the category of "the common reader."

Like most Nigerians, I have more than a nodding acquaintance with Igbo, which happens to be the first language I spoke, though only to the age of four. I am grateful to Mrs. Nneka Agba and to Dr. Esiaba Irobi for their help in building upon the remnants of this linguistic foundation in the notes and for their guidance on aspects of Igbo custom and belief. I'm also very grateful to Dr. Chidi Achebe, the writer's son, who provided valuable information on his father's life and career.

Thanks are due to Indiana University Press for permission to reproduce a short passage from my homage entitled "Chinua Achebe at Seventy," published in *Research in African Literatures* 32.3 (2001).

Finally, I wish to express warm thanks to Carol Bemis and Rivka Genesen, both of Norton, for their forbearance while the edition was in preparation and for their professionalism while seeing the book through to publication.

F. Abiola Irele
Cambridge, Massachusetts
June 2008

Introduction

The chronicler is the history-teller.

—Walter Benjamin[1]

The publication in 1958 of Chinua Achebe's *Things Fall Apart* was a significant literary and cultural event in Africa, no more so than in Achebe's own country, Nigeria. At his *alma matter*, University College, Ibadan, the novel received an enthusiastic reception by the Nigerian intellectual elite, despite their reservations concerning certain aspects of Achebe's depiction of pre-colonial Igbo society. This handful of students and faculty at Ibadan represented an initial "interpretive community" for what was just beginning to emerge as a new literature in Nigeria and in Africa generally. Achebe's work could not have appeared at a more opportune moment.

The novel's appeal to the new Nigerian elite derived from the mood of nationalist self-assertion that prevailed in the country. As young, aspiring bearers of an emerging modern culture, the elite looked to a national literature that would reflect the changing shape of the African world. The thin stream of works that had been published by Nigerian writers such as Amos Tutuola and Cyprian Ekwensi—as well as by Guinean writer Camara Laye—were welcomed as pointers to new cultural and intellectual possibilities. Within this context, *Things Fall Apart* profoundly re-ordered the imaginative consciousness. It depicted an Africa that was delivering itself from the colonial yoke while drawing upon a new register of expression that the influence of European languages had made possible. Immediately upon its publication, *Things Fall Apart* was invested with an epochal meaning. Its appeal has since broadened in Africa and beyond, and the novel has lost none of that compelling force that derives not only from its engagement with the colonial encounter, but also from its reformulation of the inherited imperial language.

Achebe has often recounted how the reaction provoked by the negative representation of Africa in European literature led to his writing of *Things Fall Apart*. Although the novel's significance extends far

---

1. *Illuminations: Essays and Reflections.* Ed. and intro. Hannah Arendt (New York: Schocken Books, 1968), p. 95.

beyond its initial character as a response to the western literary image of Africa, it is here that any consideration of this novel must begin. To judge by his own essays and pronouncements, which stand as testimonies of the ideological and creative project that presided at the birth of the work, Achebe came to fiction with as a sense of his responsibility as a writer in the context of the colonial experience. This is the burden of one of his best-known essays, "The Novelist as Teacher" in which, taking the term "teacher" in its broad African meaning as one who not only imparts knowledge and provides enlightenment, but also shapes consciousness ("Mwalimu"), Achebe sets himself against a certain conception of the writers who are detached from the concerns of their society, when they are not openly antagonistic to it. He rejects the view that limits the role of literature to mere aesthetic contemplation, without an urgent connection to the communal life. His argument for the African writer's commitment hinges largely on the demoralizing impact of the colonial experience, an effect that imposes upon the writer an obligation to take on what he calls "the task of re-education and regeneration." He sums up this task in these terms:

> I would be quite satisfied if my novels (especially the ones I set in the past) did no more than teach my readers that their past— with all its imperfections—was not one long night of savagery from which the first Europeans acting on God's behalf delivered them.[2]

It is important, however, to note that the purpose Achebe ascribes here to his work was formulated as the outcome of a reconversion of consciousness by which he came to reject the negative view of his African, Igbo background that his upbringing in a Christian, Protestant environment had instilled in his young mind, and which his early education within the colonial system had reinforced. Achebe has described the narrow character of this early education, and the damage to his self-image it implied. As he puts it, "I did not see myself as an African to begin with."[3]

Given this testimony of an alienation produced by his colonial education, there is a sense in which Achebe's writing of *Things Fall Apart* was not merely an act of cultural affirmation, an effort to rehabilitate what he was later to call "the tarnished image of Africa," but was also a deeply personal affair, a process by which he came to recover a less conflicted relation to his indigenous cultural inheritance and thus to achieve a renovated perception of his self. He has singled out as a major factor in this process the effect of his reading the works of Eu-

---

2. *Hopes and Impediments* (New York: Anchor Books, 1989), p. 45.
3. "African Literature as Restoration or Celebration." In Anna Rutherford and Kirsten Holst-Peterson, eds., *Chinua Achebe: A Celebration* (Portsmouth, NH: Heinemann, 1991), p. 7

ropean authors Joyce Cary and especially Joseph Conrad, whom he has attacked in a celebrated essay, "An Image of Africa." This reading provoked Achebe to restate and revaluate, through his novels, the literary representation of the pre-colonial African world and of the indigenous modes of social organization and cultural expression.

While this theme of cultural reclamation provides an entry into Achebe's first novel, it is important to read *Things Fall Apart* not merely as testimony of the colonial encounter and as a repudiation of the discourse of empire, but as the complex work of fiction that it is, a work marked by its full panoply of credible characters—and a memorable one in the case of Okonkwo—and by its narrative poise, sustained by an assured deployment of a language appropriated, ironically enough, from the colonial master.

From a formal point of view, the most striking feature of *Things Fall Apart* is its triadic structure. The novel follows the conventional pattern of a drama in three acts, with the first part devoted to an extended development of the narrative material, organized around the figure of the principal character Okonkwo and the portrayal of his personality as a factor of his eventual fate, marked by all the vicissitudes attendant upon the progression of an individual existence. The second part serves as an interlude in the unfolding of this existence and its historic implications for Okonkwo's world, leading to the final catastrophe, the tragic *dénouement* that is enacted in the third part.

The ordering of the novel's narrative movement at the double level of individual and collective experience is apparent from the first part, devoted not only to the story of Okonkwo but also to the fictional elaboration of the lived context in which his fortunes evolve. The village of Umuofia, the sphere of his individual destiny, is firmly located in space and time: as a precise geography of communal being, and as a recognizable historical entity. Achebe's novel registers the temporal trajectory of the village's destiny, in which the distant memory of the pattern of settlement that led to its founding—encoded in a myth of origin that is evoked at the beginning of the novel and recalled in the rituals that punctuate collective life—expands into a narrative of its dislocation and of its uncertain future at its historic point of contact with an alien force.

In order to ground the narrative of Okonkwo's lowly beginnings and dogged ascension, Achebe presents a comprehensive picture of pre-colonial Igbo society in terms of structure, kinship system, economic life, governance, social and ethical values, and ultimately, world vision. The original state of this society is one of coherence and order, achieved as much through a remarkable adjustment to the natural world within which it is enclosed, as by the constraining force of a social compact by which the collective existence is regulated—a social compact sustained by religious feeling and re-enacted in ritual and yearly festivals, thus imparting to the communal life the quality of one long and uninterrupted ceremonial. The name Achebe gives to the village—"Umuofia," literally, "people of the forest"—attests to the rustic way of life associated with the pre-colonial and pre-modern estate. Here the forest denotes a sylvan realm, an ecological sphere of existence of a people fully integrated into the natural environment.[4] We need to bear in mind, however, that this image of Igbo society is not an idyllic one, that the forest environment, constantly foregrounded in the various references to its fauna and flora, is one that is, if not hostile to, at least resistant to domestication, a situation that determines the society's dominant scale of values and attitude to the world.

No element of Achebe's representation of Igbo society conveys this feature of its collective life and apprehension more than the pride of place accorded to yam, the principal crop of its agriculture and mainstay of the diet. More than an item in the society's material order of life, yam assumes a centrality in the culture such that it comes to be endowed with a symbolic value that projects and underwrites the dominant values of the society: "Yam, the king of crops, was a very exacting king. For three or four moons, it demanded hard work and constant attention from cock-crow till the chickens went back to roost" (21). Achebe presents an agrarian society, one that has patiently worked out a relation with the land from which it draws sustenance, a fact that is emphasized by the nature deities that inhabit its system of belief and the dominance in the collective imaginary of sacred spaces, in particular the caves and hills consecrated to the deity Agbala.

Against this background we come to appreciate the vitality of family life and of the entire structure of personal relationships, founded as they are upon a system of obligations and solidarities that are charged with moral significance, to which the elder, Nwakibie, gives expression:

> We pray for life, children, a good harvest and happiness. You will have what is good for you and I will have what is good for me. Let the kite perch and let the eagle perch too. If one says no to the other, let his wing break. (13)

---

4. At the time Achebe was writing his novel, Cyprian Ekwensi's *People of the City* had been published to great acclaim and success. Written in the racy style of American popular novels exemplified by Peter Cheney, Ekwensi's novel is set in the new urban milieu of Lagos. Achebe may have intended the name of the village to convey a sense of opposition in reference and language between the urban setting of Ekwensi's novel and the rural hinterland depicted in his own novel.

At the same time, despite its collective emphasis, this is a society that affords considerable scope for individuality. While it is not a perfectly egalitarian society, the hierarchy established within it is based on achievement, recognized by outward signs that indicate the differentiated role and status of its members. It is thus an image of an organic community, tightly knit by custom and well-attested rules and conventions, that Achebe presents in this first part of *Things Fall Apart*.

A remarkable feature of Achebe's novel is the procession of characters, even within the reduced compass of its village setting: the world of *Things Fall Apart* is one teeming with life. To create this environment, Achebe uses Igbo terms to designate the specific context and expressive culture of the people, and to individualize his array of characters. These names they bear do not merely reflect their provenance but also, through the meanings they inscribe and their specific cultural grounding, they contribute to what one might term the novel's density of reference.

It is within this highly particularized world that Okonkwo has his being. Achebe casts him in what is clearly a heroic mold, as befits his warrior status. The portrait we have of him is that of "a man of action," in deliberate contrast to the reflective character of his friend Obierika. Although the narrator speaks of a "fear deep within his heart," we are not offered an extended exploration of Okonkwo's inner disposition, for he belongs more to the world of legend than to that of the modern novel.[5] The few brush strokes by which he is portrayed are enough to establish his personality and his resolute pursuit of distinction, the consuming project of self-affirmation that results in the erosion of his emotional life. However, this one-dimensional view of Okonkwo may be too summary to account for Achebe's construction of his character, for we are offered several occasions to witness Okonkwo as also a man of feeling. The profound depression that overcomes him after he kills Ikemefuna provides evidence that he is not an altogether insensitive man. The affection Okonkwo has developed for Ikemefuna while he was a member of his household opens a crack in his severe exterior that is haunted, as it were, by the image of the boy after a ritual killing in which Okonkwo has had an unnatural part: "He tried not to think about Ikemefuna, but the more he tried the more he thought about him" (38).

More conventional is Okonkwo's closeness to his favorite wife Ekwefi, which conditions the warmth of his relationship with Ezinma, their daughter, demonstrated by his concern for the child during her bout with malaria and especially the episode in which she

---

5. We might note in this respect Walter Benjamin's observation on the economical style of the traditional storyteller, to whom Achebe can be compared: "There is nothing that commends a story to memory more effectively than that chaste compactness which precludes psychological analysis" ("The Storyteller," in *Illuminations* [1940; 1986], p. 91).

is abducted by Chielo. These references point to an affective disposition that accords with his role as the head of his family. Even the disaffection toward his father and his son Nwoye can be read as inversions of this fundamental sense of family attachment. But beyond the natural bond of kinship, Okonkwo's friendship with Obierika constitutes a major current of the novel's narrative and discursive path, offering evidence of Okonkwo's sociability on a broad front.

The extraordinary manner in which Okonkwo bestrides the world of Achebe's novel raises the question of his representative status. There is clearly a sense in which he functions as a paradigmatic figure, intended to stand as an embodiment of certain human traits and social and moral values essential to the life of his society. The cult of "manliness" that Okonkwo espouses reflects a collective passion for survival, bred in its members by their precarious situation in the world of nature. At the same time, Okonkwo's singular way of conforming to the ideals of his society constitutes a perversion that takes him to the limits of acceptable conduct, even by the norms of his society. In the tension between his intense concern for self-validation and the dynamics of collective life, Okonkwo emerges ultimately as a problematic hero,[6] whose existential posture threatens the interests and sense of coherence of his society. It is this conundrum that is at the heart of Achebe's conception of his hero, one that is only resolved by the tragic outcome of his life adventure. For what may be termed Okonkwo's predicament resides in the difficulty of reconciling the ethical imperatives of the collective compact with the natural aspiration for individual fulfillment.

Despite its comprehensiveness, Achebe's imaginative reconstruction of pre-colonial Igbo life is largely a formal requirement rather than an ethnographic demonstration. It serves the referential direction of the narrative, specifically the necessity Achebe felt to delineate the socio-economic and cultural framework that conditions Okonkwo's personality and his wrestling with fate. Achebe's recreation of this world thus conforms with the diegetic function of the modern novel. From this point of view, *Things Fall Apart* can be considered a regional novel, presenting within an established canon and literary tradition a mode of life that is unfamiliar to most readers in that tradition.[7]

6. The notion of the "problematic hero" as a factor of the modern novel was first expounded by Georg Lukacs in *The Theory of the Novel* (Cambridge: The MIT Press, 1971) and has been further developed by Lucien Goldmann in *Towards a Sociology of the Novel* (London: Tavistock, 1975).

7. It is in this sense that Achebe's work has been compared to that of Thomas Hardy, whose picture of a disappearing rural world in England implies a strong valorization of the "country" and its measured pace of life. This image is presumed by the title of Hardy's novel *Far from the Madding Crowd*, with its rural countryside dominated by sheep rearing and profoundly marked by the culture around it. See Raymond Williams, *The Country and The City* (New York: Oxford University Press, 1973).

The nature of Achebe's material, the implied distance of his novel from the central tradition of English fiction, compels what might be called an ethnographic approach, in which the documentary impulse often comes to the fore, even at the cost of authorial intervention. Such is the case with the passage in which Achebe points to the significance of the *egwugwus* as masked representatives of the ancestors:

> The land of the living was not far removed from the domain of the ancestors. There was coming and going between them, especially when an old man died, because an old man was very close to the ancestors. (73)

Other passages, notably the description of the new yam festival that opens Chapter Five, assume this documentary character.[8] However, the ethnographic material is more often integrated into the narrative, dramatized in visual and evocative terms. This is indeed the case with the procession of the *egwugwu* when they perform a judicial function that is legitimized by a sacred sanction. Even more dramatic is the episode of Ezinma and the search for her birth stone (*iyi-uwa*), an episode in which the belief in *ogbanje* and the responses it calls forth are left to emerge from the narrative, without the intrusion of authorial commentary.

The fact that the Igbo system of belief often seems contested and even ironized in *Things Fall Apart* poses a question that is fundamental to our reception of the novel, for it creates an ambiguous tone that underlines the novel's narrative development. The matter-of-fact style that Achebe often adopts suggests a neutral stance on the part of the novelist, that he seems intent merely to relate the facts as they are, as in the description of the recovery of Ezinma's *ogbanje* stone or the report of an *egwugwu* having been transfixed to the spot for two days by a more powerful rival. Even more striking is the way in which Achebe presents the death of the Christian convert Okoli as a just retribution for his killing of the sacred python. But it is not always that we are required to suspend our disbelief, for a note of irony often comes through the narrator's account, betraying an ambivalence that is made evident in the following passage, detailing what we are clearly meant to regard as absurd superstitions:

> The night was very quiet. It was always quiet except on moonlight nights. Darkness held a vague terror for these people, even the bravest among them. Children were warned not to whistle at night for fear of evil spirits. Dangerous animals became even more sinister and uncanny in the dark. A snake was never called

---

8. This kind of explicit background information, which belongs to a different order of writing, is exemplified by Achebe's essay on *chi* (see pp. 159–69 of the present volume), which explains an aspect of Igbo belief that has an immediate relevance to his novel.

by its name at night, because it would hear. It was called a string. (7)

Here, Achebe marks a distance from the indigenous culture that rarely surfaces with such clarity but that nonetheless colors his writing and threatens to undermine his ideological project. It is precisely on this account that he has been taken to task by the Nigerian scholar Ode Ogede when he writes: "Achebe accepts the modes of discourse dictated by the European novel of Africa rather than rejecting them." Ogede goes on to observe:

> Things Fall Apart can be located within the tradition of the European colonial novel. We need to scrutinize the view of European colonization depicted within its pages, instead of being over-awed by its linguistic power. . . . or by its ability to employ culture to showcase the fundamental worth of the African as a human being.[9]

Achebe has always been sensitive to criticism that elements of his portrayal of Igbo society are at odds with his project for the vindication of Africa, and he has responded in several interviews by clarifying his purpose in writing the novel. As he says, it was not his intention to offer a unilateral view of Igbo society and culture as one of perfection but to present an image that is authentic and credible, one that recognizes both its strengths and its weaknesses. Although this image is sometimes grim, highlighted by the ritual killing of Ikemefuna and the fate of twins abandoned in the Evil Forest, at the same time, Achebe's novel need not be construed as a nostalgic celebration of the past for a grasp of its significance. For an essential part of its purpose is its reappraisal of this past from the privileged standpoint that his western education affords him. This critical perspective is reflected in the self-questioning and the internal debates related to the culture that Achebe attributes to several characters in the novel.

There is thus no hint of self-hate in Achebe's depiction of his indigenous background, and his stance is not comparable to what, in his essay "An Image of Africa," he perceives as a pernicious racism that permeates Conrad's fiction of Africa in his novella *Heart of Darkness*.[1] For while Achebe is not blind to the anti-colonial theme of Conrad's novella, he is concerned with the way this theme is totally obscured by the racism that clouds Conrad's fictional treatment of European colonialism. In no way then does Achebe's portrayal of pre-

9. Ode Ogede, *Chinua Achebe and the Politics of Representation* (Trenton, NJ: Africa World Press, 2001), pp. 17, 18.
1. This essay has had a considerable impact on postcolonial studies. As John G. Peters remarks, "Achebe forever forced Conrad scholars to consider Conrad's stance on issues of race and imperialism." *The Cambridge Introduction to Joseph Conrad* (Cambridge: Cambridge University Press, 2006) 9. For selected responses to Achebe's essay, see pp. 182–208 of this volume.

colonial Igbo society diminish the force of his objections to Conrad. The point is that Achebe's novel engages a fully human society, and not the caricatures we encounter in the works that constitute the colonial canon and the European writers' deprecatory tone that is an inevitable part of their rendering of African life and experience. In contrast, *Things Fall Apart* displays, in its ample scope, a profound understanding of the modes of life and expression among the Igbo, and thus establishes a more complete perspective on African life than was available before its publication.

The atmosphere that prevails in Part Two of *Things Fall Apart* contrasts markedly with that of the first part. The change of scene from Umuofia to Okonkwo's maternal village of Mbanta ushers in a period of respite from the tension that has so far marked his existence; the years of exile thus constitute an interlude in his life adventure. The festive air, marked by scenes of feasting and sensuous delight, that surrounds his welcome by his maternal kin, led by his uncle Uchendu, the sense of intimacy these scenes communicate, conveyed by the civility and tenderness displayed by all the characters toward their host—all this contributes to the impression that Okonkwo is relaxing his strict perspective, even while he is seen to fret about what he considers his diminished circumstances.

This part of the novel is particularly interesting for the way it focuses on gender, an issue that has been running as an undercurrent to the narrative. For it is at Mbanta that the values associated with the feminine principle are finally given explicit formulation in the novel: values that Okonkwo's whole inclination and all his actions have emphatically repudiated. For instance, Uchendu's admonition of Okonkwo with the expression *Nneka* ("Mother is supreme") is expressed in grave tones that emphasize his purpose: to educate his nephew on a point of vital interest to the culture. For this expression is not merely an affectionate tribute but more profoundly a recognition of the fundamental role of women in the biological grounding of society, their essential status in the natural order. In the second part of *Things Fall Apart*, with its emphasis on the special bond that unites members of the female lineage (*umu-ada,*) this recognition finds expression in overtly social and affective terms.

Although certain feminist circles have objected to what they have interpreted as Achebe's masculine bias, which they read as promoting a "patriarchal" conception of social relations, it has to be stressed that what appears to be an insistence on masculinity in the novel is simply a reflection of the ideological practices that are inherent in pre-colonial Igbo society, in which, as we've seen, "manliness" functioned as a survival strategy. Women's relegation to a subordinate status thus appears to be an immediate consequence of its ruling ideology, a constant factor of social organization that is faithfully reported by the novelist. Achebe cannot be said therefore to endorse this feature of Igbo tradition that he undertakes to depict, one that conforms to the ethnographic data and is indeed a near universal phenomenon.

But it is even more important to attend to the tension in Achebe's novel between the masculine and the feminine inherent in a dichotomy rooted in nature. For the subjugation of women as a social practice is compensated for by the high valuation of the feminine principle in the symbolic sphere—the awe and respect accorded to Chielo, the priestess of Agbala, illustrates the institutional inversion of gender role and status she embodies at this level. The feminine theme is thus counterpoised to the masculine, of which Okonkwo is the incarnation. Achebe exploits the tension involved in managing the natural opposition of male and female in order to suggest a reversal of the hierarchical values, one in which the male principle is no longer privileged in the general economy of the collective life and consciousness. This reversal is fully enacted, as it were, in the second part of the novel, in a celebration of the feminine principle as generative of life and as a summation of its sustaining values. In other words, the feminine theme, so far secondary to the main thrust of the narrative, is rung here in an assertive reversal of the theme of masculinity that has been so dominant in the first part of the novel.

As against the joyous mood that, paradoxically, surrounds Okonkwo's life in exile, the news of the white man's arrival in Umuofia and the echo of the transformations that are beginning to occur there sound a dissonant note that is aggravated for Okonkwo by the report of his son's defection to the Christians. It is essential to the tragedy awaiting him that, as Okonkwo comes to the end of his sojourn at Mbanta and contemplates what he envisions as a triumphant return to Umuofia, he remains unprepared to absorb the historic import of these events. With the narration of these events and the catastrophe in which they culminate, *Things Fall Apart* begins to engage directly with the theme of the colonial encounter.

The focus in Part Three of the novel on the trauma to which the indigenous society and culture are subjected lends a polemical significance to the narrative and justifies the description of *Things Fall Apart* as a novel of colonial protest. Achebe's account of the brutal methods of colonial occupation, exemplified by the punitive expedition to Abame, and the perfidy of the colonial officer that leads to the arrest of Okonkwo and the elders of Umuofia and to their ordeal in prison—all these read like an indictment expressive of a deep resentment on the part of the colonized writer. It must be said, however, that the protest theme is articulated in a rather detached manner, in nothing like the harshly dissident tone of the francophone novelists such as Ferdinand Oyono in *Houseboy* or Ousmane Sembene in *God's*

Bits of Wood. The role Achebe assumes here is not so much that of the colonial rebel as that of a dispassionate chronicler of history in its objective manifestation.

Central to Achebe's preoccupation in the third part of the novel is the conflict of cultures provoked by the introduction of Christianity in Igboland. It is important to consider his treatment of this question in the light of the discourse that developed around the Christian evangelical effort, which was tied to the propagation of western education and the "civilizing mission" it was supposed to accomplish, an effort that in our own day would be described as a humanitarian enterprise.[2] The novel's powerful evocation of the vibrant quality of the pre-colonial culture represents a counterdiscourse that challenges this ideology. Achebe depicts the human and intellectual limitations of the Christian missionaries, especially Mr Smith, whose aggressive and uncompromising approach to his mission is at first presented in a satirical mode. But the satire is soon abandoned, as its ominous consequences become evident, a situation that the narrator sums up tersely: "There was a saying in Umuofia that as a man danced so the drums were beaten for him. Mr Smith danced a furious step, and so the drums went mad."

But while its anti-colonial intent is evident, the novel also registers the appeal of the Christian religion and its transformative impact on Igbo society. For the victims and unfortunate members of the clan, such as the *osu* and the mothers of twins, and for sensitive souls like Nwoye, it meant emancipation from the harsh impositions of the indigenous society and culture. More than this, we witness the historic progression the Christian religion sets in motion, leading to a far-reaching reversal of the traditional order, a reversal symbolized by the flourishing of the church in the Evil Forest, which is destined to supplant the village as the new boundary of collective life and focus of consciousness. Even more significantly, we are informed that the people are receptive to this development. The introduction of literacy and modern medicine as well as the growth of trade in commodities are welcomed as benefits, as signs of a western-derived modernity whose attractions are acknowledged.

The breathless pace of the narrative in this last part of the novel thus reflects the sense of momentous changes that are felt to be afoot. Stylistically, the quickening of tempo in Achebe's writing marks a change of register that corresponds to the historical turn of the narrative, in which the language reflects the movement from the poetry

---

2. Thus, in Samuel Ajayi Crowther's diary of the mission he led along the Lower Niger, the emphasis is on the delivery of the indigenous population from slavery and human sacrifice. Mary Slessor, an intrepid adventurer who worked in the latter part of the nineteenth century among the Efiks, neighbors to the Igbos in Eastern Nigeria, took it as her special vocation to rescue twins who were similarly abandoned by Efiks.

of the pre-colonial traditional life to the prose of a new and gathering history of colonial experience and its attendant process of westernization.

An ironic aspect of Achebe's novel is that the unhappy story of Ikemefuna is closely associated with the poetry of the traditional culture. The dominant mode of *Things Fall Apart* is realism: the novel creates the illusion that its content corresponds to the outer world of experience, which becomes essential for re-creating the milieu in which events occur and characters act out their destiny. As against this realist mode, however, the novel's expressive idiom derives from the oral tradition, grounding the aesthetic current by which the narrative development is sustained. The centrality of the folk tale tradition is apparent here, and in this connection the association with Ikemefuna assumes a particular intensity, eliciting some of Achebe's most accomplished writing:

> Nwoye always wondered who Nnadi was and why he should live all by himself, cooking and eating. In the end he decided that Nnadi must live in the land of Ikemefuna's favorite story where the ant holds court in splendor and the sands dance forever. (23)

Passages like this illustrate the constant interaction between Achebe's handling of the literate medium of the modern novel and his conscious transposition into English of the folktale tradition, informed as this is by the aesthetics of orality. As in the oral tradition, the proverbs, aphorisms, and songs interspersed throughout the novel serve not only to endow the language with a pronounced aesthetic function—as "the palm-oil with which words are eaten" (6)—but also as repositories of the ancestral wisdom derived from an enduring experience of the community: a pragmatism of which *eneke* the bird has come to represent the proverbial image. As in the tradition, the proverb emerges in the novel both as a genre in its own right and in its auxiliary role within the folk tale, within which it serves to point up and thus to extend the narrative's range of reference. Achebe's integration of these oral forms into his novel lends complexity to its mode of signification, for beyond what may appear as a picturesque pattern of allusions, they establish within the work an indigenous sensibility conductive to its reception as a written work. Thus, the oral tradition can be said to function in Achebe's novel in a dual capacity: as both an authentic representation of the culture that serves as the reference of the manifest content, and at the same time, as an integral component of the narrative mode, endowing the fictional discourse with a peculiar resonance.

Franco Moretti has called *Things Fall Apart* "a world text."[3] We can take this term to refer not only to its world-wide reception but also to its character as a work whose imaginative compass extends through a range of conceptual categories, including nature, myth, and history. In its specific reference to the African experience, *Things Fall Apart* has assumed a historical significance, for although it is not a historical novel in the usual sense of the term—that is, of a fictional re-enactment of real facts—it is a work that is governed by an acute sense of the determining power of events. This observation applies to all of Achebe's fiction, in which the African experience assumes its full human and narrative scope in the modern novel. In all his work, from *Things Fall Apart* and *Arrow of God* to *Anthills of the Savannah*, Achebe has sought not merely to explore the African experience as shaped by the colonial encounter, but also to re-create in imaginative terms the complex dimensions of the African world, and thus to restore to the continent its character as a theater of human endeavour and cultural accomplishment.

But his fiction represents as well a mode of reflection on the African becoming; indeed, it is in Achebe's work that the introspective function of the novel as a modern genre emerges most forcefully in its African circumstances. His work enacts a double movement of consciousness and sensibility which he describes in these terms: "A travelling away from an old self towards a cosmopolitan modern identity at the same time as a journeying back to regain a threatened past and selfhood."[4] This dual aspect of his work comes directly into view in his first novel, in which Achebe begins to elaborate a historical vision that encompasses both a revaluation of the African past and its critical appraisal. And it is the tension between these two perspectives of the novel—the celebratory and the reflective—that makes for the fullness of meaning in *Things Fall Apart,* and, ultimately, its moral weight.

3. *Modern Epic* (London: Verso, 1996), p. 237.
4. From "What Has Literature Got to Do with It?" in *Hopes and Impediments*, p. 110.

The Text of
THINGS FALL APART

Turning and turning in the widening gyre
The falcon cannot hear the falconer;
Things fall apart; the centre cannot hold;
Mere anarchy is loosed upon the world.

—W. B. Yeats: 'The Second Coming'

Part One

Chapter One

Okonkwo was well known throughout the nine villages[1] and even beyond. His fame rested on solid personal achievements. As a young man of eighteen he had brought honour to his village by throwing Amalinze the Cat.[2] Amalinze was the great wrestler who for seven years was unbeaten, from Umuofia to Mbaino.[3] He was called the Cat because his back would never touch the earth. It was this man that Okonkwo threw in a fight which the old men agreed was one of the fiercest since the founder of their town engaged a spirit of the wild for seven days and seven nights.[4]

The drums beat and the flutes sang and the spectators held their breath. Amalinze was a wily craftsman, but Okonkwo was as slippery as a fish in water. Every nerve and every muscle stood out on their arms, on their backs and their thighs, and one almost heard them stretching to breaking point. In the end Okonkwo threw the Cat.

That was many years ago, twenty years or more, and during this time Okonkwo's fame had grown like a bush-fire in the harmattan.[5] He was tall and huge, and his bushy eyebrows and wide nose gave him a very severe look. He breathed heavily, and it was said that,

---

1. In pre-colonial times, each Igbo village was an autonomous polity, often federated and bound in a sacred compact with other villages for mutual protection against common enemies, and especially in later times, slave raiders. *Okonkwo*: a day name: "born on Nkwo," one of the four market days in Igboland; the other days are Afo, Eke, and Oye. As in most African societies, the market is a major institution not only as a sphere of economic activity but also as a social and cultural space, and often, as a sacred area.
2. A praise name (possibly made up by Chinua Achebe), appropriate for a hero or warlord; the sobriquet indicates that the quality admired here is agility rather than brute strength.
3. "The fourth village"; Mbano in the central dialect and standard orthography. Mbaino is a local dialect, much more interior and perhaps more indigenous. *Umuofia*: "people of the forest" (see Introduction, p. xii). Umuofia is next to the village of Mbaino, and the tense relations between them provides the background to the story of Ikemefuna, a significant element of the narrative.
4. Seven is a symbolic number, evoked continuously throughout the novel. The full week is made up of seven days, including the major market days (*ukwu*) and the minor ones (*nta*). Note how, in this passage, Okonkwo is directly associated with the founding myth of his community.
5. The season marked by a cold, sharp wind that blows down from the Sahara over the west coast of Africa, mostly during the months of November and December, bringing with it a dry dust from the desert.

when he slept, his wives and children in their out-houses could hear him breathe. When he walked, his heels hardly touched the ground and he seemed to walk on springs, as if he was going to pounce on somebody. And he did pounce on people quite often. He had a slight stammer and whenever he was angry and could not get his words out quickly enough, he would use his fists. He had no patience with unsuccessful men. He had had no patience with his father.

Unoka,[6] for that was his father's name, had died ten years ago. In his day he was lazy and improvident and was quite incapable of thinking about tomorrow. If any money came his way, and it seldom did, he immediately bought gourds of palm-wine,[7] called round his neighbours and made merry. He always said that whenever he saw a dead man's mouth he saw the folly of not eating what one had in one's lifetime. Unoka was, of course, a debtor, and he owed every neighbour some money, from a few cowries[8] to quite substantial amounts.

He was tall but very thin and had a slight stoop. He wore a haggard and mournful look except when he was drinking or playing on his flute. He was very good on his flute, and his happiest moments were the two or three moons after the harvest when the village musicians brought down their instruments, hung above the fireplace. Unoka would play with them, his face beaming with blessedness and peace. Sometimes another village would ask Unoka's band and their dancing *egwugwu*[9] to come and stay with them and teach them their tunes. They would go to such hosts for as long as three or four markets,[1] making music and feasting. Unoka loved the good fare and the good fellowship, and he loved this season of the year, when the rains had stopped and the sun rose every morning with dazzling beauty. And it was not too hot either, because the cold and dry harmattan wind was blowing down from the north. Some years the harmattan was very severe and a dense haze hung on the atmosphere. Old men and children would then sit round log fires, warming their bodies. Unoka loved it all, and he loved the first kites that returned with the dry season, and the children who sang songs of welcome to them. He would remember his own childhood, how he had often wandered around looking for a kite[2] sailing leisurely against the blue sky. As soon as he found one he would sing with his whole being, welcoming it

6. The name derives from a proverbial saying: "One's home is the ultimate refuge."
7. The sap of the oil palm tree, which grows straight and tall; when drawn and left to ferment, it produces a strong alcoholic drink.
8. Small oblong shells used as units of money in pre-colonial times. Great quantities were required for even minor transactions, so that they had to be carried in bags, as here.
9. Masked men, here, members of a dancing group; on solemn civil and religious occasions, they form masquerades representing ancestral spirits (see p. xv). It is a profanation to catch sight of the faces behind the masks (see p. 105).
1. Since markets were held every four days, the period here is twelve days.
2. A hawk; also, a migratory bird.

back from its long, long journey, and asking it if it had brought home any lengths of cloth.

That was years ago, when he was young. Unoka, the grown-up, was a failure. He was poor and his wife and children had barely enough to eat. People laughed at him because he was a loafer, and they swore never to lend him any more money because he never paid back. But Unoka was such a man that he always succeeded in borrowing more, and piling up his debts.

One day a neighbour called Okoye[3] came in to see him. He was reclining on a mud bed in his hut playing on the flute. He immediately rose and shook hands with Okoye, who then unrolled the goatskin[4] which he carried under his arm, and sat down. Unoka went into an inner room and soon returned with a small wooden disc containing a kola nut, some alligator pepper and a lump of white chalk.[5]

"I have kola," he announced when he sat down, and passed the disc over to his guest.

"Thank you. He who brings kola brings life. But I think you ought to break it," replied Okoye passing back the disc.

"No, it is for you, I think," and they argued like this for a few moments before Unoka accepted the honour of breaking the kola. Okoye, meanwhile, took the lump of chalk, drew some lines on the floor, and then painted his big toe.[6]

As he broke the kola, Unoka prayed to their ancestors for life and health, and for protection against their enemies. When they had eaten they talked about many things: about the heavy rains which were drowning the yams,[7] about the next ancestral feast and about the impending war with the village of Mbaino. Unoka was never happy when it came to wars. He was in fact a coward and could not bear the sight of blood. And so he changed the subject and talked about music, and his face beamed. He could hear in his mind's ear the blood-stirring and intricate rhythms of the *ekwe* and the *udu* and the *ogene*,[8] and he could hear his own flute weaving in and out of

---

3. Born on Oye market day.
4. From which many household objects were made, as with the mat here.
5. Or *nzu*, offered to assure Okoye that he is welcome in his home; *kola nut*: a bitter fruit consisting of three, sometimes four lobes, which can be neatly pried open; in the latter case, this is a sign of good luck. Due to its high caffeine content, the kola nut produces a bracing effect when chewed. Apart from being offered as a sign of hospitality, it also features regularly in ritual ceremonies; *alligator pepper*: small black grains nestled in a brown pod; although very hot, they are always chewed raw.
6. As a sign that he holds the *ozo* title, the highest in the land.
7. The African yams—not to be confused with sweet potatoes—are tubers that often grow to a large size; a staple of the Igbo diet, they require sustained effort to cultivate; the various phases of their growth mark the progression of the year among the Igbo, hence their centrality to the culture.
8. Or polyrhythm, a characteristic feature of African drum music. Unoka plays the flute in a small orchestra: *ekwe* is a wooden drum; *udu* a pot which resonates when the mouth is beaten with the open palm; *ogene* a bell-shaped gong with a high metallic sound.

them, decorating them with a colourful and plaintive tune. The total effect was gay and brisk, but if one picked out the flute as it went up and down and then broke up into short snatches, one saw that there was sorrow and grief there.

Okoye was also a musician. He played on the *ogene*. But he was not a failure like Unoka. He had a large barn full of yams and he had three wives. And now he was going to take the Idemili[9] title, the third highest in the land. It was a very expensive ceremony and he was gathering all his resources together. That was in fact the reason why he had come to see Unoka. He cleared his throat and began:

"Thank you for the kola. You may have heard of the title I intend to take shortly."

Having spoken plainly so far, Okoye said the next half a dozen sentences in proverbs. Among the Ibo the art of conversation is regarded very highly, and proverbs are the palm-oil[1] with which words are eaten. Okoye was a great talker and he spoke for a long time, skirting round the subject and then hitting it finally. In short, he was asking Unoka to return the two hundred cowries he had borrowed from him more than two years before. As soon as Unoka understood what his friend was driving at, he burst out laughing. He laughed loud and long and his voice rang out clear as the *ogene*, and tears stood in his eyes. His visitor was amazed, and sat speechless. At the end, Unoka was able to give an answer between fresh outbursts of mirth.

"Look at that wall," he said, pointing at the far wall of his hut, which was rubbed with red earth so that it shone. "Look at those lines of chalk;" and Okoye saw groups of short perpendicular lines drawn in chalk. There were five groups, and the smallest group had ten lines. Unoka had a sense of the dramatic and so he allowed a pause, in which he took a pinch of snuff and sneezed noisily, and then he continued: "Each group there represents a debt to someone, and each stroke is one hundred cowries. You see, I owe that man a thousand cowries. But he has not come to wake me up in the morning for it. I shall pay you, but not today. Our elders say that the sun will shine on those who stand before it shines on those who kneel under them. I shall pay my big debts first." And he took another pinch of snuff, as if that was paying the big debts first. Okoye rolled his goatskin and departed.

When Unoka died he had taken no title at all and he was heavily in debt. Any wonder then that his son Okonkwo was ashamed of

---

9. The deity (*ide*) of rivers and streams, sometimes thought of as a wall of water holding up the sky; the deity's sacred emblem is the python, which is thus revered.
1. Bright red oil pressed from the fleshy palm nuts which are usually bunched around the leaves, at the very top of the oil palm tree. Palm oil is used principally for cooking and other domestic purposes. The nuts also contain hard kernels which are cracked and pressed to produce a valuable vegetable oil. *Ibo*: the term *Igbo* is now more commonly used.

him? Fortunately, among these people a man was judged according to his worth and not according to the worth of his father. Okonkwo was clearly cut out for great things. He was still young but he had won fame as the greatest wrestler in the nine villages. He was a wealthy farmer and had two barns full of yams, and had just married his third wife. To crown it all he had taken two titles and had shown incredible prowess in two inter-tribal wars. And so although Okonkwo was still young, he was already one of the greatest men of his time. Age was respected among his people, but achievement was revered. As the elders said, if a child washed his hands he could eat with kings. Okonkwo had clearly washed his hands and so he ate with kings and elders. And that was how he came to look after the doomed lad who was sacrificed to the village of Umuofia by their neighbours to avoid war and bloodshed. The ill-fated lad was called Ikemefuna.[2]

Chapter Two

Okonkwo had just blown out the palm-oil lamp and stretched himself on his bamboo bed when he heard the *ogene* of the town-crier piercing the still night air. *Gome, gome, gome, gome,* boomed the hollow metal. Then the crier gave his message, and at the end of it beat his instrument again. And this was the message. Every man of Umuofia was asked to gather at the market-place tomorrow morning. Okonkwo wondered what was amiss, for he knew certainly that something was amiss. He had discerned a clear overtone of tragedy in the crier's voice, and even now he could still hear it as it grew dimmer and dimmer in the distance.

The night was very quiet. It was always quiet except on moonlight nights. Darkness held a vague terror for these people, even the bravest among them. Children were warned not to whistle at night for fear of evil spirits. Dangerous animals became even more sinister and uncanny in the dark. A snake was never called by its name at night, because it would hear. It was called a string. And so on this particular night as the crier's voice was gradually swallowed up in the distance, silence returned to the world, a vibrant silence made more intense by the universal trill of a million million forest insects.

On a moonlight night it would be different. The happy voices of children playing in open fields would then be heard. And perhaps those not so young would be playing in pairs in less open places,[2] and

2. "My strength (*ike*) will abide." A name given to an only son, who is therefore especially cherished; his being given up as hostage is thus a great sacrifice on the part of his family.
1. Makes the round of the village and cries out all public announcements; he strikes a bell or *ogene* to signal his approach or presence.
2. Suggesting furtive love play, leading to sexual encounters.

old men and women would remember their youth. As the Ibo say: "When the moon is shining the cripple becomes hungry for a walk."

But this particular night was dark and silent. And in all the nine villages of Umuofia a town-crier with his *ogene* asked every man to be present tomorrow morning. Okonkwo on his bamboo bed tried to figure out the nature of the emergency—war with a neighbouring clan? That seemed the most likely reason, and he was not afraid of war. He was a man of action, a man of war. Unlike his father he could stand the look of blood. In Umuofia's latest war he was the first to bring home a human head. That was his fifth head; and he was not an old man yet. On great occasions such as the funeral of a village celebrity he drank his palm-wine from his first human head.

In the morning the market-place was full. There must have been about ten thousand men there, all talking in low voices. At last Ogbuefi Ezeugo stood up in the midst of them and bellowed four times, "Umuofia kwenu,"[3] and on each occasion he faced a different direction and seemed to push the air with a clenched fist. And ten thousand men answered *"Yaa!"* each time. Then there was perfect silence. Ogbuefi Ezeugo was a powerful orator and was always chosen to speak on such occasions. He moved his hand over his white head and stroked his white beard. He then adjusted his cloth, which was passed under his right arm-pit and tied above his left shoulder.

"Umuofia kwenu," he bellowed a fifth time, and the crowd yelled in answer. And then suddenly like one possessed he shot out his left hand and pointed in the direction of Mbaino, and said through gleaming white teeth firmly clenched: "Those sons of wild animals have dared to murder a daughter of Umuofia." He threw his head down and gnashed his teeth, and allowed a murmur of suppressed anger to sweep the crowd. When he began again, the anger on his face was gone and in its place a sort of smile hovered, more terrible and more sinister than the anger. And in a clear unemotional voice he told Umuofia how their daughter had gone to market at Mbaino and had been killed. That woman, said Ezeugo, was the wife of Ogbuefi Udo,[4] and he pointed to a man who sat near him with a bowed head. The crowd then shouted with anger and thirst for blood.

---

3. Formulaic greeting that is both a call ("Umuofia, listen") and an appeal to the collective spirit of the clan. *Ogbuefi Ezeugo: Ogbuefi* means "one who has killed a cow" and is a term of address to a man who has attained the rank of *ozo*, the highest title in the land, and who must sacrifice a cow at his induction ceremony. *Eze* is usually a priestly title; because of its earlier designation of kingship, before the Igbos abandoned the monarchical system, it can also function as a mark of recognition, as here, where Ezeugo's name identifies him as one entitled to wear an eagle feather in his cap.
4. Ironically, the name means "Peace."

Many others spoke, and at the end it was decided to follow the normal course of action. An ultimatum was immediately dispatched to Mbaino asking them to choose between war on the one hand, and on the other the offer of a young man and a virgin as compensation.

Umuofia was feared by all its neighbours. It was powerful in war and in magic, and its priests and medicine-men were feared in all the surrounding country. Its most potent war-medicine was as old as the clan itself. Nobody knew how old. But on one point there was general agreement—the active principle in that medicine had been an old woman with one leg. In fact, the medicine itself was called *agadi-nwayi,* or old woman.[5] It had its shrine in the centre of Umuofia, in a cleared spot. And if anybody was so foolhardy as to pass by the shrine after dusk he was sure to see the old woman hopping about.

And so the neighbouring clans who naturally knew of these things feared Umuofia, and would not go to war against it without first trying a peaceful settlement. And in fairness to Umuofia it should be recorded that it never went to war unless its case was clear and just and was accepted as such by its Oracle—the Oracle of the Hills and the Caves.[6] And there were indeed occasions when the Oracle had forbidden Umuofia to wage a war. If the clan had disobeyed the Oracle they would surely have been beaten, because their dreaded *agadi-nwayi* would never fight what the Ibo call *a fight of blame*.

But the war that now threatened was a just war. Even the enemy clan knew that. And so when Okonkwo of Umuofia arrived at Mbaino as the proud and imperious emissary of war, he was treated with great honour and respect, and two days later he returned home with a lad of fifteen and a young virgin. The lad's name was Ikemefuna, whose sad story is still told in Umuofia unto this day.

The elders, or *ndichie,*[7] met to hear a report of Okonkwo's mission. At the end they decided, as everybody knew they would, that the girl should go to Ogbuefi Udo to replace his murdered wife. As for the boy, he belonged to the clan as a whole, and there was no hurry to decide his fate. Okonkwo was, therefore, asked on behalf of the clan to look after him in the interim. And so for three years Ikemefuna lived in Okonkwo's household.

Okonkwo ruled his household with a heavy hand. His wives, especially the youngest, lived in perpetual fear of his fiery temper, and so

---

5. The popular belief conveys a hint that the old woman may have been sacrificed in order to ensure the charm's potency.
6. The dwelling sites of the deity Agbala. It is to his shrine—one of these hills or caves—that Chielo takes Okonkwo's daughter (see pp. 60–65).
7. Council of the old and titled men; the word originally denoted the ancestors and came to be applied to men whose advanced age brought them close the ancestors, to whom libation is poured at all formal occasions.

did his little children. Perhaps down in his heart Okonkwo was not a cruel man. But his whole life was dominated by fear, the fear of failure and of weakness. It was deeper and more intimate than the fear of evil and capricious gods and of magic, the fear of the forest, and of the forces of nature, malevolent, red in tooth and claw.[8] Okonkwo's fear was greater than these. It was not external but lay deep within himself. It was the fear of himself, lest he should be found to resemble his father. Even as a little boy he had resented his father's failure and weakness, and even now he still remembered how he had suffered when a playmate had told him that his father was *agbala*. That was how Okonkwo first came to know that *agbala* was not only another name for a woman, it could also mean a man who had taken no title. And so Okonkwo was ruled by one passion—to hate everything that his father Unoka had loved. One of those things was gentleness and another was idleness.

During the planting season Okonkwo worked daily on his farms from cock-crow until the chickens went to roost. He was a very strong man and rarely felt fatigue. But his wives and young children were not as strong, and so they suffered. But they dared not complain openly. Okonkwo's first son, Nwoye,[9] was then twelve years old but was already causing his father great anxiety for his incipient laziness. At any rate, that was how it looked to his father, and he sought to correct him by constant nagging and beating. And so Nwoye was developing into a sad-faced youth.

Okonkwo's prosperity was visible in his household. He had a large compound enclosed by a thick wall of red earth. His own hut, or *obi*,[1] stood immediately behind the only gate in the red walls. Each of his three wives had her own hut, which together formed a half moon behind the *obi*. The barn was built against one end of the red walls, and long stacks of yam stood out prosperously in it. At the opposite end of the compound was a shed for the goats, and each wife built a small attachment to her hut for the hens. Near the barn was a small house, the 'medicine house' or shrine where Okonkwo kept the wooden symbols of his personal god and of his ancestral spirits. He worshipped them with sacrifices of kola nut, food and palm-wine, and offered prayers to them on behalf of himself, his three wives and eight children.

---

8. An echo of the English philosopher, Thomas Hobbes, whose *Leviathan* represents the state of nature as one of constant strife and danger, as demonstrated by the life of wild animals. The immediate reference is to Alfred Lord Tennyson's *In Memoriam*.
9. Born on Oye market day.
1. The structure of the Igbo village is thus determined by the men's huts, each serving as a "hub" of a family unit and linked to other units, in a pattern that extends to the rest of the village (see Victor Uchendu, 1965).

So when the daughter of Umuofia was killed in Mbaino, Ikemefuna came into Okonkwo's household. When Okonkwo brought him home that day he called his most senior wife and handed him over to her.

"He belongs to the clan," he told her. "So look after him."

"Is he staying long with us?" she asked.

"Do what you are told, woman," Okonkwo thundered, and stammered. "When did you become one of the *ndichie* of Umuofia?"

And so Nwoye's mother took Ikemefuna to her hut and asked no more questions.

As for the boy himself, he was terribly afraid. He could not understand what was happening to him or what he had done. How could he know that his father had taken a hand in killing a daughter of Umuofia? All he knew was that a few men had arrived at their house, conversing with his father in low tones, and at the end he had been taken out and handed over to a stranger. His mother had wept bitterly, but he had been too surprised to weep. And so the stranger had brought him, and a girl, a long, long way from home, through lonely forest paths. He did not know who the girl was, and he never saw her again.

Chapter Three

Okonkwo did not have the start in life which many young men usually had. He did not inherit a barn from his father. There was no barn to inherit. The story was told in Umuofia of how his father, Unoka, had gone to consult the Oracle of the Hills and the Caves to find out why he always had a miserable harvest.

The Oracle was called Agbala,[1] and people came from far and near to consult it. They came when misfortune dogged their steps or when they had a dispute with their neighbours. They came to discover what the future held for them or to consult the spirits of their departed fathers.

The way into the shrine was a round hole at the side of a hill, just a little bigger than the round opening into a hen-house. Worshippers and those who came to seek knowledge from the god crawled on their belly through the hole and found themselves in a dark, endless space in the presence of Agbala. No one had ever beheld Agbala, except his priestess. But no one who had ever crawled into his awful shrine had come out without the fear of his power. His priestess stood by the sacred fire which she built in the heart of the cave and proclaimed the will of the god. The fire did not burn with a flame. The glowing logs only served to light up vaguely the dark figure of the priestess.

Sometimes a man came to consult the spirit of his dead father or

---

1. Here, the deity, not to be confused with *agbala*, "old woman" (*agbala nwayi*).

relative. It was said that when such a spirit appeared, the man saw it vaguely in the darkness, but never heard its voice. Some people even said that they had heard the spirits flying and flapping their wings against the roof of the cave.

Many years ago when Okonkwo was still a boy his father, Unoka, had gone to consult Agbala. The priestess in those days was a woman called Chika.[2] She was full of the power of her god, and she was greatly feared. Unoka stood before her and began his story.

"Every year," he said sadly, "before I put any crop in the earth, I sacrifice a cock to Ani,[3] the owner of all land. It is the law of our fathers. I also kill a cock at the shrine of Ifejioku, the god of yams. I clear the bush and set fire to it when it is dry. I sow the yams when the first rain has fallen, and stake them when the young tendrils appear. I weed—"

"Hold your peace!" screamed the priestess, her voice terrible as it echoed through the dark void. "You have offended neither the gods nor your fathers. And when a man is at peace with his gods and his ancestors, his harvest will be good or bad according to the strength of his arm. You, Unoka, are known in all the clan for the weakness of your matchet and your hoe. When your neighbours go out with their axe to cut down virgin forests, you sow your yams on exhausted farms that take no labour to clear. They cross seven rivers to make their farms; you stay at home and offer sacrifices to a reluctant soil. Go home and work like a man."

Unoka was an ill-fated man. He had a bad *chi*[4] or personal god, and evil fortune followed him to the grave, or rather to his death, for he had no grave. He died of the swelling which was an abomination to the earth goddess. When a man was afflicted with swelling in the stomach and the limbs he was not allowed to die in the house. He was carried to the Evil Forest[5] and left there to die. There was the story of a very stubborn man who staggered back to his house and had to be carried again to the forest and tied to a tree. The sickness was an abomination to the earth, and so the victim could not be buried in her bowels. He died and rotted away above the earth, and was not given the first or the second burial.[6] Such was Unoka's fate. When they carried him away, he took with him his flute.

---

2. "God is supreme." The name stresses the all-powerful nature of the deity whose will the priestess interprets. Chika is the predecessor of Chielo or Chinelo ("God is mindful of us"), whose role as priestess of Agbala is developed in one the most significant episodes later in the novel (see below, pp. 60–65).
3. A dialectal variant of Ala, the earth goddess, supreme expression of the female principle. Ezeani is a common Igbo surname.
4. A fundamental concept of Igbo belief, denoting a personal spirit involved with the fate of every individual. For further elucidation, see Achebe's essay in this volume, pp. 159–69.
5. *Ajo Ofia* in Ananbra, *Ohia* in other dialects of Igbo. The "Evil Forest" is a geographical feature of the traditional Igbo village; it marked the realm of the wild, inhabited by malevolent spirits, separate from and opposed to the space of human habitation and communal life.
6. Usually performed on the anniversary of the person's death, the second burial is often as elaborate as the first burial.

With a father like Unoka, Okonkwo did not have the start in life which many young men had. He neither inherited a barn nor a title, nor even a young wife. But in spite of these disadvantages, he had begun even in his father's lifetime to lay the foundations of a prosperous future. It was slow and painful. But he threw himself into it like one possessed. And indeed he was possessed by the fear of his father's contemptible life and shameful death.

There was a wealthy man in Okonkwo's village who had three huge barns, nine wives and thirty children. His name was Nwakibie[7] and he had taken the highest but one title which a man could take in the clan. It was for this man that Okonkwo worked to earn his first seed yams.[8]

He took a pot of palm-wine and a cock to Nwakibie. Two elderly neighbours were sent for, and Nwakibie's two grown-up sons were also present in his *obi*. He presented a kola nut and an alligator pepper, which was passed round for all to see and then returned to him. He broke it, saying: "We shall all live. We pray for life, children, a good harvest and happiness. You will have what is good for you and I will have what is good for me. Let the kite perch and let the egret perch too. If one says no to the other, let his wing break."

After the kola nut had been eaten Okonkwo brought his palm-wine from the corner of the hut where it had been placed and stood it in the centre of the group. He addressed Nwakibie, calling him 'Our father'.

"*Nna ayi*,"[9] he said. "I have brought you this little kola. As our people say, a man who pays respect to the great paves the way for his own greatness. I have come to pay you my respects and also to ask a favour. But let us drink the wine first."

Everybody thanked Okonkwo and the neighbours brought out their drinking horns[1] from the goatskin bags they carried. Nwakibie brought down his own horn, which was fastened to the rafters.[2] The younger of his sons, who was also the youngest man in the group, moved to the centre, raised the pot on his left knee and began to pour out the wine. The first cup went to Okonkwo, who must taste his wine before anyone else.[3] Then the group drank, beginning with the eldest man. When everyone had drunk two or three horns, Nwakibie sent for his wives. Some of them were not at home and only four came in.

7. A title name, contracted form of "Nwaka-ibe-ya," literally, "greater than the other person."
8. the head of the mature yam tuber, from which, when replanted, new yams sprouted and grew.
9. Literally, "our father," a term of reverence used to address a male elder.
1. Cowhorns cleaned out and treated so they can be used as drinking vessels.
2. Wooden ledges built high up the wall and used to store personal belongings.
3. Any food or drink offered must first be tasted by the host as assurance that it is not poisoned.

"Is Anasi[4] not in?" he asked them. They said she was coming. Anasi was the first wife and the others could not drink before her, and so they stood waiting.

Anasi was a middle-aged woman, tall and strongly built. There was authority in her bearing and she looked every inch the ruler of the womenfolk in a large and prosperous family. She wore the anklet[5] of her husband's titles, which the first wife alone could wear.

She walked up to her husband and accepted the horn from him. She then went down on one knee, drank a little and handed back the horn. She rose, called him by his name and went back to her hut. The other wives drank in the same way, in their proper order, and went away.

The men then continued their drinking and talking. Ogbuefi Idigo was talking about the palm-wine tapper, Obiako,[6] who suddenly gave up his trade.

"There must be something behind it," he said, wiping the foam of wine from his moustache with the back of his left hand. "There must be a reason for it. A toad does not run in the daytime for nothing."

"Some people say the Oracle warned him that he would fall off a palm tree and kill himself," said Akukalia.[7]

"Obiako has always been a strange one," said Nwakibie. "I have heard that many years ago, when his father had not been dead very long, he had gone to consult the Oracle. The Oracle said to him, 'Your dead father wants you to sacrifice a goat to him.' Do you know what he told the Oracle? He said, 'Ask my dead father if he ever had a fowl when he was alive.'" Everybody laughed heartily except Okonkwo, who laughed uneasily because, as the saying goes, an old woman is always uneasy when dry bones are mentioned in a proverb. Okonkwo remembered his own father.

At last the young man who was pouring out the wine held up half a horn of the thick, white dregs and said, "What we are eating is finished." "We have seen it," the others replied. "Who will drink the dregs?" he asked. "Whoever has a job in hand," said Idigo, looking at Nwakibie's elder son Igwelo[8] with a malicious twinkle in his eye.

Everybody agreed that Igwelo should drink the dregs. He accepted the half-full horn from his brother and drank it. As Idigo had said, Igwelo had a job in hand because he had married his first wife a

---

4. "Let them say." An uncommon name, probably made up by Achebe.
5. Bright beads worn around the ankle as mark of the woman's high status deriving from her husband's position as a titled man.
6. "My compound/household will never perish"; *palm-wine tapper*: one who climbs up to the very top of the palm tree with the help of a rope, in order to collect the sap; the operation requires great skill and is very dangerous—palm wine tappers often fell to their deaths, as in Amos Tutuola's novel, *The Palm-Wine Drinkard.*
7. "One who is richly endowed"; here, in wealth reckoned in livestock and yam barns.
8. "God in the sky (*igwe*) is mindful of us"; a variant of the name Chielo.

month or two before. The thick dregs of palm-wine were supposed to be good for men who were going in to their wives.

After the wine had been drunk Okonkwo laid his difficulties before Nwakibie.

"I have come to you for help," he said. "Perhaps you can already guess what it is. I have cleared a farm but have no yams to sow. I know what it is to ask a man to trust another with his yams, especially these days when young men are afraid of hard work. I am not afraid of work. The lizard that jumped from the high iroko tree[9] to the ground said he would praise himself if no one else did. I began to fend for myself at an age when most people still suck at their mothers' breasts. If you give me some yam seeds I shall not fail you."

Nwakibie cleared his throat. "It pleases me to see a young man like you these days when our youth have gone so soft. Many young men have come to me to ask for yams but I have refused because I knew they would just dump them in the earth and leave them to be choked by weeds. When I say no to them they think I am hard-hearted. But it is not so. Eneke the bird says that since men have learnt to shoot without missing, he has learnt to fly without perching. I have learnt to be stingy with my yams. But I can trust you. I know it as I look at you. As our fathers said, you can tell a ripe corn by its look. I shall give you twice four hundred yams. Go ahead and prepare your farm."

Okonkwo thanked him again and again and went home feeling happy. He knew that Nwakibie would not refuse him, but he had not expected he would be so generous. He had not hoped to get more than four hundred seeds. He would now have to make a bigger farm. He hoped to get another four hundred yams from one of his father's friends at Isiuzo.[1]

Share-cropping was a very slow way of building up a barn of one's own. After all the toil one only got a third of the harvest. But for a young man whose father had no yams, there was no other way. And what made it worse in Okonkwo's case was that he had to support his mother and two sisters from his meagre harvest. And supporting his mother also meant supporting his father. She could not be expected to cook and eat while her husband starved. And so at a very early age when he was striving desperately to build a barn through share-cropping Okonkwo was also fending for his father's house. It was like pouring grains of corn into a bag full of holes. His mother and sisters worked hard enough, but they grew women's crops, like

9. A hard-wood tree that grows large and tall, towering over the vegetation in the forest; it is also long-lived, and thus often compared to the oak; *lizard that jumped*: lizards landing from a great height can often be observed shaking their heads several times, as if in self congratulation.
1. "Top (end) of the road." The term can also be used of a doorway.

coco-yams, beans and cassava.[2] Yam, the king of crops, was a man's crop.

The year that Okonkwo took eight hundred seed-yams from Nwak-ibie was the worst year in living memory. Nothing happened at its proper time; it was either too early or too late. It seemed as if the world had gone mad. The first rains were late, and, when they came, lasted only a brief moment. The blazing sun returned, more fierce than it had ever been known, and scorched all the green that had appeared with the rains. The earth burned like hot coals and roasted all the yams that had been sown. Like all good farmers, Okonkwo had begun to sow with the first rains. He had sown four hundred seeds when the rains dried up and the heat returned. He watched the sky all day for signs of rain-clouds and lay awake all night. In the morn-ing he went back to his farm and saw the withering tendrils. He had tried to protect them from the smouldering earth by making rings of thick sisal[3] leaves around them. But by the end of the day the sisal rings were burnt dry and grey. He changed them every day, and prayed that the rain might fall in the night. But the drought contin-ued for eight market weeks[4] and the yams were killed.

Some farmers had not planted their yams yet. They were the lazy easy-going ones who always put off clearing their farms as long as they could. This year they were the wise ones. They sympathised with their neighbours with much shaking of the head, but inwardly they were happy for what they took to be their own foresight.

Okonkwo planted what was left of his seed-yams when the rains finally returned. He had one consolation. The yams he had sown before the drought were his own, the harvest of the previous year. He still had the eight hundred from Nwakibie and the four hundred from his father's friend. So he would make a fresh start.

But the year had gone mad. Rain fell as it had never fallen before. For days and nights together it poured down in violent torrents, and washed away the yam heaps. Trees were uprooted and deep gorges appeared everywhere. Then the rain became less violent. But it went on from day to day without a pause. The spell of sunshine which always came in the middle of the wet season[5] did not appear. The yams put on luxuriant green leaves, but every farmer knew that with-out sunshine the tubers would not grow.

2. A tuber ("manioc") that requires straining to remove arsenic before it can be eaten. It can be boiled or pounded into paste (*akpu*); it can also be fermented, as described on p. 94; *coco-yams*: also known as "taro," small edible tubers of a somewhat harder variety than yam; their cultivation is reserved for women.
3. A valuable plant whose stem and branches consist of strands that are made into a very strong rope.
4. Counting the major and minor market days, these add up to about three months.
5. Or rainy season, lasting from late April or early May to late October, marked by steady and abundant rainfall.

That year the harvest was sad, like a funeral, and many farmers wept as they dug up the miserable and rotting yams. One man tied his cloth to a tree branch and hanged himself.

Okonkwo remembered that tragic year with a cold shiver throughout the rest of his life. It always surprised him when he thought of it later that he did not sink under the load of despair. He knew he was a fierce fighter, but that year had been enough to break the heart of a lion.

"Since I survived that year," he always said, "I shall survive anything." He put it down to his inflexible will.

His father, Unoka, who was then an ailing man, had said to him during that terrible harvest month: "Do not despair. I know you will not despair. You have a manly and a proud heart. A proud heart can survive a general failure because such a failure does not prick its pride. It is more difficult and more bitter when a man fails *alone*."

Unoka was like that in his last days. His love of talk had grown with age and sickness. It tried Okonkwo's patience beyond words.

Chapter Four

"Looking at a king's mouth," said an old man, "one would think he never sucked at his mother's breast." He was talking about Okonkwo, who had risen so suddenly from great poverty and misfortune to be one of the lords of the clan. The old man bore no ill-will towards Okonkwo. Indeed he respected him for his industry and success. But he was struck, as most people were, by Okonkwo's brusqueness in dealing with less successful men. Only a week ago a man had contradicted him at a kindred meeting which they held to discuss the next ancestral feast. Without looking at the man Okonkwo had said: "This meeting is for men." The man who had contradicted him had no titles. That was why he had called him a woman. Okonkwo knew how to kill a man's spirit.

Everybody at the kindred meeting took sides with Osugo[1] when Okonkwo called him a woman. The oldest man present said sternly that those whose palm-kernels were cracked for them by a benevolent spirit should not forget to be humble. Okonkwo said he was sorry for what he had said, and the meeting continued.

But it was really not true that Okonkwo's palm-kernels had been cracked for him by a benevolent spirit. He had cracked them himself. Anyone who knew his grim struggle against poverty and misfortune could not say he had been lucky. If ever a man deserved his success,

---

1. The name is not an indication of low caste (*osu*) because persons belonging to this caste are strictly barred from mixing with other members of the clan.

that man was Okonkwo. At an early age he had achieved fame as the greatest wrestler in all the land. That was not luck. At the most one could say that his *chi* or personal god was good. But the Ibo people have a proverb that when a man says yes his *chi* says yes also. Okonkwo said yes very strongly; so his *chi* agreed. And not only his *chi* but his clan too, because it judged a man by the work of his hands. That was why Okonkwo had been chosen by the nine villages to carry a message of war to their enemies unless they agreed to give up a young man and a virgin to atone for the murder of Udo's wife. And such was the deep fear that their enemies had for Umuofia that they treated Okonkwo like a king and brought him a virgin who was given to Udo as wife, and the lad Ikemefuna.

The elders of the clan had decided that Ikemefuna should be in Okonkwo's care for a while. But no one thought it would be as long as three years. They seemed to forget all about him as soon as they had taken the decision.

At first Ikemefuna was very much afraid. Once or twice he tried to run away, but he did not know where to begin. He thought of his mother and his three-year-old sister and wept bitterly. Nwoye's mother was very kind to him and treated him as one of her own children. But all he said was: "When shall I go home?" When Okonkwo heard that he would not eat any food he came into the hut with a big stick in his hand and stood over him while he swallowed his yams, trembling. A few moments later he went behind the hut and began to vomit painfully. Nwoye's mother went to him and placed her hands on his chest and on his back. He was ill for three market weeks, and when he recovered he seemed to have overcome his great fear and sadness.

He was by nature a very lively boy and he gradually became popular in Okonkwo's household, especially with the children. Okonkwo's son, Nwoye, who was two years younger, became quite inseparable from him because he seemed to know everything. He could fashion out flutes from bamboo stems and even from the elephant grass. He knew the names of all the birds and could set clever traps for the little bush rodents. And he knew which trees made the strongest bows.

Even Okonkwo himself became very fond of the boy—inwardly of course. Okonkwo never showed any emotion openly, unless it be the emotion of anger. To show affection was a sign of weakness; the only thing worth demonstrating was strength. He therefore treated Ikemefuna as he treated everybody else—with a heavy hand. But there was no doubt that he liked the boy. Sometimes when he went to big village meetings or communal ancestral feasts he allowed Ikemefuna to accompany him, like a son, carrying his stool and his goatskin bag. And, indeed, Ikemefuna called him father.

Ikemefuna came to Umuofia at the end of the carefree season between harvest and planting. In fact he recovered from his illness only a few days before the Week of Peace began. And that was also the year Okonkwo broke the peace, and was punished, as was the custom, by Ezeani,[2] the priest of the earth goddess.

Okonkwo was provoked to justifiable anger by his youngest wife, who went to plait her hair at her friend's house and did not return early enough to cook the afternoon meal. Okonkwo did not know at first that she was not at home. After waiting in vain for her dish he went to her hut to see what she was doing. There was nobody in the hut and the fireplace was cold.

"Where is Ojiugo?" he asked his second wife, who came out of her hut to draw water from a gigantic pot in the shade of a small tree in the middle of the compound.

"She has gone to plait her hair."

Okonkwo bit his lips as anger welled up within him.

"Where are her children? Did she take them?" he asked with unusual coolness and restraint.

"They are here," answered his first wife, Nwoye's mother. Okonkwo bent down and looked into her hut. Ojiugo's children were eating with the children of his first wife.

"Did she ask you to feed them before she went?"

"Yes," lied Nwoye's mother, trying to minimise Ojiugo's thoughtlessness.

Okonkwo knew she was not speaking the truth. He walked back to his *obi* to await Ojiugo's return. And when she returned he beat her very heavily. In his anger he had forgotten that it was the Week of Peace. His first two wives ran out in great alarm pleading with him that it was the sacred week. But Okonkwo was not the man to stop beating somebody half-way through, not even for fear of a goddess.

Okonkwo's neighbours heard his wife crying and sent their voices over the compound walls to ask what was the matter. Some of them came over to see for themselves. It was unheard-of to beat somebody during the sacred week.

Before it was dusk Ezeani, who was the priest of the earth goddess, Ani, called on Okonkwo in his *obi*. Okonkwo brought out kola nut and placed it before the priest.

"Take away your kola nut. I shall not eat in the house of a man who has no respect for our gods and ancestors."

Okonkwo tried to explain to him what his wife had done, but Ezeani seemed to pay no attention. He held a short staff in his hand which he brought down on the floor to emphasise his points.

---

2. Chief of the land; leader or ruler.

"Listen to me," he said when Okonkwo had spoken. "You are not a stranger in Umuofia. You know as well as I do that our forefathers ordained that before we plant any crops in the earth we should observe a week in which a man does not say a harsh word to his neighbour. We live in peace with our fellows to honour our great goddess of the earth without whose blessing our crops will not grow. You have committed a great evil." He brought down his staff heavily on the floor. "Your wife was at fault, but even if you came into your *obi* and found her lover on top of her, you would still have committed a great evil to beat her." His staff came down again. "The evil you have done can ruin the whole clan. The earth goddess whom you have insulted may refuse to give us her increase, and we shall all perish." His tone now changed from anger to command. "You will bring to the shrine of Ani tomorrow one she-goat, one hen, a length of cloth and a hundred cowries." He rose and left the hut.

Okonkwo did as the priest said. He also took with him a pot of palm-wine. Inwardly, he was repentant. But he was not the man to go about telling his neighbours that he was in error. And so people said he had no respect for the gods of the clan. His enemies said his good fortune had gone to his head. They called him the little bird *nza*[3] who so far forgot himself after a heavy meal that he challenged his *chi*.

No work was done during the Week of Peace. People called on their neighbours and drank palm-wine. This year they talked of nothing else but the *nso-ani*[4] which Okonkwo had committed. It was the first time for many years that a man had broken the sacred peace. Even the oldest men could only remember one or two other occasions somewhere in the dim past.

Ogbuefi Ezeudu, who was the oldest man in the village, was telling two other men who came to visit him that the punishment for breaking the Peace of Ani had become very mild in their clan.

"It has not always been so," he said. "My father told me that he had been told that in the past a man who broke the peace was dragged on the ground through the village until he died. But after a while this custom was stopped because it spoilt the peace which it was meant to preserve."

"Somebody told me yesterday," said one of the younger men, "that in some clans it is an abomination for a man to die during the Week of Peace."

"It is indeed true," said Ogbuefi Ezeudu. "They have that custom in Obodoani.[5] If a man dies at this time he is not buried but cast into the Evil Forest. It is a bad custom which these people observe

---

3. A small bird akin to the blue jay, known for its singing.
4. An abomination, an offense against the earth itself (*ani*).
5. The name of this village is vague as it means only "land."

because they lack understanding. They throw away large numbers of men and women without burial. And what is the result? Their clan is full of the evil spirits of these unburied dead, hungry to do harm to the living."

After the Week of Peace every man and his family began to clear the bush to make new farms. The cut bush was left to dry and fire was then set to it. As the smoke rose into the sky kites[6] appeared from different directions and hovered over the burning field in silent vale-diction. The rainy season was approaching when they would go away until the dry season returned.

Okonkwo spent the next few days preparing his seed-yams. He looked at each yam carefully to see whether it was good for sowing. Sometimes he decided that a yam was too big to be sown as one seed and he split it deftly along its length with his sharp knife. His eldest son, Nwoye, and Ikemefuna helped him by fetching the yams in long baskets from the barn and in counting the prepared seeds in groups of four hundred. Sometimes Okonkwo gave them a few yams each to prepare. But he always found fault with their effort, and he said so with much threatening.

"Do you think you are cutting up yams for cooking?" he asked Nwoye. "If you split another yam of this size, I shall break your jaw. You think you are still a child. I began to own a farm at your age. And you," he said to Ikemefuna, "do you not grow yams where you come from?"

Inwardly Okonkwo knew that the boys were still too young to understand fully the difficult art of preparing seed-yams. But he thought that one could not begin too early. Yam stood for manliness, and he who could feed his family on yams from one harvest to another was a very great man indeed. Okonkwo wanted his son to be a great farmer and a great man. He would stamp out the disquieting signs of laziness which he thought he already saw in him.

"I will not have a son who cannot hold up his head in the gather-ing of the clan. I would sooner strangle him with my own hands. And if you stand staring at me like that," he swore, "Amadiora[7] will break your head for you!"

Some days later, when the land had been moistened by two or three heavy rains, Okonkwo and his family went to the farm with baskets of seed-yams, their hoes and matchets, and the planting began. They made single mounds of earth in straight lines all over the field and sowed the yams in them.

Yam, the king of crops, was a very exacting king. For three or four

---

6. The passage describes the seasonal pattern of the birds' migration.
7. God of thunder, equivalent to Shango of the Yoruba or the Germanic Thor.

moons it demanded hard work and constant attention from cock-crow till the chickens went back to roost. The young tendrils were protected from earth-heat with rings of sisal leaves. As the rains became heavier the women planted maize, melons and beans between the yam mounds. The yams were then staked, first with little sticks and later with tall and big tree branches. The women weeded the farm three times at definite periods in the life of the yams, nei-ther early nor late.

And now the rains had really come, so heavy and persistent that even the village rain-maker no longer claimed to be able to intervene. He could not stop the rain now, just as he would not attempt to start it in the heart of the dry season, without serious danger to his own health. The personal dynamism required to counter the forces of these extremes of weather would be far too great for the human frame.

And so nature was not interfered with in the middle of the rainy season. Sometimes it poured down in such thick sheets of water that earth and sky seemed merged in one grey wetness. It was then uncer-tain whether the low rumbling of Amadiora's thunder came from above or below. At such times, in each of the countless thatched huts of Umuofia, children sat around their mother's cooking fire telling stories, or with their father in his *obi* warming themselves from a log fire, roasting and eating maize. It was a brief resting period between the exacting and arduous planting season and the equally exacting but light-hearted month of harvests.

Ikemefuna had begun to feel like a member of Okonkwo's family. He still thought about his mother and his three-year-old sister, and he had moments of sadness and depression. But he and Nwoye had become so deeply attached to each other that such moments became less frequent and less poignant. Ikemefuna had an endless stock of folk tales. Even those which Nwoye knew already were told with a new freshness and the local flavour of a different clan. Nwoye remembered this period very vividly till the end of his life. He even remembered how he had laughed when Ikemefuna told him that the proper name for a corn-cob with only a few scattered grains was *eze-agadi-nwayi*, or the teeth of an old woman. Nwoye's mind had gone immediately to Nwayieke, who lived near the udala[8] tree. She had about three teeth and was always smoking her pipe.

Gradually the rains became lighter and less frequent, and earth and sky once again became separate. The rain fell in thin, slanting showers through sunshine and quiet breeze. Children no longer stayed indoors but ran about singing:

---

8. A fruit the size of an egg and very sweet, usually yellow or red in color when ripe; *Nwayieke*: female born on *eke* market day.

"The rain is falling, the sun is shining,
Alone Nnadi is cooking and eating."[9]

Nwoye always wondered who Nnadi was and why he should live all by himself, cooking and eating. In the end he decided that Nnadi must live in that land of Ikemefuna's favourite story where the ant holds his court in splendour and the sands dance forever.

Chapter Five

The Feast of the New Yam[1] was approaching and Umuofia was in a festival mood. It was an occasion for giving thanks to Ani, the earth goddess and the source of all fertility. Ani played a greater part in the life of the people than any other deity. She was the ultimate judge of morality and conduct. And what was more, she was in close communion with the departed fathers of the clan whose bodies had been committed to earth.

The Feast of the New Yam was held every year before the harvest began, to honour the earth goddess and the ancestral spirits of the clan. New yams could not be eaten until some had first been offered to these powers. Men and women, young and old, looked forward to the New Yam Festival because it began the season of plenty—the new year. On the last night before the festival, yams of the old year were all disposed of by those who still had them. The new year must begin with tasty, fresh yams and not the shrivelled and fibrous crop of the previous year. All cooking-pots, calabashes and wooden bowls were thoroughly washed, especially the wooden mortar in which yam was pounded. Yam foo-foo[2] and vegetable soup was the chief food in the celebration. So much of it was cooked that, no matter how heavily the family ate or how many friends and relations they invited from neighbouring villages, there was always a huge quantity of food left over at the end of the day. The story was always told of a wealthy man who set before his guests a mound of foo-foo so high that those who sat on one side could not see what was happening on the other, and it was not until late in the evening that one of them saw for the first time his in-law who had arrived during the course of the meal and had fallen to on the opposite side.

9. It is unusual for the sun to shine when it's raining; the song registers Nnadi's pensive mood. *Nnadi*: "Father is alive, awake," therefore watching over his children, in life as in death (see Introduction, p. xv for the role of folktales and songs as essential element of narrative).
1. Held to mark a rebirth of life in nature and renewal of the community. In this sense, the festival has the same significance as Easter. The central importance of the new yam to Igbo culture and communal existence provides the source of the tragic denouement in Chinua Achebe's *Arrow of God*.
2. Boiled yam pounded into a paste and eaten with meat or fish sauce.

It was only then that they exchanged greetings and shook hands over what was left of the food.

The New Yam Festival was thus an occasion for joy throughout Umuofia. And every man whose arm was strong, as the Ibo people say, was expected to invite large numbers of guests from far and wide. Okonkwo always asked his wives' relations, and since he now had three wives his guests would make a fairly big crowd.

But somehow Okonkwo could never become as enthusiastic over feasts as most people. He was a good eater and he could drink one or two fairly big gourds[3] of palm-wine. But he was always uncomfortable sitting around for days waiting for a feast or getting over it. He would be very much happier working on his farm.

The festival was now only three days away. Okonkwo's wives had scrubbed the walls and the huts with red earth until they reflected light. They had then drawn patterns on them in white, yellow and dark green.[4] They then set about painting themselves with cam wood[5] and drawing beautiful black patterns on their stomachs and on their backs. The children were also decorated, especially their hair, which was shaved in beautiful patterns. The three women talked excitedly about the relations who had been invited, and the children revelled in the thought of being spoilt by these visitors from the mother-land. Ike-mefuna was equally excited. The New Yam Festival seemed to him to be a much bigger event here than in his own village, a place which was already becoming remote and vague in his imagination.

And then the storm burst. Okonkwo, who had been walking about aimlessly in his compound in suppressed anger, suddenly found an outlet.

"Who killed this banana tree?" he asked.

A hush fell on the compound immediately.

"Who killed this tree? Or are you all deaf and dumb?"

As a matter of fact the tree was very much alive. Okonkwo's second wife had merely cut a few leaves off it to wrap some food, and she said so. Without further argument Okonkwo gave her a sound beating and left her and her only daughter weeping. Neither of the other wives dared to interfere beyond an occasional and tentative, "It is enough, Okonkwo," pleaded from a reasonable distance.

His anger thus satisfied, Okonkwo decided to go out hunting. He had an old rusty gun made by a clever blacksmith who had come to live in Umuofia long ago. But although Okonkwo was a great man

---

3. Large fruits of a vine, with large round bodies and hollow necks, normally used as recep-
   tacles for storing palm wine and other fluids.
4. Offering a sharp contrast of colors; white is derived from chalk, and the other colors from
   plants and other organic material.
5. This reddish substance is obtained from the bark of a tree and serves as adornment, rubbed
   by women on the palms of the hand and soles of the feet.

whose prowess was universally acknowledged, he was not a hunter. In fact he had not killed a rat with his gun. And so when he called Ikemefuna to fetch his gun, the wife who had just been beaten murmured something about guns that never shot. Unfortunately for her, Okonkwo heard it and ran madly into his room for the loaded gun, ran out again and aimed at her as she clambered over the dwarf wall of the barn. He pressed the trigger and there was a loud report accompanied by the wail of his wives and children. He threw down the gun and jumped into the barn, and there lay the woman, very much shaken and frightened but quite unhurt. He heaved a heavy sigh and went away with the gun.

In spite of this incident the New Yam Festival was celebrated with great joy in Okonkwo's household. Early that morning as he offered a sacrifice of new yam and palm-oil to his ancestors he asked them to protect him, his children and their mothers in the new year.

As the day wore on his in-laws arrived from three surrounding villages, and each party brought with them a huge pot of palm-wine. And there was eating and drinking till night, when Okonkwo's in-laws began to leave for their homes.

The second day of the new year was the day of the great wrestling match between Okonkwo's village and their neighbours. It was difficult to say which the people enjoyed more—the feasting and fellowship of the first day or the wrestling contest of the second. But there was one woman who had no doubt whatever in her mind. She was Okonkwo's second wife, Ekwefi, whom he nearly shot. There was no festival in all the seasons of the year which gave her as much pleasure as the wrestling match. Many years ago when she was the village beauty Okonkwo had won her heart by throwing the Cat in the greatest contest within living memory. She did not marry him then because he was too poor to pay her bride-price. But a few years later she ran away from her husband and came to live with Okonkwo. All this happened many years ago. Now Ekwefi was a woman of forty-five who had suffered a great deal in her time. But her love of wrestling contests was still as strong as it was thirty years ago.

It was not yet noon on the second day of the New Yam Festival. Ekwefi and her only daughter, Ezinma,[6] sat near the fireplace waiting for the water in the pot to boil. The fowl Ekwefi had just killed was in the wooden mortar. The water began to boil, and in one deft movement she lifted the pot from the fire and poured the boiling water onto the fowl. She put back the empty pot on the circular pad

6. "My compound (or household) is beautiful." The name is a transferred epithet, in which the girl's attribute is extended to her entire family; the diminutive, Nma, connotes both beauty and affection.

in the corner, and looked at her palms, which were black with soot. Ezinma was always surprised that her mother could lift a pot from the fire with her bare hands.

"Ekwefi," she said, "is it true that when people are grown up, fire does not burn them?" Ezinma, unlike most children, called her mother by her name.

"Yes," replied Ekwefi, too busy to argue. Her daughter was only ten years old but she was wiser than her years.

"But Nwoye's mother dropped her pot of hot soup the other day and it broke on the floor."

Ekwefi turned the hen over in the mortar and began to pluck the feathers.

"Ekwefi," said Ezinma, who had joined in plucking the feathers, "my eyelid is twitching."

"It means you are going to cry," said her mother.

"No," Ezinma said, "it is this eyelid, the top one."

"That means you will see something."

"What will I see?" she asked.

"How can I know?" Ekwefi wanted her to work it out herself.

"Oho," said Ezinma at last. "I know what it is—the wrestling match."

At last the hen was plucked clean. Ekwefi tried to pull out the horny beak but it was too hard. She turned round on her low stool and put the beak in the fire for a few moments. She pulled again and it came off.

"Ekwefi!" a voice called from one of the other huts. It was Nwoye's mother, Okonkwo's first wife.

"Is that me?" Ekwefi called back. That was the way people answered calls from outside. They never answered yes for fear it might be an evil spirit calling.

"Will you give Ezinma some fire to bring to me?" Her own children and Ikemefuna had gone to the stream.

Ekwefi put a few live coals into a piece of broken pot and Ezinma carried it across the clean-swept compound to Nwoye's mother.

"Thank you, Nma," she said. She was peeling new yams, and in a basket beside her were green vegetables and beans.

"Let me make the fire for you," Ezinma offered.

"Thank you, Ezigbo," she said. She often called her Ezigbo, which means "the good one."

Ezinma went outside and brought some sticks from a huge bundle of firewood. She broke them into little pieces across the sole of her foot and began to build a fire, blowing it with her breath.

"You will blow your eyes out," said Nwoye's mother, looking up from the yams she was peeling. "Use the fan." She stood up and pulled out the fan which was fastened into one of the rafters. As soon as she got up, the troublesome nanny-goat,[7] which had been dutifully eating yam peelings, dug her teeth into the real thing, scooped out two mouthfuls and fled from the hut to chew the cud in the goats' shed. Nwoye's mother swore at her and settled down again to her peeling. Ezinma's fire was now sending up thick clouds of smoke. She went on fanning it until it burst into flames. Nwoye's mother thanked her and she went back to her mother's hut.

Just then the distant beating of drums began to reach them. It came from the direction of the *ilo*,[8] the village playground. Every village had its own *ilo* which was as old as the village itself and where all the great ceremonies and dances took place. The drums beat the unmistakable wrestling dance—quick, light and gay, and it came floating on the wind.

Okonkwo cleared his throat and moved his feet to the beat of the drums. It filled him with fire as it had always done from his youth. He trembled with the desire to conquer and subdue. It was like the desire for woman.

"We shall be late for the wrestling," said Ezinma to her mother.

"They will not begin until the sun goes down."

"But they are beating the drums."

"Yes. The drums begin at noon but the wrestling waits until the sun begins to sink. Go and see if your father has brought out yams for the afternoon."

"He has. Nwoye's mother is already cooking."

"Go and bring our own, then. We must cook quickly or we shall be late for the wrestling."

Ezinma ran in the direction of the barn and brought back two yams from the dwarf wall.[9]

Ekwefi peeled the yams quickly. The troublesome nannygoat sniffed about, eating the peelings. She cut the yams into small pieces and began to prepare a pottage, using some of the chicken.

At that moment they heard someone crying just outside their compound. It was very much like Obiageli,[1] Nwoye's sister.

"Is that not Obiageli weeping?" Ekwefi called across the yard to Nwoye's mother.

"Yes," she replied. "She must have broken her water-pot."

The weeping was now quite close and soon the children filed in, carrying on their heads various sizes of pots suitable to their years. Ikemefuna came first with the biggest pot, closely followed by Nwoye and his two younger brothers. Obiageli brought up the rear, her face streaming with tears. In her hand was the cloth pad on which the pot should have rested on her head.

7. Young female goat.
8. Cleared open square at the center of the village where all public gatherings take place.
9. Lower wall of the barn where yam is stored.
1. "Destined for prosperity."

"What happened?" her mother asked, and Obiageli told her mournful story. Her mother consoled her and promised to buy her another pot.

Nwoye's younger brothers were about to tell their mother the true story of the accident when Ikemefuna looked at them sternly and they held their peace. The fact was that Obiageli had been making *inyanga*[2] with her pot. She had balanced it on her head, folded her arms in front of her and began to sway her waist like a grown-up young lady. When the pot fell down and broke she burst out laughing. She only began to weep when they got near the iroko tree outside their compound.

The drums were still beating,[3] persistent and unchanging. Their sound was no longer a separate thing from the living village. It was like the pulsation of its heart. It throbbed in the air, in the sunshine, and even in the trees, and filled the village with excitement.

Ekwefi ladled her husband's share of the pottage into a bowl and covered it. Ezinma took it to him in his *obi*.

Okonkwo was sitting on a goatskin already eating his first wife's meal. Obiageli, who had brought it from her mother's hut, sat on the floor waiting for him to finish. Ezinma placed her mother's dish before him and sat with Obiageli.

"Sit like a woman!" Okonkwo shouted at her. Ezinma brought her two legs together and stretched them in front of her.

"Father, will you go to see the wrestling?" Ezinma asked after a suitable interval.

"Yes," he answered. "Will you go?"

"Yes." And after a pause she said: "Can I bring your chair for you?"

"No, that is a boy's job." Okonkwo was specially fond of Ezinma. She looked very much like her mother, who was once the village beauty. But his fondness only showed on very rare occasions.

"Obiageli broke her pot today," Ezinma said.

"Yes, she has told me about it," Okonkwo said between mouthfuls.

"Father," said Obiageli, "people should not talk when they are eating or pepper may go down the wrong way."

"That is very true. Do you hear that, Ezinma? You are older than Obiageli but she has more sense."

He uncovered his second wife's dish and began to eat from it. Obiageli took the first dish and returned to her mother's hut. And then Nkechi came in, bringing the third dish. Nkechi was the daughter of Okonkwo's third wife.

In the distance the drums continued to beat.

---

2. Bravado, showing off; the word has become the standard term for this attitude in Nigerian pidgin.
3. Besides its ethnographic interest, the omnipresence of the drums is an outward manifestation of the community's vitality.

Chapter Six

The whole village turned out on the *ilo*, men, women and children. They stood round in a huge circle leaving the centre of the playground free. The elders and grandees of the village sat on their own stools brought there by their young sons or slaves. Okonkwo was among them. All others stood except those who came early enough to secure places on the few stands which had been built by placing smooth logs on forked pillars.

The wrestlers were not there yet and the drummers held the field. They too sat just in front of the huge circle of spectators, facing the elders. Behind them was the big and ancient silk-cotton tree which was sacred. Spirits of good children lived in that tree waiting to be born. On ordinary days young women who desired children came to sit under its shade.

There were seven drums[1] and they were arranged according to their sizes in a long wooden basket. Three men beat them with sticks, working feverishly from one drum to another. They were possessed by the spirit of the drums.

The young men who kept order on these occasions dashed about, consulting among themselves and with the leaders of the two wrestling teams, who were still outside the circle, behind the crowd. Once in a while two young men carrying palm fronds ran round the circle and kept the crowd back by beating the ground in front of them or, if they were stubborn, their legs and feet.

At last the two teams danced into the circle and the crowd roared and clapped. The drums rose to a frenzy. The people surged forward. The young men who kept order flew around, waving their palm fronds. Old men nodded to the beat of the drums and remembered the days when they wrestled to its intoxicating rhythm.

The contest began with boys of fifteen or sixteen. There were only three such boys in each team. They were not the real wrestlers; they merely set the scene. Within a short time the first two bouts were over. But the third created a big sensation even among the elders who did not usually show their excitement so openly. It was as quick as the other two, perhaps even quicker. But very few people had ever seen that kind of wrestling before. As soon as the two boys closed in, one of them did something which no one could describe because it had been as quick as a flash. And the other boy was flat on his back. The crowd roared and clapped and for a while drowned the frenzied drums. Okonkwo sprang to his feet and quickly sat down again. Three young men from the victorious boy's team ran forward, carried him shoulder-high and danced

---

1. Again, seven as mystic number. The sizes of the drums determine their varying degrees of pitch and resonance, hence the tonal color of the ensemble.

through the cheering crowd. Everybody soon knew who the boy was. His name was Maduka, the son of Obierika.[2]

The drummers stopped for a brief rest before the real matches. Their bodies shone with sweat, and they took up fans and began to fan themselves. They also drank water from small pots and ate kola nuts. They became ordinary human beings again, talking and laughing among themselves and with others who stood near them. The air, which had been stretched taut with excitement, relaxed again. It was as if water had been poured on the tightened skin of a drum. Many people looked around, perhaps for the first time, and saw those who stood or sat next to them.

"I did not know it was you," Ekwefi said to the woman who had stood shoulder to shoulder with her since the beginning of the matches.

"I do not blame you," said the woman. "I have never seen such a large crowd of people. Is it true that Okonkwo nearly killed you with his gun?"

"It is true indeed, my dear friend. I cannot yet find a mouth with which to tell the story."

"Your *chi* is very much awake, my friend. And how is my daughter, Ezinma?"

"She has been very well for some time now. Perhaps she has come to stay."[3]

"I think she has. How old is she now?"

"She is about ten years old."

"I think she will stay. They usually stay if they do not die before the age of six."

"I pray she stays," said Ekwefi with a heavy sigh.

The woman with whom she talked was called Chielo. She was the priestess of Agbala, the Oracle of the Hills and the Caves. In ordinary life Chielo was a widow with two children. She was very friendly with Ekwefi and they shared a common shed in the market. She was particularly fond of Ekwefi's only daughter, Ezinma, whom she called "my daughter". Quite often she bought bean-cakes[4] and gave Ekwefi

---

2. "My household (*obi*) is supreme"; *Maduka*: "The human being (as person and member of a family) is supreme." The value of the person is considered here in comparison to wealth or worldly prosperity. Maduka is expected to be the next wrestling champion of the clan, though his father, Obierika, shows little interest in the matter.

3. The child is an *ogbanje*, who, in the belief system of the Igbo and other African peoples, plagues her mother and her family by dying and returning to earth in successive births; the idea is further developed later in the novel (see pp. 47 ff and notes). Among the Yoruba, the child is known as *abiku*. See pp. 221 and 224 of this volume for two poems on this theme by the Nigerian poets J. P. Clark and Wole Soyinka, in which, as here, the capricious and willful character of the child is emphasized. See also Ben Okri's novel, *The Famished Road*, an extended development of the *abiku* or *ogbanje* theme in narrative terms.

4. Handfuls of beans ground into a fine paste and fried in palm oil. Also known in the New World by its West African name, *akara*.

some to take home to Ezinma. Anyone seeing Chielo in ordinary life would hardly believe she was the same person who prophesied when the spirit of Agbala was upon her.

The drummers took up their sticks again and the air shivered and grew tense like a tightened bow.

The two teams were ranged facing each other across the clear space. A young man from one team danced across the centre to the other side and pointed at whomever he wanted to fight. They danced back to the centre together and then closed in.

There were twelve men on each side and the challenge went from one side to the other. Two judges walked around the wrestlers and when they thought they were equally matched, stopped them. Five matches ended in this way. But the really exciting moments were when a man was thrown. The huge voice of the crowd then rose to the sky and in every direction. It was even heard in the surrounding villages.

The last match was between the leaders of the teams. They were among the best wrestlers in all the nine villages. The crowd wondered who would throw the other this year. Some said Okafo was the better man; others said he was not the equal of Ikezue.[5] Last year neither of them had thrown the other even though the judges had allowed the contest to go on longer than was the custom. They had the same style and one saw the other's plans beforehand. It might happen again this year.

Dusk was already approaching when their contest began. The drums went mad and the crowds also. They surged forward as the two young men danced into the circle. The palm fronds were helpless in keeping them back.

Ikezue held out his right hand. Okafo seized it, and they closed in. It was a fierce contest. Ikezue strove to dig in his right heel behind Okafo so as to pitch him backwards in the clever *ege* style.[6] But the one knew what the other was thinking. The crowd had surrounded and swallowed up the drummers, whose frantic rhythm was no longer a mere disembodied sound but the very heart-beat of the people.

The wrestlers were now almost still in each other's grip. The muscles on their arms and their thighs and on their backs stood out and twitched. It looked like an equal match. The two judges were already moving forward to separate them when Ikezue, now desperate, went

5. "I'm filled with strength (*ike*)"; the idea is that this suffices for both himself and his community. *Okafo*: Sometimes written "Okafor"; born on Afo market day. Cf. Okoye.
6. This is a fast-paced style of wrestling; it involves stretching out the leg and swinging the opponent across it to destabilize him. The word also refers to the frenetic character of the drumming that accompanies the wrestling contest.

down quickly on one knee in an attempt to fling his man backwards over his head. It was a sad miscalculation. Quick as the lightning of Amadiora, Okafo raised his right leg and swung it over his rival's head.[7] The crowd burst into a thunderous roar. Okafo was swept off his feet by his supporters and carried home shoulder-high. They sang his praise and the young women clapped their hands:

> "Who will wrestle for our village?
>   Okafo will wrestle for our village.
> Has he thrown a hundred men?
>   He has thrown four hundred men.
> Has he thrown a hundred Cats?
>   He has thrown four hundred Cats.
> Then send him word to fight for us."[8]

Chapter Seven

For three years Ikemefuna lived in Okonkwo's household and the elders of Umuofia seemed to have forgotten about him. He grew rapidly like a yam tendril in the rainy season, and was full of the sap of life. He had become wholly absorbed into his new family. He was like an elder brother to Nwoye, and from the very first seemed to have kindled a new fire in the younger boy. He made him feel grown-up; and they no longer spent the evenings in mother's hut while she cooked, but now sat with Okonkwo in his *obi*, or watched him as he tapped his palm tree for the evening wine. Nothing pleased Nwoye now more than to be sent for by his mother or another of his father's wives to do one of those difficult and masculine tasks in the home, like splitting wood, or pounding food. On receiving such a message through a younger brother or sister, Nwoye would feign annoyance and grumble aloud about women and their troubles.

Okonkwo was inwardly pleased at his son's development, and he knew it was due to Ikemefuna. He wanted Nwoye to grow into a tough young man capable of ruling his father's household when he was dead and gone to join the ancestors.[1] He wanted him to be a prosperous man, having enough in his barn to feed the ancestors with regular sacrifices. And so he was always happy when he heard him grumbling about women. That showed that in time he would be able to control his women-folk. No matter how prosperous a man

---

7. Thus gaining supremacy over him, as the head is considered the seat of a person's being.
8. The song points to the role of the champion wrestler, who embodies the heroic ideal of the community.
1. See p. 73 and Introduction, p. xv, for the full significance of this phrase.

was, if he was unable to rule his women and his children (and especially his women) he was not really a man. He was like the man in
the song who had ten and one wives and not enough soup for his
foo-foo.

So Okonkwo encouraged the boys to sit with him in his *obi*, and he
told them stories of the land—masculine stories of violence and
bloodshed. Nwoye knew that it was right to be masculine and to be
violent, but somehow he still preferred the stories that his mother
used to tell, and which she no doubt still told to her younger
children—stories of the tortoise and his wily ways, and of the bird
eneke-nti-oba[2] who challenged the whole world to a wrestling contest
and was finally thrown by the cat. He remembered the story she often
told of the quarrel between Earth and Sky long ago, and how Sky
withheld rain for seven years, until crops withered and the dead could
not be buried because the hoes broke on the stony Earth. At last Vulture was sent to plead with Sky, and to soften his heart with a song
of the suffering of the sons of men. Whenever Nwoye's mother sang
this song he felt carried away to the distant scene in the sky where
Vulture, Earth's emissary, sang for mercy. At last Sky was moved to
pity, and he gave to Vulture rain wrapped in leaves of coco-yam. But
as he flew home his long talon pierced the leaves and the rain fell as
it had never fallen before. And so heavily did it rain on Vulture that
he did not return to deliver his message but flew to a distant land,
from where he had espied a fire. And when he got there he found it
was a man making a sacrifice. He warmed himself in the fire and ate
the entrails.[3]

That was the kind of story that Nwoye loved. But he now knew that
they were for foolish women and children, and he knew that his
father wanted him to be a man. And so he feigned that he no longer
cared for women's stories. And when he did this he saw that his father
was pleased, and no longer rebuked him or beat him. So Nwoye and
Ikemefuna would listen to Okonkwo's stories about tribal wars, or
how, years ago, he had stalked his victim, overpowered him and
obtained his first human head. And as he told them of the past they
sat in darkness or the dim glow of logs, waiting for the women to finish their cooking. When they finished, each brought her bowl of foo-
foo and bowl of soup to her husband. An oil lamp was lit and
Okonkwo tasted from each bowl, and then passed two shares to
Nwoye and Ikemefuna.

In this way the moons and the seasons passed. And then the

2. A bird that is reputed to be deaf to the world during its flight, so that it flies straight to its
   home or destination without being distracted.
3. An example of the large body of aetiological folk tales in Africa, told to explain the origin
   of phenomena. In this case, it provides an explanation for the vulture's habit of feeding on
   carcasses.

locusts[4] came. It had not happened for many a long year. The elders said locusts came once in a generation, reappeared every year for seven years and then disappeared for another lifetime. They went back to their caves in a distant land, where they were guarded by a race of stunted men. And then after another lifetime these men opened the caves again and the locusts came to Umuofia.

They came in the cold harmattan season after the harvests had been gathered, and ate up all the wild grass in the fields.

Okonkwo and the two boys were working on the red outer walls of the compound. This was one of the lighter tasks of the after-harvest season. A new cover of thick palm branches and palm leaves was set on the walls to protect them from the next rainy season. Okonkwo worked on the outside of the wall and the boys worked from within. There were little holes from one side to the other in the upper levels of the wall, and through these Okonkwo passed the rope, or *tie-tie*,[5] to the boys and they passed it round the wooden stays and then back to him; and in this way the cover was strengthened on the wall.

The women had gone to the bush to collect firewood, and the little children to visit their playmates in the neighbouring compounds. The harmattan was in the air and seemed to distil a hazy feeling of sleep on the world. Okonkwo and the boys worked in complete silence, which was only broken when a new palm frond was lifted on to the wall or when a busy hen moved dry leaves about in her ceaseless search for food.

And then quite suddenly a shadow fell on the world, and the sun seemed hidden behind a thick cloud. Okonkwo looked up from his work and wondered if it was going to rain at such an unlikely time of the year. But almost immediately a shout of joy broke out in all directions, and Umuofia, which had dozed in the noon-day haze, broke into life and activity.

"Locusts are descending," was joyfully chanted everywhere, and men, women and children left their work or their play and ran into the open to see the unfamiliar sight. The locusts had not come for many, many years, and only the old people had seen them before.

At first, a fairly small swarm came. They were the harbingers sent to survey the land. And then appeared on the horizon a slowly-moving mass like a boundless sheet of black cloud drifting towards Umuofia. Soon it covered half the sky, and the solid mass was now broken by tiny eyes of light like shining star-dust. It was a tremendous sight, full of power and beauty.

---

4. The appearance of these insects is dreaded, for they are capable of devouring whole fields of food crops in a single day, thus causing widespread famine. The positive association here is thus unusual. For the association of the insect with calamity, see p. 80.
5. Presumably, pidgin for a rope made from branches of the palm tree.

Everyone was now about, talking excitedly and praying that the locusts should camp in Umuofia for the night. For although locusts had not visited Umuofia for many years, everybody knew by instinct that they were very good to eat. And at last the locusts did descend. They settled on every tree and on every blade of grass; they settled on the roofs and covered the bare ground. Mighty tree branches broke away under them, and the whole country became the brown-earth colour of the vast, hungry swarm.

Many people went out with baskets trying to catch them, but the elders counselled patience till nightfall. And they were right. The locusts settled in the bushes for the night and their wings became wet with dew. Then all Umuofia turned out in spite of the cold harmattan, and everyone filled his bags and pots with locusts. The next morning they were roasted in clay pots and then spread in the sun until they became dry and brittle. And for many days this rare food was eaten with solid palm-oil.

Okonkwo sat in his *obi* crunching happily with Ikemefuna and Nwoye, and drinking palm-wine copiously, when Ogbuefi Ezeudu came in. Ezeudu was the oldest man in this quarter of Umuofia. He had been a great and fearless warrior in his time, and was now accorded great respect in all the clan. He refused to join in the meal, and asked Okonkwo to have a word with him outside. And so they walked out together, the old man supporting himself with his stick. When they were out of ear-shot, he said to Okonkwo:

"That boy calls you father. Do not bear a hand in his death." Okonkwo was surprised, and was about to say something when the old man continued:

"Yes, Umuofia has decided to kill him. The Oracle of the Hills and the Caves has pronounced it. They will take him outside Umuofia as is the custom, and kill him there. But I want you to have nothing to do with it. He calls you his father."

The next day a group of elders from all the nine villages of Umuofia came to Okonkwo's house early in the morning, and before they began to speak in low tones Nwoye and Ikemefuna were sent out. They did not stay very long, but when they went away Okonkwo sat still for a very long time supporting his chin in his palms. Later in the day he called Ikemefuna and told him that he was to be taken home the next day. Nwoye overheard it and burst into tears, whereupon his father beat him heavily. As for Ikemefuna, he was at a loss. His own home had gradually become very faint and distant. He still missed his mother and his sister and would be very glad to see them. But somehow he knew he was not going to see them. He remembered once when men had talked in low tones with his father; and it seemed now as if it was happening all over again.

Later, Nwoye went to his mother's hut and told her that Ikemefuna was going home. She immediately dropped the pestle with which she was grinding pepper, folded her arms across her breast and sighed, "Poor child".

The next day, the men returned with a pot of wine. They were all fully dressed as if they were going to a big clan meeting or to pay a visit to a neighbouring village. They passed their cloths under the right arm-pit, and hung their goatskin bags and sheathed matchets[6] over their left shoulders. Okonkwo got ready quickly and the party set out with Ikemefuna carrying the pot of wine. A deathly silence descended on Okonkwo's compound. Even the very little children seemed to know. Throughout that day Nwoye sat in his mother's hut and tears stood in his eyes.

At the beginning of their journey the men of Umuofia talked and laughed about the locusts, about their women, and about some effeminate men who had refused to come with them. But as they drew near to the outskirts of Umuofia silence fell upon them too.

The sun rose slowly to the centre of the sky, and the dry, sandy footway began to throw up the heat that lay buried in it. Some birds chirruped in the forests around. The men trod dry leaves on the sand. All else was silent. Then from the distance came the faint beating of the *ekwe*. It rose and faded with the wind—a peaceful dance from a distant clan.

"It is an *ozo* dance,"[7] the men said among themselves. But no one was sure where it was coming from. Some said Ezimili, others Abame or Aninta. They argued for a short while and fell into silence again, and the elusive dance rose and fell with the wind. Somewhere a man was taking one of the titles of his clan, with music and dancing and a great feast.

The footway had now become a narrow line in the heart of the forest. The short trees and sparse undergrowth which surrounded the men's village began to give way to giant trees and climbers which perhaps had stood from the beginning of things, untouched by the axe and the bush-fire. The sun breaking through their leaves and branches threw a pattern of light and shade on the sandy footway.

Ikemefuna heard a whisper close behind him and turned round sharply. The man who had whispered now called out aloud, urging the others to hurry up.

"We still have a long way to go," he said. Then he and another man went before Ikemefuna and set a faster pace.

Thus the men of Umuofia pursued their way, armed with sheathed matchets, and Ikemefuna, carrying a pot of palm-wine on his head, walked in their midst. Although he had felt uneasy at first, he was not

6. Machete.
7. Stately, as befits titled men, who are conscious of the great respect they are accorded.

afraid now. Okonkwo walked behind him. He could hardly imagine
that Okonkwo was not his real father. He had never been fond of his
real father, and at the end of three years he had become very distant
indeed. But his mother and his three-year-old sister . . . of course she
would not be three now, but six. Would he recognise her now? She
must have grown quite big. How his mother would weep for joy, and
thank Okonkwo for having looked after him so well and for bringing
him back. She would want to hear everything that had happened to
him in all these years. Could he remember them all? He would tell
her about Nwoye and his mother, and about the locusts. . . . Then
quite suddenly a thought came upon him. His mother might be dead.
He tried in vain to force the thought out of his mind. Then he tried
to settle the matter the way he used to settle such matters when he
was a little boy. He still remembered the song;

> Eze elina, elina!
>   Sala
> Eze ilikwa ya
> Ikwaba akwa oligholi
> Ebe Danda nechi eze
> Ebe Uzuzu nete egwu
>   Sala[8]

He sang it in his mind, and walked to its beat. If the song ended
on his right foot, his mother was alive. If it ended on his left, she was
dead. No, not dead, but ill. It ended on the right. She was alive and
well. He sang the song again, and it ended on the left. But the second time did not count. The first voice gets to Chukwu,[9] or God's
house. That was a favourite saying of children. Ikemefuna felt like a
child once more. It must be the thought of going home to his
mother.

One of the men behind him cleared his throat. Ikemefuna looked
back, and the man growled at him to go on and not stand looking

---

8. *King, do not eat*
        Sala
   King, do not eat,
   If you eat this
   Where Danda is being crowned
   Where the dust is dancing
   It is people (that is, who are raising the dust)
        Sala

   Sala: a refrain taken up by the audience in a rhythmic response to the narrative; *eze*:
   "ruler"; *Danda*: the ant, a trickster figure in Igbo folk tale tradition, celebrated as a folk hero
   in Nkem Nwakwo's novel of that name.
9. Term adopted by the Christian missions and now generally used in Igbo for "God,"
   although the Igbo scholar Donatus Nwoga has argued that the concept of the Supreme
   God is a western, Christian importation (see Nwoga, 1981). Chukwu is also referred to as
   obasi; this word and *chineke* cover the same range of meaning.

back. The way he said it sent cold fear down Ikemefuna's back. His hands trembled vaguely on the black pot he carried. Why had Okonkwo withdrawn to the rear? Ikemefuna felt his legs melting under him. And he was afraid to look back.

As the man who had cleared his throat drew up and raised his matchet, Okonkwo looked away. He heard the blow. The pot fell and broke in the sand. He heard Ikemefuna cry, "My father, they have killed me!" as he ran towards him. Dazed with fear, Okonkwo drew his matchet and cut him down. He was afraid of being thought weak.

As soon as his father walked in, that night, Nwoye knew that Ikemefuna had been killed, and something seemed to give way inside him, like the snapping of a tightened bow. He did not cry. He just hung limp. He had had the same kind of feeling not long ago, during the last harvest season. Every child loved the harvest season. Those who were big enough to carry even a few yams in a tiny basket went with grown-ups to the farm. And if they could not help in digging up the yams, they could gather firewood together for roasting the ones that would be eaten there on the farm. This roasted yam soaked in red palm-oil and eaten in the open farm was sweeter than any meal at home. It was after such a day at the farm during the last harvest that Nwoye had felt for the first time a snapping inside him like the one he now felt. They were returning home with baskets of yams from a distant farm across the stream when they had heard the voice of an infant crying in the thick forest. A sudden hush had fallen on the women, who had been talking, and they had quickened their steps. Nwoye had heard that twins were put in earthenware pots and thrown away in the forest, but he had never yet come across them. A vague chill had descended on him and his head had seemed to swell, like a solitary walker at night who passes an evil spirit on the way. Then something had given way inside him. It descended on him again, this feeling, when his father walked in, that night after killing Ikemefuna.

Chapter Eight

Okonkwo did not taste any food for two days after the death of Ikemefuna. He drank palm-wine from morning till night, and his eyes were red and fierce like the eyes of a rat when it was caught by the tail and dashed against the floor. He called his son, Nwoye, to sit with him in his *obi*. But the boy was afraid of him and slipped out of the hut as soon as he noticed him dozing.

He did not sleep at night. He tried not to think about Ikemefuna, but the more he tried the more he thought about him. Once he got

up from bed and walked about his compound. But he was so weak
that his legs could hardly carry him. He felt like a drunken giant walking with the limbs of a mosquito. Now and then a cold shiver
descended on his head and spread down his body.

On the third day he asked his second wife, Ekwefi, to roast plantains for him. She prepared it the way he liked—with slices of oil-
bean[1] and fish.

"You have not eaten for two days," said his daughter Ezinma when
she brought the food to him. "So you must finish this." She sat down
and stretched her legs in front of her. Okonkwo ate the food absent-
mindedly. 'She should have been a boy,' he thought as he looked at
his ten-year-old daughter. He passed her a piece of fish.

"Go and bring me some cold water," he said. Ezinma rushed out of
the hut, chewing the fish, and soon returned with a bowl of cool
water from the earthen pot in her mother's hut.

Okonkwo took the bowl from her and gulped the water down. He
ate a few more pieces of plantain and pushed the dish aside.

"Bring me my bag," he asked, and Ezinma brought his goatskin bag
from the far end of the hut. He searched in it for his snuff-bottle. It
was a deep bag and took almost the whole length of his arm. It contained other things apart from his snuff-bottle. There was a drinking
horn in it, and also a drinking gourd,[2] and they knocked against each
other as he searched. When he brought out the snuff-bottle he
tapped it a few times against his knee-cap before taking out some
snuff on the palm of his left hand. Then he remembered that he had
not taken out his snuff-spoon. He searched his bag again and brought
out a small, flat, ivory spoon, with which he carried the brown snuff
to his nostrils.

Ezinma took the dish in one hand and the empty water bowl in the
other and went back to her mother's hut. 'She should have been a
boy,' Okonkwo said to himself again. His mind went back to Ikemefuna and he shivered. If only he could find some work to do he would
be able to forget. But it was the season of rest between the harvest
and the next planting season. The only work that men did at this time
was covering the walls of their compound with new palm fronds. And
Okonkwo had already done that. He had finished it on the very day
the locusts came, when he had worked on one side of the wall and
Ikemefuna and Nwoye on the other.

'When did you become a shivering old woman,' Okonkwo asked

1. Or *Ugba*, a tree that often bears a legume-like fruit, which is sliced into small slivers, fermented and used to make a very tasty spice salad, which is eaten mainly at festivals and is
   therefore highly prized. Its significance as symbol of spiritual experience is evoked in the
   poetry of the Igbo writer Christopher Okigbo.
2. Smaller in size than the palm gourd (see note 3, p. 24 above). The neck of the calabash
   can also be fashioned into a cup (*iko*).

himself, 'you, who are known in all the nine villages for your valour in war? How can a man who has killed five men in battle fall to pieces because he has added a boy to their number? Okonkwo, you have become a woman indeed.'

He sprang to his feet, hung his goatskin bag on his shoulder and went to visit his friend, Obierika.

Obierika was sitting outside under the shade of an orange tree making thatches from leaves of the raffia-palm. He exchanged greetings with Okonkwo and led the way into his *obi*.

"I was coming over to see you as soon as I finished that thatch," he said, rubbing off the grains of sand that clung to his thighs.

"Is it well?" Okonkwo asked.

"Yes," replied Obierika. "My daughter's suitor is coming today and I hope we will clinch the matter of the bride-price. I want you to be there."

Just then Obierika's son, Maduka, came into the *obi* from outside, greeted Okonkwo and turned towards the compound.

"Come and shake hands with me," Okonkwo said to the lad. "Your wrestling the other day gave me much happiness." The boy smiled, shook hands with Okonkwo and went into the compound.

"He will do great things," Okonkwo said. "If I had a son like him I should be happy. I am worried about Nwoye. A bowl of pounded yams can throw him in a wrestling match. His two younger brothers are more promising. But I can tell you, Obierika, that my children do not resemble me. Where are the young suckers[3] that will grow when the old banana tree dies? If Ezinma had been a boy I would have been happier. She has the right spirit."

"You worry yourself for nothing," said Obierika. "The children are still very young."

"Nwoye is old enough to impregnate a woman. At his age I was already fending for myself. No, my friend, he is not too young. A chick that will grow into a cock can be spotted the very day it hatches. I have done my best to make Nwoye grow into a man, but there is too much of his mother in him."

'Too much of his grandfather,' Obierika thought, but he did not say it. The same thought also came to Okonkwo's mind. But he had long learnt how to lay that ghost. Whenever the thought of his father's weakness and failure troubled him he expelled it by thinking about his own strength and success. And so he did now. His mind went to his latest show of manliness.

"I cannot understand why you refused to come with us to kill that boy," he asked Obierika.

---

3. Small shoots that grow out of the banana plant at its base; each develops later into a full plant. They are thus likened in a proverb to children growing to replace their parents.

"Because I did not want to," Obierika replied sharply. "I had something better to do."

"You sound as if you question the authority and the decision of the Oracle, who said he should die."

"I do not. Why should I? But the Oracle did not ask me to carry out its decision."

"But someone had to do it. If we were all afraid of blood, it would not be done. And what do you think the Oracle would do then?"

"You know very well, Okonkwo, that I am not afraid of blood; and if anyone tells you that I am, he is telling a lie. And let me tell you one thing, my friend. If I were you I would have stayed at home. What you have done will not please the Earth. It is the kind of action for which the goddess wipes out whole families."

"The Earth cannot punish me for obeying her messenger," Okonkwo said. "A child's fingers are not scalded by a piece of hot yam which its mother puts into its palm."

"That is true," Obierika agreed. "But if the Oracle said that my son should be killed I would neither dispute it nor be the one to do it."

They would have gone on arguing had Ofoedu[4] not come in just then. It was clear from his twinkling eyes that he had important news. But it would be impolite to rush him. Obierika offered him a lobe of the kola nut he had broken with Okonkwo. Ofoedu ate slowly and talked about the locusts. When he finished his kola nut he said;

"The things that happen these days are very strange."

"What has happened?" asked Okonkwo.

"Do you know Ogbuefi Ndulue?"[5] Ofoedu asked.

"Ogbuefi Ndulue of Ire village," Okonkwo and Obierika said together.

"He died this morning," said Ofoedu.

"That is not strange. He was the oldest man in Ire," said Obierika.

"You are right," Ofoedu agreed. "But you ought to ask why the drum has not been beaten to tell Umuofia of his death."

"Why?" asked Obierika and Okonkwo together.

"That is the strange part of it. You know his first wife who walks with a stick?"

"Yes. She is called Ozoemena."[6]

"That is so," said Ofoedu. "Ozoemena was, as you know, too old to attend Ndulue during his illness. His younger wives did that. When he died this morning, one of these women went to Ozoemena's hut

---

4. "The ancestors are our guide." *Ofo* is an emblem of divine justice used in swearing or indicting one's enemy at a shrine or before a deity.
5. "The life is here."
6. "May we be spared another sorrow/tragedy." See p. 47 for its adoption as the name of a child. Ozoemena's death is kept secret until the burial so as not to cast suspicion on her wife.

and told her. She rose from her mat, took her stick and walked over to the *obi*. She knelt on her knees and hands at the threshold and called her husband, who was laid on a mat. 'Ogbuefi Ndulue,' she called, three times, and went back to her hut. When the youngest wife went to call her again to be present at the washing of the body, she found her lying on the mat, dead."

"That is very strange indeed," said Okonkwo. "They will put off Ndulue's funeral until his wife has been buried."

"That is why the drum has not been beaten to tell Umuofia."

"It was always said that Ndulue and Ozoemena had one mind," said Obierika. "I remember when I was a young boy there was a song about them. He could not do anything without telling her."

"I did not know that," said Okonkwo. "I thought he was a strong man in his youth."

"He was indeed," said Ofoedu.

Okonkwo shook his head doubtfully.

"He led Umuofia to war in those days," said Obierika.

Okonkwo was beginning to feel like his old self again. All that he required was something to occupy his mind. If he had killed Ikemefuna during the busy planting season or harvesting it would not have been so bad; his mind would have been centred on his work. Okonkwo was not a man of thought but of action. But in the absence of work, talking was the next best.

Soon after Ofoedu left, Okonkwo took up his goatskin bag to go.

"I must go home to tap my palm trees for the afternoon," he said.

"Who taps your tall trees for you?" asked Obierika.

"Umezulike," replied Okonkwo.

"Sometimes I wish I had not taken the *ozo* title," said Obierika. "It wounds my heart to see these young men killing palm trees in the name of tapping."[7]

"It is so indeed," Okonkwo agreed. "But the law of the land must be obeyed."

"I don't know how we got that law," said Obierika. "In many other clans a man of title is not forbidden to climb the palm tree. Here we say he cannot climb the tall tree but he can tap the short ones standing on the ground. It is like Dimaragana, who would not lend his knife for cutting up dog-meat because the dog was taboo to him, but offered to use his teeth."

"I think it is good that our clan holds the *ozo* title in high esteem," said Okonkwo. "In those other clans you speak of, *ozo* is so low that every beggar takes it."

---

7. See note 6, p. 14. It is essential to make the incision at the right spot of the palm tree, so it is not damaged irreparably and thus "killed."

"I was only speaking in jest," said Obierika. "In Abame and Aninta the title is worth less than two cowries. Every man wears the thread of title on his ankle, and does not lose it even if he steals."

"They have indeed soiled the name of *ozo*," said Okonkwo as he rose to go.

"It will not be very long now before my in-laws come," said Obierika.

"I shall return very soon," said Okonkwo, looking at the position of the sun.[8]

There were seven men in Obierika's hut when Okonkwo returned. The suitor was a young man of about twenty-five, and with him were his father and uncle. On Obierika's side were his two elder brothers and Maduka, his sixteen-year-old son.

"Ask Akueke's[9] mother to send us some kola nuts," said Obierika to his son. Maduka vanished into the compound like lightning. The conversation at once centred on him, and everybody agreed that he was as sharp as a razor.

"I sometimes think he is too sharp," said Obierika, somewhat indulgently. "He hardly ever walks. He is always in a hurry. If you are sending him on an errand he flies away before he has heard half of the message."

"You were very much like that yourself," said his eldest brother. "As our people say, 'When mother-cow is chewing grass its young ones watch its mouth.' Maduka has been watching your mouth."

As he was speaking the boy returned, followed by Akueke, his half-sister, carrying a wooden dish with three kola nuts and alligator pepper. She gave the dish to her father's eldest brother and then shook hands, very shyly, with her suitor and his relatives. She was about sixteen and just ripe for marriage. Her suitor and his relatives surveyed her young body with expert eyes as if to assure themselves that she was beautiful and ripe.

She wore a coiffure which was done up into a crest in the middle of the head. Cam wood was rubbed lightly into her skin, and all over her body were black patterns drawn with *uli*.[1] She wore a black necklace which hung down in three coils just above her full, succulent breasts. On her arms were red and yellow bangles, and on her waist four or five rows of *jigida*, or waist-beads.

---

8. To determine the time of day, indicated by the length and direction of one's shadow; at noon, the sun is directly overhead and casts no shadow.
9. "Pride of the python" (*eke*). Women were often identified by their children's name, often their first born, as mother of "so and so."
1. A kind of dye applied to the skin to form tattoo-like patterns. *Jigida* (below): Beads strewn along fine string and worn around the waist, representing therefore the most intimate form of female adornment.

When she had shaken hands, or rather held out her hand to be shaken, she returned to her mother's hut to help with the cooking.

"Remove your *jigida* first," her mother warned as she moved near the fireplace to bring the pestle resting against the wall. "Every day I tell you that *jigida* and fire are not friends. But you will never hear. You grew your ears for decoration, not for hearing. One of these days your *jigida* will catch fire on your waist, and then you will know."

Akueke moved to the other end of the hut and began to remove the waist-beads. It had to be done slowly and carefully, taking each string separately, else it would break and the thousand tiny rings would have to be strung together again. She rubbed each string downwards with her palms until it passed the buttocks and slipped down to the floor around her feet.

The men in the *obi* had already begun to drink the palm-wine which Akueke's suitor had brought. It was a very good wine and powerful, for in spite of the palm fruit hung across the mouth of the pot to restrain the lively liquor, white foam[2] rose and spilled over.

"That wine is the work of a good tapper," said Okonkwo.

The young suitor, whose name was Ibe,[3] smiled broadly and said to his father: "Do you hear that?" He then said to the others: "He will never admit that I am a good tapper."

"He tapped three of my best palm trees to death," said his father, Ukegbu.

"That was about five years ago," said Ibe, who had begun to pour out the wine, "before I learnt how to tap." He filled the first horn and gave to his father. Then he poured out for the others. Okonkwo brought out his big horn from the goatskin bag, blew into it to remove any dust that might be there, and gave it to Ibe to fill.

As the men drank, they talked about everything except the thing for which they had gathered. It was only after the pot had been emptied that the suitor's father cleared his voice and announced the object of their visit.

Obierika then presented to him a small bundle of short broomsticks. Ukegbu counted them.

"They are thirty?" he asked.

Obierika nodded in agreement.

"We are at last getting somewhere," Ukegbu said, and then turning to his brother and his son he said: "Let us go out and whisper together." The three rose and went outside. When they returned Ukegbu handed the bundle of sticks back to Obierika. He counted them; instead of thirty there were now only fifteen. He passed them over to his eldest brother, Machi, who also counted them and said:

---

2. Froth caused by the fermenting process in the palm wine.
3. A relation, member of the extended family.

"We had not thought to go below thirty. But as the dog said, 'If I fall down for you and you fall down for me, it is play'. Marriage should be a play and not a fight; so we are falling down again." He then added ten sticks to the fifteen and gave the bundle to Ukegbu.

In this way Akueke's bride-price was finally settled at twenty bags of cowries. It was already dusk when the two parties came to this agreement.

"Go and tell Akueke's mother that we have finished," Obierika said to his son, Maduka. Almost immediately the woman came in with a big bowl of foo-foo. Obierika's second wife followed with a pot of soup, and Maduka brought in a pot of palm-wine.

As the men ate and drank palm-wine they talked about the customs of their neighbours.

"It was only this morning," said Obierika, "that Okonkwo and I were talking about Abame and Aninta, where titled men climb trees and pound foo-foo for their wives."

"All their customs are upside-down. They do not decide bride-price as we do, with sticks. They haggle and bargain as if they were buying a goat or a cow in the market."

"That is very bad," said Obierika's eldest brother. "But what is good in one place is bad in another place. In Umunso they do not bargain at all, not even with broomsticks. The suitor just goes on bringing bags of cowries until his in-laws tell him to stop. It is a bad custom because it always leads to a quarrel."

"The world is large," said Okonkwo. "I have even heard that in some tribes a man's children belong to his wife and her family."

"That cannot be," said Machi. "You might as well say that the woman lies on top of the man when they are making the children."

"It is like the story of white men[4] who, they say, are white like this piece of chalk," said Obierika. He held up a piece of chalk, which every man kept in his *obi* and with which his guests drew lines on the floor before they ate kola nuts. "And these white men, they say, have no toes."

"And have you never seen them?" asked Machi.

"Have you?" asked Obierika.

"One of them passes here frequently," said Machi. "His name is Amadi."

Those who knew Amadi laughed. He was a leper, and the polite name for leprosy was 'the white skin'.

---

4. The first mention of the white man in the novel. The reference to his having no toes (kept out of view by his shoes) is immediately associated by Machi with leprosy, whose victims often lose their fingers and toes.

Chapter Nine

For the first time in three nights, Okonkwo slept. He woke up once in the middle of the night and his mind went back to the past three days without making him feel uneasy. He began to wonder why he had felt uneasy at all. It was like a man wondering in broad daylight why a dream had appeared so terrible to him at night. He stretched himself and scratched his thigh where a mosquito had bitten him as he slept. Another one was wailing near his right ear. He slapped the ear and hoped he had killed it. Why do they always go for one's ears? When he was a child his mother had told him a story about it. But it was as silly as all women's stories. Mosquito, she had said, had asked Ear to marry him, whereupon Ear fell on the floor in uncontrollable laughter. "How much longer do you think you will live?" she asked. "You are already a skeleton." Mosquito went away humiliated, and any time he passed her way he told Ear that he was still alive.

Okonkwo turned on his side and went back to sleep. He was roused in the morning by someone banging on his door.

"Who is that?" he growled. He knew it must be Ekwefi. Of his three wives Ekwefi was the only one who would have the audacity to bang on his door.

"Ezinma is dying," came her voice, and all the tragedy and sorrow of her life were packed in those words.

Okonkwo sprang from his bed, pushed back the bolt on his door and ran into Ekwefi's hut.

Ezinma lay shivering on a mat beside a huge fire that her mother had kept burning all night.

"It is *iba*,"[1] said Okonkwo as he took his matchet and went into the bush to collect the leaves and grasses and barks of trees that went into making the medicine for *iba*.

Ekwefi knelt beside the sick child, occasionally feeling with her palm the wet, burning forehead.

Ezinma was an only child and the centre of her mother's world. Very often it was Ezinma who decided what food her mother should prepare. Ekwefi even gave her such delicacies as eggs, which children were rarely allowed to eat because such food tempted them to steal. One day as Ezinma was eating an egg Okonkwo had come in unexpectedly from his hut. He was greatly shocked and swore to beat Ekwefi if she dared to give the child eggs again. But it was impossible to refuse Ezinma anything. After her father's rebuke she developed an even keener appetite for eggs. And she enjoyed above all the secrecy in which she now ate them. Her mother always took her into their bedroom and shut the door.

---

1. Malarial fever.

Ezinma did not call her mother *Nne*[2] like all children. She called her by her name, Ekwefi, as her father and other grown-up people did. The relationship between them was not only that of mother and child. There was something in it like the companionship of equals, which was strengthened by such little conspiracies as eating eggs in the bedroom.

Ekwefi had suffered a good deal in her life. She had borne ten children and nine of them had died in infancy, usually before the age of three. As she buried one child after another her sorrow gave way to despair and then to grim resignation. The birth of her children, which should be a woman's crowning glory, became for Ekwefi mere physical agony devoid of promise. The naming ceremony after seven market weeks became an empty ritual. Her deepening despair found expression in the names she gave her children. One of them was a pathetic cry, Onwumbiko—'Death, I implore you.' But Death took no notice; Onwumbiko died in his fifteenth month. The next child was a girl, Ozoemena—'May it not happen again.' She died in her eleventh month, and two others after her. Ekwefi then became defiant and called her next child Onwuma—'Death may please himself.' And he did.

After the death of Ekwefi's second child, Okonkwo had gone to a medicine-man, who was also a diviner of the Afa[3] Oracle, to inquire what was amiss. This man told him that the child was an *ogbanje*,[4] one of those wicked children who, when they died, entered their mothers' wombs to be born again.

"When your wife becomes pregnant again," he said, "let her not sleep in her hut. Let her go and stay with her people. In that way she will elude her wicked tormentor and break its evil cycle of birth and death."

Ekwefi did as she was asked. As soon as she became pregnant she went to live with her old mother in another village. It was there that her third child was born and circumcised on the eighth day. She did not return to Okonkwo's compound until three days before the naming ceremony. The child was called Onwumbiko.

Onwumbiko was not given proper burial when he died. Okonkwo had called in another medicine-man[5] who was famous in the clan for his great knowledge about *ogbanje* children. His name was Okagbue Uyanwa.[6] Okagbue was a very striking figure, tall, with a full beard

---

2. "Mother."
3. Part of the system of divination in West Africa, which includes *Ifa* among the Yoruba in Nigeria and *Fa* among the Gun and Fon in the Benin Republic (formerly Dahomey). Among the Igbo, Afa was controlled by the priests of the ancient Nri-Kingdom to ensure its hegemony over its neighbors (see Onwuejeogwu, 1981).
4. See note 3, p. 30. We are presented here in detail with the mental agony caused by the child and the desperate measures taken to prevent its return.
5. *Dibia*, in Igbo; healer and diviner, thought to be endowed with supernatural powers.
6. *Okagbue* means: "I have put a stop to evil and all forms of ill omen." *Uyanwa* suggests that he looks after children (*nwa*).

and a bald head. He was light in complexion and his eyes were red and fiery. He always gnashed his teeth as he listened to those who came to consult him. He asked Okonkwo a few questions about the dead child. All the neighbours and relations who had come to mourn gathered round them.

"On what market-day was it born?" he asked.

"*Oye*," replied Okonkwo.

"And it died this morning?"

Okonkwo said yes, and only then realised for the first time that the child had died on the same market-day as it had been born. The neighbours and relations also saw the coincidence and said among themselves that it was very significant.

"Where do you sleep with your wife, in your *obi* or in her own hut?" asked the medicine-man.

"In her hut."

"In future call her into your *obi*."

The medicine-man then ordered that there should be no mourning for the dead child. He brought out a sharp razor from the goatskin bag slung from his left shoulder and began to mutilate the child.[7] Then he took it away to bury in the Evil Forest, holding it by the ankle and dragging it on the ground behind him. After such treatment it would think twice before coming again, unless it was one of the stubborn ones who returned, carrying the stamp of their mutilation—a missing finger or perhaps a dark line where the medicine-man's razor had cut them.

By the time Onwumbiko died Ekwefi had become a very bitter woman. Her husband's first wife had already had three sons, all strong and healthy. When she had borne her third son in succession, Okonkwo had slaughtered a goat for her, as was the custom. Ekwefi had nothing but good wishes for her. But she had grown so bitter about her own *chi* that she could not rejoice with others over their good fortune. And so, on the day that Nwoye's mother celebrated the birth of her three sons with feasting and music, Ekwefi was the only person in the happy company who went about with a cloud on her brow. Her husband's wife took this for malevolence, as husband's wives were wont to. How could she know that Ekwefi's bitterness did not flow outwards to others but inwards into her own soul; that she did not blame others for their good fortune but her own evil *chi* who denied her any?

At last Ezinma was born, and although ailing she seemed determined to live. At first Ekwefi accepted her, as she had accepted

---

7. So it cannot be recognized and thus to discourage it from returning to earth. Note the deliberate character of the *dibia*'s action, suggesting his experience and confidence in his own powers.

others—with listless resignation. But when she lived on to her fourth, fifth and sixth years, love returned once more to her mother, and, with love, anxiety. She determined to nurse her child to health, and she put all her being into it. She was rewarded by occasional spells of health during which Ezinma bubbled with energy like fresh palm-wine. At such times she seemed beyond danger. But all of a sudden she would go down again. Everybody knew she was an *ogbanje*. These sudden bouts of sickness and health were typical of her kind. But she had lived so long that perhaps she had decided to stay. Some of them did become tired of their evil rounds of birth and death, or took pity on their mothers, and stayed. Ekwefi believed deep inside her that Ezinma had come to stay. She believed because it was that faith alone that gave her own life any kind of meaning. And this faith had been strengthened when a year or so ago a medicine-man had dug up Ezinma's *iyi-uwa*.[8] Everyone knew then that she would live because her bond with the world of *ogbanje* had been broken. Ekwefi was reassured. But such was her anxiety for her daughter that she could not rid herself completely of her fear. And although she believed that the *iyi-uwa* which had been dug up was genuine, she could not ignore the fact that some really evil children sometimes misled people into digging up a specious one.

But Ezinma's *iyi-uwa* had looked real enough. It was a smooth pebble wrapped in a dirty rag. The man who dug it up was the same Okagbue who was famous in all the clan for his knowledge in these matters. Ezinma had not wanted to co-operate with him at first. But that was only to be expected. No *ogbanje* would yield her secrets easily, and most of them never did because they died too young—before they could be asked questions.

"Where did you bury your *iyi-uwa*?" Okagbue had asked Ezinma. She was nine then and was just recovering from a serious illness.

"What is *iyi-uwa*?" she asked in return.

"You know what it is. You buried it in the ground somewhere so that you can die and return again to torment your mother."

Ezinma looked at her mother, whose eyes, sad and pleading, were fixed on her.

"Answer the question at once," roared Okonkwo, who stood beside her. All the family were there and some of the neighbours too.

"Leave her to me," the medicine-man told Okonkwo in a cool, confident voice. He turned again to Ezinma. "Where did you bury your *iyi-uwa*?"

"Where they bury children," she replied, and the quiet spectators murmured to themselves.

---

8. Or mark of reincarnation. An aspect of Igbo belief is foregrounded in this episode for its dramatic significance.

"Come along then and show me the spot," said the medicine-man.

The crowd set out with Ezinma leading the way and Okagbue following closely behind her. Okonkwo came next and Ekwefi followed him. When she came to the main road, Ezinma turned left as if she was going to the stream.

"But you said it was where they bury children?" asked the medicine-man.

"No," said Ezinma, whose feeling of importance was manifest in her sprightly walk. She sometimes broke into a run and stopped again suddenly. The crowd followed her silently. Women and children returning from the stream with pots of water on their heads wondered what was happening until they saw Okagbue and guessed that it must be something to do with *ogbanje*. And they all knew Ekwefi and her daughter very well.

When she got to the big udala tree Ezinma turned left into the bush, and the crowd followed her. Because of her size she made her way through trees and creepers more quickly than her followers. The bush was alive with the tread of feet on dry leaves and sticks and the moving aside of tree branches. Ezinma went deeper and deeper and the crowd went with her. Then she suddenly turned round and began to walk back to the road. Everybody stood to let her pass and then filed after her.

"If you bring us all this way for nothing I shall beat sense into you," Okonkwo threatened.

"I have told you to let her alone. I know how to deal with them," said Okagbue.

Ezinma led the way back to the road, looked left and right and turned right. And so they arrived home again.

"Where did you bury your *iyi-uwa*?" asked Okagbue when Ezinma finally stopped outside her father's *obi*. Okagbue's voice was unchanged. It was quiet and confident.

"It is near that orange tree," Ezinma said.

"And why did you not say so, you wicked daughter of Akalogoli?"[9] Okonkwo swore furiously. The medicine-man ignored him.

"Come and show me the exact spot," he said quietly to Ezinma.

"It is here," she said when they got to the tree.

"Point at the spot with your finger," said Okagbue.

"It is here," said Ezinma touching the ground with her finger. Okonkwo stood by, rumbling like thunder in the rainy season.

"Bring me a hoe," said Okagbue.

When Ekwefi brought the hoe, he had already put aside his goatskin bag and his big cloth and was in his underwear, a long and

9. Literally, "good for nothing." The name seems to be satirical.

thin strip of cloth wound round the waist like a belt and then passed between the legs to be fastened to the belt behind. He immediately set to work digging a pit where Ezinma had indicated. The neighbours sat around watching the pit becoming deeper and deeper. The dark top-soil soon gave way to the bright-red earth with which women scrubbed the floor and walls of huts. Okagbue worked tirelessly and in silence, his back shining with perspiration. Okonkwo stood by the pit. He asked Okagbue to come up and rest while he took a hand. But Okagbue said he was not tired yet.

Ekwefi went into her hut to cook yams. Her husband had brought out more yams than usual because the medicine-man had to be fed. Ezinma went with her and helped in preparing the vegetables.

"There is too much green vegetable," she said.

"Don't you see the pot is full of yams?" Ekwefi asked.

"And you know how leaves become smaller after cooking."

"Yes," said Ezinma, "that was why the snake-lizard killed his mother."

"Very true," said Ekwefi.

"He gave his mother seven baskets of vegetables to cook and in the end there were only three. And so he killed her," said Ezinma.

"That is not the end of the story."

"Oho," said Ezinma. "I remember now. He brought another seven baskets and cooked them himself. And there were again only three. So he killed himself too."

Outside the *obi* Okagbue and Okonkwo were digging the pit to find where Ezinma had buried her *iyi-uwa*. Neighbours sat around, watching. The pit was now so deep that they no longer saw the digger. They only saw the red earth he threw up mounting higher and higher. Okonkwo's son, Nwoye, stood near the edge of the pit because he wanted to take in all that happened.

Okagbue had again taken over the digging from Okonkwo. He worked, as usual, in silence. The neighbours and Okonkwo's wives were now talking. The children had lost interest and were playing.

Suddenly Okagbue sprang to the surface with the agility of a leopard.

"It is very near now," he said. "I have felt it."

There was immediate excitement and those who were sitting jumped to their feet.

"Call your wife and child," he said to Okonkwo. But Ekwefi and Ezinma had heard the noise and run out to see what it was.

Okagbue went back into the pit, which was now surrounded by spectators. After a few more hoe-fuls of earth he struck the *iyi-uwa*. He raised it carefully with the hoe and threw it to the surface. Some women ran away in fear when it was thrown. But they soon returned and everyone was gazing at the rag from a reasonable distance. Okagbue emerged and without saying a word or even looking at the spectators he went to his goatskin bag, took out two leaves and began to chew them.[1] When he had swallowed them, he took up the rag with his left hand and began to untie it. And then the smooth, shiny pebble fell out. He picked it up.

"Is this yours?" he asked Ezinma.

"Yes," she replied. All the women shouted with joy because Ekwefi's troubles were at last ended.

All this had happened more than a year ago and Ezinma had not been ill since. And then suddenly she had begun to shiver in the night. Ekwefi brought her to the fireplace, spread her mat on the floor and built a fire. But she had got worse and worse. As she knelt by her, feeling with her palm the wet, burning forehead, she prayed a thousand times. Although her husband's wives were saying that it was nothing more than *iba*, she did not hear them.

Okonkwo returned from the bush carrying on his left shoulder a large bundle of grasses and leaves, roots and barks of medicinal trees and shrubs. He went into Ekwefi's hut, put down his load and sat down.

"Get me a pot," he said, "and leave the child alone."

Ekwefi went to bring the pot and Okonkwo selected the best from his bundle, in their due proportions, and cut them up. He put them in the pot and Ekwefi poured in some water.

"Is that enough?" she asked when she had poured in about half of the water in the bowl.

"A little more . . . I said a *little*. Are you deaf?" Okonkwo roared at her.

She set the pot on the fire and Okonkwo took up his matchet to return to his *obi*.

"You must watch the pot carefully," he said as he went, "and don't allow it to boil over. If it does its power will be gone." He went away to his hut and Ekwefi began to tend the medicine pot almost as if it was itself a sick child. Her eyes went constantly from Ezinma to the boiling pot and back to Ezinma.

Okonkwo returned when he felt the medicine had cooked long enough. He looked it over and said it was done.

"Bring a low stool for Ezinma," he said, "and a thick mat."

He took down the pot from the fire and placed it in front of the stool. He then roused Ezinma and placed her on the stool, astride the steaming pot. The thick mat was thrown over both. Ezinma struggled to escape from the choking and overpowering steam, but she was held down. She started to cry.

---

1. Ritual leaves meant to afford him protection against malevolent forces, a precaution he takes given the danger his profession is believed to involve.

When the mat was at last removed she was drenched in perspiration. Ekwefi mopped her with a piece of cloth and she lay down on a dry mat and was soon asleep.

Chapter Ten

Large crowds began to gather on the village *ilo* as soon as the edge had worn off the sun's heat and it was no longer painful on the body. Most communal ceremonies took place at that time of the day, so that even when it was said that a ceremony would begin "after the mid-day meal" everyone understood that it would begin a long time later, when the sun's heat had softened.

It was clear from the way the crowd stood or sat that the ceremony was for men. There were many women, but they looked on from the fringe like outsiders. The titled men and elders sat on their stools waiting for the trials to begin. In front of them was a row of stools on which nobody sat. There were nine of them. Two little groups of people stood at a respectable distance beyond the stools. They faced the elders. There were three men in one group and three men and one woman in the other. The woman was Mgbafo[1] and the three men with her were her brothers. In the other group were her husband, Uzowulu,[2] and his relatives. Mgbafo and her brothers were as still as statues into whose faces the artist has moulded defiance. Uzowulu and his relative, on the other hand, were whispering together. It looked like whispering, but they were really talking at the top of their voices. Everybody in the crowd was talking. It was like the market. From a distance the noise was a deep rumble carried by the wind.

An iron gong sounded, setting up a wave of expectation in the crowd. Everyone looked in the direction of the *egwugwu* house. *Gome, gome, gome, gome* went the gong, and a powerful flute blew a high-pitched blast. Then came the voices of the *egwugwu*, guttural and awesome. The wave struck the women and children and there was a backward stampede. But it was momentary. They were already far enough where they stood and there was room for running away if any of the *egwugwu* should go towards them.

The drum sounded again and the flute blew. The *egwugwu* house was now a pandemonium of quavering voices: *Aru oyim*[3] *de de de dei!* filled the air as the spirits of the ancestors, just emerged from the

1. Born on Afo market day.
2. "The road that I built."
3. "My friend's body." The expression stresses the masquerade's spiritual essence as opposed to the human being who is made of mere animal or vegetable matter. The words are meant to send shivers down the spines of the onlookers.

earth, greeted themselves in their esoteric language. The *egwugwu*
house into which they emerged faced the forest, away from the
crowd, who saw only its back with the many-coloured patterns and
drawings done by specially chosen women at regular intervals. These
women never saw the inside of the hut. No woman ever did. They
scrubbed and painted the outside walls under the supervision of men.
If they imagined what was inside, they kept their imagination to
themselves. No woman ever asked questions about the most powerful and the most secret cult in the clan.

Aru oyim de de de dei! flew around the dark, closed hut like
tongues of fire. The ancestral spirits of the clan were abroad. The
metal gong beat continuously now and the flute, shrill and powerful,
floated on the chaos.

And then the *egwugwu* appeared. The women and children sent up
a great shout and took to their heels. It was instinctive. A woman fled
as soon as an *egwugwu* came in sight. And when, as on that day, nine
of the greatest masked spirits in the clan came out together it was a
terrifying spectacle. Even Mgbafo took to her heels and had to be
restrained by her brothers.

Each of the nine *egwugwu* represented a village of the clan. Their
leader was called Evil Forest. Smoke poured out of his head.

The nine villages[4] of Umuofia had grown out of the nine sons of
the first father of the clan. Evil Forest represented the village of
Umueru, or the children of Eru, who was the eldest of the nine sons.

"*Umuofia kwenu!*" shouted the leading *egwugwu*, pushing the air
with his raffia arms. The elders of the clan replied, "*Yaa!*"

"*Umuofia kwenu!*"

"*Yaa!*"

"*Umuofia kwenu!*"

"*Yaa!*"

Evil Forest then thrust the pointed end of his rattling staff into the
earth. And it began to shake and rattle, like something agitating with
a metallic life. He took the first of the empty stools and the eight
other *egwugwu* began to sit in order of seniority after him.

Okonkwo's wives, and perhaps other women as well, might have
noticed that the second *egwugwu* had the springy walk of Okonkwo.
And they might also have noticed that Okonkwo was not among the
titled men and elders who sat behind the row of *egwugwu*. But if they
thought these things they kept them within themselves. The
egwugwu with the springy walk was one of the dead fathers of the
clan. He looked terrible with the smoked raffia body, a huge wooden
face painted white except for the round hollow eyes and the charred

---

4. The full clan in conclave, as it were.

teeth that were as big as a man's fingers. On his head were two powerful horns.

When all the *egwugwu* had sat down and the sound of the many
tiny bells and rattles on their bodies had subsided, Evil Forest
addressed the two groups of people facing them.

"Uzowulu's body, I salute you," he said. Spirits always addressed
humans as 'bodies'. Uzowulu bent down and touched the earth with
his right hand as a sign of submission.

"Our father, my hand has touched the ground," he said.

"Uzowulu's body, do you know me?" asked the spirit.

"How can I know you, father? You are beyond our knowledge."

Evil Forest then turned to the other group and addressed the eldest of the three brothers.

"The body of Odukwe,[5] I greet you," he said, and Odukwe bent
down and touched the earth. The hearing then began.

Uzowulu stepped forward and presented his case.

"That woman standing there is my wife, Mgbafo. I married her with
my money and my yams. I do not owe my in-laws anything. I owe them
no yams. I owe them no coco-yams. One morning three of them came
to my house, beat me up and took my wife and children away. This
happened in the rainy season. I have waited in vain for my wife to
return. At last I went to my in-laws and said to them, 'You have taken
back your sister. I did not send her away. You yourselves took her. The
law of the clan is that you should return her bride-price.' But my wife's
brothers said they had nothing to tell me. So I have brought the matter to the fathers of the clan. My case is finished. I salute you."

"Your words are good," said the leader of the *egwugwu*. "Let us hear
Odukwe. His words may also be good."

Odukwe was short and thick-set. He stepped forward, saluted the
spirits and began his story.

"My in-law has told you that we went to his house, beat him up and
took our sister and her children away. All that is true. He told you that
he came to take back her bride-price and we refused to give it him.
That also is true. My in-law, Uzowulu, is a beast. My sister lived with
him for nine years. During those years no single day passed in the sky
without his beating the woman. We have tried to settle their quarrels
time without number and on each occasion Uzowulu was guilty—"

"It is a lie!" Uzowulu shouted.

"Two years ago," continued Odukwe, "when she was pregnant, he
beat her until she miscarried."

"It is a lie. She miscarried after she had gone to sleep with her
lover."

5. A formal or ceremonial form of address.

"Uzowulu's body, I salute you," said Evil Forest, silencing him. "What kind of lover sleeps with a pregnant woman?" There was a loud murmur of approbation from the crowd. Odukwe continued:

"Last year when my sister was recovering from an illness, he beat her again so that if the neighbours had not gone in to save her she would have been killed. We heard of it, and did as you have been told. The law of Umuofia is that if a woman runs away from her husband her bride-price is returned. But in this case she ran away to save her life. Her two children belong to Uzowulu. We do not dispute it, but they are too young to leave their mother. If, on the other hand, Uzowulu should recover from his madness and come in the proper way to beg his wife to return she will do so on the understanding that if he ever beats her again we shall cut off his genitals for him."

The crowd roared with laughter. Evil Forest rose to his feet and order was immediately restored. A steady cloud of smoke rose from his head. He sat down again and called two witnesses. They were both Uzowulu's neighbours, and they agreed about the beating. Evil Forest then stood up, pulled out his staff and thrust it into the earth again. He ran a few steps in the direction of the women; they all fled in terror, only to return to their places almost immediately. The nine *egwugwu* then went away to consult together in their house. They were silent for a long time. Then the metal gong sounded and the flute was blown. The *egwugwu* had emerged once again from their underground home.[6] They saluted one another and then reappeared on the *ilo*.

"*Umuofia kwenu!*" roared Evil Forest, facing the elders and grandees of the clan.

"*Yaa!*" replied the thunderous crowd; then silence descended from the sky and swallowed the noise.

Evil Forest began to speak and all the while he spoke everyone was silent. The eight other *egwugwu* were as still as statues.

"We have heard both sides of the case," said Evil Forest. "Our duty is not to blame this man or to praise that, but to settle the dispute." He turned to Uzowulu's group and allowed a short pause.

"Uzowulu's body, I salute you," he said.

"Our father, my hand has touched the ground," replied Uzowulu, touching the earth.

"Uzowulu's body, do you know me?"

"How can I know you, father? You are beyond our knowledge," Uzowulu replied.

"I am Evil Forest. I kill a man on the day that his life is sweetest to him."

6. The abode of the ancestors.

"That is true," replied Uzowulu.

"Go to your in-laws with a pot of wine and beg your wife to return to you. It is not bravery when a man fights with a woman." He turned to Odukwe, and allowed a brief pause.

"Odukwe's body, I greet you," he said.

"My hand is on the ground," replied Odukwe.

"Do you know me?"

"No man can know you," replied Odukwe.

"I am Evil Forest, I am Dry-meat-that-fills-the-mouth, I am Fire-that-burns-without-faggots. If your in-law brings wine to you, let your sister go with him. I salute you." He pulled his staff from the hard earth and thrust it back.

"*Umuofia kwenu!*" he roared, and the crowd answered.

"I don't know why such a trifle should come before the *egwugwu*," said one elder to another.

"Don't you know what kind of man Uzowulu is? He will not listen to any other decision," replied the other.

As they spoke two other groups of people had replaced the first before the *egwugwu*, and a great land case began.

Chapter Eleven

The night was impenetrably dark. The moon had been rising later and later every night until now it was seen only at dawn. And whenever the moon forsook evening and rose at cock-crow the nights were as black as charcoal.

Ezinma and her mother sat on a mat on the floor after their supper of yam foo-foo and bitter-leaf soup. A palm-oil lamp gave out yellowish light. Without it, it would have been impossible to eat; one could not have known where one's mouth was in the darkness of that night. There was an oil lamp in all the four huts on Okonkwo's compound, and each hut seen from the others looked like a soft eye of yellow half-light set in the solid massiveness of night.

The world was silent except for the shrill cry of insects, which was part of the night, and the sound of wooden mortar and pestle as Nwayieke pounded her foo-foo. Nwayieke lived four compounds away, and she was notorious for her late cooking. Every woman in the neighbourhood knew the sound of Nwayieke's mortar and pestle. It was also part of the night.

Okonkwo had eaten from his wives' dishes and was now reclining with his back against the wall. He searched his bag and brought out his snuff-bottle. He turned it on to his left palm, but nothing came out. He hit the bottle against his knee to shake up the tobacco. That was always the trouble with Okeke's snuff. It very quickly went damp,

and there was too much saltpetre[1] in it. Okonkwo had not bought
snuff from him for a long time. Idigo was the man who knew how to
grind good snuff. But he had recently fallen ill.

Low voices, broken now and again by singing, reached Okonkwo
from his wives' huts as each woman and her children told folk stories.
Ekwefi and her daughter, Ezinma, sat on a mat on the floor. It was
Ekwefi's turn to tell a story.

"Once upon a time," she began, "all the birds were invited to a feast
in the sky. They were very happy and began to prepare themselves for
the great day. They painted their bodies with red cam wood and drew
beautiful patterns on them with *uli*.

"Tortoise saw all these preparations and soon discovered what it all
meant. Nothing that happened in the world of the animals ever
escaped his notice; he was full of cunning. As soon as he heard of the
great feast in the sky his throat began to itch at the very thought.
There was a famine in those days and Tortoise had not eaten a good
meal for two moons. His body rattled like a piece of dry stick in his
empty shell. So he began to plan how he would go to the sky."

"But he had no wings," said Ezinma.

"Be patient," replied her mother. "That is the story. Tortoise had no
wings, but he went to the birds and asked to be allowed to go with
them.

" 'We know you too well,' said the birds when they had heard him.
'You are full of cunning and you are ungrateful. If we allow you to
come with us you will soon begin your mischief.'

" 'You do not know me,' said Tortoise. 'I am a changed man. I have
learnt that a man who makes trouble for others is also making it for
himself.'

"Tortoise had a sweet tongue, and within a short time all the birds
agreed that he was a changed man, and they each gave him a feather,
with which he made two wings.

"At last the great day came and Tortoise was the first to arrive at
the meeting-place. When all the birds had gathered together, they set
off in a body. Tortoise was very happy and voluble as he flew among
the birds, and he was soon chosen as the man to speak for the party
because he was a great orator.

" 'There is one important thing which we must not forget,' he said
as they flew on their way. 'When people are invited to a great feast like
this, they take new names for the occasion. Our hosts in the sky will
expect us to honour this age-old custom.'

"None of the birds had heard of this custom but they knew that
Tortoise, in spite of his failings in other directions, was a widely-

---

1. A naturally occurring compound (potassium nitrate) also used as a condiment.

travelled man who knew the customs of different peoples. And so they each took a new name. When they had all taken, Tortoise also took one. He was to be called *All of you*.

"At last the party arrived in the sky and their hosts were very happy to see them. Tortoise stood up in his many-coloured plumage and thanked them for their invitation. His speech was so eloquent that all the birds were glad they had brought him, and nodded their heads in approval of all he said. Their hosts took him as the king of the birds, especially as he looked somewhat different from the others.

"After kola nuts had been presented and eaten, the people of the sky set before their guests the most delectable dishes Tortoise had ever seen or dreamt of. The soup was brought out hot from the fire and in the very pot in which it had been cooked. It was full of meat and fish. Tortoise began to sniff aloud. There was pounded yam and also yam pottage cooked with palm-oil and fresh fish. There were also pots of palm-wine. When everything had been set before the guests, one of the people of the sky came forward and tasted a little from each pot. He then invited the birds to eat. But Tortoise jumped to his feet and asked: 'For whom have you prepared this feast?'

"'For all of you,' replied the man.

"Tortoise turned to the birds and said: 'You remember that my name is *All of you*. The custom here is to serve the spokesman first and the others later. They will serve you when I have eaten.'

"He began to eat and the birds grumbled angrily. The people of the sky thought it must be their custom to leave all the food for their king. And so Tortoise ate the best part of the food and then drank two pots of palm-wine, so that he was full of food and drink and his body filled out in his shell.

"The birds gathered round to eat what was left and to peck at the bones he had thrown all about the floor. Some of them were too angry to eat. They chose to fly home on an empty stomach. But before they left each took back the feather he had lent to Tortoise. And there he stood in his hard shell full of food and wine but without any wings to fly home. He asked the birds to take a message for his wife, but they all refused. In the end Parrot, who had felt more angry than the others, suddenly changed his mind and agreed to take the message.

"'Tell my wife,' said Tortoise, 'to bring out all the soft things in my house and cover the compound with them so that I can jump down from the sky without very great danger.'

"Parrot promised to deliver the message, and then flew away. But when he reached Tortoise's house he told his wife to bring out all the hard things in the house. And so she brought out her husband's hoes, matchets, spears, guns and even his cannon. Tortoise looked down from the sky and saw his wife bringing things out, but it was too far to see what they were. When all seemed ready he let himself go. He fell and fell and fell until he began to fear that he would never stop falling. And then like the sound of his cannon he crashed on the compound."

"Did he die?" asked Ezinma.

"No," replied Ekwefi. "His shell broke into pieces. But there was a great medicine-man in the neighbourhood. Tortoise's wife sent for him and he gathered all the bits of shell and stuck them together. That is why Tortoise's shell is not smooth."

"There is no song in the story," Ezinma pointed out.

"No," said Ekwefi. "I shall think of another one with a song. But it is your turn now."

"Once upon a time," Ezinma began, "Tortoise and Cat went to wrestle against Yams—no, that is not the beginning. Once upon a time there was a great famine in the land of animals. Everybody was lean except Cat, who was fat and whose body shone as if oil was rubbed on it . . ."

She broke off because at that very moment a loud and high-pitched voice broke the outer silence of the night. It was Chielo, the priestess of Agbala, prophesying. There was nothing new in that. Once in a while Chielo was possessed by the spirit of her god and she began to prophesy. But tonight she was addressing her prophecy and greetings to Okonkwo, and so everyone in his family listened. The folk stories stopped.

"*Agbala do-o-o-o! Agbala ekeneo-o-o-o*," came the voice like a sharp knife cutting through the night. "*Okonkwo! Agbala ekene gio-o-o-o! Agbala cholu ifu ada ya Ezinmao-o-o-o!*"[2]

At the mention of Ezinma's name Ekwefi jerked her head sharply like an animal that had sniffed death in the air. Her heart jumped painfully within her.

The priestess had now reached Okonkwo's compound and was talking with him outside his hut. She was saying again and again that Agbala wanted to see his daughter, Ezinma. Okonkwo pleaded with her to come back in the morning because Ezinma was now asleep. But Chielo ignored what he was trying to say and went on shouting that Agbala wanted to see his daughter. Her voice was as clear as metal, and Okonkwo's women and children heard from their huts all that she said. Okonkwo was still pleading that the girl had been ill of late and was asleep. Ekwefi quickly took her to their bedroom and placed her on their high bamboo bed.

The priestess suddenly screamed. "Beware, Okonkwo!" she warned. "Beware of exchanging words with Agbala. Does a man speak when a god speaks? Beware!"

2. "Agbala wants to see his daughter Ezinma."

She walked through Okonkwo's hut into the circular compound and went straight towards Ekwefi's hut. Okonkwo came after her.

"Ekwefi," she called, "Agbala greets you. Where is my daughter,[3] Ezinma? Agbala wants to see her."

Ekwefi came out from her hut carrying her oil lamp in her left hand. There was a light wind blowing, so she cupped her right hand to shelter the flame. Nwoye's mother, also carrying an oil lamp, emerged from her hut. Her children stood in the darkness outside their hut watching the strange event. Okonkwo's youngest wife also came out and joined the others.

"Where does Agbala want to see her?" Ekwefi asked.

"Where else but in his house in the hills and the caves?" replied the priestess.

"I will come with you, too," Ekwefi said firmly.

"*Tufia-a!*"[4] the priestess cursed, her voice cracking like the angry bark of thunder in the dry season. "How dare you, woman, to go before the mighty Agbala of your own accord? Beware, woman, lest he strike you in his anger. Bring me my daughter."

Ekwefi went into her hut and came out again with Ezinma.

"Come, my daughter," said the priestess. "I shall carry you on my back. A baby on its mother's back does not know that the way is long."

Ezinma began to cry. She was used to Chielo calling her 'my daughter'. But it was a different Chielo she now saw in the yellow half-light.

"Don't cry, my daughter," said the priestess, "lest Agbala be angry with you."

"Don't cry," said Ekwefi, "she will bring you back very soon. I shall give you some fish to eat." She went into the hut again and brought down the smoke-black basket in which she kept her dried fish and other ingredients for cooking soup. She broke a piece in two and gave it to Ezinma, who clung to her.

"Don't be afraid," said Ekwefi, stroking her head, which was shaved in places, leaving a regular pattern of hair. They went outside again. The priestess bent down on one knee and Ezinma climbed on her back, her left palm closed on her fish and her eyes gleaming with tears.

"*Agbala do-o-o-o! Agbala ekeneo-o-o-o!* . . ." Chielo began once again to chant greetings to her god. She turned round sharply and walked through Okonkwo's hut, bending very low at the eaves. Ezinma was crying loudly now, calling on her mother. The two voices disappeared into the thick darkness.

A strange and sudden weakness descended on Ekwefi as she stood gazing in the direction of the voices like a hen whose only chick has

3. In a mystical sense; already, Chielo sees Ezinma as the successor to her priestly function.
4. An exclamation of revulsion before a taboo.

been carried away by a kite. Ezinma's voice soon faded away and only Chielo was heard moving farther and farther into the distance.

"Why do you stand there as though she had been kidnapped?" asked Okonkwo as he went back to his hut.

"She will bring her back soon," Nwoye's mother said.

But Ekwefi did not hear these consolations. She stood for a while, and then, all of a sudden, made up her mind. She hurried through Okonkwo's hut and went outside. "Where are you going?" he asked.

"I am following Chielo," she replied and disappeared in the darkness. Okonkwo cleared his throat, and brought out his snuff-bottle from the goatskin bag by his side.

The priestess's voice was already growing faint in the distance. Ekwefi hurried to the main footpath and turned left in the direction of the voice. Her eyes were useless to her in the darkness. But she picked her way easily on the sandy footpath hedged on either side by branches and damp leaves. She began to run, holding her breasts with her hands to stop them flapping noisily against her body. She hit her left foot against an outcropped root, and terror seized her. It was an ill omen. She ran faster. But Chielo's voice was still a long way away. Had she been running too? How could she go so fast with Ezinma on her back? Although the night was cool, Ekwefi was beginning to feel hot from her running. She continually ran into the luxuriant weeds and creepers that walled in the path. Once she tripped up and fell. Only then did she realise, with a start, that Chielo had stopped her chanting. Her heart beat violently and she stood still. Then Chielo's renewed outburst came from only a few paces ahead. But Ekwefi could not see her. She shut her eyes for a while and opened them again in an effort to see. But it was useless. She could not see beyond her nose.

There were no stars in the sky because there was a rain-cloud. Fire-flies went about with their tiny green lamps, which only made the darkness more profound. Between Chielo's outbursts the night was alive with the shrill tremor of forest insects woven into the darkness.

"*Agbala do-o-o-o!* . . . *Agbala ekeneo-o-o-o!* . . ." Ekwefi trudged behind, neither getting too near nor keeping too far back. She thought they must be going towards the sacred cave. Now that she walked slowly she had time to think. What would she do when they got to the cave? She would not dare to enter. She would wait at the mouth, all alone in that fearful place. She thought of all the terrors of the night. She remembered the night, long ago, when she had seen *Ogbu-agali-odu*,[5] one of those evil essences loosed upon the world by

5. "The one who kills."

the potent 'medicines' which the tribe had made in the distant past
against its enemies but had now forgotten how to control. Ekwefi had
been returning from the stream with her mother on a dark night like
this when they saw its glow as it flew in their direction. They had
thrown down their water-pots and lain by the roadside expecting the
sinister light to descend on them and kill them. That was the only
time Ekwefi ever saw *Ogbu-agali-odu*. But although it had happened
so long ago, her blood still ran cold whenever she remembered that
night.

The priestess's voice came at longer intervals now, but its vigour
was undiminished. The air was cool and damp with dew. Ezinma
sneezed. Ekwefi muttered, "Life to you." At the same time the priestess also said, "Life to you, my daughter." Ezinma's voice from the
darkness warmed her mother's heart. She trudged slowly along.

And then the priestess screamed. "Somebody is walking behind
me!" she said. "Whether you are spirit or man, may Agbala shave your
head with a blunt razor! May he twist your neck until you see your
heels!"

Ekwefi stood rooted to the spot. One mind said to her: 'Woman, go
home before Agbala does you harm.' But she could not. She stood until
Chielo had increased the distance between them and she began to follow again. She had already walked so long that she began to feel a slight
numbness in the limbs and in the head. Then it occurred to her that
they could not have been heading for the cave. They must have bypassed it long ago; they must be going towards Umuachi,[6] the farthest
village in the clan. Chielo's voice now came after long intervals.

It seemed to Ekwefi that the night had become a little lighter. The
cloud had lifted and a few stars were out. The moon must be preparing to rise, its sullenness over. When the moon rose late in the night,
people said it was refusing food, as a sullen husband refuses his wife's
food when they have quarrelled.

"*Agbala do-o-o-o! Umuachi! Agbala ekene unuo-o-o!*" It was just as
Ekwefi had thought. The priestess was now saluting the village of
Umuachi. It was unbelievable, the distance they had covered. As they
emerged into the open village from the narrow forest track the darkness was softened and it became possible to see the vague shape of
trees. Ekwefi screwed her eyes up in an effort to see her daughter and
the priestess, but whenever she thought she saw their shape it immediately dissolved like a melting lump of darkness. She walked numbly
along.

Chielo's voice was now rising continuously, as when she first set
out. Ekwefi had a feeling of spacious openness, and she guessed they

---

6. The town's landmark is a special tree (*achi*) whose seeds are used in soup.

must be on the village *ilo*, or playground. And she realised too with
something like a jerk that Chielo was no longer moving forward. She
was, in fact, returning. Ekwefi quickly moved away from her line of
retreat. Chielo passed by, and they began to go back the way they had
come.

It was a long and weary journey and Ekwefi felt like a sleep-walker
most of the way. The moon was definitely rising, and although it had
not yet appeared on the sky its light had already melted down the
darkness. Ekwefi could now discern the figure of the priestess and
her burden. She slowed down her pace so as to increase the distance
between them. She was afraid of what might happen if Chielo suddenly turned round and saw her.

She had prayed for the moon to rise. But now she found the half-
light of the incipient moon more terrifying than darkness. The world
was now peopled with vague, fantastic figures that dissolved under
her steady gaze and then formed again in new shapes. At one stage
Ekwefi was so afraid that she nearly called out to Chielo for companionship and human sympathy. What she had seen was the shape
of a man climbing a palm tree, his head pointing to the earth and his
legs skywards. But at that very moment Chielo's voice rose again in
her possessed chanting, and Ekwefi recoiled, because there was no
humanity there. It was not the same Chielo who sat with her in the
market and sometimes bought bean-cakes for Ezinma, whom she
called her daughter. It was a different woman—the priestess of
Agbala, the Oracle of the Hills and Caves. Ekwefi trudged along
between two fears. The sound of her benumbed steps seemed to
come from some other person walking behind her. Her arms were
folded across her bare breasts. Dew fell heavily and the air was cold.
She could no longer think, not even about the terrors of night. She
just jogged along in a half-sleep, only waking to full life when Chielo
sang.

At last they took a turning and began to head for the caves. From
then on, Chielo never ceased in her chanting. She greeted her god in
a multitude of names—the owner of the future, the messenger of
earth, the god who cut a man down when his life was sweetest to him.
Ekwefi was also awakened and her benumbed fears revived.

The moon was now up and she could see Chielo and Ezinma
clearly. How a woman could carry a child of that size so easily and for
so long was a miracle. But Ekwefi was not thinking about that. Chielo
was not a woman that night.

"*Agbala do-o-o-o! Agbala ekeno-o-o-o! Chi negbu madu ubosi ndu ya
nato ya uto daluo-o-o!* . . ."[7]

---

7. "The deity that kills a man on the day his life is sweetest to him." *daluo-o-o:* a greeting—
"How are you?" "Are you well?" It also means, in other contexts, "Thank you."

Ekwefi could already see the hills looming in the moon-light. They formed a circular ring with a break at one point through which the foot-track led to the centre of the circle.

As soon as the priestess stepped into this ring of hills her voice was not only doubled in strength but was thrown back on all sides. It was indeed the shrine of a great god. Ekwefi picked her way carefully and quietly. She was already beginning to doubt the wisdom of her coming. Nothing would happen to Ezinma, she thought. And if anything happened to her could she stop it? She would not dare to enter the under ground caves. Her coming was quite useless, she thought.

As these things went through her mind she did not realise how close they were to the cave mouth. And so when the priestess with Ezinma on her back disappeared through a hole hardly big enough to pass a hen, Ekwefi broke into a run as though to stop them. As she stood gazing at the circular darkness which had swallowed them, tears gushed from her eyes, and she swore within her that if she heard Ezinma cry she would rush into the cave to defend her against all the gods in the world. She would die with her.

Having sworn that oath, she sat down on a stony ledge and waited. Her fear had vanished. She could hear the priestess's voice, all its metal taken out of it by the vast emptiness of the cave. She buried her face in her lap and waited.

She did not know how long she waited. It must have been a very long time. Her back was turned on the footpath that led out of the hills. She must have heard a noise behind her and turned round sharply. A man stood there with a matchet in his hand. Ekwefi uttered a scream and sprang to her feet.

"Don't be foolish," said Okonkwo's voice. "I thought you were going into the shrine with Chielo," he mocked.

Ekwefi did not answer. Tears of gratitude filled her eyes. She knew her daughter was safe.

"Go home and sleep," said Okonkwo. "I shall wait here."

"I shall wait too. It is almost dawn. The first cock has crowed."

As they stood there together, Ekwefi's mind went back to the days when they were young. She had married Anene because Okonkwo was too poor then to marry. Two years after her marriage to Anene she could bear it no longer and she ran away to Okonkwo. It had been early in the morning. The moon was shining. She was going to the stream to fetch water. Okonkwo's house was on the way to the stream. She went in and knocked at his door and he came out. Even in those days he was not a man of many words. He just carried her into his bed and in the darkness began to feel around her waist for the loose end of her cloth.

Chapter Twelve

On the following morning the entire neighbourhood wore a festive air because Okonkwo's friend, Obierika, was celebrating his daughter's *uri*.[1] It was the day on which her suitor (having already paid the greater part of her bride-price) would bring palm-wine not only to her parents and immediate relatives but to the wide and extensive group of kinsmen called *umunna*.[2] Everybody had been invited—men, women and children. But it was really a woman's ceremony and the central figures were the bride and her mother.

As soon as day broke, breakfast was hastily eaten and women and children began to gather at Obierika's compound to help the bride's mother in her difficult but happy task of cooking for a whole village.

Okonkwo's family was astir like any other family in the neighbourhood. Nwoye's mother and Okonkwo's youngest wife were ready to set out for Obierika's compound with all their children. Nwoye's mother carried a basket of coco-yams, a cake of salt[3] and smoked fish which she would present to Obierika's wife. Okonkwo's youngest wife, Ojiugo, also had a basket of plantains and coco-yams and a small pot of palm-oil. Their children carried pots of water.

Ekwefi was tired and sleepy from the exhausting experiences of the previous night. It was not very long since they had returned. The priestess, with Ezinma sleeping on her back, had crawled out of the shrine on her belly like a snake. She had not as much as looked at Okonkwo and Ekwefi or shown any surprise at finding them at the mouth of the cave. She looked straight ahead of her and walked back to the village. Okonkwo and his wife followed at a respectful distance. They thought the priestess might be going to her house, but she went to Okonkwo's compound, passed through his *obi* and into Ekwefi's hut and walked into her bedroom. She placed Ezinma carefully on the bed and went away without saying a word to anybody.

Ezinma was still sleeping when everyone else was astir, and Ekwefi asked Nwoye's mother and Ojiugo to explain to Obierika's wife that she would be late. She had got ready her basket of coco-yams and fish, but she must wait for Ezinma to wake.

"You need some sleep yourself," said Nwoye's mother. "You look very tired."

As they spoke Ezinma emerged from the hut, rubbing her eyes and stretching her spare frame. She saw the other children with their water-pots and remembered that they were going to fetch water for Obierika's wife. She went back to the hut and brought her pot.

---

1. The ceremony as well as the dance that concludes it.
2. The community of all relatives belonging to the male lineage (see Victor Uchendu, 1965).
3. A very precious commodity.

"Have you slept enough?" asked her mother.

"Yes," she replied. "Let us go."

"Not before you have had your breakfast," said Ekwefi. And she went into her hut to warm the vegetable soup she had cooked last night.

"We shall be going," said Nwoye's mother. "I will tell Obierika's wife that you are coming later." And so they all went to help Obierika's wife—Nwoye's mother with her four children and Ojiugo with her two.

As they trooped through Okonkwo's *obi* he asked: "Who will prepare my afternoon meal?"

"I shall return to do it," said Ojiugo.

Okonkwo was also feeling tired and sleepy, for although nobody else knew it, he had not slept at all last night. He had felt very anxious but did not show it. When Ekwefi had followed the priestess, he had allowed what he regarded as a reasonable and manly interval to pass and then gone with his matchet to the shrine, where he thought they must be. It was only when he had got there that it had occurred to him that the priestess might have chosen to go round the villages first. Okonkwo had returned home and sat waiting. When he thought he had waited long enough he again returned to the shrine. But the Hills and the Caves were as silent as death. It was only on his fourth trip that he had found Ekwefi, and by then he had become gravely worried.

Obierika's compound was as busy as an ant-hill.[4] Temporary cooking tripods were erected on every available space by bringing together three blocks of sun-dried earth and making a fire in their midst. Cooking pots went up and down the tripods, and foo-foo was pounded in a hundred wooden mortars. Some of the women cooked the yams and the cassava, and others prepared vegetable soup. Young men pounded the foo-foo or split firewood. The children made endless trips to the stream.

Three young men helped Obierika to slaughter the two goats with which the soup was made. They were very fat goats, but the fattest of all was tethered to a peg near the wall of the compound. It was as big as a small cow. Obierika had sent one of his relatives all the way to Umuike[5] to buy that goat. It was the one he would present alive to his in-laws.

"The market of Umuike is a wonderful place," said the young man

---

4. Mound of red earth built up by a colony of ants, often to impressive heights, within which they swarm. This is a prominent feature of the landscape in the African savannah (cf. title of Achebe's last novel, *Anthills of the Savannah*).

5. As a community (*umu*) of people who consider themselves as specially endowed with power (*ike*).

who had been sent by Obierika to buy the giant goat. "There are so many people on it that if you threw up a grain of sand it would not find a way to fall to earth again."

"It is the result of a great medicine,"[6] said Obierika. "The people of Umuike wanted their market to grow and swallow up the markets of their neighbours. So they made a powerful medicine. Every market-day, before the first cock-crow, this medicine stands on the market-ground in the shape of an old woman with a fan. With this magic fan she beckons to the market all the neighbouring clans. She beckons in front of her and behind her, to her right and to her left."

"And so everybody comes," said another man, "honest men and thieves. They can steal your cloth from off your waist in that market."

"Yes," said Obierika. "I warned Nwankwo[7] to keep a sharp eye and a sharp ear. There was once a man who went to sell a goat. He led it on a thick rope which he tied round his wrist. But as he walked through the market he realised that people were pointing at him as they do to a madman. He could not understand it until he looked back and saw that what he led at the end of the tether was not a goat but a heavy log of wood."

"Do you think a thief can do that kind of thing single-handed?" asked Nwankwo.

"No," said Obierika. "They use medicine."

When they had cut the goats' throats and collected the blood in a bowl, they held them over an open fire to burn off the hair, and the smell of burning hair blended with the smell of cooking. Then they washed them and cut them up for the women who prepared the soup.

All this ant-hill activity was going smoothly when a sudden inter-ruption came. It was a cry in the distance: *Oji odu achu ijiji-o-o!* (*The one that uses its tail to drive flies away!*) Every woman immediately abandoned whatever she was doing and rushed out in the direction of the cry.

"We cannot all rush out like that, leaving what we are cooking to burn in the fire," shouted Chielo, the priestess. "Three or four of us should stay behind."

"It is true," said another woman. "We will allow three or four women to stay behind."

Five women stayed behind to look after the cooking-pots, and all the rest rushed away to see the cow that had been let loose. When they saw it they drove it back to its owner, who at once paid the heavy fine which the village imposed on anyone whose cow was let loose on

6. Charm, talisman.
7. "Child born on Nkwo day"; a variant on "Okonkwo."

his neighbours' crops. When the women had exacted the penalty they checked among themselves to see if any woman had failed to come out when the cry had been raised.

"Where is Mgbogo?" asked one of them.

"She is ill in bed," said Mgbogo's next-door neighbour. "She has *iba*."

"The only other person is Udenkwo," said another woman, "and her child is not twenty-eight days yet."

Those women whom Obierika's wife had not asked to help her with the cooking returned to their homes, and the rest went back, in a body, to Obierika's compound.

"Whose cow was it?" asked the women who had been allowed to stay behind.

"It was my husband's," said Ezelagbo.[8] "One of the young children had opened the gate of the cow-shed."

Early in the afternoon the first two pots of palm-wine arrived from Obierika's in-laws. They were duly presented to the women, who drank a cup or two each, to help them in their cooking. Some of it also went to the bride and her attendant maidens, who were putting the last delicate touches of razor to her coiffure and cam wood on her smooth skin.

When the heat of the sun began to soften, Obierika's son, Maduka, took a long broom and swept the ground in front of his father's *obi*. And as if they had been waiting for that, Obierika's relatives and friends began to arrive, every man with his goatskin bag hung on one shoulder and a rolled goatskin mat under his arm. Some of them were accompanied by their sons bearing carved wooden stools. Okonkwo was one of them. They sat in a half-circle and began to talk of many things. It would not be long before the suitors came.

Okonkwo brought out his snuff-bottle and offered it to Ogbuefi Ezenwa,[9] who sat next to him. Ezenwa took it, tapped it on his knee-cap, rubbed his left palm on his body to dry it before tipping a little snuff into it. His actions were deliberate, and he spoke as he performed them:

"I hope our in-laws will bring many pots of wine. Although they come from a village that is known for being close-fisted, they ought to know that Akueke is the bride for a king."

"They dare not bring fewer than thirty pots," said Okonkwo. "I shall tell them my mind if they do."

At that moment Obierika's son, Maduka, led out the giant goat from the inner compound, for his father's relatives to see. They all

---

8. The term *eze* in this woman's name does not indicate a title.
9. "Child with the bearing of a king."

admired it and said that that was the way things should be done. The goat was then led back to the inner compound.

Very soon after, the in-laws began to arrive. Young men and boys in single file, each carrying a pot of wine, came first. Obierika's relatives counted the pots as they came in. Twenty, twenty-five. There was a long break, and the hosts looked at each other as if to say, 'I told you.' Then more pots came. Thirty, thirty-five, forty, forty-five. The hosts nodded in approval and seemed to say, 'Now they are behaving like men.' Altogether there were fifty pots of wine. After the pot-bearers came Ibe, the suitor, and the elders of his family. They sat in a half-moon, thus completing a circle with their hosts. The pots of wine stood in their midst. Then the bride, her mother and half a dozen other women and girls emerged from the inner compound, and went round the circle shaking hands with all. The bride's mother led the way, followed by the bride and the other women. The married women wore their best cloths and the girls wore red and black waist-beads and anklets of brass.

When the women retired, Obierika presented kola nuts to his in-laws. His eldest brother broke the first one. "Life to all of us," he said as he broke it. "And let there be friendship between your family and ours."

The crowd answered: *"Ee-e-e!"*

"We are giving you our daughter today. She will be a good wife to you. She will bear you nine sons like the mother of our town."

"Ee-e-e!"

The oldest man in the camp of the visitors replied: "It will be good for you and it will be good for us."

"Ee-e-e!"

"This is not the first time my people have come to marry your daughter. My mother was one of you."

"Ee-e-e!"

"And this will not be the last, because you understand us and we understand you. You are a great family."

"Ee-e-e!"

"Prosperous men and great warriors." He looked in the direction of Okonkwo. "Your daughter will bear us sons like you."

"Ee-e-e!"

The kola was eaten and the drinking of palm-wine began. Groups of four or five men sat round with a pot in their midst. As the evening wore on, food was presented to the guests. There were huge bowls of foo-foo and steaming pots of soup. There were also pots of yam pottage. It was a great feast.

As night fell, burning torches were set on wooden tripods and the young men raised a song. The elders sat in a big circle and the singers went round singing each man's praise as they came before him. They had something to say for every man. Some were great farmers, some were orators who spoke for the clan; Okonkwo was the greatest wrestler and warrior alive. When they had gone round the circle they settled down in the centre, and girls came from the inner compound to dance. At first the bride was not among them. But when she finally appeared holding a cock[1] in her right hand, a loud cheer rose from the crowd. All the other dancers made way for her. She presented the cock to the musicians and began to dance. Her brass anklets rattled as she danced and her body gleamed with cam wood in the soft yellow light. The musicians with their wood, clay and metal instruments went from song to song. And they were all gay. They sang the latest song in the village:

> "If I hold her hand
> She says, 'Don't touch!'
> If I hold her foot
> She says, 'Don't touch!'
> But when I hold her waist-beads
> She pretends not to know."

The night was already far spent when the guests rose to go, taking their bride home to spend seven market weeks with her suitor's family.[2] They sang songs as they went, and on their way they paid short courtesy visits to prominent men like Okonkwo, before they finally left for their village. Okonkwo made a present of two cocks to them.

Chapter Thirteen

Go-di-di-go-go-di-go. Di-go-go-di-go. It was the *ekwe* talking to the clan. One of the things every man learned was the language of the hollowed-out wooden instrument. Diim! Diim! Diim! boomed the cannon[1] at intervals.

The first cock had not crowed, and Umuofia was still swallowed up in sleep and silence when the *ekwe* began to talk, and the cannon shattered the silence. Men stirred on their bamboo beds and listened anxiously. Somebody was dead. The cannon seemed to rend the sky. Di-go-go-di-go-di-di-go-go floated in the message-laden night air. The faint and distant wailing of women settled like a sediment of

---

1. A highly valued gift.
2. This is customary; the purpose of the ceremony is to enable the family to get to know the future bride; if they are not satisfied with her, the marriage can be stopped.
1. As with other firearms, the cannon was introduced into West Africa by European slave dealers, primarily to protect the forts where slaves were herded before being transported across the Atlantic.

sorrow on the earth. Now and again a full-chested lamentation rose
above the wailing whenever a man came into the place of death. He
raised his voice once or twice in manly sorrow and then sat down
with the other men listening to the endless wailing of the women
and the esoteric language of the *ekwe*. Now and again the cannon
boomed. The wailing of the women would not be heard beyond the
village, but the *ekwe* carried the news to all the nine villages and
even beyond. It began by naming the clan: *Umuofia obodo dike*, 'the
land of the brave.' *Umuofia obodo dike! Umuofia obodo dike!* It said
this over and over again, and as it dwelt on it, anxiety mounted in
every heart that heaved on a bamboo bed that night. Then it went
nearer and named the village: *Iguedo of the yellow grinding-stone!*[2] It
was Okonkwo's village. Again and again Iguedo was called and men
waited breathlessly in all the nine villages. At last the man was
named and people sighed "E-u-u, Ezeudu is dead." A cold shiver ran
down Okonkwo's back as he remembered the last time the old man
had visited him. "That boy calls you father," he had said. "Bear no
hand in his death."

Ezeudu was a great man, and so all the clan was at his funeral. The
ancient drums of death beat, guns and cannon were fired, and men
dashed about in frenzy, cutting down every tree or animal they saw,
jumping over walls and dancing on the roof. It was a warrior's funeral,
and from morning till night warriors came and went in their age-
groups. They all wore smoked raffia skirts and their bodies were
painted with chalk and charcoal.[3] Now and again an ancestral spirit
or *egwugwu* appeared from the underworld, speaking in a tremulous,
unearthly voice and completely covered in raffia. Some of them were
very violent, and there had been a mad rush for shelter earlier in the
day when one appeared with a sharp matchet and was only prevented
from doing serious harm by two men who restrained him with the
help of a strong rope tied round his waist.[4] Sometimes he turned
round and chased those men, and they ran for their lives. But they
always returned to the long rope he trailed behind. He sang, in a terrifying voice, that Ekwensu, or Evil Spirit, had entered his eye.

But the most dreaded of all was yet to come. He was always alone
and was shaped like a coffin. A sickly odour hung in the air wherever
he went, and flies went with him. Even the greatest medicine-men
took shelter when he was near. Many years ago another *egwugwu* had

---

2. Block of granite over which pepper and corn were ground; *iguedo*: yellow palm frond.
3. Obtained from burnt wood; the black color contrasts with the white chalk; *raffia*: a plant
   normally used as roofing for dwellings. It also produces a sweet juice akin to palm wine but
   milder; indeed, in Igboland, the raffia palm (*ngwo*) is the primary source of palm wine.
4. The rope had to be tied round the waist of each masquerade to restrain them, as they often
   became excited and violent.

dared to stand his ground before him and had been transfixed to the spot for two days. This one had only one hand and with it carried a basket full of water.

But some of the *egwugwu* were quite harmless. One of them was so old and infirm that he leaned heavily on a stick. He walked unsteadily to the place where the corpse was laid, gazed at it a while and went away again—to the underworld.

The land of the living was not far removed from the domain of the ancestors. There was coming and going between them, especially at festivals and also when an old man died, because an old man was very close to the ancestors. A man's life from birth to death was a series of transition rites which brought him nearer and nearer to his ancestors.

Ezeudu had been the oldest man in his village, and at his death there were only three men in the whole clan who were older, and four or five others in his own age-group. Whenever one of these ancient men appeared in the crowd to dance unsteadily the funeral steps of the tribe, younger men gave way and the tumult subsided.

It was a great funeral, such as befitted a noble warrior. As the evening drew near, the shouting and the firing of guns, the beating of drums and the brandishing and clanging of matchets increased.

Ezeudu had taken three titles in his life. It was a rare achievement. There were only four titles in the clan, and only one or two men in any generation ever achieved the fourth and highest. When they did, they became the lords of the land. Because he had taken titles, Ezeudu was to be buried after dark with only a glowing brand to light the sacred ceremony.

But before this quiet and final rite, the tumult increased tenfold. Drums beat violently and men leaped up and down in frenzy. Guns were fired on all sides and sparks flew out as matchets clanged together in warriors' salutes. The air was full of dust and the smell of gunpowder. It was then that the one-handed spirit came, carrying a basket full of water. People made way for him on all sides and the noise subsided. Even the smell of gunpowder was swallowed in the sickly smell that now filled the air. He danced a few steps to the funeral drums and then went to see the corpse.

"Ezeudu!" he called in his guttural voice. "If you had been poor in your last life I would have asked you to be rich when you come again. But you were rich. If you had been a coward, I would have asked you to bring courage. But you were a fearless warrior. If you had died young, I would have asked you to get life. But you lived long. So I shall ask you to come again the way you came before. If your death was the death of nature, go in peace. But if a man caused it, do not allow him a moment's rest." He danced a few more steps and went away.

The drums and the dancing began again and reached fever-heat. Darkness was around the corner, and the burial was near. Guns fired

the last salute and the cannon rent the sky. And then from the centre of the delirious fury came a cry of agony and shouts of horror. It
was as if a spell had been cast. All was silent. In the centre of the
crowd a boy lay in a pool of blood. It was the dead man's sixteen-year-
old son, who with his brothers and half-brothers had been dancing
the traditional farewell to their father. Okonkwo's gun had exploded
and a piece of iron had pierced the boy's heart.

The confusion that followed was without parallel in the tradition
of Umuofia. Violent deaths were frequent, but nothing like this had
ever happened.

The only course open to Okonkwo was to flee from the clan. It was
a crime against the earth goddess to kill a clansman, and a man who
committed it must flee from the land. The crime was of two kinds,
male and female. Okonkwo had committed the female, because it
had been inadvertent. He could return to the clan after seven years.

That night he collected his most valuable belongings into head-
loads. His wives wept bitterly and their children wept with them without knowing why. Obierika and half a dozen other friends came to
help and to console him. They each made nine or ten trips carrying
Okonkwo's yams to store in Obierika's barn. And before the cock
crowed Okonkwo and his family were fleeing to his motherland. It
was a little village called Mbanta,[5] just beyond the borders of Mbaino.

As soon as the day broke, a large crowd of men from Ezeudu's quarter stormed Okonkwo's compound, dressed in garbs of war. They set
fire to his houses, demolished his red walls, killed his animals and
destroyed his barn. It was the justice of the earth goddess, and they
were merely her messengers. They had no hatred in their hearts
against Okonkwo. His greatest friend, Obierika, was among them.
They were merely cleansing the land which Okonkwo had polluted
with the blood of a clansman.

Obierika was a man who thought about things. When the will of
the goddess had been done, he sat down in his *obi* and mourned his
friend's calamity. Why should a man suffer so grievously for an
offence he had committed inadvertently? But although he thought
for a long time he found no answer. He was merely led into greater
complexities. He remembered his wife's twin children, whom he had
thrown away. What crime had they committed? The Earth had
decreed that they were an offence on the land and must be destroyed.
And if the clan did not exact punishment for an offence against the
great goddess, her wrath was loosed on all the land and not just on
the offender. As the elders said, if one finger brought oil it soiled the
others.

5. The name suggests a small settlement.

Part Two

Chapter Fourteen

Okonkwo was well received by his mother's kinsmen in Mbanta. The old man who received him was his mother's younger brother, who was now the eldest surviving member of that family. His name was Uchendu,[1] and it was he who had received Okonkwo's mother twenty and ten years before when she had been brought home from Umuofia to be buried with her people. Okonkwo was only a boy then and Uchendu still remembered him crying the traditional farewell: "Mother, mother, mother is going."

That was many years ago. Today Okonkwo was not bringing his mother home to be buried with her people. He was taking his family of three wives and eleven children to seek refuge in his motherland. As soon as Uchendu saw him with his sad and weary company he guessed what had happened, and asked no questions. It was not until the following day that Okonkwo told him the full story. The old man listened silently to the end and then said with some relief: "It is a female *ochu*."[2] And he arranged the requisite rites and sacrifices.

Okonkwo was given a plot of ground on which to build his compound, and two or three pieces of land on which to farm during the coming planting season. With the help of his mother's kinsmen he built himself an *obi* and three huts for his wives. He then installed his personal god and the symbols of his departed fathers. Each of Uchendu's five sons contributed three hundred seed-yams to enable their cousin to plant a farm, for as soon as the first rain came farming would begin.

At last the rain came. It was sudden and tremendous. For two or three moons the sun had been gathering strength till it seemed to breathe a breath of fire on the earth. All the grass had long been scorched brown, and the sands felt like live coals to the feet. Evergreen trees wore a dusty coat of brown. The birds were silenced in the forests, and the world lay panting under the live, vibrating heat. And then came the clap of thunder. It was an angry, metallic and thirsty clap, unlike

---

1. "One experienced in life."
2. Murder or manslaughter.

the deep and liquid rumbling of the rainy season. A mighty wind arose and filled the air with dust. Palm trees swayed as the wind combed their leaves into flying crests like strange and fantastic coiffure.

When the rain finally came, it was in large, solid drops of frozen water which the people called 'the nuts of the water of heaven'. They were hard and painful on the body as they fell, yet young people ran about happily picking up the cold nuts and throwing them into their mouths to melt.

The earth quickly came to life and the birds in the forests fluttered around and chirped merrily. A vague scent of life and green vegetation was diffused in the air. As the rain began to fall more soberly and in smaller liquid drops, children sought for shelter, and all were happy, refreshed and thankful.

Okonkwo and his family worked very hard to plant a new farm. But it was like beginning life anew without the vigour and enthusiasm of youth, like learning to become left-handed in old age. Work no longer had for him the pleasure it used to have, and when there was no work to do he sat in a silent half-sleep.

His life had been ruled by a great passion—to become one of the lords of the clan. That had been his life-spring. And he had all but achieved it. Then everything had been broken. He had been cast out of his clan like a fish on to a dry, sandy beach, panting. Clearly his personal god or *chi* was not made for great things. A man could not rise beyond the destiny of his *chi*. The saying of the elders was not true—that if a man said yea his *chi* also affirmed. Here was a man whose *chi* said nay despite his own affirmation.

The old man, Uchendu, saw clearly that Okonkwo had yielded to despair and he was greatly troubled. He would speak to him after the *isa-ifi* ceremony.[3]

The youngest of Uchendu's five sons, Amikwu, was marrying a new wife. The bride-price had been paid and all but the last ceremony had been performed. Amikwu and his people had taken palm-wine to the bride's kinsmen about two moons before Okonkwo's arrival in Mbanta. And so it was time for the final ceremony of confession.

The daughters of the family were all there, some of them having come a long way from their homes in distant villages. Uchendu's eldest daughter had come from Obodo, nearly half a day's journey away. The daughters of Uchendu's brothers were also there. It was a full gathering of *umuada*,[4] in the same way as they would meet if a death occurred in the family. There were twenty-two of them.

3. The purpose of the ceremony is explained in the passage that follows; the term means a cleaning of the face, "coming clean."
4. The female lineage, made up of the first girls or first daughters; equivalent to *umunna*.

They sat in a big circle on the ground and the bride sat in the centre with a hen in her right hand. Uchendu sat by her, holding the ancestral staff of the family. All the other men stood outside the circle, watching. Their wives watched also. It was evening and the sun was setting.

Uchendu's eldest daughter, Njide, asked the questions.

"Remember that if you do not answer truthfully you will suffer or even die at child-birth," she began. "How many men have lain with you since my brother first expressed the desire to marry you?"

"None," she replied simply.

"Answer truthfully," urged the other women.

"None?" asked Njide.

"None," she answered.

"Swear on this staff of my fathers," said Uchendu.

"I swear," said the bride.

Uchendu took the hen from her, slit its throat with a sharp knife and allowed some of the blood to fall on his ancestral staff.

From that day Amikwu took the young bride to his hut and she became his wife. The daughters of the family did not return to their homes immediately but spent two or three days with their kinsmen.

On the second day Uchendu called together his sons and daughters and his nephew, Okonkwo. The men brought their goatskin mats, with which they sat on the floor, and the women sat on a sisal mat spread on a raised bank of earth. Uchendu pulled gently at his grey beard and gnashed his teeth. Then he began to speak, quietly and deliberately, picking his words with great care:

"It is Okonkwo that I primarily wish to speak to," he began. "But I want all of you to note what I am going to say. I am an old man and you are all children. I know more about the world than any of you. If there is any one among you who thinks he knows more let him speak up." He paused, but no one spoke.

"Why is Okonkwo with us today? This is not his clan. We are only his mother's kinsmen. He does not belong here. He is an exile, condemned for seven years to live in a strange land. And so he is bowed with grief. But there is just one question I would like to ask him. Can you tell me, Okonkwo, why it is that one of the commonest names we give our children is Nneka, or 'Mother is Supreme'? We all know that a man is the head of the family and his wives do his bidding. A child belongs to its father and his family and not to its mother and her family. A man belongs to his fatherland and not to his motherland. And yet we say Nneka—'Mother is Supreme.' Why is that?"

There was silence. "I want Okonkwo to answer me," said Uchendu.

"I do not know the answer," Okonkwo replied.

"You do not know the answer? So you see that you are a child. You

have many wives and many children—more children than I have. You
are a great man in your clan. But you are still a child, *my* child. Listen to me and I shall tell you. But there is one more question I shall
ask you. Why is it that when a woman dies she is taken home to be
buried with her own kinsmen? She is not buried with her husband's
kinsmen. Why is that? Your mother was brought home to me and
buried with my people. Why was that?"

Okonkwo shook his head.

"He does not know that either," said Uchendu, "and yet he is full
of sorrow because he has come to live in his motherland for a few
years." He laughed a mirthless laughter, and turned to his sons and
daughters. "What about you? Can you answer my question?"

They all shook their heads.

"Then listen to me," he said and cleared his throat. "It's true that
a child belongs to its father. But when a father beats his child, it
seeks sympathy in its mother's hut. A man belongs to his fatherland
when things are good and life is sweet. But when there is sorrow
and bitterness he finds refuge in his motherland. Your mother is
there to protect you. She is buried there. And that is why we say
that mother is supreme. Is it right that you, Okonkwo, should bring
to your mother a heavy face and refuse to be comforted? Be careful or you may displease the dead. Your duty is to comfort your
wives and children and take them back to your fatherland after
seven years. But if you allow sorrow to weigh you down and kill you,
they will all die in exile." He paused for a long while. "These are
now your kinsmen." He waved at his sons and daughters. "You
think you are the greatest sufferer in the world. Do you know that
men are sometimes banished for life? Do you know that men sometimes lose all their yams and even their children? I had six wives
once. I have none now except that young girl who knows not her
right from her left. Do you know how many children I have
buried—children I begot in my youth and strength? Twenty-two. I
did not hang myself, and I am still alive. If you think you are the
greatest sufferer in the world ask my daughter, Akueni, how many
twins she has borne and thrown away. Have you not heard the song
they sing when a woman dies?

"'For whom is it well, for whom is it well?
There is no one for whom it is well.'[5]

"I have no more to say to you."

5. The song expresses both a stoic view of life and the necessity for human solidarity.

Chapter Fifteen

It was in the second year of Okonkwo's exile that his friend, Obierika, came to visit him. He brought with him two young men, each of them carrying a heavy bag on his head. Okonkwo helped them put down their loads. It was clear that the bags were full of cowries.

Okonkwo was very happy to receive his friend. His wives and children were very happy too, and so were his cousins and their wives when he sent for them and told them who his guest was.

"You must take him to salute our father," said one of the cousins.

"Yes," replied Okonkwo. "We are going directly." But before they went he whispered something to his first wife. She nodded, and soon the children were chasing one of their cocks.

Uchendu had been told by one of his grandchildren that three strangers had come to Okonkwo's house. He was therefore waiting to receive them. He held out his hands to them when they came into his *obi*, and after they had shaken hands he asked Okonkwo who they were.

"This is Obierika, my great friend. I have already spoken to you about him."

"Yes," said the old man, turning to Obierika. "My son has told me about you, and I am happy you have come to see us. I knew your father, Iweka.[1] He was a great man. He had many friends here and came to see them quite often. Those were good days when a man had friends in distant clans. Your generation does not know that. You stay at home, afraid of your next-door neighbour. Even a man's motherland is strange to him nowadays." He looked at Okonkwo. "I am an old man and I like to talk. That is all I am good for now." He got up painfully, went into an inner room and came back with a kola nut.

"Who are the young men with you?" he asked as he sat down again on his goatskin. Okonkwo told him.

"Ah," he said. "Welcome, my sons." He presented the kola nut to them, and when they had seen it and thanked him, he broke it and they ate.

"Go into that room," he said to Okonkwo, pointing with his finger. "You will find a pot of wine there."

Okonkwo brought the wine and they began to drink. It was a day old, and very strong.

"Yes," said Uchendu after a long silence. "People travelled more in those days. There is not a single clan in these parts that I do not know very well. Aninta, Umuazu, Ikeocha, Elumelu, Abame—I know them all."

---

1. "Anger is great"; a warrior's name.

"Have you heard," asked Obierika, "that Abame is no more?"

"How is that?" asked Uchendu and Okonkwo together.

"Abame has been wiped out," said Obierika. "It is a strange and terrible story. If I had not seen the few survivors with my own eyes and heard their story with my own ears, I would not have believed. Was it not on an Eke day[2] that they fled into Umuofia?" he asked his two companions, and they nodded their heads.

"Three moons ago," said Obierika, "on an Eke market-day a little band of fugitives came into our town. Most of them were sons of our land whose mothers had been buried with us. But there were some too who came because they had friends in our town, and others who could think of nowhere else open to escape. And so they fled into Umuofia with a woeful story." He drank his palm-wine, and Okonkwo filled his horn again. He continued:

"During the last planting season a white man had appeared in their clan."

"An albino," suggested Okonkwo.

"He was not an albino. He was quite different." He sipped his wine. "And he was riding an iron horse. The first people who saw him ran away, but he stood beckoning to them. In the end the fearless ones went near and even touched him. The elders consulted their Oracle and it told them that the strange man would break their clan and spread destruction among them." Obierika again drank a little of his wine. "And so they killed the white man and tied his iron horse to their sacred tree because it looked as if it would run away to call the man's friends. I forgot to tell you another thing which the Oracle said. It said that other white men were on their way. They were locusts,[3] it said, and that first man was their harbinger sent to explore the terrain. And so they killed him."

"What did the white man say before they killed him?" asked Uchendu.

"He said nothing," answered one of Obierika's companions.

"He said something, only they did not understand him," said Obierika. "He seemed to speak through his nose."

"One of the men told me," said Obierika's other companion, "that he repeated over and over again a word that resembled Mbaino. Perhaps he had been going to Mbaino and had lost his way."

"Anyway," resumed Obierika, "they killed him and tied up his iron horse. This was before the planting season began. For a long time nothing happened. The rains had come and yams had been sown. The iron horse was still tied to the sacred silk-cotton tree. And then one morning three white men led by a band of ordinary men like us

---

2. Market day.
3. See p. 34. The allusion here is a reversal of the earlier mention of these insects.

came to the clan. They saw the iron horse and went away again. Most of the men and women of Abame had gone to their farms. Only a few of them saw these white men and their followers. For many market weeks nothing else happened. They have a big market in Abame on every other Afo day and, as you know, the whole clan gathers there. That was the day it happened. The three white men and a very large number of other men surrounded the market. They must have used a powerful medicine to make themselves invisible until the market was full. And they began to shoot. Everybody was killed, except the old and the sick who were at home and a handful of men and women whose *chi* were wide awake and brought them out of that market."[4] He paused.

"Their clan is now completely empty. Even the sacred fish in their mysterious lake have fled and the lake has turned the colour of blood.[5] A great evil has come upon their land as the Oracle had warned."

There was a long silence. Uchendu ground his teeth together audibly. Then he burst out:

"Never kill a man who says nothing. Those men of Abame were fools. What did they know about the man?" He ground his teeth again and told a story to illustrate his point. "Mother Kite once sent her daughter to bring food. She went, and brought back a duckling. 'You have done very well,' said Mother Kite to her daughter, 'but tell me, what did the mother of this duckling say when you swooped and carried its child away?' 'It said nothing,' replied the young kite. 'It just walked away.' 'You must return the duckling,' said Mother Kite. 'There is something ominous behind the silence.' And so Daughter Kite returned the duckling and took a chick instead. 'What did the mother of this chick do?' asked the old kite. 'It cried and raved and cursed me,' said the young kite. 'Then we can eat the chick,' said her mother. 'There is nothing to fear from someone who shouts.' Those men of Abame were fools."

"They were fools," said Okonkwo after a pause. "They had been warned that danger was ahead. They should have armed themselves with their guns and their matchets even when they went to market."

"They have paid for their foolishness," said Obierika. "But I am greatly afraid. We have heard stories about white men who made the powerful guns and the strong drinks and took slaves away across the seas, but no one thought the stories were true."

---

4. Punitive expeditions of this type were not uncommon in the early days of the colonial administration. Wren describes such an expedition undertaken in 1905 to avenge the killing of a white man, during which two Igbo towns were wiped out, and speculates that this may have served as the specific historical reference for the destruction of Abame in Achebe's novel (see Wren, pp. 26–29).
5. Not so much in a literal as in a symbolic sense.

"There is no story that is not true," said Uchendu. "The world has no end, and what is good among one people is an abomination with others. We have albinos among us. Do you not think that they came to our clan by mistake, that they have strayed from their way to a land where everybody is like them?"

Okonkwo's first wife soon finished her cooking and set before their guests a big meal of pounded yams and bitter-leaf[6] soup. Okonkwo's son, Nwoye, brought in a pot of sweet wine tapped from the raffia palm.

"You are a big man now," Obierika said to Nwoye. "Your friend Anene asked me to greet you."

"Is he well?" asked Nwoye.

"We are all well," said Obierika.

Ezinma brought them a bowl of water with which to wash their hands. After that they began to eat and to drink the wine.

"When did you set out from home?" asked Okonkwo.

"We had meant to set out from my house before cock-crow," said Obierika. "But Nweke did not appear until it was quite light. Never make an early morning appointment with a man who has just married a new wife." They all laughed.

"Has Nweke married a wife?" asked Okonkwo.

"He has married Okadigbo's second daughter," said Obierika.

"That is very good," said Okonkwo. "I do not blame you for not hearing the cock crow."

When they had eaten, Obierika pointed at the two heavy bags.

"That is the money from your yams," he said. "I sold the big ones as soon as you left. Later on I sold some of the seed-yams and gave out others to share-croppers. I shall do that every year until you return. But I thought you would need the money now and so I brought it. Who knows what may happen tomorrow? Perhaps green men will come to our clan and shoot us."

"God will not permit it," said Okonkwo. "I do not know how to thank you."

"I can tell you," said Obierika. "Kill one of your sons for me."

"That will not be enough," said Okonkwo.

"Then kill yourself," said Obierika.

"Forgive me," said Okonkwo, smiling. "I shall not talk about thanking you any more."

---

6. A vegetable that tastes bitter when first chewed, but leaves a sweetish aftertaste.

Chapter Sixteen

When nearly two years later Obierika paid another visit to his friend in exile the circumstances were less happy. The missionaries had come to Umuofia. They had built their church there, won a handful of converts and were already sending evangelists to the surrounding towns and villages. That was a source of great sorrow to the leaders of the clan; but many of them believed that the strange faith and the white man's god would not last. None of his converts was a man whose word was heeded in the assembly of the people. None of them was a man of title. They were mostly the kind of people that were called *efulefu*, worthless, empty men. The imagery of an *efulefu*[1] in the language of the clan was a man who sold his matchet and wore the sheath to battle. Chielo, the priestess of Agbala, called the converts the excrement of the clan, and the new faith was a mad dog that had come to eat it up.[2]

What moved Obierika to visit Okonkwo was the sudden appearance of the latter's son, Nwoye, among the missionaries in Umuofia.

"What are you doing here?" Obierika had asked when after many difficulties the missionaries had allowed him to speak to the boy.

"I am one of them," replied Nwoye.

"How is your father?" Obierika asked, not knowing what else to say.

"I don't know. He is not my father," said Nwoye, unhappily.

And so Obierika went to Mbanta to see his friend. And he found that Okonkwo did not wish to speak about Nwoye. It was only from Nwoye's mother that he heard scraps of the story.

The arrival of the missionaries had caused a considerable stir in the village of Mbanta. There were six of them and one was a white man. Every man and woman came out to see the white man. Stories about these strange men had grown since one of them had been killed in Abame and his iron horse tied to the sacred silk-cotton tree. And so everybody came to see the white man. It was the time of the year when everybody was at home. The harvest was over.

When they had all gathered, the white man began to speak to them. He spoke through an interpreter who was an Ibo man, though his dialect was different and harsh to the ears of Mbanta. Many people laughed at his dialect and the way he used words strangely. Instead of saying 'myself' he always said 'my buttocks.'[3] But he was a man of commanding presence and the clansmen listened to him. He said he was one of them, as they could see from his colour and his

---

1. Fool, idiot, ne'er-do-well.
2. Dogs were often used in this way, as agents of personal hygiene.
3. The confusion is caused by the wrong use of tone, which determines meaning in Igbo.

language. The other four black men were also their brothers, although one of them did not speak Ibo. The white man was also their brother because they were all sons of God. And he told them about this new God, the Creator of all the world and all the men and women. He told them that they worshipped false gods, gods of wood[4] and stone. A deep murmur went through the crowd when he said this. He told them that the true God lived on high and that all men when they died went before Him for judgment. Evil men and all the heathen who in their blindness bowed to wood and stone were thrown into a fire that burned like palm-oil. But good men who worshipped the true God lived for ever in His happy kingdom. "We have been sent by this great God to ask you to leave your wicked ways and false gods and turn to Him so that you may be saved when you die," he said.

"Your buttocks understand our language," said someone lightheartedly and the crowd laughed.

"What did he say?" the white man asked his interpreter. But before he could answer, another man asked a question: "Where is the white man's horse?" he asked. The Ibo evangelists consulted among themselves and decided that the man probably meant bicycle. They told the white man and he smiled benevolently.

"Tell them," he said, "that I shall bring many iron horses when we have settled down among them. Some of them will even ride the iron horse themselves." This was interpreted to them but very few of them heard. They were talking excitedly among themselves because the white man had said he was going to live among them. They had not thought about that.

At this point an old man said he had a question. "Which is this god of yours," he asked, "the goddess of the earth, the god of the sky, Amadiora of the thunderbolt, or what?"

The interpreter spoke to the white man and he immediately gave his answer. "All the gods you have named are not gods at all. They are gods of deceit who tell you to kill your fellows and destroy innocent children. There is only one true God and He has the earth, the sky, you and me and all of us."

"If we leave our gods and follow your god," asked another man, "who will protect us from the anger of our neglected gods and ancestors?"

"Your gods are not alive and cannot do you any harm," replied the white man. "They are pieces of wood and stone."

When this was interpreted to the men of Mbanta they broke into derisive laughter. These men must be mad, they said to themselves.

---

4. This reproduces the standard rhetoric of Christian missionaries.

How else could they say that Ani and Amadiora were harmless? And Idemili and Ogwugwu[5] too? And some of them began to go away.

Then the missionaries burst into song. It was one of those gay and rollicking tunes of evangelism which had the power of plucking at silent and dusty chords in the heart of an Ibo man. The interpreter explained each verse to the audience, some of whom now stood enthralled. It was a story of brothers who lived in darkness and in fear, ignorant of the love of God. It told of one sheep out on the hills, away from the gates of God and from the tender shepherd's care.

After the singing the interpreter spoke about the Son of God whose name was Jesu Kristi. Okonkwo, who only stayed in the hope that it might come to chasing the men out of the village or whipping them, now said:

"You told us with your own mouth that there was only one god. Now you talk about his son. He must have a wife, then." The crowd agreed.

"I did not say He had a wife," said the interpreter, somewhat lamely.

"Your buttocks said he had a son," said the joker. "So he must have a wife and all of them must have buttocks."

The missionary ignored him and went on to talk about the Holy Trinity. At the end of it Okonkwo was fully convinced that the man was mad. He shrugged his shoulders and went away to tap his afternoon palm-wine.

But there was a young lad who had been captivated. His name was Nwoye, Okonkwo's first son. It was not the mad logic of the Trinity that captivated him. He did not understand it. It was the poetry of the new religion, something felt in the marrow. The hymn about brothers who sat in darkness and in fear seemed to answer a vague and persistent question that haunted his young soul—the question of the twins crying in the bush and the question of Ikemefuna who was killed. He felt a relief within as the hymn poured into his parched soul. The words of the hymn were like the drops of frozen rain melting on the dry palate of the panting earth. Nwoye's callow mind was greatly puzzled.

Chapter Seventeen

The missionaries spent their first four or five nights in the market-place, and went into the village in the morning to preach the gospel. They asked who the king of the village was, but the villagers told them that there was no king. "We have men of high title and the chief priests and the elders," they said.

5. Considered the deadliest of all the Igbo deities.

It was not very easy getting the men of high title and the elders together after the excitement of the first day. But the missionaries persevered, and in the end they were received by the rulers of Mbanta. They asked for a plot of land to build their church.

Every clan and village had its 'evil forest'. In it were buried all those who died of the really evil diseases, like leprosy and smallpox. It was also the dumping ground for the potent fetishes of great medicine-men when they died. An 'evil forest' was, therefore, alive with sinister forces and powers of darkness. It was such a forest that the rulers of Mbanta gave to the missionaries. They did not really want them in their clan, and so they made them that offer which nobody in his right senses would accept.

"They want a piece of land to build their shrine," said Uchendu to his peers when they consulted among themselves. "We shall give them a piece of land." He paused, and there was a murmur of surprise and disagreement. "Let us give them a portion of the Evil Forest. They boast about victory over death. Let us give them a real battlefield in which to show their victory." They laughed and agreed, and sent for the missionaries, whom they had asked to leave them for a while so that they might 'whisper together'. They offered them as much of the Evil Forest as they cared to take. And to their greatest amazement the missionaries thanked them and burst into song.

"They do not understand," said some of the elders. "But they will understand when they go to their plot of land tomorrow morning." And they dispersed.

The next morning the crazy men actually began to clear a part of the forest and to build their house. The inhabitants of Mbanta expected them all to be dead within four days. The first day passed and the second and third and fourth, and none of them died. Everyone was puzzled. And then it became known that the white man's fetish had unbelievable power. It was said that he wore glasses on his eyes so that he could see and talk to evil spirits. Not long after, he won his first three converts.

Although Nwoye had been attracted to the new faith from the very first day, he kept it secret. He dared not go too near the missionaries for fear of his father. But whenever they came, to preach in the open market-place or the village playground, Nwoye was there. And he was already beginning to know some of the simple stories they told.

"We have now built a church," said Mr Kiaga, the interpreter, who was now in charge of the infant congregation. The white man had gone back to Umuofia, where he built his headquarters and from where he paid regular visits to Mr Kiaga's congregation at Mbanta.

"We have now built a church," said Mr Kiaga, "and we want you all to come in every seventh day to worship the true God."

On the following Sunday, Nwoye passed and re-passed the little

red-earth and thatch building without summoning enough courage
to enter. He heard the voice of singing and although it came from a
handful of men it was loud and confident. Their church stood on a
circular clearing that looked like the open mouth of the Evil Forest.
Was it waiting to snap its teeth together? After passing and re-passing
by the church, Nwoye returned home.

It was well known among the people of Mbanta that their gods and
ancestors were sometimes long-suffering and would deliberately
allow a man to go on defying them. But even in such cases they set
their limit at seven market weeks or twenty-eight days. Beyond that
limit no man was suffered to go. And so excitement mounted in the
village as the seventh week approached since the impudent missionaries built their church in the Evil Forest. The villagers were so certain about the doom that awaited these men that one or two converts
thought it wise to suspend their allegiance to the new faith.

At last the day came by which all the missionaries should have
died. But they were still alive, building a new red-earth and thatch
house for their teacher, Mr Kiaga. That week they won a handful
more converts. And for the first time they had a woman. Her name
was Nneka, the wife of Amadi,[6] who was a prosperous farmer. She
was very heavy with child.

Nneka had had four previous pregnancies and childbirths. But
each time she had borne twins, and they had been immediately
thrown away. Her husband and his family were already becoming
highly critical of such a woman and were not unduly perturbed when
they found she had fled to join the Christians. It was a good riddance.

One morning Okonkwo's cousin, Amikwu,[7] was passing by the
church on his way from the neighbouring village, when he saw
Nwoye among the Christians. He was greatly surprised, and when he
got home he went straight to Okonkwo's hut and told him what he
had seen. The women began to talk excitedly, but Okonkwo sat
unmoved.

It was late afternoon before Nwoye returned. He went into the *obi*
and saluted his father, but he did not answer. Nwoye turned round to
walk into the inner compound when his father, suddenly overcome
with fury, sprang to his feet and gripped him by the neck.

"Where have you been?" he stammered.

Nwoye struggled to free himself from the choking grip.

---

6. "My compound is here." He is possibly an Ikwere, an ethnic group in the Delta related to
   the Igbos.
7. "Amikwu" is an unusual name and means "compound of curses." The word is made up of
   /ama, /("compound") and /ikwu /("curse"). Achebe seems to have made up this unflattering name to reflect a certain authorial distance he adopts toward the character.

"Answer me," roared Okonkwo, "before I kill you!" He seized a heavy stick that lay on the dwarf wall and hit him two or three savage blows.

"Answer me!" he roared again. Nwoye stood looking at him and did not say a word. The women were screaming outside, afraid to go in.

"Leave that boy at once!" said a voice in the outer compound. It was Okonkwo's uncle, Uchendu. "Are you mad?"

Okonkwo did not answer. But he left hold of Nwoye, who walked away and never returned.

He went back to the church and told Mr Kiaga that he had decided to go to Umuofia, where the white missionary had set up a school to teach young Christians to read and write.

Mr Kiaga's joy was very great. "Blessed is he who forsakes his father and his mother for my sake," he intoned. "Those that hear my words are my father and my mother."

Nwoye did not fully understand. But he was happy to leave his father. He would return later to his mother and his brothers and sisters and convert them to the new faith.

As Okonkwo sat in his hut that night, gazing into a log fire, he thought over the matter. A sudden fury rose within him and he felt a strong desire to take up his matchet, go to the church and wipe out the entire vile and miscreant gang. But on further thought he told himself that Nwoye was not worth fighting for. Why, he cried in his heart, should he, Okonkwo, of all people, be cursed with such a son? He saw clearly in it the finger of his personal god or *chi*. For how else could he explain his great misfortune and exile and now his despicable son's behaviour? Now that he had time to think of it, his son's crime stood out in its stark enormity. To abandon the gods of one's father and go about with a lot of effeminate men clucking like old hens was the very depth of abomination. Suppose when he died all his male children decided to follow Nwoye's steps and abandon their ancestors? Okonkwo felt a cold shudder run through him at the terrible prospect, like the prospect of annihilation. He saw himself and his fathers crowding round their ancestral shrine waiting in vain for worship and sacrifice and finding nothing but ashes of bygone days, and his children the while praying to the white man's god. If such a thing were ever to happen, he, Okonkwo, would wipe them off the face of the earth.

Okonkwo was popularly called the "Roaring Flame." As he looked into the log fire he recalled the name. He was a flaming fire. How then could he have begotten a son like Nwoye, degenerate and effeminate? Perhaps he was not his son. No! he could not be. His wife had played him false. He would teach her! But Nwoye resembled his grandfather, Unoka, who was Okonkwo's father. He pushed the thought out of his mind. He, Okonkwo, was called a flaming fire.

How could he have begotten a woman for a son? At Nwoye's age Okonkwo had already become famous throughout Umuofia for his wrestling and his fearlessness.

He sighed heavily, and as if in sympathy the smouldering log also sighed. And immediately Okonkwo's eyes were opened and he saw the whole matter clearly. Living fire begets cold, impotent ash. He sighed again, deeply.

Chapter Eighteen

The young church in Mbanta had a few crises early in its life. At first the clan had assumed that it would not survive. But it had gone on living and gradually becoming stronger. The clan was worried, but not overmuch. If a gang of *efulefu* decided to live in the Evil Forest it was their own affair. When one came to think of it, the Evil Forest was a fit home for such undesirable people. It was true they were rescuing twins from the bush, but they never brought them into the village. As far as the villagers were concerned, the twins still remained where they had been thrown away. Surely the earth goddess would not visit the sins of the missionaries on the innocent villagers?

But on one occasion the missionaries had tried to overstep the bounds. Three converts had gone into the village and boasted openly that all the gods were dead and impotent and that they were prepared to defy them by burning all their shrines.

"Go and burn your mothers' genitals," said one of the priests. The men were seized and beaten until they streamed with blood. After that nothing happened for a long time between the church and the clan.

But stories were already gaining ground that the white man had not only brought a religion but also a government.[1] It was said that they had built a place of judgment in Umuofia to protect the followers of their religion. It was even said that they had hanged one man who killed a missionary.

Although such stories were now often told they looked like fairy-tales in Mbanta and did not as yet affect the relationship between the new church and the clan. There was no question of killing a missionary here, for Mr Kiaga, despite his madness, was quite harmless. As for his converts, no one could kill them without having to flee from the clan, for in spite of their worthlessness they still belonged to the clan. And so nobody gave serious thought to the stories about the white man's government or the consequences of killing the

---

1. The observation stresses the connection between the advent of Christianity and colonial domination.

Christians. If they became more troublesome than they already were they would simply be driven out of the clan.

And the little church was at that moment too deeply absorbed in its own troubles to annoy the clan. It all began over the question of admitting outcasts.

These outcasts, or osu,[2] seeing that the new religion welcomed twins and such abominations, thought that it was possible that they would also be received. And so one Sunday two of them went into the church. There was an immediate stir; but so great was the work the new religion had done among the converts that they did not immediately leave the church when the outcasts came in. Those who found themselves nearest to them merely moved to another seat. It was a miracle. But it only lasted till the end of the service. The whole church raised a protest and were about to drive these people out, when Mr Kiaga stopped them and began to explain.

"Before God," he said, "there is no slave or free. We are all children of God and we must receive these our brothers."

"You do not understand," said one of the converts. "What will the heathen say of us when they hear that we receive osu into our midst? They will laugh."

"Let them laugh," said Mr Kiaga. "God will laugh at them on the judgment day. Why do the nations rage and the peoples imagine a vain thing? He that sitteth in the heavens shall laugh. The Lord shall have them in derision."

"You do not understand," the convert maintained. "You are our teacher, and you can teach us the things of the new faith. But this is a matter which we know." And he told him what an osu was.

He was a person dedicated to a god, a thing set apart—a taboo for ever, and his children after him. He could neither marry nor be married by the free-born. He was in fact an outcast, living in a special area of the village, close to the Great Shrine. Wherever he went he carried with him the mark of his forbidden caste—long, tangled and dirty hair. A razor was taboo to him. An osu could not attend an assembly of the free-born, and they, in turn, could not shelter under his roof. He could not take any of the four titles of the clan, and when he died he was buried by his kind in the Evil Forest. How could such a man be a follower of Christ?

"He needs Christ more than you and I," said Mr Kiaga.

"Then I shall go back to the clan," said the convert. And he went. Mr Kiaga stood firm, and it was his firmness that saved the young church. The wavering converts drew inspiration and confidence from

---

2. Member of a low caste in Igbo society; originally destined to be sacrificed, they were held in contempt, and it was taboo to mix with them.

his unshakable faith. He ordered the outcasts to shave off their long, tangled hair. At first they were afraid they might die.

"Unless you shave off the mark of your heathen belief I will not admit you into the church," said Mr Kiaga. "You fear that you will die. Why should that be? How are you different from other men who shave their hair? The same God created you and them. But they have cast you out like lepers. It is against the will of God, who has promised everlasting life to all who believe in His holy name. The heathen say you will die if you do this or that, and you are afraid. They also said I would die if I built my church on this ground. Am I dead? They said I would die if I took care of twins. I am still alive. The heathen speak nothing but falsehood. Only the word of our God is true."

The two outcasts shaved off their hair,[3] and soon they were among the strongest adherents of the new faith. And what was more, nearly all the *osu* in Mbanta followed their example. It was in fact one of them who in his zeal brought the church into serious conflict with the clan a year later by killing the sacred python, the emanation of the god of water.

The royal python was the most revered animal in Mbanta and all the surrounding clans. It was addressed as 'Our Father', and was allowed to go wherever it chose, even into people's beds. It ate rats in the house and sometimes swallowed hens' eggs. If a clansman killed a royal python accidentally, he made sacrifices of atonement and performed an expensive burial ceremony such as was done for a great man. No punishment was prescribed for a man who killed the python knowingly. Nobody thought that such a thing could ever happen.

Perhaps it never did happen. That was the way the clan at first looked at it. No one had actually seen the man do it. The story had arisen among the Christians themselves.

But, all the same, the rulers and elders of Mbanta assembled to decide on their action. Many of them spoke at great length and in fury. The spirit of war was upon them. Okonkwo, who had begun to play a part in the affairs of his motherland, said that until the abominable gang was chased out of the village with whips there would be no peace.

But there were many others who saw the situation differently, and it was their counsel that prevailed in the end.

"It is not our custom to fight for our gods," said one of them. "Let us not presume to do so now. If a man kills the sacred python in the secrecy of his hut, the matter lies between him and the god. We did not see it. If we put ourselves between the god and his victim we may receive blows intended for the offender. When a man blasphemes,

3. Which they were forced to leave unkempt, as a sign of their degraded status.

what do we do? Do we go and stop his mouth? No. We put our fingers into our ears to stop us hearing. That is a wise action."

"Let us not reason like cowards," said Okonkwo. "If a man comes into my hut and defecates on the floor, what do I do? Do I shut my eyes? No! I take a stick and break his head. That is what a man does. These people are daily pouring filth over us, and Okeke says we should pretend not to see." Okonkwo made a sound full of disgust. This was a womanly clan, he thought. Such a thing could never happen in his fatherland, Umuofia.

"Okonkwo has spoken the truth," said another man. "We should do something. But let us ostracise these men. We would then not be held accountable for their abominations."

Everybody in the assembly spoke, and in the end it was decided to ostracise the Christians. Okonkwo ground his teeth in disgust.

That night a bell-man went through the length and breadth of Mbanta proclaiming that the adherents of the new faith were thenceforth excluded from the life and privileges of the clan.

The Christians had grown in number and were now a small community of men, women and children, self-assured and confident. Mr Brown, the white missionary, paid regular visits to them. "When I think that it is only eighteen months since the Seed was first sown among you," he said, "I marvel at what the Lord hath wrought."

It was Wednesday in Holy Week and Mr Kiaga had asked the women to bring red earth and white chalk and water to scrub the church for Easter; and the women had formed themselves into three groups for this purpose. They set out early that morning, some of them with their water-pots to the stream, another group with hoes and baskets to the village red-earth pit, and the others to the chalk quarry.

Mr Kiaga was praying in the church when he heard the women talking excitedly. He rounded off his prayer and went to see what it was all about. The women had come to the church with empty water-pots. They said that some young men had chased them away from the stream with whips. Soon after, the women who had gone for red earth returned with empty baskets. Some of them had been heavily whipped. The chalk women also returned to tell a similar story.

"What does it all mean?" asked Mr Kiaga, who was greatly perplexed.

"The village has outlawed us," said one of the women. "The bell-man announced it last night. But it is not our custom to debar anyone from the stream or the quarry."

Another woman said, "They want to ruin us. They will not allow us into the markets. They have said so."

Mr Kiaga was going to send into the village for his men-converts when he saw them coming on their own. Of course they had all heard the bell-man, but they had never in all their lives heard of women being debarred from the stream.

"Come along," they said to the women. "We will go with you to meet those cowards." Some of them had big sticks and some even matchets.

But Mr Kiaga restrained them. He wanted first to know why they had been outlawed.

"They say that Okoli killed the sacred python,"[4] said one man.

"It is false," said another. "Okoli told me himself that it was false."

Okoli was not there to answer. He had fallen ill on the previous night. Before the day was over he was dead. His death showed that the gods were still able to fight their own battles. The clan saw no reason then for molesting the Christians.

Chapter Nineteen

The last big rains of the year were falling. It was the time for treading red earth with which to build walls. It was not done earlier because the rains were too heavy and would have washed away the heap of trodden earth; and it could not be done later because harvesting would soon set in, and after that the dry season.

It was going to be Okonkwo's last harvest in Mbanta. The seven wasted and weary years were at last dragging to a close. Although he had prospered in his motherland Okonkwo knew that he would have prospered even more in Umuofia, in the land of his fathers where men were bold and warlike. In these seven years he would have climbed to the utmost heights. And so he regretted every day of his exile. His mother's kinsmen had been very kind to him, and he was grateful. But that did not alter the facts. He had called the first child born to him in exile Nneka—'Mother is Supreme'—out of politeness to his mother's kinsmen. But two years later when a son was born he called him Nwofia—'Begotten in the Wilderness'.

As soon as he entered his last year in exile Okonkwo sent money to Obierika to build him two huts in his old compound where he and his family would live until he built more huts and the outside wall of his compound. He could not ask another man to build his own *obi* for him, nor the walls of his compound. Those things a man built for himself or inherited from his father.

As the last heavy rains of the year began to fall, Obierika sent word

4. Okoli's killing of the python is as much an expression of the convert's religious zeal as an act of disavowal of the indigenous culture and religion. Compare his gesture to that of Oduche in *Arrow of God*, marked, however, in this case by a profound ambiguity. *Okoli:* "Strong man."

that the two huts had been built and Okonkwo began to prepare for his return, after the rains. He would have liked to return earlier and build his compound that year before the rains stopped, but in doing so he would have taken something from the full penalty of seven years. And that could not be. So he waited impatiently for the dry season to come.

It came slowly. The rain became lighter and lighter until it fell in slanting showers. Sometimes the sun shone through the rain and a light breeze blew. It was a gay and airy kind of rain. The rainbow began to appear, and sometimes two rainbows, like a mother and her daughter, the one young and beautiful, and the other an old and faint shadow. The rainbow was called the python of the sky.

Okonkwo called his three wives and told them to get things together for a great feast. "I must thank my mother's kinsmen before I go," he said.

Ekwefi still had some cassava left on her farm from the previous year. Neither of the other wives had. It was not that they had been lazy, but that they had many children to feed. It was therefore understood that Ekwefi would provide cassava for the feast. Nwoye's mother and Ojiugo would provide the other things like smoked fish, palm-oil and pepper for the soup. Okonkwo would take care of meat and yams.

Ekwefi rose early on the following morning and went to her farm with her daughter, Ezinma, and Ojiugo's daughter, Obiageli, to harvest cassava tubers. Each of them carried a long cane basket, a matchet for cutting down the soft cassava stem, and a little hoe for digging out the tuber. Fortunately, a light rain had fallen during the night and the soil would not be very hard.

"It will not take us long to harvest as much as we like," said Ekwefi.

"But the leaves will be wet," said Ezinma. Her basket was balanced on her head, and her arms folded across her breasts. She felt cold. "I dislike cold water dropping on my back. We should have waited for the sun to rise and dry the leaves."

Obiageli called her "Salt" because she said that she disliked water. "Are you afraid you may dissolve?"

The harvesting was easy, as Ekwefi had said. Ezinma shook every tree violently with a long stick before she bent down to cut the stem and dig out the tuber. Sometimes it was not necessary to dig. They just pulled the stump, and earth rose, roots snapped below, and the tuber was pulled out.

When they had harvested a sizeable heap they carried it down in two trips to the stream, where every woman had a shallow well for fermenting her cassava.

"It should be ready in four days or even three," said Obiageli. "They are young tubers."

"They are not all that young," said Ekwefi. "I planted the farm nearly two years ago. It is a poor soil and that is why the tubers are so small."

Okonkwo never did things by halves. When his wife Ekwefi protested that two goats were sufficient for the feast he told her that it was not her affair.

"I am calling a feast because I have the wherewithal. I cannot live on the bank of a river and wash my hands with spittle. My mother's people have been good to me and I must show my gratitude."

And so three goats were slaughtered and a number of fowls. It was like a wedding feast. There was foo-foo and yam pottage, egusi soup and bitter-leaf soup and pots and pots of palm-wine.

All the *umunna* were invited to the feast, all the descendants of Okolo,[1] who had lived about two hundred years before. The oldest member of this extensive family was Okonkwo's uncle, Uchendu. The kola nut was given to him to break, and he prayed to the ancestors. He asked them for health and children. "We do not ask for wealth because he that has health and children will also have wealth. We do not pray to have more money but to have more kinsmen. We are better than animals because we have kinsmen. An animal rubs its itching flank against a tree, a man asks his kinsman to scratch him." He prayed especially for Okonkwo and his family. He then broke the kola nut and threw one of the lobes on the ground for the ancestors.

As the broken kola nuts were passed round, Okonkwo's wives and children and those who came to help them with the cooking began to bring out the food. His sons brought out the pots of palm-wine. There was so much food and drink that many kinsmen whistled in surprise. When all was laid out, Okonkwo rose to speak.

"I beg you to accept this little kola," he said. "It is not to pay you back for all you did for me in these seven years. A child cannot pay for its mother's milk. I have only called you together because it is good for kinsmen to meet."

Yam pottage was served first because it was lighter than foo-foo and because yam always came first. Then the foo-foo was served. Some kinsmen ate it with egusi[2] soup and others with bitter-leaf soup. The meat was then shared so that every member of the *umunna* had a portion. Every man rose in order of years and took a share. Even the few kinsmen who had not been able to come had their shares taken out for them in due turn.

---

1. The maternal ancestor was also probably a champion wrestler and warrior.
2. Melon seed, used as vegetable in stew; the festive atmosphere here evokes the deliberate extravagance typical of a "potlatch."

As the palm-wine was drunk one of the oldest members of the *umunna* rose to thank Okonkwo:

"If I say that we did not expect such a big feast I will be suggesting that we did not know how open-handed our son, Okonkwo, is. We all know him, and we expected a big feast. But it turned out to be even bigger than we expected. Thank you. May all you took out return again tenfold. It is good in these days when the younger generation consider themselves wiser than their sires to see a man doing things in the grand, old way. A man who calls his kinsmen to a feast does not do so to save them from starving. They all have food in their own homes. When we gather together in the moonlit village ground it is not because of the moon. Every man can see it in his own compound. We come together because it is good for kinsmen to do so. You may ask why I am saying all this. I say it because I fear for the younger generation, for you people." He waved his arm where most of the young men sat. "As for me, I have only a short while to live, and so have Uchendu and Unachukwu and Emefo. But I fear for you young people because you do not understand how strong is the bond of kinship. You do not know what it is to speak with one voice. And what is the result? An abominable religion has settled among you. A man can now leave his father and his brothers. He can curse the gods of his fathers and his ancestors, like a hunter's dog that suddenly goes mad and turns on his master. I fear for you; I fear for the clan." He turned again to Okonkwo and said, "Thank you for calling us together."

Part Three

Chapter Twenty

Seven years was a long time to be away from one's clan. A man's place was not always there, waiting for him. As soon as he left, someone else rose and filled it. The clan was like a lizard; if it lost its tail it soon grew another.

Okonkwo knew these things. He knew that he had lost his place among the nine masked spirits who administered justice in the clan. He had lost the chance to lead his warlike clan against the new religion, which he was told, had gained ground. He had lost the years in which he might have taken the highest titles in the clan. But some of these losses were not irreparable. He was determined that his return should be marked by his people. He would return with a flourish, and regain the seven wasted years.

Even in his first year in exile he had begun to plan for his return. The first thing he would do would be to rebuild his compound on a more magnificent scale. He would build a bigger barn than he had had before and he would build huts for two new wives. Then he would show his wealth by initiating his sons into the *ozo* society. Only the really great men in the clan were able to do this. Okonkwo saw clearly the high esteem in which he would be held, and he saw himself taking the highest title in the land.

As the years of exile passed one by one it seemed to him that his *chi* might now be making amends for the past disaster. His yams grew abundantly, not only in his motherland but also in Umuofia, where his friend gave them out year by year to share-croppers.

Then the tragedy of his first son had occurred. At first it appeared as if it might prove too great for his spirit. But it was a resilient spirit, and in the end Okonkwo overcame his sorrow. He had five other sons and he would bring them up in the way of the clan.

He sent for the five sons and they came and sat in his *obi*. The youngest of them was four years old.

"You have all seen the great abomination of your brother. Now he is no longer my son or your brother. I will only have a son who is a man, who will hold his head up among my people. If any one of you

97

prefers to be a woman, let him follow Nwoye now while I am alive so that I can curse him. If you turn against me when I am dead I will visit you and break your neck."

Okonkwo was very lucky in his daughters. He never stopped regretting that Ezinma was a girl. Of all his children she alone understood his every mood. A bond of sympathy had grown between them as the years had passed.

Ezinma grew up in her father's exile and became one of the most beautiful girls in Mbanta. She was called Crystal of Beauty, as her mother had been called in her youth. The young ailing girl who had caused her mother so much heartache had been transformed, almost overnight, into a healthy buoyant maiden. She had, it was true, her moments of depression when she would snap at everybody like an angry dog. These moods descended on her suddenly and for no apparent reason. But they were very rare and short-lived. As long as they lasted, she could bear no other person but her father.

Many young men and prosperous middle-aged men of Mbanta came to marry her. But she refused them all, because her father had called her one evening and said to her: "There are many good and prosperous people here, but I shall be happy if you marry in Umuofia when we return home."

That was all he had said. But Ezinma had seen clearly all the thought and hidden meaning behind the few words. And she had agreed.

"Your half-sister, Obiageli, will not understand me," Okonkwo said. "But you can explain to her."

Although they were almost the same age, Ezinma wielded a strong influence over her half-sister. She explained to her why they should not marry yet, and she agreed also. And so the two of them refused every offer of marriage in Mbanta.

"I wish she were a boy," Okonkwo thought within himself. She understood things so perfectly. Who else among his children could have read his thought so well? With two beautiful grown-up daughters his return to Umuofia would attract considerable attention. His future sons-in-law would be men of authority in the clan. The poor and unknown would not dare to come forth.

Umuofia had indeed changed during the seven years Okonkwo had been in exile. The church had come and led many astray. Not only the low-born and the outcast but sometimes a worthy man had joined it. Such a man was Ogbuefi Ugonna,[1] who had taken two titles, and who like a madman had cut the anklet of his titles and cast it away to join

---

1. "Pride of his father."

the Christians. The white missionary was very proud of him and he was one of the first men in Umuofia to receive the sacrament of Holy Communion, or Holy Feast as it was called in Ibo. Ogbuefi Ugonna had thought of the Feast in terms of eating and drinking, only more holy than the village variety. He had therefore put his drinking-horn into his goatskin bag for the occasion.

But apart from the church, the white men had also brought a government. They had built a court where the District Commissioner judged cases in ignorance. He had court messengers who brought men to him for trial. Many of these messengers came from Umuru on the bank of the Great River,[2] where the white men first came many years before and where they had built the centre of their religion and trade and government. These court messengers were greatly hated in Umuofia because they were foreigners and also arrogant and high-handed. They were called *kotma*,[3] and because of their ash-coloured shorts they earned the additional name of Ashy-Buttocks. They guarded the prison, which was full of men who had offended against the white man's law. Some of these prisoners had thrown away their twins and some had molested the Christians. They were beaten in the prison by the *kotma* and made to work every morning clearing the government compound and fetching wood for the white Commissioner and the court messengers. Some of these prisoners were men of title who should be above such mean occupation. They were grieved by the indignity and mourned for their neglected farms. As they cut grass in the morning the younger men sang in time with the strokes of their matchets:

> "Kotma of the ash buttocks,
> He is fit to be a slave.
> The white man has no sense,
> He is fit to be a slave."[4]

The court messengers did not like to be called Ashy-Buttocks, and they beat the men. But the song spread in Umuofia.

Okonkwo's head was bowed in sadness as Obierika told him these things.

"Perhaps I have been away too long," Okonkwo said, almost to himself. "But I cannot understand these things you tell me. What is it that has happened to our people? Why have they lost the power to fight?"

2. The Niger, which flows southward along the western side of Igbo land (see maps, pp. 222 and 223).
3. Court interpreters; they were the first indigenous civil servants in the colonial system, serving as go-betweens for the white administrators and the indigenous populations. In this role, they proved indispensable for the consolidation of the colonial system.
4. The derisive tone of the prisoners' work song reflects the suspicion with which Africans in the service of the administration were viewed throughout the colonial period.

"Have you not heard how the white man wiped out Abame?" asked Obierika.

"I have heard," said Okonkwo. "But I have also heard that Abame people were weak and foolish. Why did they not fight back? Had they no guns and matchets? We would be cowards to compare ourselves with the men of Abame. Their fathers had never dared to stand before our ancestors. We must fight these men and drive them from the land."

"It is already too late," said Obierika sadly. "Our own men and our sons have joined the ranks of the stranger. They have joined his religion and they help to uphold his government. If we should try to drive out the white men in Umuofia we should find it easy. There are only two of them. But what of our own people who are following their way and have been given power? They would go to Umuru and bring the soldiers, and we would be like Abame." He paused for a long time and then said: "I told you on my last visit to Mbanta how they hanged Aneto."

"What has happened to that piece of land in dispute?" asked Okonkwo.

"The white man's court has decided that it should belong to Nnama's family, who had given much money to the white man's messengers and interpreter."

"Does the white man understand our custom about land?"

"How can he when he does not even speak our tongue? But he says that our customs are bad; and our own brothers who have taken up his religion also say that our customs are bad. How do you think we can fight when our own brothers have turned against us? The white man is very clever. He came quietly and peaceably with his religion. We were amused at his foolishness and allowed him to stay. Now he has won our brothers, and our clan can no longer act like one. He has put a knife on the things that held us together and we have fallen apart."

"How did they get hold of Aneto to hang him?" asked Okonkwo.

"When he killed Oduche in the fight over the land, he fled to Aninta to escape the wrath of the earth. This was about eight days after the fight, because Oduche had not died immediately from his wounds. It was on the seventh day that he died. But everybody knew that he was going to die and Aneto got his belongings together in readiness to flee. But the Christians had told the white man about the accident, and he sent his *kotma* to catch Aneto. He was imprisoned with all the leaders of his family. In the end Oduche died and Aneto was taken to Umuru and hanged. The other people were released, but even now they have not found the mouth with which to tell of their suffering."

The two men sat in silence for a long while afterwards.

Chapter Twenty-One

There were many men and women in Umuofia who did not feel as strongly as Okonkwo about the new dispensation. The white man had indeed brought a lunatic religion, but he had also built a trading store and for the first time palm-oil and kernel became things of great price, and much money flowed into Umuofia.

And even in the matter of religion there was a growing feeling that there might be something in it after all, something vaguely akin to method in the overwhelming madness.

This growing feeling was due to Mr Brown, the white missionary, who was very firm in restraining his flock from provoking the wrath of the clan. One member in particular was very difficult to restrain. His name was Enoch and his father was the priest of the snake cult. The story went around that Enoch had killed and eaten the sacred python, and that his father had cursed him.

Mr Brown preached against such excess of zeal. Everything was possible, he told his energetic flock, but everything was not expedient. And so Mr Brown came to be respected even by the clan, because he trod softly on its faith. He made friends with some of the great men of the clan and on one of his frequent visits to the neighbouring villages he had been presented with a carved elephant tusk, which was a sign of dignity and rank. One of the great men in that village was called Akunna[1] and he had given one of his sons to be taught the white man's knowledge in Mr Brown's school.

Whenever Mr Brown went to that village he spent long hours with Akunna in his *obi* talking through an interpreter about religion. Neither of them succeeded in converting the other but they learnt more about their different beliefs.

"You say that there is one supreme God who made heaven and earth," said Akunna on one of Mr Brown's visits. "We also believe in Him and call Him Chukwu. He made all the world and the other gods."

"There are no other gods," said Mr Brown. "Chukwu is the only God and all others are false. You carve a piece of wood—like that one" (he pointed at the rafters from which Akunna's carved *Ikenga*[2] hung), "and you call it a god. But it is still a piece of wood."

"Yes," said Akunna. "It is indeed a piece of wood. The tree from which it came was made by Chukwu, as indeed all minor gods were. But He made them for His messengers so that we could approach Him through them. It is like yourself. You are the head of your church."

1. "Father's wealth."
2. Carved image of a deity that expresses an individual's power (*ike*).

"No," protested Mr Brown. "The head of my church is God Himself."

"I know," said Akunna, "but there must be a head in this world
among men. Somebody like yourself must be the head here."

"The head of my church in that sense is in England."

"That is exactly what I am saying. The head of your church is in
your country. He has sent you here as his messenger. And you have
also appointed your own messengers and servants. Or let me take
another example, the District Commissioner. He is sent by your
king."

"They have a queen,"[3] said the interpreter on his own account.

"Your queen sends her messenger, the District Commissioner. He
finds that he cannot do the work alone and so he appoints *kotma* to
help him. It is the same with God, or Chukwu. He appoints the
smaller gods to help Him because His work is too great for one person."

"You should not think of him as a person," said Mr Brown. "It is
because you do so that you imagine He must need helpers. And the
worst thing about it is that you give all the worship to the false gods
you have created."

"That is not so. We make sacrifices to the little gods, but when they
fail and there is no one else to turn to we go to Chukwu. It is right to
do so. We approach a great man through his servants. But when his
servants fail to help us, then we go to the last source of hope. We
appear to pay greater attention to the little gods but that is not so. We
worry them more because we are afraid to worry their Master. Our
fathers knew that Chukwu was the Overlord and that is why many of
them gave their children the name Chukwuka—'Chukwu is
Supreme'."

"You said one interesting thing," said Mr Brown. "You are afraid of
Chukwu. In my religion Chukwu is a loving Father and need not be
feared by those who do His will."

"But we must fear Him when we are not doing His will," said
Akunna. "And who is to tell His will? It is too great to be known."

In this way Mr Brown learnt a good deal about the religion of the
clan and he came to the conclusion that a frontal attack on it would
not succeed. And so he built a school and a little hospital in Umuofia.
He went from family to family begging people to send their children
to his school. But at first they only sent their slaves or sometimes their
lazy children. Mr Brown begged and argued and prophesied. He said
that the leaders of the land in the future would be men and women
who had learnt to read and write. If Umuofia failed to send her chil-

---

3. An allusion to Queen Victoria of England, who reigned from 1837 to 1901; this mention
   of her dates the passage.

dren to the school, strangers would come from other places to rule them. They could already see that happening in the Native Court, where the D.C. was surrounded by strangers who spoke his tongue. Most of these strangers came from the distant town of Umuru on the bank of the Great River where the white man first went.

In the end Mr Brown's arguments began to have an effect. More people came to learn in his school, and he encouraged them with gifts of singlets and towels.[4] They were not all young, these people who came to learn. Some of them were thirty years old or more. They worked on their farms in the morning and went to school in the afternoon. And it was not long before the people began to say that the white man's medicine was quick in working. Mr Brown's school produced quick results. A few months in it were enough to make one a court messenger or even a court clerk. Those who stayed longer became teachers; and from Umuofia labourers went forth into the Lord's vineyard. New churches were established in the surrounding villages and a few schools with them. From the very beginning religion and education went hand in hand.

Mr Brown's mission grew from strength to strength, and because of its link with the new administration it earned a new social prestige. But Mr Brown himself was breaking down in health. At first he ignored the warning signs. But in the end he had to leave his flock, sad and broken.

It was in the first rainy season after Okonkwo's return to Umuofia that Mr Brown left for home. As soon as he had learnt of Okonkwo's return five months earlier, the missionary had immediately paid him a visit. He had just sent Okonkwo's son, Nwoye, who was now called Isaac,[5] to the new training college for teachers in Umuru. And he had hoped that Okonkwo would be happy to hear of it. But Okonkwo had driven him away with the threat that if he came into his compound again, he would be carried out of it.

Okonkwo's return to his native land was not as memorable as he had wished. It was true his two beautiful daughters aroused great interest among suitors and marriage negotiations were soon in progress, but, beyond that, Umuofia did not appear to have taken any special notice of the warrior's return. The clan had undergone such profound change during his exile that it was barely recognisable. The new religion and government and the trading stores were very much in the people's eyes and minds. There were still many who saw these

---

4. At the time, singlets (undershirts) and towels were new and tawdry items of western industrial production.
5. In the Old Testament story, Isaac is saved by God at the last minute from being sacrificed by Abraham, his father. Nwoye assumes this name as a conscious tribute to Ikemefuna, killed by Okonkwo, his adopted father.

new institutions as evil, but even they talked and thought about little else, and certainly not about Okonkwo's return.

And it was the wrong year too. If Okonkwo had immediately initiated his two sons into the *ozo* society as he had planned he would have caused a stir. But the initiation rite was performed once in three years in Umuofia, and he had to wait for nearly two years for the next round of ceremonies.

Okonkwo was deeply grieved. And it was not just a personal grief. He mourned for the clan, which he saw breaking up and falling apart, and he mourned for the warlike men of Umuofia, who had so unaccountably become soft like women.

Chapter Twenty-Two

Mr Brown's successor was the Reverend James Smith, and he was a different kind of man. He condemned openly Mr Brown's policy of compromise and accommodation. He saw things as black and white. And black was evil. He saw the world as a battlefield in which the children of light were locked in mortal conflict with the sons of darkness. He spoke in his sermons about sheep and goats and about wheat and tares. He believed in slaying the prophets of Baal.

Mr Smith was greatly distressed by the ignorance which many of his flock showed even in such things as the Trinity and the Sacraments. It only showed that they were seeds sown on a rocky soil. Mr Brown had thought of nothing but numbers. He should have known that the kingdom of God did not depend on large crowds. Our Lord Himself stressed the importance of fewness. Narrow is the way and few the number. To fill the Lord's holy temple with an idolatrous crowd clamouring for signs was a folly of everlasting consequence. Our Lord used the whip only once in His life—to drive the crowd away from His church.

Within a few weeks of his arrival in Umuofia Mr Smith suspended a young woman from the church for pouring new wine into old bottles. This woman had allowed her heathen husband to mutilate her dead child. The child had been declared an *ogbanje*, plaguing its mother by dying and entering her womb to be born again. Four times this child had run its evil round. And so it was mutilated to discourage it from returning.

Mr Smith was filled with wrath when he heard of this. He disbelieved the story which even some of the most faithful confirmed, the story of really evil children who were not deterred by mutilation, but came back with all the scars. He replied that such stories were spread in the world by the Devil to lead men astray. Those who believed such stories were unworthy of the Lord's table.

There was a saying in Umuofia that as a man danced so the drums were beaten for him. Mr Smith danced a furious step and so the drums went mad. The over-zealous converts who had smarted under Mr Brown's restraining hand now flourished in full favour. One of them was Enoch, the son of the snake-priest who was believed to have killed and eaten the sacred python. Enoch's devotion to the new faith had seemed so much greater than Mr Brown's that the villagers called him the outsider who wept louder than the bereaved.

Enoch was short and slight of build, and always seemed in great haste. His feet were short and broad, and when he stood or walked his heels came together and his feet opened outwards as if they had quarrelled and meant to go in different directions. Such was the excessive energy bottled up in Enoch's small body that it was always erupting in quarrels and fights. On Sundays he always imagined that the sermon was preached for the benefit of his enemies. And if he happened to sit near one of them he would occasionally turn to give him a meaningful look, as if to say, 'I told you so'. It was Enoch who touched off the great conflict between church and clan in Umuofia which had been gathering since Mr Brown left.

It happened during the annual ceremony which was held in honour of the earth deity. At such times the ancestors of the clan who had been committed to Mother Earth at their death emerged again as *egwugwu* through tiny ant-holes.

One of the greatest crimes a man could commit was to unmask an *egwugwu* in public, or to say or do anything which might reduce its immortal prestige in the eyes of the uninitiated. And this was what Enoch did.

The annual worship of the earth goddess fell on a Sunday, and the masked spirits were abroad. The Christian women who had been to church could not therefore go home. Some of their men had gone out to beg the *egwugwu* to retire for a short while for the women to pass.[1] They agreed and were already retiring, when Enoch boasted aloud that they would not dare to touch a Christian. Whereupon they all came back and one of them gave Enoch a good stroke of the cane, which was always carried. Enoch fell on him and tore off his mask. The other *egwugwu* immediately surrounded their desecrated companion, to shield him from the profane gaze of women and children, and led him away. Enoch had killed an ancestral spirit, and Umuofia was thrown into confusion.

That night the Mother of the Spirits walked the length and breadth of the clan, weeping for her murdered son. It was a terrible night. Not even the oldest man in Umuofia had ever heard such a strange and

1. To avoid the profanation of being seen by women.

fearful sound, and it was never to be heard again. It seemed as if the very soul of the tribe wept for a great evil that was coming—its own death.

On the next day all the masked *egwugwu* of Umuofia assembled in the market-place. They came from all the quarters of the clan and even from the neighbouring villages. The dreaded Otakagu came from Imo, and Ekwensu, dangling a white cock, arrived from Uli.[2] It was a terrible gathering. The eerie voices of countless spirits, the bells that clattered behind some of them, and the clash of matchets as they ran forwards and backwards and saluted one another, sent tremors of fear into every heart. For the first time in living memory the sacred bull-roarer[3] was heard in broad daylight.

From the market-place the furious band made for Enoch's compound. Some of the elders of the clan went with them, wearing heavy protections of charms and amulets. These were men whose arms were strong in *ogwu*, or medicine. As for the ordinary men and women, they listened from the safety of their huts.

The leaders of the Christians had met together at Mr Smith's parsonage on the previous night. As they deliberated they could hear the Mother of Spirits wailing for her son. The chilling sound affected Mr Smith, and for the first time he seemed to be afraid.

"What are they planning to do?" he asked. No one knew, because such a thing had never happened before. Mr Smith would have sent for the District Commissioner and his court messengers, but they had gone on tour[4] on the previous day.

"One thing is clear," said Mr Smith. "We cannot offer physical resistance to them. Our strength lies in the Lord." They knelt down together and prayed to God for delivery.

"O Lord save Thy people," cried Mr Smith.

"And bless Thine inheritance," replied the men.

They decided that Enoch should be hidden in the parsonage for a day or two. Enoch himself was greatly disappointed when he heard this, for he had hoped that a holy war was imminent; and there were a few other Christians who thought like him. But wisdom prevailed in the camp of the faithful and many lives were thus saved.

The band of *egwugwu* moved like a furious whirlwind to Enoch's compound and with matchet and fire reduced it to a desolate heap. And from there they made for the church, intoxicated with destruction.

2. A town in Anambra State, made famous for its landing strip that served as a vital link for the secessionist government to the outside world during the Biafra war; *Otakagu*: "one who bites like a tiger"; *Imo*: the great river in Central Igboland; *Ekwensu*: the Igbo word for Satan or Devil.
3. A wooden device that produces a roaring noise to warn the uninitiated of the approach or presence of secret societies.
4. Standard expression for periodic journey into the interior by a colonial administrative officer.

Mr Smith was in his church when he heard the masked spirits coming. He walked quietly to the door which commanded the approach to the church compound, and stood there. But when the first three or four *egwugwu* appeared on the church compound he nearly bolted. He overcame this impulse and instead of running away he went down the two steps that led up to the church and walked towards the approaching spirits.

They surged forward, and a long stretch of the bamboo fence with which the church compound was surrounded gave way before them. Discordant bells clanged, matchets clashed and the air was full of dust and weird sounds. Mr Smith heard a sound of footsteps behind him. He turned round and saw Okeke, his interpreter. Okeke had not been on the best of terms with his master since he had strongly con demned Enoch's behaviour at the meeting of the leaders of the church during the night. Okeke had gone as far as to say that Enoch should not be hidden in the parsonage, because he would only draw the wrath of the clan on the pastor. Mr Smith had rebuked him in very strong language, and had not sought his advice that morning. But now, as he came up and stood by him confronting the angry spirits, Mr Smith looked at him and smiled. It was a wan smile, but there was deep gratitude there.

For a brief moment the onrush of the *egwugwu* was checked by the unexpected composure of the two men. But it was only a momentary check, like the tense silence between blasts of thunder. The second onrush was greater than the first. It swallowed up the two men. Then an unmistakable voice rose above the tumult and there was immediate silence. Space was made around the two men, and Ajofia began to speak.

Ajofia[5] was the leading *egwugwu* of Umuofia. He was the head and spokesman of the nine ancestors who administered justice in the clan. His voice was unmistakable and so he was able to bring immediate peace to the agitated spirits. He then addressed Mr Smith, and as he spoke clouds of smoke rose from his head.

"The body of the white man, I salute you," he said, using the language in which immortals spoke to men.

"The body of the white man, do you know me?" he asked.

Mr Smith looked at his interpreter, but Okeke, who was a native of distant Umuru, was also at a loss.

Ajofia laughed in his guttural voice. It was like the laugh of rusty metal. "They are strangers," he said, "and they are ignorant. But let that pass." He turned round to his comrades and saluted them, calling them the fathers of Umuofia. He dug his rattling spear into the

5. "Spirit of the forest," or "Evil Forest." See pp. 54–57.

ground and it shook with metallic life. Then he turned once more to
the missionary and his interpreter.

"Tell the white man that we will not do him any harm," he said to
the interpreter. "Tell him to go back to his house and leave us alone.
We liked his brother who was with us before. He was foolish, but we
liked him, and for his sake we shall not harm his brother. But this
shrine which he built must be destroyed. We shall no longer allow it
in our midst. It has bred untold abominations and we have come to
put an end to it." He turned to his comrades. "Fathers of Umuofia, I
salute you;" and they replied with one guttural voice. He turned again
to the missionary. "You can stay with us if you like our ways. You can
worship your own god. It is good that a man should worship the gods
and the spirits of his fathers. Go back to your house so that you may
not be hurt. Our anger is great but we have held it down so that we
can talk to you."

Mr Smith said to his interpreter: "Tell them to go away from here.
This is the house of God and I will not live to see it desecrated."

Okeke interpreted wisely to the spirits and leaders of Umuofia:
"The white man says he is happy you have come to him with your
grievances, like friends. He will be happy if you leave the matter in
his hands."

"We cannot leave the matter in his hands because he does not
understand our customs, just as we do not understand his. We say he
is foolish because he does not know our ways, and perhaps he says
we are foolish because we do not know his. Let him go away."

Mr Smith stood his ground. But he could not save his church.
When the *egwugwu* went away the red-earth church which Mr
Brown had built was a pile of earth and ashes. And for the moment
the spirit of the clan was pacified.

Chapter Twenty-Three

For the first time in many years Okonkwo had a feeling that was akin
to happiness. The times which had altered so unaccountably during
his exile seemed to be coming round again. The clan which had
turned false on him appeared to be making amends.

He had spoken violently to his clansmen when they had met in the
market-place to decide on their action. And they had listened to him
with respect. It was like the good old days again, when a warrior was
a warrior. Although they had not agreed to kill the missionary or drive
away the Christians, they had agreed to do something substantial.
And they had done it. Okonkwo was almost happy again.

For two days after the destruction of the church, nothing happened. Every man in Umuofia went about armed with a gun or a

matchet. They would not be caught unawares, like the men of Abame.

Then the District Commissioner returned from his tour. Mr Smith went immediately to him and they had a long discussion. The men of Umuofia did not take any notice of this, and if they did, they thought it was not important. The missionary often went to see his brother white man. There was nothing strange in that.

Three days later the District Commissioner sent his sweet-tongued messenger to the leaders of Umuofia asking them to meet him in his headquarters. That also was not strange. He often asked them to hold such palavers,[1] as he called them. Okonkwo was among the six leaders he invited.

Okonkwo warned the others to be fully armed. "An Umuofia man does not refuse a call," he said. "He may refuse to do what he is asked; he does not refuse to be asked. But the times have changed, and we must be fully prepared."

And so the six men went to see the District Commissioner, armed with their matchets. They did not carry guns, for that would be unseemly. They were led into the courthouse where the District Commissioner sat. He received them politely. They unslung their goatskin bags and their sheathed matchets, put them on the floor, and sat down.

"I have asked you to come," began the Commissioner, "because of what happened during my absence. I have been told a few things but I cannot believe them until I have heard your own side. Let us talk about it like friends and find a way of ensuring that it does not happen again."

Ogbuefi Ekwueme rose to his feet and began to tell the story.

"Wait a minute," said the Commissioner. "I want to bring in my men so that they too can hear your grievances and take warning. Many of them come from distant places and although they speak your tongue they are ignorant of your customs. James! Go and bring in the men." His interpreter left the court-room and soon returned with twelve men. They sat together with the men of Umuofia, and Ogbuefi Ekwueme began again to tell the story of how Enoch murdered an *egwugwu*.[2]

It happened so quickly that the six men did not see it coming. There was only a brief scuffle, too brief even to allow the drawing of a sheathed matchet. The six men were handcuffed and led into the guardroom.

"We shall not do you any harm," said the District Commissioner to them later, "if only you agree to co-operate with us. We have brought a peaceful administration to you and your people so that you may be happy. If any man ill-treats you we shall come to your rescue. But we

1. Formal discussions, negotiations.
2. By unmasking him; *Ekwueme*: "man of his word."

will not allow you to ill-treat others. We have a court of law where we judge cases and administer justice just as it is done in my own country under a great queen. I have brought you here because you joined together to molest others, to burn people's houses and their place of worship. That must not happen in the dominion of our queen, the most powerful ruler in the world. I have decided that you will pay a fine of two hundred bags of cowries. You will be released as soon as you agree to this and undertake to collect that fine from your people. What do you say to that?"

The six men remained sullen and silent and the Commissioner left them for a while. He told the court messengers, when he left the guardroom, to treat the men with respect because they were the leaders of Umuofia. They said, "Yes, sir," and saluted.

As soon as the District Commissioner left, the head messenger, who was also the prisoners' barber, took down his razor and shaved off all the hair on the men's heads.[3] They were still handcuffed, and they just sat and moped.

"Who is the chief among you?" the court messengers asked in jest. "We see that every pauper wears the anklet of title in Umuofia. Does it cost as much as ten cowries?"

The six men ate nothing throughout that day and the next. They were not even given any water to drink, and they could not go out to urinate or go into the bush when they were pressed. At night the messengers came in to taunt them and to knock their shaven heads together.

Even when the men were left alone they found no words to speak to one another. It was only on the third day, when they could no longer bear the hunger and the insults, that they began to talk about giving in.

"We should have killed the white man if you had listened to me," Okonkwo snarled.

"We could have been in Umuru now waiting to be hanged," someone said to him.

"Who wants to kill the white man?" asked a messenger who had just rushed in. Nobody spoke.

"You are not satisfied with your crime, but you must kill the white man on top of it." He carried a strong stick, and he hit each man a few blows on the head and back. Okonkwo was choked with hate.

As soon as the six men were locked up, court messengers went into Umuofia to tell the people that their leaders would not be released unless they paid a fine of two hundred and fifty bags of cowries.

---

3. The prisoners' heads are shaved as a sign of their humiliation; this, as well as the whipping of adults, was a regular feature of the penal system in British colonies.

"Unless you pay the fine immediately," said their head-man, "we will take your leaders to Umuru before the big white man, and hang them."

This story spread quickly through the villages, and was added to as it went. Some said that the men had already been taken to Umuru and would be hanged on the following day. Some said that their families would also be hanged. Others said that soldiers were already on their way to shoot the people of Umuofia as they had done in Abame.

It was the time of the full moon. But that night the voice of children was not heard. The village *ilo* where they always gathered for a moon-play was empty. The women of Iguedo did not meet in their secret enclosure to learn a new dance to be displayed later to the village. Young men who were always abroad in the moonlight kept their huts that night. Their manly voices were not heard on the village paths as they went to visit their friends and lovers. Umuofia was like a startled animal with ears erect, sniffing the silent, ominous air and not knowing which way to run.

The silence was broken by the village crier beating his sonorous *ogene*. He called every man in Umuofia, from the Akakanma age-group[4] upwards, to a meeting in the marketplace after the morning meal. He went from one end of the village to the other and walked all its breadth. He did not leave out any of the main footpaths.

Okonkwo's compound was like a deserted homestead. It was as if cold water had been poured on it. His family was all there, but everyone spoke in whispers. His daughter Ezinma had broken her twenty-eight-day visit to the family of her future husband, and returned home when she heard that her father had been imprisoned, and was going to be hanged. As soon as she got home she went to Obierika to ask what the men of Umuofia were going to do about it. But Obierika had not been home since morning. His wives thought he had gone to a secret meeting. Ezinma was satisfied that something was being done.

On the morning after the village crier's appeal the men of Umuofia met in the market-place and decided to collect without delay two hundred and fifty bags of cowries to appease the white man. They did not know that fifty bags[5] would go to the court messengers, who had increased the fine for that purpose.

---

4. Children born in the same year or who were roughly the same age underwent initiation rites together and thereafter met regularly and organized activities as a defined group throughout their lifetime. The age group system thus helped to identify generations and their specific interests within the larger society.
5. Points to the early onset of corruption in the modern system.

Chapter Twenty-Four

Okonkwo and his fellow prisoners were set free as soon as the fine was paid. The District Commissioner spoke to them again about the great queen, and about peace and good government. But the men did not listen. They just sat and looked at him and at his interpreter. In the end they were given back their bags and sheathed matchets and told to go home. They rose and left the courthouse. They neither spoke to anyone nor among themselves.

The court-house, like the church, was built a little way outside the village. The footpath that linked them was a very busy one because it also led to the stream, beyond the court. It was open and sandy. Footpaths were open and sandy in the dry season. But when the rains came the bush grew thick on either side and closed in on the path. It was now dry season.

As they made their way to the village the six men met women and children going to the stream with their waterpots. But the men wore such heavy and fearsome looks that the women and children did not say *'nno'* or 'welcome' to them, but edged out of the way to let them pass. In the village little groups of men joined them until they became a sizeable company. They walked silently. As each of the six men got to his compound, he turned in, taking some of the crowd with him. The village was astir in a silent, suppressed way.

Ezinma had prepared some food for her father as soon as news spread that the six men would be released. She took it to him in his *obi*. He ate absent-mindedly. He had no appetite; he only ate to please her. His male relations and friends had gathered in his *obi*, and Obierika was urging him to eat. Nobody else spoke, but they noticed the long stripes on Okonkwo's back where the warder's whip had cut into his flesh.

The village crier was abroad again in the night. He beat his iron gong and announced that another meeting would be held in the morning. Everyone knew that Umuofia was at last going to speak its mind about the things that were happening.

Okonkwo slept very little that night. The bitterness in his heart was now mixed with a kind of child-like excitement. Before he had gone to bed he had brought down his war dress, which he had not touched since his return from exile. He had shaken out his smoked raffia skirt and examined his tall feather head-gear and his shield. They were all satisfactory, he had thought.

As he lay on his bamboo bed he thought about the treatment he had received in the white man's court, and he swore vengeance. If Umuofia decided on war, all would be well. But if they chose to be cowards he would go out and avenge himself. He thought about wars in the past. The noblest, he thought, was the war against Isike. In those days Okudo[1] was still alive. Okudo sang a war song in a way that no other man could. He was not a fighter, but his voice turned every man into a lion.

'Worthy men are no more,' Okonkwo sighed as he remembered those days. 'Isike will never forget how we slaughtered them in that war. We killed twelve of their men and they killed only two of ours. Before the end of the fourth market week they were suing for peace. Those were days when men were men.'

As he thought of these things he heard the sound of the iron gong in the distance. He listened carefully, and could just hear the crier's voice. But it was very faint. He turned on his bed and his back hurt him. He ground his teeth. The crier was drawing nearer and nearer until he passed by Okonkwo's compound.

'The greatest obstacle in Umuofia,' Okonkwo thought bitterly, 'is that coward, Egonwanne.[2] His sweet tongue can change fire into cold ash. When he speaks he moves our men to impotence. If they had ignored his womanish wisdom five years ago, we would not have come to this.' He ground his teeth. 'Tomorrow he will tell them that our fathers never fought a "war of blame". If they listen to him I shall leave them and plan my own revenge.'

The crier's voice had once more become faint, and the distance had taken the harsh edge off his iron gong. Okonkwo turned from one side to the other and derived a kind of pleasure from the pain his back gave him. 'Let Egonwanne talk about a "war of blame" tomorrow and I shall show him my back and head.'[3] He ground his teeth.

The market-place began to fill as soon as the sun rose. Obierika was waiting in his *obi* when Okonkwo came along and called him. He hung his goatskin bag and his sheathed matchet on his shoulder and went out to join him. Obierika's hut was close to the road and he saw every man who passed to the market-place. He had exchanged greetings with many who had already passed that morning.

When Okonkwo and Obierika got to the meeting-place there were already so many people that if one threw up a grain of sand it would not find its way to the earth again. And many more people were coming from every quarter of the nine villages. It warmed Okonkwo's heart to see such strength of numbers. But he was looking for one man in particular, the man whose tongue he dreaded and despised so much.

1. The praise singer was an essential member of pre-colonial armies in Africa; as indicated by this name, Okudo is distinguished by his wearing an eagle feather.
2. "Money of my sibling."
3. As a sign of contempt.

"Can you see him?" he asked Obierika.

"Who?"

"Egonwanne," he said, his eyes roving from one corner of the huge market-place to the other. Most of the men were seated on goatskins on the ground. A few of them sat on wooden stools they had brought with them.

"No," said Obierika, casting his eyes over the crowd. "Yes, there he is, under the silk-cotton tree.[4] Are you afraid he would convince us not to fight?"

"Afraid? I do not care what he does to *you*. I despise him and those who listen to him. I shall fight alone if I choose."

They spoke at the top of their voices because everybody was talking, and it was like the sound of a great market.

'I shall wait till he has spoken,' Okonkwo thought. 'Then I shall speak.'

"But how do you know he will speak against war?" Obierika asked after a while.

"Because I know he is a coward," said Okonkwo. Obierika did not hear the rest of what he said because at that moment somebody touched his shoulder from behind and he turned round to shake hands and exchange greetings with five or six friends. Okonkwo did not turn round even though he knew the voices. He was in no mood to exchange greetings. But one of the men touched him and asked about the people of his compound.

"They are well," he replied without interest.

The first man to speak to Umuofia that morning was Okika,[5] one of the six who had been imprisoned. Okika was a great man and an orator. But he did not have the booming voice which a first speaker must use to establish silence in the assembly of the clan. Onyeka[6] had such a voice; and so he was asked to salute Umuofia before Okika began to speak.

"*Umuofia kwenu!*" he bellowed, raising his left arm and pushing the air with his open hand.

"*Yaa!*" roared Umuofia.

"*Umuofia kwenu!*" he bellowed again, and again and again, facing a new direction each time. And the crowd answered, "*Yaa!*"

There was immediate silence as though cold water had been poured on a roaring flame.

Okika sprang to his feet and also saluted his clansmen four times. Then he began to speak:

---

4. Or kapok, from which the cotton silk is obtained.
5. "Okika" is another unusual name, probably a shortened form of "okikachukwu," one who has an appointment with God or destiny.
6. "The one who excels."

"You all know why we are here, when we ought to be building our barns or mending our huts, when we should be putting our compounds in order. My father used to say to me: 'Whenever you see a toad jumping in broad daylight, then know that something is after its life.' When I saw you all pouring into this meeting from all the quarters of our clan so early in the morning, I knew that something was after our life." He paused for a brief moment and then began again:

"All our gods are weeping. Idemili is weeping, Ogwugwu is weeping, Agbala is weeping, and all the others. Our dead fathers are weeping because of the shameful sacrilege they are suffering and the abomination we have all seen with our eyes." He stopped again to steady his trembling voice.

"This is a great gathering. No clan can boast of greater numbers or greater valour. But are we all here? I ask you: Are all the sons of Umuofia with us here?" A deep murmur swept through the crowd.

"They are not," he said. "They have broken the clan and gone their several ways. We who are here this morning have remained true to our fathers, but our brothers have deserted us and joined a stranger to soil their fatherland. If we fight the stranger we shall hit our brothers and perhaps shed the blood of a clansman. But we must do it. Our fathers never dreamt of such a thing, they never killed their brothers. But a white man never came to them. So we must do what our fathers would never have done. Eneke the bird was asked why he was always on the wing and he replied: 'Men have learnt to shoot without missing their mark and I have learnt to fly without perching on a twig.' We must root out this evil. And if our brothers take the side of evil we must root them out too. And we must do it *now*. We must bale this water now that it is only ankle-deep. . . ."

At this point there was a sudden stir in the crowd and every eye was turned in one direction. There was a sharp bend in the road that led from the market place to the white man's court, and to the stream beyond it. And so no one had seen the approach of the five court messengers until they had come round the bend, a few paces from the edge of the crowd. Okonkwo was sitting at the edge.

He sprang to his feet as soon as he saw who it was. He confronted the head messenger, trembling with hate, unable to utter a word. The man was fearless and stood his ground, his four men lined up behind him.

In that brief moment the world seemed to stand still, waiting. There was utter silence. The men of Umuofia were merged into the mute backcloth of trees and giant creepers, waiting.

The spell was broken by the head messenger. "Let me pass!" he ordered.

"What do you want here?"

"The white man whose power you know too well has ordered this meeting to stop."

In a flash Okonkwo drew his matchet. The messenger crouched to avoid the blow. It was useless. Okonkwo's matchet descended twice and the man's head lay beside his uniformed body.

The waiting backcloth jumped into tumultuous life and the meeting was stopped. Okonkwo stood looking at the dead man. He knew that Umuofia would not go to war. He knew because they had let the other messengers escape. They had broken into tumult instead of action. He discerned fright in that tumult. He heard voices asking: "Why did he do it?"

He wiped his matchet on the sand and went away.

Chapter Twenty-Five

When the District Commissioner arrived at Okonkwo's compound at the head of an armed band of soldiers and court messengers he found a small crowd of men sitting wearily in the *obi*. He commanded them to come outside, and they obeyed without a murmur.

"Which among you is called Okonkwo?" he asked through his interpreter.

"He is not here," replied Obierika.

"Where is he?"

"He is not here!"

The Commissioner became angry and red in the face. He warned the men that unless they produced Okonkwo forthwith he would lock them all up. The men murmured among themselves, and Obierika spoke again.

"We can take you where he is, and perhaps your men will help us."

The Commissioner did not understand what Obierika meant when he said, "Perhaps your men will help us." One of the most infuriating habits of these people was their love of superfluous words, he thought.

Obierika with five or six others led the way. The Commissioner and his men followed, their firearms held at the ready. He had warned Obierika that if he and his men played any monkey tricks they would be shot. And so they went.

There was a small bush behind Okonkwo's compound. The only opening into this bush from the compound was a little round hole in the red-earth wall through which fowls went in and out in their endless search for food. The hole would not let a man through. It was to this bush that Obierika led the Commissioner and his men. They skirted round the compound, keeping close to the wall. The only sound they made was with their feet as they crushed dry leaves.

Then they came to the tree from which Okonkwo's body was dangling, and they stopped dead.

"Perhaps your men can help us bring him down and bury him," said Obierika. "We have sent for strangers from another village to do it for us, but they may be a long time coming."

The District Commissioner changed instantaneously. The resolute administrator in him gave way to the student of primitive customs.

"Why can't you take him down yourselves?" he asked.

"It is against our custom," said one of the men. "It is an abomination for a man to take his own life. It is an offence against the Earth, and a man who commits it will not be buried by his clansmen. His body is evil, and only strangers may touch it. That is why we ask your people to bring him down, because you are strangers."

"Will you bury him like any other man?" asked the Commissioner.

"We cannot bury him. Only strangers can. We shall pay your men to do it. When he has been buried we will then do our duty by him. We shall make sacrifices to cleanse the desecrated land."

Obierika, who had been gazing steadily at his friend's dangling body, turned suddenly to the District Commissioner and said ferociously: "That man was one of the greatest men in Umuofia. You drove him to kill himself; and now he will be buried like a dog. . . ." He could not say any more. His voice trembled and choked his words.

"Shut up!" shouted one of the messengers, quite unnecessarily.

"Take down the body," the Commissioner ordered his chief messenger, "and bring it and all these people to the court."

"Yes, sah," the messenger said, saluting.

The Commissioner went away, taking three or four of the soldiers with him. In the many years in which he had toiled to bring civilisation to different parts of Africa he had learnt a number of things. One of them was that a District Commissioner must never attend to such undignified details as cutting down a hanged man from the tree. Such attention would give the natives a poor opinion of him. In the book which he planned to write he would stress that point. As he walked back to the court he thought about that book. Every day brought him some new material. The story of this man who had killed a messenger and hanged himself would make interesting reading. One could almost write a whole chapter on him. Perhaps not a whole chapter but a reasonable paragraph, at any rate. There was so much else to include, and one must be firm in cutting out details. He had already chosen the title of the book, after much thought: *The Pacification of the Primitive Tribes of the Lower Niger.*[1]

1. The author is identified in *Arrow of God* as George Allen; the device links *Things Fall Apart* thematically to the latter novel, which can thus be considered its sequel.

CONTEXTS AND CRITICISM

Chinua Achebe—Interviews

LEWIS NKOSI, DONATUS NWOGA, DENNIS DUERDEN, AND ROBERT SERUMAGA

Interview with Chinua Achebe[†]

Interviewed by Lewis Nkosi in Lagos, August 1962. At the time of recording this interview Chinua Achebe was Director of the External Service of the Nigerian Broadcasting Corporation. He had already published with Heinemann *Things Fall Apart* (1958) and *No Longer at Ease* (1960), and was working on *Arrow of God*, which was published in 1964.

* * *

NKOSI Well, Chinua Achebe, you are one of the leading novelists in Nigeria, you're famous in America, and England, as well as Europe. When did you really being to write?

ACHEBE I wrote *Things Fall Apart* in 1958, or rather it was published in '58—I started work on it around '56—towards the end of '56. But the story itself had been sort of maturing in my mind for about two years previously.

NKOSI When did you really become interested in writing as an art, something that you might use throughout your life? Did you start this at school?

ACHEBE Well, I think at the university at Ibadan, I can't say definitely when it was but I know around '51, '52, I was quite certain that I was going to try my hand at writing, and one of the things that set me thinking was Joyce Carey's novel set in Nigeria, *Mr Johnson*, which was praised so much, and it was clear to me that this was a most superficial picture of—not only of the country, but even of the Nigerian character and so I thought if this was famous, then perhaps someone ought to try and look at this from the inside.

NKOSI Yes; well, according to the blurb in one of your books, you had been sent to the university to study medicine, is that correct?

---

† From *African Writers Talking*. Ed. Cosmo Pieterse and Dennis Duerden (New York: Africana Publishing Corporation, 1972). Reprinted by permission of Lewis Nkosi.

ACHEBE   Yes, that's right, it's just one of those things: you see, when I left school I didn't really know what I wanted to do and medicine was very glamorous—it was either medicine or engineering—but I soon discovered that it wasn't really my cup of tea, so I changed.

NKOSI   Of the two books you have written, which gives you the greatest satisfaction?

ACHEBE   That's very difficult—it's really quite impossible to say, it depends on when I am asked this question: some days I feel happier with *Things Fall Apart,* some days with the other one. They are so different, you see; I think it's rather like one's children, perhaps—you know, you like one for certain things and the other for other things. *Things Fall Apart* I wrote with more affection, but that doesn't mean I prefer it, I wrestled a lot more with *No Longer at Ease,* and so I think that probably, *No Longer at Ease* is better, technically, but that's as far as I can go.

NKOSI   Yes, well, most of us would probably differ with the author himself since lots of us like the first one very much; the texture of the writing seems to be so much more finished and syntactically finished. What are you working on at the moment?

ACHEBE   I'm trying to, you see, what I've decided to do really is to oscillate between the past—the immediate past—and the present: *Things Fall Apart* is about a hundred years ago; *No Longer at East* is today; and I want to go back now to not quite the time of *Things Fall Apart,* but a little later, because I think there's a lot of interesting material there; and the fourth one would be present day. And that's the way I intend to work.

NKOSI   There is quite a community of writers in Nigeria. Could you tell us something about this, whether there is any social intercourse between you and younger writers writing at the moment or do you lead an isolated life?

ACHEBE   Well, you see there are so few—that's the thing, so it's quite easy to get to know one another and I think most of the younger writers have been students at the University College, Ibadan—so it's community. In Lagos here we are trying to start a writers' club, well, a society of authors really, but it's not so that we can get acquainted but to have a platform, you know, to do battle if necessary.

NKOSI   Yes; now, as a professional broadcaster do you find much time to do your own writing, and what hours do you use for writing?

ACHEBE   Well, I find that if I have a story that I badly want to tell I can always find the time. Of course, it is becoming increasingly difficult for me to write as quickly as I would want. The novel on which I am working now is taking me much longer than I had thought. But it doesn't matter: I don't think the speed is all that important.

NKOSI   Is this latest novel that you are working on centred around Lagos or does it deal with the urban community?

ACHEBE   No, it goes back to the village. You see, it goes back to what I've said before: if I want to write about Nigeria, say a hundred years ago, seventy-five years ago, it has to be the village society. The present day would be Lagos and the towns.

NKOSI   Yes. It is very interesting how well you are able to capture the nuances of tribal life. Have you lived in the rural areas yourself?

ACHEBE   Yes. I was brought up in a village, went to school there; I didn't really get into any big town until I went to Ibadan, and you see, in the villages in Nigeria—well where I come from in the Eastern Region, life is still—well things are changing very fast but if one is interested, one can still see signs of what life used to look like.

NKOSI   Do you yourself find this ambivalent? Did you, at the time when you were growing up, have the feeling that you were no longer at ease with the rural scene and at the same time find that you had a tremendous affection for the life of your people in the rural setting. How did you reconcile this within yourself?

ACHEBE   Well, as a little boy it didn't worry me at all. I took most of these things for granted. I was born into a Christian family, you see my father was a missionary and that was the life of the . . . You know, the sort of civilized life of the village was us, but it was only later—even though I was brought up as a Christian, the life of the village was there for you to see—it was only later that I began to evaluate, so to speak.

NKOSI   Yes. Were you overseas very long?

ACHEBE   No, I've only been out once to Britain in '56 for a short period at the BBC.

NKOSI   What would you say are the main influences on your life, say, from the point of view of literature? Whom do you admire most amongst writers?

ACHEBE   That again is very difficult. I don't really think that there's any one I can say I admire all that much. I used to like Hemingway; and I used to like Conrad, I used to like Conrad particularly; and I like Graham Greene, I find him a bit heavy going now and again but I do like him; and some of the younger people like Kingsley Amis and—well, I don't have any special favourites.

NKOSI   Now, if we may just ask this rather peculiar question, just how much power does a professional artist, a professional writer, have in a society like Lagos or the Nigerian society as a whole?

ACHEBE   Not much, because writing is so new and we are only just beginning to be known but I think by power you don't mean—

NKOSI   I mean influence.

ACHEBE   Influence, yes, well I think that will come; if one writes good novels or writes good poetry, he's bound to have an influence but I don't see much of it at present, only the beginnings, you see, in the schools and that sort of thing, which shows that perhaps the next generation will be influenced by what we write today.

NKOSI   Yes. Do you set yourself any particular time schedule for your writing: how many novels, for instance, you have to do within a year, you know, that sort of thing?

ACHEBE   No, no, I don't; you see, I think writing is such a serious thing that one ought to take it fairly easily and slowly, you know, at its own pace. I don't like forcing a story. Some days, weeks even, I can't write anything, and I don't want to go to the table and start scribbling, you see, I feel it's—it is an important thing and ought to be taken seriously.

This interview was recorded in the year that Chinua Achebe published *Arrow of God*. The interview, with Donatus Nwoga, took place during the Conference on Commonwealth Literature, held at Leeds University in September 1964.

NWOGA   I was fortunate to listen to Mr Achebe address the Conference on Commonwealth Literature recently and he made certain statements about the duty of the author, or the responsibilities of the author, which, I suppose, you could also accept as a privilege in a developing society. I wonder, Mr Achebe, would you indicate what you think is the duty, the privilege, the responsibility of the author, in the situation in which you find yourself?

ACHEBE   Well, what I was trying to get at is this—it's difficult to put in a very few words, but what I wanted to put across was this: that we writers in—say a writer like myself in Nigeria—should not take for granted the relationships which exist between writers and their audience in another society, like, say, Britain; because we tend to do this and I think we might be neglecting our proper function if we take anything for granted instead of thinking what exactly is our society, what are its needs, what can I do, what can I contribute; this is what I was trying to get at, and I think we have a very important function. In this paper I saw my role, this is only one of the roles of the writer, as a teacher.

NWOGA   As a teacher, this of course differentiates the purpose of literature in societies which have been so well established that literature is an exercise of those who have the time for it, and a society like ours where people don't read so much that they can afford to waste the time they spend in reading. They tend to think of literature as a source of some sort of education, some sort of learning.

ACHEBE   I was using teacher there, not in the narrow sense of teaching a scale or teaching to pass an examination. I was thinking primarily more of a deeper meaning of teaching and what I had in

mind, what I think a novelist can teach is something very fundamental, namely to indicate to his readers, to put it crudely, that we
in Africa did not hear of culture for the first time from Europeans.

NWOGA I wonder, instead of making a long comment myself,
whether you could repeat some of the stories I've heard you tell of
letters you got from people who have enjoyed your stories?

ACHEBE Well, I think I'll give two or three illustrations. One was
from Northern Nigeria, which I was very pleased to get, because
one doesn't usually get reaction from that part. This was a letter
from someone who had just left school, and he said something like,
'I don't usually write to writers, no matter how good their work is
or how interesting, but I thought I should write to you because you,
I think, you teach us young people a lot, you see, and I hope you
will carry on teaching us.' Now this is one of them, and then there
was the other one, which was rather pathetic, from a student in
Ghana who said I had neglected to include questions and answers
at the end of *Things Fall Apart*, and could I rectify this position so
that he would pass his school certificate next year.

NWOGA You mentioned earlier that you wanted to tell the people
that we didn't first hear about culture when the Europeans came.
I wonder whether you could develop this a bit?

ACHEBE Yes, what I think is the basic problem of a new African
country like Nigeria is really what you might call a 'crisis in the
soul'. We have been subjected—we have subjected ourselves
too—to this period during which we have accepted everything
alien as good and practically everything local or native as inferior.
I could give you illustrations of when I was growing up, the attitude of our parents, the Christian parents, to Nigerian dances, to
Nigerian handicrafts; and the whole society during this period
began to look down on itself, you see, and this was a very bad
thing; and we haven't actually, even now with the independence,
we still haven't got over this period. I can give again the example
of the boy in my wife's class who said he wouldn't write about
the harmattan because it was 'bush', you see: he would rather
write about winter. Now things like this show one that the writer
has the responsibility to teach his audience that there is nothing
shameful about the harmattan, that it is not only daffodils that
can make a fit subject for poetry, but the palm tree and so on. This
is what I was getting at.

NWOGA You have even pointed this out in your novel *No Longer at
Ease*; there is the politician, Honourable Sam Okoli, who keeps
saying he once had a graduate from Ibadan who wouldn't call him
'Sir', but he was pleased he had as his secretary somebody who
went to Cambridge, an English person, who was calling him 'Sir'
and he appeared to be extremely excited about all this.

ACHEBE   Oh yes, yes I know the aspect of this whole complex, colonial complex which you cannot eradicate overnight. You see, a writer has a responsibility to try and stop this because unless our culture begins to take itself seriously it will never sort of get off the ground.

NWOGA   Yes. I remember one self-styled critic suggesting that you were opposing colonialism while at the same time enjoying the fruits of colonialism: living in Lagos, writing and all that. Do you think he was right in assessing you as being opposed to colonialism as such?

ACHEBE   Well, that is a very stupid comment. I mean, to oppose colonialism does not mean that one does not appreciate the values of Western technological civilization. I mean the two things don't come in as necessarily conflicting and such a comment should be beneath notice.

NWOGA   I thought so myself. There's another thing too I think I would like to mention: maybe I shouldn't say it's the same person, but it was the same person, who said something about your misunderstanding of African religion. He referred in particular to this word 'chi' which was translated as one's personal God and he thought that he had studied Ibo religion enough to indicate this wasn't a personal God, but the God within. Do you see any distinction between . . .

ACHEBE   I think the man was talking through his hat. I know who you are talking about now and I wouldn't normally spend any time discussing him but in this particular case I think he was completely wrong. I saw this article[1] and he was talking about 'chi' as the God with the capital G. I take it you are using the equivalent of the Christian God, perhaps God Almighty within. I mean this is complete balderdash, because trying to translate a word like 'chi' into English always carries its own problems. When I say 'personal God' it's not perfect but it's as close as I could get. Now I think the best translation would be 'personal spirit', not 'personal God', but 'God within' is just trash.

NWOGA   I thought so, because it rather felt like the imposition on the African of a certain Western, possibly Christian, metaphysics.

The next interview was recorded with Dennis Duerden talking to Chinua Achebe in Lagos, in September 1965.

DUERDEN   Chinua, one has the feeling after reading your novel *Things Fall Apart* that the contemporary Nigerian Society from

---

1. Cf. *Transition*, Vol. 3, No. 13, Mar.–Apr. 1964, p. 36f. 'The Offended *Chi* in Achebe's Novels' by Austin J. Shelton. Nwoga's letter in reply, 'The *Chi* Offended' is in Vol. 4, No. 15, 1964, p. 5.

which you spring must have preserved the patterns of African traditional life to a large degree, if not in the cities, at least in the villages. Is this true?

ACHEBE   Yes, I think it is true to a large extent; certainly it was true
when I was growing up. I think it's not quite so true today because
the change is sort of accelerating, but when I was growing up in my
village, it was still possible to catch glimpses of what the complete
traditional society must have looked like and one supplemented
these impressions with accounts, stories told by old people—like
my father. Now, my father, although he was a Christian convert,
was very useful to me in this way because he told me how things
were in the past. And I'd like to say, too, it's not only in the villages;
even in the cities, if you look carefully enough, you can see patterns of the past too; it depends on how closely you look. If you
take Lagos, for instance, today: you will find that many villages
from the hinterland are presented here as units—what you might
call the improvement societies. Each village has its own meeting,
perhaps the women have their dances and so on and the men hold
some traditional celebrations and so on. So, the patterns although
much paler today, the patterns are still there.

DUERDEN   Yes, when you wrote *Things Fall Apart* did you actually do
it from a historical point of view, describing history, or was it from
these experiences of yours when you were growing up?

ACHEBE   It was purely from the experience and of course a bit of
imagination. I didn't have to do any research as such. The festivals
were still there, most of them were still there, the whole attitude,
really it's the attitude of the people; their philosophy of life was still
there. I mean, you could see it; and the rest really was using your
own imagination to create the details of the story.

DUERDEN   What village actually did you live in?

ACHEBE   A place called Ogidi, which is six miles from the Niger.

DUERDEN   This was during the thirties, was it?

ACHEBE   That's right.

DUERDEN   I've heard that there was a big wave of Christian conversion in the thirties which destroyed a number of the traditional
places and things which went on there. Like ritual plays. Is this
true?

ACHEBE   Well, actually this may have been before the thirties because
when I was growing up it was not very common to see people converted. I know we used to go out every fourth Sunday into the village, the Christians, I mean, and sing and preach and the pagans,
as they were called, would assemble and listen; you see, the
idea was that we could convert a few others. I don't remember
that we met with any great success. In fact many of the people
who turned up, were what you might call 'back-sliders,' some

who had been in the Church and had given it up, and they put some rather embarrassing questions to the catechist or the pastor. So in all I think the peak of conversion was much earlier than the thirties.

DUERDEN   Yes. When I was in Ibadan I saw this film J. P. Clark has made about a play which takes place amongst his own people, the Ijaw, and it's about a seven day play which was performed about twenty or thirty years ago which hasn't been performed since, which he got them to revive. He got an old man who told the story, and he got local actors to do it. Do you know anything about it?

ACHEBE   Well I know J. P.'s play. In fact, I have read his, sort of, modern version of it, which is extremely good. I do not think we did have that kind of extended drama in my area, not as far as I know, but what I do remember were skits, you know, short skits performed by masks or masqueraders, usually at the expense of some members of the community, those who had fallen out of favour, rather short satirical pieces, but nothing of the extent of J. P.'s Ijaw play.

DUERDEN   They'd be like Egungun.[2]

ACHEBE   Yes.

DUERDEN   And these still exist, do they?

ACHEBE   Not really now, no. I think perhaps the only thing remaining is the night masquerades which were often very powerful in the past. You see, they came out at night and went from house to house, and sang, and also indulged in gossip, you see, again at the expense of anyone who was not toeing the line of the village. This is pure entertainment and this still happens, apart from masquerades at festivals, not only at traditional ones but at Christmas and Easter and so on: all this, the whole trend, is really towards a light-hearted version of our old entertainment.

DUERDEN   What are the night masquerades? What were they called?

ACHEBE   They were called Egwugwu and they were really beyond the law practically. They could sing what they liked, they went from A's house to B's house and they would say some nasty things about A in B's house, and then go to C and say some nasty things about B. Usually things based in fact, you see, but normally things people would not say in the daytime, and this was the way that—just for amusement.

When this interview was recorded with Chinua Achebe, his fourth novel, A Man of the People, had just been published. He had left his post as Director of External Service of the Nigerian Broadcasting Corporation in the same year, 1966.

---

2. Originally dancers wearing ancestral-spirit masks. Now masked dancer-actors who perform generally satirical episodes and poems. The masks worn are of social stereotypes.

The interview was conducted by Robert Serumaga in the studios of the Transcription Centre in London, in February 1967.

SERUMAGA   Chinua, you were born in Nigeria at a place called Ogidi which is near Onitsha?

ACHEBE   That's right.

SERUMAGA   Now, when you were born I think Captain Lugard had been and gone and there had been changes brought about by the British invasion of Africa. How did you manage at that particular time to get so much insight into the kind of society, pre-colonial society you write about?

ACHEBE   Well actually the pre-colonial society in Africa had not completely disappeared. I was brought up in a village and looking around you could see not the whole society, but you could see enough of what was left to be able to fill in the gaps. And if you were interested in the old Africa—as I was instinctively: I mean, this was something that came to me naturally, I just was interested—you could see it and you could ask questions.

SERUMAGA   Did you have any specific kind of role in the society which would have given you advantages in gaining certain kinds of information about rituals and things like that?

ACHEBE   No, on the contrary I was almost excluded from it. On looking back, if I had any advantage, this was it: that my father had been a missionary, he was retired when I was growing up; and we were Christians and in our village you had two sides—the 'people of the Church', as we were called, and the 'people of the world', the others. And there was a certain amount of distance; although we were in the same village there was a certain distance, which I think made it possible for me not to take things for granted you see. I say this because as for some of the people who grew up with me, whose parents were heathen, as we called them, these things did not strike them. This is what they tell me today: they took things for granted. Whereas I went to church on Sunday, we prayed every morning and so on, and the rest of the village I could see from a slight distance.

SERUMAGA   Now this distance in your part of the country, did it produce any real conflict in the sense that, for example in James Ngugi's book *The River Between*, there is this kind of cultural conflict. Did it create any conflict between the heathen and the Christians?

ACHEBE   No, not really. I think they had come to co-exist quite peacefully, and the Church and the world co-existed. In the same family, an extended family, you had some members belonging to this side and some others to the other side; there was certainly no violent conflict at all.

SERUMAGA   What about the conflict of one's own character? The sort of person who'd grown up with parents in that kind of traditionally based family, and then be Christianized at the same time? Did it happen on an individual basis that one experienced this conflict between one's belief and traditions?

ACHEBE   Yes, for me, it did. When I was growing up I didn't obviously think of it in those terms—I was merely curious. When there was a festival in the village we were supposed not to visit our neighbours because they were likely to give us food offered to idols. Now we always managed to visit—my sister and I—we were curious. And it was only later, when you came to think of it in terms of philosophy and so on, that you begin to react against this. But at that stage I was merely curious to see what was going on on the other side.

SERUMAGA   In at least two of your books you create situations where you have a character who has a son who has been Christianized while he is not and they come into conflict about certain things, like for example, the killing of the python. Now were there any specific instances, that you might have known from the point of view of history in your part of the country where these things happened—where a family was split by the teachings of two different cultures?

ACHEBE   Oh yes there were such stories, yes, certainly, because the first generations of Christians (this is what I heard), had to demonstrate their faith in a very aggressive manner, and this often took the form of violating the customs of the village. At that stage there were skirmishes. But this was before my time. I heard of them, but on the whole I think the village accepted the new faith with humour. You see my great-grandfather for instance, was the man who had initially received the missionaries in my village. And he let them stay around and sing their songs; and eventually he said they must leave, not because of any conflict in religion, but because their singing sounded so mournful that his neighbours might think he was dead! And so they moved. But this was the kind of—I mean—good humour. After all, he even let my father join them.

SERUMAGA   In your books you present the society as it is. Now in Africa there has been change to a certain extent, from the values of *Things Fall Apart* to the values of *A Man of the People*. Has this change been in the direction that you would have envisaged should be the right one?

ACHEBE   Oh no, no, no, certainly not. Although you see life is not simple—it's often so complex. There have been gains—I mean let's not forget that, there have been gains, I am not one of those who would say that Africa has gained nothing at all during the colonial period, I mean this is ridiculous—we gained a lot. But unfortunately when two cultures meet, you would expect, if we were angels shall we say, we could pick out the best in the other and retain the best in our own, and this would be wonderful. But this doesn't happen often. What happens is that some of the worst elements of the old are retained and some of the worst of the new are added on to them. So if it were for me to order society I would be very unhappy about the way things have turned out. But again, I see this as the way life is. Every society has to grow up, every society has to learn its own lesson, so I don't despair. *A Man of the People* is a rather serious indictment—if you like—of post-independence Africa. But I don't give up because I think this is a necessary stage in our growth.

SERUMAGA   You have hope. But do you see any agents of change; do you see bows behind the arrows of the gods, at the moment, to turn us into the right direction?

ACHEBE   Oh yes, of course. I mean the coups, themselves, are bows shooting the arrows of God. If you take the example of Nigeria, which is the place I know best, things had got to such a point politically that there was no other answer—no way you could resolve this impasse politically. The political machine had been so abused that whichever way you pressed it, it produced the same results; and therefore you wanted another force, another force just had to come in. Now when I was writing *A Man of the People* it wasn't clear to me that this was going to be necessarily a military intervention. It could easily have been civil war, which in fact it very nearly was in Nigeria. But I think that all these things the next generation of politicians in Nigeria, when we do have them, will have experienced, and they'll have learned one or two lessons, I hope, from what happened to the First Republic. This is the only hope I have and if this turns out to be vain, it would really be terrible . . .

SERUMAGA   Of course, you did almost uncannily predict the course of Nigerian events in *A Man of the People*, and in the earlier book, *Things Fall Apart*, it seemed to me that it was not the society itself that fell apart—the society was progressing or changing, if you like, in a dynamic sort of way culturally—and what fell apart, it seemed, was Okonkwo in his obstinacy; in his refusal to change at all it is Okonkwo who did completely break down. Would you agree with that?

ACHEBE   Yes, I think this is a reasonable interpretation. I mean my sympathies were not entirely with Okonkwo—this is what I think you're getting at. Life just has to go on and if you refuse to accept changes, then tragic though it may be, you are swept aside.

SERUMAGA   Of course the changes that came to the society in *Things Fall Apart* would have produced a situation where characters are no longer at ease, as in your next book. Now I must emphasize this because I'm terribly optimistic myself, I think that if we are going to change again, veer into another right direction, it's going to take us a long time. You don't agree with this at all?

ACHEBE   I would neither agree nor disagree because I don't know how long it's going to take. I am not really concerned so much with whether it takes ten years or twenty years but with the final thing, and I am not being so naïve as to think that the progress is in one direction. You see, there are halts, there are even backward steps and so on, but I think in the final analysis writing is learning. Even if, mark you, this means a society breaks up, it may well be that this society had no basis for being together in the first place and this in itself is a lesson. We are learning for instance on the African scene that it's not enough to talk about unity and so on; you've got to work for it, you see, and 1966 was a disappointing year on the African scene. This I think is a necessary lesson.

SERUMAGA   Now, going on to the other point about your writing: my assessment is that whereas earlier we had books that were almost apologetics of African culture, and then we had negritude which was a complete protest against Europe and the romanticization, almost, of African values, now you come with a kind of very confident approach whereby you present your society as it is, and therefore show us what is good in it and what is bad in it.

ACHEBE   I don't, in fact, remember consciously saying to myself that I must be confident. I saw that the kind of people I was writing about did not suffer any of these complexes—that brought about their excessive protestation or excessive whatever went on before. I found a number of people that were all around me who just lived their lives the way they wanted to live them, and these were the people I wanted to write about. It may be that at the back of my mind was this kind of decision that now we have had grovelling, we have had protest, now we must have something in between—I don't know, but I don't remember taking the decision consciously. That was the way I saw the story I was going to write, so that's how I wrote it.

SERUMAGA   Would it be that because the people in the society—and in a sense you yourself, say, writing about them—were in conditions where they hadn't been affected by the cultural changes which produced the writers of negritude, would it be that after your society of *Things Fall Apart* has been affected by these changes, that then these people themselves would have made the logical progression into a kind of negritude, a kind of protest against Europe, for the impositions Europe had made against them?

ACHEBE   Yes, I think in retrospect, I think I would agree. The working of the colonial period on Nigeria was rather different from its effect on, shall we say, Senegal. I think there is a certain difference in the way that Europe worked on Africa in various areas, and this is bound to create different responses.

SERUMAGA Now, you mentioned earlier about how you work, you did not have this definite conception that you were going away from protest. How do you work when you are writing a novel like *Things Fall Apart* for instance; did you do a lot of research in the history of the society, or is it something you picked up from experience?

ACHEBE This is largely picked up. As I said at the beginning this was the life that interested me, partly the life I lived and the life that was lived around me, supported by what I heard in conversation—I was very keen on listening to old people—and what I learned from my father, so it was all sort of picked up here and there. There was no research in the library if that's what you mean.

SERUMAGA And how do you work with the language because you seem to get in all the authenticity of your particular language—in the way they speak, and transliterate it so beautifully into English. Now can you describe exactly how you do this, if you can?

ACHEBE No, it's not easy. I feel consciously that if you were going to write about a certain character and I put down the dialogue between A and B, that somehow it would sound right or wrong and there's no way I can describe it except that it sounds wrong to my ear. If A talks like this and this is not right, I immediately feel it, that this is not right. I don't really see how else I can. . . .

SERUMAGA There is no conscious intellectual process in transposing one language into another on your part?

ACHEBE No, no, no. I just feel that this is the right way to convey this atmosphere, this speech or this idiom, this kind of language, you see. If you put in modern slang for instance, it would jar immediately.

SERUMAGA It is said that you wrote *Things Fall Apart* in one go, with no revisions; is that true?

ACHEBE Not altogether. My original conception of the story was really a combination of *Things Fall Apart* and *No Longer at Ease*. It was one story originally, not even long, it was short but it covered the whole period of *Things Fall Apart* and *No Longer at Ease*. And having done it I immediately felt that it was not right—that the time covered was too long and therefore the story was going to be too thin. So what I did was simply mechanically to cut it in two and blow up the first part. So there was that amount of rewriting, but not in detail. You see I work very slowly and carefully with my writing, so I don't have to do a first draft, a second draft and a third draft.

SERUMAGA How long on average does it take you to finish a novel?

ACHEBE Oh, it's varied from a year, even fourteen months, to five months.

SERUMAGA   And this is very interesting about your *Things Fall Apart* and *No Longer at Ease,* because I, as a reader, having read *Things Fall Apart* and *Arrow of God* and seen the references in *Things Fall Apart* to the python and the killing of the python and then seen this as the main theme of *Arrow of God,* I thought that *Arrow of God* was almost a continuation of the story of *Things Fall Apart* in a different context—with a different village. Would you say that this is so?

ACHEBE   Well, no, I don't think so. It is the same area—the supporting scenery is the same—it's got to be the same because I'm writing about the same people. So the supporting thing, the background is the same. But the story itself is not—in fact I see it as the exact opposite: Ezeulu the chief character in *Arrow of God* is a different kind of man from Okonkwo. He is an intellectual. He thinks about why things happen—of course as a priest; you see, his office requires this—so he goes into things, to the roots of things, and he's ready to accept change, intellectually. He sees the value of change and therefore his reaction to Europe is different, completely different, from Okonkwo's. He is ready to come to terms with the new—up to a point—except where his dignity is involved. This he could not accept; he is very proud. So you see it's really the other side of the coin, and the tragedy is that they come to the same end, the same sort of sticky end. So there's really no escape whether you accept change or whether you don't—which is rather pessimistic, which I think should please you, although it is in fact not the same story.

SERUMAGA   Well, does this then conflict with your own personal view of society?

ACHEBE   It does only if you see it sort of fixed at one point. But if you take a long view of society, you will see that I think that it doesn't contradict what I said earlier, namely that if you take a long enough view, that society is, in fact, adjusting. Because life must go on, no matter what we say, no matter how many people suffer or how many people are killed, life does go on. This is really what I was saying at the beginning. But if you take a short episode, it may be full of tragedy. I mean if you take the situation in Nigeria today, it's full of tragedy—in Uganda even. But I think the long view, at least to me, holds out some element of hope.

SERUMAGA   Well now, Chinua, you are no longer working with the radio of Nigeria. This presumably releases more of your time for writing, but why did you resign, and what are you going to do now?

ACHEBE   I left radio in August last year as a result of the political situation—when it became unsafe to live in Lagos and I was terribly distressed with the turn of events, so I decided that the best thing was to leave. This decision was, of course, merely hastened by the political situation because I was already thinking that I had perhaps done enough in radio and I should be thinking of setting up as a full-time writer. And this is what I would like to do ultimately, although maybe for the next year or so I will probably work at the University of Nigeria at Nsukka, to help in setting up the Institute of African Literature which they're thinking about.

BIODUN JEYIFO

Literature and Conscientization: Interview with Chinua Achebe†

JEYIFO Well, as I told you, this interview is essentially meant to reminisce on the past and examine the present and perhaps look forward to the future. So I suppose we should start by going back to the beginnings. If one may state what is now a commonplace, when you started writing, there were not too many other Nigerian literary artists on the scene. Of course there *were* literary artists in the oral tradition. But there were no *writers,* so to speak. What started you on this vocation? One has read in fact that you went to Ibadan initially to read medicine.

ACHEBE Yes. Well, you know, what you went into a university to read in those days was not really very much related to what your real interests were. Well, sometimes, if you were lucky, the two might coincide, but I do know that the university existed mainly to raise you from one class to another. It had little relationship to such things as what your *real* interests might be—literary, philosophical, whatever. You were simply looking for the shortest, the quickest avenue into the "senior service." Well, I'm putting it a bit crudely and of course there is no way of knowing whether if I'd gone into medicine and become a doctor I would still have written my novels. I mean it's not the first time that such a thing has happened. But I gave up my study of medicine because I discovered that I hadn't really thought about it. And being an average student in both the arts and the sciences at that time—in fact I think I did a little better in the sciences than in the arts—it was a question of following that advantage and I thought I would get a degree in medicine. But after one year in Ibadan, I matured a bit, and knew that although I could have gone on and become a doctor, I wouldn't have enjoyed that vocation.

---

† From *Conversations with Chinua Achebe.* Ed. Bernth Lindfors (Jackson: University Press of Mississippi, 1997), 110–23. Reprinted by permission of the author.

So I moved into the liberal arts. Of course at that point I wasn't thinking of writing at all.

JEYIFO   Although you had written at Umuahia.

ACHEBE   Yes, I was the editor of my house magazine and the school magazine, and I'd written a few odd things here and there. But as I said, those were not such "literary" things. I enjoyed stories and read novels a lot. The decision to become a writer—it's difficult for me to say when it happened because, as you said, there were no writers. Well, there were a few names. Cyprian was beginning to write. And then while I was in the university, Tutuola came out.

JEYIFO   Had you actually heard of Tutuola by the time you were writing *Things Fall Apart*?

ACHEBE   Oh yes, of course, I was in my penultimate year at Ibadan when *The Palm-Wine Drinkard* was published, and I was also a student of Parrinder who played a role in connecting Tutuola with Faber and wrote an introduction or something for Tutuola's second book, *My Life in the Bush of Ghosts*. So I did hear of him, although I didn't meet him until years later. These were however marginal. So it wasn't like now, and it's difficult to imagine how different it was. I mean now, every child I meet tells me he or she is going to write!

JEYIFO   So, later on, when you decided to be a writer—you've since then formulated some very clear ideas, some very clear purposes which impel you to write. For instance, to write a truer and more meaningful and relevant story about the way our people lived in the past as a corrective to some of the things which had been written by others before you started to write. So were these ideas conscious at that point?

ACHEBE   They were not very conscious at the beginning. You know, the way a writer works—a lot of his motivations are instinctive and subconscious. It's easier to perceive after the event, which is not to say the ideas were absent. It's only that I didn't sit back and say I'm going to write ABCD, you see. It's more like an urge to express yourself—self-expression, which is a human thing. I think this is something which is basic to our nature, whether you do it in painting or music, or whether you just talk. I mean people who dramatise themselves. I'll tell you something. When I was in the BBC staff school, I'd just finished *Things Fall Apart* and my friend then who was in the same course with me, Bisi Onabanjo . . .

JEYIFO   The present Governor of Ogun State?

ACHEBE   Yes, he was urging me to show this thing to our teacher at the BBC staff school, a novelist. But I was very shy—I envy some of the children today who are so sure they want to be writers!—I was hesitant, but Bisi kept urging me until one day I walked up timidly to the man and said I'd written a novel. This man was a well-known novelist himself in Britain . . .

JEYIFO   Who was he, by the way?

ACHEBE   Gilbert Phelps. And like every other writer, you know, you don't want an invasion of your privacy by anybody, so he said rather evasively that he would look at it, and I then showed it to him and, well, he liked it. And from that moment, I was launched because it was published by Heinemann, and he showed it to them. So the story got around—and this is really what I'm talking about—and one of the instructors said, "I hear you are writing a novel; is it going to be like Cyprian Ekwensi's?" And I said, without meaning to be rude, "I hope not!" And then, you know the British, he said, "I hope not too!" Well, you know, everybody has his own idea—I mean Cyprian had developed one style and kind of writing and I had no intention to imitate or repeat what he had done. Tutuola was a total world of his own, too. And I must say, I was completely impressed by Tutuola from the word go. I mean, this thing about Nigerians not liking him at the *beginning;* that did not apply to me. It just did not apply to me—although I didn't go about shouting anything about him. But that was one different style and approach and everything, and Cyprian was another, and I wanted something of my own.

JEYIFO   So in that case, still on this subject of *writing* as a vocation, is it possible to date *when* you actually began to see writing—I hesitate to use the word "mission"—you know, as a vocation?

ACHEBE   Yes. Well, I will say yes and no. Because you see, the moment I became conscious of the possibilities of representing somebody from a certain standpoint, from that moment I realised that there must be misrepresentation, there must be misjudgment, there must be even straightforward discrimination and distortion, and this was clear from European literature which I read as a student. In secondary school, one didn't feel that way. For some reason, maybe one simply had not grown up sufficiently. Reading Alan Paton and other writers, you know, you tended even to identify with Europeans. Because this is the thing really: a writer controls . . .

JEYIFO   Can seduce . . .

ACHEBE   Yes, controls your response by the way he stacks the evidence for or against, you see. We should have immediately identified with the Africans but this was impossible because the dice were loaded against them, the way the story was told, the way the author took sides. And being children, you could not perceive this, you simply didn't want the adventurers to be harmed by the savages!

JEYIFO   That still happens by the way, as unfortunate as it may sound. Tarzan films and Kung Fu films . . .

ACHEBE   Yes, and on many different levels. I mean, I've heard a student, a third-year student, saying that if the whites (this is talking
from the Christian angle), that if the missionaries had not come
here, we would all be slaves still. I mean, you're right; it's not as if
we've emancipated ourselves. Individuals can, of course, if they
have the kind of exposure and intelligence that one should have in
our situation. I think one can emancipate oneself and see that the
story you are reading is written by somebody with a point of view,
with a position. I think once you discover that, you are on your way.
  So that's the kind of beginning I had. It's quite difficult to say,
but I'm quite sure that by the time we were reading our set-books
at Ibadan we were not as innocent as we had been in secondary
school—just enjoying adventure stories. We were able to say: I
don't think this is fair or right! I remember one of the brightest students in my class, Olumide, saying something to the effect that the
only moment he enjoyed Joyce Cary's *Mister Johnson* was the
moment when Johnson was shot! This horrified our English
teacher. But you can see that we were beginning to struggle out of
the position into which we had been placed. And if one exaggerated, that should be understood.
  So I think it was at Ibadan that my feeling about literature, the
vocation, began to form.

JEYIFO   There's also an element that—although one can say that
your development, your beginnings, also marked a point of beginning for contemporary Nigerian literature, not in an absolute
sense but in a relative sense—it also seems that, in your writings,
one perceives there to be other beginnings too, in the sense that
one sees that you show a certain sensibility, an awareness of oral
resources, which you exploit and use a lot. How did this emerge?
For instance, were you quite conscious of the story-telling art in
the oral context?

ACHEBE   Oh yes, I was always fascinated by our traditional stories as
a child. I was always fascinated by the stories of my people, always
intrigued and fascinated by our festivals. You know, when there was
a new dance, a new masquerade coming out, I would want to see
it. Now we were not supposed to be eager to see all this, you know,
as Christians. My father was a very staunch evangelist, he had
taken the church and education, missionary education, to, oh,
practically everywhere in our part of the country and on both sides
of the Niger.
  So we were very proper Christians; we were not supposed to be
interested or excited by the things of the "heathens"! But I should
say here that my father, who should have shown the example,
showed sometimes he was ambivalent; he would be offended if a
masquerade came out improperly set up. Now, you wouldn't think

that he had any interest in whether a masquerade was properly done up or not. But it was later, after he had died, in fact only in the last couple of years, that I realised that before he became a Christian, he had been a sensational masquerader himself, and that the masquerade which he carried was so famous, for its agility and its dance . . .

JEYIFO   How was it that you only stumbled on this fact after he had died?

ACHEBE   Because he never told us! He never mentioned anything about that. But you see, it shows that, although he had turned his back on those things for whatever reason, he instinctively responded to good form, to the artistic element in our tradition. So it was that element, particularly the artistic element in our culture that attracted me; a good story, a good dance, a good piece of music, anything that was done well, won my respect.

And that was just an alternative to what the Christians were saying. I mean, I did not doubt the Christians' theology or anything like that; it seemed very obscure, but I didn't have any reason, at that stage anyway, to query it. But it seemed one reality, and another reality was that in the village.

JEYIFO   As all of this developed—well, you've done other things all along apart from writing—you were in the external service of the old NBC. Did you at any time consider writing as a full-time activity, as an option?

ACHEBE   Well, again, you see, I couldn't have because there were no precedents, really. Okay, Cyprian had written books, but he was a pharmacist, and then he came into broadcasting. And Tutuola was in the Labour Department and somebody, in fact, the Director-General of NBC, brought him in to give him a break, and he put him in the stores of NBC. Hence, writing was something you did in your spare time; it was not supposed to be a profession in that sense. It never occurred to me that you could earn a living from it. Indeed, it never occurred to me that you could make any money at all out of it. I was not very well informed about the American situation at that time where a few writers perhaps could become quite wealthy. That sort of thing didn't cross my mind. And even if it did, I wouldn't have had the confidence to launch myself into it. I enjoyed the other things I was doing as well. Broadcasting at that point was a very exciting thing to do. And I learnt a lot by handling scripts; I was involved with the spoken word programmes. I was never an announcer, I was a producer. So I learnt a lot. We did short stories, short talks, fifteen-minute talks, debates, current affairs, and so on. But the short story was really my special talent, and I encountered a lot of ideas just handling that, converting what is written on paper to what you can speak.

In a way that's pretty close to having to deal with dialogue in the novel. And even "tongue twisters"—there are things you don't think about until you put somebody on the air. I remember one day (I think it was the man in charge of the Nigerian Ports Authority who wrote a very fine script), and when we started recording him, he got to a point where he just stopped! He just couldn't go on and the whole thing was ruined!

JEYIFO   Because it was a live broadcast?

ACHEBE   Yes. And, you see, what was down on the script was something like "six storied shed," you know, a lot of "s" piled up, and this was a thing which when you read with the eye you can't see it, but in reading aloud you are tied in knots, you can't say the word! So, the profession of a producer in radio was very useful to me, very useful.

JEYIFO   Also, at that point in time, although you didn't go on to become a full-time writer—I'm talking now of the early sixties to the mid-sixties—there began to emerge something of a community of writers and critics, all being part of the general intellectual class, the intelligentsia, but occupying a rather special place within this emergent national intelligentsia. And of course, with hindsight, one can see that writers have played a very crucial role in contemporary Nigerian history. Can you reminisce about this—your colleagues, the Mbari, *Black Orpheus,* a lot of activity . . .

ACHEBE   I think what was happening then was an indication that there was a certain ferment in the society. It was not just one person or two people, but something general, something in the air, something that had to do with the fact that we were about to become independent—I'm now talking of around 1958 when *Things Fall Apart* was published.

I actually wrote it while I was in Lagos. I started broadcasting in Lagos, then I was promoted Controller, Eastern Region, at the very young age of 28, because the whites were leaving in a hurry. So I went as Controller to Enugu and I was there when *Things Fall Apart* was published, and within two years, you know, we were independent and we wanted to set up our own international broadcasting, external broadcasting and all of the three Controllers, Badejo in Ibadan, Ladan, he's dead now . . .

JEYIFO   Umaru Ladan?

ACHEBE   Yes, that was his name; he was in the North, he was the most junior. Badejo was already moving to become Director-General, so I was made Director of External Broadcasting. I therefore went back to Lagos which was closer to the centre of activities in those days, the real "production centre" being Ibadan, the university, and Lagos being a sort of periphery. But there was a general atmosphere of optimism which was created by this independence which came in 1960.

JEYIFO   Almost a sense of a renaissance—apart from the *political* independence, also a *cultural* renaissance.

ACHEBE   Oh yes. We were rediscovering ourselves, we were about to take our lives into our own hands again. You see, we were going to take the initiative again in our history, because this is what colonialism and all that meant: a loss of initiative and you just have no say in who you were, your own self-development and all that. And there was this feeling that at long last all this was coming to an end and one was intoxicated and it produced this feeling of euphoria. We had a story to tell, we were a different people, we must tell this story, and we insist on being listened to.

JEYIFO   If I may generalise a little on your works, especially the earlier ones from this period, something strikes me immediately from what you say now, which would seem to be that there's a displacement somewhat in the sense that your works from that period—I'm thinking of *Things Fall Apart, No Longer at Ease, Arrow of God*— were not so optimistic! Maybe the sense of a new beginning shows in the energy of the writing—that is, in the sense of form—but in the themes you were exploring, you were not so optimistic.

ACHEBE   Well, this is a very interesting angle. I don't think I've ever had to answer it in this form! Okay, if you were so enthusiastic, why didn't you write enthusiastic novels? Well, I suspect that has to do with my own nature and character; but also I think it has to do with what I consider the proper role of art, you see. I think that art is an alternative in the imagination to the reality all around us. And I think all artists, whatever may be their particular strengths and weaknesses, are doing that. They are giving us something that is not already given, something which is not flying around the life of the community, the life of the individual, as they see it in reality, and something else which we see through the imagination, which mixes, interpenetrates the two realities. I think this is our role. I think this is what happens when there is *optimism.*

I think the writer must retreat instinctively into this kind of reserve. Because he knows, through his imagination, through his intelligence, that it can't all be that sweet. The writer instinctively says that this is very good, that we should be happy and gay and optimistic, but from this reserve which comes from all kinds of sources—your intelligence, your experience, other people's experience that you have absorbed—that something must be lurking, some danger must be lying in wait. I think this is one of our roles— we just don't get lost in the celebration, like everybody else, you see. The prophets come up when things are going very well and they start proclaiming doom! I think this is partly the answer to your question. This is our role, and I think it is proper too, to always call attention to it because humanity is not new; we've been around for ages, we've made the same mistakes over and over again. History is full of periods when we are carried away by optimism, and in reverse there are periods when we suffer great hardships and we are crushed morally, mentally and psychologically, and the writer comes up, an artist, somebody, and he holds up some hope of a greater tomorrow, whatever it is. And I think these things are essential for keeping a kind of even keel so that society doesn't lose its head in enjoyment or is not crushed in despair.

JEYIFO   Within that general pattern, critics on the left have pointed out something which may be an *Achebe dimension,* a personal dimension: that there is a pervasive sense of irony. You seem to be particularly sensitive and responsive to the unintended consequences in human affairs and history, a detachment from history. What do you say to this?

ACHEBE   I think this is part of my awareness of the complexity of reality. There is a dimension to things which I don't know exactly how to explain. And that's what you might call the unintended. I've used the phrase *"powers of event"* in the *Arrow of God,* when the *"powers of event"* achieve their own logic. For instance, you've already worked out things in considerable detail and you expect this to happen and that to happen, and then suddenly these things don't happen as you planned them. Something else, the unforeseen, chance, whatever it is, intervenes.

I don't think we should ignore this force or phenomenon, whatever it is, maybe providence. If you are religious, you will call it God. But there is that dimension over which you have no control. So I make allowance for that, because my view of reality is that it is at once simple and extremely complex.

Again, talking of this ambivalence of the writer, to simplify it by showing that this relates to that, this has happened before, this is like this, by even the use of metaphor one then begins to see that this complexity is actually not so terrifying.

If this has happened before, and our ancestors have coped with it, then there's no reason why we of this generation could not deal with it. So that's a kind of simplification. We are not then crushed; because if we are dealing with something you've never seen before, never heard of before—nobody has ever seen it—how do you begin to handle it? So, you simplify by metaphor and analogy. That's one rule.

Now, when something is too simple, on the other hand, it's the job of the writer to complicate it! Because it cannot be as simple as that. If it was, then there would be no problem in the world, but you see, a writer comes into the relationship and dredges up all kinds of frightening possibilities. And then what seems a simple thing is made not so simple. And it's the same artist even dealing with these realities. And I think this is the proper role of art.

JEYIFO   May I ask you a question which I've always wanted to ask you? I know it's always a little too bold to see a writer in terms of his fictional characters, but I personally have always wanted to ask if there is something of Achebe in Obierika in *Things Fall Apart?*

ACHEBE   Yes, that is very bold indeed! Well, the answer is yes, in the sense that at the crucial moment when things are happening, he represents this other alternative. This is a society in *Things Fall Apart* that believes in strength and manliness and the masculine ideals. Okonkwo accepts them, in a rather literal sense.

JEYIFO   And quite disastrously too.

ACHEBE   Yes, quite. Actually the culture "betrays" him. He is "betrayed" because he's doing exactly what the culture preaches. But, you see, the culture is devious and flexible, because if it wasn't, it wouldn't survive. The culture says you must be strong, you must be this and that, but when the moment comes for absolute strength, the culture says, "No, no, hold it!"

So, Okonkwo says, "Where is this coming from? I mean, you've said it's good to be strong, and so on!" The culture has to be ambivalent, so it immediately raises the virtues of the women, of love, of tenderness and so on, and holds up abominations. You cannot do this; even though the cultural norm says you must do it, you cannot. So you evade, you leave it for somebody else to do! Obierika is therefore more subtle and more in tune with the danger, the impending betrayal by the culture, and he's not likely to be crushed, because he holds something in reserve. You therefore find me more in him, than in Okonkwo. Although I think every character that a writer creates ultimately comes from himself, his experience, his own imagination, and therefore also represents some aspect of the writer, even if the writer says this part of me is something to avoid, to keep at a distance. Because we really have no facility for exploring what we don't know. It doesn't need to have happened to us physically but in the imagination.

JEYIFO   On the question of the imagination, you once gave a lecture in Ife, a convocation lecture titled "The Truth of Fiction," in which you assigned to literature something a little different from what you had said in other essays—for instance, in "The Novelist as Teacher." Here, you assigned to literature a conscientizing capability, a means to imaginatively project oneself into a reality which is not immediately coincident with one's own situation. Do you think this is adequate for the kind of society that Nigeria is now?

ACHEBE   Well, it has to be because I think our failure as a nation is
a failure of the imagination, if you think deeply about it. Whatever
ills you care to take up and explore, you would see that if our imagination was working properly, our own self-interest would stop us
from doing many of the things we are perpetrating, such as injustice
to other people. In the long run we are digging our own graves. If
we really could project into the skin of the beggar under the bridge
in Lagos, we would immediately start doing something to bring
about a just society. It is that lack of imagination which I think is
at the root of cruelty. One is cruel because one is not imaginative
enough.
       Now I see what you mean. How can we wait until every com-
missioner, every politician, has become imaginative? No, I don't
think we can wait, and society doesn't have that kind of patience.
If one still says what one wants to say, or still does what one must
do, it's not because we expect people to start behaving like oneself or accept what one says. Even if they accept, they'll say you
are a man of the future, or something like that. But our imagination is faulty. Now, we may never be allowed to correct our imagination before we are overtaken by something else. This is the
tragedy of it.
       We may be so crass and cruel that the man on whose back we
are sitting will cut off our heads before we've had a chance to mend
our ways. I'm not holding for preventing that from happening at
all. I'm merely saying that, barring revolution—which I cannot say
will come tomorrow or the day after, I do not know—we still have
an option to improve our situation, even if this means that when
the danger comes, it will not be so brutal, because they will say we
give you some credit for your goodwill. That's not impossible and
that's not to be underrated. I mean, it's rather like what was said
by Malraux in *Man's Fate*. There's one image which he uses there
which I think is very effective for me. There's a man who needs surgery; he is very ill, he's also running a very high temperature. There
is really no conflict between the nurse who comes in and gives him
aspirin to lower the temperature and the surgeon who is getting
ready for the surgery, you see. The surgery may be inevitable, I
don't know; but there's really no conflict, unless the nurse is saying aspirin is all that is required.
JEYIFO   Yes, that is the crucial distinction, the crucial element which
I wanted to indicate, because it does seem that if, as you say, a large
part of the problem is a failure of the imagination, a large part of
it is also due to *imaginative* exploitation of downright cynicism.
There are a lot of very cynical people who control our lives and are
very imaginative.
ACHEBE   Yes, yes. People's vile imagination.

JEYIFO   In fact, you do make a distinction in that essay, "The Truth of Fiction," between what you call malevolent fictions and beneficent fictions.

ACHEBE   Yes. You see, one is really talking in metaphors. You know, we are dealing now with areas we cannot really be absolutely sure about. We are now sinking into the subconscious and all that kind of thing. But it seems to me that a really imaginative person cannot be evil—a man in my view of the imagination, who can put himself in the shoes of his neighbour. I mean, this is what all the religions are teaching—that man is your brother; you are not of the same parents and all that, but you have to imagine, you have to bring your own imagination into play. As we say in our own languages, this is your mother's son, which is nearer than "brother." And once you've said that, you accept that it is very difficult to be the way you were before. So I think this is the area where art with its ameliorative, curative powers can operate.

JEYIFO   Moving to more specific areas of your total activities, you've also at various times, including now, been an editor. In fact, you are the editor of perhaps the most stable journal so far—*Okike,* and also you've been a publisher at different times. What I see in this, perhaps simplifying a lot and also generalising a lot, is an attempt to define yourself as an intellectual, an artist, in relation to an immediate audience. And this audience wasn't there when you started—an immediate audience, a community of letters. Do you have any reflections to offer on this, any opinions on this problem, which is really a vast one. You've also been the editorial adviser to Heinemann's African Writers Series.

ACHEBE   Yes, I think I can reflect, in the sense that a lot of what's happened here, a good part of it, has simply happened. Some of it I've then decided to promote. And I've been learning as I go along. Our society is a "new" one; writing of the kind we do is also new, as we were saying earlier on, and so one cannot come to it fully sure of all the answers.

Which is not to say that a writer's basic instincts are changing. No, I think a writer's basic instincts must be inviolate; there must be complete integrity there. So this is why when I hear writers say, "Before I used to do this; now I've seen that my ways are wrong," I feel that's too much like born-again Christians! And I have great suspicion of people who have these instant conversions; I think there is something specious about it. I think the basic thing in the equipment of the writer, which is his integrity, is there from the beginning. He doesn't learn it half-way through his career. Your soul as an artist cannot be something which you are tinkering with along the way. You may say the emphasis has changed. It's really a matter of emphasis rather than of absolute distinctions.

Again we are talking of ambivalences. Things come in twos, nothing is absolute. It's the man of action, the politician, who is allowed to see things in their absoluteness. And he's usually quite wrong and dangerous. A writer must keep that reserve, recognizing that although this is true, but . . . That "but" is terribly important and while we are experiencing our contemporary history and so on, we are seeing mistakes—maybe not mistakes—wrong emphases or even emphases that become outdated, because things move very fast in our situation. I mean, the twenty-first century is almost sixteen years away and we are running like mad. So what was the right emphasis yesterday may not be quite right today, so we must be agile and flexible and imaginative. I'm not saying we should be different people from what we were yesterday. And one of the areas where this flexibility is called for, is in our relationships; how do we get to the people, to our audience, to our nation, to our country. If I was writing novels and I thought that, well, novels only reach a certain number of people after five years or something, it is quite permissible to say "well, what else is there to do which might get my voice across as quickly as possible?" It might be an essay, it might be a play on the stage, it might be radio or television or whatever; I think these are simply "dresses" you can change, "shoes" you can change. But your basic integrity demands that you don't lie about what you see; you shouldn't. You don't touch it up so that it looks acceptable because somebody else is saying so, because America is saying so, because Russia is saying so. You may be right or you may be wrong, but this is what you see. You may say what you see, but it's not for you to start monitoring and censoring what you see, maybe in keeping with what somebody else sees.

JEYIFO One final question. You have been honoured as a writer, an artist, around the world. One particular honour, and this is a paradox, one that came late, relative to the others, was the Nigerian national honours, and even that was highly controversial. A few people thought that you should not have accepted the honour, since, in their view, the people who were giving the honour were not much different from Chief Nanga. How do you react to this? And if I may sum it all up: what is Nigeria to you? I sense that your acceptance of that honour had a lot to do with this question—what Nigeria is.

ACHEBE That's a very important question and I am aware of the doubt expressed by people, especially by my colleagues in the writing profession. I should state that I did not feel that the moment somebody offers this and you say yes, there is a certain compromise. You don't accept with the right hand and slap the person with the left hand. But my view of this is really quite simple. I am a Nigerian. Nigeria, with all its faults, is the country where it pleased providence to put me. Now, I am not one of those who will say

Nigeria is an absolute good, that even if Nigeria is cutting my throat, I should be singing the national anthem. That's not my kind of patriotism. But this is where I am. There was a time, as you know, when I was quite vocal in my condemnation, in fact my absolute rejection of Nigeria. That's one individual's action. Now, I do not then become a stateless United Nations citizen. Okay, I wanted to break out of Nigeria, not because I didn't like Nigeria, because I was always fond of this country. But the experience one went through at a particular period was so bad, that one really had to say no. That was not to be; so we reconciled ourselves with this experiment—it's still an experiment—called Nigeria. It is not a great country. In fact I've got a book which should be out in a short while, called *The Trouble with Nigeria*. I do not think Nigeria is a great country, contrary to what Shagari and others may be saying. It's not true, you see. I listed all kinds of things about Nigeria which in my view would make it one of the worst countries in the whole world, one of the least attractive places on earth. But it's my country and since, as I said, providence put me here, my role is to make this place more habitable than I met it. That's our role, that's the role of every generation, and that's what civilisation is about. I do not think that I have any right to move to America or Britain or France or the Soviet Union and then live there because those societies work better than mine. Because I know that those societies were created by human ingenuity, by human intelligence, by good leaders, by writers. So I have to deal with Nigeria.

Now one of the weaknesses of Nigeria is failure to accept merit and quality, in various areas—in the sciences, in the arts, in everything. Politics is all that matters here. If you seek the political kingdom, everything else will be added unto you.

JEYIFO   A failure to establish a criterion of achievement.

ACHEBE   Yes, we don't know it. So when, in a fit of absent-mindedness, or whatever, the Nigerian nation says we recognise your achievements as a writer and we give you a medal, I don't see that I should reject it. Not that I need that medal. In fact, it was Femi Osofisan who said I didn't need it. Of course, I didn't need it and this was all the more reason why I thought I could take it, because I really didn't need it. But for me, it meant that for the first time literature was being accorded a certain recognition. And while I was going to receive it, I was also writing a speech—this was before anybody else knew that this was going to happen—a speech in which I was going to say precisely this: that nobody is going to buy me with honours, and that I think that this will not be the end because we should have a situation in which national honours are given to writers, given to painters, given to sculptors, given to journalists.

What we have here—if you go round this campus, you'll find student hostels are named after politicians that you cannot remember one year after they leave office. Statues are raised to politicians the first year they are in office; universities are named after living politicians. Now, I think this kind of thing is wrong. And if we can change the emphasis ever so little by bringing in scientists and writers, we will be encouraging other scientists, other writers. Politics is not the only way. And I want a situation in which literature, as a matter of routine, becomes something which Nigerians talk about and recognise. Now if my accepting national honours will do anything in this connection I will be quite satisfied. There should be recognition of the arts in our political culture.

JAMES CURREY, ALAN HILL, AND KEITH SAMBROOK

Working with Chinua Achebe: In Conversation with Kirsten Holst Petersen†

The following contribution is based on two interviews * * * both recorded in August 1990 in London.

On 17 June 1958 Heinemann published *Things Fall Apart,* written by an unknown Nigerian. They played safe and printed only 2,000 copies. The book went on to sell upwards of 3,000,000 copies in the U.K. edition alone, not counting the American editions, the reprints throughout Africa, and the translations into forty-five different languages; but apart from achieving such international acclaim it also gave the impetus to a new publishing venture which came to be the springboard for the astonishing new wave of writing from independent Africa. Alan Hill tells the story of its way to publication.

ALAN HILL   I was the educational books director of Heinemann when Achebe's manuscript came into the office. I don't think he had any idea of the importance of what he had done. It did not occur to him that he was the first great African writer in the English language. He had just sat down and written a novel—in manuscript as he didn't have a typewriter; and there were no carbon copies, neither was there a photocopier in those days. He just parcelled up the one copy of the manuscript in brown paper and sent it by ordinary mail to London, in response to an advertisement in *The Spectator*: 'Authors' manuscripts typed.' He got an acknow-

† From *Chinua Achebe: A Celebration* (Oxford; Portsmouth, NH: Heinemann, 1991). Reprinted by permission of Pearson Education.

ledgment and a request for a £32 fee, which he sent by British postal order, and he heard nothing more for a year. He sent follow-ups but nothing happened and he was getting very depressed. So one of his colleagues in the Nigerian Broadcasting Service, who was on a visit to London, went to this typing agency and found the manuscript lying in a corner gathering dust. They eventually typed it and sent the manuscript back to him with one typed copy. Years later, I asked Chinua what he would have done if the manuscript had in fact been lost. 'I would have been so discouraged,' he replied, 'that I would probably have given up writing altogether . . . and if I had rewritten it, it would have been a different book.'

Shortly afterwards he came to London on a course at the BBC. He showed it to his course officer who sent it round to Heinemann's. Heinemann's normal fiction reader read it and did a long report, but the firm was still hesitating whether to accept it. Would anyone possibly buy a novel by an African? There were no precedents. So the rather doubting bunch at the top of Heinemann's thought of the educational department, who after all sold books to Africa and were supposed to know about Africans. So they showed it to one of our educational advisers, Professor Donald MacRae, who was just back from West Africa. He read it in the office and ended the debate with an eleven-word report: 'This is the best first novel I have read since the war.' We took the book and printed 2,000 copies.

KIRSTEN HOLST PETERSEN   How about editing the book. Was there any editing?

AH   No, we didn't touch a word of it. We brought it out and it was very well reviewed in *The Times Literary Supplement,* and C.P. Snow reviewed it and all round it had very good and respectful reviews.

This led Alan Hill to look further into publishing possibilities in Africa.

AH   Achebe could not be unique. I felt there must be other potential authors among the new university-educated generation in Nigeria. So the following year, 1959, I went to West Africa and I took the book around with me. Everywhere I was greeted with total scepticism that a recent student from the University of Ibadan should have written a novel that was of any significance at all. I then went on to travel round the whole of sub-Saharan Africa, and when I got back it was clear I needed specialised help if we were to find and publish new African authors—a feat which none of the famous British publishers who were long-established in Africa had ever attempted.

Fortune favoured me. In 1960 Nelson's talented West African specialist Van Milne had a flaming row with his boss and resigned. I at once invited him to join me. Though he was only to stay two years, his contribution was crucial. We decided to make a really cheap paperback of *Things Fall Apart*—25p in fact—and look for some other books to go with it so that we could put out a package. Achebe by now had written a second book, and Van picked up Kenneth Kaunda who was just out of prison and was writing a book about the independence struggle in Zambia. Van finally approached Cyprian Ekwensi who had made something of a name for himself by writing for Hutchinson, and he dug out a manuscript from his bottom drawer called *Burning Grass*. This made a group of four books, and by 1962 we were able to launch them as the first of 'The African Writers Series.'

Both Alan Hill and Keith Sambrook emphasise the pioneering work done by Van Milne.

KEITH SAMBROOK   The African Writers Series was started by Van Milne who had joined Heinemann to develop their African publishing; he persuaded Alan Hill to back the idea in 1961, and was able to do this because Heinemann already had the copyright of the two earlier Achebe novels, *Things Fall Apart* and *No Longer At Ease,* and he got Cyprian Ekwensi to write a simple novel about Northern Nigeria, *Burning Grass,* and worked with Kenneth Kaunda on *Zambia Shall Be Free.* Those were the first four titles launched in 1962. Van had left Heinemann, when I joined in January 1963, and left behind him four manuscripts, one of which was Ngugi's *Weep Not, Child.* That had come to Van through Achebe at a writers' conference in Makerere in 1962.

However, Achebe's role soon became crucial.

AH   Van's early departure back to Nelson's—his old boss having retired—left us in only a mild quandary. We just didn't realise the scale and importance of what we had embarked upon, as was exemplified in Van's reasons for leaving us: 'So far as Africa is concerned, Heinemann is cottage industry. I want to get back to the big time!' Suitably humbled, I invited Keith Sambrook to join us in 1963 as Van's replacement, and he worked with me until I retired.

But before he arrived I felt the need for a General Editor 'on the ground' to develop the series. So in November 1962 I sent out my number two, Tony Beal, to Nigeria to meet Chinua to invite him to be general editor. The two met in Lagos, in the Bristol Hotel, and Chinua at once said 'yes.' For the next ten years, Chinua edited the series—we published 100 titles in ten years, an average of ten per year. He read them all, commented on them, said whether he thought they were worth publishing or not, and in addition to the hundred there were many more that we didn't accept. In many cases he did major editorial work, recommending to authors important improvements to their work.

KS Achebe had told Van Milne that Ngugi was a very promising young writer. What I think you must remember is that Van Milne and I were academic and school book publishers. This was our entire training and background, and we thought in terms of books for use by students. Van also had strong political interests in Africa, and that explained the Zambia/Kaunda book. Achebe clearly didn't think first and foremost in terms of educational books and when he directed Van towards Ngugi, the slant of the series changed somewhat. It was no longer viewed simply as an extension of educational publishing, but as a series that launched new writing.

AH By this time you may be wondering why a major creative writing series was being handled by an educational publisher. I must emphasise that, from the very start, we knew we were not now in the business of publishing school textbooks. Van and I had long discussions as to what our publishing role should properly be. Looking back on a list of 300 titles, it is easily answered in retrospect. But in 1961 we had just two novels by Achebe, and beyond that we faced the unknown . . . complete darkness. We decided in the end to be guided by literary quality—to publish anything of real merit which came our way, irrespective of its 'category.' In point of fact, the great majority of the first titles were new fiction, interspersed with poetry and drama. The fact that some of the titles were set for school and university examinations was an incidental, though very welcome, bonus.

Then why Heinemann Educational Books? The reason is simple. We were the only firm with the faith—the passion almost—and the will to do the job; and we had Chinua Achebe's first two novels to give us a flying start. Also—and this was quite essential—we had the necessary business set-up to sell books within Africa itself. The big fiction houses were useless; they just didn't reach black Africa, for the book trade in that continent was almost entirely educational. William Heinemann, our fiction and general company, had never sold books in Africa outside the European communities. Only the educational company had the know-how and the marketing organisation to bring the African Writers Series to the ordinary African.

For the first ten years Achebe was editor of the series and he did all this work for nothing. He did it for the good of African literature. And, you know, this is what the younger generation of critics just don't realize, that he made an enormous contribution to the African Writers Series. His name was the magnet that brought everything in, and his critical judgement was the decisive factor in what we published. And in addition to that, the fantastic sales of his own books selling by the million provided the economic basis for the rest of the series. I did a calculation in 1984, by which time we had published getting on for three hundred titles, and one third of the sales revenue from the entire list came from Achebe's four novels. And so his freely offered literary judgement plus his own tremendous sales were the backbone of the African Writers series.

In those early days I used to go out to see Achebe in Nigeria, in Lagos. He was the very image of a modern Nigerian 'yuppie' in those days. He had a very handsome British colonial-type house, he used to wear a sharp suit, dark glasses, and he had a Jaguar car. At first sight he was a perfect Nigerian 'yuppie.' But of course, once one started to talk to him, one realized that there was something very different below the surface. We had a very agreeable relationship, he was a very understanding and accommodating author.

KHP   What was the pattern of this working relationship? What role did Achebe play?

JAMES CURREY   Here again, I think that Achebe is very important. He of course read most of the manuscripts, and he was a very very strong encourager of the other potential writers. Another important thing was that he was very well regarded by Alan Hill, the founding chairman of Heinemann Educational, so if Chinua said a book ought to be published, Alan tended to agree and side with us against the rest of our colleagues.

KS   I think that from very early on, when the new manuscripts came in, particularly from Nigeria, we automatically consulted Achebe, and once Aig Higo became manager of Heinemann's office in Nigeria in 1965, we more or less put everything through him if it was Nigerian or West African, indeed increasingly from anywhere in Africa, because he has such a very good literary judgment and insight. So between them, Achebe and Higo were filters for everything we published and in this way we found a lot of new writing by new authors.

AH   Keith has already mentioned a very good example of how Chinua attracted a new author. It happened like this: I was at a board meeting at our offices in Kingswood in Surrey and I had a telephone call from Van Milne in Makerere. There was a symposium going on in Makerere, organized by the Council for Cultural Freedom, a CIA-funded outfit which was a mixture of the British Council and the Pentagon. They were running this thing, and Wole Soyinka and Chinua Achebe were both there. Anyhow, Van Milne phoned me up and said a young student at Makerere had shown to Achebe an almost finished manuscript of a novel he'd written. Achebe was very impressed with it and he'd shown it at once to Van Milne. Van Milne read it and told me over the telephone: 'I think it's terrific, and I want your agreement to take on this book sight unseen.' And I said, 'You've got it,' and went back to the meeting. The book was Ngugi's *Weep Not, Child*. Now that would never have come to us in that way if the author hadn't taken it and shown it to Achebe. And that is how the African Writers Series was built up.

By 1967 it was clear we were onto something big, and we could no longer run the African Writers Series as an 'add-on' to our educational publishing. So I invited James Currey of the Oxford University Press to join us and run the African Writers Series as his specialism.

KHP   Did Achebe's involvement with the crisis in the East affect your working relationship?

JC   Yes, definitely communication became more difficult during the Biafran War. During the war, Chinua Achebe came to London from time to time, but less frequently as the war progressed because he was visiting the United States as unofficial Biafran fund-raising ambassador. I do remember him occasionally coming through, and this was exciting because he had this tremendous enthusiasm and vision of the new Biafran state. This meant that he found it more and more difficult to have a regular dialogue with us on the African Writers Series, but nevertheless he was tremendously supportive and we, who were becoming more and more confident, would say, 'We've got this and this which looks interesting, and these are the reports.' And Chinua had more and more an overview and less and less reading of the individual manuscripts of that time. We would talk things through with him, and as a sympathetic ear he was very very good. Then the Biafran war ended, and that was obviously an extremely difficult period for Chinua Achebe because he was in the East, and the recently re-opened university at Nsukka was struggling. In 1971 I remember visiting him in his house on the university campus which, like all the other houses on the campus, had blackened walls—there was no electric light, the whole university was a shell and had been through various military occupations. It was then that Chinua said, 'Look, during this period I've been unable to give you as much advice as I would have liked to have done. I think it should be handed over to another writer, and I would suggest that Ngugi should be the advisor.'

KHP   You published his collection of short stories, *Beware, Soul Brother,* which were about the Nigerian Civil War. Did this not cause some difficulties as Britain supported the other side?

AH   Oh, no. There were no problems there. During the Civil War he used to come over to London. He used to get into a clapped-out Super Constellation aircraft at the Uli-Ihiala airstrip and he'd fly to Lisbon; then he'd transfer to an ordinary commercial aircraft and come to London. And he'd come strolling into the office as cool and as humorous as if he'd just come from Chelsea or Kensington. We used to hold parties and receptions for him. When Chinua finished ten years as general editor, the event coincided with the publication of the one hundredth book—which was his own book, *Girls at War*. So we celebrated with a party at the Athenaeum Club, attended by many literary celebrities. Chinua now (1972) resigned his position as general editor, and decisions were taken in London, James Currey being editorially in charge of the series.

KHP   You were originally educational publishers. Did this change represent a 'drift' into fiction, or was it a definite policy?

KS   Well, very little had been published at that time, so to continue the series Chinua encouraged us to look for new writers and writing. This was to some extent resisted at Heinemann Educational Books, and in order to obtain any kind of general trade marketing for books outside Africa we had to enlist William Heinemann, our general publishing colleagues, and persuade them, often against their will, to publish hardbacks of these early novels. In this way, the new books stood a chance of being noticed in the trade.

KHP   Why did you want hardbacks?

KS   Well, that was the only way you get them into the trade. Otherwise they were simply going to be seen as school textbooks.

JC   Paperbacks hardly existed in Britain at that time, except for Penguin. Also they did not get reviewed.

KS   The authors, of course, wanted that kind of exposure. And there was a growing interest in African literature at the time.

KHP   You must have faced some opposition.

KS   Well, scepticism and certainly cynicism from some of our colleagues. But to be fair, Alan Hill had great enthusiasm for the African Writers Series. Alan was outgoing, and he wanted to establish Heinemann in Africa because he believed in Africa and in African progress. But I think that he was the only one amongst our colleagues who had anything but profound scepticism. They tended to regard it as an obligation and a waste of time. Later on, they changed their minds, because the second Ngugi novel, *The River Between*, began to sell, and in 1964 it was reviewed by people whom they regarded highly. Also Achebe's *Arrow of God* was widely acclaimed in 1964 and did very well.

JC   Another thing against us was that whilst our colleagues at Heinemann were happy about creative writing as long as the author was dead (D. H. Lawrence) they found it very hard to come to terms with an educational series by living writers. The other important factor that happened during the period of decolonisation—and this is the period we're talking about—was the establishment of examination boards in both East and West

Africa. These boards were all part of the enthusiastic decolonisation process, and they insisted quite rightly that everything needed to be more African oriented. When it came to literature, initially they were pretty conservative—Shakespeare, etc. But there was a great interest in and enthusiasm for things that were African, and fairly rapidly they realized that there were interesting works being produced by young Africans and examination questions could be asked about these works.

But as publishers we came up against a general problem: what was appropriate for an educational publisher to publish? Fiction was for a general publisher. William Heinemann had the proud record of being one of the most enterprising London-based fiction publishers. But even they needed their arms twisted a bit to publish these books. Meanwhile there was a demand building up in Africa for 'set' books. As publishers who were interested in literature, as both Keith and I were, we managed to override our colleagues' initial scepticism and get away with it because of the sales success of the series as a whole. However, one of the great pleasures of the African Writers Series was all the different books which one published in hope, and publishing in hope is always a risky business. It turned out, however, within the context of the '60s that Heinemann with its growing educational market, with mailings to schools, contact with inspectors and universities, etc. was actually able to get these books into the educational network in Africa.

KS However, it is still true that initially the African Writers Series attracted more interest outside Africa than it did inside Africa. That was not the intention. Our original intention was to provide books at a price which readers in Africa could afford. But they hadn't heard of Achebe in Nigeria, so it took a little while to establish him in his own country. The interesting thing is that it happened in a surprisingly short space of time. It started in 1962 when the first four volumes came out, and by 1965 we were selling quite a large number of the first ten titles in Africa itself. Publishing policy was obviously important.

KHP Would Heinemann's reasons for doing the series and Achebe's coincide? Obviously Heinemann was in it for the market and the money.

AH Well, Heinemann was me.

KHP All right, you, then. As a British publisher you would be thinking in terms of a market and money . . .

AH That's right.

KHP . . . and Achebe would be thinking of furthering Nigerian writing.

AH   Yes, but you have to remember that we were not dominated by a money-grabbing ideology in those days. Publishing has changed a lot since then, and I don't really care for the accountancy-ridden profit-making of present-day publishing firms which are now in the grip of big corporations who are only interested in the profits which the products make.

As I said, in the earlier days, like Achebe whose ten years' editorship was entirely unpaid, we were very idealistic. Africa was an immensely exciting country. Independence was coming, we published *Things Fall Apart* when Nigeria was still an English colony moving towards independence, and there seemed to be a tremendous dawn, 'the wind of change,' as everyone said, and this was something we wanted to be in on, and if splendid writing was being written in these countries we were going to publish it. Whether it was profitable or not wasn't really our major consideration. The fact that the overall series was profitable, of course, meant that nobody interfered with us. We later on published a whole lot of books that weren't profitable. But these were carried by the profits generated by some 'big-selling' authors: Achebe, Ngugi, etc.

KHP   Many of the later titles can't have sold many copies. There was a whole spate of intermediate books.

AH   Yes, quite. We have been criticized by people who have said, 'You should not have published these books.' But when you're pioneering in an unknown field, I felt that we should cast the net as wide as possible, rather than try to be over-meticulous and over-selective. So we cast the net wide, and we had some real surprises.

KS   Quite consciously we decided that if we were going to publish new writers we had to take on people who were not in the Achebe and Ngugi class. This built up the Series and encouraged good writers like Kofi Awoonor to come and give us his novel and Lenrie Peters his poetry. In the meantime Clive Wake and John Reed encouraged us to look at writing from Francophone Africa, either works already in translation or works which could be translated.

JC   Thirty titles in the Series sold over 100,000 copies each. I think that Chinua Achebe was very important in encouraging us in treating the African Writers Series not just as an educational series, but as a series which could sustain sufficient sales on the open market, and that school teachers would just have to be careful about what they selected. An important factor in this transition was the question of s-e-x. One of the early titles which Chinua strongly supported in the African Writers Series was the translation of Mongo Beti's *Mission to Kala*. The translation was published in 1964 and it was set in East Africa for the old East African Examination Council in the early '70s. They ordered the book—*Mission to Kala* sounded quite a safe bet in a mission school—but they were absolutely horrified by it when it actually arrived. It was a fully adult novel written by Mongo Beti in the '50s for the French fiction market.

S-e-x was a very important thing, but the other thing was s-h-i-t. *The Beautyful Ones Are Not Yet Born* is very scatological. In fact, it would have been too way out for an English school at the time. But by the time I started working for the series in 1967, it was so successful that there need be no holds barred, the best fiction or poetry there was could be published, and we would find a market for it. After all, even though the African market was an educational market, there were people like Sam Cofie running the University bookshop in Legon, and he provided a cultural centre for school teachers, peace-corps volunteers, African students, etc. They wanted to buy paperbacks, and you must remember that Penguin paperbacks were orange in England, and we used the colour unashamedly, so the series became known as 'the orange series.' One could say that the Allan Lane, Penguin revolution begat the African Writers Series, in a way. Paperbacks were still comparatively rare in 1960–61.

KHP   Would you say that Achebe's opinions have altered the direction of the series?

AH   No. It didn't alter the direction. I think, principally, having him was the magnet which drew all the writers to the series. That was really the thing.

KHP   How did the rest of the publishing world in London look at this new venture?

AH   Well, they were astonished. They were glad that someone had done it. Some of them wished *they* had done it.

There wasn't a vast field of writing from which you could pick and choose to fit some ideological preconception. Whatever it was, if it was good, we would take it.

KHP   This 'goodness,' was this a literary criterion?

AH   Yes, basically it would be a literary criterion. The intention was to publish African literature wherever it sprang up and wherever we could find it. It was simply a trade matter. The books were sold through the educational book system because there wasn't any other in West Africa.

JC   Although Heinemann Educational was an educational publisher it published a general fiction and poetry series. I think Chinua Achebe gave us enormous support in publishing fiction. This is so much the matter of the publisher's self image, which is related to the thrust of the publisher's marketing, and by then we could sell a general series in Africa. With Chinua's help and encouragement the series was a general series rather than an educational one, because of the cultural, educational and social context in which we were operating. Meanwhile, the strength of Heinemann's own marketing and distribution in Africa was always growing. But the most important thing was that people in Africa had an intrinsic part in choosing and recommending titles, and Chinua Achebe, more than anyone else, re-shaped the literary map of Africa.

Essays and Responses

CHINUA ACHEBE

Chi in Igbo Cosmology†

There are two clearly distinct meanings of the word *chi* in Igbo.[1] The first is often translated as god, guardian angel, personal spirit, soul, spirit-double, etc. The second meaning is day or daylight but is most commonly used for those transitional periods between day and night or night and day. Thus we speak of *chi ofufo* meaning daybreak and *chi ojiji*, nightfall. We also have the word *mgbachi* for that most potent hour of noon that splits the day in two, a time favoured in folklore by itinerant spirits and feared by children.

I am chiefly concerned here with the first meaning of *chi*, a concept so central in Igbo psychology and yet so elusive and enigmatic. The great variety of words and phrases which has been put forward at different times by different people as translations of this concept attests to its great complexity and lends additional force to the famous plea of Dr J. B. Danquah that we pay one another's gods the compliment of calling them by their proper name.

In a general way we may visualise a person's *chi* as his other identity in spiritland—his *spirit being* complementing his terrestrial *human being*; for nothing can stand alone, there must always be another thing standing beside it.

Without an understanding of the nature of *chi* one could not begin to make sense of the Igbo world-view; and yet no study of it exists that could even be called preliminary. What I am attempting here is not to fill that gap but to draw attention to it in a manner appropriate to one whose primary love is literature and not religion, philosophy or linguistics. I will not even touch upon such tantalising speculations as what happens to a person's *chi* when the person dies, and its shrine

† From *Morning Yet on Creation Day: Essays* (London: Heinemann, 1975), 93–103. Copyright © 1975 by Chinua Achebe. Used by permission of Doubleday, a division of Random House, Inc. and The Wylie Agency.
1. The Igbo people (called Ibo by the English) inhabit south-eastern Nigeria. They caught world attention for a while as chief protagonists of the Biafran tragedy. Igbo is both the people (about 10 million) and their language.

is destroyed. Does it retreat completely back to its old home? And finally what happens at the man's reincarnation?

But before we embark on a consideration of the nature and implication of this concept which is so powerful in Igbo religion and thought let us examine briefly what connection there may be between it and the other meaning of *chi*. For a long time I was convinced that there couldn't possibly be any relationship between *chi* (spirit being) and *chi* (daylight) except as two words that just happened to sound alike. But one day I stumbled on the very important information that among the Igbo of Awka a man who has arrived at the point in his life when he needs to set up a shrine to his *chi* will invite a priest to perform a ritual of bringing down the spirit from the face of the sun at daybreak. Thereafter it is represented physically in the man's compound until the day of his death when the shrine must be destroyed.

The implication of this is that a person's *chi* normally resides with the sun, bringer of daylight, or at least passes through it to visit the world. Which itself may have an even profounder implication for it is well known in Igbo cosmology that the Supreme Deity, Chukwu Himself, is in close communion with the sun. But more on that later.

Since Igbo people did not construct a rigid and closely argued system of thought to explain the universe and the place of man in it, preferring the metaphor of myth and poetry, anyone seeking an insight into their world must seek it along their own way. Some of these ways are folk-tales, proverbs, proper names, rituals and festivals. There is of course the 'scientific' way as well—the tape-recorded interview with old people. Unfortunately it is often more impressive than useful. The old people who have the information we seek will not often bare their hearts to any passer-by. They will give answers, and true answers too. But there is truth and there is truth. To get to the inner truth will often require more time than the recording interviewer can give—it may require a whole lifetime. In any case no one talks naturally into a strange box of tricks!

It is important to stress what I said earlier: the central place in Igbo thought of the notion of duality. Wherever Something stands, Something Else will stand beside it. Nothing is absolute. *I am the truth, the way and the life* would be called blasphemous or simply absurd for is it not well known that a man may worship Ogwugwu to perfection and yet be killed by Udo? The world in which we live has its double and counterpart in the realm of spirits. A man lives here and his *chi* there. Indeed the human being is only one half (and the weaker half at that) of a person. There is a complementary spirit being, *chi*. (The word *spirit* though useful does create serious problems of its own, however, for it is used to describe many different orders of non-human being.) Thus the abode of *chi* may be confused with *ani mmo* where the dead who encounter no obstacles in their passage go to live. But *ani mmo* is thought to be not above like the realm of *chi*, but below, inside the earth. Considerable confusion and obscurity darken the picture at this point because there is a sense in which the two supernatural worlds are both seen as parallel to the land of the living. In an early anthropological study of the Igbo Major A. G. Leonard at the opening of this century reported the following account from one of his Igbo informants:

> We Ibo look forward to the next world as being much the same as this . . . we picture life there to be exactly as it is in this world. The ground there is just the same as it is here, the earth is similar. There are forests and hills and valleys with rivers flowing and roads leading from one town to another . . . People in spiritland have their ordinary occupations, the farmer his farm.[2]

This 'spiritland' where dead ancestors recreate a life comparable to their earthly existence is not only parallel to the human world but is also similar and physically contiguous with it for there is constant coming and going between them in the endless traffic of life, death and reincarnation. The masked spirits who often grace human rituals and ceremonies with their presence are representative visitors from this underworld and are said to emerge from their subterranean home through ant-holes. At least that is the story as told to the uninitiated. To those who know, however, the masked 'spirits' are only *symbolic* ancestors. But this knowledge does not in any way diminish their validity or the awesomeness of their presence.

These ancestral spirits which may be personified by man are, however, of a very different order from *chi* and so is their place of abode. There is a story of how a proud wrestler, having thrown every challenger in the world, decides to go and wrestle in the world of spirits. There he also throws challenger after challenger, including many multiple-headed ones—so great was his prowess. At last there is no one left to fight. But the wrestler refuses to leave. The spirits beg him to go; his companion praise-singer on the flute pleads with him. But it is all in vain. *There must be somebody left; surely the famed land of spirits can do better than this*, he said. Again everyone begs him to collect his laurels and go but again he refuses. Finally his own *chi* appears, reluctant, thin as a rope. The wrestler laughs at this miserable-looking contender and moves forward contemptuously to knock him down whereupon the other lifts him clear off the ground with his little finger and smashes him to death.

This cautionary tale is concerned mainly, I think, with setting a limit to man's aspirations. The limit is not the sky; it is somewhere much closer to earth. A sensible man will turn round at the frontiers

2. A. G. Leonard, *The Lower Niger and Its Tribes* (London: Cass, 1968). 185–6.

of absolutism and head for home again. There is, however, around the story as well a vague intimation that the place where *chi* inhabits is forbidden to man in a way that *ani mmo*, the abode of his dead fathers, does not appear to be. For we have, at least, a description of the landscape of *ani mmo*; nothing comparable exists for the territory of *chi*.

There is another cautionary tale about *chi*, this time involving the little bird, *nza*, who ate and drank somewhat more than was good for him and in a fit of recklessness which inebriation alone would explain taunted his *chi* to come and get him if he could. Whereupon a hawk swooped down from the clear sky and carried him away. Which shows the foolishness of counting on *chi's* remoteness, for *chi* need not come in person or act directly but may use one's enemy who is close by.

The story of the headstrong wrestler in addition to all the other things it tells us makes also the important point that a man's *chi* does have a special hold over him such as no other powers can muster. This is why, for instance, it can dispense with the physical endowments and terrors of the multiple-headed spirits. This special power that *chi* has over its man (or the man's special vulnerability to his *chi*) is further exemplified in a proverb: 'No matter how many divinities sit together to plot a man's ruin it will come to nothing unless his chi is there among them.' Clearly *chi* has unprecedented veto powers over man's destiny.

But power so complete, even in the hands of *chi*, is abhorrent to the Igbo imagination. Therefore the makers of proverbs went to work again, as it were, to create others that would set a limit to its exercise. Hence the well-known *Onye kwe chie ekwe*. If a man agrees his *chi* agrees. And so the initiative, or some of it at least, is returned to man.

If you want to know how life has treated an Igbo man, a good place to look is the names his children bear. His hopes, his fears, his joys and sorrows; his grievances against his fellows, or complaints about the way he has been used by fortune; even straight historical records, are all there. And because *chi* is so central to Igbo thought we will also find much about it in proper names—more, I think, than from any other single source.

Chika (*chi* is supreme); Chibuzo (*chi* is in front); Nebechi (look to *chi*) are only a few examples of the large number of names that show the general primacy of *chi* over mankind. Chinwuba asserts *chi's* special responsibility for increase and prosperity; Chinwendu its power over life and Chikadibia over health. A man who suffers from false accusations or calumnies heaped on him by his fellows may call his child Chiebonam (may *chi* not accuse me) meaning that the moral justification which *chi* can give is what counts in the end. It is, however, unusual to link *chi* in this way with moral sanction, a responsibility that belongs normally to Ani, the Earth Goddess and proper source of moral law—a fact recognised in the name Aniebonam which is analogous to Chiebonam.

The Igbo believe that a man receives his gifts or talents, his character—indeed his portion in life generally—before he comes into the world. It seems there is an element of choice available to him at that point; and that his *chi* presides over the bargaining. Hence the saying *Obu etu nya na chie si kwu*, which we often hear when a man's misfortune is somehow beyond comprehension and so can only be attributable to an agreement he himself must have entered into, at the beginning, alone with his *chi*, for there is a fundamental justice in the universe and nothing so terrible can happen to a person for which he is not somehow responsible. A few other names suggest this role of *chi* as the great dealer out of gifts: Nkechinyelu and Chijioke, for example.

As we have seen the Igbo believe that when a man says yes his *chi* will also agree; but not always. Sometimes a man may struggle with all his power and say yes most emphatically and yet nothing he attempts will succeed. Quite simply the Igbo say of such a man: *Chie ekwero*, his *chi* does not agree. Now, this could mean one of two things: either the man has a particularly intransigent *chi* or else it is the man himself attempting too late to alter that primordial bargain he had willingly struck with his *chi*, saying yes now when his first unalterable word had been no, forgetting that 'the first word gets to Chukwu's house'.

But of course the idea of an intransigent *chi* does exist in Igbo: *ajo chi*, literally 'bad chi'. We must remember, however, when we hear that a man has a bad *chi* that we are talking about his fortune rather than his character. A man of impeccable character may yet have a bad *chi* so that nothing he puts his hand to will work out right. *Chi* is therefore more concerned with success or failure than with righteousness and wickedness. Which is not to say that it is totally indifferent to morality. For we should know by now that nothing is *totally* anything in Igbo thinking; everything is a question of measure and degree. We have already seen in the name Chiebonam that *chi* shares a little of the moral concerns of Ani, the earth goddess. But in addition there is a hint of moral attribution to *chi* in the way the Igbo sometimes explain differences in human character. For maximum dramatisation they pick two brothers who are dissimilar in character: one good, the other bad. And they say: *ofu nne n'amu, ma ofu chi adeke*, a very neat and tight statement which can only be approximately interpreted as: one mother gives birth, different *chi* create.

This statement apart from reiterating the idea of 'one man, one *chi*' goes further to introduce the fundamental notion of *chi* as creator which is of the utmost importance: a man does not only have his own *chi* but is created by it and no two people, not even blood brothers, it seems, are created by the same *chi*. What we know of *chi* can thus be summed up as follows: every person has an individual *chi* who created him, its natural home is somewhere in the region of the sun but it may be induced to visit an earthly shrine; a person's fortunes in life are controlled more or less completely by his *chi*. (Perhaps this is a good place to point out that there are many minor—and occasionally even major—divergences of perception about *chi* from different parts of Igbo land so that one can at best only follow what appears to be the dominant and persistent concepts. For example, although communities exist which assert categorically that *chi* lives with Chukwu, in most places such closeness can only be deduced indirectly.)

There are many names and sayings in Igbo which confirm the creative role of *chi*. When we name a child Chiekezie we imply that *chi* has restored a certain balance by that particular creation, or has at last apportioned shares equitably. Of a man unattractive or deficient in character we might say: *chi ya kegbulu ya ekegbu*. Here again there are two possible interpretations to our statement: either the man in question was created badly or else was cheated of his full share of things. Or both interpretations may even be intended; for what else is creation but the imparting of distinguishing characteristics and bestowing of gifts? Certainly the Igbo language by having the same root-word *ke* for *create* and *share* does encourage this notion.

The idea of individualism is sometimes traced to the Christian principle that God created all men and consequently every one of them is presumed worthy in His sight. The Igbo do better than that. They postulate the concept of every man as both a unique creation and the work of a unique creator. Which is as far as individualism and uniqueness can possibly go! And we should naturally expect such a cosmogony to have far-reaching consequences in the psychology and institutions of the people. This is not the place, however, to go into that. But we should at least notice in passing the fierce egalitarianism (less charitable people would have other names for it, of course) which was such a marked feature of Igbo political organisation, and may justifiably speculate on its possible derivation from this concept of every man's original and absolute uniqueness. An American anthropologist who studied the Igbo community of Onitsha in recent years called his book *The King in Every Man*.[3]

All this might lead one to think that among the Igbo the individual would be supreme, totally free and existentially alone. But the Igbo are unlikely to concede to the individual an absolutism they deny even to *chi*. The obvious curtailment of a man's power to walk alone and do as he will is provided by another potent force—the will of his community. For wherever Something stands, no matter what, Some-

3. Richard Henderson, *The King in Every Man* (New Haven, CT: Yale University Press, 1971).

thing Else will stand beside it. No man however great can win judgment against all the people.

We must now turn to the all-important relationship between *chi* and Chi Ukwu, one of the names by which the Supreme Deity is known in Igbo. The most obvious link is the name itself. Chi Ukwu (or simply, Chukwu) means literally Great Chi. Thus whatever *chi* may be it does seem to partake of the nature of the Supreme God. Another link is provided by the sun, bringer of daylight. As we saw earlier, among the Igbo of Awka a man's *chi* may be invoked to descend from the solar realm. As it happens, the Igbo also see the sun as an agent of Chukwu to whom it is said to bear those rare sacrifices offered as man's last desperate resort. It would seem then that wherever the abode of Chukwu happens to be in the heavens it cannot be distant from the place of *chi*.

In Yoruba[4] cosmology the Supreme God, Olodumare (one of whose titles is, incidentally, Owner of the Sun) sent the god, Obatala, on a mission of creation to make man. The Igbo are not so specific about Chukwu's role in the creation of man, but may be suggesting a similar delegation of power by the Supreme Overlord to a lesser divinity except that in their case every act of creation is the work of a separate and individual agent, *chi*, a personified and unique manifestation of the creative essence.

Still further west, the Akan of Ghana believe in a Moon Goddess whom they call Ngame, Mother of the World who gives a 'soul' to every human being at birth by shooting lunar rays into him. The Igbo, seemingly more reticent about such profound events may yet be hinting at a comparable cosmic relationship between their *chi* and solar rays. This would explain the invocation of *chi* from the face of the sun at the consecration of its shrine and account also for the second meaning of the word: daylight. And, of course, the Igbo being patrilineal (as anthropologists tell us) where the Akan are matrilineal a preference by them for the sun over the moon would be completely in character!

The significance of the sun in Igbo religion though subtle and unobtrusive is nonetheless undeniable and may even be called pervasive. If we are to believe the *New Larousse Encyclopaedia of Mythology* it seems that two-times-two-times-two is everywhere the sun's mystical figure (just as three-times-three is the moon's). Certainly the Igbo have a lot of use for fours and eights. The basic unit of their calendar is the four-day 'small' week and an eight-day 'great' week; the circumcision of their male child takes place on the eighth day after which it is accounted a human being; they compute largeness in units of four hundred, *nnu*, etc., etc.

---

4. The Yoruba of Western Nigeria are, in size and achievement, among the great peoples of Africa.

The exact relationship between the Supreme God (Chukwu), the sun and *chi* in Igbo cosmology will probably never be (and perhaps was intended not to be) unravelled. But if Chukwu means literally Great Chi one is almost tempted to borrow the words of Christian dogma and speak of *chi* as being of the same 'substance' as and 'proceeding' from Chukwu. Or is *chi* an infinitesimal manifestation of Chukwu's infinite essence given to each of us separately and uniquely, a single ray from the sun's boundless radiance? Or does Chukwu have a separate existence as ruler over a community of *chi*, countless as the stars and as endless in their disparate identities, holding anarchy at bay with His will?

One last word about Chineke which we have come to interpret as 'God who creates' and use as an alternative name for Chukwu. If our interpretation and use were supported by Igbo language and religious tradition the role of Chukwu as *the* Creator would be established and the activity of *chi* in their multiplicity relegated to the status of mere figures of speech. Unfortunately the early missionaries who appropriated Chineke as the Creator-God of Christianity acted a little hastily, unaware that the Igbo language was capable of treachery to hasty users on account of its tonality. (The story of the white preacher who kept saying that God had great buttocks when he meant great strength may be apocryphal, but it makes an important point.)

Chineke consists of three words: *chi na eke*. In assigning a meaning to it the crucial word is *na* which itself has three possible meanings. Let us examine each meaning in turn and see what it does to Chineke:

(a) said with a high tone *na* means *who* or *which*. Chineke will then mean '*chi* which creates';

(b) said with a low tone *na* can mean the auxiliary verb *does*, in which case Chineke will mean '*chi* does create'; and finally

(c) again said with a low tone *na* can mean the conjunctive *and*. Here something fundamental changes because *eke* is no longer a verb but a noun. Chineke then becomes '*chi* and *eke*'. And that, in my opinion, is the correct version.

Chineke, which we have come to interpret as '*chi* who creates' is nothing of the sort, but rather is a dual deity '*chi* and *eke*'. The early missionaries by putting the wrong tone on that little word *na* escorted a two-headed, pagan god into their holy of holies!

Now what are the grounds for making such a terrible assertion? Quite simply I have looked at traditional Igbo usage. But before I give the examples that will make this clear let us take a quick look at *eke*, this mysterious second member of the duality. What is it? I do not know for certain, but it does seem to have more or less the same attributes as *chi*; also it is sometimes called *aka*.

We have already referred to the common name Chinwuba (*chi* has increase) earlier on. Another version of this name is Ekejiuba (*Eke* holds increase). We have also mentioned the name Nebechi (look to *chi*). Now, there is also Lemeke (Leweke) which would appear to be exactly the same name except that *eke* occurs instead of *chi*. It is interesting to note that the *chi* versions of these names occur more in the northern and western parts of Igbo land while the *eke* names tend to occur more in the southern and eastern parts.

Let us turn for a moment from proper names to other sayings in which *chi* and *eke* are yoked together. If you want to curse a man in the most thorough fashion you curse his *chi* and his *eke* (or *aka*). That really takes care of him!

There is also the well-known little anecdote about the hen. Someone once asked her why it was that from daybreak to sunset she was always scratching the ground for food; was she never satisfied? To which she replied: 'You see, my dear fellow, when I wake up in the morning I begin to look for food for my *chi*. When I am through with that I must then find some for my *eke*. By the time I finish with that too it is already sunset and I haven't catered for myself!'

From the foregoing it would appear that *chi* and *eke* are very closely related deities, perhaps the same god in a twofold manifestation, such as male or female; or the duality may have come into being for the purpose of bringing two dialectal tributaries of Igbo into liturgical union. This last is particularly attractive because there exists a small number of similar 'double-headed' phrases each comprising two words and the conjunctive, both words being of identical meaning but drawn from two basic dialectal areas. Used in this conjunction the words immediately introduce the element of totality into their ordinary meaning. Thus *ikwu na ibe* stands for the entire community of kinsmen and women; *ogbo na uke* for the militant and aggressive band of spirit adversaries; *okwu na uka* for endless wranglings; *nta na imo* for odds and ends, etc. If indeed *chi na eke* should turn out to belong to this group of phrases the idea of using it to curse a man absolutely would then make a lot of sense! Which might be bad news indeed for the Christian Church in Igbo land. But it may surely draw consolation from the fact that the Book of the Old Testament itself, in all its glory and dignity, ends 'with a curse'!

Far be it from me, however, to suggest that Chineke should be dropped at this late hour as an alternative name for Chukwu. That would be futile pedantry; for whatever doubts we may entertain about its antecedents it has certainly served generations of Christians and non-Christians in Igbo land in contemplating the nature of the all-distant Supreme Deity, whose role in the world is shrouded in mystery and metaphor. The attraction of Chineke for the early evangelists must have been its seeming lack of ambiguity on the all-important question of creation. They needed a 'God who creates' and Chineke stood ready at hand. But Igbo traditional thought in its own way and style did recognise Chukwu as the Supreme Creator speculating only on the modalities, on *how* He accomplished the work and through what agencies and intermediaries. As we have seen He appears to work through *chi* to create man. Similarly there are numerous suggestions in Igbo lore of Him working with man to make the world— or rather to enhance its habitability, for the work of creation was not ended in one monumental effort but goes on still, Chukwu and man talking things over at critical moments, sometimes agreeing, sometimes not. Two examples will suffice:

> When Death first came into the world men sent a messenger to Chukwu to beg Him to remove the terrible scourge. Although He was disposed to consider the matter the first request that actually got through to Him from mankind was the wrong one and once He had granted it there was no way it could be altered.

In a study of Igbo people published in 1913 Northcote Thomas recorded the following story about Ezenri, that fascinating priest/king whose spiritual pre-eminence was acknowledged over considerable parts of Igbo land:

> Ezenri and Ezadama came from heaven and rested on an ant heap; all was water. Cuku (Chukwu) asked who was sitting there and they answered 'We are the kings of Nri and Adama', thereupon Cuku and the kings talked. After some conversation Cuku gave them each a piece of yam; yams were at that time unknown to man, for human beings walked in the bush like animals. . . . [5]

Later on Chukwu tells Ezenri how to plant and tend the yam but Ezenri complains that the ground is too wet; and Chukwu advises him to send for Awka people—workers in iron—to blow on the earth with their bellows and make it dry.

There is a very strong suggestion here and also in the story about the coming of death that at crucial cosmological moments Chukwu will discuss His universe with man. The moment of man's first awareness of the implications of death was such a time; but so also was the great turning point when man ceased wandering in the bush and became a settled agriculturist calling upon the craft of the blacksmith to effect this momentous transition.

And finally, at the root of it all lies that very belief we have already seen: a belief in the fundamental worth and independence of every man and of his right to speak on matters of concern to him and, flowing from it, a rejection of any form of absolutism which might endan-

---

5. Northcote W. Thomas, *Ibo-speaking Peoples of Nigeria* (London: Harrison & Sons, 1913; reprinted Negro Universities Press, New York, 1969, Vol. I), p. 50.

ger those values. It is not surprising that the Igbo held discussion and consensus as the highest ideals of the political process. This made them 'argumentative' and difficult to rule. But how could they suspend for the convenience of a ruler limitations which they impose even on their gods? For as we have seen a man may talk and bargain even with his *chi* at the moment of his creation. And what was more, Chukwu Himself in all His power and glory did not make the world by fiat. He held conversations with mankind; he talked with those archetypal men of Nri and Adama and even enlisted their good offices to make the earth firm and productive.

CHINUA ACHEBE

An Image of Africa:
Racism in Conrad's *Heart of Darkness*†

In the fall of 1974 I was walking one day from the English Department at the University of Massachusetts to a parking lot. It was a fine autumn morning such as encouraged friendliness to passing strangers. Brisk youngsters were hurrying in all directions, many of them obviously freshmen in their first flush of enthusiasm. An older man going the same way as I turned and remarked to me how very young they came these days. I agreed. Then he asked me if I was a student too. I said no, I was a teacher. What did I teach? African literature. Now that was funny, he said, because he knew a fellow who taught the same thing, or perhaps it was African *history*, in a certain community college not far from here. It always surprised him, he went on to say, because he never had thought of Africa as having that kind of stuff, you know. By this time I was walking much faster. "Oh well," I heard him say finally, behind me: "I guess I have to take your course to find out."

A few weeks later I received two very touching letters from high school children in Yonkers, New York, who—bless their teacher—had just read *Things Fall Apart*. One of them was particularly happy to learn about the customs and superstitions of an African tribe.

I propose to draw from these rather trivial encounters rather heavy conclusions which at first sight might seem somewhat out of proportion to them. But only, I hope, at first sight.

The young fellow from Yonkers, perhaps partly on account of his age, but I believe also for much deeper and more serious reasons, is

† From *Hopes and Impediments: Selected Essays* (London: Heinemann, 1990), 1–20. Copyright © 1988 by Chinua Achebe. Used by permission of Doubleday, a division of Random House, Inc., and the Emma Sweeney Agency. This is an amended version of the second Chancellor's Lecture at the University of Massachusetts, Amherst, February 1975; later published in the *Massachusetts Review*, vol. 18, no. 4, winter 1977, Amherst.

obviously unaware that the life of his own tribesmen in Yonkers, New York, is full of odd customs and superstitions and, like everybody else in his culture, imagines that he needs a trip to Africa to encounter those things.

The other person being fully my own age could not be excused on the grounds of his years. Ignorance might be a more likely reason; but here again I believe that something more wilful than a mere lack of information was at work. For did not that erudite British historian and Regius Professor at Oxford, Hugh Trevor-Roper, also pronounce that African history did not exist?

If there is something in these utterances more than youthful inexperience, more than a lack of factual knowledge, what is it? Quite simply it is the desire—one might indeed say the need—in Western psychology to set Africa up as a foil to Europe, as a place of negations at once remote and vaguely familiar, in comparison with which Europe's own state of spiritual grace will be manifest.

This need is not new; which should relieve us all of considerable responsibility and perhaps make us even willing to look at this phenomenon dispassionately. I have neither the wish nor the competence to embark on the exercise with the tools of the social and biological sciences but do so more simply in the manner of a novelist responding to one famous book of European fiction: Joseph Conrad's *Heart of Darkness,* which better than any other work that I know displays that Western desire and need which I have just referred to. Of course there are whole libraries of books devoted to the same purpose but most of them are so obvious and so crude that few people worry about them today. Conrad, on the other hand, is undoubtedly one of the great stylists of modern fiction and a good story-teller into the bargain. His contribution therefore falls automatically into a different class—permanent literature—read and taught and constantly evaluated by serious academics. *Heart of Darkness* is indeed so secure today that a leading Conrad scholar has numbered it "among the half-dozen greatest short novels in the English language."[1] I will return to this critical opinion in due course because it may seriously modify my earlier suppositions about who may or may not be guilty in some of the matters I will now raise.

Heart of Darkness projects the image of Africa as "the other world," the antithesis of Europe and therefore of civilization, a place where man's vaunted intelligence and refinement are finally mocked by triumphant bestiality. The book opens on the River Thames, tranquil, resting peacefully "at the decline of day after ages of good service done to the race that peopled its banks." But the actual story will take

---

1 Albert J. Guerard, Introduction to *Heart of Darkness* (New York: New American Library, 1950), p. 9

place on the River Congo, the very antithesis of the Thames. The River Congo is quite decidedly not a River Emeritus. It has rendered no service and enjoys no old-age pension. We are told that "going up that river was like travelling back to the earliest beginning of the world."

Is Conrad saying then that these two rivers are very different, one good, the other bad? Yes, but that is not the real point. It is not the differentness that worries Conrad but the lurking hint of kinship, of common ancestry. For the Thames too "has been one of the dark places of the earth." It conquered its darkness, of course, and is now in daylight and at peace. But if it were to visit its primordial relative, the Congo, it would run the terrible risk of hearing grotesque echoes of its own forgotten darkness, and falling victim to an avenging recrudescence of the mindless frenzy of the first beginnings.

These suggestive echoes comprise Conrad's famed evocation of the African atmosphere in *Heart of Darkness*. In the final consideration, his method amounts to no more than a steady, ponderous, fake-ritualistic repetition of two antithetical sentences, one about silence and the other about frenzy. We can inspect samples of this on pages 103 and 105 of the New American Library edition: (a) "It was the stillness of an implacable force brooding over an inscrutable intention" and (b) "The steamer toiled along slowly on the edge of a black and incomprehensible frenzy." Of course, there is a judicious change of adjective from time to time, so that instead of "inscrutable," for example, you might have "unspeakable," even plain "mysterious," etc., etc.

The eagle-eyed English critic F. R. Leavis drew attention long ago to Conrad's "adjectival insistence upon inexpressible and incomprehensible mystery." That insistence must not be dismissed lightly, as many Conrad critics have tended to do, as a mere stylistic flaw; for it raises serious questions of artistic good faith. When a writer while pretending to record scenes, incidents, and their impact is in reality engaged in inducing hypnotic stupor in his readers through a bombardment of emotive words and other forms of trickery, much more has to be at stake than stylistic felicity. Generally, normal readers are well armed to detect and resist such underhand activity. But Conrad chose his subject well—one which was guaranteed not to put him in conflict with the psychological predisposition of his readers or raise the need for him to contend with their resistance. He chose the role of purveyor of comforting myths.

The most interesting and revealing passages in *Heart of Darkness* are, however, about people. I must crave the indulgence of my reader to quote almost a whole page from about the middle of the story when representatives of Europe in a steamer going down the Congo encounter the denizens of Africa:

We were wanderers on a prehistoric earth, on an earth that wore the aspect of an unknown planet. We could have fancied ourselves the first of men taking possession of an accursed inheritance, to be subdued at the cost of profound anguish and of excessive toil. But suddenly, as we struggled round a bend, there would be a glimpse of rush walls, of peaked grass-roofs, a burst of yells, a whirl of black limbs, a mass of hands clapping, of feet stamping, of bodies swaying, of eyes rolling, under the droop of heavy and motionless foliage. The steamer toiled along slowly on the edge of the black and incomprehensible frenzy. The prehistoric man was cursing us, praying to us, welcoming us—who could tell? We were cut off from the comprehension of our surroundings; we glided past like phantoms, wondering and secretly appalled, as sane men would be before an enthusiastic outbreak in a mad-house. We could not understand because we were too far and could not remember because we were travelling in the night of first ages, of those ages that are gone, leaving hardly a sign—and no memories.

The earth seemed unearthly. We are accustomed to look upon the shackled form of a conquered monster, but there—there you could look at a thing monstrous and free. It was unearthly, and the men were—No, they were not inhuman. Well, you know, that was the worst of it—this suspicion of their not being inhuman. It would come slowly to one. They howled and leaped, and spun, and made horrid faces; but what thrilled you was just the thought of their humanity—like yours—the thought of your remote kinship with this wild and passionate uproar. Ugly. Yes, it was ugly enough; but if you were man enough you would admit to yourself that there was in you just the faintest trace of a response to the terrible frankness of that noise, a dim suspicion of there being a meaning in it which you—you so remote from the night of first ages—could comprehend.

Herein lies the meaning of *Heart of Darkness* and the fascination it holds over the Western mind: "What thrilled you was just the thought of their humanity—like yours . . . Ugly."

Having shown us Africa in the mass, Conrad then zeros in, half a page later, on a specific example, giving us one of his rare descriptions of an African who is not just limbs or rolling eyes:

And between whiles I had to look after the savage who was fire-man. He was an improved specimen; he could fire up a vertical boiler. He was there below me, and, upon my word, to look at him was as edifying as seeing a dog in a parody of breeches and a feather hat, walking on his hind legs. A few months of training had done for that really fine chap. He squinted at the steam gauge and at the water gauge with an evident effort of intrepidity—and he had filed his teeth, too, the poor devil, and the wool of his pate shaved into queer patterns, and three ornamental scars on each of his cheeks. He ought to have been clapping his hands and stamping his feet on the bank, instead of which he was hard at work, a thrall to strange witchcraft, full of improving knowledge.

As everybody knows, Conrad is a romantic on the side. He might not exactly admire savages clapping their hands and stamping their feet but they have at least the merit of being in their place, unlike this dog in a parody of breeches. For Conrad, things being in their place is of the utmost importance.

"Fine fellows—cannibals—in their place," he tells us pointedly. Tragedy begins when things leave their accustomed place, like Europe leaving its safe stronghold between the policeman and the baker to take a peep into the heart of darkness.

Before the story takes us into the Congo basin proper we are given this nice little vignette as an example of things in their place:

> Now and then a boat from the shore gave one a momentary contact with reality. It was paddled by black fellows. You could see from afar the white of their eyeballs glistening. They shouted, sang; their bodies streamed with perspiration; they had faces like grotesque masks—these chaps; but they had bone, muscle, a wild vitality, an intense energy of movement, that was as natural and true as the surf along their coast. They wanted no excuse for being there. They were a great comfort to look at.

Towards the end of the story Conrad lavishes a whole page quite unexpectedly on an African woman who has obviously been some kind of mistress to Mr. Kurtz and now presides (if I may be permitted a little liberty) like a formidable mystery over the inexorable imminence of his departure:

> She was savage and superb, wild-eyed and magnificent. . . . She stood looking at us without a stir and like the wilderness itself, with an air of brooding over an inscrutable purpose.

This Amazon is drawn in considerable detail, albeit of a predictable nature, for two reasons. First, she is in her place and so can win Conrad's special brand of approval; and second, she fulfils a structural requirement of the story; a savage counterpart to the refined, European woman who will step forth to end the story:

> She came forward, all in black with a pale head, floating toward me in the dusk. She was in mourning . . . She took both my hands in hers and murmured, "I had heard you were coming" . . . She had a mature capacity for fidelity, for belief, for suffering.

The difference in the attitude of the novelist to these two women is conveyed in too many direct and subtle ways to need elaboration. But perhaps the most significant difference is the one implied in the author's bestowal of human expression to the one and the withholding of it from the other. It is clearly not part of Conrad's purpose to confer language on the "rudimentary souls" of Africa. In place of speech they made "a violent babble of uncouth sounds." They "exchanged short grunting phrases" even among themselves. But most of the time they were too busy with their frenzy. There are two occasions in the book, however, when Conrad departs somewhat from his practice and confers speech, even English speech, on the savages. The first occurs when cannibalism gets the better of them:

> "Catch 'im," he snapped, with a bloodshot widening of his eyes and a flash of sharp white teeth—"catch 'im. Give 'im to us." "To you, eh?" I asked; "what would you do with them?" "Eat 'im!" he said curtly.

The other occasion was the famous announcement: "Mistah Kurtz—he dead."

At first sight these instances might be mistaken for unexpected acts of generosity from Conrad. In reality they constitute some of his best assaults. In the case of the cannibals the incomprehensible grunts that had thus far served them for speech suddenly proved inadequate for Conrad's purpose of letting the European glimpse the unspeakable craving in their hearts. Weighing the necessity for consistency in the portrayal of the dumb brutes against the sensational advantages of securing their conviction by clear, unambiguous evidence issuing out of their own mouths, Conrad chose the latter. As for the announcement of Mr. Kurtz's death by the "insolent black head in the doorway," what better or more appropriate *finis* could be written to the horror story of that wayward child of civilization who wilfully had given his soul to the powers of darkness and "taken a high seat amongst the devils of the land" than the proclamation of his physical death by the forces he had joined?

It might be contended, of course, that the attitude to the African in *Heart of Darkness* is not Conrad's but that of his fictional narrator, Marlow, and that far from endorsing it Conrad might indeed be holding it up to irony and criticism. Certainly, Conrad appears to go to considerable pains to set up layers of insulation between himself and the moral universe of his story. He has, for example, a narrator behind a narrator. The primary narrator is Marlow, but his account is given to us through the filter of a second, shadowy person. But if Conrad's intention is to draw a cordon sanitaire between himself and the moral and psychological *malaise* of his narrator, his care seems to me totally wasted because he neglects to hint, clearly and adequately, at an alternative frame of reference by which we may judge the actions and opinions of his characters. It would not have been beyond Conrad's power to make that provision if he had thought it necessary. Conrad seems to me to approve of Marlow, with only minor reservations—a fact reinforced by the similarities between their two careers.

Marlow comes through to us not only as a witness of truth, but one holding those advanced and humane views appropriate to the English liberal tradition which required all Englishmen of decency to be deeply shocked by atrocities in Bulgaria or the Congo of King Leopold of the Belgians or wherever.

Thus, Marlow is able to toss out such bleeding-heart sentiments as these:

> They were all dying slowly—it was very clear. They were not enemies, they were not criminals, they were nothing earthly now—nothing but black shadows of disease and starvation, lying confusedly in the greenish gloom. Brought from all the recesses of the coast in all the legality of time contracts, lost in uncongenial surroundings, fed on unfamiliar food, they sickened, became inefficient, and were then allowed to crawl away and rest.

The kind of liberalism espoused here by Marlow/Conrad touched all the best minds of the age in England, Europe and America. It took different forms in the minds of different people but almost always managed to sidestep the ultimate question of equality between white people and black people. That extraordinary missionary Albert Schweitzer, who sacrificed brilliant careers in music and theology in Europe for a life of service to Africans in much the same area as Conrad writes about, epitomizes the ambivalence. In a comment which has often been quoted Schweitzer says: "The African is indeed my brother but my junior brother." And so he proceeded to build a hospital appropriate to the needs of junior brothers with standards of hygiene reminiscent of medical practice in the days before the germ theory of disease came into being. Naturally he became a sensation in Europe and America. Pilgrims flocked, and I believe still flock even after he has passed on, to witness the prodigious miracle in Lambaréné, on the edge of the primeval forest.

Conrad's liberalism would not take him quite as far as Schweitzer's, though. He would not use the word "brother" however qualified; the farthest he would go was "kinship." When Marlow's African helmsman falls down with a spear in his heart he gives his white master one final disquieting look:

And the intimate profundity of that look he gave me when he
received his hurt remains to this day in my memory—like a claim
of distant kinship affirmed in a supreme moment.

It is important to note that Conrad, careful as ever with his words,
is concerned not so much about "distant kinship" as about someone
laying a claim on it. The black man lays a claim on the white man
which is well-nigh intolerable. It is the laying of this claim which
frightens and at the same time fascinates Conrad, "the thought of
their humanity—like yours . . . Ugly."

The point of my observations should be quite clear by now, namely
that Joseph Conrad was a thoroughgoing racist. That this simple
truth is glossed over in criticisms of his work is due to the fact that
white racism against Africa is such a normal way of thinking that its
manifestations go completely unremarked. Students of *Heart of
Darkness* will often tell you that Conrad is concerned not so much
with Africa as with the deterioration of one European mind caused
by solitude and sickness. They will point out to you that Conrad is, if
anything, less charitable to the Europeans in the story than he is to
the natives, that the point of the story is to ridicule Europe's civilizing mission in Africa. A Conrad student informed me in Scotland
that Africa is merely a setting for the disintegration of the mind of
Mr. Kurtz.

Which is partly the point. Africa as setting and backdrop which
eliminates the African as human factor. Africa as a metaphysical
battlefield devoid of all recognizable humanity, into which the wandering European enters at his peril. Can nobody see the preposterous and perverse arrogance in thus reducing Africa to the role
of props for the break-up of one petty European mind? But that is
not even the point. The real question is the dehumanization of
Africa and Africans which this age-long attitude has fostered and
continues to foster in the world. And the question is whether a
novel which celebrates this dehumanization, which depersonalizes
a portion of the human race, can be called a great work of art. My
answer is: No, it cannot. I do not doubt Conrad's great talents.
Even *Heart of Darkness* has its memorably good passages and
moments:

> The reaches opened before us and closed behind, as if the for-
> est had stepped leisurely across the water to bar the way for our
> return.

Its exploration of the minds of the European characters is often
penetrating and full of insight. But all that has been more than fully
discussed in the last fifty years. His obvious racism has, however, not
been addressed. And it is high time it was!

Conrad was born in 1857, the very year in which the first Anglican missionaries were arriving among my own people in Nigeria. It was certainly not his fault that he lived his life at a time when the reputation of the black man was at a particularly low level. But even after due allowances have been made for all the influences of contemporary prejudice on his sensibility, there remains still in Conrad's attitude a residue of antipathy to black people which his peculiar psychology alone can explain. His own account of his first encounter with a black man is very revealing:

> A certain enormous buck nigger encountered in Haiti fixed my conception of blind, furious, unreasoning rage, as manifested in the human animal to the end of my days. Of the nigger I used to dream for years afterwards.[2]

Certainly Conrad had a problem with niggers. His inordinate love of that word itself should be of interest to psychoanalysts. Sometimes his fixation on blackness is equally interesting, as when he gives us this brief description: "A black figure stood up, strode on long black legs, waving long black arms"—as though we might expect a black figure striding along on black legs to wave white arms! But so unrelenting is Conrad's obsession.

As a matter of interest, Conrad gives us in *A Personal Record* what amounts to a companion piece to the buck nigger of Haiti. At the age of sixteen Conrad encountered his first Englishman in Europe. He calls him "my unforgettable Englishman" and describes him in the following manner:

> [his] calves exposed to the public gaze . . . dazzled the beholder by the splendour of their marble-like condition and their rich tone of young ivory . . . The light of a headlong, exalted satisfaction with the world of men . . . illumined his face . . . and triumphant eyes. In passing he cast a glance of kindly curiosity and a friendly gleam of big, sound, shiny teeth . . . his white calves twinkled sturdily.[3]

Irrational love and irrational hate jostling together in the heart of that talented, tormented man. But whereas irrational love may at worst engender foolish acts of indiscretion, irrational hate can endanger the life of the community. Naturally, Conrad is a dream for psychoanalytic critics. Perhaps the most detailed study of him in this direction is by Bernard C. Meyer, M.D. In his lengthy book, Dr. Meyer follows every conceivable lead (and sometime inconceivable

2. Jonah Raskin, *The Mythology of Imperialism* (New York: Random House, 1971), p. 143.
3. Bernard C. Meyer, M.D., *Joseph Conrad: A Psychoanalytic Biography* (Princeton: Princeton UP, 1967), p. 30.

ones) to explain Conrad. As an example, he gives us long disquisitions on the significance of hair and hair-cutting in Conrad. And yet not even one word is spared for his attitude to black people. Not even the discussion of Conrad's antisemitism was enough to spark off in Dr. Meyer's mind those other dark and explosive thoughts. Which only leads one to surmise that Western psychoanalysts must regard the kind of racism displayed by Conrad as absolutely normal despite the profoundly important work done by Frantz Fanon in the psychiatric hospitals of French Algeria.

Whatever Conrad's problems were, you might say he is now safely dead. Quite true. Unfortunately, his heart of darkness plagues us still. Which is why an offensive and deplorable book can be described by a serious scholar as "among the half-dozen greatest short novels in the English language." And why it is today perhaps the most commonly prescribed novel in twentieth-century literature courses in English departments of American universities.

There are two probable grounds on which what I have said so far may be contested. The first is that it is no concern of fiction to please people about whom it is written. I will go along with that. But I am not talking about pleasing people. I am talking about a book which parades in the most vulgar fashion prejudices and insults from which a section of mankind has suffered untold agonies and atrocities in the past and continues to do so in many ways and many places today. I am talking about a story in which the very humanity of black people is called in question.

Secondly, I may be challenged on the grounds of actuality. Conrad, after all, did sail down the Congo in 1890 when my own father was still a babe in arms. How could I stand up more than fifty years after his death and purport to contradict him? My answer is that as a sensible man I will not accept just any traveller's tales solely on the grounds that I have not made the journey myself. I will not trust the evidence even of a man's very eyes when I suspect them to be as jaundiced as Conrad's. And we also happen to know that Conrad was, in the words of his biographer, Bernard C. Meyer, "notoriously inaccurate in the rendering of his own history."[4]

But more important by far is the abundant testimony about Conrad's savages which we could gather if we were so inclined from other sources and which might lead us to think that these people must have had other occupations besides merging into the evil forest or materializing out of it simply to plague Marlow and his dispirited band. For as it happened, soon after Conrad had written his book an event of far greater consequence was taking place in the art

4. Meyer, p. 30.

world of Europe. This is how Frank Willett, a British art historian, describes it:

> Gauguin had gone to Tahiti, the most extravagant individual act of turning to a non-European culture in the decades immediately before and after 1900, when European artists were avid for new artistic experiences, but it was only about 1904–5 that African art began to make its distinctive impact. One piece is still identifiable; it is a mask that had been given to Maurice Vlaminck in 1905. He records that Derain was "speechless" and "stunned" when he saw it, bought it from Vlaminck and in turn showed it to Picasso and Matisse, who were also greatly affected by it. Ambroise Vollard then borrowed it and had it cast in bronze . . . The revolution of twentieth century art was under way.[5]

The mask in question was made by other savages living just north of Conrad's River Congo. They have a name too: the Fang people, and are without a doubt among the world's greatest masters of the sculptured form. The event Frank Willett is referring to marked the beginning of cubism and the infusion of new life into European art that had run completely out of strength.

The point of all this is to suggest that Conrad's picture of the peoples of the Congo seems grossly inadequate even at the height of their subjection to the ravages of King Leopold's International Association for the Civilization of Central Africa.

Travellers with closed minds can tell us little except about themselves. But even those not blinkered, like Conrad, with xenophobia, can be astonishingly blind. Let me digress a little here. One of the greatest and most intrepid travellers of all time, Marco Polo, journeyed to the Far East from the Mediterranean in the thirteenth century and spent twenty years in the court of Kublai Khan in China. On his return to Venice he set down in his book entitled *Description of the World* his impressions of the peoples and places and customs he had seen. But there were at least two extraordinary omissions in his account. He said nothing about the art of printing, unknown as yet in Europe but in full flower in China. He either did not notice it at all or, if he did, failed to see what use Europe could possibly have for it. Whatever the reason, Europe had to wait another hundred years for Gutenberg. But even more spectacular was Marco Polo's omission of any reference to the Great Wall of China, nearly four thousand miles long and already more than one thousand years old at the time of his visit. Again, he may not have seen it; but the Great Wall of China is the only structure built by

5. Frank Willet, *African Art* (New York: Praeger, 1971), pp. 35–36.

man which is visible from the moon![6] Indeed, travellers can be blind.

As I said earlier Conrad did not originate the image of Africa which we find in his book. It was and is the dominant image of Africa in the Western imagination and Conrad merely brought the peculiar gifts of his own mind to bear on it. For reasons which can certainly use close psychological inquiry, the West seems to suffer deep anxieties about the precariousness of its civilization and to have a need for constant reassurance by comparison with Africa. If Europe, advancing in civilization, could cast a backward glance periodically at Africa trapped in primordial barbarity it could say with faith and feeling: There go I but for the grace of God. Africa is to Europe as the picture is to Dorian Gray—a carrier on to whom the master unloads his physical and moral deformities so that he may go forward, erect and immaculate. Consequently, Africa is something to be avoided just as the picture has to be hidden away to safeguard the man's jeopardous integrity. Keep away from Africa, or else! Mr. Kurtz of *Heart of Darkness* should have heeded that warning and the prowling horror in his heart would have kept its place, chained to its lair. But he foolishly exposed himself to the wild irresistible allure of the jungle and lo! the darkness found him out.

In my original conception of this essay I had thought to conclude it nicely on an appropriately positive note in which I would suggest from my privileged position in African and Western cultures some advantages the West might derive from Africa once it rid its mind of old prejudices and began to look at Africa not through a haze of distortions and cheap mystifications but quite simply as a continent of people—not angels, but not rudimentary souls either—just people, often highly gifted people and often strikingly successful in their enterprise with life and society. But as I thought more about the stereotype image, about its grip and pervasiveness, about the wilful tenacity with which the West holds it to its heart; when I thought of the West's television and cinema and newspapers, about books read in its schools and out of school, of churches preaching to empty pews about the need to send help to the heathen in Africa, I realized that no easy optimism was possible. And there was in any case something totally wrong in offering bribes to the West in return for its good opinion of Africa. Ultimately the abandonment of unwholesome thoughts must be its own and only reward. Although I have used the word "wilful" a few times here to characterize the West's view of Africa, it may

6. For the omission of the Great Wall of China, I am indebted to *The Journey of Marco Polo* as re-created by the artist Michael Foreman, published by *Pegasus Magazine*, 1974.

well be that what is happening at this stage is more akin to reflex action than calculated malice. Which does not make the situation more but less hopeful.

The *Christian Science Monitor*, a paper more enlightened than most, once carried an interesting article written by its Education Editor on the serious psychological and learning problems faced by little children who speak one language at home and then go to school where something else is spoken. It was a wide-ranging article taking in Spanish-speaking children in America, the children of migrant Italian workers in Germany, the quadrilingual phenomenon in Malaysia and so on. And all this while the article speaks unequivocally about language. But then out of the blue sky comes this:

> In London there is an enormous immigration of children who speak Indian or Nigerian dialects, or some other native language.

I believe that the introduction of "dialects," which is technically erroneous in the context, is almost a reflex action caused by an instinctive desire of the writer to downgrade the discussion to the level of Africa and India. And this is quite comparable to Conrad's withholding of language from his rudimentary souls. Language is too grand for these chaps; let's give them dialects!

In all this business a lot of violence is inevitably done not only to the image of despised peoples but even to words, the very tools of possible redress. Look at the phrase "native language" in the *Christian Science Monitor* excerpt. Surely the only *native* language possible in London is Cockney English. But our writer means something else—something appropriate to the sounds Indians and Africans make!

Although the work of redressing which needs to be done may appear too daunting, I believe it is not one day too soon to begin. Conrad saw and condemned the evil of imperial exploitation but was strangely unaware of the racism on which it sharpened its iron tooth. But the victims of racist slander who for centuries have had to live with the inhumanity it makes them heir to have always known better than any casual visitor, even when he comes loaded with the gifts of a Conrad.

GERALD GRAFF

Teaching the Politics of *Heart of Darkness*†

Since I started teaching in the mid-1960s, a work I have assigned frequently is Joseph Conrad's classic *Heart of Darkness*, published in 1899. When I first assigned the novella in 1966 or 1967, I taught it in much the way it had been taught to me in college in the late 1950s, as a profound meditation on a universal moral theme. I presented Conrad's story of the destruction of the idealistic trader Mr. Kurtz as a universal parable of the precarious status of civilized reason in a world overly confident of its having outgrown the primitive and the irrational.

My reading of *Heart of Darkness* as a universal parable of reason and unreason pointed up something in the novel that I still think is important. But this reading also depended on my not seeing certain things or not treating them as worth thinking about. Of little interest to me were the facts that Conrad sets his novella in the Congo in the high period of European colonialism and that he chooses subjugated black Africans to represent the primitive, irrational forces that are Mr. Kurtz's undoing. Conrad, after all, could have chosen any number of ways to symbolize the forces of primitive unreason. That he happened to choose black Africa seemed incidental to his main intention, which was to make a statement about the human condition that would transcend mere questions of nationality and race.

Like Mark Helprin, * * * I had been trained to believe that literature is "an impartial phenomenon that addresses essential questions beyond and apart from politics," and I assumed that these transcendent concerns were what the teaching of literature is all about. The subjugation of black Africans was the sort of thing that might interest historians, sociologists, and political scientists, but if the job was to treat literature *as* literature, it was at best of ancillary interest. After all, if God had wanted us to raise political questions in teaching literature, why had he put the departments of English and sociology in separate buildings?

It never occurred to me to ask how a black person might read the story, and the fact that only a small number of black students appeared in my classes helped assure that the question did not come up. Had it come up, however, I would have found it beside the point.

---

† From *Beyond the Culture Wars: How Teaching the Conflicts Can Revitalize American Education*. Copyright © 1992 by Gerald Graff. Used by permission of W. W. Norton & Company, Inc.

What difference did it make who you were and what your history was when you read a literary work? The point of studying literature was to rise above those traces of your upbringing and history. It was Conrad and his vision that mattered, and reflecting on the position from which you read Conrad could only distract attention from his vision to your own narcissistic special interests.

Today I teach *Heart of Darkness* very differently. One critical work that caused me to change my approach was an essay by the Nigerian novelist Chinua Achebe, entitled "An Image of Africa: Racism in Conrad's *Heart of Darkness*."[1] Achebe argues that Conrad's presentation of black Africa is thoroughly racist. And he is able to accumulate a painfully large number of quotations from both the novel and Conrad's letters and diaries that do reveal how cruelly stereotyped Conrad's thinking about the black African is. Here, for example, is a part of one of the passages quoted by Achebe in which Conrad's narrator, Charlie Marlow, reflects on the position of himself and his shipmates:

> We were wanderers on a prehistoric earth, on an earth that wore the aspect of an unknown planet. We could have fancied ourselves the first of men taking possession of an accursed inheritance, to be subdued at the cost of profound anguish and of excessive toil. But suddenly as we struggled round a bend there would be a glimpse of rush walls, of peaked grass-roofs, a burst of yells, a whirl of black limbs, a mass of hands clapping, of feet stamping, of bodies swaying, of eyes rolling under the droop of heavy and motionless foliage. The steamer toiled along slowly on the edge of a black and incomprehensible frenzy. The prehistoric man was cursing us, praying to us, welcoming us—who could tell? . . . .[2]

Achebe observes that in this passage and often elsewhere in the novel black Africans appear as an undifferentiated mass of eye-rolling, tomtom-beating savages, "a black and incomprehensible frenzy" representing a primitive and "prehistoric" stage of humanity. One is a bit startled to realize that passages of apparent eloquence that have sent chills down the spine of Western readers sound worse than comic when read from Achebe's point of view (though Achebe notes that F. R. Leavis also found the prose of this novel comically bathetic).[3]

---

1. Chinua Achebe, "An Image of Africa: Racism in Conrad's *Heart of Darkness*," in Joseph Conrad, *Heart of Darkness*, 3d ed., ed. Robert Kimbrough (New York: Norton, 1988). [Also, see above, pp. 169–81.]
2. Joseph Conrad, *Heart of Darkness*, p. 37; quoted by Achebe, Ibid., p. 253.
3. Ibid., p. 253; Leavis's discussion appears in *The Great Tradition* (London: George W. Stewart, 1948; reprinted 1954), pp. 211–21.

Achebe acknowledges that Conrad expresses compassion for the exploited Africans and that he "condemn[s] the evil of imperial exploitation."[4] Yet Achebe argues that ultimately Conrad reduces Africa to a mere "foil for Europe," a mere "setting and backdrop which eliminates the African as human factor," and directs the reader's attention instead to the tragedy of the white imperialist Kurtz. More important and disturbing for Achebe than Conrad's stereotyped portrayal of black Africans is his unspoken assumption about whose point of view counts. As Achebe puts it, "Can nobody see the preposterous and perverse arrogance in thus reducing Africa to the role of props for the break-up of one petty European mind?"[5]

In short, according to Achebe, what Conrad does to black Africa at the level of representation is something like what European imperialism was doing to it. Even in the process of satirizing European imperialism, Conrad uses Africa as a "backdrop" for the implied superiority of European civilization. The real question, Achebe says, "is the dehumanization of Africa and Africans which this age-long attitude has fostered and continues to foster in the world. And the question is whether a novel which celebrates this dehumanization, which depersonalizes a portion of the human race, can be called a great work of art. My answer is: No, it cannot."[6]

I suspect it would be hard for anyone of whatever political persuasion to read Achebe's essay and still read and teach *Heart of Darkness* in quite the same way he or she did before. I at least found I could not. It was not that Achebe's essay convinced me that *Heart of Darkness* is completely racist; in fact, it did not. What Achebe did convince me was that Conrad's assumptions about race are not, as I had imagined, simply an extraneous or nonliterary element of the novel but something that the novel's literary and aesthetic effect depends upon. It had obviously been far easier for me to suspend disbelief in Conrad's assumptions about race and to turn the story into a purely aesthetic experience than it was for Achebe, for whom the way a novel represents black Africans could be truly a matter of life and death.

Then, too, black and third world students were beginning to show up more frequently in my university and my classes—still in pitiful proportions, to be sure, but enough to make it harder for me to take for granted that Conrad's outlook and my own were the natural and normal one. This is not to say that how we read is determined by our color (or gender or ethnic origin). But it would be foolish to deny that the social composition of the students sitting in front of you

4. Ibid., p. 256.
5. Ibid., p. 257.
6. Ibid.

has an influence on the way you teach. If it did not, we all would still be teaching Greek and Latin instead of English and American literature.

Even if Achebe's interpretation of Conrad is unfair, as I think it is, it forced me to rethink my assumptions about art and politics. For according to Achebe, Conrad's novel is not simply a disinterested work of art, but a text that played and may still be playing an active role in constructing the Western image of black Africa. "Conrad did not originate the image of Africa which we find in his book," Achebe writes. "It was and is the dominant image of Africa in the Western imagination and Conrad merely brought the peculiar gifts of his own mind to bear on it. For reasons which can certainly use close psychological inquiry the West seems to suffer deep anxieties about the precariousness of its civilization and to have a need for constant reassurance by comparison with Africa."[7] Achebe's point is one that recent literary and cultural "theory" has been making, though I think with more complications and qualifications: that literary representations are not simply neutral aesthetic descriptions but interventions that act upon the world they describe. This, in fact, is the point underlying many recent critiques of the idea of *objectivity*, critiques that are poorly understood by their critics; the point is not that there is no truth but that descriptions influence the situations they describe, thereby complicating the problem of truth.

In short, I was forced to rethink not just my interpretation of *Heart of Darkness* but my theoretical assumptions about literature. First, I was forced to recognize that I *had* theoretical assumptions. I had previously thought I was simply teaching the truth about *Heart of Darkness*, "the text itself." I now had to recognize that I had been teaching an interpretation of the text, one that was shaped by a certain *theory* that told me what was and was not worth noticing and emphasizing in my classroom. I had been unable to see my theory *as* a theory because I was living so comfortably inside it.

When I teach *Heart of Darkness* now, as I have in several undergraduate courses for the last few years, I assign Achebe's essay. I do not simply teach Achebe's interpretation as the correct one, however, but ask my students to weigh it against other interpretations. Nor do I discard my earlier reading of the novel as a contemplation of universal truths about the human soul. I assign another critical essay that argues for that interpretation. I also assign several essays (all these materials are included in the Norton Critical Edition of Conrad's novel) by critics who take issue with Achebe. These critics—and

7. Ibid., p. 261.

I agree with them—grant Achebe's thesis up to a point about Conrad's racism and colonialism but argue that Achebe ignores or minimizes the powerful critique of racism and colonialism that coexists in the novel with these more sinister attitudes.

After Conrad my class reads Achebe's novel *Things Fall Apart*, which presents a counterview of Africa to Conrad's, as if Achebe were trying to wrest the power to represent Africa away from the great European. I supplement these materials with short essays representing opposing sides in the past and present debate over the place, or nonplace, of politics in the arts, illustrating the fact that the debate has a long history dating back to Plato's founding of the history of criticism in an act of political correctness, his expulsion of the poets from his republic for corrupting the morals of the state. Also included in the reading list are several recent neoconservative polemics, some of which say unflattering things about me, impressing my students that their instructor has been abused by so many prominent people. I also invite conservative colleagues into my class to debate the issues with me and my students. To make sure my students enter the debate rather than watch passively from the sidelines, I assign a paper on it or ask them to prepare class presentations in which they give their views.

In short, I now teach *Heart of Darkness* as part of a critical debate about how to read it, which in turn is part of a larger theoretical debate about how politics and power affect the way we read literature. Without claiming to be neutral or disguising my own leanings, I try to help students adjudicate between competing arguments and make informed choices on the key points of contention: Is literature a realm of universal experience that transcends politics, or is it inevitably political, and in what sense of "political," a word too often brandished today without being defined?

I also raise the question of the extent to which a work like *Heart of Darkness* is itself a conflict of theories. Contrary to their opponents, the point of current politically oriented theorists is not that literary works are simple expressions of racism or colonialism but that literature is an arena of conflicting and contradictory social values, a struggle of utopian and dystopian visions.[8] The point needs underscoring: The dominant trend in contemporary theory is *not* to reduce literary works to transparent expressions of ideology, whether for good or bad. This is the impression that has been presented by critics whose dislike of recent theory exceeds their willingness to read it.

---

8. See, for example, the treatments of Conrad and *Heart of Darkness* in two influential works of Marxist criticism, Terry Eagleton's *Criticism and Ideology: A Study in Marxist Literary Theory* (London: New Left Books, 1977), pp. 130–40; and Fredric Jameson's *The Political Unconscious: Narrative as a Socially Symbolic Act* (Ithaca, N.Y.: Cornell University Press, 1983), pp. 206–80.

The most powerful and influential of recent theories argue that literature is a scene of contradictions that cannot be subsumed under any "totalizing" ideology.

The only prominent critic of theory I know who gets this right is Frederick Crews of the University of California at Berkeley. As Crews concisely and accurately sums it up, the primary message of recent theory is "that literature is a site of struggle whose primary conflicts, both intrapsychic and social, deserve to be brought to light rather than homogenized into notions of fixed authorial 'values.'"[9] Crews has provided what seems to me a model of what a scrupulous critique of current theory would look like: He shows how at its worst this kind of theory simply replaces the clichés and predictable readings of earlier critical schools with a new set of clichés and predictable readings, but how at its best it has revitalized whole fields such as Faulkner studies.

Far from debasing the academic standards of my courses, teaching *Heart of Darkness* as I now teach it seems to me to have made my courses considerably *more* challenging than they were previously. For my students now have to be more reflective about their assumptions than they had to be before, and they are now asked to take part in a set of complex debates that I previously did not expect them to. Nor, I think, do the critical and theoretical debates I teach distract students from the close reading of literary works in themselves. When it seemed to me at one point that my students were agreeing too easily with Achebe, I corrected by restating the aesthetic reading of *Heart of Darkness* and the need to return constantly to the verbal particulars of the text.

In the end I think Achebe's critique pushes my students to a closer reading of the verbal and stylistic particularity of *Heart of Darkness* than they would achieve through an exclusively aesthetic approach. Then, too, I think it also enables them to understand more clearly just what an "aesthetic approach" is, since they now have something to compare it with. Before, students would look blank when I used words like "aesthetic" (or "traditional," "humanistic," etc.), as if to say, "'Aesthetic' as opposed to *what*?" Introducing a challenge to traditional values helps students understand what is at stake in embracing or rejecting them.

Was I really being less "political" when I taught *Heart of Darkness* without mentioning the issue of race than I am now when I put that issue in the foreground? In today's climate of hysterical accusation and denunciation, merely to raise the question for debate is for some of us enough to convict a teacher of the crime

---

9. Frederick Crews, "The Strange Fate of William Faulkner," *New York Review of Books* XXXVIII, no. 5 (March 7, 1989): 49.

of political correctness. Yet it seems to me reasonable to argue
that something political is at stake in whose representation of black
Africa, Conrad's or Achebe's, gets into the debate, just as something political is at stake in whether other representations of the
culture war get into the national media besides the ones favored by
those who see nothing on the scene but the takeover of "urban
guerillas."

The way of teaching I have described will obviously not recommend itself to all teachers. Not all teachers will be comfortable dealing with political conflicts, nor is there any reason why they should
have to. I choose to deal with these political conflicts not because I
take them to be the only ones worth teaching but because they do
have a good deal of urgency in our culture today and because I think
frank discussion of these conflicts is more likely to improve our handling of them than pretending they do not exist.

In this, I like to think I am moving toward a solution to the current
controversies that other teachers are also finding today, which is to
incorporate the controversies themselves into my reading list and
course framework. Instead of choosing between the Western Conrad
and the non-Western Achebe, I teach the conflict between their novels and between competing views of literature.

One dividend of this approach I did not expect. Teaching *Things
Fall Apart*, I found the novel not only first-rate literature and a source
of insight into a culture unfamiliar to me but a means of illuminating *Heart of Darkness* that I had not previously had. When I had
taught Conrad's novel as a universal statement, my students seemed
to find the concept of universality difficult and elusive—or perhaps
they simply could not see the point of insisting on it. Again, "Universality as opposed to what?" seemed to be their unspoken thought.
Once I introduced Achebe, however, with his sharp challenge to the
idea that Conrad's world view is the universal one, the concept of
universality came into much clearer focus for my students. The
"Western" aspect of Conrad suddenly became a less mystifying quality now that students had something to contrast it with. And this led
in turn to the question of whether "Western" and "non-Western" are
really mutually exclusive.

*   *   *

OLUSEGUN ADEKOYA

Criticising the Critic: Achebe on Conrad†

To the criticism by a distinguished and lettered lady—name not given—that the "literature which preys on strange people and prowls in far-off countries", "decivilized the tales, the strange people and the far-off countries", Conrad (1895: vii–viii) gave the following reply:

> The picture of life, there as here, is drawn with the same elaboration of detail, coloured with the same tints. Only in the cruel serenity of the sky, under the merciless brilliance of the sun, the dazzled eye misses the delicate detail, sees only the strong outlines . . . Nevertheless it is the same picture . . . And there is a bond between us and that humanity so far away . . . Their hearts—like ours—must endure the load of the gifts from Heaven: the curse of facts and the blessing of illusions, the bitterness of our wisdom and the deceptive consolation of our folly.

Surely, the voice does not sound as that of "a thoroughgoing racist" (Achebe, 1988:8). One trembles at the thought of what the reply of a V. S. Naipaul would have been to the lady's question. We join issue with Chinua Achebe in this essay on some of the serious but largely erroneous allegations made against Joseph Conrad in "An Image of Africa: Racism in Conrad's *Heart of Darkness*". Unlike in its first version (1978:1–15), Achebe grudgingly acknowledges Conrad's negative criticism of Imperialism perhaps in reaction to Wilson Harris' remark (1981:88–89) that "At no point in his essay does Achebe turn upon the crucial parody of the proprieties of established order that mask corruption in all societies". However, Achebe is yet to accept the full implications of the parody. Our argument is that Conrad's consciousness in *Heart of Darkness* (1973) is rooted in primal nature and quickened by the oneness of humanity. His central concern is the moral and spiritual blindness that leads man to engage nature in the strife for conquest. Confronted by the immense stillness of primeval forest in a moonlight night in Central Africa, Marlow ponders: "Could we handle that dumb thing, or would it handle us?" (Conrad, 1973:38). Conrad affirms in the novel, through a subtle exploration of the Christian myth of Creation, that in the relentless struggle between man and nature, it is man—the quester, the adventurer—who is bound to lose in the end. It detracts enormously from Conrad's creative imagination to reduce his thematic pre-occupation in *Heart of Darkness* to the ranking of cultures.

† From *Eagle on Iroko: Selected Papers from the Chinua Achebe International Symposium 1990.* Ed. Edith Ihekweazu (Ibadan: Heinemann, 1996), 526–41.

Achebe interprets the novel as "a story in which the very humanity of black people is called in question" (1988:10). I, on the contrary,
perceive it as an examination of the totality of humanity. It holds up
a mirror, not of distortion, but of reflection and refraction, to nature,
and erodes the surface of things in order to expose the bitter truth
hidden underneath. Civilized or primitive, man is stood naked before
the mirror. "The expectations the reader brings to the text", Elizabeth
Wright theorizes about reader-text relation, "are challenged by the
encounter" (1982:117).

Conrad challenges our settled ideas of civilization, as represented
by industrialized Europe, and of primitivism, as represented by pre-
colonial Africa. He removes the illusion of reality from both "primitive culture" and "modern culture" in order to reveal the bitter truth
that, although Africans and Europeans can technologically be centuries apart in *Heart of Darkness*, yet they share emotionally, physically and spiritually a common ancestry. Marlow affirms the oneness
of humanity in the passage below:

> The earth seemed unearthly. We are accustomed to look upon
> the shackled form of a conquered monster, but there—there
> you could look at a thing monstrous and free . . . They howled
> and leaped, and spun, and made horrid faces; but what thrilled
> you was just the thought of their humanity—like yours—the
> thought of your remote kinship with this wild and passionate
> uproar. Ugly. Yes, it was ugly enough; but if you were man
> enough you would admit to yourself that there was in you just
> the faintest trace of a response to the terrible frankness of that
> noise, a dim suspicion of there being a meaning in it which
> you—you so remote from the night of first ages—could
> comprehend. And why not? The mind of man is capable of
> anything—because everything is in it, all the past as well as all
> the future. What was there after all? Joy, fear, sorrow, devotion,
> valour, rage—who can tell?—but truth—truth stripped of its
> cloak of time. (51–52)

The truth takes the form of man's acquisitive drive, especially for
power over other people and for property, in *Heart of Darkness*. Even
though analytic consciousness can categorize a set of emotions in
one culture as civilized and refined and condemn same in another as
crude, barbaric and inferior, human emotions are basically the same
throughout the ages. The universality of these emotions—under the
general rubric of human nature—makes a mockery of any attempt to
rank the cultures of the world. The builders of technological culture
have succeeded to a large extent in mastering matter, but have failed
woefully in dispelling the darkness in the human heart. It is as if

material nature employed passion to take vengeance on humanity for all its acts of hubris.

In the passage cited above the "shackled form of a conquered monster" refers to industrialized Europe that has lost its simplicity, innocence and animal freedom, while the "thing monstrous and free" is primitive, materially under-nourished Africa in which it was still possible to live intuitively and establish a kinship with nature. The bestial vitality and barbaric frenzy, which unsettles Achebe and incurs his wrath, is perceived by Conrad as positive but unsavory qualities of primitive society, the absence of which makes all mechanized societies appear dead and sterile. The irony is that industrial civilization hampers the free expression of feelings, depersonalizes man, and tends to reduce man to a mindless robot, while primitive, unconscious subjection to the vagaries of nature, arising from powerlessness, stifles intellectual creativity, animalizes man and limits human efficiency. The paradox of human nature is reflected in every aspect of all the cultures of the world. Neither a mechanized society nor a primitive society is whole, but the ascendancy of materialism over spiritualism makes the former attractive and irresistible.

Nevertheless, it would be deceptive and ludicrous to place Africa and Europe on the same level of socio-economic development. That Africa is technologically backward is a fact. Conrad, however, does not celebrate this fact. For him, there is nothing to choose between the blindman that is the mechanical man and the mute that is the primitive man. Neither does he create a new vision of human possibility: of being. Hence Wilson Harris concluded that Conrad reached the furthest limit of imagination, but did not cross it, because he did not go beyond despair. The problem is that a world ontology without strife is inconceivable. What humanity really needs but cannot come by is perfect love and genuine co-operation.

Moreover, consciousness, the tool of culture and scientific analysis, breeds division and, therefore, is evil. In the Christian myth of Creation, it is the acquisition of consciousness, consequent upon the eating of the forbidden fruit, the fruit of knowledge, that separates man from the paradisiac state of the Beginning. It is, as hinted at by Conrad in his reply to the lettered lady, one of the dazzling but deceptive gifts that fall on the human race and weigh it down.

The charge that the *Heart of Darkness* serves the need "in Western psychology to set Africa up as a foil to Europe, as a place of negations at once remote and vaguely familiar, in comparison with which Europe's own state of spiritual grace will be manifest" (Achebe, 1988:2) is challenged by the enormous evidence supplied in the text, for example, by the painting by Kurtz of "a woman, draped and blindfolded, carrying a lighted torch" (Conrad, 1973:36). A mordant self-criticism by an evil genius, the painting questions the possibility of a blindman leading another blindman, without the two of them falling into a perilous pit. Rather than make manifest "Europe's own state of spiritual grace", Conrad doubts or denies outright its existence in *Heart of Darkness*.

Bestiality is manifested in the novel by both Africans and Europeans. If anything, the European bestiality is more savage. Whereas material impoverishment imposes a low form of existence on Africans, moral and spiritual impoverishment reduces the European pilgrims to beasts and savages. The bestiality, on the part of Europeans, can be traced to the factor of human depravity: the animal compulsion that drives the powerful to prey upon the weak. The most politically powerful and the most economically developed states in the world today are constructed on the philosophy of social Darwinism: the theory of survival of the fittest. It is this despicable theory or its practical realization which reduces human beings to beasts and savages—and not the feet stamping and the eyes rolling—that is parodied in *Heart of Darkness*. To overlook this important dimension of Conrad's vision is to miss the message of the novel. Dennis Lee avers in *Savage Fields* (1977:44) that "*Strife is amoral*".

The amorality of strife forms the basis of Conrad's condemnation of Imperialism. He sees the whole colonial enterprise as "robbery with violence, aggravated murder on a great scale, and men going at it blind—as is very proper for those who tackle a darkness. The conquest of the earth, which mostly means the taking it away from those who have a different complexion or slightly flatter noses than ourselves, is not a pretty thing when you look into it too much. What redeems it is the idea only" (1973:10). Conrad is not only indignant at the deceit in the gratuitous and self-serving idea of civilizing the savages which is used to justify the rape and subjugation of Africa, he does not believe in the colonial administration. He, therefore, cannot be accused of exhibiting a paternalizing attitude towards Africans.

Even then, the "ultimate question of equality between white people and black people" (1988:7), with which Achebe is primarily concerned can neither be raised nor answered in a coherent way outside of Conrad's cogent critique of Imperialism. Otherwise the subject of racism would become a mere abstraction, as it in fact tends to be in Achebe's essay. Let us face it, not until Africa can feed, clothe, house and educate herself will she be accorded equal respect in a world that is becoming more and more materialistic. The imperialist exploiters employ psychological terrorism as a weapon of conquest. There are political and economic motives behind the myth of white superiority.

Situating Conrad's moral vision in its proper context of that particular greed which breaks out in form of imperial exploitation reduces to the barest minimum, if it does not remove entirely, what racism there is in the novel and its author. It is this profound moral vision, apart from the superb artistry, that makes *Heart of Darkness* a great novel. Hence, in spite of Achebe's rebuttal, the novel continues to appeal to all hearts who yearn for the moral improvement and spiritual health of man.

In "The Method of Nature", an oration delivered before the Society of Alephi, in 1841, Emerson declared: "Let there be worse cotton and better men" (1963:40). In Conrad's understanding of the multidimensionality of culture and civilization, equal emphasis is placed in *Heart of Darkness* on the moral, spiritual and material aspects. One may even argue that the moral and spiritual dimensions are given greater emphasis in the novel. Therefore, using a cultural artifact as evidence of black civilization, as Achebe does with the Fang carving, is a waste of time. White racists base their myth of racial superiority on nothing other than the higher level of material development in the West. Affected by the same attitude of using material progress as the determinant of human civilization, Kurtz writes in his report for the International Society for the Suppression of Savage Customs, "we whites, from the point of development we had arrived at, must necessarily appear to them (savages) in the nature of supernatural beings—we approach them with the might as of a deity" (Conrad, 1973:71–72). It is no exaggeration to claim that Conrad calls in the novel for a total re-examination of our definitions of terms like civilization, humanity, progress, and truth.

Achebe misses in its entirety the ironic and sardonic thrust of the novel. He writes of the Thames and the Congo: "It (the Thames) conquered its darkness, of course, and is now in daylight and at peace. But if it were to visit its primordial relative, the Congo, it would run the terrible risk of hearing grotesque echoes of its own forgotten darkness, and falling victim to an avenging recrudescence of the mindless frenzy of the first beginnings" (1988:3). Another hermeneutic explication of the text shows that the Thames has conquered its darkness in certain respects, while in others it has merely replaced darkness with darkness. London, we are told, "has been one of the dark places of the earth". Marlow meditates on this monstrous town, which is represented as "a brooding gloom in sunshine, a lurid glare under the stars" (Conrad 1973:7), from which the sparks of the fire of civilization were taken to light the dark corners of the world. The "running blaze" has dwindled to a "flicker"—a Conradian metaphor for decadence and degeneration. The metaphor holds up to ridicule his sardonic wish: "We live in the flicker—may it last as long as the old earth keeps rolling!" (1973:8). It is not a mere coincidence, then, that the novel begins at sunset, a metaphor for the fall of the British Empire. The arrogant, short-sighted slogan that "The Sun Never Set on British Soil" has had its day.

Marlow's description of the conquest of Britain by the Romans parallels the subjugation of Africa by the European emissaries of death, light, pity and trade. Marlow projects history as cyclic progression. When power left the hands of the Romans, they ceased referring to the British as barbarians. Today, Britain seeks protection under the powerful arms of her Big Brother: the United States of America. Who knows, tomorrow, as the wheel of history continues in its circuitous path, America might turn out to be a loser in the power game. Conrad wrestles with the wheel of history in *Heart of Darkness*, but does not succeed in breaking it. Aided by the cyclic method of nature which informs his cyclic vision of history, he would readily agree with Frantz Fanon (1967:10–11) that "the man who adores the Negro is as 'sick' as the man who abominates him . . . and truly what is to be done is to set man free". To overcome that sickness, Conrad presents Africa as he saw it: a primitive land that was further underdeveloped by Europe; and searching for that freedom, he presents the story of Kurtz as an archetypal example of how not to live and love. Is it ironical that Kurtz who killed Africans recklessly in his heyday to satisfy his lust for ivory can towards the close of his life "want no more than justice?" (Conrad, 1973:106). His fall is not effected by the Africans, or through his participation in any unspeakable rites, but by the moral law of nature. The "wilderness . . . had taken on him a terrible vengeance for the fantastic invasion" (Conrad, 1973:83).

Achebe is embittered by the description of Africans as "rudimentary souls", but is silent on the description of the European pilgrims in the very next line as "small souls" (Conrad, 1973:72). Is Conrad's worldview also anti-humanist? By "rudimentary souls", Conrad means simple souls that have not been cluttered up with debilitating details and bewildering complexities—primordial hearts that have not been fuddled up with false meretricious sophistication. There is a subtle suggestion of a form of child-like innocence that is shielded from corruption in the expression, especially the corruption of facts. However, since simplicity has come to be regarded as a mark of under-development, the expression may be taken as utterly negative: as racial abuse. The expression reveals Conrad's ambiguous attitude to Africa. He is enamored of the people's vitality and harmonious existence with nature, but is appalled by the ugliness in this particular way of life, the strength of which ironically is its weakness. Conrad's paradoxical apprehension of life in its totality reminds one of the Romantic irony that there is loftiness in lowliness, and *vice versa*. Indeed, there is an undercurrent of a distinctively Romantic temper running through *Hear of Darkness*. It was probably the force that propelled Conrad to the Congo.

One may even be tempted to take umbrage at Conrad's idea that the "savages" have no "clear idea of time" (1973:58). However, the adjective "clear" absolves Conrad, for the primitive conception of time as cyclic and mythical sharply contradicts the scientific conception of it as linear and transparent. Such is the mastery of time that science has turned this god that is measured by events in traditional African society into an abstraction. Time is fragmented mechanically into minuscule units that cannot even be reckoned by the human brain. One can then understand why a European who has got accustomed to relying on the wrist-watch for time precision would perceive the African idea of time as foggy. The remark does not stem from the author's racism, but from sheer bewilderment which, of course, is bred by culture shock. A little sympathetic understanding is required in explicating a work like *Heart of Darkness*. It would, for example, reveal that the statement that the "amazing words" of Kurtz's adorers "resembled no sounds of human language" (Conrad, 1973:96) does not place the language of the Africans on Saussure's "indefinite plane of jumbled ideas", that is, in a pre-linguistic stage, what Lacan calls "the mirror stage" (Wright, 1982:119). Rather, it is a frank assessment which issues out of a spontaneous reaction to a foreign tongue. Every foreign language, to a non-speaker, sounds ghostly and weird. Even if Conrad places the language of the people in a primordial state, it is all for their good, for there is nothing edifying or ennobling in the truncation of language in the modern society, in the blunting of its cutting edge to an obtuse dullness, which unfortunately is aggravated by the expansion of technology. The problem is further exacerbated by the intrusion of machines like the telephone and the telex into inter-personal communication in modern society. An examination of the growth of human language reveals that language generally decays and loses its charm with the passage of time. However, language recovers its coruscation and sharpness as time recedes into the past. "As we go back in history, language becomes", in the words of Emerson, "more picturesque, until its infancy, when it is all poetry; or all spiritual facts are represented by natural symbols" (1963:13). It is also noticed that the boundary between the subject and the object becomes increasingly dark and nebulous, and man merges with the natural setting. The naturalization of man is a major priority in our atomic age. It can break the fetters forged by reason to imprison man's mind and by urbanization to obliterate the dependence of language on nature. Conrad's merging of the Africans with their surrounding natural environment should not be interpreted as a form of dehumanization. In any case, the separation of man from nature, which was brought about by industrialization and urbanization in Europe, was largely unknown in Black Africa at the time Conrad visited the Congo.

"For Conrad", Achebe writes in a satirical vein, "things being in their place is of the utmost importance" (1988:5). Conrad certainly was painfully aware of the enormous damage done by Europeans' violent transplantation of peoples. Among the tragic consequences of the Great Explorations are death on a massive scale, identity crises, psychic disorientation, racial hatred, loss of faith, rootlessness and slavery. Europeans went beyond transplantation and almost wiped out the entire population of the Caribs, the Arawaks and the Amerindians. The body of Africa was battered with weapons of war and the mind of Europe was bruised by fear and guilt. The point is that the psycho-social problems engendered by colonization, especially the loss by black Africans of confidence and faith in themselves, far outweigh its salutary material effects. Psychological problems are the most pathetic. The moving description of miserable Africans who have been uprooted from their homes, "lost in uncongenial surroundings, fed on unfamiliar food, overworked, reduced by disease and starvation" (Conrad: 1973:24) to mere skeletons and horrid shapes and, after becoming inefficient and totally useless, abandoned on the coast, like waste matter, to despair, pain and slow death, is a graphic representation of the evil in the forceful transplantation of people. A sardonic commentary on the so-called Western Civilization, the description contrasts sharply with that of the jolly black fellows with "a wild vitality, an intense energy of movement, that was as natural and true as the surf along their coast", who are having a rollicking time, as they paddle their boat gracefully and with tremendous confidence amidst shouts and songs; for they want "no excuse for being there" (1973:20).

Also sardonic are the passages parodying European Civilization, the destructive power of the invading man-of-war ship shelling the bush, the rapacious greed and crass materialism of the Eldorado Exploring Expedition that manifests itself as the inhuman lust for ivory, the crippling intrigues and petty jealousies among the European wanderers over privileged positions and promotion, the hollowness of Kurtz's insatiable appetite for lying fame, sham distinction, fouled success, untrammeled but corrupt power and vain-glory, and indeed the total loss of vision which reduces the whole colonial affair to a grand delusion. Conrad saw nothing that was really beneficial to the "savages" in the coming of Europeans to Africa. If anything, he saw their presence in Africa as the beginning of the dehumanization of Africans and the underdevelopment of their land. In none of the passages of indictment mentioned above does Conrad celebrate the civilizing power of Europe. Had things been in their place, perhaps South Africa would not have been mangled by the monster of apartheid.

Achebe argues that *Heart of Darkness* is not a great work of art because it "eliminates the African as human factor" (1988:8) in an African setting. Surely Africans are represented in the novel, as towers of boat, crewmen, carriers, prisoners, messengers, wood-cutters and helpers in the road construction work. Conrad presents such African characters as would enhance his indictment of the phil-anthropic pretence of the colonialists. Besides, Marlow's contacts with the natives are momentary and fragmentary, if not distant. The only exception is the relatively prolonged contact with the thirty crew members on the steamer bound for the Inner Station. Even then, Conrad had another major problem, the problem of incommunica-bility, which had to do with understanding the language(s) of the natives, and which his four-month sojourn in the Congo made prac-tically impossible. The problem bears direct relation on Achebe's crit-icism that Africans are portrayed as not capable of making coherent, intelligible speeches. "They 'exchanged short grunting phrases' even among themselves" (Achebe, 1988:6). Achebe cites the two instances in which Africans use the English language in the novel. The first is the headman's request for human flesh to eat, while the second is the announcement by the manager's boy of Kurtz's death.

Had Conrad attempted to represent socio-cultural details and ver-ities, it would certainly have produced the kind of distortion of which he is charged by Achebe; for the culture appears profoundly mysteri-ous and incomprehensible to the novelist who is expected to repre-sent verbally what he does not understand, what is yet to be absorbed, what appears to him like a dream. The glow of fires as Kurtz's wor-shippers keep vigil, the throb of their drums, and the drone of their incantations—all impinge on Marlow's mind as bewildering sense impressions. In such a situation, silence is golden. The resort to the non-verbal modes of communication in the novel is not accidental. Two examples will suffice. The first is Marlow's "speech in English with gestures" (Conrad, 1973:29) to the porters. Conrad recorded in his diary on Wednesday, 30th July, 1880: "Expect lots of bother with carriers tomorrow. Had them all called and made a speech, which they did not understand. They promise good behaviour." (1955:169–170). The second is the look that the helmsman gives Marlow when the former receives his mortal wound. Achebe sees in the simile "like a claim of distant kinship" (Conrad, 1973:73), that is, between a white employer and an African employee dying in the service of Western Imperialism, the white man's pride of race. Conrad, on the contrary, hints at the bond that binds the two men in toil and myste-rious origin. It is the profundity of the look that establishes for the reader the great partnership between the two men, Marlow's great sense of loss, the quality of the helmsman's hurt, and, above all, the oneness of human biological nature, for flesh is neither clay nor wood!

We begin to appreciate the enormity of the problem that confronts Conrad when we realize that Kurtz's mind disintegrates partly out of sheer loneliness. To exemplify the problem posed by the absence of verbal communication, we quote Marlow's remark on Kurtz: "this initiated wraith from the back of Nowhere honoured me with its amazing confidence before it vanished altogether. This was because it could speak English to me" (1973:71). The fact that the African characters do not use language profusely in *Heart of Darkness* is not intended by Conrad as evidence of the people's lack of the natural capacity for language. Even the vision of Kurtz who is said to be a talented orator is given in broken phrases and fragmented sentences. Yet, the meaning is not lost on the reader. There is no amount of words that can express vividly what Marlow feels in his body and mind when he flings his shoe into the serpentine Congo, on which the drama of the Fall is re-enacted, because of the fear that he might not meet Kurtz alive. Besides, a profuse use of the English Language by the African characters, who had not mastered the language, would have violated the law of verisimilitude and diminished the truthfulness of Conrad's art. Conrad, intuitively, through unalloyed fidelity to his own immediate sensations, translated language into action and magic in the scenes depicting Africans in *Heart of Darkness*, a feat that might not have been possible if he had found linguistic access to the mind of Africa.

"Certainly", Achebe wrote, "Conrad had a problem with niggers" (1988:9). As proof, he cited the following sentence: "A black figure stood up, strode on long black legs, waving long black arms" (Conrad 1973:94). In these dark days lighted by skin tone creams and hair tints it is quite possible for a black figure to have blue hairs, yellow arms and black legs. It is a sign of cultural bastardization and psychic disorientation. Conrad's expression, therefore, darkly hints at the idea of cultural and psychic integrity. With the hyperbolic repetitions, descriptive epiphets and grandiloquent, sesquipedalian images and nouns in the novel, Conrad is groping for a new mythopoeic prose style. He is struggling vaguely and unwittingly to wrest language from staleness and perversion and to restore words to their poetic origin.

Achebe argues that the description of the old African woman as "savage and superb, wild-eyed and magnificent" and of Kurtz's white fiancee as having "a mature capacity for fidelity, for belief, for suffering" exposes Conrad's racial bias (5–6). It is clear that Achebe misses the elaborate irony in Conrad's portraiture of Kurtz's girl friend: a dance of illusion and reality which is beautifully orchestrated during the long conversation between Marlow and Kurtz's fiancee, with which the novel ends. Like the other blind "civilized" folk, Kurtz's mistress lives in a delicate but false dream-world of belief, of illusion, of hope, and of love. Her knowledge of Kurtz, as a great, generous, good and noble man, is completely false. Marlow keeps her in the dark, in order not to shatter her dream-world or shake her strong belief that Kurtz is good-natured. He says: "I could not tell her. It would have been too dark—too dark altogether . . ." (1973:111). The African woman may be wild, but she has integrity. The European woman's refinement is artificial, deceptive and hollow.

Having seen the devilish side of human nature, the darkness in the human heart, as manifested in its utter nakedness by Kurtz in a colonial situation that shields the aggressor from the fear of the law and of punishment for his atrocities, Marlow knows better than the conceited, self-centred, hypocritical and materialistic white people he meets in the streets, after his return to Europe, to think that one race is biologically and morally superior to another, or that one race is destined to lead and salvage another. Conrad's brief sojourn in the Congo opened his mind to the sad facts of life. His remark to his friend Edward Garnett (in Jean-Aubry, 1957:175) that "Before the Congo, I was just a mere animal" testifies to that and reveals the degree of blindness to the hidden truth of life in Europe then. Hence Europe is shown in the novel as a vast cemetery and its civilization as sham sophistication. She is rotten at the core, but glows outside. If Conrad depicts Africans as barbaric and uncivilized, but full of life, vigour and vitality, he presents Europeans as the living-dead. African "culture" is portrayed as a crude and low form of existence, while European "culture" is depicted as embodying the germs of corruption and decay. Conrad exposes the weaknesses perceptible in the two cultures.

Beyond that, he uses the story of Kurtz to teach man a lesson in humility and restraint. Greed, fuelled by power, destroys Kurtz. Defeated in the struggle with mute matter, all-possessing, all-conquering Kurtz recognizes the limits of human power and admonishes man on his death-bed to live rightly. Conrad's vision in *Heart of Darkness* transcends the dubious division of the world into black and white. Achebe's reading of the novel is no doubt coloured by his concern for African "culture" and by the anger bred by the burden placed on the Black man because of skin pigmentation. His interpretation of the text is totally uncharitable. It is writers like Conrad who have the courage to tell us the bitter truth about our deplorable socio-economic condition who, ultimately, are our best friends. Africans and African cultures can do with a little criticism.

REFERENCES

Achebe, Chinua, "An Image of Africa: Racism in Conrad's *Heart of Darkness*," *Hopes and Impediments: Selected Essays (1965–1987)*, London: Heinemann, 1988).
———, "An Image of Africa", *Research in African Literatures* Vol. 9, No. 1 (Spring 1978).

Conrad, Joseph, "Author's Note" to *Almayer's Folly* (London: J. M. Dent and Sons Ltd., 1895).

―――, *Heart of Darkness* (Middlesex, England: Penguin Books Ltd., 1973).

―――, "The Congo Diary" in *Tales of Hearsay and Last Essays* (London: J.M. Dent and Sons Ltd., 1955).

Emerson, Ralph, Waldo, "The Method of Nature" in *Nature, The Conduct of Life and Other Essays* (London: J. M. Dent and Sons Ltd., 1963).

Fanon, Frantz, *Black Skin, White Masks: The Experience of a Black Man in a White World* (New York: Grove Press, Inc., 1967).

Harris, Wilson, "The Frontier on which *Heart of Darkness* Stands", *Research in African Literatures* Vol. 12, No. 1 (Spring 1981).

Jean-Aubry, Gerald, *The Sea Dreamer: A Biography of Joseph Conrad*, trans. Helen Sebba (London: George Allen and Unwin Ltd., 1957).

Lee, Dennis, *Savage Fields: An Essay in Literature and Cosmology* (Toronto: House of Anansi Press Limited, 1977).

Wright, Elizabeth, "Modern Psychoanalytic Criticism" in *Modern Literary Theory: A Comparative Introduction*, ed. Ann Jefferson and David Robey (London: Batsford Academic and Educational Ltd., 1982).

CARYL PHILLIPS

Was Joseph Conrad Really a Racist?[†]

Chinua Achebe leans forward to make his point. He raises a gentle finger in the manner of a benevolent schoolmaster. "But you have to understand. Art is more than just good sentences; this is what makes this situation tragic. The man is a capable artist and as such I expect better from him. I mean, what is his point in that book? Art is not intended to put people down. If so, then art would ultimately discredit itself."

Achebe does not take his eyes from me, and I stare back at him. The face is familiar and marked with the heavy lines of aging that one would expect to find on a 72-year-old man's face. But Achebe's lines are graceful whorls that suggest wisdom. He leans back now and looks beyond me, through the window at the snowy landscape.

We are sitting in his one-story house in upstate New York, deep in the wooded campus of Bard College. For the past thirteen years,

† From *Philosophia Africana* 10.1 (2007).

Achebe has been a professor at this well-known liberal arts college, which has had writers such as Mary McCarthy and Norman Mailer on the faculty. His house is decorated with African art and artifacts, but the landscape and the climate could not be further removed from Nigeria and the world of Achebe's fiction and non-fiction. As though tiring of the wintry landscape, Achebe turns and returns to our conversation.

"The man would appear to be obsessed with 'that' word."

"Nigger."

Achebe nods.

"He has an admiration of the white skin. It is the whiteness that he likes, and he is obsessed with the physicality of the negro."

Again Achebe falls silent, but this time he lowers his eyes as though suddenly overcome with fatigue. I continue to look at him, the father of African literature in the English language and undoubtedly one of the most important writers of the second half of the twentieth century. What I find difficult to fathom is just why Conrad's short novel, *Heart of Darkness*, should exercise such a hold on him.

Achebe has taught term-long university courses dedicated to this one slim volume first published in 1902. As long ago as February 1975, while a visiting professor at the University of Massachusetts in Amherst, Achebe delivered a public lecture entitled "An Image of Africa: Racism in Conrad's *Heart of Darkness*." The lecture has since come to be recognized as one of the most important and influential treatises in post-colonial literary discourse. However, the problem is, I disagree with Achebe's response to the novel, and have never viewed Conrad—as Achebe states in his lecture—as simply "a thoroughgoing racist." Yet at the same time, I hold Achebe in the highest possible esteem, and therefore, a two-hour drive up the Hudson River Valley into deepest upstate New York would seem a small price to pay to resolve this conundrum.

Achebe's lecture quickly establishes his belief that Conrad deliberately sets Africa-up as "the other world" so that he might examine Europe. According to Achebe, Africa is presented to the reader as "the antithesis of Europe and therefore of civilization, a place where man's vaunted intelligence and refinement are finally mocked by triumphant bestiality."

Achebe sees Conrad mocking both the African landscape and the African people. The story begins on the "good" River Thames which, in the past, "has been one of the dark places of the earth." The story soon takes us to the "bad" River Congo, presently one of those "dark places." It is a body of water upon which the steamer toils "along slowly on the edge of a black and incomprehensible frenzy."

According to Achebe, Conrad's long and famously hypnotic sentences are mere "trickery," designed to induce a hypnotic stupor in the reader. Achebe drafts the support of "the eagle-eyed English critic FR Leavis," who many years ago noted Conrad's "adjectival insistence upon inexpressible and incomprehensible mystery," whose cumulative effect is to suggest that poor Africa is inexplicable.

But it is when Achebe turns to Conrad's treatment of African humanity that he is most disparaging of Conrad's vision. He quotes from the moment in the novel when the Europeans on the steamer encounter real live Africans in the flesh:

> We are accustomed to look upon the shackled form of a conquered monster, but there—there you could look at a thing monstrous and free. It was unearthly, and the men were. No, they were not inhuman. Well, you know, that was the worst of it—this suspicion of their not being inhuman. It would come slowly to one. They howled and leaped, and spun, and made horrid faces; but what thrilled you was just the thought of their humanity—like yours—the thought of your remote kinship with this wild and passionate uproar. Ugly. Yes, it was ugly enough; but if you were man enough you would admit to yourself that there was in you just the faintest trace of a response to the terrible frankness of that noise, a dim suspicion of there being a meaning in it which you—and you so remote from the night of first ages—could comprehend.[1]

These people are "ugly," but what is even more disturbing is that they are in some way also human. A half-page later, Conrad focuses on one particular African who, according to Achebe, is rare, for he is not presented as "just limbs or rolling eyes." The problem is that the African man is, most disturbingly, not "in his place."

> And between whiles I had to look after the savage who was a fireman. He was an improved specimen; he could fire up a vertical boiler. He was there below me, and, upon my word, to look at him was as edifying as seeing a dog in a parody of breeches and a feather hat, walking on his hind legs.[2]

Those critics who have defended *Heart of Darkness* against charges of racism have often pointed to both the methodology of narration and Conrad's anti-colonial purpose. The narrator of the novel is Marlow, who is simply retelling a story that was told to him by a shadowy second figure. However, in his lecture Achebe makes it clear he is not fooled by this narrative gamesmanship or the claims of those who would argue that the complex polyphony of the storytelling is Conrad's way of trying to deliberately distance himself from the views of his characters.

1. Joseph Conrad, *Heart of Darkness* (New York: Dover, 1990).
2. Conrad, *Heart of Darkness*.

. . . If Conrad's intention is to draw a cordon sanitaire between himself and the moral and psychological malaise of his narrator, his care seems to me to be totally wasted because he neglects to hint, clearly and adequately, at an alternative frame of reference by which we may judge the actions and opinions of his characters. It would not have been beyond Conrad's power to make that provision if he had thought it necessary. Conrad seems to me to approve of Marlow. . . . [3]

Achebe is, however, aware of Conrad's ambivalence toward the colonizing mission, and he concedes that the novel is, in part, an attempt to examine what happens when Europeans come into contact with this particular form of economic and social exploitation. In the lecture he remembers that a student in Scotland once informed him that Africa is "merely a setting for the disintegration of the mind of Mr Kurtz," which is an argument that many teachers and critics, let alone students, have utilized to defend the novel. But to read the book in this way is to further stir Achebe's outrage.

> Africa as setting and backdrop, which eliminates the African as human factor. Africa as a metaphysical battlefield devoid of all recognizable humanity, into which the wandering European enters at his peril. Can nobody see the preposterous and perverse arrogance in thus reducing Africa to the role of props for the break-up of one petty European mind?[4]

Achebe has no problem with a novel that seeks to question both European ambivalence toward the colonizing mission and her own "system" of civilization. What he has a huge problem with is a novelist—in fact, an artist—who attempts to resolve these important questions by denying Africa and Africans their full and complex humanity.

During the two-hour drive up the Hudson through a snow-bound and icy landscape, I thought again of my own response to the novel. There are three remarkable journeys in *Heart of Darkness*. First, Marlow's actual journey up-river to Kurtz's inner station. Second, the larger journey that Marlow takes us on from civilized Europe, back to the beginning of creation when nature reigned, and then back to civilized Europe. And finally, the journey that Kurtz undergoes as he sinks down through the many levels of the self to a place where he discovers unlawful and repressed ambiguities of civilization.

---

3. Chinua Achebe, "An Image of Africa: Racism in Conrad's *Heart of Darkness,*" *Massachusetts Review* 18 (1977); reprinted in Robert Kimbrough, ed., *Heart of Darkness: An Authoritative Text, Background and Sources, Criticism,* 3rd edition (London: Norton, 1988), 251–62. See also Lisa Honaker, "The Lecture Heard around the World," available on-line at http//:caxtonstockton.edu/hod/achebe (visited 11 Dec. 2006).
4. Achebe, "An Image of Africa."

In all three journeys, Conrad's restless narrative circles back on itself as though trapped in the complexity of the situation. The over-arching question is, what happens when one group of people, sup-posedly more humane and civilized than another group, attempts to impose itself upon its "inferiors"? In such circumstances will there always be an individual who, removed from the shackles of "civilized" behavior, feels compelled to push at the margins of conventional "morality?" What happens to this one individual who imagines him-self to be released from the moral order of society and therefore free to behave as "savagely" or as "decently" as he deems fit? How does this man respond to chaos?

Conrad uses colonization, and the trading intercourse that flour-ished in its wake, to explore these universal questions about man's capacity for evil. The end of European colonization has not rendered *Heart of Darkness* any less relevant, for Conrad was interested in the making of a modern world in which colonization was simply one facet. The uprootedness of people, and their often disquieting encounter with the "other," is a constant theme in his work, and par-ticularly so in this novel. Conrad's writing prepares us for a new world in which modern man has had to endure the psychic and physical pain of displacement and all the concomitant confusion of watching imagined concrete standards become mutable. Modern descriptions of twentieth century famines, war, and genocide all seem to be eerily prefigured by Conrad, and *Heart of Darkness* abounds with passages that seem terrifyingly contemporary in their descriptive accuracy.

> Near the same tree two more bundles of acute angles sat with their legs drawn up. One, with his chin propped on his knees, stared at nothing, in an intolerable and appalling manner: his brother phantom rested its forehead, as if overcome with a great weariness; and all about others were scattered in every pose of contorted collapse, as in some picture of a massacre or a pesti-lence.[5]

As my car moved ever closer to Bard College, I constantly asked myself, was Conrad really a racist? If so, how did I miss this? Writ-ten in the wake of the 1884 Berlin Conference, which saw the con-tinent of Africa carved into a "magnificent cake" and divided among European nations, *Heart of Darkness* offers its readers an insight into the "dark" world of Africa.

The European world produced the narrator, produced Marlow, and certainly produced the half-French, half-English Kurtz ("All Europe contributed to the making of Kurtz"), but set against the glittering "humanity" of Europe, Conrad presents us with a late nineteenth

5. Conrad, *Heart of Darkness*.

century view of a primitive African world that has produced very little and is clearly doomed to irredeemable savagery. This world picture would have troubled few of Conrad's original readers, for Conrad was merely providing them with the descriptive "evidence" of the bestial people and the fetid world that they "knew" lay beyond Europe. However, by the end of the twentieth, and beginning of the twenty-first century, Conrad's readers are living in a decolonized—indeed post-colonial–world, and Conrad's brutal depiction of African humanity, so that he might provide a "savage" mirror into which the European might gaze and measure his own tenuous grip on civilization, is now regarded by some, including Achebe, as deeply problematic.

But is it not ridiculous to demand of Conrad that he imagine an African humanity that is totally out of line with both the times in which he was living and the larger purpose of his novel? In his lecture, even Achebe wistfully concedes that the novel reflects "the dominant image of Africa in the Western imagination."

And the novel does assert European infamy, for there are countless examples throughout the text that point to Conrad's recognition of the illegitimacy of this trading mission and the brutalizing effect it is having on the Africans. However, the main focus of the novel is the Europeans, and the effect upon them of their encountering another, less "civilized," world.

The novel proposes no program for dismantling European racism or imperialistic exploitation, and as a reader I have never had any desire to confuse it with an equal opportunity pamphlet. I have always believed that Conrad's only program is doubt; in this case, doubt about the supremacy of European humanity and the ability of this supposed humanity to maintain its imagined status beyond the high streets of Europe. However, as I pull my car up outside Achebe's house, I already sense I had better shore up my argument with something more resilient than this.

For a moment Achebe has me fooled. He looks as though he has nodded off, but he has just been thinking. This mild-mannered man looks up now and smiles. He returns to the subject we were talking about as though he has merely paused to draw breath.

> Conrad didn't like black people. Great artists manage to be bigger than their times. In the case of Conrad you can actually show that there were people at the same time as him, and before him, who were not racists with regard to Africa.

"Who?" I ask. Achebe says nothing for a moment, and so I continue. "I find it difficult to think of any European writers who have had a benevolent view of Africa. Surely they've all used Africa as a foil."

"Well, Livingstone," suggests Achebe. "He is not a writer, but he is an explorer, and Conrad admired explorers. When asked what he thought of Africans, Livingstone replied that he found them 'infuriating.' In other words, they were just like everybody else."

We both fall silent and I think back to Achebe's lecture. That Conrad had some "issues" with black people is beyond doubt. Achebe quotes Conrad who, when recalling his first encounter with a black person, remembers it thusly:

> A certain enormous buck nigger encountered in Haiti fixed my conception of blind, furious, unreasoning rage, as manifested in the human animal to the end of my days. Of the nigger I used to dream for years afterwards.[6]

Conversely, when the sixteen-year-old Conrad encounters his first Englishman in Europe, he calls him "my unforgettable Englishman" and describes him in the following manner:

> [His] calves exposed to the public gaze . . . dazzled the beholder by the splendour of their marble-like condition and their rich tone of young ivory. . . . The light of a headlong, exalted satisfaction with the world of men . . . illumined his face . . . and triumphant eyes. In passing he cast a glance of kindly curiosity and a friendly gleam of big, sound, shiny teeth . . . his white calves twinkled sturdily.[7]

However, despite Achebe's compelling "evidence," I am still finding it difficult to dismiss this man and his short novel. Are we to throw all racists out of the canon? Are we, as Achebe suggests, to ignore the period in which novels are written and demand that the artist rise above the prejudices of his times? As much as I respect the man sitting before me, something does not ring true. We both agree that Conrad was not the originator of this disturbing image of Africa and Africans. And we both appear to agree that Conrad had the perception to see that this encounter with Africa exposed the fissures and instabilities in so-called European civilization. Further, we both agree that in order to expose European fragility, Conrad pandered to a certain stereotype of African barbarity that, at the time, was accepted as the norm. Finally, we both agree that this stereotype is still with us today. Achebe speaks quickly, as though a thought has suddenly struck him.

> You see, those who say that Conrad is on my side because he is against colonial rule do not understand that I know who is on my side. And where is the proof that he is on my side? A few statements about it not being a very nice thing to exploit people who

---

6. Joseph Conrad, *Nigger of the Narcissus* (New York: Kessinger, 2004). See also Conrad, "Youth," in *Youth, Heart of Darkness, the End of the Tether*, John Lyon, ed. (New York: Penguin Classics, 1995).
7. Conrad, *Nigger of the Narcissus*.

have flat noses? This is his defence against imperial control? If so it is not enough. It is simply not enough. If you are going to be on my side what is required is a better argument. Ultimately you have to admit that Africans are people. You cannot diminish a people's humanity and defend them.

I feel as though I am walking around an impregnable fortress. However, I am losing interest in the problem of breaching the ramparts and becoming more concerned with the aesthetics of its construction.

"Which European or American writers do you feel have best represented the continent of Africa and African people?"

Achebe looks at me for a long while and then slowly begins to shake his head.

"This is difficult. Not many."

I suggest Graham Greene.

"Yes, perhaps. Graham Greene would be one because he knew his limitations. He didn't want to explain Africans to the world. He made limited claims and wasn't attempting to be too profound. After all, we can't be too profound about somebody whose history and language and culture is beyond our own."

"But you're not suggesting that outsiders should not write about other cultures?"

"No, no. This identification with the other is what a great writer brings to the art of story-making. We should welcome the rendering of our stories by others, because a visitor can sometimes see what the owner of the house has ignored. But they must visit with respect and not be concerned with the color of skin, or the shape of nose, or the condition of the technology in the house."

It is now my turn to stare out of the window at the six-foot snow drifts and the bare, rickety arms of the trees. The light is beginning to fade, and soon I will have to leave. I avert my eyes and turn to face my host.

"Chinua, I think Conrad offends you because he was a disrespectful visitor."

"I am an African. What interests me is what I learn in Conrad about myself. To use me as a symbol may be bright or clever, but if it reduces my humanity by the smallest fraction, I don't like it."

"Conrad does present Africans as having 'rudimentary' souls."

Achebe draws himself upright.

"Yes, you will notice that the European traders have 'tainted' souls, Marlow has a 'pure' soul, but I am to accept that mine is 'rudimentary'?" He shakes his head. "Towards the end of the nineteenth century, there was a very short-lived period of ambivalence about the certainty of this colonizing mission, and *Heart of Darkness* falls into this period. But you cannot compromise my humanity in order that you explore your own ambiguity. I cannot accept that. My humanity is not to be debated, nor is it to be used simply to illustrate European problems."

The realization hits me with force. I am not an African. Were I an African, I suspect I would feel the same way as my host. But I was raised in Europe, and although I have learned to reject the stereotypically reductive images of Africa and Africans, I am undeniably interested in the break-up of a European mind and the health of European civilization. I feel momentarily ashamed that I might have become caught up with this theme and subsequently overlooked how offensive this novel might be to a man such as Chinua Achebe and to millions of other Africans. Achebe is right; to the African reader, the price of Conrad's eloquent denunciation of colonization is the recycling of racist notions of the "dark" continent and her people. Those of us who are not from Africa may be prepared to pay this price, but this price is far too high for Achebe. However lofty Conrad's mission, he has, in keeping with times past and present, compromised African humanity in order to examine the European psyche. Achebe's response is understandably personal:

> "Conrad's presentation of me is my problem and I have a responsibility to deal with it, you understand?" I nod. "I don't come from a 'half-made' society as your 'friend' Naipaul would say. We're not 'half-made' people, we're a very old people. We've seen lots of problems in the past. We've dealt with these problems in Africa, and we're older than the problems. Drought, famine, disease, this is not the first time that we're dealing with these things in Africa."

He takes a deep breath. Beyond him, and through the window, the blanket of night begins to descend over the woods.

> "You know," he continues, "I think that to some extent it is how you must feel about your 'friend.' You take it to heart because a man with such talent should not behave in this way. My people, we say one palm nut does not get lost in the fire, for you must know where it is. But if you have twenty, you may lose sight of some and they will get burned, but you have others. Well, as you know, we have very few who have the talent and who are in the right place, and to lose even one is a tragedy. We cannot afford to lose such artists. It is sheer cussedness to wilfully turn and walk away from the truth, and for what? Really, for what? I expect a great artist, a man who has explored, a man who is interested in Africa, not to make life more difficult for us. Why do this? Why make our lives more difficult? In this sense Conrad is a disappointment."

CHINUA ACHEBE

Africa's Tarnished Image[†]

It is a great irony of history and geography that Africa, whose land mass is closer than any other to the mainland of Europe, should come to occupy in European psychological disposition the farthest point of otherness, should indeed become Europe's very antithesis. The French-African poet and statesman Leopold Sedar Senghor, in full awareness of this paradox, chose to celebrate that problematic proximity in a poem, "Prayer to Masks," with the startling imagery of one of nature's most profound instances of closeness: "joined together at the navel." And why not? After all, the shores of northern Africa and southern Europe enclose, like two cupped hands, the waters of the world's most famous sea, perceived by the ancients as the very heart and center of the world. Senghor's metaphor would have been better appreciated in the days of ancient Egypt and Greece than today.

History aside, geography has its own kind of lesson in paradox for us. This lesson, which was probably lost on everyone else except those of us living in West Africa in the last days of the British Raj, was the ridiculous fact of longitudinal equality between London, mighty imperial metropolis, and Accra, rude rebel camp of colonial insurrection— so that, their unequal stations in life notwithstanding, they were bisected by the same Greenwich meridian and thus doomed together to the same time of day!

But longitude is not all there is in life. There is also latitude, which gives London and Accra very different experiences of midday temperature, for example, and perhaps gave their inhabitants over past eons of time radically different complexions. So differences are there, if those are what one is looking for. But there is no way in which such differences as do exist could satisfactorily explain the profound perception of alienness that Africa has come to represent for Europe.

This perception problem is not in its origin a result of ignorance, as we are sometimes inclined to think. At least it is not ignorance entirely, or even primarily. It was in general a deliberate *invention* devised to facilitate two gigantic, historical events: the Atlantic slave trade and the colonization of Africa by Europe, the second event following closely on the heels of the first, and the two together stretching across almost half a millennium from about A.D. 1500. In an important and authoritative study of this invention, two American scholars, Dorothy Hammond and Alta Jablow, show how the content

† From *Another Africa,* with Robert Lyons (New York: Anchor, 1998), pp. 103–17. Copyright essays and poems © 1998 by Chinua Achebe. Used by permission of Doubleday, a division of Random House, Inc.

of British writing about Africa changed dramatically at the height of
the slave trade in the eighteenth century and

> . . . shifted from almost indifferent and matter-of-fact reports of
> what the voyagers had seen to judgmental evaluation of the
> Africans. . . . The shift to such pejorative comment was due in
> large measure to the effects of the slave trade. A vested interest
> in the slave trade produced a literature of devaluation, and since
> the slave trade was under attack, the most derogatory writing
> about Africa came from its literary defenders. Dalzel, for
> instance, prefaced his work with an apologia for slavery: "What-
> ever evils the slave trade may be attended with . . . it is
> mercy . . . to poor wretches, who . . . would otherwise suffer
> from the butcher's knife." Numerous proslavery tracts appeared,
> all intent upon showing the immorality and degradation of
> Africans. . . . Enslavement of such a degraded people was thus
> not only justifiable but even desirable. The character of Africans
> could change only for the better through contact with their Eu-
> ropean masters. Slavery, in effect, became the means of the
> Africans' salvation, for it introduced them to Christianity and
> civilization.[1]

The vast arsenal of derogatory images of Africa amassed to defend
the slave trade and, later, colonization, gave the world not only a literary tradition that is now, happily, defunct, but also a particular way
of looking (or rather *not* looking) at Africa and Africans that endures,
alas, into our own day. And so, although those sensational "African"
novels that were so popular in the nineteenth century and early part
of the twentieth have trickled to a virtual stop, their centuries-old
obsession with lurid and degrading stereotypes of Africa has been
bequeathed to the cinema, to journalism, to certain varieties of anthropology, even to humanitarianism and missionary work itself.

About two years ago, I saw an extraordinary program on television
about the children of the major Nazi war criminals whose lives had
been devastated by the burden of the guilt of their fathers. I felt quite
sorry for them. And then, out of nowhere, came the information that
one of them had gone into the Church and would go as a missionary
to the Congo.

"What has the Congo got to do with it?" I asked of my television
screen. Then I remembered the motley parade of adventurers, of
saints and sinners from Europe that had been drawn to that region
since it was first discovered by Europe in 1482—Franciscan monks,
Jesuit priests, envoys from the kings of Portugal, agents of King

---

1. *The Africa That Never Was: Four Centuries of British Writing about Africa* (Prospect
Heights: Waveland Press, 1992), pp. 22–23.

Leopold of the Belgians, H. M. Stanley, Roger Casement, Joseph Conrad, Albert Schweitzer, ivory hunters and rubber merchants, slave traders, explorers. They all made their visit and left their mark for good or ill. And the Congo, like the ancient tree by the much-used farm road, bears on its bark countless scars of the machete.

A saint like Schweitzer can give one a lot more trouble than King Leopold II, a villain of unmitigated guilt, because along with doing good and saving African lives, Schweitzer also managed to say that the African was indeed his brother, but only his *junior* brother.

But of all the hundreds and thousands of European visitors to the Congo region in the last five hundred years, there was perhaps no other with the deftness and sleight-of-hand of Joseph Conrad or the depth of the wound he gave that roadside tree. In his Congo novella, *Heart of Darkness*, Conrad managed to transform elements from centuries of generally crude and fanciful writing about Africans into a piece of "serious" literature.

Halfway through his story, Conrad describes a journey up the River Congo in the 1890s as though it were the very first encounter between conscious humanity coming from Europe and an unconscious, primeval hegemony that had apparently gone nowhere since the world was created. Naturally, it is the conscious party that tells the story:

> We were wanderers on a prehistoric earth, on the earth that wore the aspect of an unknown planet. We could have fancied ourselves the first of men taking possession of an accursed inheritance.[2]

Prehistoric earth . . . unknown planet . . . fancied ourselves . . . the first of men . . . This passage, which is Conrad at his best, or his worst, according to the reader's predilection, goes on at some length through *a burst of yells, a whirl of black limbs*, of *hands clapping, feet stamping, bodies swaying, eyes rolling*, through *a black incomprehensible frenzy* to *the prehistoric man* himself, *in the night of first ages*. And then Conrad delivers his famous coup de grâce. Were these prehistoric creatures really human? And he answers the question with the most sophisticated ambivalence of double negatives:

> No they were not inhuman. Well, you know that was the worst of it—this suspicion of their not being inhuman.[3]

Perhaps this is a good point for me to anticipate the kind of objection some people expressed when I first spoke about Conrad and *Heart of Darkness* in 1975. It was not my intention then or now to

---

2. *Heart of Darkness*, ed. Robert Kimbrough (New York: Norton), p. 37.
3. Ibid.

spend the rest of my life in Conrad controversy, and so I have generally kept away from both critics and defenders of my 1975 argument.
But my present purpose requires that I take up one particular line of
objection, one which presumes to teach me how to distinguish a book
of fiction from, say, a book of history or sociology. My critics do not put
it as brutally as that; they are very kind. One of them actually took the
trouble to write a letter to me and offer his good offices to reconcile me
with Conrad because, as he said, Conrad was actually *on my side!* I did
not, however, take up this kind mediation offer because I was not talking about *sides*. For me there is only one, *human*, side. Full stop!

But to return to Conrad and the word *fancy*, which his genius had
lit upon:

> We could have fancied ourselves the first of men taking posses-
> sion of an accursed inheritance.

I suggest that *fancied* is the alarm-word insinuated into Conrad's
dangerously highfalutin account by his genius, as well as by reason
and sanity, but almost immediately crowded out, alas, by the emotional and psychological fascination he had for the long-established
and well-heeled tradition of writing about Africa. Conrad was at once
prisoner of this tradition and one of its most influential purveyors; he
more than anyone else secured its admission into the hall of fame of
"canonical" literature. Fancy, sometimes called Imagination, is not
inimical to Fiction. On the contrary, they are bosom friends. But they
observe a certain protocol around each other's property and around
the homestead of their droll and difficult neighbor, Fact.

Conrad was a writer who kept much of his fiction fairly close to the
facts of his life as a sailor. He had no obligation to do so, but that was
what he chose to do—to write about places that actually exist and
about people who live in them. He confessed in his 1917 "Author's
Note" that

> *Heart of Darkness* is experience too, but it is experience pushed
> a little (and only very little) beyond the actual facts of the case
> for the perfectly legitimate, I believe, purpose of bringing it
> home to the minds and bosoms of the readers.[4]

One fact of the case about the River Congo which Conrad may not
have known was how much traffic it had seen before it saw Conrad
in the 1890s. Even if one discounts the Africans who lived on its
banks and would presumably have sailed up and down it through the
millennia before Conrad, there was even a European sailing ship on
the Congo four hundred years before our man made his journey and
wrote his book. Yes, four hundred!

---

4. Ibid., p. 4.

The Portuguese captain Diogo Cao, who discovered the river for Europe in 1482, was actually looking for something else when he stumbled on it; he was looking for a passage around Africa into the Indian Ocean. On his second voyage he went further up the river and heard from the inhabitants of the area about a powerful ruler whose capital was still further up. Cao left four Franciscan monks to study the situation and resumed the primary purpose of his expedition. On his way back he once more detoured into the Congo to pick up his monks; but they were gone! He seized in retaliation a number of African hostages, carried them off to Lisbon, and delivered them to King Manuel of Portugal.[5] This unpropitious beginning of Europe's adventure in the heart of Africa was quickly mended when Cao returned to the Congo for the third time in 1487, bringing back his African hostages who had meanwhile learned the Portuguese language and Christian religion. Cao was taken to see the king, Mweni-Congo, seated on an ivory throne surrounded by his courtiers. Cao's monks were returned to him, and all was well.

An extraordinary period ensued in which the king of Congo became a Christian with the title of King Afonso I. Before very long,

> the royal brothers of Portugal and Congo were writing letters to each other that were couched in terms of complete equality of status. Emissaries went back and forth between them. Relations were established between Mbanza[6] and the Vatican. A son of the Mweni-Congo was appointed in Rome itself as bishop of his country.[7]

This bishop, Dom Henrique, had studied in Lisbon, and when he led a delegation of Congo noblemen to Rome for his consecration, he had addressed the Pope in Latin.

Nzinga Mbemba, baptized as Dom Afonso, was a truly extraordinary man. He learned in middle life to read and speak Portuguese, and it was said that when he examined the legal code of Portugal he was surprised by its excessive harshness. He asked the Portuguese envoy what the penalty was in his country for a citizen who dared to put his feet on the ground! This criticism was probably reported back to the king of Portugal, for in a 1511 letter to his "royal brother," Dom Afonso, he made defensive reference to differing notions of severity between the two nations.[8] Can we today imagine a situation in which an African ruler is giving, rather than receiving, admonition on law and civilization?

---

5. I am indebted to Basil Davidson's *The African Slave Trade* (Boston: Little, Brown and Company, 1980) for the outline of this story.
6. The capital of the kingdom of Congo, which the king soon renamed San Salvador.
7. Davidson, p. 136.
8. Ibid., p. 152.

The Christian kingdom of Dom Afonso I in Congo did not fare well
and was finally destroyed two centuries later after a long struggle with
the Portuguese. The source of the problem was the determination of
the Portuguese to take out of Congo as many slaves as their vast new
colony in Brazil demanded, and the Congo kings' desire to limit or
end the traffic. There was also a dispute over mining rights. In the
war that finally ended the independence of the kingdom of Congo
and established Portuguese control over it, the armies of both nations
marched under Christian banners. But that is another story, for
another time.

Even the sketchiest telling of this story such as I have done here
still reads like a fairy tale, not because it did not happen but because
we have become all too familiar with the Africa of Conrad's *Heart of
Darkness*, its predecessors going back to the sixteenth century and its
successors today in print and electronic media. This tradition has
invented an Africa where nothing good happens or ever happened, an
Africa that has not been discovered yet and is waiting for the first European visitor to explore it and explain it and straighten it up.

In Conrad's boyhood, explorers were the equivalent of today's Hol-
lywood superstars. As a child of nine, Conrad pointed at the center
of Africa on a map and said: *When I grow up I shall go there!* Among
his heroes were Mungo Park, who drowned exploring the River
Niger; David Livingstone, who died looking for the source of the Nile;
and Dr. Barth, the first white man to approach the gates of the walled
city of Kano. Conrad tells a memorable story of Barth "approaching
Kano which no European eye had seen till then," and an excited population of Africans streaming out of the gates "to behold the wonder."

And Conrad also tells us how much better he liked Dr. Barth's
"first-white-man" story than the story of Sir Hugh Clifford, British
governor of Nigeria, traveling in state to open a college in Kano forty
years later. Even though Conrad and Hugh Clifford were friends, the
story and pictures of this second Kano event left Conrad "without any
particular elation. Education is a great thing, but Doctor Barth gets
in the way."[9]

That is neatly and honestly put. Africa of colleges is of little interest to avid lovers of unexplored Africa. In one of his last essays, Conrad describes the explorers he admired as "fathers of militant
geography" or "the blessed of militant geography." Too late on the
scene himself to join their ranks, did he become merely an adept con-
jurer of militant geography and history?

It is not a crime to prefer the Africa of explorers to the Africa of colleges. There have been some good people who did. When I was a
young radio producer in Lagos in the early 1960s, a legendary figure

9. Ibid., p. 147.

from the first decade of British colonial rule in Nigeria returned for a final visit in her eighties. Sylvia Leith-Ross had made a very important study of Igbo women in her pioneering work *African Women*,[1] in which she established from masses of personal interviews of Igbo women that they did not fit European stereotypes of downtrodden slaves and beasts of burden.[2] She graciously agreed to do a radio program for me about Nigeria at the turn of the century. It was a wonderful program. What has stuck to my mind was when she conceded the many good, new things in the country, like Ibadan University College, and asked wistfully: "But where is my beloved bush?"

Was this the same hankering for the exotic which lay behind Conrad's preference for a lone European explorer over African education? I could hear a difference in tone. Sylvia Leith-Ross was gentle, almost self-mocking in her choice, and without the slightest hint of hostility. At worst, you might call her a starry-eyed conservationist!

Conrad is different. At best you are uncertain about the meaning of his choice. That is, until you encounter his portrait, in *Heart of Darkness*, of an African who has received the rudiments of education:

> And between whiles I had to look after the savage who was fireman. He was an improved specimen; he could fire up a vertical boiler. He was there below me and, upon my word, to look at him was as edifying as seeing a dog in a parody of breeches and a feather hat walking on his hind legs. A few months of training had done for that really fine chap. He squinted at the steam-gauge and at the water-gauge with an evident effort of intrepidity—and he had filed teeth too, the poor devil, and the wool of his pate shaved into queer patterns, and three ornamental scars on each of his cheeks. He ought to have been clapping his hands and stamping his feet on the bank, instead of which he was hard at work, a thrall to strange witchcraft, full of improving knowledge.[3]

This is poisonous writing and in full consonance with the tenets of the slave trade-inspired tradition of European portrayal of Africa. There are endless variations in that tradition of the "problem" of education for Africa; for example, a highly educated African might be shown sloughing off his veneer of civilization along with his Oxford blazer when the tom-tom begins to beat. The moral: Africa and education do not mix. Or: Africa will revert to type.

And what is this type? Something dark and ominous and alien. At the center of all the problems Europe has had in its perception of Africa lies the simple question of African humanity: *Are they or are they not? Are they truly like us?*

1. *African Women: A Study of the Ibo of Nigeria* (London: Faber & Faber, 1938).
2. Ibid., p. 19.
3. Conrad, pp. 38–39.

Conrad devised a simple hierarchical order of souls for the characters in *Heart of Darkness*. At the bottom are the Africans whom he calls "rudimentary souls." Above them are the European ivory traders—petty, vicious, morally obtuse; he calls them "tainted souls" or "small souls." At the top are regular Europeans, and they don't seem to have the need for an adjective. The gauge for measuring a soul turns out to be the evil character, Mr. Kurtz, himself; how he affects that particular soul.

> He had the power to charm or frighten rudimentary souls into an aggravated witch-dance in his honor, he could also fill the small souls of the pilgrims with bitter misgivings—he had one devoted friend at least and he had conquered one soul in the world that was neither rudimentary nor tainted with self-seeking.[4]

The tendency of Africans to offer worship to any European who comes along is another recurrent theme in European writing about Africa. Variations on it include the veneration of an empty Coca-Cola bottle that falls out of an airplane. Even children's stories are not spared this insult, as I once learned from foolishly buying an expensive colorful book for my little girl without first checking it out.

The aggravated witch-dance for a mad white man by hordes of African natives may accord with the needs and desires of the fabulists of the Africa that never was, but the experience of Congo was different. Far from falling over themselves to worship their invaders, the people of this region of Africa have a long history of resistance to European control. In 1687 an Italian priest, Father Cavazzi, complained:

> These nations think themselves the foremost men in the world. They imagine that Africa is not only the greatest part of the world, but also the happiest and most agreeable. . . . [Their King] is persuaded that there is no other monarch in the world who is his equal.[5]

Between Father Cavazzi's words and Joseph Conrad's images of gyrating and babbling savages there was indeed a hiatus of two harsh centuries. Did the people of the Congo region deteriorate beyond recognition in this period and lose even the art of being human? No, they remained human through it all, to this day. I know some of them.

People are wrong when they tell you that Conrad was on the side of the Africans because his story showed great compassion toward them. Africans are not really interested in compassion, whatever it

---

4. Ibid., p. 51.
5. Davidson, p. 29.

means; they ask for one thing alone—to be seen for what they are: human beings. Conrad does not grant them this favor in *Heart of Darkness*. Apparently some people can read it without seeing any problem. We simply have to be patient. But a word may be in order for the last-ditch defenders who fall back on the excuse that the racial insensitivity of Conrad was normal in his time. Even if that were so, it would still be a flaw in a serious writer—a flaw that responsible criticism today could not gloss over. But it is not even true that everybody in Conrad's day was like him. David Livingstone, an older contemporary, and by no means a saint, was different. Ironically he was also Conrad's great hero, whom he placed

> among the blessed of militant geography . . . a notable European figure and the most venerated perhaps of all the objects of my early geographical enthusiasm.[6]

And yet his hero's wise, inclusive humanity eluded Conrad. What did he think of Livingstone's famous judgment of Africans?

> I have found it difficult to come to a conclusion on their [African] character. They sometimes perform actions remarkably good, and sometimes as strangely the opposite. . . . After long observation, I came to the conclusion that they are just a strange mixture of good and evil as men are everywhere else.[7]

Joseph Conrad was forty-four years *younger* than David Livingstone. If his times were responsible for his racial attitude we should expect him to be more advanced than Livingstone, not more backward. Without doubt the times in which we live influence our behavior, but the best, or merely the better, among us, like Livingstone, are never held hostage by their times.

An interesting analogy may be drawn here with the visual arts imagery of Africans in eighteenth-century Britain. In 1997, an exhibition was held by the National Portrait Gallery in London on the subject of Ignatius Sancho, an African man of letters, and his contemporaries. The centerpiece of the exhibition was the famous painting of Ignatius Sancho by Thomas Gainsborough in 1768. Reyahn King describes the painting in these words:

> Gainsborough's skill is clearest in his treatment of Sancho's skin colour. Unlike Hogarth, whose use of violet pigments when painting black faces results in a greyish skin tone, the brick-red of Sancho's waistcoat in Gainsborough's portrait, combined with the rich brown background and Sancho's own skin colour make the painting unusually warm in tone as well as feeling.

6. Conrad, p. 147.
7. *Missionary Travels,* quoted by Hammond and Jablow, p. 43.

Gainsborough has painted thinly over a reddish base with shading in a chocolate tone and minimal colder lights on Sancho's
nose, chin and lips. The resulting face seems to glow and contrasts strongly with the vanishing effect so often suffered by the
faces of black servants in the shadows of 18th-century portraits
of their masters.[8]

Evidently Gainsborough put care and respect into his painting; and
he produced a magnificent portrait of an African who had been born
on a slave ship and, at the time of his sitting, was still a servant in an
aristocratic household. But neither of these facts was allowed to take
away from him his human dignity in Gainsborough's portrait.

There were other portraits of Africans in Britain painted at the
same time. One of them provides a study in contrast with Gainsborough's rendering of Ignatius Sancho. The African portrayed in this
other picture was one Francis Williams, a graduate of Cambridge, a
poet and founder of a school in Jamaica; an amazing phenomenon in
those days.[9] A portrait of him by an anonymous artist shows a man
with a big, flat face lacking any distinctiveness, standing in a cluttered library on tiny broomstick legs. It was clearly an exercise in
mockery. Perhaps Francis Williams aroused resentment because of
his rare accomplishments. Certainly the anonymous scarecrow portrait was intended to put him in his place in much the same way as
the philosopher, David Hume, was said to have dismissed Williams's
accomplishments and compared the admiration people had for him
to the praise they might give "a parrot who speaks a few words
plainly."

It is clear, then, that in eighteenth-century Britain there were
Britons like the painter Gainsborough who were ready to accord
respect to an African, even an African who was a servant; and there
were other Britons like the anonymous painter of Francis Williams,
or the eminent philosopher, Hume, who would sneer at a black man's
achievement. And it was not so much a question of the times in
which they lived as the kind of people they were. It was the same in
the times of Joseph Conrad a century later, and it is the same today!

Things have not gone well in Africa for quite a while. The era of
colonial freedom that began so optimistically with Ghana in 1957
would soon be captured by Cold War manipulators and skewed into
a deadly season of ostensible ideological conflicts, encouraging the
emergence of all kinds of evil rulers able to count on limitless sup-
plies of military hardware from their overseas patrons, no matter how
atrociously they ruled their peoples.

8. King, Reyahn, et al., *Ignatius Sancho: An African Man of Letters* (London: National Portrait Gallery, 1997), p. 28.
9. Ibid., p. 30.

With the sudden end of the Cold War, these rulers or their successor regimes have lost their value to their sponsors and have been
cast on the rubbish heap and forgotten, along with their nations.

Disaster parades today with impunity through the length and
breadth of much of Africa: war, genocide, dictatorship, military government, corruption, collapsed economy, poverty, disease, and every
ill attendant upon political and social chaos!

It is necessary for these sad conditions to be reported because evil
thrives best in quiet, untidy corners. In many African countries, however, the local news media cannot report these events without
unleashing serious and sometimes fatal consequences. And so the
foreign correspondent is frequently the only means of getting an
important story told, or of drawing the world's attention to disasters
in the making or being covered up. Such an important role is risky in
more ways than one. It can expose the correspondent to actual physical danger; but there is also the moral danger of colonizing another's
story. This will immediately raise the question of the character and
attitude of the correspondent. For the same qualities of mind that
separated a Conrad from a Livingstone, or a Gainsborough and an
anonymous painter of Francis Williams, are still present and active
today. Perhaps this difference can best be put in one phrase: the presence or absence of respect for the human person.

In a 1997 calendar issued by Amnesty International USA jointly
with the International Center of Photography, a brief but important
editorial message criticizes some current journalistic practices:

> The apocalyptic vision of the newsmakers [does not] accurately
> document the world community. Nor are they particularly help-
> ful in forming a picture of our common humanity.[1]

And it goes on to set down the principles that guided its own selection of twelve photographs in the calendar as follows:

> [They] document an authentic humanity. They also communi-
> cate the fact that every person, everywhere, possesses an inalien-
> able rightness and an imperishable dignity—two qualities that
> must be respected and protected."[2]

Robert Lyons's photographs of Africa seem to me to possess these
qualities of respect. I wish I could say the same of a documentary film
that I have seen twice in the last three years or so on PBS. It was
about sex and reproduction through the entire gamut of living things,

---

1. Schulz, William F., and Willis Hartshorn, *1997 Amnesty International: Photographs from
   the Collection of the International Center of Photography* (New York: Universe Publishing),
   p. 1.
2. Ibid.

from the simplest single-cell creatures in the water to complex organisms like fishes and birds and mammals. It was a very skillful scientific program that pulled no punches when it came to where babies came from. It was all there in its starkness. Was it necessary to conclude this graphic reproductive odyssey with man (or rather woman)? I did not think so. The point (whatever it was) had already been made with apes, including, I believe, those that invented the "missionary position."

But the producers of the documentary were quite uncompromising in their exhaustiveness. And so a woman in labor *was* exposed to show the baby coming out of her. But the real shock was that everybody in that labor room was white except the Ghanaian (by her accent) mother in childbirth. Why were all the rest white? Because it was all happening in a hospital in London, not in Accra.

I am sure that the producers of that program would reject with indignation any suggestion that their choice of candidate was influenced in any way by race. And they might even be right, in the sense that they would not have had a meeting of their production team to decide that a white woman would not be an appropriate subject. But the fact is that such deliberation would not be necessary today, except perhaps in the crude caucuses of the lunatic fringe. Race is no longer a visible member of the boardroom. That much progress must be conceded; and it is not to be sniffed at. But an invisible member with a vote is still a deadly threat to justice. The lesson for that production team, and for the rest of us, is that when we are comfortable and inattentive, we run the risk of committing grave injustices absentmindedly.

The Igbo-African Background

J. P. CLARK
Abiku[†]

Coming and going these several seasons,
Do stay out on the baobab tree,
Follow where you please your kindred spirits
If indoors is not enough for you.
True, it leaks through the thatch
When floods brim the banks,
And the bats and the owls
Often tear in at night through the eaves,
And at harmattan, the bamboo walls
Are ready tinder for the fire
That dries the fresh fish up on the rack.
Still, it has been the healthy stock
To several fingers, to many more will be
Who reach to the sun.
No longer then bestride the threshold
But step in and stay
For good. We know the knife scars
Serrating down your back and front
Like the beak of the sword-fish,
And both your ears, notched
As a bondsman to this house,
Are all relics of your first comings.
Then step in, step in and stay,
For her body is tired,
Tired, her milk going sour
Where many more mouths gladden the heart.

Nigeria, showing the Igbo area

Igboland, showing the major places listed in *Things Fall Apart*

WOLE SOYINKA

Abiku[†]

Wanderer child. It is the same child who dies and returns again and
again to plague the mother—Yoruba belief.

In vain your bangles cast
Charmed circles at my feet
I am Abiku, calling for the first
And the repeated time.

Must I weep for goats and cowries
For palm oil and the sprinkled ash?
Yams do not sprout in amulets
To earth Abiku's limbs.

So when the snail is burnt in his shell,
Whet the heated fragment, brand me
Deeply on the breast—you must know him
When Abiku calls again.

I am the squirrel teeth, cracked
The riddle of the palm; remember
This, and dig me deeper still into
The god's swollen foot.

Once and the repeated time, ageless
Though I puke, and when you pour
Libations, each finger points me near
The way I came, where

The ground is wet with mourning
White dew suckles flesh-birds
Evening befriends the spider, trapping
Flies in wine-froth;

Night, and Abiku sucks the oil
From lamps. Mothers! I'll be the
Suppliant snake coiled on the doorstep
Yours the killing cry.

† From *Idanre & Other Poems* (London: Methuen, 1967), 28–30. Reprinted by permission.

The ripest fruit was saddest;
Where I crept, the warmth was cloying.
In silence of webs, Abiku moans, shaping
Mounds from the yolk.

VICTOR C. UCHENDU

The Igbo World[†]

To know how a people view the world around them is to understand
how they evaluate life; and a people's evaluation of life, both temporal and nontemporal, provides them with a "charter" of action, a
guide to behavior. The Igbo world, in all its aspects—material, spiritual, and sociocultural—is made intelligible to Igbo by their cosmology, which explains how everything came into being. Through it, the
Igbo know what functions the heavenly and earthly bodies have and
how to behave with reference to the gods, the spirits, and the ancestors. In their conception, not only is cosmology an explanatory device
and a guide to conduct; it is also an action system. As an explanatory
device, Igbo cosmology theorizes about the origin and character of
the universe. I am not concerned with this aspect of the Igbo world
view here. Rather, I am concerned with two other aspects: cosmology as a system of prescriptive *ethics*, which defines what the Igbo
ought to do and what they ought to avoid; and cosmology as an *action
system*, which reveals what the Igbo actually do as manifested in their
overt and covert behavior. The latter is very important if we are to
understand the dynamic factors in Igbo culture. But the three aspects
of Igbo cosmology must not be regarded as isolated phenomena. They
are interrelated. I have isolated them for analytical purposes, as a way
of organizing the data and illustrating this well-accepted fact: that
cosmological ideas express the basic notions underlying cultural
activities and define cultural goals and social relations.

The World of Man and the World of Spirits

The Igbo world is a "real" one in every respect. There is the world of
man peopled by all created beings and things, both animate and inam-
inate. The spirit world is the abode of the creator, the deities, the disembodied and malignant spirits, and the ancestral spirits. It is the
future abode of the living after their death. There is constant interaction between the world of man and the world of the dead; the visible

† From *The Igbo of Southeast Nigeria* (International Thomson Publishing, 1965), 11–21.
© 1965 Wadsworth, a part of Cengage Learning, Inc. Reproduced by permission.

and invisible forces. Existence for the Igbo, therefore, is a dual but interrelated phenomenon involving the interaction between the material and the spiritual, the visible and the invisible, the good and the bad, the living and the dead. The latter are a part of the Igbo social world.

In the Igbo conception, the world of the "dead" is a world full of activities; its inhabitants manifest in their behavior and thought processes that they are "living." The dead continue their lineage system; they are organized in lineages with patrilineal emphasis just as are those on earth. The principle of seniority makes the ancestors the head of the lineage; it gives the lineage its stability and continuity. An Igbo without *emenna*—a patrilineage—is an Igbo without citizenship both in the world of man and in the world of the ancestors. In the Igbo view, there is a constant interaction between the dead and the living: the dead are reincarnated, death making the transition from the corporeal to the incorporeal life of the ancestors possible. An illustration of the reality of the Igbo dual but interrelated world is provided by this dialogue. Father Shanahan, a great Roman Catholic missionary among the Igbo (who later became a bishop), wanted to baptize a condemned murderer before his death.

MURDERER: If I accept baptism, Father, will it prevent me from meeting my enemy in the next life?

FATHER: Well, no, you will probably meet him one way or the other.

MURDERER: Then baptize me by all means, and as soon as I do meet him, I'll knock his head off a second time (Jordan, 1949:137).

Apparent in this dialogue is the Igbo conviction that there is a carry-over of social status and other personal qualities from the world of man to the world of the dead. The murderer accepted baptism, not because he believed that it would cleanse his sins but rather because of the reassurance that the baptism was not meant to prevent a face-to-face meeting with his enemy, whose head he wanted to "knock off a second time," thus demonstrating his physical superiority over his enemy in the world of man and the world of the dead.

For the Igbo, death is a necessary precondition for joining the ancestors, just as reincarnation is necessary for the peopling of the temporal segment of the lineage. Therefore death which occurs at a ripe age is a cause for joy, being an index of high status among the ancestors. But since the young as well as the old die, death is received with mixed feelings. Death is personified and dealt with as a powerful spirit which gains mastery over *Nde*, the life-giving principle. It is the severance of this life-giving principle from the human, corporeal body. Without death, there will be no population increase in the ancestral households and correspondingly, no change in social status for the living Igbo.

Maintaining Cosmological Balance

The world as a natural order which inexorably goes on its ordained way according to a "master plan" is foreign to Igbo conceptions. Rather, their world is a dynamic one—a world of moving equilibrium. It is an equilibrium that is constantly threatened, and sometimes actually disturbed by natural and social calamities. The events which upset it include natural disasters like long, continuous droughts, long periods of famine, epidemic diseases, as well as sorcery and other antisocial forces; litigation, homicide, violation of taboo, and other incidents which the Igbo define as Nsɔ or Ale—taboo.

But the Igbo believe that these social calamities and cosmic forces which disturb their world are controllable and should be "manipulated" by them for their own purpose. The maintenance of social and cosmological balance in the world becomes, therefore, a dominant and pervasive theme in Igbo life. They achieve this balance, for instance, through divination, sacrifice, appeal to the countervailing powers of their ancestors (who are their invisible father-figures) against the powers of the malignant, and nonancestral spirits, and, socially, through constant realignment in their social groupings.

Death, for example, disturbs the existing social and ritual relationships and demands a new mode of adjustment for the bereaved family. The status goal of the one who dies young seems frustrated, and in his family creates a vacuum in its role structure through the loss of a member. The uncertainty about the cause of such an untimely death is a source of concern for all. Divination settles this uncertainty by specifying the cause of death and recommending ritual remedies. The diviner's verdicts follow a culturally expected pattern: the deaths of young people are usually blamed on the sins committed during their previous life on earth; deaths of adults may be attributed to "ripe" age, or senility, a breach of taboo or other antisocial behavior, such as sorcery, false oath, or theft committed in his previous or present life. Whatever the verdict, the loss of ritual balance is implicit and ritual remedies are recommended. If sorcery is involved, the deceased adult is denied "ground" burial (a privilege accorded only to those who die without blemish), and the corpse is cast into ɔhia ɔjɔɔ—a "bad bush" fit only for the outcast. The ritual purifications are primarily designed to dissociate the living from the deceased's blemish and thus reestablish the ritual balance his breach of taboo has destroyed.

Indeed, whatever threatens the life of the individual or his security as well as society is interpreted by the Igbo as a sign of warning that things must be set right before they get out of hand. Losses in trade indicate to the trader that his *Mbataku*—the wealth-bringing deity—

is threatening action for being neglected, while drought or too long a rainy season is a warning that society has lost its balance with nature.

Not only deities and spiritual forces are manipulated. Human beings and social relations are also subject to manipulation. * * * [T]he Igbo individual balances his conflicts in one agnatic group with his privileges in another. His *umunɛ* (mother's agnates[1] among whom he enjoys okɛnɛ privileges) stand with him against the perennial conflicts he faces among his ɵmɵnna (his own agnates). Although he is exposed to physical danger among his ɵmɵnna, his person is sacred in his *umunɛ*. It is the place of his exile should he be convicted of sorcery by his ɵmɵnna. Assured of the support of a strong *umunɛ*, the Igbo can challenge his ɵmɵnna successfully; with the support of both his ɵmɵnna and his *umunɛ*, he can move his world.

When we come to the domain of Igbo legal process, the same principle of balance of forces is seen at work. Legal procedures aim essentially at readjusting social relations. Social justice is more than law, and the spirit of the law is more important than the letter of the law: this seems to be the Igbo juridicial principle. The resolution of a case does not have to include a definite victory for one of the parties involved. Judgment among the Igbo ideally involves a compromise. They insist that a good judgment "cuts into the flesh as well as the bone" of the matter under dispute. This implies a "hostile" compromise in which there is neither victor nor vanquished; a reconciliation to the benefit of—or a loss to—both parties.

Those relationships not considered mutually beneficial tend to remain fragile. Parties to a relationship, whether they are human or spiritual, are expected to fulfill some obligation and to derive some reward. Each party is expected to be motivated by self-interest. The relationship lasts as long as the parties are satisfied with the terms of the contract. As the Igbo proverb puts it, "It is only proper that the left and right palms should wash each other so that both might be clean."

Underlying the maxim that social life demands "beneficial reciprocity" is the realization that no individual or spirit is self-sufficient. Human interdependence is a constant theme in the folklore of the Igbo. It is the greatest of all values for them. As another proverb has it: "A man is never so stout that flesh covers his nails." "To help one to get up" is an ever-recurring theme in their social life. A man who "helps others to get up" commands much prestige. He is the "big" man, the popular man who deserves much respect and obedience. Since the need to get along well with everyone is such a major concern in interpersonal relations, a properly socialized Igbo is one who

---

1. Agnates are patrilateral kinsfolk. They are men and women to whom one is related through males only. In other words, a descent link from a man to a child is called an *agnatic* link while a descent link from a woman to a child is called an *uterine* link. A social group tracing descent through males only is an *agnatic group*.

is able to interact with others, to speak out his mind freely even if it hurts to do so. Getting on well with neighbors does not mean "letting them alone." What one person does is of great concern to others. It is the Igbo way to associate with people who will give one advice, to have friends "who can hear one's cry." Secretive persons who "bury injuries in their minds" are held in contempt; they are often the victims of unwarranted aggression and targets of sorcery accusations. They hinder social adjustment through human interdependence.

*　*　*

Because reciprocity is the organizing principle of Igbo social relationship, near equality is their ideal. Domination by a few powerful men or spirits is deeply resented. A relationship that is one-sided, either in its obligation or in its reward system, does not last long among them. Imbalance, either in the social or in the spiritual world, is considered a trouble indicator. Through mutual interdependence and his ability to manipulate his world, the Igbo individual tries to achieve equality or near equality in both the world of man and the world of the spirits.

Manipulating His World

The Igbo world is not only a world in which people strive for equality; it is one in which change is constantly expected. Its contractual character makes it a constantly changing world. Since the relationship between the social world and the spiritual world is contractual, there is always the fear that the terms of the contract might not be fully honored by either party: the spirits often change their mind as do men. Each tries to get the better part of the other, a source of uncertainty in Igbo social relations. This uncertainty is not critical for the Igbo. It simply keeps him alert since he believes that social relations can be manipulated. For every force, he tries to provide a countervailing force. He achieves this either through shifting his alliance or by invoking the aid of a more powerful force.

If you ask the Igbo why he believes that the world should be manipulated, he will reply "The world is a marketplace and it is subject to bargain." In his view, neither the world of man alone nor the world of the spirits is a permanent home. The two worlds together constitute a home. Each world is peopled with "interested" individuals and groups and much buying and selling goes on in each. People go to the marketplace for different reasons, but the common motivation is the desire to make a profit. Although the profit motive is the guiding factor, there are occasional losses. From the Igbo point of view, a person does not abandon trading because he suffers losses. It would be cowardly to do so, but he cannot carry on indefinitely if he does not balance his losses with gains. The Igbo would advise the perennially unsuccessful trader to change his line of merchandise. Instead of trading in yams, he should try pepper; eventually he will find his line. But if all else fails, magic will not.

This description of life in the idiom of market exchange is not a mere theoretical formulation of mine; it is the Igbo way and is manifested in their everyday behavior. This idiom is dramatized every time a mother goes to the village market. She has packed her wares in a rectangular wicker basket. As she is helped to put the load on her head, her children, who are hanging around to give her the "market wish," come up one after the other and say:

> Nnɛ zugbuo ndi ahia;
> Ndi ahia azugbula gi.

This may be rendered as:

> Mother, gain from market people;
> Market people, lose to mother.

As each child gives his market wish, he spits into the mother's cupped palms. When this ritual is over, mother rubs her palms together and ritually cleanses her face, thus symbolically, ensuring "good face" for the day's bargaining operations. An interesting feature of the market wish ritual is that it conforms to the principle of social balance. Among the Igbo, market prices are determined by a rigorous system of bargaining, a time-consuming operation from the Westerner's point of view. It is a bargain between a buyer and a seller, each of whom is consciously dramatizing the market wish.

Cyclical Nature of Status Seeking

It is a fair assessment of the Igbo world to say that the most important commodity it offers and for which the Igbo strive is the ɔzɔ, or title system. The Igbo are status seekers. To use a market metaphor, they believe that the world is a marketplace where status symbols can be bought.

For the Igbo, life on earth is a link in the chain of status hierarchy which culminates in the achievement of ancestral honor in the world of the dead. In this view, those who die young suffer much frustration in *Ala Mmɔ—the spirit land.* They remain "boys" in both worlds—most repugnant to Igbo youth. Fortunately for the low-status person, this is temporary because the Igbo believe in reincarnation. A person's social position is such an important thing that even on his deathbed the individual Igbo thinks more of his status in the hereafter than of his death. His most important injunctions to his heir and family are: Do not shame my spirit. Do not let my enemies see my corpse. Give me good burial. For the Igbo, status-seeking is a cyclical process of death, individual role bargaining with the creator, reincarnation, birth, and then death.

The social importance of reincarnation is that it provides the "idea system" that rationalizes, interprets, accommodates, or rejects changes and innovations as well as tolerates certain character traits. Furthermore, it is at reincarnation that the individual works out a proper role for himself through face-to-face interaction with the creator. Guided by his *chi*—the Igbo form of guardian spirit—the reincarnating soul makes a choice from two parcels that *chinɛkɛ*, the creator, presents. Of these two parcels, one is believed to contain the desired social positions that the individual predicted in his *ɛbibi* (prereincarnation social position that the individual predicts during his lifetime on earth). In their *ɛbibi*, most Igbo predict long life, intelligence, wealth, "having mouth," that is, the power of oratory and wisdom. What the Igbo seldom realize is that these desirable traits are not genetically or spiritually transmitted but are the result of conditioning through their child-rearing practices, which are constantly reinforced by rewards and sanctions of adults as well as by the general demands made on the individual Igbo by his culture.

Not all Igbo are able to make the "right" choice in their role bargaining with the creator. A "wrong" choice, however, does not spell the social doom of the reincarnating Igbo. He can still make the most of his choice while on earth and hope for better luck during the next cycle.

Transparent Living

In a world where life processes are delicately balanced, and where the individual has a wide latitude in manipulating human and nonhuman elements to his possible advantage, it is necessary for people to live *transparent lives*. We have mentioned earlier that secretive persons are held in contempt as not being properly socialized; that the Igbo group-oriented value system does not imply a "let alone" policy in interpersonal relations. There are conflicts. To resolve them, adjustment through compromise is the accepted way. To achieve this compromise the cause of the conflict must be made known to arbitrators. Anybody can play this role.

Igbo are a people who tend to wash their dirty linen in public. Anyone who has overheard Igbo co-wives quarreling will appreciate this point. The compact household units, the matter-of-fact approach to sex, the symbolic way "transparency" is conveyed by tasting food or drink meant for the visitor or neighbor, the respect accorded to the leader who has "strong eyes" to see "hidden things" and the "mouth" to expose them are indicative of their "transparent" orientation. The concept of the good life among the Igbo is so built on the transparency theme that the individual dreads any form of loss of face. The major deterrent to crime is not guilt-feeling but shame-feeling.

The qualities demanded of Igbo leaders emphasize their transparent orientation. The leader should be accessible to all. If he holds *ɔfɔ*—the symbol of ritual authority—he is required to vindicate his innocence regularly through the rite of *iju ogu*—the affirmation of innocence. This is generally regarded as a formal indication that he maintains his ritual status—a necessary condition for his high office. To dispel suspicion and reassure themselves that no evil is planned, two friends whose relations are strained may resort to *igbandu*—a formal oath for re-establishing confidence—in which one may drink the blood of the other. A stranger may be required to swear repeatedly to his host, a husband will swear with his wife's lover (concubinage is one of the institutions for sexual expression among Igbo), and patron-client relationships as well as doctor-patient relationships may be strengthened by repeated swearing of fidelity. In this context, the experience of a female British anthropologist who worked in an Igbo village-group is worth citing: "The elders of the village, in spite of the fact that some of them were nervous lest a white woman might have designs upon their land and palm trees, were nonetheless convinced that if she decided to decamp they would be ridiculed by the surrounding villages. They were therefore always urging me to swear with them that I would not go away" (Green 1947:252). This demonstrable evidence of good faith is the pattern of behavior one would expect from a people who put so much value on transparent living and who are realistic enough to believe that some people will not live up to the ideal behavior unless they are constrained to do so.

Furthermore, the period of nudity, which once extended into adolescence for both boys and girls, was a symbolic expression of their "transparent" character, since girls were expected to be virgins at marriage. Most personal acts like *iyiɔgwɵ*—the acquisition of protective medicine, and the borrowing or lending of money—are usually done in the presence of witnesses. To hide these facts would lead to the suspicion that dangerous medicine was being acquired and that money was being borrowed for antisocial purposes. As I have mentioned in a different context earlier, solitude is regarded as a mark of wickedness, of evil design. Of course, not every Igbo lives up to this ideal. To be a properly socialized Igbo is to approximate "as far as the eye can see"—the Igbo way.

"A Country Is Spoiled by Men"

A proverb often cited by Igbo elders and judges is *Madu bɵ njɔ ala*—"Man makes the country wicked." It is man who "spoils" the country and not the spirits, the people emphasize.

An Igbo anecdote gives the basis of this maxim and its implication for their transparent orientation. It is told of an Igbo leader and philosopher who was engaged in an informal discussion with a distinguished foreign visitor who made some disparaging remark about his host's country. This comment upset the philosopher, who thought about it for a while and then made this reply:

> "Do you say that my country is bad? Can the earth or trees or mud walls speak? How do they offend?"
>
> "No," the visitor answered. "As far as I know, they don't."
>
> "Well answered," the philosopher replied. "Never speak badly of my country again. Should any of my people offend you, accuse them directly."

As if to leave no doubt in the mind of the visitor, the philosopher called one of his sons, by name Madubunjɔala, and requested him to bring ɔkwa—a carved wooden bowl for presenting pepper and kola nut. After his son had left, the philosopher explained: "To mark the intrigues of some of my enemies in this country, I named that child (pointing after his son) *Madubunjɔala* ('Man makes a country wicked'). It is people and not spirits who make a country 'wicked.'"

This anecdote clearly indicates the direction of scapegoating among the Igbo. When things go wrong, people of "shady" character—solitary and secretive persons—are accused. This logically follows from the transparency theme. The reasoning may be briefly stated: The ideal of a transparent life is incompatible with antisocial behavior. Those who live a "dark" life are the enemies of society because they commit most crimes.

A World of Change

The Igbo world is one in which change is expected. Change is accepted as a realistic adjustment to the status and role structure, as an adjustment to the world around them. I mentioned earlier the Igbo belief in reincarnation and its implication for the individual role bargaining with the creator. It appears to me that the latter is the most important ideological factor making for internally induced change among the Igbo. Believing that he chose his roles, the Igbo is constrained to make a success of his social position or career. This belief, too, imposes on his family the obligation of providing the sociocultural environment for the realization of his status goals. In effect, the Igbo stress on the success goal is ideologically rooted in the reincarnation dogma.

Though the quest for success goals is full of hazards and sometimes a threat to life, this fact does not deter the Igbo. "One who is overcautious of his life is always killed by the fall of a dry leaf," they say. It is their view that life must be faced and its problems overcome. Facing life's challenges may involve physical aggression, the use of protective medicine, or even bribery. To protect one's rights in a changing world requires perpetual vigilance. "An absentee child," they say, "eats his yam half roasted." In a world of equals like the Igbo, where all the people are competing for the same goal, the rule of the game is that competitors must be alert if they hope to win.

The individual freedom of choice fostered by Igbo culture allows innovation. There is opportunity for experimentation as well as tolerance for failure and admiration for success. The most important factor for the acceptance or rejection of an innovation is its status implication for the individuals and groups concerned. The crucial question is this: Will the acceptance of this innovation "make the individual or the town get up"? If the answer is in the affirmative, there is a great possibility of immediate acceptance; but to be retained, the innovation "must work," the material and symbolic evidence of "getting up" must be demonstrated.

Equalitarianism

The Igbo world is based on an equalitarian principle. Equality or near equality ensures that no one person or group of persons acquires too much control over the life of others. This is an ideological obstacle to the development of a strong central authority. However, no human society achieves absolute equality among its citizens and Igbo society is no exception. There are distinctions of age, sex, and wealth. The Igbo realize this quite well and, in fact, stress these factors in their stratification model. What the Igbo mean by an equalitarian society is that which gives to all its citizens an equal opportunity to achieve success. The stress is on achievement. They recognize that "a child who washes his hands clean deserves to eat with his elders."

The Igbo achievement orientation has two important social effects. In the first place, it makes the Igbo world a highly competitive one in which the rules of competition may be manipulated by the status seeker in order to attain his goals. Second, it fosters a sociopolitical system which is conciliar and democratic. A forward-moving and talented young man who can acquire wealth and "convert" it into the traditionally valued status symbols (such as title taking) is allowed to wield political power over his peers and elders. This is a further demonstration of the Igbo saying that "no one knows the womb that bears the chief." It is not surprising that chiefship among the Igbo must not only be achieved, but be constantly validated to be retained.

The Igbo leader "emerges": he is not born or made. The Igbo saying that "everyone is a chief in his hut" must be understood in its proper context. What is meant is that a dictatorial leader of the Igbo is inconceivable. A leader may be a dictator if he likes, but his leadership must be restricted to his household. A leader is supported by his followers as

long as "he does not govern too much." To govern too much is to alienate them. As long as a leader behaves as if he is making it possible for
everyone "to get up," that is, to advance their social status, so long will
he remain an ideal leader. Within this context, indeed, a leader may
have his way as well as enjoy the support of followers. This is the typical situation which makes the Igbo hero worshipers.

Igbo leadership depends on the concept of public service and the
realization of dreams: high status for the individual and progress for
the community. The town is a small village-group in which the leader
operates. His ability to influence any other similar unit is minimal.
Each village-group is suspicious of, and often hostile to, the neighboring village-groups. "A tall tree does not span two towns" is an Igbo
proverb that makes sense in a highly segmented society. Since political office is not remunerative, an aggressive expansionist policy does
not have much meaning for the Igbo. Their expansion has been small
and predatory. Dwelling units are villages rather than semiurban
units; sociopolitical integration is achieved through decentralization
rather than through hierarchical organization.

Summary

The Igbo world is a world peopled by the invisible and visible forces,
by the living, the dead, and those yet to be born. It is a world in which
all these forces interact, affecting and modifying behavior; a world
that is delicately balanced between opposing forces, each motivated
by its self-interest; a world whose survival demands some form of
cooperation among its members, although that cooperation may be
minimal and even hostile in character. It is a world in which others
can be manipulated for the sake of the individual's status
advancement—the goal of Igbo life. It conceives reincarnation as not
only the bridge between the living and the dead, but a necessary precondition for the transaction and transfer of social status from the
world of man to the world of the dead. It is a world of constant struggle which recognizes that conflict situations exist and therefore
demands from the individual constant adjustments; and, although
leaving some of the rules of adjustment rather vague, still insists that
"good citizenship" demands "transparent" living and that human
interdependence is the greatest of all values. It is a world that is
spoiled by man and not by spirits; yet man is allowed a wide latitude
in his behavior—an important factor in the dynamics of Igbo culture.
Finally, it is a world in which the leader is given minimal power and
yet is expected to give maximum service in return—the hallmark of
which is "to make the town get up." This is the Igbo world.

DON C. OHADIKE

Igbo Culture and History[†]

Early Igbo History

The Igbo (or Ibo) people form one of the largest ethnic groups in Africa, with about 15 million living in Nigeria and another million living outside. Their farming communities are broadly situated between the Niger River in the west and the Cross River in the east, stretching from delta swampland near the southern coast through tropical rain forest to open grasslands to the north. The Igbo language has dozens of dialects, which developed because Igboland was an aggregation of self-contained towns and villages, separated from each other by dense bush. Before the twentieth century, it would have been incorrect to speak of the Igbo as a single people; they were made up of over two hundred separate groups. Although their customs and languages were clearly related, each group could have been considered a distinct society, encompassing perhaps twenty or thirty villages. An Igbo person who traveled thirty miles in Igboland might have had great difficulty making himself or herself understood. However, during the colonial period (1900–1960) many Igbo people ventured far from home and congregated in urban centers, at the work place, and in institutions of higher learning. Many realized that what they thought were distinct languages were different dialects of the same language and that all Igbo-speaking people had the same basic culture and sociopolitical organization. In that sense, the concept of a common Igbo identity is a product of the twentieth century.

An Igbo creation myth relates that in the beginning the surface of the earth was covered by water and no humans lived on it. Then one day Chukwu (God) created the first human family, composed of Eze Nri, his wife, his sons, and his daughters. Eze Nri and his family stood on the top of an anthill and had nowhere to go because the land was submerged. They were also hungry. Chukwu looked down and took pity on their condition. He gave Eze Nri a piece of yam and said, 'Take this, it is edible.' Eze Nri and his family ate the yam and found it was good.

The following morning, they were hungry again and Eze Nri prayed to God for more yam. Chukwu listened attentively and then gave him some yam seeds, saying, 'Plant these and you will have an abundance of yams.' Eze Nri accepted the yam seeds with gratitude. He looked

† From Chinua Achebe, Things Fall Apart: Classics in Context (Portsmouth, NH: Heinemann, 1996), xix–xlix.

around him and said to Chukwu, 'But the land is covered with water.' Chukwu instructed him to send for Awka blacksmiths, who came with their bellows and blew until the land was dry. Chukwu then asked Eze Nri to sacrifice his first son and his first daughter and plant the yam seeds in their graves. Eze Nri obeyed. Shortly afterwards, yam and cocoyam tendrils sprouted from his children's graves. Eventually, Eze Nri harvested yams and cocoyams and shared them among the Igbo people.

This story establishes the Igbo people's belief in a supreme god (Chukwu) who created all things and demanded obedience. It also suggests that religion has long been an integral part of Igbo life. The myth points to the origins of agriculture, the antiquity of the family, and the importance of iron working in shaping the Igbo community. Above all, since this myth makes no mention of migrations from distant places—as opposed to the majority of African traditions of origin—it suggests that the Igbo people have occupied their present locale for a very long time, a suggestion that is confirmed by archaeology.

Archaeological evidence shows today's Igbo people and their ancestors have been settled in roughly the same geographical region for two thousand years or more. Much of the material culture of present-day Igbo people resembles that of the people who occupied certain locations in Igboland around 1,000 BC. At Afikpo, present-day pottery resembles that produced about 3,000 years ago. At one of the Afikpo sites, the number of stone implements gradually decreased as the amount and variety of pottery increased, showing the transition from hunting and gathering to agriculture.

Igbo people have smelted and forged iron for centuries, and their oral traditions are rich with accounts of iron working and iron use. At Lejja, a small town situated about ten miles south of Nsukka, an ancient iron-working settlement existed where smelting was done in a pit or bowl furnace, initially using rather primitive techniques. Over time, the Igbo improved their technological skills and began to produce sophisticated metal tools such as spearheads, arrowheads, swords, hoes, knives, earrings, finger rings, bracelets, anklets, hammers, anvils, tweezers, scissors, and cooking pots. By the first millennium of the Christian era, they were already producing bronze masks and figurines, of the types that archaeologists discovered in Igbo-Ukwu.

The widespread use of iron tools enabled the Igbo people to make better use of the forest. With iron tools they grew yams (their principal staple food), cocoyams, bananas, and plantains. Iron tools also helped them to cut down fruits from the tall palm trees, and process them into edible and medicinal oils. Scholars have attributed the current high density of the Igbo population to the antiquity and effectiveness of yam cultivation and their skills at exploiting the oil palm.

At its fully developed stage, the Igbo agricultural system was based on shifting cultivation, a type of rotating cultivation where the same fields were planted for several years in succession and then were left fallow to regain their fertility. Crops did best on forest land cleared for the first time, but some people, either unwilling or unable to handle the back-breaking amount of work required to clear virgin forest, planted their yams continuously on old farm lands and reaped poor harvests as a result. In *Things Fall Apart*, Okonkwo's father is portrayed as too lazy to clear forest land; he prays to the spirits to grant him a better harvest but is rebuked for his own lack of initiative.

Social and Political Structures

A striking feature of Igbo society was the lack of centralized political structures. The Igbo lived in autonomous villages and towns, ruled by their elders. With a few exceptions, they organized themselves in patrilineages—lineage groups organized along lines of descent from father to son. Relationships were based on blood ties, and each person traced his or her descent to three groups. First, a person belonged to the smallest social unit known as *uno*, or house. This was a natural family, consisting of a man, his wife or wives, and their children. The second group was the *umunna*, or lineage, composed of a number of related houses. Finally, a group of lineages formed a compact village or town, *obodo*. This was the highest territorially defined authority of the Igbo. A town or compact village was sometimes named after its founder, or after a striking geographical feature that best described its location. It might also be named after the most important sociological circumstances that surrounded its foundation. It is important to recognize that the members of a lineage were blood relatives and that each lineage was a semi-autonomous unit within a town. Each house, lineage, and town was headed by a headman, *onyisi*, who acquired the position by virtue of his age. Town meetings were usually held in the town square, but the most important lineage and house meetings were held in the *obi* (meeting shed) of the most senior elders. Interaction between towns was limited and was regulated by goodwill, mutual respect, and diplomacy. Wars often broke out when these failed.

CROSS-CUTTING TIES

The Igbo communities were known as extremely democratic, yet they had no centralized governments. How, then, did they achieve democracy?

The Igbo subscribed to the principle of direct participation in government. Their entire social and political structures revolved around the idea of cross-cutting ties. The five most important cross-cutting institutions were the councils of elders, age-groups, councils of chiefs, women's associations, and secret societies. Without them, the Igbo society would be starved of its essence and would disintegrate. As we shall presently see, the traditional Igbo communities did indeed fall apart in the twentieth century when the Europeans destroyed their cross-cutting ties in the process of colonial rule.

COUNCIL OF ELDERS

Matters affecting lineage members were discussed at the meetings of its elders, *ndisi* or *indichie*, with the assistance of the adult members of the lineage. In inter-lineage disputes, elders from the affected lineages met to discuss solutions, with the oldest man in the gathering presiding.

The authority of the lineage head derived from the group's respect for him as the oldest living representative of the founding ancestors. He was the custodian of ancestral lands, the keeper of the ritual objects that symbolized political authority, and the group's spiritual and temporal head. Even though he was the religious, executive, and judicial head of his lineage, he would not act without their approval. No action would be taken until an issue had been fully argued at a lineage meeting and some degree of consensus achieved.

AGE-GROUPS

An age-group association, known as *ogbo* or *otu*, was composed of men (or women) who were of about the same age. All residents of a town born within a few years of each other belonged to the same age-group, with separate sections for men and women. The association was named after a major event that was taking place at the time of its members' birth. For example, there were the Biafran War age-group, *ogbo aya Biafra* (those born between 1967 and 1970), the Second World War age-group, *ogbo aya Hitler* (1939–1945), and the influenza age-group, *ogbo ifelunza* (1918–1921). The exact age-span in an age-group varied from town to town, but the most common were the three and five-year intervals.

The age-group system enabled societies without written records to remember past events. It also helped them assign special duties and responsibilities to the different segments of the community, in accordance with the principle of seniority.

The junior age-groups (age 15 and below) did minor jobs like fetching water, cleaning footpaths, sweeping the streets and town squares, and running errands.

Men in the middle age-groups (from about age 16 to about 40) formed the fighting forces. If five years separated one age-group from the next, there would be up to five distinct age-groups in this category. In the event of a war, each age-group acted as a separate regiment, under a leader who belonged to an older age-group. The middle age-groups also felled trees and cleared the bush at the beginning of each planting season. They functioned as the executive arm of the government and would apprehend fugitives, for example. After marriage, young women would become active in the appropriate women's association (see below).

The senior male age-groups (those aged 40 and above) were responsible for judicial matters. They usually decided when a town should go to war, how an offender should be punished, when the various agricultural cycles would open and close, and when the annual festivals would be held.

The age-group system promoted respect. Juniors deferred to seniors and expected the same treatment when they advanced to higher grades. The members of a group acted together, and the friendships they cultivated in childhood remained intact throughout life.

THE ACQUISITION OF TITLES AND THE COUNCIL OF CHIEFS

The Igbo people emphasized personal achievement; hereditary succession to titles would have contradicted notions of leadership and fair play. Some Igbo men managed to acquire prestigious titles, enabling them to be acknowledged as great men or chiefs. Titled chiefs formed their own councils and represented their communities to outsiders.

Most Igbo men eagerly sought admission into the council of chiefs, but not all could succeed. Every Igbo man began his life as an apprentice. A young boy accompanied his father or uncle to the farm and rendered as much assistance as he could. As he grew older he learned that marriage, wealth, and the acquisition of titles enabled individuals to advance socially. Until a man was initiated into certain titles, he could not dress in certain ways, or wear hats of certain colors, or shake hands in certain ways, or take a piece of kola nut before other people.

Titles cost money; only men with exceptional abilities and good luck ever bought all the available titles. The taking of the higher titles demanded the payment of expensive initiation fees, accompanied by elaborate feasting and dancing. Throughout Igboland, a man who failed to progress beyond the most junior titles was a man without status in the eyes of his people. Whatever his age, they looked upon him as a boy. His age mates might make him run errands for them. In Awka he might be termed *agbala*, a woman. In Illah, he was taunted, *isi igwu*, meaning, 'head full of lice,' or 'louse breeder.' When he died, they buried him without dignity, and the mourning period was brief. Status attainment was clearly linked to the acquisition of wealth through hard work.

The highest title in many Igbo communities (and the one alluded to in Okonkwo's village) was *ozo* (or any of its variants: *eze, nze, alo,* and *ichie*). To qualify for the *ozo* title, a man must have acquired the junior titles and discharged all the duties normally assigned to members of the junior title groups. He must have accumulated enough wealth and completed the ceremonies connected with the second burial of his father. Thus, no man could attain a status that might equal or exceed his father's while the latter was still alive.

The Igbo believed that no man could inherit immortality; it must be acquired through a process of title-taking called *ichi-echichi*, 'to secure the breath of life', to attain immortality or godship. The Igbo word *chi* represents invisible forces, spirits, and personal gods; it is the root of such words as Chukwu (God), *ichie*, an immortal or a titled person, and *ndi ichie*, title holders.

Only men who achieved this ritual death and resurrection could attain immortality; an *ozo* man was a person who had received the gift of immortality. He was no longer an ordinary human, but a god. To purchase the highest title was, therefore, to be born again, to be admitted into the association of rulers, *otu ochichi*, and to be initiated into the cult of the ancestors, *otu ndichie*.

At the secular level, the highest title spared its holder the indignity of manual labor. It guaranteed him a seat in the council of chiefs. It reserved for him portions of fees paid by new initiates into the title association and gave him rights to certain portions of livestock slaughtered in his lineage. A titled man was greeted with high-sounding salutations such as *igwe* (His Highness) and *ogbu efi* (he who slaughters bulls). The *ozo* title lost its appeal in the twentieth century when colonial officers stripped traditional Igbo chiefs of their power and then subordinated them to British-appointed warrant chiefs and Western-educated Africans.

WOMEN'S ASSOCIATIONS

Igbo women had their own clubs, age-group associations, and title associations that complemented those of men. Women controlled certain spheres of community life, just as men controlled other spheres. Women were perceived to possess superior spiritual well-being and headed many of the traditional cults and shrines. In Achebe's novel, for example, the oracle is served by a priestess.

Women also gained status by amassing wealth through trading, farming, or weaving, and were treated as *ndi ogalanya*, wealthy persons. In certain districts, wealthy women married other women, and 'fathered' their own children.

Like an Igbo man, every Igbo woman began her life as an apprentice. From a very young age a girl assisted her mother at home, on the farm, or in the marketplace. As she grew older she learned from experience that hard work, marriage, and membership of certain associations enabled women to advance socially. One of the most important women's associations was *otu omu* (the Omu society), headed by a female functionary, known as Omu. The desire to join this prestigious association acted as an incentive for hard work and thrift, for only women who had enough wealth to pay for the initiation ceremonies were admitted. The members of the Omu society acted as a pressure group in political matters and imposed fines on men and women who disturbed the peace of the marketplace. They punished quarrelsome women and those who broke certain taboos, like those prohibiting incest and adultery. It was perilous for any man, no matter how influential, to provoke the anger of this association.

The leaders of the Omu society attended the meetings of the councils of chiefs and elders and participated in discussions affecting the welfare of the citizens. Though they would not themselves take part in wars, they could decide when to urge the male warrior chiefs to start one.

The Omu society, and several other women's associations, acted as checks and balances in the social and political organization of Igbo communities. The *otu umu ada* was an association of women born to a lineage or town, while *otu inyeme di* was an association of women married to the men of a lineage or town. In theory, every married woman belonged to both associations, while an unmarried woman belonged only to *otu umu ada*. Whereas men participated in the politics of their home towns alone, women exercised influence in the politics of both their home towns and the towns of their marriage.

Of special importance was the control women exercised over local trade. In the Igbo world view, a marketplace was not simply a place to buy and sell goods; it was also a ritual, political, and social center. The power women exercised over the organization of local trade derived from the fact that most local traders were women. They alone could best serve the needs of those who converged in the marketplace for commercial and other purposes. Caravans of long-distance traders made their way to local markets, often accompanied by a large number of noncommercial specialists, such as the agents of important oracles, smiths, carvers, priests, diviners, and doctors. Although most long-distance traders were men, their prosperity depended upon the careful regulation of local markets. Igbo women's associations upheld gender balance and equality. Their political and social activities were very useful, though men occasionally felt they were contentious.

SECRET SOCIETIES

Some secret societies were exclusively for men, some for women, and others for both sexes. Very little is known about the secret societies because the men and women who joined them took their oath of secrecy very seriously. Besides, the Igbo were averse to divulging information that might hinder the effectiveness of their secret societies; many of them functioned as the mouthpieces of ancestors, oracles, and spirits. In important judicial matters, masked ancestors (the *egwugwu*, or *egungun*) might appear and pronounce a verdict. In Chapter Ten of *Things Fall Apart*, for example, we see the *egwugwu* emerge to hear a series of legal cases. When that happened, no one contested their judgment, because no one could pretend to be wiser than the ancestors or the spirits. And no one ever disclosed the identity of the individual behind the mask, even if he happened to recognize the voice or the walk of a particular elder.

IGBO MARRIAGE CUSTOMS

Marriage also served to bring households, lineages, and even towns together. The Igbo regarded it as the cornerstone of their whole social structure. Discussions leading to marriage were taken seriously, and they involved not just the immediate families of the bride and groom but also their entire lineages. The Igbo believed that every adult male and female must marry and build their own household. They valued children very highly, and marriage was a requisite first step towards bringing them into the world.

The key unit of agricultural production was the household. In the absence of mechanization, the size of a household was crucial in providing enough labor. Realizing that monogamy was a sure avenue to poverty, most husbands practiced polygamy. If a man failed to act promptly to increase the size of his household, his wife might bring additional wives to him.

Having several women in a household enhanced not only a man's status but also the prestige of the first wife. As the head woman of the household, she shared every title that the man might acquire. She presided over household deliberations, most men preferring not to get personally involved, except in emergencies. Junior wives enjoyed the security and prosperity that large households provided. In addition, Igbo women had rights and freedoms that they jealously guarded. They lived in their own separate houses, cooked for themselves, and raised their own children. They grew crops, part of which they sold in the marketplace, and kept the proceeds. Moreover, Igbo laws and customs permitted an unhappy wife to leave.

Igbo Religion

The line that separated the religious life from the secular in Igbo culture was as thin as air. The Igbo believed in the Supreme Being (Chukwu) and in life after death. Chukwu lived far away in the sky; he was the origin of all things and directed the activities of all things. The names the Igbo gave their children expressed these beliefs. For example, an Igbo family might name a baby Amaogechukwu ('God's time is the best'), or Chukwukelu ('God is the creator'), or Chukwunyelu ('God gave me this wonderful gift').

Moreover, Igbo proverbs, folk tales, and incantations testified to their belief in the existence of God. Since nothing happened by chance, everything—good health or illness, fortune or misfortune— was attributed to the will of God. They also believed that one must live in peace with one's ancestors to be rewarded with good health, good luck and many children. Misfortune and untimely death were consequences of living in disharmony with the higher beings.

Igbo people had no symbols of Chukwu because no one knew what he looked like. They rarely kept special altars or shrines for his worship, since he was everywhere at the same time. Every transgression was ultimately an offense against him, and they constantly prayed that those trespasses that they might unknowingly have committed be forgiven them. The Igbo people nursed a deep reverence for the mysterious nature of Chukwu. They were not sure how to approach him, but they knew that he was a spirit and that those who worshipped him must do so in spirit. They therefore communed with him through the major spirits and ancestors.

The Igbo also believed in the existence of the Ekwensu, the equivalent of Satan, whose prime occupation was to lead people astray. Ekwensu had several servants who helped him carry out his evil thoughts. One of them was death itself, the malicious being who would visit a man on the day he enjoyed life the most.

Ekwensu used people to commit crimes against other people and would then turn around and punish the same people who served him. Ekwensu was Chukwu's principal enemy and at the same time his faithful servant. Acting on the powers bestowed on him by Chukwu, he would cause an evil doer to suffer or die in a strange manner. Should a man meet with an unexpected misfortune, it was a punishment for some crime he had committed. The crime might have escaped the attention of his neighbors but not the watchful eyes of the higher forces. Until a sinner atoned for a transgression he might not even remember committing, he remained in a state of conflict with the higher forces, who would punish him continuously. When a person felt disturbed by certain inexplicable misfortunes, he would approach a diviner, who might recommend that the unseen forces be propitiated. Fear of unconsciously offending the higher beings was responsible for the large number of propitiation rites.

The Igbo also approached the higher forces when they wanted special favors. Should a family want to have many children, it would approach a diviner who might recommend some sacrificial offerings. Sacrifice was an important element in Igbo religious ceremony.

Igbo people had a wide range of spirit symbols that often took the form of natural phenomena. Among these were spirits of the rivers, streams, lakes, rain, hills, caves, lightning, iron, the farm, the earth, strength, fertility, and witchcraft. A spirit symbol might have its own priest or priestess. Certain professions had their own patron gods who assisted them in their endeavors. A patron god might be connected to rain making, hunting, farming, trading, or iron working. For example, by offering the right sacrifices, prayers and invocations, a rain maker could persuade the rain god to produce rain.

Rivers, streams, lakes, and rain had life-sustaining qualities, and symbolized purity, cleanliness, coolness, freshness, fertility, and longevity. The water spirits were important deities. With water, the Igbo washed away evil and uncleanness. Important cleansing rituals were performed near, or in, rivers and streams.

The most dreaded spirits were associated with fire (*oku*) and thunder (*amadioha* or *akpala*). Fire symbolized raging flames, burning heat, burning forests, dryness, drought, bad harvest, high fever, miscarriage in pregnant women, and death. When a community indulged in excessive sin, its territory might become a fiery surface, and humans, livestock and plants might die. Only qualified doctors could cool the land again.

Any object could be turned into an object of worship if consecrated. Even after its consecration, the object would never acquire the qualities of a god, nor would it ever become a god; instead it would become a religious object, assuming the name of the spirit it represented. Its power would depend on the strength of the spirit that lived in it. A body of water, a piece of metal, a stone, or even a piece of bone might serve as an object of worship; however, it is not the stone or bone that is being worshipped; but rather the spirit that it represented. Many outsiders have jumped to the conclusion that the object is the god itself.

The most common object of worship was *ikenga*, a wooden carving, that symbolized a man's strength and success, distinguished by its prominent horns. Anyone could buy an *ikenga* in the marketplace and have a qualified priest invoke the right spirit into it, after which it would acquire the strength of the spirit it held. Until the necessary act of invocation had been performed, it remained a mere object. Every Igbo household had an *ikenga*. A man never parted with his *ikenga*, although he might replace one destroyed by fire, for example. He consulted his *ikenga* before he embarked on any project, and he would offer libation in its name whenever he served palm wine in his house.

Of equal standing was a man's personal god, *chi*. *Chi* was similar to the Christian concept of a guardian angel. A person's *chi* followed him or her throughout life, and could be either benevolent or malignant. A person with a good *chi* was always successful in his or her endeavors, while a person with a bad *chi* was an unfortunate person, who would labor without reaping.

The Igbo people did not believe that a man's *chi* controlled his entire destiny. No matter how 'good' his *chi* was, a person would achieve success only if he worked hard and led an upright life. They emphasized the importance of hard work in the saying 'If a person says "yes", that person's *chi* says "yes".' In addition, the Igbo believed that diviners and other medicine men and women could intervene on behalf of an unfortunate person to change his or her malignant *chi* into a benevolent one. Most private prayers, sacrifices, and invocations were directed toward chasing off misfortune and keeping oneself in a state of harmony with one's *chi*.

At the group level, one of the chief deities of the Igbo people was Ani, the earth deity, the great mother goddess, and the spirit of fertility. Every lineage and, indeed, every homestead had a shrine dedicated to her. Ani had her own special priestesses, who played leading roles in many aspects of community life. They officiated during all religious ceremonies that concerned Ani and presided over all matters involving crime against the earth goddess. Their presence was vital when matters concerning incest, birth, death, and burial were being discussed. The ultimate resting place for all men and women who had led a good life was in the bosom of Ani. On the other hand, all men and women who practiced witchcraft or died a shameful death, including those who committed suicide, had no place in Ani's abode. Usually their corpses were left unburied in the 'bad bush.'

Like some other belief systems, the entire religious system of the Igbo people revolved around the idea of birth, death, and reincarnation. The Igbo believed that when elders died their spirits did not go away for good, but prowled unseen, looking after the welfare of the living members of the lineage. An elder would pour libations to his departed forebears before he drank his palm wine. He would also give a piece of kola nut in their name as he asked for their protection and guidance. The Igbo often offered animal sacrifices in the names of departed ancestors. If a baby boy was born soon after the death of his grandfather, this child could have been no other person than the old man reincarnated and might be named Nnamdi or Nnadi ('Father is back'). If a baby girl was born soon after the death of her grandmother, she might be named Nnenna.

The Igbo people believed that infants could also be reincarnated, but these babies usually put their parents through unnecessary pain. Babies often died soon after birth only to come back again to the same parents, as a result of which they were called *ogbanje*, meaning those who 'come and go.' Some women were known to have lost up to five children, none of them living long enough to witness the birth of the next child. To break this circle of birth and death, a diviner would have to be consulted. In Achebe's novel, Ezinma's mother has buried nine of her ten children; she is desperately afraid that Ezinma too will prove to be an *ogbanje*.

THE ENIGMA OF TWINSHIP

Until the beginning of the twentieth century, the Igbo threw away twin babies soon after they were born. People today are very reluctant to talk about it, for they cannot explain why they often prayed to God (Chukwu) for many children, yet when twins or triplets were born, the infants were left in the forest to die. This was not an Igbo phenomenon alone, however. Many African groups regarded the birth of twins as supernaturally charged and took different steps to deal with it. For example, the San people of southern Africa would destroy one or both babies. Among the Ashanti, the babies would be forfeited to the chief; their parents would place them in a brass basin, and then carry them to the chief's palace soon after birth. On the other hand, twins born into the royal family were killed at once to prevent the confusion and turmoil their birth might cause in terms of succession and inheritance.

The Igbo believed that there was something abnormal and mystical about twins. When people ask for rain, they do not expect a flood; twin birth represented excessive fertility and had to be kept in check. After leaving the babies in the bush to die, the mother would undergo extensive rituals intended to prevent her from bearing more twins. If appropriate measures were not immediately taken, not only the parents of twins but the entire community might suffer harm.

HOMICIDE

Spilling the blood of a townsman or townswoman was a serious offense against the earth goddess. However, criminal justice systems varied, especially in regard to how law breakers were punished. For example, whereas most Igbo groups would hang a murderer, in certain towns a husband who killed his wife was hanged, while a woman who killed her husband was not. In some towns a woman who killed her co-wife was not hanged, because both women belonged to the same man.

If a murder occurred in precolonial times, certain age-groups might seize the property of the murderer and destroy his house. If he ran away, they might hold his relatives hostage until the murderer was brought in and hanged. In other areas, if a murderer escaped, a waiting period of three or more years was allowed, after which his lineage paid a fine and gave one of their daughters to the family of the dead man. These examples demonstrate the Igbo people's abhorrence for blood-letting. Accidental homicide might attract a lighter punishment, but no killing ever went unpunished. Of equal importance was the principle that restitution must be made to the victim's relatives.

Killing was permitted only during war, but combatants made every effort to keep casualties to the minimum. Even in war, killing another was a transgression against the earth goddess, Ani. Cutting off the heads of one's enemies, practiced by certain Igbo groups and bragged about by Okonkwo in the novel, was neither accepted nor practiced by the majority of Igbo people. When men returned from war, they performed elaborate cleansing rituals before they could rejoin their lineages. Homicide was only one item in a long list of acts treated as abomination, *nso*. When an act of abomination was committed, a qualified doctor had to be brought in at once to remove it. An offender, together with his or her kin group and the wider community, would remain in a state of ritual turbulence until these rituals were completed.

IGBO ORACLES

Straddling the religious and secular worlds were the Igbo oracles. Oracles were religious shrines that discharged both judicial and oracular functions and acted as centers for divination. They received messages from dead relatives and passed them on to the living. They explained to curious relatives why a person had died. They warned individuals and whole communities about impending danger and offered advice on ritual matters. A community might consult an oracle if disturbed by a high death rate, or an unduly high rate of twin births, or successive bad harvests. Oracles also acted as courts of appeal in judicial matters. Individuals might take their dispute to an oracle if they failed to reconcile their differences. If a man felt that he had been wrongfully accused of a crime, he might take the matter to an oracle, who might exonerate him or confirm the guilt.

Oracles were feared and respected for miles around; one example was that of the Aro oracle, known to Europeans as the Long Juju. The Aro oracle was consulted by traders from many areas to settle business disputes. Oracles were housed in secret groves, surrounded by thick bush. The home of an oracle was a forbidden territory, for the Igbo believed that anyone who saw an oracle would surely die. Only the chief priestess (or priest) ever looked upon the face of the oracle; supplicants never approached an oracle directly. The chief priestess of an oracle served as the mouthpiece of the deity that dwelt in the shrine. Her words were final in all matters, because the forces she represented were higher than all secular powers. To disobey the orders of the priestess was to disobey the deity she represented. The chief priestess might combine her oracular services with other vocations like trading or farming. She and her agents received gifts of money, foodstuffs, and livestock for their services, and they might demand certain sacrifices as well.

The Igbo believed that their oracles would offer impartial decisions in judicial matters. So great was the confidence they reposed in their oracles that they would willingly pay large sums of money to consult them and accept whatever verdict they might pronounce. Most of the agents of the oracles traveled far and wide as medicine men, diviners, traders, smiths, or carvers. They used their knowledge of the communities they visited to direct litigants to the oracles they represented.

Up to this point, I have presented a rather generalized description of Igbo society before the coming of the Europeans. We must remember that the Igbo clans were numerous and autonomous, and there were many variations in culture and political systems deriving from their relative isolation from one another and their different relations with such neighboring kingdoms as Benin, Igala, Ijo, Efik, and Urhobo. What one town permitted might be forbidden in another. Despite these variations, the Igbo people shared certain basic cultural attributes that set them apart from other groups in West Africa. Isolation ceased to be a factor in the twentieth century, following the spread of wage labor and the construction of motor roads and railway lines, but even before that external influence intensified when Igboland was flooded with European immigrants and their African employees. In the pages that follow we examine how the European presence drastically modified Igbo society.

The Igbo People Meet the Europeans:
The Era of Informal Empire

The Igbo people's meeting with the Europeans in the nineteenth century would change their history. European slave traders had exported substantial numbers of Igbo people from the Bight of Biafra to the New World. Nonetheless, no European had penetrated the interior of Igboland before 1830.

The events that led to the establishment of a European presence in Igboland were tied to the politics of abolition. Realizing that the slave trade was no longer consistent with their economic interests, the British, who had dominated the trade, championed the movement that eventually brought it to a close. While the abolition debate raged on, however, certain interest groups in Europe and America formed societies to push European cultural, commercial, and political influence into the African interior. One of the most famous was the African Association, which sponsored many expeditions into Africa. Expeditions such as those led by Mungo Park, Hugh Clapperton, and Richard and John Lander reassured the British public that the Niger River emptied itself into the Atlantic Ocean and that European traders had done business in the coastal towns at the mouth of the river for over three centuries. Encouraged by these successes, the British government and private organizations sent further expeditions up the Niger River to establish contacts with the Africans of that region. These Niger expeditions were undertaken by missionaries and traders, sometimes accompanied by government officials.

Between 1832 and 1854, expeditions up the Niger River risked devastation by tropical diseases. The West African interior came to be described as the 'white man's grave'. The expeditions continued despite these risks. In 1854 medical workers confirmed that the use of quinine minimized death from malaria, and other advances in medicine and technology facilitated further European penetration.

The increasing European demand for palm oil and an expanding African demand for imported European goods encouraged the British to establish trading posts in Aboh, Onitsha, and Lokoja in 1857. Pleased with the booming trade, some Igbo communities invited European traders and missionaries to come and live among them.

Friendly relations began to crumble after 1875, however, when the palm oil business entered a long period of economic depression. Palm oil prices fell in Europe while the prices of manufactured goods were on the rise, leading to trade disputes between European and African traders. Conflict also developed around the question of security on the Niger. African chiefs had developed a system of trade that guaranteed peace along the Niger River and on the mainland. The chiefs of the various states collected tolls, duties, or tributes from passing traders; European traders initially paid the tributes because they needed the protection of local chiefs. When British gunboats began to ply the Niger River more frequently in the 1880s, however, European traders began to refuse to pay these tolls, arguing that the chiefs did not provide adequate protection. The chiefs relaxed security, and some private citizens took advantage of the situation to organize widespread robberies, sometimes attacking European trading posts and vessels. Obviously, such actions and the retaliation they often provoked strained relationships and generated violence along the river. This period is often described in terms of 'gunboat diplomacy'.

For some time the British government ignored the appeal of British traders for military assistance. In October 1879, however, in response to a complaint that some citizens of Onitsha had attacked British citizens, the British War Office authorized Captain Burr to bombard the town. Captain Burr anchored the warship *Pioneer* midstream and opened fire. After bombarding Onitsha for two days, Captain Burr led his men into the town, where they 'destroyed every object' they could find. The warriors of Onitsha bravely defended their town but were no match for the better-armed British.

The British justified their action on the grounds that the chiefs were unable to control their subjects, and that it was appropriate for British 'moral force' to curb acts of violence against British subjects. Again in 1883, three British warships shelled and destroyed Aboh, on the charge that some Aboh citizens had attacked a British trader.

THE MISSIONARY FACTOR

Having protected its traders with warships, the British government could no longer ignore the plight of its missionaries, who also demanded assistance. Protecting the missionaries was far more difficult, however; while traders confined their activities to the banks of the Niger River, Christian missionaries carried their propaganda further inland, provoking indignation among the inhabitants.

The role of Christian missionaries in the conquest of Africa is sometimes underestimated. Missionaries were the first foreigners to venture inland in fairly large numbers, and their accounts of what they found helped stimulate imperial ambitions. Such missionaries played an important role in the establishment of British domination over the Igbo people.

The first Christian missionaries to work in Igboland were agents of the Church Missionary Society (CMS), a branch of the Anglican Church. The CMS established a mission at Onitsha in 1857, and soon after in Alenso, Asaba, and other neighbouring towns. They subsequently opened more stations within a forty-mile radius of Onitsha and Asaba. The fiercest conflicts between the Igbo people and the Europeans raged throughout that same region, conflicts that form the backdrop of Achebe's classic novel.

CMS missionaries were soon joined in the Onitsha and Asaba areas by two different Roman Catholic societies, the Holy Ghost Fathers and the priests of the Société des Missions Africaines (SMA). The Holy Ghost Fathers worked in Igboland east of the Niger River, while the SMA worked on the area west of the river. The CMS worked on both sides of the river. The three most memorable missionaries of that period were Reverend Samuel Ajayi Crowther of the CMS, Father Joseph Shanahan of the Holy Ghost Fathers, and Father Carlo Zappa of the SMA. It is interesting to note that many of the most effective CMS missionaries were in fact Africans. Rev. John Christopher Taylor was an Igbo man, born in Sierra Leone to freed slave parents. Rev. Crowther, later appointed bishop, was a former Yoruba slave. The Roman Catholics, on the other hand, relied entirely on European priests for their missionary work.

The Igbo had adopted a conciliatory stance in their early dealings with the missionaries, because the Igbo religion was pacific and the Igbo themselves respected the religious views of other people. The Igbo usually listened patiently to the Christians and then expected the missionaries to pay equal attention to their own viewpoints. Some Igbo saw the missionaries as essentially harmless, and shrugged at the uncomprehending priests who fraternized with outcasts and gainlessly occupied themselves with preaching.

Yet, if necessary, missionaries were prepared to destroy the entire system of Igbo customs and beliefs in order to convert the people to Christianity. Bishop Crowther himself saw Igbo society as evil, his ministry as a battle between light and darkness. Father Zappa criticized the 'foolishness' of following the religion of their forefathers. Father Shanahan described his mission as a battle against a 'baffling brick wall of failure'. Most missionaries painted ghastly pictures of Igbo society, which they sent back to Europe, and incited European governments and traders against the Igbo.

Missionaries expected British colonial agents to protect them, and, ignoring possible provocation, the British raided many Igbo towns on the grounds that they had harassed the missionaries. Some foreign missionaries actually provided strategic information about the villages where they worked for colonial armies on punitive expeditions. Encouraged by the British military presence, missionaries intensified their attack on Igbo customs. The new converts themselves became bolder and more intractable.

It took the Igbo a long while to realize that the missionaries were more dangerous than they appeared. In Obosi, the chiefs accosted Bishop Crowther and protested the tendency of the Christians to ignore the objects of worship of their forefathers, to kill and eat sacred snakes and fishes, and to pull down objects of worship and shrines. The chiefs demanded that Christian converts should confess the wrongs done to Igbo gods, pay for the damage, and promise not to repeat those wrongs in the future. In Alenso they murdered several Christians; in Illah and other villages to the south they burned down churches and drove the Christians away. Feeling cornered between missionary intransigence and a reckless imperial drive, the Igbo people fought back.

At this point, we can see a vicious cycle: the forces of the British Royal Company responded to these acts of violence with greater violence. The Royal Niger Company agreed to give official protection to Christians and to attack local communities who threatened them. Incited by missionary complaints that the people of Asaba still practiced human sacrifice, for example, Company forces raided Asaba in 1888 and destroyed half of it.

Despite their official backing, and their initial welcome, the first Christian missionaries made slow progress in Igboland. They had encountered a strong traditionalist society prepared to defend its customs.

The British Annexation of Igboland: The Era of Formal Empire

The actual British conquest of Igboland began in January 1900, following a growing intervention in Igbo affairs. The bombardments of Onitsha and Aboh in 1879 and 1883, respectively, had been authorized to protect British traders, and the destruction of half of Asaba in 1888 was intended to protect Christians. It was only in 1900 that the British imperial government declared Igboland a protectorate and embarked upon formal conquest.

IGBO RESISTANCE TO COLONIAL RULE: THE EKUMEKU MOVEMENT

Some Igbo communities rejected British annexation and backed this up by preparing for war. Even before colonial rule was imposed, many Western Igbo towns had suffered economic, military, and political decline as a result of the combined activities of British traders, imperial agents, and Christian missionaries. This may well explain why the earliest and the fiercest military clashes took place in Western Igboland. Many of these battles were fought under the umbrella of the Ekumeku movement.

Western Igbo communities launched the Ekumeku movement in 1898 to resist the disintegration of their society and to halt the advance of British imperialism. The Ekumeku wars were not a sudden outburst but the climax of a long period of political disturbances touched off by British cultural, commercial, and political ambitions on the Niger. Organized under the leadership of a union of titled chiefs, the movement achieved 'a far-flung coalition' against British military pressure. The Ekumeku warriors were young men, drawn from the town clubs and secret societies. They accepted silence and guerrilla tactics as their military strategies. Only men who took the oath of secrecy enrolled for service. Summoned through coded messages, they held their meetings in secret places. They selected several targets and attacked them simultaneously, creating panic among the European and Christian communities. They earned the nickname 'the Silent Ones' because of the unique way they silently carried out their activities. The Western Igbo resistance was finally crushed in 1914.

RESISTANCE MOVEMENTS EAST OF THE NIGER RIVER: THE ARO EXPEDITION

British operations in Eastern Igboland began in 1901. The best documented of these operations was the Aro expedition of 1901–02. The Aro were great traders and entrepreneurs, and had long met the needs of the hinterland peoples for imported European goods. They commanded widespread influence and respect among their neighbors, both because of their commercial expertise, and because of the role that the Aro oracle played in the judicial systems of the region. These economic interests motivated the Aro trading chiefs to unite several Igbo towns and to finance a war of resistance against Britain.

British activities in the Niger Delta and in the Cross River estuary had destroyed the communities with whom the Aro did business. For example, the Efik chiefs of the Cross River valley suffered a severe loss of trade and prestige as a result of the British intrusion. In the Niger Delta, British military forces destroyed Brass and treacherously kidnapped King Jaja of Opobo, exiling him to the West Indies. The vibrant commercial city-state of Opobo then entered a decline from which it never recovered. One finds a direct relationship between British incursions and the eclipse of the indigenous entrepreneurial classes in southeastern Nigeria. The British intention was to subordinate African business interests to European interests, as had happened during the era of the Atlantic slave trade; it was the refusal of Nigerian communities to accept that subordinate position that precipitated further military intervention.

Having defeated the Niger Delta and Cross River estuary communities, the British moved further inland to confront the Aro in 1901.

They destroyed the Long Juju oracle and went on to punish neigh-boring Igbo communities. Somewhat surprisingly, it was neither the Aro nor the dreaded Abam warriors who put up the strongest resis-tance to the British. Other Igbo communities engaged the colonial forces in a running battle that lasted until after the First World War.

THE CONSOLIDATION OF BRITISH RULE IN IGBOLAND

British officials recognized that administering the Igbo people would be even more difficult than conquering them. The greatest challenge was how to rule the hundreds of Igbo towns and villages that recog-nized no centralized governments. In the Muslim parts of Northern Nigeria, by contrast, the British maintained much of the structure of the pre-existing Sokoto Caliphate; they simply reinforced the power and authority of the ruling classes of *emirs*, and then governed through them. But Igbo political structures were fragmented and small in scale; British officials could not comprehend the democratic genius of Igbo political organization, and felt more comfortable with the familiar hierarchies of kingdoms and empires.

Shortly after the British conquest of Igboland, officials moved to set up a system of African courts. Their aim was to replace indigenous institutions with a new structure of appointed officials called 'war-rant chiefs—so-called because their sole legitimacy derived from a colonial legal document, the warrant. These warrant chiefs and the British resident commissioners made bylaws and regulated local affairs. They controlled the local police and punished anyone who resisted colonial rule. These men were the tools with which the colo-nial government hoped to centralize the autonomous political insti-tutions of the Igbo.

The system of warrant chiefs and native courts introduced dra-matic changes into Igbo society. The laws that set them up brushed aside traditional judicial institutions. Cases that should have been decided by lineage and village elders—for example, Okonkwo's pun-ishment for manslaughter in Achebe's novel—would now be tried by strangers. The district officers who controlled these native courts might have been trained in English law, but they had little or no knowledge of native laws and customs. As a result, many of their decisions contradicted Igbo ideas of justice.

The Igbo people protested against the warrant chief and native court systems, but their protests resulted only in punitive expeditions. The crisis came to a head in the late 1920s, when the British extended the principle of direct taxation into the 'untaxed provinces' of south-ern Nigeria. This policy sparked anti-tax riots in 1927–28, and the famous Aba women's riots of 1929. These widespread protests ulti-mately compelled the colonial administration to reorganize the native authority government in the 1930s and 1940s, leading to an improved system of native administration. British officials finally recognized that the poorly trained, and mostly illiterate, warrant chiefs, together with their small army of court clerks and messengers, could not be relied upon to collect taxes and discharge a host of administrative and judicial functions. Tied more closely to indigenous political institutions, the new administrative system remained operative until 1952, when it gave way to a regional government system that paved the way for constitutional reform and prepared Nigerians for political independence. In October 1960, the Igbo people joined other Nigerians in celebrating national independence.

Conclusions

The ancient Igbo communities were similar to other peoples who lived in the difficult environments of the premodern world. Their major preoccupations were to live free from crime and sickness, to live in harmony with unseen higher forces, to live in peace with themselves and their neighbors, to have many children and grandchildren, and to produce enough food. Some observers may argue that the Igbo methods were primitive, forgetting that the methods that other societies adopted were equally primitive. We must remember that the England, France, and Russia of today are totally different from the England, France, and Russia of five hundred years ago, just as Igboland of today is totally different from premodern Igboland. The careful reader should avoid making false comparisons between premodern African societies and modern European and American societies.

Still, it is quite striking how rapidly the Igbo people, despite their attachment to their customs, succumbed to European civilization. The fact that it took barely a hundred years (1857—1960) for the British to tear apart a society that had taken thousands of years to evolve suggests that European colonialism was a potent agent of change. Even more puzzling is the speed with which Christianity and Western education swept the Igbo people off their feet. In the long run, even those chiefs and community leaders who had organized and financed the wars of resistance converted to Christianity and helped the missionaries build schools and churches.

One explanation for this sudden rush to embrace Western civilization is that the Igbo were quick to perceive the importance of Western education in the new colonial structure. A second explanation is that the Igbo people were, and still are, often very eager to accept change. A third is that, as the ties that bound the communities disintegrated, the Igbo found new ones in Christianity and Western education. The result is that Igboland now has an unusually high concentration of Christian and Western-educated Africans. The Igbo seek membership in school and church organizations with as much enthusiasm as their forebears sought admission into the ancient age-groups, town clubs, and title associations. Barely a hundred years ago, Igbo people could hardly read or write. Today, Igbo professors occupy important faculty positions in universities in Africa, Europe, and America. Igbo medical practitioners work in hospitals around the globe, and their scientists, engineers, lawyers, and other professionals render useful services on every continent. Obviously the Igbo people have made material progress. It remains to be seen to what extent they will continue to barter their culture for material progress and be completely devoured by Western civilization.

General Essays on Chinua Achebe

A. G. STOCK

Yeats and Achebe[†]

Perhaps human nature has always felt the need to interpret history, to find a guiding idea which makes an acceptable pattern of the past and extends it into the future. Not that any idea can change what has happened, but the pattern affects the mind that contemplates it, the more deeply the more its owner cares about the destiny of mankind. He may be lifted from passion to compassion, from anxiety to serenity; he may, in a Yeatsian phrase, be enabled to hold in a single glance reality and justice.

Christianity has one such idea of history, Marxism a different one, and both fortify their disciples by assuring them of ultimate victory. The Yeatsian idea, on the other hand, takes the bitterness out of defeat, by representing defeat as inevitable, victory as impermanent, and the contending forces as phases of a single, inexhaustible creative energy.

For Yeats the whole of potential being is a vast chaos, a 'fabulous formless darkness'. Every civilization is an ordered structure which mind builds up, the cumulative mind that is in tradition, by defining a hierarchy of values and imposing it on experience. The chaos is always beating on its walls, but is kept out so long as the hierarchy holds its own integrity—which shapes its artefacts, its speculative thought, its codes of conduct, and moulds its children by giving a language to their experience. But to define is to limit, and mind cannot be contained for ever within any one enclosed order; mind belongs also to the outer darkness. In every hierarchy there are some impulses made shameful because others are exalted, some types of personality frustrated which would have been fulfilled in a different mould, beliefs made nonsensical which could have made sense in another context of thought. In the end these negligible-seeming cracks make up the 'opposing gyre' which becomes its nemesis: they

† From *Journal of Commonwealth Literature* 5 (1968): 105–11. Reprinted by permission of SAGE.

widen, coalesce, form a breach in the walls letting in the 'mere anarchy' of the kingdom of darkness. Thus, no civilization can either
remain static or evolve for ever towards a more inclusive perfection.
It must both collapse from within and be overwhelmed from without,
and what replaces it will appear most opposite to itself, being built
from all that it overlooked or undervalued.

This in brief is the view of history that is expounded in *A Vision* and
is the frame of reference of such poems as *The Second Coming*. I
have compressed it because my theme is less Yeats's philosophy than
Achebe's first novel, *Things Fall Apart*.[1]

> Things fall apart; the centre cannot hold;
> Mere anarchy is loosed upon the world;
> The blood dimmed tide is loosed, and everywhere
> The ceremony of innocence is drowned.

It is startling to find the Yeatsian pattern traced most closely where
Yeats himself was least likely to look for it, in an imaginary but typical village of the lower Niger. Not that *Things Fall Apart* smells of dis-
cipleship; the two minds, their perspectives and their fields of vision,
are too different for that. For Yeats the pattern is an instrument of
prophecy. He looks at Europe with its two-thousand-year-old tradition of Christian civilization, which itself once made chaos of the values that preceded it and is now collapsing before the onset of
something new, something all the more frightening because it is
nameless, being all that our inherited civilization has incapacitated
us from understanding. Achebe is not interested in prophecy but in
analysing the way things happen. Nor is he primarily interested in
Europe; from the standpoint of Umuofia the western world is itself
the fabulous formless darkness. But his instrument of interpretation
is the same; his Umuofia is a civilization in miniature, and the chaos
finds its way in through slight flaws in its structure, murmurs that
might have remained inaudible if they had not found an echo in the
darkness.

Achebe's title insists on the analogy. Two things happen when it is
taken seriously: the Yeatsian idea becomes more than a subjective
fantasy, for it is seen to have validity for other minds in other contexts
and the coherence of structure and depth of analysis in the novel
become much more evident.

The first part depicts 'the ceremony of innocence' in Umuofia—
those customary ways of doing things which, because they have always
been accepted, are able to embody man's whole sense of his relationship to the present and the past, the natural and the supernatural

---

1. Chinua Achebe, *Things Fall Apart*, Wm. Heinemann, 1958.

worlds. Achebe gives some commentary, enough to make it intelligible to an outsider, but not the commentary of a social anthropologist, who would probably focus on the peculiarities of Umuofian religious beliefs till he gave the impression that they were more obsessed with the supernatural and less aware of the actual than most Europeans. He writes like a son of the tribe for whom this way of life is the norm, though wider knowledge has made him aware that it is not everyone's. The result is that in watching the procedures of seed-time and harvest, courtship and marriage and death, the reader grows into the life; he comes to accept the characteristic way (for every civilization has its own) in which the natural world is penetrated by the supernatural. Spirits mix with men at solemn festivals, they give judgement in disputes likely to endanger the unity of the tribe. The adult Umuofian knows, if he chooses to think about it, that their forms are those of respected living counsellors, but why should this make their authority any less? It would in fact be a kind of sacrilege to draw attention to it. The man, in the disguise that depersonalizes him, speaks with the supernatural wisdom of the ancestors, much as the Catholic priest saying mass ceases to be himself and becomes a channel of the divine.

The village is held together by a network of relationships, with a common recognition, much stronger than in modern European civilization, that the community is greater than the individual and is the source and means of his self-fulfilment. They do not cease on that account to be individuals; they break the law, as Okonkwo himself does, in bursts of momentary passion, but never in deliberate nonconformity. When they break it they accept the penalty. Okonkwo violates the peace of the village by pure accident when his gun kills Ezeudu's son, but although everyone knows it was an accident he never dreams of pleading special hardship or special merit against the inflexibility of the law.

Nevertheless the seeds of disintegration are there and become gradually visible. Within this general set-up, with its provision for everything and its fairly exacting discipline, the qualities commanding most respect are toughness, courage, self-reliance; without them, whatever else you may have you will not win a place of honour, for the accepted values are hard on weakness. Okonkwo's father Unoka was a failure. He had many endearing gifts; he was a flute-player of genius and a gay companion filled with the joy of life. In the whole book there is nothing so nearly lyrical as Unoka's response to the return of the sun:

> Unoka loved it all, and he loved the first kites that returned with the dry season, and the children who sang songs of welcome to them. He would remember his own childhood, how he

had wandered around looking for a kite sailing leisurely against the blue sky. As soon as he found one he would sing with his whole being, welcoming it back from its long, long journey and asking if it had brought home any lengths of cloth.

That was years ago, when he was young.[2]

A boy can be whatever he naturally is, but Unoka the grown man would not fit into the mould of Umuofia. His talents might make him a welcome guest at parties, but he was lazy and improvident and no fighter, and his son was ashamed of him. Unoka himself seems to have acquiesced in his status. He once says wistfully that the hardest of misfortunes is to fail alone when other men succeed—a remark in which there is pathos, but not rebellion. Okonkwo, however, reacts over-violently against his father's incompetence, cultivating in himself all the qualities of success and suppressing everything that is like his father. He is hard to himself and merciless to his family, and has no forbearance for the soft strain in his eldest son Nwoye.

It was not that the manners of Umuofia had no place for tenderness, but Okonkwo did not dare give way to it. There was no need for him to take part in the killing of Ikemefuna, who had been like one of his sons, except that he gloried in trampling on his private feelings in the name of public virtue. The thing is to be done, he argues, and why should I be exempt more than another? Some of his friends, who thought it would have been graceful in the circumstances for him to stay away, were perturbed by this ruthless rectitude, but Okonkwo lost no public esteem. Only his son Nwoye could not forgive the deed: he had loved Ikemefuna, and was the kind of youth to whom personal feeling meant more than public spirit, which was one reason that he was a nonentity in Umuofia. Such an outrage must have clarified the issue, making him see where he stood in relation to the ideals of his society, and prepared him for articulate revolt when the time came.

When Okonkwo was exiled he took refuge, as was right and proper, with his mother's kinsfolk. It might have been a healing experience, as his uncle Uchenda gently showed him, if he had understood how it symbolized man's need of the tender and consoling qualities which are the woman's side of his nature; but he submitted without humility, as an act of will. Consequently he was not chastened or subdued by exile, it was nothing but seven years out of his life, at the end of which, with the same unfaltering will, he returned to build his reputation in Umuofia over again.

In the meantime the Christian missionaries had arrived in the region. They made no sense to Okonkwo, but for Nwoye their teaching gave articulate expression to much that he had felt and never

2. Ibid., p. 3.

dared to think aloud; his simmering resentment of his father's harsh code, his need to be recognized and valued as a person. Nwoye was an easy convert, and Okonkwo, true to his character, disowned him.

Nwoye was not the only one. It is always the failures and misfits who are the first converts, and others like him found in Christianity the strength that springs from clear statement of their rejected values. So for the first time Umuofia, whose unity was its life, was divided against itself. How could it take common action against its own sons when a man like Okonkwo, merely for accidental breach of the peace, had gone without demur to seven years' exile?

Even then the centre might have held if all the Christians had been as tolerant and wise as Mr Brown, the first missionary to come, and none of the others as obstinate as Okonkwo. Lacking the democratic machinery of western device, Umuofia was nevertheless perfectly sensitive to the popular will and capable of accommodating minorities, and because a section of the people clearly desired the new religion it looked for a while as if it might be fitted in. But misfits, although they may be honest are seldom wise, and Mr Smith who succeeded Mr Brown was an arrogant militant, while on the other side diehards like Okonkwo were spoiling for a fight. When it came Okonkwo was happy, thinking that the destruction of the church was a victory. It appeared so in the battle of gods, but behind the church was a force they only dimly knew about—the white government, incomprehensible, uncomprehending, invincible.

To a European mind the British raj, however monstrous, is not 'mere anarchy', but Achebe's angle of vision makes it just that, as meaningless as it is invincible. No orgies of bloodshed are needed to make the point clear; it is all in the concentrated irony of the scene where the Commissioner, having arrested the six leaders by barefaced treachery without even listening to what they have to say, proceeds to harangue them:

> We have brought a peaceful administration to you and your people so that you may be happy. If any man ill-treats you we shall come to your rescue . . . [3]

They are up against a monster so powerful and so blind that it cannot see what it treads on: too powerful and too blind to be dealt with as men deal with men, and they are not its match in brute force.

When Okonkwo killed the messenger he knew he was right. He acted without hesitation like the embodiment of all the forefathers; but not a hand was raised in his support. He had too much courage to know or care to know what had dawned on all the others: that they confronted something too big for them and could only submit.

3. Ibid., p. 173.

Okonkwo, seeing that the world he belonged to was dead, went away and hanged himself.

Up to this point the story has been told so unemotionally that its impact on first reading is uncertain. One sees exactly how and why it has happened, but what it is that has happened has not fully come home. But when in a flash of insight Obierika bursts out: 'That man was one of the greatest men in Umuofia. You drove him to kill himself and now he will be buried like a dog', one suddenly realizes it. Okonkwo's end was not only that of an obstinate hero running his head against a machine too big for him, it was the end of a way of life.

The Commissioner, evidently one of the enlightened kind, knows nothing about it:

> The story of this man who had killed a messenger and hanged himself would make interesting reading. One could almost write a whole chapter on him. Perhaps not a chapter, but a reasonable paragraph at any rate.[4]

The other characters in the book are shadowy, but Okonkwo comes vividly to life in all his failings and excesses. He is also the epitome of a process: in himself he is at once the strength of Umuofia and the reason for its downfall, that imbalance in one particular direction which leaves something frustrated. 'His whole life was dominated by fear—the fear of failure and weakness.' Achebe states this as a recognizable fact, not thinking it necessary to establish the point like a psychological novelist with interior monologues and elaborately analysed incidents of childhood. The code of Umuofia might tolerate gentleness but it expected strength, and because of his father's inadequacy Okonkwo was afraid to live by his merely natural strength; he must be strong to the repression of all patience with weakness. So it came about that his own son was driven from mere mediocrity to conscious alienation, and found in the white man's religion a different code which turned his weakness into a kind of strength. But in the whole confused impact of the whites on Umuofia one element could not be taken apart from another. They have their perplexingly subversive religion, they have their total ignorance of the very meaning of tradition and reverence, they have physical force on a scale that makes them inaccessible to reason; they are in fact mere anarchy let loose on the Umuofian world.

Like Yeats, but in a very different framework of feeling, T. S. Eliot was aware

> How twenty centuries of stony sleep
> Were vexed to nightmare by a rocking cradle.

4. Ibid., p. 185.

His Magi having seen the cradle return home changed, half-citizens of a country not yet born, alienated from their own people and no longer at ease. Achebe took his next title from *The Journey of the Magi*, and translated it no less appositely into the terms of modern African society. He has assimilated the vision of history of the two most detached of the poets, accurately but not in the least subserviently. He has taken the abstract idea of a historical process out of the two thousand years of history and replanted it on African soil with no damage to its historical validity. He has stripped away the metaphysics, and Eliot's belief in the Christian revelation transcending all others for all time has vanished as completely as Yeats's doctrine of eternal recurrence and his nostalgia for the lost Hellenic world. What remains is the analysis of fact. 'This is how a historical process works in the lives of men.' Unless an abstract formula can be thus retranslated convincingly into concrete happenings, it has no place among what Aristotle called the laws of probability and necessity.

JAMES SNEAD

European Pedigrees/African Contagions: Nationality, Narrative, and Communality in Tutuola, Achebe, and Reed†

Languages are the pedigree of nations. (Samuel Johnson)

A nation, says Bloom. A nation is the same people living in the same place. . . . By God, then, says Ned, laughing, if that's so I'm a nation for I'm living in the same place for the past five years. (James Joyce, *Ulysses*)

Our true nationality is mankind. (H. G. Wells)

The unclarity about the real nature of 'African' or 'European' writing participates in a more general quandary over the indefatigable, yet ultimately indefinable word 'nation'. There is no consensus about what a nation is. Arising in the late eighteenth century, and particularly in the French Revolution, the political theory of 'nation', as developed by Diderot and Condorcet and recorded by Abbé Siéyès in 1789 ('a union of individuals governed by *one* law, and represented by the same lawgiving assembly') speaks of a collection of individuals united in supporting a perceived interest; the hierarchical or privileging connotations of 'realm', 'country', 'kingdom', 'territory', and 'race' are smelted into the usage 'nation'. Yet a purely political definition of 'nation' would seem

† From *Nation and Narration*. Ed. Homi K. Bhabha (New York: Routledge, 1990), 231–49. Copyright © 1990 by Routledge. Reproduced by permission of Taylor and Francis Books UK.

inadequate to cover the territorial and constitutional fragilities of nineteenth- and twentieth-century history. Even adding other criteria, such as 'common heritage', leaves things all too vague.

Johnson's idea of language as a nation's 'pedigree' does not so much define 'nation' in the present as call upon the already existing aura of other concepts, such as 'history' and 'race', to produce the sense that there are now lost, but recoverable, distinctions between disparate races of people. The full quote comes from Johnson's 1773 journey to the Hebrides, and it reads: 'What can a nation that has not letters tell of its original? . . . There is no tracing ancient nations but by language, and therefore I'm always sorry when language is lost, because languages are the pedigree of nations.'[1] Such a use of linguistic traits to recover a 'lost' national identity is contemporaneous with the enunciation of a German nationalist ideology by Herder and Novalis, which Fichte and Schleiermacher later heightened to a frankly metaphysical level: language and nation express aspects of Divine Truth. A 'nation' was an irreducible and original quality, an almost transcendent reality, which we could best grasp through 'mother tongue' and national literature. Schleiermacher, anticipating twentieth-century theorists such as Whorf, was among the first to suggest such a notion: 'what is cogitated in one language can never be repeated in the same way in another'.[2] In this way, whatever else a group of people had since become, its 'nationhood' could be identified backwards to its linguistic source, a relatively well-defined form of distinction.[3]

'Language' here must be taken not merely in philological and etymological terms, but also as an entire pool of resources at the disposal of narrators, from the raw materials (vocabulary and syntax, as well as the repertoire of myths, rituals, folklore), to the processing tools (formal and structural devices, such as repetition or withholding, types of address, tropes of arrangement), to considerations of narrative reception (audience composition and feedback, marketplace). At each of these stages, Johnson's 'language' can be, and often is, usurped by the prerogatives of 'nation', particularly by literary historians. It will be the aim of this article to show that, despite the intermittent adoption of black nationalist credos by some African and Afro-American writers, many African and Afro-American (and indeed, many western) narratives often aggressively out-scheme any

1. James Boswell, *Boswell's Journal of A Tour to the Hebrides With Samuel Johnson, LL.D.*, ed. Frederick A. Pottle and Charles H. Bennett (New York: Viking, 1936), '18 September 1773', p. 186.
2. Quoted in Stanley I. Benn, 'Nationalism', *The Encyclopedia of Philosophy*, ed. Paul Edwards, vol. 5 (New York: Macmillan, 1967), p. 443.
3. A modern version of this notion may be found in contemporary debates over whether to establish an 'official language' for countries such as the United States, where a shared 'mother tongue' is less and less to be taken for granted.

attempt at narrow nationalistic definition. These African and Afro-American texts exhibit a different approach to what new criticism, speaking of western European literature, often has called 'universality'. Writers in the African tradition seem inclined to display a certain linguistic and cultural eclecticism or *miscegenation*—even as their critical apologists, finding in African writers a 'universal appeal', still seek to assert the radical difference of black thinking and black writing from the racially-based, pure pedigrees of western European tradition. I shall use as my chief examples some texts by the Nigerians Amos Tutuola and Chinua Achebe, and by the black American, Ishmael Reed.

The National and the Universal

It is no accident that the epigraphs' three improvisations on the theme of 'nation', taken together, delineate the almost humorous instability of the concept. By taking 'nation' as a form of spatial coherence, one inadequately addresses the problem of defining 'people'. Leopold Bloom, displaced Jew, has good reason to define his 'Irishness' by place instead of race. Yet he quickly encounters an objection to his words 'same people'. For, as Joyce's Ned Lambert wittily shows, the term 'nation' itself embodies a paradox: a 'nation' is coherent, specific, and local; yet a person, the atomic essence of a nation ('I'm a nation'), does not constitute a *population*. Nations require plurality, yet plurality dilutes all strict standards of differentiation: 'Civilization is a re-agent, and eats away the old traits'.[4] There seems a principle of necessary dilution whereby the 'nation' must apply increasingly more general rubrics to its population, while at the same time continuing to include an ever widening spectrum of people.

Imperialism—the accumulation of diverse 'nations' under a single flag—may be seen as an almost semantic imperative; 'force' replaces 'nature' in forging alliances; selective assimilation, rather than aggressive exclusion, allows the national concept to survive, despite the relative distance between concept and reality. For instance, the more successful the British Empire became, the less it was racially and linguistically pure 'British'. Indeed, from almost any starting point, national definitions include more than they exclude, precisely because of the internal contradictions of the term 'nation' itself, which, as the H. G. Wells quote shows, can sustain an almost self-annulling level of generality (one's 'true nationality is mankind').

As a result, the concept of 'nation' finds its meaning on the broadest, rather than on the most detailed, levels, even as it pretends to furnish

---

4. Ralph Waldo Emerson, 'Race', in *The Portable Emerson*, ed. Carl Bode and Malcolm Cowley (New York: Penguin, 1981), p. 407.

us with the most specific segregations. It might be predicted, then, that the study of national literatures would involve similar contradictions. The temptation to regard 'language' or 'literature' as the guarantor of a nation's 'pedigree' (remember that *natio* has in Latin an almost eugenic connotation) recalls the similar (and frequently more destructive) employment of the concept of 'color'. In both cases an apparently exclusionary process is meant somehow to isolate the pure 'pedigree' of a race, a language, or a literature, even as that process ends up in a compensating search for some emblem of universality.[5] Johnson's remark is perhaps more understandable against this background, though his linguistic definition of 'nation' raises as many problems as Leopold Bloom's topographical one.

We are familiar enough with the practice whereby literary history or literary canons stand in for a notion of national spirit or character, but a countervailing tendency also needs to be discussed, one already implicit in Wells' comment. This tendency would valorize particular national authors not just to the extent that they speak for themselves or for their 'race', but also to the extent that they speak for 'mankind'. Authors such as Homer, Dante, Rabelais, Cervantes, Shakespeare, and Goethe are often seen as 'consummate geniuses' of a given national spirit, or 'founding fathers' of their respective national literatures, yet ultimately attract even greater interest because they seem in some way to have embodied 'universal truths'. Nation and nationalism, then, begin to dissolve their hegemonies with the formation of this larger grouping, defined by 'genius'. The Romantic conception of 'universal genius' has not waned even in the present day—in all cases, the favored designees of 'universal genius' are drawn not from a particular country, nor even from a given colonial power, but in fact from the 'nation' of Europe itself; this conception serves to proclaim the superiority of white thinking, white writing, and white culture.

Despite the general use of these authorial 'founding fathers' to stand for a white European cultural ideal, the actual texts they have written seem radically *mixed*, even syncretistic. *The Odyssey, The Divine Comedy, Don Quixote, King Lear*, or *Faust* would seem the last possible proof-texts for any *separationist* or *exclusionary* brand of racial or cultural hubris. It might seem a paradox, but the language of such texts—that subsequent literary canons have taken as the quintessence of 'Greek', 'Italian', 'Spanish', 'English', 'German', or simply 'European' genius—is radically heterogeneous and eclectic. These texts are extraordinary, not by virtue of the skill and confidence

---

5. Few authors have described the simultaneous and contradictory processes of racial inclusion and exclusion as well as William Faulkner, whose novels show the inevitable linguistic, sexual, and psychological mixtures consequent upon any systematic social rhetoric of division. See my *Figures of Division: William Faulkner's Major Novels* (New York: Methuen, 1986).

with which they *exemplify* a particular style or vernacular, but by the way in which their language *mixes* a variety of styles and vernaculars; they are not so much *universal* as *hybrid*, unifying previously scattered or dispersed dialects, colloquialisms, and oral traditions. They reach beyond the standard set of materials proper to a local sense of group cohesion, and make assimilationist gestures which abruptly break the mold of national languages. By such a liberal inclusiveness—indeed, by their impurity—even the major texts of western European literature have been able to furnish general reference points to other cultures, creating rich semantic fields within the common places of what were once canonized as national and European classics.[6]

Yet neither the new critical quest for texts embodying 'universal truths, nor even the formalist (Propp) or structuralist (Lévi-Strauss and Greimas) project to find 'deep structures' or 'grammars' which would describe a transnational level of narration have eliminated literary chauvinism. Albeit Edward Said has seen signs recently that 'contemporary criticism . . . has no faith in traditional continuities (nation, family, biography, period)' in most places literary studies still designate themselves by nationalistic terms, with even the least naive of critics believing, with varying degrees of irony, in the essence of a particular body of literary works produced by people speaking the same language.[7]

As distinguished a scholar as Erich Köhler can begin a recent article on French literature by saying: 'whoever wishes to clarify the nature of the "French spirit" need only, as a first step, interrogate French Literature.'[8] The tradition of literary territorialism finds tautological expression in the first paragraph of *The Concise Cambridge History of English Literature*: 'Though echoes from Celtic Britain must have lingered in men's minds, English literature begins,

6. Vernacular translations of the Bible by Tyndall in the English tradition or by Luther in the German tradition (Nietzsche called Luther's Bible 'the best German book', compared to which 'almost everything else is mere "literature"') are perhaps the pre-eminent versions of using texts as commonplaces for group cohesion. Religious texts configure a narrative about the Divine—absolute universality—into an enduring set of words which by their peculiar magnetism can be subjected to the narrower claims of competing language communities. The Koran provides an even more extreme example, being a religious text which interweaves religious belief, the historical standardization of Arabic writing systems, the primary inventory of tropes of literary expression, and a certain supra-national identification into a broad discursive fabric shared by all speakers and writers of Arabic. It is not uncommon, however, for an 'outsider' precisely to uncover the hybridizing possibilities of a text which had hitherto been used only to consolidate a particular nationalist prerogative. The case of Wole Soyinka's 1973 translation and production of Euripides' 'classic', *The Bacchae*, at London's Old Vic is exemplary here.

7. Edward Said, 'Roads taken and not taken', in *The World, The Text, and the Critic* (Cambridge, Mass.: Harvard University Press, 1983), p. 146.

8. Wer sich berät das Wesen des "französschen Geistes" klarzuwerden sucht, braucht zunächst nur die französische Literatur zu befragen'. See *Kindlers Literatur Lexikon im dtv,* *Band 1, Essays* (Munich: Deutscher Taschenbuch Verlag, 1974), p. 153.

at least, by being English'.[9] The notion suggested here of an abrupt break or alteration leading to an original, founding moment—while indispensable to a certain sense of literary historical plotting—is neither logically nor philologically plausible. The beginning is and must be arbitrary—pedigrees, linguistic or otherwise, never find a first instance: it is precisely out of the *loss* of absolute beginnings that the *need* for arbitrary beginnings flows.[1]

Just as the modern comparative philologist posits only provisional forms, marking them with an asterisk to denote that the forms are hypothetical, so too do these provisional and ultimately unprovable beginnings serve a crucial rhetorical and definitional aim. The *Concise Cambridge History* admits that indeed 'we do not know where or what the beginning is . . . the earliest forms of English literature, like the earliest forms of other national literatures, have perished'.[2] Yet this gap in the narrative of literary nationalism makes even more imperative the mandate to find, or manufacture, a moment at which particular national literatures seem to have become distinctive, if only to guarantee the coherence of a now dispersed center of identity. An earlier philologist, who was both a beneficiary and a victim of this kind of performative nationalism, well diagnosed the problem in 1886: 'What is called a "nation" in Europe today, and is really rather a *res facta* than a *res nata* (and occasionally can hardly be told from a *res ficta et picta*) is in any case something evolving, young, and easily changed, not yet a race'.[3]

European nationalism, particularly in the nineteenth century, seemed to depend increasingly for its definition upon *cultural* criteria. Dedication to the idea of culture provided a kind of generalized *coverage*, insuring a group's identity against external or internal threats of usurpation, assimilation, or denaturement. One could classify various national cultures both in terms of the tenacity with which the coverage was maintained and the extent to which one culture projected an image of radical *difference*—defined as 'national' and 'natural' *superiority*—from another culture. Freud suggests, with

---

9. George Sampson, *The Concise Cambridge History of English Literature* (Cambridge: Cambridge University Press, 1959), p. 1.
1. Freud, in the 'wolf man' case, reconstructed a *primal scene*, triangulating backwards, as it were, to plot a hypothetical 'original' moment important for the understanding of later events, but one whose reality he was always careful to leave in question. He begins his proof by saying 'I will only ask [the reader] to join me in adopting a *provisional* belief in the reality of the scene', and by the end, he still has no 'proof' of that fateful original moment: 'I intend on this occasion to close the discussion of the reality of the primal scene with a *non liquet*'. He has construed, not found, the starting point for his later case 'history': Sigmund Freud, *Three Case Histories* (New York: Macmillan, 1963), 'From the history of an infantile neurosis' (1918), pp. 224, 248.
2. Sampson, op. cit., pp. xi, 1.
3. Friedrich Nietzsche, *Beyond Good and Evil*, trans. Walter Kaufmann (New York: Vintage, 1966), sec. 251, p. 188. German title: *Jenseits von Gut and Böse*.

Nieztsche, that the entire idea of national differences, far from natural or original, gratifies more immediate desires:

> Closely related races keep one another at arm's length; the South German cannot endure the North German, the Englishman casts every kind of aspersion upon the Scot, the Spaniard despises the Portuguese. We are no longer astonished that greater differences should lead to an almost insuperable repugnance, such as the Gallic people feel for the German, the Aryan for the Semite, and the white races for the coloured. . . . In the undisguised antipathies and aversions which people feel towards strangers with whom they have to do we may recognize the expression of self-love—of narcissism.[4]

When confronted with non-western cultures, European 'narcissism', at first a mere 'repugnance' towards other peoples, develops into a myth of the past whose now embarrassing aspects non-industrialized cultures may be seen to represent.

Particularly in the nineteenth century—precisely the point at which colonialism and imperialism were making their most brutal inroads into Third World cultures—aesthetic nationalism and progressivism were keen factors in the European's narcissistic self-presentation, both within Europe and in the rest of the world. The progressivist conception of European history, in its ecumenical appraisal of non-western cultures as potential and primitive versions of European society, achieved a vision of global cultural development that elevated and separated white Europeans from the 'backward' cultures that they devalued. Yet this notion also, by a peculiar kind of magnanimity, needed to include the primitive within its imperial hoard. For eventually, the presumably flattering model of linear improvement tends to undermine itself. European artists and scholars began to suggest that if the non-western aesthetic is a potential, or primitive, or aboriginal manifestation of that which western man has brought to maturity, then it follows that potency, primacy, and originality themselves represent radically regenerative attributes that the mature post-Enlightenment west has already lost. Linearity, then, might as easily imply decay as progress.

While Diderot's *Encyclopédie* made sense as a chronicle of Europe's mature achievements through the late eighteenth century, the very notions of 'maturity' and 'accumulation' upon which it concentrated must have reminded the observant reader of their concomitants in the organic metaphor, 'senescence' and 'obesity'. Almost from the beginning, both incipient and full-blown modernism expressed a

4. Sigmund Freud, *Group Psychology and the Analysis of the Ego*, trans. James Strachey (New York: Norton, 1959), pp. 33–4. German title: *Massen-psychologie und Ich-Analyse* (1921).

wish to return to primal roots as well as a somewhat troubling awareness that this return was inconsistent with the claims to 'newness'
and 'progress' and often 'national genius' that had for so long been
made about the history of western cultures, independently and as a
whole.

Jean-Paul Sartre expresses these anxieties best in his 1948 preface
to Leopold Senghor's anthology of French West African poetry: 'It is
almost impossible for our poets to realign themselves with popular
tradition. Ten centuries of erudite poetry separate them from it. And,
further, the folkloric inspiration is dried up; at most we could merely
contrive a sterile facsimile.'[5] Given the assumption of linear conti-
nuity between origin and maturity in western culture, it came to be
suspected in the late nineteenth century that primitive states might
possess greater power and energy than sterile nations, or that, in
other words, western material progress had amounted to spiritual and
artistic decadence.[6]

Major European artists began to have doubts about the linear
model for purely formal reasons, as well. Richard Wagner, Gustav
Mahler, Igor Stravinsky, James Joyce, Henry James, Thomas Mann,
and others, in testing the quantitative capacities of aesthetic forms,
and indulging early modernism's predisposition towards encyclopedic art, were also indirectly challenging the European nationalisms
and even imperialisms that had allowed for only token levels of
hybridization. These and other artists found it necessary to undermine the entire notion of formal and material accumulation and
development—crucial to western historical, as well as musical and
fictional plots—in favor of significant cycles and structural *repetitions* in their scores and texts. So the paradox of cultural coverage
became clear: the more retrospective, encyclopedic, weighty,
mature—indeed, *western*—the work of art became, the more it had
to incorporate elements of futurist, non-western, primitive, repetitive, and minimal structuration, if it were at all to remain comprehensible.

Despite attempts to apply evolutionary terminology to art forms, it
became clear that there could be no approach to human sensations
and response that had a progressivist nationalism as its basis. Long
before Freud, it had been noted that if inclusion were the working
principle for much modern art, then 'primitive' repetition rather than
'mature' development had to be a corollary structural feature. Even

5. Jean-Paul Sartre, Preface to *Anthologie de la Nouvelle Poèsie Nègre et Malgache de Langue
   Française*, ed. Leopold Sedar Senghor (Paris: Presses Universitaires de France, 1948).
6. For more on the relationship between philosophical progressivism and some formal characteristics of modernist European art, as compared with black artistic forms, see my article,
   'Repetition as a figure of black culture', in Henry L. Gates (ed.), *Black Literature and Literary Theory* (New York: Methuen, 1984).

if an art form developed within a national culture as the outpouring of some necessary racial vigor, who could guarantee that such an art form would continue to appeal to that same 'race'? The more complex the art work, the more vexing the problem of comparative reception between cultures becomes. That is to say: even if the European and the African respond differently to Benin bronze or Bayeux Tapestry, can there be a question here either of nationalism or of progress?

Versions of universality: collections versus contagions

When African literature is in question, literary critics use terms such as 'national', 'progress', and 'tradition' quite differently than in their discussions of European texts. In the first place, there is a flattening of the entire concept of 'nation'—and for all the wrong reasons. Although African poets and politicians have been keen to borrow political and linguistic criteria from Europe's repertoire (as in the only partially successful concept *négritude*), European literary critics and historians for the most part have been reluctant to deal with Africa in all its dazzling racial, tribal, and regional multiplicity.

A standard German encyclopedia of world literature for example— one which includes articles on Flemish and Serbian literature, and dozens on European and Asian literature overall—compresses its comments about Africa into two articles: 'The traditional literature of black Africa', and 'Neo-African literature' (which includes Afro-American writers as well!). Extravagant generalizations about 'the African' follow. Although the distinction, based on writing, between 'traditional' (oral) and 'modern' (written) African literature is common, more recent overviews have broken the continent down into more specific though scarcely more enlightening divisions such as 'West' and 'East' African, 'Anglophone' and 'Francophone', or even national ('Nigerian') or tribal ('Ibo') units. The conclusion that 'today there are at least two distinctive prose styles in African literature in English, the Yoruba and the Ibo' is either reductive or imprecise, or both.[7]

Despite their hesitancy about coming to terms with the specificity of African literature, few western readers seem unwilling to talk about its 'universality'. The new critical valorization of 'universal appeal', which we have seen conflicts somewhat with the literary historian's insistence on strict national delineations, is frequently applied to African works—where the issue of 'nation' is even less clear than in Europe—even though the word 'universality' seems often merely to function as a code-word meaning 'comprehensibility for the

---

7. Bernth Lindfors, *Folklore in Nigerian Literature* (New York: Africana, 1973), p. 173.

European reader'. As 'one non-African reader' puts it, in trying to assert his qualifications for interpreting African literature:

> . . . accomplished works of art communicate in such a universal human idiom that they are capable of transcending their particular time and place and speaking to all mankind. One does not have to be Greek to understand Homer, Hindu to appreciate Kalidasa, or Japanese to enjoy Chikamatsu. So why should a person have to be black to respond to James Baldwin, George Lamming or Amos Tutuola?[8]

In some instances, the search for the 'universal' in the 'African' takes extreme forms:

> Like any other artist, the Nigerian novelist must achieve universality through a sensitive interpretation of his own culture. . . . [T]he African writer [must retain] that international standard of English which is required if his work is to be other than merely local in its effects.
>
> Using his African background, [Wole Soyinka] explores the human condition . . .
>
> *The Lion and the Jewel*, as comedy, depends on seeing humans in terms of their universal motivations of pride, power and sex . . .
>
> Soyinka's writing, although firmly set in Africa, is universal in its themes.
>
> Amos Tutuola's *The Palm-Wine Drinkard* is [among the] marvellous works of the human imagination . . . the impact of much of what he writes is supracultural.[9]

Attributing 'universality' to African writers—or expecting to find it in them—can merely be a question of (as in the case of political imperialism) a given observer projecting onto a neutral space a wish for power. That power, in turn, may be defined as the power to comprehend and systematize within a European scheme a wide and often perplexing range of non-European cultures and writings.

In his article 'Neo-African literature', the well-known Africanologist Jahnheinz Jahn brings a flattened perspective to modern African literature, further compressing variety into identity. Jahn's over-reliance

---

8. Lindfors, op. cit., p. 2.
9. See Douglas Killam, 'Cyprian Ekwensi', p. 78; John Povey, 'The novels of Chinua Achebe', p. 98; Eldred D. Jones, 'The essential Soyinka', p. 113; all in Bruce King (ed.), *Introduction to Nigerian Literature* (Ibadan: University of Lagos and Evans, 1971); J. Z. Kronenfeld, 'The "communalistic" African and the "individualistic" westerner: some comments on misleading generalizations in western criticism of Soyinka and Achebe', in Bernth Lindfors (ed.), *Critical Perspectives on Nigerian Literatures* (Washington, DC: Three Continents Press, 1976), pp. 252–3; Bruce King, op. cit., 'Introduction', p. 6, and Robert P. Armstrong, 'The narrative and intensive continuity: *The Palm-Wine Drinkard*', in Lindfors, op. cit., p. 110.

on concepts such as 'the African way of thinking' or 'the African conceptual world' leads him to ostensibly laudatory, but occasionally outrageous conclusions, such as 'In traditional Africa, everyone who speaks is a magician of words, a poet'. As one observer comments:

> Critics of African literature tend to be either racists, nationalists or individualists. The racists devoutly believe *africanité* of African Literature and usually seek to demonstrate that black African writers think alike, feel alike, and therefore write alike . . . so long as he is black and African his writing is regarded as an expression of *négritude*, a verbal manifestation of the negro African soul. . . . Nationalist critics, on the other hand, are preoccupied with mapping the geography of African literature . . . a literature conveniently contained within the arbitrary territorial boundaries drawn by the former colonial powers.[1]

In describing the 'African's' spontaneous poetry, Jahn comments on what he sees as an unusual juxtaposition of images in an African poem—and in doing so exposes his own ethnocentrism: 'An image like "black innocence" is not an oxymoron for the neo-African poet, but an imperative image that creates a new reality'.[2] Jahn never even seems to question his own culture's assumption that 'black' and 'innocence' are oxymoronic opposites here, seeming to think that the belief is universally held, even by black African poets.

In much western writing about African literature, theorizing about 'progression' of narrative forms is replaced by discussion of 'derivation'. The journey from 'traditional' to 'modern' African literature, for this mentality, was entirely due to contact with Arabic and European cultures, the adoption of writing systems, and, most significantly, the transcription of African languages to European writing conventions: 'All languages of this giant area are originally unwritten. The first known written form in black Africa was Arabic'. Traditional narration included songs, improvisations ('forgotten as soon as they arose'!), myths, epics and sagas, riddles, prayers, incantations, panegyrics, drama, and so on.[3] These are often dismissed as either irretrievable or unworthy of serious discussion, while the introduction of 'writing' and European language prototypes gives us a beginning, a 'pedigree', at the same time less remote and more familiar than would be possible for European language and literature. Note comments such as 'A standard orthography for the Yoruba language was established by the missionaries of the Church Missionary Society of London

---

1. Jahnheinz Jahn, 'Die Neo-Afrikanische Literatur', in *Kindlers Literatur Lexicon*, p. 695, my translation. Also, Lindfors, *Folklore*, p. 153.
2. Jahn, op. cit., p. 695, my translation.
3. See Jürgen Zwernemann, 'Die Traditionelle Literatur des Schwarzen Afrika', in *Kindlers Literatur Lexikon*, pp. 684–5.

working in Yorubaland in the period 1842–82', or 'it was only at the start of the twentieth century that written Hausa literature came into being'.[4]

The European, whose intervention 'begins' African literature, once more finds himself flatteringly represented as the 'author of progress', and it is now possible to speak of first-and second-generation African writers, who are alternately beatified and villified, depending upon their closeness or remoteness to this primal, 'traditional', African source, or what one writer calls 'the African personality of this literature'.[5] The notion of 'progress', then, seems tied not to any internal logic, but to a sense of closeness or distance from European influence: 'There may be traditional Nigerian dramatic forms such as the masquerade or various ceremonies, but outside [read European!] infusion is obviously needed if local forms are to be developed and given artistic permanence'.[6] The assumption that the novel as we know it is a European form—coupled with the notion that for the most part, Europeans changed African oral traditions into written traditions—permits a new progressivist thesis tailored to 'African realities': 'The modern Nigerian novel . . . follows the main historical development of the English novel'; 'Just as each European nation has its own literature so each nation in Africa can be expected to produce its own literary tradition.'[7]

The critical reception of Amos Tutuola, and particularly of his first novel, *The Palm-Wine Drinkard* (1952), furnishes us with an interesting example of these critical habits. Tutuola, a Yoruba writer born in 1920, has presented us in his first work with an extraordinary text, a memoir of a search through fantastic terrains to 'find out where my palm-wine tapster who had died was':

> When I saw that there was no palm-wine for me again, and nobody could tap it for me, then I thought within myself that old people were saying that the whole people who had died in this world, did not go to heaven directly, but they were living in one place somewhere in this world. . . . One fine morning, I took all my native juju and also my father's juju with me and I left my father's hometown to find out whereabouts was my tapster who had died.[8]

Often dream-like, often a hugely successful meditation on the syntactical possibilities of the English language, *The Palm-Wine*

4. Adeboye Babalola, 'A survey of modern literature in the Yoruba, Efik and Hausa Languages', in King, op. cit., pp. 57, 50.
5. Lindfors, *Folklore*, p. 4.
6. King, op. cit., 'Introduction', p. 9.
7. Killam, op. cit., p. 77; King, op. cit., p. 11.
8. Amos Tutuola, *The Palm-Wine Drinkard* (New York: Grove, 1980), p. 9. All subsequent page references are from this text.

Drinkard is the quest-narrative of a disembodied 'I', through both physical and cultural terrains. In his astute and humorous mixing of African and European reference points—such as linking 'juju' with that all too English cliché 'one fine morning'—Tutuola both plays with and against the expectations of African and European readers.

Critics have had difficulties with Tutuola's decidedly non-Aristotelian narrative structure, as well as with his idiosyncratic style—or, more precisely, they have been uncertain whether Tutuola's style was an individual creation or rather an expression of a 'West African' or 'Yoruba' 'spirit'. When Tutuola's style has been in question, the typical response has been, as in the discussion of 'modern African literature' generally, to search for European or African precursors, but rarely to give the artist credit for willed craftsmanship:[9]

> It is obvious that *The Palm-Wine Drinkard* . . . is reminiscent of other works in world literature . . . Bunyan and Dante . . . Orpheus. . . . The two works with which *The Palm-Wine Drinkard* has most in common . . . are the *Odyssey* and *The Canterbury Tales*. . . . The last chapter of *The Palm-Wine Drinkard* shows Tutuola using a final blend of African and European myth.

Tutuola, borrowing from European or African models, depending on the critic, is seen as closer to the 'source' of 'Yoruba' than such writers as Soyinka or Achebe, who have been 'spoiled' by Western influence:

> There can be no doubt that Amos Tutuola is closer to the traditional esthetic of the Yoruba. . . . One would expect therefore, upon further study, to perceive a continuum of 'Yorubaness,' extending from Tutuola at the deeply Yoruba end to Wole Soyinka at the more Europeanized, modernized end.[1]

Yet this praise quickly reveals itself as an oblique denigration. Some readers say that Tutuola's more 'deeply Yoruba' narrative is closer to the 'African genesis', 'like drumming', and better than the writing of the 'more Westernized African . . . [whose] writing is more in the nature of a gloss; in Tutuola, it is intrinsic'.[2] Other readers compare Tutuola unfavorably to Soyinka, and on the same grounds: '[Soyinka's] English is impeccable; one would search his works in vain for the unconscious West Africanisms and innocent barbarisms that crowd

9. See Armstrong, op. cit., pp. 112–13, and Anne Tibble, *African/English Literature*, quoted in Lindfors, op. cit., p. 10.
1. Armstrong, op. cit., p. 128.
2. Armstrong, op. cit., p. 127; O. R. Dathorne, 'Amos Tutuola: the nightmare of the tribe', in King, op. cit., p. 66.

every page of Tutuola's writing'. It is not uncommon to read of
Tutuola's 'bad English. . . . No doubt Tutuola stumbled on his style
accidentally at first by translating Yoruba expressions into English;
but it has become a conscious technique in his later novels'.[3] 'Conscious' artistic technique (a sign of healthy, individualistic, artistic
vigor) vies with the 'unconscious' influence of 'proletariat' diction
(the same communal 'popular tradition' lauded by Sartre and now
criticized as 'clumsy' and 'ungrammatical'). Once more we see the
paradox whereby the evolutionary model, applied to writing, both
reveres and demeans sources of literary originality, especially when
they are writers and poets.

Like Tutuola, Chinua Achebe has suffered from the imposition of
national and even tribal categories. His novels—in particular *Things
Fall Apart* (1958), *No Longer at Ease* (1960), and *Arrow of God*
(1964)—have Nigerian settings, and employ storytelling devices
(myths, proverbs, songs) from the Ibo oral tradition. In depicting the
first encounters between black African tribes and white European
colonialists, they already stake out a supra-national territory. They
have variously been praised and derided as 'sociological' or 'anthropological', but their most interesting aspect is the almost casual
manner in which they present African norms to primarily non-
African readers. As in the case of Tutuola's works, Achebe's novels
provide an unexpectedly tricky reading experience for their western
audience, using wily narrative stratagems to undermine national
and racial illusions. One wonders whether either author was prepared for the interpretive confusions resulting from their unexpected disregard of literature's earlier segregations. For Achebe's
novels do not merely insinuate the unaware reader into a foreign
and putatively inferior consciousness; they suggest a natural and
indeed actual place for African cultures alongside or even admixed
with European ones. The presence of 'anthropological' detail in
Achebe might represent verisimilitude for a reader fluent in Ibo customs, but for a European reader, it constitutes a veritable declaration of war on the practice of dividing cultures and fictions into
strict national groupings.

For one thing, Achebe consistently leaves crucial Ibo words
untranslated (some editions append a 'Glossary of Ibo words and
phrases', which, in its terse inadequacy, reminds one of the parodis-
tic 'Partial bibliography' at the end of Ishmael Reed's *Mumbo Jumbo*).
Many words can only be deciphered from the context:

> He could hear in his mind's ear the blood-stirring and intricate
> rhythms of the *ekwe* and the *udu* and the *ogene*, and he could

3. Lindfors, op. cit., 'Yoruba and Ibo prose styles', p. 161; King, op. cit., 'Introduction', p. 2.

hear his own flute weaving in and out of them, decorating them with a colorful and plaintive tune.[4]

Moreover, similes are based on African, not European realities: 'Okonkwo's fame had grown like a bush-fire in the harmattan' (p. 7). What is being defined here is not so much 'tribal' or even a 'national' language or sensibility, but a black sense of cultural prerogative, the converse of the normal relations of power between Europe and Africa. The European reader, feeling at the outset at home in a literary form that Europe has developed, is made to assume, without warning, the vulnerable position of the African in a European culture which he or she is expected to understand and absorb. Whites, perhaps for the first time, see themselves as Africans see them: 'It is like the story of white men who, they say, are white like this piece of chalk, . . . And these white men, they say, have no toes' (p. 71). The words 'white body' are no longer synonymous with 'innocence' (as Jahn might suggest), but (in the Ibo conception reported in *Arrow of God*) with 'leprosy'.[5]

Perhaps most importantly, Achebe's ability to shift points of view and narrative centering between white and black characters (there is no longer any question of simply peering into the machinations of a putative 'African mind') increases the ironic distance from both perspectives, and intensifies Achebe's ongoing elegy to segregationist discourse and narrative. The ill-fated assumptions of superiority in both black and white realms are the problem: interpreting between whites and the leaders of Umuofia village in *Things Fall Apart*, Okeke says 'We say he is foolish because he does not know our ways, and perhaps he says we are foolish because we do not know his' (p. 175). The segregation of black and white viewpoints in the novel's early chapters simply replicates a wider cultural gap, one which leads to an outcome of which the reader is already all too aware. *Things Fall Apart* expropriates and pre-empts (albeit only in fiction) the written form in which the English language has assaulted an unwritten Ibo reality. The ironic ending, in which the district commissioner decides to capture the entire tale in 'the book which he planned to write', recapitulates the ongoing process of cultural interpretation and redefinition which typically worked to the detriment of blacks:

> The story of this man who had killed a messenger and hanged himself would make interesting reading. One could almost write a whole chapter on him. Perhaps not a whole chapter but a reasonable paragraph, at any rate . . . one must be firm in cutting out details. He had already chosen the title of the book, after

4. Chinua Achebe, *Things Fall Apart* (New York: Fawcett Crest, 1984), p. 10. All subsequent references are from this text.
5. Chinua Achebe, *Arrow of God* (London: Heinemann, 1964), p. 177.

much thought: *The Pacification of the Primitive Tribes of the Lower Niger.* (p. 191)

Yet it is Achebe who, through writing *Things Fall Apart*, pre-empts an attempted white usurpation of his story and his culture, trapping the 'official version' within a more sympathetic history.[6]

By borrowing his title from Yeats' pessimistically cyclical poem 'The Second Coming', Achebe similarly rewrites the text both of European historicism and of the cyclical view that was its hopeful antidote (the title of his second novel, *No Longer at Ease*, performs a similar operation on T. S. Eliot's 'The Journey of the Magi'). If, for Yeats (as for Spengler and other modernist philosophers of history), the transition from barbarism (or paganism) to the Christian era would be followed by an unknown, presumably negative cycle, in which 'things fall apart', Achebe reverses this view to highlight the negative impact that this hypothetically 'positive' Christian phase has already had upon the 'falling-apart' of African culture:

> in evoking Yeats's themes, Achebe implies that the sense of history and tradition, the burdens of cultural continuity, decay, rebirth, have all been the African's lot as well as the Westerner's . . . the novelist has exploited the European's cultural criteria . . . in order to reverse the white man's exclusivist definitions of history and culture.[7]

Even as the west is bemoaning the internal collapse of some of its structures, Achebe is showing the British subversion of Ibo customs (already endangered by their own decrepitude). Achebe hereby does more than merely 'exploit' the 'European's cultural criteria'. Far more than merely borrowing the notion of historical cycles from Yeats, he is in fact reclaiming an age-old non-western cyclical conception that European writers had only recently annexed.

In *Arrow of God*, the intersection of narrative form and literary revision is even clearer. In Achebe's third novel, as in *Things Fall Apart*, we see the collapse of a certain traditional Ibo culture under both internal and external assault. There is no glossary of Ibo words this time, and African proverbs (and even entire fables) interlace the narrative. The *New York Times* reviewer called it 'long on native customs and idiom, and short on narrative interest', and yet this appraisal is a

6. A similar literary reversal takes place in Ferdinand Oyono's *Un Vie de Boy* (1960), in which by gaining literacy from the French Camerounian missionaries, he both registers the acts of colonialist cruelty that he can now read from written diaries, and keeps a diary in his own dialect (Ewondo) that comments on the colonizers' ethnocentrism and ruthlessness. The literary device of the diary—borrowed from those who tried to oppress him by limiting his access to writing—becomes the text of the novel itself; writing, once the tool of oppression, has become a tool of liberation.

7. Lloyd W. Brown, 'Cultural norms and modes of perception in Achebe's fiction', in Lindfors, *Critical Perspectives*, p. 135.

sort of inverse testimony to the seriousness and subtlety of Achebe's narrative design.[8] For this novel (in a way that parallels Wole Soyinka's 1980 film *Blues for a Prodigal*) gives a deeper analysis of both the black and the white worlds than Achebe had ever attempted before. It alternates rapidly between events in chief priest Ezeulu's village and the machinations of the imperious white man, 'Wintabota' (Captain T. K. Winterbottom), culminating in their tragic collision.

Achebe's 'white' narrative often assumes a disarmingly familiar modernist shading. For this accommodation, Achebe has been much praised by certain critics, happy to find that Achebe's 'voice' seems as authentic in the white chapters as it does in Ezeulu's 'tribal' scenes. Jamesian passages ('The vehemence with which she said this seemed so much greater than the cause of her annoyance', p. 152) vie with passages of Woolfian streams of consciousness ('From this point Clarke speculated briefly on the nature of knowledge. Did knowledge of one's friends and colleagues impose a handicap on one? Perhaps it did,' p. 131), convincing us (if his titles already had not) that Achebe is fully aware of the modernist project, and fluent in its craft.

Yet perhaps the more important and typically unnoticed thing about this novel is not the to-and-fro between the mutually interpolating versions of African and English reality, interesting as it is. Far more striking is the increasing velocity with which the 'white' narrative constantly interrupts and undermines the 'African' one, in a way perhaps not unrelated to the historical effects of slavery and colonialism on African village life and culture. Political appropriation and co-optation as historical fact here are mirrored in the insistence of white discourse: the attempt of the 'white' narrative to usurp or 'universalize' the 'black' one, with all its quaint heritage of 'native customs and idiom'. At best, one has single chapters (as in 13) in which blacks and whites vie, as it were, for the control of their own history.

As we have seen, a similar struggle leads Achebe in *Things Fall Apart* to pre-empt a proposed white version of the plot (the district commissioner's report mentioned at the end—*The Pacification of the Primitive Tribes of the Lower Niger*) by ironically encircling it within his own, African narrative. In *Arrow of God*, we see Tony Clarke reading the same report (p. 39), so in a sense, Achebe's initial gambit has not worked. Achebe, again in the second novel, feels obliged to inscribe possibly biased white readings within an African narrative framework. The repetition of the attempt seems to indicate a suspicion of its ultimate futility. Indeed, as the novel progresses, the number of chapters written in 'white' discourse (as in chapters 3, 5, 10, 13, 14, and 15) increases. In only a few chapters (which have both black and white narrative) is chapter-based segregation broken down,

8. Ronald Christ, *New York Times Book Review*, 17 December 1967, p. 22.

yet the final victory of white discourse in a more global sense is already foretokened in the immediate material conditions of Achebe's literary products: written in English; published in England. Thus the fateful historical intervention of the European in Ibo society, and the effects on the Nigerian village life and culture of slavery and colonialism, here find a striking and unsettling narrational and institutional resonance.

* * *

JAMES OLNEY

The African Novel in Transition: Chinua Achebe[†]

Chinua Achebe, who is probably the most highly regarded novelist of West Africa and perhaps of all of black Africa, presents the student of African literature with an interesting, and I should say paradigmatic, case. If we take his novels as a single, coherent body (and I think Achebe encourages this when he occasionally re-uses settings and characters), then his themes read like an epitome of African fiction from its beginning to the present time. Nor is it in theme alone that Achebe's fiction seems to summarize the history of the African novel: in the progress of his thematic and technical concerns as well, or in the historic development that his career traces, Achebe is, for the non-African reader, representative and characteristic. One might say, adapting the idea from C. G. Jung's notion of psychological development in the individual and in the race, that the ontogenetic, private curve of Achebe's career repeats in small the phylogenetic, historic pattern of the African novel. Being thus representative, the body of Achebe's work tells us much not only about him and about the African novel, but a great deal also about the society and the civilization that the novel reflects and in which it has its roots.

In the introduction to *Africa in Prose*,[1] O. R. Dathorne speaks of two stages of development in African fiction, but he outlines, in fact, and conveniently for our purposes, three: the earliest fiction, given over for the most part to preserving tribal customs and dramatizing cultural conflicts with the white invaders; an intermediate fiction that shows the individual breaking away from the tribal group; and contemporary fiction that concerns itself with personal fulfillment in a world divided and confused by the European/African encounter.

[†] From *South Atlantic Quarterly* 70 (1970): 299–316. Copyright © 1970 by Duke University Press. All rights reserved. Used by permission of the publisher.
1. O. R. Dathorne and Willfried Feuser, eds., *Africa in Prose* (Baltimore: Penguin Books, 1969), pp. 13–14.

I should like to suggest that almost exactly this same progress is to be discovered in the fiction of Achebe, with a novel devoted to each stage of thematic development:[2] "At the start," as Dathorne puts it, "there was the anthropological concern with tribe, and later with the coming of the white man" (thus, *Things Fall Apart*); more recently, "there emerges the theme of the individual struggling against the pressures of the tribe and breaking out of the enclave in which custom would seek to restrict him" (thus, *No Longer at Ease*); "Latterly there has been a concern in depth with the person, his private predicament in a world he seeks to salvage from the chaos of a divided inheritance" (thus, *A Man of the People*). In Ogbuefi Okonkwo, Obi Okonkwo, and Odili Samalu, the figures in and around whom the various conflicts focus in these three novels, Achebe embodies and dramatizes, in a sort of summary form, African experience of the past century as seen by the African novelist. That experience, as Achebe imagines and represents it, is one of progressive cultural disintegration and moral confusion; at the same time, however, Achebe's drama hints at new, if difficult, possibilities and seems to suggest almost a new morality. The movement, in largest outline, is from cultural tragedy to personal tragedy to personal comedy.

Achebe writes from within; we read, in hopes of understanding, from without. Obvious dangers attend such a situation. It is a principle of cultural anthropology, and undoubtedly a valid principle, that one should not try to judge the works of one civilization by the standards of another or try to understand the culture of one people in the philosophical terms of another. Thus, to view the tribal dance of Africa through the assumptions of European ballroom dancing is, at best, misguided and, at worst, vicious. So also with other art forms or cultural manifestations that have shaped themselves out of the African experience over those centuries when Africa had no essential contact with other, and especially European, civilizations. But is not the case somewhat different with the novel? The novel is primarily and in origin a Western, as distinguished from African, art form, which of course is not true, for example, of the dance, of poetry, of song in general, of sculpture; and the comments that one makes about novels are, I am certain, fortunately or unfortunately, colored by this fact. We often judge the African novel by standards and ideals that are non-African. The African writer who chooses the novel form thereby commits himself to a mode of expression developed by the Western world and

<hr />

2. Achebe has in fact published four novels to date: *Things Fall Apart* (1958); *No Longer at Ease* (1960); *Arrow of God* (1964); and *A Man of the People* (1966). I am excluding *Arrow of God* from these remarks because it deals with essentially the same world as *Things Fall Apart* and because the curve I am concerned with can be more precisely traced by considering *Things Fall Apart* than *Arrow of God*. References are to the following editions: *Things Fall Apart* (New York: Astor-Honor, Inc., n.d.); *No Longer at Ease* (London: Heinemann, 1963); *A Man of the People* (Garden City, N.Y.: Doubleday Anchor, 1967).

hence, probably, to some of the ideas and ideals of that Western world—ideas and ideals, after all, that have shaped the novel form and to which it gives expression. At least, I think this is importantly true with Achebe, and in his novels one sees a paradigm of the African novel.

The ideal that we find embodied countless times in the characters and the actions of Western fiction is, of course, what we call love. Love may or may not make the world go round, but it undoubtedly keeps the novelist in business. The question, then, is whether, in drawing his characters, in setting his men and women in relation to one another, the African novelist will incline to do the same sort of thing as a Western writer, or something quite different. To see how Achebe handles his characters, both in themselves and in interrelation, it will be well to place the question in context by reminding ourselves of what love is, of where sex figures, of what place procreation occupies in the Western world. Thus we shall be in a position to see where Achebe resembles and where he differs from the Western novelist in this matter of love.

The fable that Aristophanes relates in Plato's *Symposium*, to explain the origin of sexual desire and the nature of love, gives a clear and finely ironic picture of the idea of love (leaving practice out of consideration) in the Western world. From an original state of circular wholeness and perfection, according to Aristophanes, man has fallen into his present condition of incompleteness and fragmentation. Zeus, so that man would learn better than to overreach himself, cut the members of the human race, as originally constituted (four arms, four legs, two faces on a circular neck, a double component of generative organs), in half. "Man's original body having thus been cut in two, each half yearned for the half from which it had been severed. When they met they threw their arms around one another and embraced, in their longing to grow together again." And this is the love, romantic and sentimental (though anything but sentimental in Aristophanes' fable)—or, again, the *idea* of love—that has obtained in the Western world for 2500 years. Man, before he was split in two, was entire in himself, the Greek equivalent of pre-Eve androgynous Adam. The instinct that remembers wholeness and yearns to have it again is the motive force that we call love, and this it is that draws the lines for the relations of the sexes.[3] Thus love, according to this Western fable,

---

3. One might note in passing that this theory of love serenely recognizes homosexual and heterosexual love as essentially the same in motive and validity (for there were originally three sexes: pure male, pure female, and hermaphrodite, only the third of which would lead to heterosexual love). I mention this sidelight on love in the Western world to point up the fact that the same is distinctly not true in African sexual theory and that, because of this, homosexuality was virtually unknown, according to many writers, in traditional African communities, such as the one Achebe describes in *Things Fall Apart*, before the arrival of Western man with his "new" ideas of love and sex. To the traditional African it would seem obvious, from the very physical make-up of man and woman, that their *raison d'être* is to reproduce.

is suprarational or irrational, going beyond or against reason and logic; it is an entirely individual matter, but leaves its victim without choice as to whom he shall love. Furthermore, there is no necessary connection between love (an individual necessity) and marriage (a social arrangement), and children are altogether incidental and secondary to love. Finally, Aristophanes' tale suggests that love is not a means to an end (pleasing society, producing children, acquiring money or a name) but is the end itself (being made whole, complete, perfect again).

Things Fall Apart, the first of Achebe's novels, both in the chronology of its events and in the chronology of its author's career, begins a story that is continued in *No Longer at Ease* and establishes a theme of African/European conflict that we find at the center of all of Achebe's works. The story told in this first novel, if we neglect the anthropologically interesting but fictionally irrelevant descriptions of traditional ceremonies spotted throughout the book, is a vastly simple tale of cultural conflict resolved in tragedy: Ogbuefi Okonkwo, a Herculean strong man and representative of the old, coherent community, is so frustrated and discouraged with the arrival of the white man and with subsequent defections among his own people (including his son Nwoye, rechristened Isaac in the new faith) that he commits suicide. Achebe complicates the action with a good many details of what happens in Iboland from day to day and year to year, but essentially this is the whole story of *Things Fall Apart*. If one examines the characters involved in Okonkwo's tragedy, one finds that they have the same exaggerated simplicity, the same representative significance as this outline of action, which might serve equally as a sketch of Achebe's plot and his theme. Internal division, the theme says, results in self-destruction, and the plot "proves" this theme dramatically. Characterization in *Things Fall Apart*, like plot and theme, is simple, rigid, and abstract: there is, indeed, really only one character in the novel—Okonkwo. Okonkwo, it is true, has three wives and a number of children; friends and townspeople move in and out of the action involving him; elders meet to judge disputes and to pronounce traditional wisdom—but there is not another distinct and distinguishable figure in the novel. His wives, his children, his friends and enemies exist only as shadow figures that help to define the character and the significance of Okonkwo. The most obvious instance would be the wives who claim none of the novelist's attention as people interesting in themselves—for, in fact, they are not people at all but mere things used (by Achebe *and* Okonkwo) to define the central male. None of the women are particularized beyond being numerically 1, 2, and 3. We never learn the name of Wife No. 1; we only hear of her as "Nwoye's mother," a designation of considerable significance when one considers the role of women in this book and in the society it describes. There is nothing in *Things Fall Apart* resembling a physical or mental description of these adjuncts to Okonkwo's masculinity: they seem simply to represent "Woman," that useful creature who fetches water, bears children, plants female crops (coco-yam and cassava), cooks, and keeps her personality (if, indeed, she has one) very much to herself. These three women are in no sense and never individuals but rather generic representatives of Ibo wives and abstractions from Ibo womanhood.

What shall we say of the character of Okonkwo himself? Achebe is at considerable pains to let us see, know, and understand his hero; yet, in spite of the fact that he sacrifices all other characters to the definition of Okonkwo, Achebe draws in him no more than the generalized portrait of a man whose character is deliberately and significantly without individualizing traits. We learn of him, and this is really about all, that Okonkwo is physically powerful, ambitious, generous and honest, proud, quick to anger, hard-working, a great wrestler. To the reader who is at all familiar with the great tribes of West Africa, this picture begins to suggest something. Any observer who names the African tribes that have unique and distinct characters unto themselves must place the Ibos near the top of the list. An Ibo will not easily lose himself in a confusion of tribes. Historically, he has resisted any blurring of tribal character, any melting down of the Ibo personality that would render it indistinct within the larger agglomeration. He refuses to be Nigerian if that should prejudice his remaining distinctly Ibo; he retains his Ibo personality and will not surrender it for the less distinct "African personality" (in the phrase made popular by Kwame Nkrumah). On the other hand, he will not go the step in particularity that lies beyond tribal character: with the assurance of tribal definition behind him, the Ibo does not insist on his own and individual, perhaps eccentric, personality. And what is this tenaciously maintained tribal identity? Here is the description by an Ibo (not, as it happens, Achebe but Onyenaekeya Udeagu) of "Ibos as They Are":[4] The Ibo is physically powerful ("He is," as Udeagu puts it, "strong and able to work or fight"); ambitious ("He likes to advance and he is quick to learn"); generous and honest ("They are very generous and approachable. . . . He likes to give rather than take"); proud ("This pride enhances the prestige of an Ibo wherever he goes"); quick to anger ("Ibos are an argumentative set of people. . . . Their expressive mentality . . . does not always allow them to gulp in false charges without defense"); hard-working ("They possess high aptitude for hard work and learning. . . . An Ibo prefers to die than to be idle"); a great wrestler ("Wrestling forms the best and most remarkable Ibo game").

4. Onyenaekeya Udeagu, "Ibos as They Are," in *An African Treasury*. ed. Langston Hughes (New York: Pyramid Books, 1961), pp. 26–29.

Now is this the Ibo character or the character of Okonkwo? The two, it becomes apparent, are coterminous, and we soon come to the conclusion that Achebe has not been concerned to create Okonkwo, any more than his wives, as a unique, living and changing human being. It is Okonkwo's inability to change, for one thing—seen otherwise as an uncompromising devotion to the ancestral past—that leads him to self-destruction. The inflexibility of his character ("inflexible" both in a moral sense and in a technical, novelistic sense) leads on inevitably to Okonkwo's tragedy, since the world, with the arrival of the white man, insists on change. But this is not the tragedy of a mere individual. Like his women, Okonkwo is an "ideal" standing for the characteristics of a whole people. He too is an abstraction: Ibo-man incarnate, Ibo manhood to the tenth power, specifically as it was before the arrival of the European. And Okonkwo's fate, he being representative and typical, one must accept as the symbolic fate of Ibo society with the advent of the white man.

With this picture of ideal Ibo-man and Ibo-woman, we are ready to question the motive and basis for sexual relations in the world of Achebe's novel. Why *do* man and woman come together in this society? Is it because "love" draws them together, even, at times, against their conscious will? Hardly. Is it, as in Aristophanes' fable, because they have an ineffable yearning to be made whole again by union with the separated half (or, in Okonkwo's case, the separated fourths)? Obviously not. Is it because the man requires a woman to do his cooking, water-fetching, cassava and coco-yam planting? Perhaps, in part. But the primary reason and the essential motive is to produce children and so to continue the line.[5] And why should he want to continue the line? In a profoundly circular response that allows no further questioning, the answer is that this is why man was created. Christianity says, in a typical formulation, "Man was created to praise, reverence and serve God Our Lord, and by so doing to save his soul." This emphasis on individual salvation would constitute virtual heresy for the Ibo of Okonkwo's character. For the pre-colonial Ibo, the truth would be: "Man was created to procreate, and by so doing to continue the ancestral line." It is the will of the ancestors or of the spirit of the clan to continue living, and that can be only if the present embodiment of the ancestral past produces a future embodiment in the form of children. "Before the European era," Onyenaekeya Udeagu claims, "there was no harlot in Iboland. Every man and woman married and perpetuated that end which nature ordains

5. Cf. the remark of a villager in *Arrow of God* during a marriage dispute: "Different people have different reasons for marrying. *Apart from children which we all want,* some men want a woman to cook their meals, some want a woman to help on the farm, others want someone they can beat." *Arrow of God* (London: Heinemann, 1964), pp. 76–77; italics are mine.

for reproduction. There is no excuse for not marrying except extreme poverty and deformity."[6] Not so, according to the Western notion. "It is better to marry than to burn," St. Paul says, and that very cautious, grudging, backhanded in fact, approval of marriage expresses well the Christian and generally Western attitude towards the non-primacy of the procreative motive in matters of the spirit. In the Western world, every man is responsible for his own soul and his own emotional needs, but only for his own; he must take on himself one burden only—getting himself together according to his individual necessities and individual conscience. This is as true of Christian doctrine as of Aristophanes' love ethic.

The picture that Achebe gives us in Part I of *Things Fall Apart* is of an "Ibo community in the past" (as he says in a note appended to the American edition), an Ibo community not atomized by the agonies, the attitudes, and the appetites of merely individual members, an Ibo community with one soul, rather than a multitude of souls, held together by the will of the ancestors speaking group wisdom and tribal desires through the mouths of the present ruling elders. It is only when foreign ideas and beliefs are imposed that this community begins to disintegrate. One of these foreign ideas is that sex and love should go together, and that love is a personal matter, an individual pleasure and necessity, a private question; that love is the end and not the means; that man seeks love because he wants love and not because he wants children in order to continue the ancestral line, or to appease and to express it. Another foreign and dangerous idea is that you can only love one person. This strange Western notion says that, of course, it is possible to produce children by several women, but love is given only to that one, unique, separated half. And love, according to the West, is the big thing—not procreation, not the ancestral voice. When these two different views of sexual relationships come into conflict, and when some members of the Ibo community start to follow one belief while others follow another, then things start to fall apart in the world of Achebe's novel. "We must all hang together, or assuredly we shall all hang separately." In becoming an individual personality or soul, or by adopting the Western ideal of individualism, the single figure separates himself from the homogeneous and coherent tribal character. In becoming uniquely himself, he ceases to be specifically Ibo. Okonkwo's son, Nwoye/Isaac (who, we later learn, takes only one wife), goes over to the other side which means symbolically that the center, both tribal and familial, "cannot hold," and from here on, the old community all hangs separately—as, in fact, Okonkwo does hang himself.

---

6. "Ibos as They Are," p. 28.

When we say that Okonkwo is not individualized or that he is a representative character, we are saying something not only about the techniques of Achebe's fiction but also, perhaps more importantly, about the society, the culture, the world that informs that fiction. Implicit in the characterization of *Things Fall Apart* is the cultural belief of the Ibos of the old order that individualism, if it is conceived of at all, is a positive evil. Describing "tribal man," Peter Abrahams, the South African novelist, says that "he is not an individual in the western sense. Psychologically and emotionally he is the present living personification of a number of forces, among the most important of which are the ancestral dead."[7] Mankind, according to African thought, includes more than the sum of those now living, for the dead, though no longer alive, continue to exist and to exert a tremendous force on and through their living descendants. Hence, in a tradition-oriented novel like Achebe's, "Man" must be understood in the sense of man in the living present and man in the ancestral ages. And just as ritual masks are not ordinarily drawn directly from life nor intended to represent particular individuals, but rather to symbolize the being or the existence of ancestral force in composite, so character in the traditional African novel is not likely to be drawn from an individual; for it is not, any more than a Dan mask or a Benin bronze, a living likeness, but rather a sum of existing, informing forces. Fictional character in *Things Fall Apart*, like ritual sculpture, is more a significant and affective or symbolic figuration than a mimetic one. Léopold Senghor, writing of "the traditional African narrative," makes a suggestive comment that applies *mutatis mutandis* to a Western-influenced yet still tradition-directed novel like *Things Fall Apart*: "None of the actors is in the European sense an individual confronting society. Every figure represents in the first instance a type, it is paradigmatic, like an African mask."[8] The whole difference, for the work of art as for the society that it reflects, turns on the question of the unique individual and the representative type; the one is a Western ideal, the other an African. And this is why *Things Fall Apart* seems, in a sense, both more and less than a novel—as an African mask seems both more and less than a portrait.

If Achebe is going to present his reader with an imitation of reality in *Things Fall Apart*, then it will be a reality transcending the particular individual and the single moment of the present; and if Abrahams and Senghor are right about tribal man, then the novelistic result will be precisely as we have discovered it in our analysis: individual characterization will give way before non-specific ancestral

---

7. "The Blacks," *Holiday*, 25 (April 1959), 120.
8. "L'esprit de la civilisation ou les lois de la culture négro-africaine," *Présence Africaine*, VIII–X (Paris, 1956), 60; quoted in Janheinz Jahn, *Muntu* (New York: Grove Press, 1961), p. 211.

embodiment or tribal representation, and character development will yield to the one great monolithic fact of cultural conflict. Until it begins to disintegrate under the impact of a foreign civilization, the old Ibo community, manifest in the person of Okonkwo, is untroubled by internal dissension or individual conscience, by moral hesitation or disunity of purpose. Conflict in such fiction as this will always be large and simple, external rather than internal, intertribal or intercultural or even international rather than interpersonal or intrapersonal. Okonkwo, though he destroys himself, does so not from individual motives, but as a representative of Iboland beaten down by something too foreign, too external to himself, even to understand.

"I am also interested," Achebe continues in the note already quoted from the American edition of *Things Fall Apart*, "in the problems of present day Nigeria and intend in my next novel to bring the story of Okonkwo's family up to date." The time of the events in *Things Fall Apart* is never specified, but would appear to be the end of the nineteenth century; *No Longer at Ease*, the sequel to *Things Fall Apart*, skips over one generation to pick up its hero in 1957, the generation it skips over being Nwoye/Isaac, the son of Ogbuefi Okonkwo, who accepts all the religious belief and the colonial system of the European white man. Whatever Christian belief and practice may do to an Ibo, and how it may change his personality, is assumed, rather than dramatically represented, in the character of Isaac. Isaac's son Obi Okonkwo is of the third-generation Nigerians after the white man. He is one of those who have been aware of Western culture all their lives, who have necessarily accommodated themselves, in a certain degree anyway, to the white man's world while living in the village of their ancestors. Education for a Nigerian of this generation and condition is like a confusion of tongues: the personality of the tribe, with all its affective power, undoubtedly remains in him as an educative and moral force, but his conscious, formal education is according to the white man's ways and values. The Western world may be able to remove the Ibo from his ancestors, but removing the ancestors from the Ibo is another matter. In passing over Isaac to concentrate on Obi, Achebe chooses a hero who is in reaction against the Christian father, who himself became a Christian by reacting against his father, a pagan of the old community. Still, however, anti-antipaganism in the third generation does not necessarily produce a pagan, and Obi Okonkwo is too many removes in experience from his grandfather, and too advanced in moral confusion, ever to inhabit a world at all like Ogbuefi Okonkwo's in *Things Fall Apart*.

This is Obi's story, a story more complicated than his grandfather's, just as Obi's character is the more complex of the two: returning to Nigeria after four years' schooling in England, financed on a loan from his Ibo compatriots, Obi Okonkwo goes to Lagos, takes a job in the civil service (on a scholarship-granting committee), and resolutely opposes the corruption and bribe taking evident all around him. In England he had met Clara Okeke, another Ibo, had met her again on the return boat, had fallen in love, and back in Lagos becomes "loving to" her, i.e., takes her as his mistress. Though they become engaged, Clara, who has always acted rather peculiarly when the question of marriage has come up, now says that they can never marry because she is "an *osu*,"—that is, a person dedicated to serve a god, "thereby setting himself apart and turning his descendants into a forbidden caste to the end of Time" (p. 72); one who is *osu* cannot marry outside the caste.[9] Obi romantically intends to marry anyway, goes back to his home village to persuade his parents, and there meets flat refusal because, though his parents are Christians, marriage to an *osu* would mean family destruction and ancestral annihilation, since any children of the marriage would automatically become *osu* to all Ibos and could never marry within the culture. Obi's mother dramatizes the refusal by telling her son that she is dying, but, if he marries before her death, her blood will be on his head for she will in that case commit suicide. Obi, stunned by this pronouncement, returns to Lagos and tries to reason with Clara and to postpone marriage; Clara, however, is both indignant and pregnant, and Obi, caught between his ancestors and his fiancée, between the African ideal of procreation and the Western ideal of love, can find no solution but to finance an illegal abortion. The abortion puts him seriously in debt, and when he learns that his mother is dead and that Clara has disappeared, Obi breaks down, takes bribes, both of love and money, is caught and convicted; and so the story ends in unqualified personal tragedy.

Obi's tragedy, though in a sense equally great with his grandfather's, is personal rather than tribal or cultural; again unlike his grandfather's, Obi's tragedy is a result not of powerful external forces but of inner confusion, and consequently the technique of Achebe's presentation is quite different in *No Longer at Ease* from what it was in *Things Fall Apart*. The two central figures of *No Longer at Ease* are more individual and distinct, more separate in themselves and more clearly characterized than the figures of *Things Fall Apart*. They stand for nothing and represent no group, but simply are, more or less successfully, themselves; they are, as it were, characters in a novel rather than symbols of a force. Clara, a modern woman at loose ends

9. To be *osu* is, in effect, to be of a slave caste; as Achebe puts it in "Chike's School Days," a short story of earlier date than *No Longer at Ease*: "Strangely enough, a slave to a god was worse than a slave to man. A slave to man could buy his freedom. But an *osu* was condemned forever, and his generation after him." *The Sacrificial Egg and Other Stories* (Onitsha: Etudo Ltd., 1962), p. 16.

in the world and thrown back on herself, has no traditional, clearly defined role in a society that knows what it is, who its women are, and how they relate to their men. Having lost her innocence to a Western education, she cannot be Ibo Woman; she has no choice but to try to be herself. Obi likewise, with his English education, is an individual, one divided and troubled by the voice of his personal conscience, that being a peculiarly modern difficulty entirely unknown to the massively simple Grandfather Okonkwo. For Obi, who is torn in two different directions—towards his Western love for Clara and towards his African loyalty to the family—the conflict that resolves itself in tragedy is an internal affair. Instead of a conflict that exists out there between representatives of two cultures, Achebe shows us a conflict that is really a projection of Obi's character. Yet the conflict is not merely personal, not simply psychological, but involves loyalty to two different and irreconcilable ways of life.

With the conflict thus internalized and his characters individualized, Achebe draws a relationship between Obi and Clara that accords with all the notions of romantic, sentimental, Western love; Clara, as Obi thinks in the best manner of any popular song of the West, is the only one for him. She is not, as Wife No. 1 was to Grandfather Okonkwo, one of several adjuncts to Obi's manhood, a sort of possession by which he is known; instead, she embodies for Obi, and she alone, the power of love—a power entirely different in effect and significance from the power of either the dead ancestors or the living family. Clara is, as it were, that separated half that can complete Obi's being. "Obi knew better than anyone else that his family would violently oppose the idea of marrying an *osu*. Who wouldn't? But for him it was either Clara or nobody. Family ties were all very well as long as they did not interfere with Clara" (p. 75). Family ties, however, prove to be not only "all very well" but, in fact, very powerful too—more powerful, indeed, than a mere momentary, Western-inspired passion for a woman. Love, as Obi experiences it in *No Longer at Ease,* is a distinctly equivocal thing: the most powerful emotion in the Western lexicon, yet, as Obi discovers, impotent in the face of opposition from the African ancestors.

In the course of the novel and at the end, Obi is "loving to" other women; but this is not at all the same as "being in love"; it is not, as the movies and songs say, "the real thing." And that his love for Clara is the genuine article, tinselly though that may be, is made eminently clear by Achebe:

> Until Obi met Clara on board the cargo boat *Sasa* he had thought of love as another grossly over-rated European invention. It was not that he was indifferent to women. On the contrary, he had been quite intimate with a few in England—a

Nigerian, a West Indian, English girls, and so on. But these intimacies which Obi regarded as love were neither deep nor sincere. There was always a part of him, the thinking part, which seemed to stand outside it all watching the passionate embrace with cynical disdain. The result was that one half of Obi might kiss a girl and murmur: "I love you," but the other half would say: "Don't be silly." And it was always this second half that triumphed in the end when the glamour had evaporated with the heat, leaving a ridiculous anti-climax.

With Clara it was different. It had been from the very first. There was never a superior half at Obi's elbow wearing a patronising smile. [p. 70]

In *No Longer at Ease* Achebe presents a sexual relationship that is motivated not by an urge to procreation and ancestral appeasement—which makes it quite different from anything in *Things Fall Apart*—but by, quite simply, an Aristophanic yearning for reunion. Indeed, the illegal abortion that Obi provides for Clara is a powerful symbol suggesting how drastically different is the motivation for sexual relations here from what it was in pre-European Ibo society. The voice of the tribal past can only be very confused, in itself and to Obi's ears, when he, the ancestral present, decides to marry an *osu* anyway, in spite of fathers and forefathers and then agrees to abort the child which would, paradoxically, both continue the ancestral line and simultaneously corrupt and destroy it. "To leave no heirs behind him," as Janheinz Jahn says, paraphrasing and quoting the Bantu writer Alexis Kagame,

> is the worst evil that can befall a man, and there is no curse more terrible to put on a man than to wish him to die childless. But the whole weight of an extinct race lies on the dead. "The worst of evils, the irremediable catastrophe falls on the dead ancestors who came before him." For they have all, for the whole time of their infinite deathlessness, "missed the goal of their existence," that is, "to perpetuate themselves through reproduction" in the living person. Thus everything is concentrated on the precious existence of the living, in whom the life that was transmitted to them from their ancestors is carried on.[1]

By a terrible irony, and in total moral confusion, it is Obi himself who pronounces the curse of childlessness not only for his own self but for the ancestors who are, by that act, not simply dead but finally, irremediably, eternally powerless and nonexistent. Obi, as he finds when he returns to the ancestral village, is "no longer at ease here, in the old dispensation,/ With an alien people clutching their gods." But

---

1. *Muntu*, p. 109.

neither is he at ease in the new dispensation, and therein lies his personal tragedy: for the Western gods withhold from him that same personal fulfillment through love with which they tempted him away from the traditional gods of the Ibos. Fittingly, it is the Western world, i.e., the British administration, that prosecutes Obi and clucks its tongue at this most recent native to have gone bad. Obi is destroyed utterly according to the notions of either Africa or the West: on the one hand childless for eternity, on the other hand love-less and incomplete.

In *A Man of the People* Achebe takes up his African/European sub-ject again, this time with new characters and in a new tone and with a decidedly different resolution. The theme is now worked out almost entirely in terms of character and character development. Instead of culturally representative, static figures set in conflict, we have one character of various desires and divided loyalties who changes and grows in understanding in the course of the novel and who comes to a happy end, even though it is qualified with consid-erable irony, in the final pages of the book. The time of the novel is 1964–65—that is, after full Nigerian independence but before the military coup of 1966. Odili Samalu, a secondary-school teacher and the hero of the novel, re-encounters, after some sixteen years, his one-time schoolmaster who, though an almost illiterate vulgarian, has in the meantime become a member of parliament, the minister of culture, a "man of the people," and an exceedingly corrupt politician—M. A. Nanga, or, as he prefers to be called, "Chief the Honourable Dr. M. A. Nanga, M.P. LL.D." (p. 18). Odili receives favor from Nanga, goes to stay with him in the capital city, and is outraged to learn, in a fine comic scene, that Nanga has stolen his mistress Elsie for a one-night affair. Odili leaves Nanga's house determined to get revenge, first by contesting Nanga's seat in par-liament, second by alienating the affections of the pretty, young girl (Edna) whom Nanga intends to take as his second or "parlor" wife. In the end, Odili is seized at a political rally for Nanga, is beaten and hospitalized, and Nanga is elected without opposition. But then a military coup turns everything around: Nanga is jailed and Odili marries Edna, whom he now loves with a true and deep, specifically Western passion.

The most notable thing about *A Man of the People* that distin-guishes it from the other novels is that it is told in the first person by Odili. There is no view in the novel over a culture or cultures. Everything is seen from within the categories. What this means, practically for the novel, is that we receive a full picture of Odili's character-in-change, his reasonings, his motives, and his ideals, and it means also that we experience the conflict, between political aggrandizement and moral rectitude, along with Odili right from inside. By the time of *A Man of the People*, everyone has his individualized character, the conflict is entirely internal, sexual relations involve either "romantic love" or "being loving to," and there is no effective community voice, speaking ancient and ancestral wisdom, to guide actions. To indicate the moral distance traveled from *Things Fall Apart*, one might point to the remark of a married, white American woman with whom Odili has a brief and casual affair. As they chat together, with a sort of inane mindlessness on her part and a restrained hostility on his, she says, "Sex means much more to a woman than to a man." (Her rationale: "It takes place *inside* her. The man uses a mere projection of himself" [p. 50].) Now, without either disputing or defending this, one can still remark that this would never have been said, or anything like it, in the world of *Things Fall Apart*. Even here it rather scandalizes Odili and could probably only have been said by an American. Anyhow, the remark would be entirely meaningless to, for example, Nwoye's nameless mother (the American's name, incidentally, is Jean, her husband is John, and they insist immediately on first names)—Wife No. 1, who lived only in the role of bearer of children for husband and ancestors. Hers could never have been a life determined by a search for personal satisfaction or pleasure, by a yearning for individual fulfillment or completion.

The novel concludes with Odili's reflection that there is no longer such a thing as community spirit or will or a community voice. In his world the only possibility lies in personal fidelity and individual loyalty, a recapture of individual wholeness and perfection through love. This is how Achebe, through Odili, says it in the fine conclusion to his novel (Odili's friend Max has been killed by Chief Koko, a corrupt politician whom Max opposed in the election; Max's lover Eunice shot Koko dead on the spot—and all for love of Max):

> Max was avenged not by the people's collective will but by one solitary woman who loved him. Had his spirit waited for the people to demand redress it would have been waiting still, in the rain and out in the sun. But he was lucky. And I don't mean it to shock or to sound clever. For I do honestly believe that in the fat-dripping, gummy, eat-and-let-eat regime just ended . . . —in such a regime, I say, you died a good death if your life had inspired someone to come forward and shoot your murderer in the chest—without asking to be paid. [pp. 140–41]

Love, in the view of the individualist Odili, love Western, romantic, and sentimental, love is great—and might conceivably, barely prevail. Sex, according to this cautiously optimistic ethic, has little or nothing to do with procreation and ancestral continuation (the traditional African view); rather, it appears either in the guise of romantic love (the Western view, perhaps the modern African also) or as "being loving to" (amalgamation and confusion of traditional African and modern Western: polygamy for pleasure rather than procreation). A society that conceives thus of love and sex will also exalt the individual, and so it is with Achebe's latest novel.

A *Man of the People* is very likely a slighter thing than the sturdy, plodding, much better-known *Things Fall Apart*; but what it lacks in massive solidity of structure, A *Man of the People* more than makes up in technical refinement: in flexibility of characterization and subtlety and delicate assurance of tone. The nature of Achebe's achievement might be made clearer if one imagined a new generic name for such a work as *Things Fall Apart*: an historical/cultural fiction, perhaps, or a sociological presentation, or a ritual, anthropological drama. (This novel, for good reason, is most popular with ethnologists and anthropologists, with social scientists in general, and with "African studies" experts.) A *Man of the People,* on the other hand, is pre-eminently a "novel," with all the dramatized complexity of human relations implied by the novel tradition. While the satire of A *Man of the People* rejects, there is a parallel movement, centering on Odili and his moral growth, that makes discoveries and accepts. A *Man of the People* takes place in a world much worse off, much more corrupt and cynical and generally nasty, than the world of *Things Fall Apart*; yet Achebe, or at least his hero, finds in this wretched world a life which is both meaningful and possible. A *Man of the People* does not merely show that a certain world of grace is lost forever—of course it is—but takes that loss for granted and attempts to say what there may be of value in this world without innocence that lies about us. This latest novel of Achebe's—and this will suggest how very different it is, and how far he has come, in theme and technique, from *Things Fall Apart*—reminds the reader, by its tone, its theme, and its conclusion, of no one so much as E. M. Forster; reminds one of Forster in its very slightness and unpretentiousness, in its humanistic spirit, in its sensitive and unheroic hero, in its humor—a light play of irony over a subject often heavy with solemnity—in its dramatic suddenness of plot action, in its emphasis on the worth of personal relations as against anything else the world can offer. Where Forster, however, ordinarily keeps to the private world of individuals, Achebe carries the theme into the public realm of political involvement—to have his hero discover in the end that it is only, after all, in the private realm that there is anything meaningful at all, specifically that the only valuable pursuit and possession is the whole self, to be found through the love of one individual person. And there, for the moment at least, on the point of individual fulfillment, Achebe seems to bring the African novel to the same conclusion as the contemporary Western novel.

SIMON GIKANDI

Chinua Achebe and the Invention of African Literature†

Although he is now considered to be the man who invented African literature, Chinua Achebe's goals were modest when he began to conceive and write *Things Fall Apart* in the early 1950s: 'I was quite certain that I was going to try my hand at writing, and one of the things that set me thinking was Joyce Cary's novel set in Nigeria, *Mister Johnson*, which was praised so much, and it was clear to me that this was a most superficial picture . . . and so I thought if this was famous, then perhaps someone ought to try and look at this from the inside' (*African Writers Talking*, 4). Achebe's project of looking at Nigerian culture from the inside was going to move more slowly than he might have expected, however. After sending the only copy of his manuscript to a typing agency in London where it was mislaid for nearly a year, he finally submitted his novel to William Heinemann, a famous British publisher of modern fiction. Heinemann did not welcome Achebe's novel without hesitation: not only was there no precedent for publishing modern African fiction, there were also concerns about its potential readership. Would there be many readers for a novel by an African writer dealing with the colonial encounter?

Ultimately, William Heinemann decided to take a chance on this new writer, and about 2,000 copies of the novel were published in 1958. The rest is history. *Things Fall Apart* is not only the most widely read African novel—the English edition alone has sold millions of copies—but is the one work of postcolonial literature that almost every student of English is bound to encounter at one time or another, often in high school, and most certainly in college and university.

But in thinking about the enormous success of this book and the influence it has had in the shaping of African and world literature, we should not forget its uncertain beginnings. Indeed, the history of this novel, which is also the history of the beginnings of modern African literature in English, is about how works of fiction create their own traditions, cultural contexts, and reading communities.

The first question any introduction to this novel must pose is this: what enabled Achebe's work to speak to its time in a way other novels could not? After all, *Things Fall Apart* was not the first African novel in English in the twentieth century. Achebe's novel was

---

† From Chinua Achebe, *Things Fall Apart: Classics in Context* (Portsmouth, NH: Heinemann, 1996), ix–xvii. Reprinted by permission of the author.

preceded by other important African novels such as Casely Hayford's *Ethiopia Unbound*, Sol Plaatje's *Mhudi*, and Amos Tutuola's *The Palm-Wine Drinkard*. If Achebe is now considered to be the man who invented African literature, it is not so much because he was a pioneer or an innovator. In the very simple and conventional story of Okonkwo, a strong individual and an Igbo hero struggling to maintain the cultural integrity of his people against the overwhelming power of colonial rule, Achebe was able to capture the anxieties of many African readers in the 1950s. We can understand these anxieties much better if we examine the important historical and psychological parallels between the years in which Okonkwo's story is set (between 1860 and 1890) and the years in which *Things Fall Apart* was conceived, written, and first published (1952–1958).

The central theme of the novel is what happens to the values that define Okonkwo's cultural community, and his own sense of moral order, when the institutions he had fought so hard to sustain collapse in the face of European colonialism. The cultural hero who had defeated Amalinze the Cat in the novel's first paragraph makes a regressive journey into exile and ultimate death. In retracing his rise and fall, we are also made aware of the collective dimension of his tragedy: Okonkwo may have failed because of his weaknesses as an individual, but his failure was inevitable because colonial rule had destabilized the values and institutions that sustained him. Indeed, there is a close relationship in the novel between Okonkwo's individual crisis—of authority and power—and the crisis of his community, which increasingly finds its defining characteristics (including notions of wealth, marriage, worship, language, and history) undermined and transplanted by the new colonial order. These issues are so powerful in the novel that attentive readers will rarely miss them.

Similarly, the period in which Achebe conceived and wrote *Things Fall Apart* was also a time of anxiety and crisis. By 1952 it had become apparent that the period of colonial rule in Nigeria was entering its final phase: after almost a hundred years of foreign domination, a period in which the culture of the country was often fashioned after that of Britain, and its destiny was often seen as somehow lying in Europe, the country was entering a period of self-government. And because this historical shift was as sudden as the initial imposition of colonial rule, critical questions arose: What was to be the nature of the Nigerian nation after colonialism? What kind of persons had colonial culture created? What was the language of the desired postcolonial culture? And, ultimately, how was the history and destiny of this new community to be charted?

Although *Things Fall Apart* may appear to be exclusively concerned with the imposition of colonial rule and the traumatic encounter between Africa and Europe, it is also a work that seeks to address the crisis of culture generated by the collapse of colonial rule. Indeed, Achebe has constantly argued that the theme of colonial domination in Africa—its rise and influence—was made imperative in his works by his concern that the culture of colonialism had had such a strong hold on African peoples, especially on a psychological level, that its consequences could continue to haunt African society long after European colonizers had left the continent. In one of his most influential statements on the role of the novelist in Africa, Achebe observed that, although decolonization had changed the African cultural landscape, it was foolish to pretend that Africans had 'fully recovered from the traumatic effects of our first confrontation with Europe' (*Morning Yet*, 44). Achebe went on to argue that his role as a writer was 'to help my society regain belief in itself and put away the complexes of the years of denigration and self-abasement' (*Morning Yet*, 44). In a situation in which colonial rule had established its authority by inventing and insisting on the racial inferiority of the African, novels set in the past, such as *Things Fall Apart*, were retrospective attempts to understand the origins of the current crisis—'to look back and try and find out what went wrong, where the rain began to beat us' (*Morning Yet*, 44).

Clearly, the crisis of the soul triggered by colonialism at the end of *Things Fall Apart*, when Okonkwo is forced to his death and his heroic life is reduced to a single paragraph in a racist European text, was very much an issue in 1958. However, unlike many other African writers of his generation, Achebe did not see colonial rule as something that could be transcended simply by an appeal to an heroic and romantic African past. And where other writers could see the culture of colonialism as the antithesis of an African identity, Achebe was interested in discovering a redemptive moment in colonialism, asking himself, in his own words, 'what possibility, what encouragement, there was in this episode of our history for the celebration of our own world, for the singing of the song of ourselves, in the din of an insistent world and song of others' (*Chinua Achebe: A Celebration*, 3).

Achebe's novel presents the colonial experience from an African perspective, but it does so without romanticizing the African past. Thus, one of the most enduring aspects of *Things Fall Apart* is Achebe's ambiguous representation of the Igbo past as heroic but, at the same time, compromised by Okonkwo's blind commitment to his culture and his obliviousness to alternative values and interpretations. This is the meaning of what is probably the definitive moment in the novel—the killing of Ikemefuna. Okonkwo strikes the fatal blow against his adopted son in the name of tradition and the moral order of his community but, as he is reminded by his friend Obierika, although the oracle of the hills (the custodian of moral authority) had decreed that the boy must be killed, she had not ordered Okonkwo, the surrogate father, to carry out the sentence. This one disturbing episode encapsulates the very essence of Achebe's philosophy, especially his concern with moral complexities and dualities. As he told Bill Moyers in a famous television interview, his values as a novelist are guided by a powerful Igbo proverb—'Wherever something stands, something else will stand beside it' (*A World of Ideas*, 333). Culture is, in other words, defined by ambivalence rather than unquestioned authority.

If *Things Fall Apart* appears to be a novel that sets out to provide important moral lessons to its readers, it is because Achebe conceives the primary function—and power—of literature to be moral or ethical in nature. The power of the storyteller, says Achebe, lies in his or her ability to appeal to the mind and to reach beyond his or her particular circumstance and thus speak to different periods and generations; the good storyteller is not bound by narrow political or personal concerns or even by the demands of specific historical moments. Achebe's sympathies, then, are not with the heroic character (in this case Okonkwo), but the witness or storyteller (Obierika) who refuses to endorse Okonkwo's commitment to the central doctrines of his culture or the European colonizer's arrogant use of power.

However, the novelist's ability to bring the historical period and his moment of writing together also depended on a notable relationship between his life and his work. As an author, Achebe may be separated from the central events in *Things Fall Apart* by a period of seventy years, but his own biography is very much a part of the story he tells and its context. Achebe's family occupies a central role in the history which his novel narrates. We know, for example, that his great-grandfather was the man who first received Christian missionaries in the village of Ogidi (Umuofia in the novel). More significantly, Achebe's father, Isaiah Okafor (like Nwoye in the novel), was one of the first converts to Christianity in the area and worked for many years as an evangelist and teacher in the Christian Missionary Society, the evangelical branch of the Church of England. This family history is important to our understanding of *Things Fall Apart* not so much because it invites us to read the author's life in the novel itself, but because it calls attention to the cross-roads of culture from which Achebe's artistry emerges. For if the African identity of the novel derives from its acute sense of the oral tradition, then this is an acknowledgment of the influences of the Igbo stories which Achebe used to hear from his non-Christian relatives. It was from the older people in his village that Achebe came to develop an awareness of the history of Igbo people before colonization, a history which is an important aspect of the first part of *Things Fall Apart*.

But it would be a mistake to assume that Achebe grew up with a profound understanding and respect for the African past. One of the ironic aspects of being born in a family of African converts to Christianity was that one's status in society depended on a certain self-alienation from the old culture. 'The line between Christian and non-Christian was much more definite in my village forty years ago than it is today,' Achebe observed in 1973. 'When I was growing up I remember we tended to look down on the others. We were called in our language "the people of the church" or "the association of God." The others we called, with the conceit appropriate to followers of the true religion, the heathen or even "the people of nothing"' (*Morning Yet*, 65). Although Achebe's first novel is a celebration of the precolonial past, it is important to emphasize this sense of superiority among African Christians for one overwhelming reason: it was out of this identification with the culture of colonialism—and his ultimate disillusionment with it—that Achebe became a writer.

Achebe grew up and came of age in the culture of colonialism. He was not only brought up in a Christian family, and thus identified with European culture, his early education was in Church schools where the influence of the Bible and biblical stories, Christian moral codes, and indeed modern civility were emphasized. (Achebe has provided us with a wonderful portrait of this culture in the house of Isaac Okonkwo in his second novel, *No Longer at Ease*.) In addition, Achebe's secondary education at the prestigious government school at Umuahia could not but draw him even further into the culture of colonialism. Such schools were modeled after British public schools (the equivalent of prep schools in the United States) which meant that the values they promoted—in scholarship, sports, and conduct—were essentially English.

When he arrived at the University of Ibadan in 1948, Achebe was expected to read the major texts of the English tradition, including most notably Shakespeare, Milton, and Wordsworth. But by 1948 this acculturation in Englishness was being challenged by African nationalism: advocates of African independence and cultural renewal were beginning to question the central notion in colonial education—the assumption that an African destiny included 'a future European identity for which the present is but an apprenticeship'; in addition, the nationalist movement had brought about 'a mental revolution that was to reconcile us to ourselves' (*Morning Yet* 7, 70).

Since this mental revolution was connected so implicitly to the writing of *Things Fall Apart*, it is important that readers consider what we may call its cultural politics. Simply put, the writing of this novel marked a radical change in Achebe's way of looking at himself and his culture and in his conception of literature itself. For if we accept the general argument that colonial rule justified itself through the process of writing and rewriting other people's histories and cultural practices, as the last paragraph of *Things Fall Apart* seems to assert, then we must pay closer attention to the fundamental relationship between the kind of reading communities in which Achebe was brought up and the kind of novel he produced in 1958. Two forms of reading communities are involved: that of the family, and that of the school.

Achebe grew up in a household in which books were revered and played an important role in the visualization of modern life: 'As the fifth in a family of six children and with parents so passionate for their children's education, I inherited many discarded books . . . I remember also my mother's *Ije Onye Kraist* which must have been an Igbo adaptation of *Pilgrim's Progress*' (*Morning Yet,* 68). Many of these books, most notably the Bible, were later to influence Achebe's literary works as much as the Igbo stories he heard as a child. The Ikemefuna episode in *Things Fall Apart*, to cite just one example, is fashioned after Abraham's aborted sacrifice of Isaac in the Old Testament.

In high school, as Achebe observed later, he was exposed to English books such as *Treasure Island* and *Oliver Twist*. The most significant impact of these books was on Achebe's view of the world: on reading these books, he observes, 'I did not see myself as an African to begin with . . . I went through my first level of schooling thinking I was of the party of white man in his hair-raising adventures and narrow escapes' (*Chinua Achebe,* 7). At University College Ibadan, Achebe was introduced to famous European writers who had set their novels in Africa, such as Joseph Conrad, Joyce Cary, and Graham Greene. But by now, instead of identifying with the European adventurers against their African counterparts, Achebe felt impelled to represent the historical encounter between Europe and Africa from an African perspective. The connection between Achebe's reading of the colonial novel and his decision to become a writer is fundamental to our understanding of the cultural function of *Things Fall Apart:* 'I suddenly saw that these books had to be read in a different light. Reading *Heart of Darkness*, for instance, . . . I realized that I was one of those savages jumping up and down on the beach. Once that kind of enlightenment comes to you, you realize that someone has to write a different story' (*A World of Ideas*, 343).

Things Fall Apart is certainly not the first African novel, but it was probably the first work in which the author set out to represent the African experience in a narrative that sought, self-consciously, to be different from the colonial novel. Since its publication in 1958, Achebe's novel has served as a model for other African writers, and indeed, for a different kind of literature in English. Achebe's goal in this novel—to indicate to his readers 'that we in Africa did not hear of culture for the first time from Europeans' (*African Writers Talking* 7)—has changed the way African readers perceive their own cultures and their relationship to colonial institutions. Achebe is the man who invented African literature because he was able to show, in the structure and language of his first novel, that the future of African writing did not lie in simple imitation of European forms but in the fusion of such forms with oral traditions. Achebe is the conscience of African literature because he has consistently insisted on the power of storytellers to appeal to the morality and humanity of their readers and to give their life fuller meaning.

AUGUSTINE C. OKERE

Achebe and Christianity†

Achebe's pioneering role in the fictional portrayal of early Christian-missionary activity in Nigeria is well known to all scholars of African literature.[1] Other Nigerians who have addressed the theme include T. M. Aluko (*One Man One Wife*, 1959), Onuora Nzekwu (*Blade Among the Boys*, 1962), John Munonye (*The Only Son*, 1966). All these can be said to have trailed after Achebe, none of them catching the fine, intricate relationships and complexities of the issues involved as Achebe does especially in *Things Fall Apart* (1958), (TFA), and *Arrow of God* (1964), (AG).

Like these writers, Achebe is a nationalist writer, in his own case, avowedly so. In his essay, "Named for Victoria, Queen of England" Achebe says that he wrote his novels "especially those set in the past" to correct the distorted accounts of Africa given by European explorers, missionaries and administrators and writers (*Morning Yet on Creation Day*, 70). Of *Things Fall Apart* he says: "I now know that my first book, *Things Fall Apart* was an act of atonement with my past, the ritual return and homage of a prodigal son ("Named for Victoria", 70).

In spite of this nationalist outlook Achebe's treatment of the colonial-missionary encounter with African (Igbo) traditional culture does not take the subjective stance of a nationalist having it back on the European castigators of his race. Militating against his adult, patriotic impulse is his background and upbringing. In the essay mentioned above he says that he "was born of devout Christian parents" who gave him "a rigid and guarded Christian upbringing" (67), including an early Christian education. In this way he was exposed to reading that was Western, Christian-oriented. Although Achebe

---

† From *Emerging Perspectives on Chinua Achebe*. Vol. 2. Ed. Ernest N. Emenyonu and Iniobong I. Uko (Trenton, NJ: Africa World Press, 2004), 115–33. Reprinted by permission of Africa World Press.
1. I am indebted to T. R. Henn's discussion of *A Vision in The Lonely Tower* (London: Methuen University Paperbacks, 1965), 191–219.

protested against this upbringing by dropping his Christian name, Albert, Christianity has so much hold on him that issues of the colonial missionary encounter dominate his first three novels. In these novels, Achebe explores the encounter as a historical event, and makes an objective appraisal of the colonial-missionary experience. It may be said that Achebe, like Ezeulu the hero of his third novel, is, in spite of himself, aware of the attractions and advantages of the new religion to his people. The significance of the title of his first novel, *Things Fall Apart*, must be taken into account in any serious discussion of Achebe's attitude to the colonial missionary experience.

The title is believed to have been taken from W. B. Yeats' poem, "The Second Coming," which is concerned with the catastrophic climax and collapse of the Christian era and the uncertain situation between it and the era succeeding it. Yeats' poem appears in *A Vision* (1925) in which he propounds his theory of the cyclic movement of history. What Achebe takes from the Yeatsian theory is the idea of the inevitability of change.

In *Things Fall Apart*, he portrays the events of the late 19th and early 20th centuries Igboland as marking the end of traditional Igbo civilization and the ushering in of another civilization, the Christian-oriented civilization of Western Europe. In his treatment of the encounter in both *Things Fall Apart* and *Arrow of God* Achebe seems to suggest that the indigenous system had reached the catastrophic climax of Yeats' formulation. He emphasizes the weaknesses inherent in the traditional system that predisposed those disadvantaged in the existing order towards embracing the new order.

The greatest shortcoming of the traditional order according to Achebe's portrayal was its failure to provide for the safety and welfare of all citizens. One example was the discrimination against the *osu* and mothers of twins and their babies. The traditional order also endorsed the killing of Ikemefuna because it had been "decreed by the Oracle of the Hills and the Caves" (*TFA* 51, 60). Achebe makes it clear that it was the feeling of insecurity and the distress of such victims of traditional religious sanctions like Enoch (an *osu*) and Nneka (mother of twin babies) as well as their sympathizers like Nwoye that predisposed them to embracing the new religion. Nwoye's alienation from his father and the traditional order starts after he knows that his father has killed Ikemefuna:

> As soon as his father walked in that night, Nwoye knew that Ikemefuna had been killed, and something seemed to give way inside him, like the snapping of a tightened bow (*TFA* 55).

The imagery here suggests both the jolt and trauma which the event causes Nwoye. Achebe does not miss any opportunity to remind us that the killing of Ikemefuna and the throwing away of twins are always associated with Nwoye's consciousness. Referring to Nwoye's feeling when he realizes that Ikemefuna had been killed, Achebe says:

> He had the same kind of feeling not long ago, during the last harvest season . . . Nwoye had felt for the first time a snapping inside him like the one he now felt. They were returning . . . from a distant farm . . . when they heard the voice of an infant crying in the thick forest . . . Nwoye had heard that twins were put in earthen-ware pots and thrown away in the forest, but he had never yet come across them. A vague chill had descended on him and his head seemed to swell . . . Then something had given way inside him (*TFA* 55–56).

In the above passage Achebe is describing a humane impulse which was beginning to vibrate in the minds of many people in Umuofia. Among the custodians of the traditional religious order doubts and questions were also beginning to emerge which suggest an element of dissatisfaction with the existing order. In *Things Fall Apart* Obierika raises fundamental issues as he thinks of, and mourns Okonkwo's calamity:

> Why should a man suffer so grievously for an offence he had committed inadvertently? But although he thought for a long time he found no answer. He was merely led into greater complexities. He remembered his wife's twin children, whom he had thrown away. What crime had they committed? The earth had decreed that they were an offence on the land and must be destroyed . . . (*TFA* 113–114).

For a person in this frame of mind resistance to the in-coming order can hardly be whole-hearted. Although he does not join the Christians his reaction to Okonkwo's call to arms at the end of the novel (181–184) lacks enthusiasm and although he blames the District Commissioner for Okonkwo's suicide he seems to be reconciled to the situation of a new order.

By stressing that Okonkwo's exile is "decreed by earth" Achebe is also insinuating that the earth-goddess inadvertently facilitated the implanting of Christianity in Umuofia by removing the rallying point of resistance to the new order. It will be recalled that the killing of Ikemefuna and the throwing away of twins, both inhuman acts, are said to be "decreed by earth."

This situation of an ailing social order making possible the implanting of Christianity is also evident in *Arrow of God*. The jealousy and rivalry between Ezeulu and Ezeidemili contributes to the weakening of the cohesion and stability of the traditional social order in Umuaro. The rivalry between the priests of the two deities (and

their gods) is such that can only end in the destruction of one or both
of the cults. This is made clear in Ulu's rebuke of Ezeulu:

> Go home and sleep and leave me to settle my quarrel with Ide-
> mili whose envy seeks to destroy me that his python may come to
> power. . . . as for me and Idemili we shall fight to finish and who-
> ever throws the other down will strip him of his anklet (*AOG*, 192).

In *Arrow of God* Achebe also points out that the nature of the traditional deities makes it possible for the people to discard them whenever there was an occasion to do so. Ogbuefi Nwaka tells the people
of Umuaro:

> And we have all heard how the people of Aninta dealt with their
> deity when he failed them. Did they not carry him to the boundary
> between them and their neighbours and set fire on him? (*AOG* 28).

There is evidence that the turbulence in Umuaro brings a situation
of unease between the priest and his deity. Ezeulu saw the death of
his son, Obika, in the midst of the struggle between him and Umuaro
as a betrayal by his God. It is significant that he interprets the
betrayal as pointing to "the collapse and ruin of all things" (*AOG* 229).

Although the people of Umuaro claim that "their god had taken
sides with them against his headstrong and ambitious priest" (230),
Achebe's comment is intended to show that the defeat of the chief
priest also means the defeat (and death) of Ulu. As he puts it, if the
claim of Umuaro were correct:

> Then Ulu had chosen a dangerous time to uphold that truth for
> in destroying his priest he had also brought disaster on himself,
> like the lizard in the fable who ruined his mother's funeral by his
> own hand. For a deity who chose a moment such as this to chas-
> tise his priest or abandon him before his enemies was inciting
> people to take liberties (215).

The moment referred to is the moment of the advent of Christianity
in Umuaro. It is at such a moment that the people can defy traditional sanctions and try the advice of Goodcountry, the catechist of
St. Mark's CMS Church, "that if they made their thank-offering to
God they could harvest their crops without fear of Ulu." At the critical moment Ezeulu seems to have reconciled himself to the situation.
As he contemplates his misfortune we get the impression that he
does realize that the game is up. This is the implication of his last
utterance in the novel:

> What could it point to but the collapse and ruin of all things?
> Then a god finding himself powerless might take flight and in one,
> final, backward glance at his abandoned worshippers cry: if the rat
> cannot flee fast enough let him make way for the tortoise (229).

Achebe's portrayal of the traditional set up in both *Things Fall Apart* and *Arrow of God* suggests that change became inevitable and desirable because of the weaknesses inherent in that set-up. But he is also interested in the performance of the missionaries and their converts. He distinguishes between two types of missionaries and converts and points out the shortcomings of each. The type of missionary represented by the Reverend Mr. Brown is prepared to dialogue with the existing traditional order. Achebe does not fail, however, to point out that the insights into traditional religion gained through such dialogue are misapplied by the missionaries.

Corresponding to this type of missionary are the moderate and less fanatical converts like Moses Unachukwu (*Arrow of God*). These types of converts are willing to respect the norms of traditional religion in the practice of their newly acquired religion. Moses is opposed to Mr. Goodcountry's insistence that killing the sacred python is the way to show the convert's belief in Christianity. Moses told the new teacher quite bluntly that neither the Bible nor the catechism asked the converts to kill the python" (AOG 48). Moses Unachukwu advises the catechist:

> If you are wise you will face the work they sent you to do here and take your hand off the python . . . nobody here has complained to you that the python ever blocked his way as he came to church. If you want to do your work in peace you will heed what I have said, but if you want to be the lizard that ruined his own mother's funeral you may carry on the way you are doing (AOG 50).

Moses Unachukwu's position is based on the Igbo philosophy of "live and let live." Achebe shows approval of such a stance and gives Moses the glory of getting Umuaro over to the Christian God at the end of the novel.

Achebe condemns the method of evangelism practiced by the Reverend Mr. Smith (*Things Fall Apart*) and Mr. Goodcountry (*Arrow of God*) which insists on the total eradication of the traditional order. The Reverend Mr. Smith, as we are told, "sees things as either white or black, and black is evil." Achebe considers as tragic a situation where the traditional religion is willing to let Christianity prove itself but the Christian missionaries and some of their converts fail to adopt the same attitude towards traditional religious practice.

One of the converts, Enoch, unmasks the *egwugwu* (TFA 68), an assault considered by the people of Umuofia as a most serious travesty of their custom. In *Arrow of God* Mr. Goodcountry encourages his converts to kill the totemic python and one of them, Oduche, actually attempts to kill it, although secretly, by suffocation. Achebe contrasts Oduche with Moses Unachukwu and makes the point that

respect for the customs of the people does not necessarily vitiate the
faith of the Christian converts.

Achebe illustrates the ideal relationship between the converts and
the non-converts in his account of the situation in his own family. His
great grandfather, Udo Osinyi-Udo, allowed the earliest missionaries
to operate from his compound. He decided to eject them only
because the "eerie songs they sang might make his neighbors think
it was his funeral dirge" ("Named for Victoria . . ." 66). According to
Achebe, the parting was "without rancour", and the old man did not
raise "any serious objections" when Achebe's father joined the missionaries (66) and although he resisted the latter's attempt to convert
him, it did not bring about a quarrel. The old man's disposition is
summarized as follows:

> I don't know for certain but I think the old man was the very
> embodiment of tolerance insisting only that whatever a man
> decided to do he should do with style ("Named for Victoria . . ."
> 66).

The essay, "Named for Victoria . . . ," must be taken seriously in any
discussion of Achebe's attitude to Christianity as portrayed in his fiction. Critics who feel that Achebe is critical of Ezeulu's performance
in *Arrow of God* may do well to read it. The spirit of tolerance is
underscored in Achebe's description of his family:

> We lived at the crossroads of cultures. On one arm of the cross
> we sang hymns and read the Bible night and day. On the other
> arm my father's brother and his family . . . offered food to the
> idols. That was how it was supposed to be anyhow ("Named for
> Victoria . . ." 67).

He goes on to describe how, in spite of the fact that he was deep in
the practice of Christianity, "those idols" had a "strange pull on" him.
His account of the effect on this pull is worth quoting in full:

> . . . despite those delusions of divine destiny (as a Christian) I
> was not past taking my little sister to our neighbour's house
> when our parents were not looking and partaking of heathen fes-
> tival meals. I never found their rice and stew to have a flavour
> of idolatry. I was about ten then. If anyone likes to believe that
> I was torn by spiritual agonies or scorched on the racks of my
> ambivalence, he certainly may suit himself. I do not remember
> any undue distress. What I do remember was a fascination for
> the ritual and the life on the other arm of the cross-roads. And
> I believe two things were in my favour—that curiosity, and the
> little distance imposed between me and it by the accident of my
> birth. The distance becomes not a separation but a bringing
> together like the necessary backward step which a judicious

viewer may take in order to see a canvas steadily and fully
("Named for Victoria . . ." 68).

The advantage of this vantage position manifests in all his works. He,
more than any other Igbo novelist of English expression, shows an in-
depth knowledge of both traditional and Christian religious practice
and although he proclaims that he has renounced the latter, he cannot divest himself of the internalized tenets which his birth, upbringing and education impose on him. Thus, we find in his works not only
chronicles of the colonial-missionary encounter but also ample evidence of the effects of this background. His subtle manipulation of
biblical material demonstrates the excellence of his craftsmanship
even better than his generally acclaimed manipulation of the English
language.

Biblical material in his fiction are in the form of echoes, casual
references, deliberate quotations used for analogies and comments.
There are casual references to, and echoes of the Bible which are
merely a manner of thinking or speaking. In *No Longer at Ease*
(*NLAE*) for example, Isaac Okonkwo calls his daughters the foolish
virgins (*NLAE* 56). The phrase "foolish virgins" is obviously taken
from the parable of the Ten Virgins in Matthew 25, 1–13 but there
is nothing in the novel to suggest that it has the implications of the
biblical original. In the same manner, commenting on the permanence of the written word, Isaac Okonkwo quotes Pilate in John 19,
22: "what is written is written" (*NLAE* 115). And in *Arrow of God* the
chief messenger tells John Nwodika, "you have already done what
you were sent to do; the rest is for me. So put your tongue into its
scabbard." We recall that in John 18, 11 Jesus tells Peter: "put your
sword into the scabbard." This kind of use is common in Nigerian
literature and is accounted for by the fact of the author's western
missionary education.

In Achebe's fiction, however, the utterances acquire significance in
the context of the novels as a whole. Isaac Okonkwo's "what is written is written" assumes the status of a prophecy when combined with
what Odogwu says later about Obi: "As it was in the beginning, is
now, and ever shall be . . ." The effect is to give the reader a deeper
insight into the nature of Obi's tragedy and we pity him as we watch
him struggling against forces that have been predestined to crush
him.

In the same way, the chief messenger's words combine with the
recurrent motif "everything has a season." John Nwodika himself is
aware of this. He abides by it and succeeds. If we apply the motif to
Ezeulu's situation, we see his alliance with Christianity as resulting
from his deeper insight and he becomes even greater than a mere
chief priest of Ulu.

Achebe's typical references and allusions to the Bible often operate at this deeper level of significance. In A Man of the People Odili refers to how Chief Nanga comes to him "in the dark like Nicodemus" and offers him "two fifty pounds" (143). This is an allusion to John 3, 1 where the Pharisee, Nicodemus, who was a member of the Jewish Sanhedrin went secretly at night to learn the truth of the ministry of Jesus. There is in the allusion an implication of the hypocrisy of Chief Nanga. It also brings out the relationship between Nanga, as a member of the ruling class, and Odili the idealist reformer. Like Nicodemus of the Bible Nanga is, on one occasion, during the political rally, in a group where Odili's popularity is on trial (156–157). Nanga judges, condemns and punishes Odili whereas in John 7, 50 Nicodemus pleads for a fair hearing for Jesus. The climax of the contrasts is that Nicodemus became so committed to the cause that Jesus espoused that he joined Joseph Arimathea to bury the body of the crucified Jesus. The allusion to Nicodemus makes the point that the ruling class of the society of A Man of the People is hypocritical and unregenerate, a situation that makes the collapse of their government inevitable and welcome. The novel states that "some political commentators have said that it was the supreme cynicism that inflamed the people and brought down the government" (161).

Often Achebe's biblical echoes, allusions or quotations give authenticity to what is said thus instilling confidence in, and eliciting belief from the person or persons addressed. This is the effect achieved by the catechist, Kiaga, when encouraging his converts to ignore the banter of the non-converts he quotes Psalm 2, 1;4:

> Why do the nations rage and the people imagine vain things . . .
> he that sitteth in the heavens shall laugh. The lord shall have
> them in derision (TFA 143).

The quotation is in itself appropriate in the context where it appears. Psalm 2 is regarded by Bible scholars as a messianic Psalm in which "the psalmist depicts the revolt of the nations against God and his anointed son" as well as God's answer "and warning given to the rebels" (New American . . . Edition 4, 95). By quoting the psalm, Kiaga also puts himself entirely into the original biblical context and becomes one with the prophets, a transfiguration which is made complete by his speaking in character when Nwoye joins the converts:

> Blessed is he who forsakes his father and his mother for my sake
> (TFA 139) (Luke 14, 26: Matthew 10, 37–38).

This mode of perception makes the missionaries see events of the present as a fulfillment of biblical prophecies and their role as missionaries a continuation of the ministry of Jesus. Thus, the Reverend

Mr. Brown expresses his satisfaction with the progress of his mission in Umuofia in a metaphor that clearly recalls Luke 8, 11.

> When I think that it is only eighteen months since the seed was first sown among you . . . I marvel at *what the Lord has wrought* (*TFA* 146).

"Seed" represents here, as it does in the Bible, the word of God. The preachers of this word are described in the biblical metaphor of "labourers in the vineyard" (Matthew 20, 1). There is also a link with the Old Testament through the echo of Numbers 2, 23: I Marvel at "*what the Lord has wrought*" (my emphasis). It will be recalled that Numbers is a book of the Bible that deals with the preparation of the Israelites to be witnesses among the nations.

In *No Longer at Ease* Reverend Samuel Ikedi refers to Obi's going to study abroad as the fulfillment of the words of the prophet Isaiah 9, 2:

> The people which sat in darkness saw a great light and to them which sat in the region and shadow of death. To them did the light spring up (*NLAE* 7).

In Matthew 4, 16, this prophecy is seen as being fulfilled in the ministry of Jesus. The people "which sat in darkness" whom Reverend Ikedi refers to are the people of Umuofia and Obi is the light that has sprung up. Reverend Ikedi also refers to "the days of darkness from which we have been delivered by the blood of the lamb of God" (9). Having been delivered it becomes Obi's duty to heed the advice "that the fear of the Lord is the beginning of wisdom" (Proverbs 1, 7; *NLAE* 9). The rest of Obi's story hinges on this. It is ironic that in spite of his attempts to live according to the principles that Reverend Ikedi prescribes for him he gets into the tragic muddle that culminates in his imprisonment.

When Obi takes delivery of his new car, Green tells him: "you will do well to remember . . . that at this time every year you will be called upon to cough up forty pounds for your insurance" (*NLAE* 87). Achebe likens Green's words to the apocalyptic warning of the coming of the "day of the Lord" in Joel. The underlying theme of preparing for the day of reckoning applies to Obi as later events show. By the analogy, Achebe gives Green's words all the eschatological weight of Joel's prophecy.

Achebe may appropriate a biblical reference, metaphor or symbol to define a situation or comment on an issue. At the reception organized for him by the Umuofia Progressive Union in Lagos, Obi says: "did not the psalmist say that it was good for brethren to meet together in harmony" (*NLAE* 73). This is a close but not exact

quotation of Psalm 133, 1, which has the word "dwell". By quoting
the Psalm Obi shows that he is aware of the "benefits of brotherly
concord," which is the subject of the Psalm. Ironically, he is the first
to break the "harmony" for he walks out on the Union when they
introduce the subject of his association with Clara. There is here an
implicit satire on the well-known divergence between ideals and
practice which is an important theme in *No Longer at Ease*. In the
novel, the only phrase Ogbuefi Odogwu appropriates from the
Christians is the concluding portion of the prayer which says, "As it
was in the beginning, is now and ever shall be world without end"
(47). He applies this his favorite phrase to Isaac Okonkwo's family.
As he puts it:

> As a man comes into this world . . . so will he go out of it. When
> a titled man dies his anklets of title are cut so he will return as
> he came. The Christians are right when they say that as it was
> in the beginning so it will be in the end (47).

Later he applies it specifically to Obi: "He is Ogbuefi Okonkwo come
back. He is Okonkwo *kpom kwem*, exact, perfect" (49). Although
Obi's father, Isaac Okonkwo, protests that "dead men do not come
back," Odogwu insists that they do, using the authority of the Christian prayer: "as it was in the beginning so it will be in the end. That
is what your religion tells us" (49).

   Taken as a whole Odogwu's speech has crucial implications for Obi
Okonkwo's story. Literally, he is referring to the physical resemblance
between Obi and Obi's grandfather. There is also a suggestion in the
latter part of his speech that Obi will achieve greatness like his grandfather. But there is a further ironic implication of his sharing his
grandfather's ultimate disgrace. The speech also defines the pattern
of consequences of the contact with Christianity in the three generations from Okonkwo through his grandson Obi, and gives structural
unity to the two novels, *Things Fall Apart* and *No Longer at Ease*,
which span these generations.

   Obi's grandfather, Okonkwo in *Things Fall Apart*, dies trying to prevent Christianity from taking root in the clan. At his death, he is
alienated from the very tradition he had labored so much to uphold.
Okonkwo's son Nwoye (Isaac) defies him and embraces Christianity.
Even if we agree that Achebe is yet to write a novel on Isaac
Okonkwo's generation, we can infer from his reaction to Obi's pro-
posal to marry Clara (an *Osu*) that he capitulates before the very tradition from which he is running away.

   Odogwu's "as it was in the beginning" also links Obi with his father
in another interesting way. When Obi refuses to go home for his
mother's funeral, one member of the Umuofia Progressive Union in
Lagos remarks:

This story that we are all talking about, what has he done? He was told that his mother died and he did not care. It is a strange and surprising thing, but I can tell you that I have seen it before. His father did it . . . when this boy's father—you all know him, Isaac Okonkwo—when Isaac Okonkwo heard of the death of his father he said that those that kill with the matchet must die by the matchet (NLAE 145).

Isaac Okonkwo himself confirms the story as he tries to tell Obi the sufferings he "went through . . . to become a Christian":

When they brought me word that he [his father Okonkwo] had hanged himself I told them that those who live by the sword must perish by the sword. Mr. Bradley, the white man who was our teacher, said it was not the right thing to say and told me to go home for the burial. I refused to go . . . (125).

Expectedly, Isaac Okonkwo's is an accurate quotation from the Bible. It is ironic that he condemns his father using the language of the Bible and is in turn condemned, in the Clara debate, by his son, Obi, who reminds him that "the Bible says that in Christ there is no bond or free" (120). This story establishes the link between Obi, his father and his grandfather, and their three generations represent Odogwu's "was", "is" and "shall be".

Obi's reaction to the news of his mother's death can only be understood by him in terms of the story in 2 Samuel 12, 15–21 "of King David who refused food when his beloved son was sick but washed and ate when he (the son) died" (149). Achebe comments that Obi too must have felt this kind of peace. "The peace that passeth all understanding" (Philippians 4,7). This peace marks the final resolution of all Obi's heartaches. He "had been utterly prostrated by the shock of his mother's death." When, after weeping, he goes to bed that night, and "he did not wake up even once in the night," unlike what had been his experience "in the last few months" when "he had hardly known any sleep at all" (146).

It is peace resulting from his reconciling himself with forces that he can neither control nor surmount. As Achebe observes, Obi's thoughts about his circumstances give him "a queer kind of pleasure" (151):

They seemed to release his spirit. He no longer felt guilt. He, too, had died. Beyond death there are no ideals and no humbug, only reality. The patient idealist says, 'give me a place to stand and I shall move the earth.' But such a place does not exist. We all have to stand on the earth itself and go with her at her pace. The most horrible sight in the world cannot put out the eye. The death of a mother is not like a palm tree bearing fruit at the end of its leaf, no matter how much we want to make it so. And that is not the only illusion we have (151).

From this we can see that Obi realizes that his ideals have been an illusion. His mother's death has brought him face to face with reality. Coming to terms with this reality has brought him peace. He has to move with the earth at her own pace. He becomes a new Obi, to use his own words, "a brand new snake just emerged from its slough" (150). The snake image here is significant. Coming to terms with the world as he sees it also means the death of the idealist in him. He is now in the world in which he can think of himself as a snake with all the satanic implications. His first action after this "reformation" is to accept bribes and compromise his position by seducing the girl who is a candidate for scholarship—a course of action that leads to his tragic fall. The biblical analogy thus works in reverse for Obi. David came to terms with God, and the peace which he found was lasting peace because, as we are told, he had a son, Solomon, who was beloved by the Lord. Obi's peace, on the other hand, is only a brief interlude before the final catastrophe.

The impression one gets after reading Achebe's novels is that of an author addressing a society in which the Christian ethic has become a dominant factor in shaping the thinking and actions of the people. But Achebe seems to be saying that the acceptance of the Christian ethic must be seen in the context of the realities of life.

In *No Longer at Ease*, Isaac Okonkwo has four daughters before Obi is born. Because of the premium which Igbo culture places on male children, Isaac Okonkwo is, as Achebe tells us, "naturally becoming a little anxious." However, we are also reminded that he would not adopt the traditional mode of solution to his problem:

> . . . Being a Christian convert—in fact a catechist—he would not marry a second wife . . . he would not let the heathen know that he is unhappy (6).

The conflict within him is implied in the name "Nwanyidimma" (girl is good) which he gives to his fourth daughter. Although Achebe comments that Isaac Okonkwo's "voice did not carry conviction" there is an implication of a struggle to adopt the Christian attitude to his dilemma.

The distinction between acceptance of the Christian ethic and the practice of the demands of that acceptance is also implicit in the story of Elsie and Odili in *A Man of the People*. Odili meets the promiscuous Elsie "at a party organized by the students' Christian Movement" (27). This organization is one that claims for its membership a higher level of religiosity. The irony of the ease with which Elsie moves from the "prayerful" party to a sexual orgy is Achebe's criticism of the depravity of the age. It may also be his cynical suggestion that people like Elsie exist in spite of the ideals of the Students' Christian Movement.

Achebe's knowledge of, and involvement with, the Bible shows best in his exploration of characterization. Sometimes he deliberately models his characters on Biblical archetypes of either the Old or the New Testament. Indications of the Biblical connection are sometimes given through the characters' names. Thus Isaac in *Things Fall Apart* and Moses in *Arrow of God* are seen to perform in the novel the roles of the biblical archetypes.

A character does not need to be a Christian to function as a type. A close examination of the circumstances of Ezeulu reveals parallels with Old Testament figures and by figuration, with Jesus. Like the Old Testament prophets, Ezeulu is gifted with mystical insight. He tells his friend Akuebue, "I can see things where other men are blind" (*AOG* 132). He uses this deeper insight to guide his people although they always disobey him and suffer as a result. He does not hesitate to assert his superior status:

> But you cannot know the thing which beats the drum to which Ezeulu dances. I can see tomorrow; that is why I can tell Umuaro: 'come out from this because there is death there or do this because there is profit in it.' If they listen to me, o-o; if they refuse to listen, o-o. I have passed the stage of dancing to receive presents (132).

He displays this insight in his decision to send his son Oduche "to learn the secrets of the white man's magic." The people of Umuaro rightly point out that this is part of Ezeulu's pact with the white man. Although he does not see his action in this way he is in-fact unconsciously allying with the new forces (religious and governmental), which eventually overthrow the very order of which he is the custodian. He does this because it has been given to him mystically to know that the "disease" which is afflicting his clan is one "that has never been seen before." Such revelation is comparable to God's manifestation of himself to such Old Testament figures as Abraham. Although Ezeulu interprets his own visions in terms of the traditional Igbo religion which he knows, he is always pointing to the "end of things" a phrase which he uses three times in his discussion of the subject of Oduche joining the Christians. He tells Akuebue:

> Shall I tell you why I sent my son? . . . A disease that has never been seen before cannot be cured with everyday herbs. When we want to make a charm we look for the animal whose blood can match its power . . . but sometimes even a bull does not suffice, then we must look for a human. Do you think it is the sound of

> the death-cry gurgling through blood that we want to hear.
> No . . . we do it because we have reached the very end of
> things . . . and our fathers have told us that it may even happen
> to an unfortunate generation that they are pushed beyond the
> end of things, . . . When this happens they may sacrifice their
> own blood . . . That was why our ancestors when they were
> pushed beyond the end of things by the Warriors of Abam sacri-
> ficed not a stranger but one of themselves and made the great
> medicine which they called Ulu (133–134).

If we apply Ezeulu's philosophy to his situation we can conclude that
sending Oduche to a missionary school is an act of sacrifice. This
raises two points. In the first place, it reminds us of the sacrifice of
Isaac by his father, Abraham (Auden 100). Ezeulu thus becomes a
figure like Abraham, willing to sacrifice his son to God. But the more
important point is that Ezeulu, the Chief Priest of Ulu, a deity of Igbo
traditional religion, is offering the sacrifice as a result of the type of
revelation normally associated with Old Testament prophets.
Ezeulu's "end of things" is obviously a reference to the end of the traditional, pre-Christian order because at the climax of his agony he
does not say that his betrayal by Ulu only points to "the collapse and
ruin of all things." At that point we feel, in retrospect, the impact of
the phrases and it becomes clear that Ezeulu has all along had, even
if unconsciously, a foreknowledge of the collapse of the traditional
order.

Obika's death marks the beginning of a new era when Umuaro is
converted to Christianity. Without his knowing it, Ezeulu is both a
prophet of this new era as well as the instrument ("the arrow of God")
used by the Christian God for the conversion of Umuaro. In this
regard, he becomes what Auden has described as a "doer of the word
who has never heard the word" (100). This is a very important aspect
of his complex personality. He is Man-God, "known" and "unknow-
able," a fact acknowledged both by custom which stipulates that he
paints one part of his body white and the other black during rituals,
and by Akuebue who says of him:

> I am your friend and I can talk to you as I like; but that does not
> mean I forget that one half of you is man and the other half spirit
> (133).

The duality places Ezeulu at a higher level than the Old Testament
figures. There is an immediate reference to the cardinal doctrine of
Christianity that Jesus Christ is "true God and true man."

Although one cannot think of Ezeulu as a Jesus figure in the usually accepted sense, the parallels with aspects of the story of Jesus are
remarkable. For example, the dream in which he confronts the elders of Umuaro echoes the experiences of Jesus before the Jewish

populace. There is the same community of opposition by the elders who shout together, "He shall not speak, we will not listen to him," (*AOG* 159). They also revile him in words that echo those used by the Jewish populace to deride the hanging Jesus: "He saved our fathers from the warriors of Abam but he cannot save us from the white man" (159). As in the case of Jesus, "some spat in his face and called him the priest of the dead God" (159).

Achebe gives significance to Ezeulu's death by linking it with an event that marks the triumph of Christianity in Umuaro. Although he lives and dies upholding the traditional order, his career is also inextricably bound up with the story of Christianity in Umuaro. Ezeulu's death is an ending, "the end" of the beginning of the Christian epoch in Umuaro.

The duality of Ezeulu's personality and the significance of his career in the history of Christianity in Umuaro make the comparison between him and the Christian Jesus inescapable. His unique position is emphasized even in his fall. His last days have the tragic grandeur, which is denied Okonkwo. The novel says that "in his last days" he lived "in the haughty splendor of a demented high priest . . ." (229). "High Priest" is a deliberate echo of Jesus as High Priest in Hebrews, 9.

In Achebe's poetry, the use of biblical material is a bit more complex. Christian analogues are juxtaposed with traditional Igbo equivalents as Achebe is trying to demonstrate the validity of the latter. For example, in the poem "Mango Seedling" (5), the fate of a mango seedling sprouting on a concrete canopy is reminiscent of both the widow of Zarepath, "the widow/of infinite faith," and the traditional Igbo fable of the old tortoise and his "dot of cocoyam." Because of its limited source of food the seedling is compared with the widow, but it is also contrasted with her because the widow's meager store was miraculously replenished by God after she had provided for Elijah (1 Kings, 17, 12–16). In the same way the seedling is compared and contrasted with old Tortoise:

> Old Tortoise's miraculous feast on the ever recurring dot of cocoyam set in a large bowl of green vegetables—this day beyond fable, beyond faith (5).

The seedling, like the bat of Igbo folklore does not belong to earth or sky. It belongs neither to the religious tradition of the Jews nor to the tradition in which the Tortoise survived. So it dies in spite of its "passionate courage":

> Dry, wire-thin in sun and dust of the dry month headstone on the tiny debris of passionate courage (6).

The seedling is denied a thunderous and disastrous end "in delirious waterfall / Toward earth below." Rather its end is uneventful, saddening but stubborn and courageous, as if nature would not let it down:

> . . . every rainy day little playful floods assembled on the slab danced, parted round its feet united again, and passed . . . (6).

The "primordial quarrel of Earth / And sky" between which according to the poem, the seedling is "poised in courageous impartiality" is the quarrel which, in Igbo folklore, led to the sky withholding rain for several months (TFA 48). Although the ensuing drought may have contributed to the death of the seedling, its problem is, specifically, its lack of rootedness in *ala*, to which, as Achebe has pointed out in "Beware Soul Brother":

> A man's
> Foot must return whatever beauties
> it may weave in air, where
> it must return for safety
> a renewal of strength . . . (29).

The seedling is "striving bravely to sink roots / into objectivity, mid-air in stone." If it had been rooted in *ala* (the soil) it would, according to the argument of the poem, have survived.

The juxtaposing of the biblical and the contemporary is sometimes so subtle that Achebe's intention is not immediately obvious. In "Non Commitment":

> . . . Pontius Pilate openly washed involvement off his white hands and became famous

And

> Judas wasn't such a fool either . . . He alone in that motley crowd had sense enough to tell a doomed movement when he saw one and get out quick, a nice little pocket bulging his coat-pocket into the bargain (31).

Here Achebe is pointing out the irony implicit in a situation where those who will not commit themselves and traitors in issues of grave moral dimensions become celebrated characters. The biblical story of the betrayal of Jesus by Judas and Pilate's hypocritical washing of his hands in the matter of the condemnation of Jesus are taken by Achebe as analogues of the contemporary situation that he is describing. The word, "white" which qualifies Pilate's hand is a clue to the Pilates that Achebe has in mind. If we interpret the poem in terms of the Nigerian situation Judas would be a symbol of the local traitors. Of greater significance, however, is Achebe's reinterpretation of the

Pilate-Judas situation which is a radical departure from the orthodox Christian interpretation.

In "Lazarus" Achebe contrasts the orthodox Christian interpretation of the raising to life of Lazarus by Jesus with the social implications of such a miracle in contemporary society. The resurrection of Lazarus is marked by:

> The breath-taking joy of his sisters when the word spread: he is risen (37).

In contemporary society, there cannot be this unqualified joy because:

> . . . a man who has lived a full life will have others to reckon with beside his sisters.

Resurrection in the modern social context will be an embarrassment to the officer who has been promoted to take the position left vacant by the dead person.

Achebe's poem is based on a contemporary event. The people of Ogbaku (in Owerri, Imo State of Nigeria) killed "the barrister" for apparently killing their kinsman (in a car accident). For this killing there could be "justification". When it turned out that their kinsman was not dead, the people then killed him to retain their plea. Achebe likens his revival to a resurrection. It brings joy to his sisters but it is a source of grave anxiety for the "luckless people" because "their kinsman avenged in murder" stirring "in wide eyed resurrection" would turn:

> Away from them in obedience to other fraternities, would turn indeed their own accuser and in one breath obliterate their plea and justification! So they killed him a second time that day on the threshold of a promising resurrection (37–38).

Achebe's "Lazarus" has affinity with the ghost scene in Shakespeare's *Macbeth* III, IV, 77 ff where, in his distress over the appearance of Banquo's ghost Macbeth says:

> The time has been that when the brains were out the man would die, and there an end; but now they rise again, with twenty mortal murders on their crowns and push us from our stools.

In both Shakespeare and Achebe resurrection is not treated in terms of orthodoxy, that is, the resurrection of all the dead on the Last Day, but resurrection particularized and coming before the Last Day, thus constituting an embarrassment to the living.

The treatment of a biblical theme in a contemporary context is also evident in the poem, "1966". This poem casts a backward look on the thoughtlessness and indolence of Nigerian rulers that led to the political turmoil in Nigeria in 1966. Because of their misrule:

> A diamond-tipped drillpoint crept closer to residual chaos to rare artesian hatred that once squirmed warm blood in God's face confirming his first disappointment in Eden (31).

The fratricidal confrontations in Nigeria are likened to the killing of Abel by his brother, Cain. Both crimes have their origin in "residual chaos . . . rare artesian hatred." God had been disappointed with the fall of Adam and Eve. The killings in Nigeria, like the crime of Cain, heighten this disappointment.

This poem is, however, weak in its logic. If, as Achebe implies, sin is inherent (residual chaos . . .) the events of 1996 in Nigeria cannot be incidental on the absent-mindedness or the thoughtlessness of Nigerian rulers, but should be seen as part of God's design.

Not only is Achebe influenced by the Bible he is fascinated by Christian religious practice and ritual. In "Christmas in Biafra" he looks closely at, and carefully describes a Christmas crib set up by Catholic nuns working in a hospital in war-torn Biafra:

> Beyond the hospital gate the good nuns had set up a manger of palms to house in fine plastercast scene at Bethlehem. The holy Family was central, serene, the child Jesus plump, wise-looking and rose-cheeked; one of the magic in keeping with legend of black Othello in sumptuous robes. Other figures of men and angels stood at well-appointed distances from the heart of the divine miracle and the usual cattle gazed on in holy wonder . . . (13).

This description emphasizes the beauty of the crib. There is implicit in it the awe and reverence of a poet who knows the full import of the mystery represented by the crib. Nevertheless, he is also mindful of its irrelevance in war-torn Biafra. The reader is directed from the "Child Jesus, plump wise-looking and plump-cheeked" to the "infant son" of the woman worshipper:

> flat like a dead lizard
> on her shoulder his arms and legs
> cauterized by famine was a miracle
> of its own kind. Large sunken eyes
> stricken past boredom to a flat
> unrecognizing glueyness moped faraway
> motionless across her shoulder . . . (14).

The figure in the crib, like the "faraway sounds of other men's carols" appears to the poet to mock the worshippers. Achebe's comments are implied in the reaction of the child when his mother:

> turned him round and pointed
> at those pretty figures of God
> and angels and men and beasts—
> a spectacle to stir the heart
> of a child (14).

The child, who, like most children in Biafra, is doomed to the slow-grinding death by kwashiorkor, represents the spirit of the Biafran nation. All he does is to cast:

> one slow deadpan look of total
> unrecognition and he began again
> to swivel his enormous head away
> to mope as before at his empty distance (24).

The "empty distance" is symbolic of the hopelessness of the child's situation, and his reaction amounts to a rejection of this gesture of the nuns; it is an expression of "pure transcendental hate" (13).

Achebe's somber description shows that neither the crib nor the faraway sounds of other/men's carols floating on crackling waves arouses the usual festive emotions associated with Christmas.

"Christmas in Biafra" is unlike "Lazarus". Whereas "Lazarus" uses the biblical story for what it is worth, "Christmas in Biafra" actually comments on the Christian situation itself. As in the poignantly ironic reference to "Madonna and Child" in the poem, "Refugee Mother and Child," Achebe seems to be saying that what the child needs in his present circumstances is not a well-laid out crib. In fact, for him, the whole idea of Christmas is rejected in Biafra, the "death-calls of the moment":

> this sunken-eyed moment wobbling
> down the rocky steepness on broken
> bones slowly fearfully to hideous
> concourse of gathering sorrows . . .

Achebe's despair is comparable to that of Mycerinus (Arnold 2–5) as the latter contemplates the decree of the oracle from the city of Buto that he had only six years more to live, in spite of his just rule. Achebe is in effect asking the Christian nuns the same questions that Mycerinus asks of the gods:

> O wherefore cheat our youth, if thus it be . . .
> stringing vain words of powers we cannot see,
> blind divinations of a will supreme;
> lost labour! When the circumambient gloom
> but hides, if Gods, Gods careless of our doom?

For Achebe the problem is not the question of believing or not believing in the meaning of Christmas, but of there being no need at all to believe in a God who is apparently unconcerned with the suffering of the people. It should be recalled that for the people on the Biafran side, the Nigerian civil war was a war of survival. Theirs was the "just position" and to many, God did not seem to have appreciated the justness of their cause. "Christmas in Biafra" is thus an eloquent expression of the resultant despair.

Achebe is a prominent writer of the conflict-protest tradition of African literature. This is literature that aims at showing Africans where the rain started to beat them; to trace the origins of an encounter that has exerted so much influence on their history and individual lives. Achebe's portrayal of the Christian missionary experience carries the message that there is need to retain what is best in both Christianity and traditional religion, a message he exemplifies in his portrayal of a character like Moses Unachukwu in *Arrow of God*. Achebe himself embodies the conflict situation which is played out in the individual writer who is aware of the benefits of the Christian missionary presence but who must also show a commitment to validating his cultural past. His is an intellectualized appraisal of the situation often through analogical use of biblical material to comment on and sometimes interpret events in contemporary Nigerian society.

WORKS CITED

Achebe, Chinua. *Things Fall Apart*. London: Heinemann, 1958.

———. *Arrow of God*. London: Heinemann, 1964.

———. *No Longer at Ease*. London: Heinemann, 1960.

———. *A Man of the People*. London: Heinemann, 1966.

———. *Beware Soul Brother*. Enugu: Nwamife Publishers Ltd., 1971.

———. "Named for Victoria, Queen of England." In *Morning Yet on Creation Day*. London: Heinemann, 1975.

Arnold, Matthew. "Mycerinus" In *Selected Poetry and Prose*. New York: Holt, Rinehart and Winston, 1962.

Auden, M. H. *The Enchanted Flood or The Romantic Iconography of the Sea*. London: Faber & Faber Ltd., 1951.

New American Catholic Bible. Fireside Edition.

NEIL TEN KORTENAAR

Chinua Achebe and the Question of Modern African Tragedy†

Chinua Achebe's *Things Fall Apart,* arguably the most influential literary text to come out of Africa, is cast in the form of a tragedy.[1] Okonkwo, already acknowledged by his community to be "the greatest wrestler and warrior alive" (*TFA,* 82), is an over-reacher who seeks the recognition of his clan, Umuofia, as its leader and, more, as the embodiment of its collective will. Okonkwo pits his will and strength against unjust and inhuman fates larger than he is, fates that take the form of the historical forces of colonialism and that eventually destroy him. The qualities that help Okonkwo rise—his ambition, his discipline, and his single-mindedness—are inseparable from the defects that will cast him down: his intolerance, his need to dominate, and, above all, his fear of weakness.

Achebe has readily spoken to Robert Wren of his own tragic sensibility, which has always responded to the dark sensibilities of Thomas Hardy and A. E. Housman.[2] Achebe, however, has become understandably defensive about the issue of European influences on his art. In an interview with Charles Rowell in 1989, he denied that he was thinking of the Aristotelian concept of tragedy when he wrote *Things Fall Apart.*[3] Achebe attributes his novel's tragic form to parallel historical developments: he writes and the ancient Greeks wrote tragedy because the Greeks owed a great deal to Egypt, which was "very close to the Sudan and Nubia which was very close to West Africa" (Rowell, 179).[4] Another explanation Achebe gives for the conjunction is that tragedy is universal (or at least "not necessarily foreign to other people" [Rowell, 179]). Achebe argues that many cultures are familiar with "the man who's larger than life, who exemplifies virtues that are admired by the community, but also a man who for all that is still human. He can have flaws, you see; all that seems to me to be very elegantly underlined in Aristotle's work. I think they are there in human nature itself, and would be found in other traditions even if they were not spelled out in the same exact way" (Rowell, 179). One

---

† From *Philosophia Africana* 9.2 (August 2006): 83–100.
1. Chinua Achebe, *Things Fall Apart* (Oxford: Heinemann, 1988). Henceforth cited as *TFA.*
2. Robert Wren, "Those Magical Years," in *Conversations with Chinua Achebe,* ed. Bernth Lindfors (Jackson: University Press of Mississippi, 1997), 104.
3. Charles H. Rowell, "An Interview with Chinua Achebe" in *Conversations with Chinua Achebe,* cited above at note 2, 165–84. Henceforth cited as Rowell.
4. Achebe is thinking here of the scholarship of Cheikh Anta Diop and Martin Bernal, who have argued that classical Greece was indebted to Egypt, which was an explicitly black civilization.

senses an anxiety in Achebe's response here: he does not want to explain the influence of classical tragedy on his work but to explain it away. His argument about common African origins or a shared human sensibility should allow the Nigerian writer to borrow from classical Greece with a clear conscience, but Achebe's point is precisely the opposite: parallels do not indicate influence and no borrowing has taken place. Clearly, he feels that borrowing would be improper.

Others find that classical influences on African literature are not only improper but pernicious. Timothy Reiss has forcefully argued that tragedy as a literary mode and the theoretical discourse about tragedy together constitute "a principal category of thought enabling . . . the 'colonization' of others."[5] His argument is that, because tragedy consolidates the human realm by emphasizing the dissonance between the human and the larger, non-human sphere, it has allowed the Western self to reject as other, and even as non-human, all that is not itself. According to Reiss, Europeans believe that, while other peoples are as yet undivided and therefore, to an extent, innocent, they themselves, precisely because they are alienated from their essential selves, from the world, and from community with others, feel the truth of fallen humanity most deeply. As Guitar Bains says in Toni Morrison's *Song of Solomon*, "For years white writers having been telling white people they are unnatural, telling them they are depraved. They call it tragedy."[6] The result is that the West sees itself as alienated from nature, but also as heroic: the West alone makes history, the record of the world as remade by humans.

Reiss argues that the West also casts others, especially Native North Americans and Africans, as tragic because the progress of history has inevitably alienated them, too, from their essential selves, as it took from them their lands and obliterated their cultures. Such peoples, however, do not make history but, rather, are deprived of history: "To set the story and stories of Native America into tragedy and the tragic is to use cultural power to remove peoples from their present," says Reiss; "Tragedy and the tragic make things destined, personally irresponsible, fated by greater nonhuman forces" (*AA*, 144). Defeated peoples are described as "tragic" by their conquerors because "they are understood as tragically disjointed from the necessary progress and 'legitimate' direction of human history": "To denominate a culture and its members as tragic, its deeds and experiences as tragedy, replaces the local ambiguities of life and the realities of particular place and time, with someone else's overlaying transparency" (*AA*, 145).

---

5. Timothy J. Reiss, *Against Autonomy: Global Dialectics of Cultural Exchange* (Stanford: Stanford University Press, 2002), 109. Henceforth cited as *AA*.
6. Toni Morrison, *Song of Solomon* (New York: Penguin, 1987), 157.

Casting Okonkwo's story as a tragedy provides Achebe's novel with unity and teleological drive but, as Ode Ogede argues, it also gives rise to a narrative contradiction: to blame historical injustice on a transhuman realm called fate or History with a capital "H" is to remove agency from the colonized and, in effect, to justify the course of events.[7] Tragedy, argue Reiss and Ogede, makes human suffering appear inevitable, part of the nature of things, and even suggests that in the terrible spectacle of suffering lies wisdom. The most obvious explanation of Achebe's adoption of tragic form—that it accords heroic status to one whose humanity has been denied by the ethnographic gaze of the British colonizer—is thereby vitiated; it seems that Okonkwo can only be recognized as a man because he is doomed. Worse, casting Okonkwo's story as a tragedy *even before the British appear on the scene* perversely suggests that the debacle of colonization fulfilled lines of development already present in Igbo society. Colonialism permanently disrupted the historical trajectories of African societies and recast them in a disadvantageous mold made elsewhere, but the focus in *Things Fall Apart* on the doomed hero gives the impression that somehow the ongoing collective disaster was brought on by fissures internal to the community.

Michael Valdez Moses reads Achebe's novel the same way Ogede does, as a tragedy in the mold of Thomas Hardy and Joseph Conrad, but with this difference: Moses approves of the genre.[8] According to Moses, who explicitly follows Hegel in assuming that history has a particular direction that involves the unification of all particular histories into a single history of humankind and the progressive increase of human freedom, the Igbo-speakers of Umuofia, like others elsewhere, are being integrated into a larger world by empire and in the process are becoming Igbos, Africans, and soon Nigerians. A traditional hierarchical society based on archaic heroic values is giving way to a more modern and egalitarian society. The process as described by Moses is not without pain and irony. He explains that irrational, cruel, and unjust practices, such as imperial conquest and colonial rule, are all part of the ruse of reason, ultimately serving the progress of human liberation.[9] Tragedy, Moses argues, "requires a collision between two moral principles or 'ethical substantives,' both

7. Ode Ogede, *Achebe and the Politics of Representation* (Trenton: Africa World Press, 2001).
8. Michael Valdez Moses, *The Novel and the Globalization of Culture* (New York: Oxford University Press, 1995). Henceforth cited as *NGC*.
9. Moses writes, "For Hegel the worst and most inhumane abuses of history—the slave trade of Africa, the tyrannical rule of the Caesars, the torture and crucifixion of Christians, the chattel existence of women and children under Mandarin rule, the degradation of the *chandala* in India, the exploitative treatment of European serfs, the religious violence of Catholic and Protestant sectarians, the Terror of the French Revolution—ultimately assume a necessary role in a historical progression that dialectically overcomes and cancels out all of these horrific practices. Humanity creates and liberates itself *through* history, but its birth and development occur only through tragic violence *in* history" (*NGC*, 11).

of which command the respect of the audience" (*NGC*, 10). A genuine good (the integrity of the community of the clan) has been lost, but that sacrifice is both inevitable and even desirable, because a greater good, the freedom of individuals and the integration of humanity, has thereby been achieved.

Moses is not wrong. A novel written in English by a Nigerian in 1957 cannot but tell the story of Igboland as a version of the coming of colonization. From the opening pages of the novel and long before the news of white men with unheard-of capacities for mass destruction has reached Umuofia, readers understand that the world we are reading about is *precolonial*, that is, it fits into a narrative of colonization that we know but the characters do not. In that sense, the novel is written from *an* end of history, not *the* end. The relation between the death of the representative hero and the survival of the chastened community is not, however, the dialectic that Moses suggests. It is not true, as Moses writes, that "For Achebe, this conflict is *inescapable*. It was impossible for the political and ethical differences between the British and the Igbo to have been mediated in a peaceful fashion. Whatever accommodation is ultimately possible between premodern Umuofia and modern Nigeria, between Igbo and European traditions in the postcolonial epoch, can occur only through the violent and comprehensive reordering of the communal life of Okonkwo's people" (*NGC*, 122). Colonization is not merely the dialectical counterweight to the premodern Igbo clan. Achebe's novel does not look back on the tragedy of modernization and globalization from a vantage point at the "end of history," as do the works of Hegel and Moses (*NGC*, 131). If at every moment *Things Fall Apart* presumes the educated nationalist writer able to produce this novel, the implied author is not located at the end but in the very midst of history. As Moses himself admits, Achebe's sequel, *No Longer at Ease,* presumes that "the tragedy of modernization in postcolonial Africa has by no means reached its end" (*NGC*, 147).

A Hegelian like Moses, who assumes not only that world history leads to himself but also that world history is a story of progress, displays what Uday Singh Mehta calls a "naked admiration of success."[1] The liberal version of globalization is that there is only one end of history and that end is known, and that, moreover, there was only ever going to be one end. If, however, that version now appears correct, if indeed there seems to be a universal end of history, it is because that history has imposed itself by force on other histories. Mehta quotes Kant: "But how is an *a priori* history possible? Answer: When the soothsayer himself causes and contrives the events that he proclaims

1. Uday Singh Mehta, *Liberalism and Empire: A Study in Nineteenth-Century British Liberal Thought* (Chicago: University of Chicago Press, 1999), 87. Henceforth cited as *LE*.

in advance" (*LE*, 210). The European narrative of progress which purported to be constative proved performative: it brought into being the world it desired merely by casting others in the roles of tragic heroes. With friends like Moses, who needs Ogede?

But what if one is not persuaded by Moses' and Hegel's reading of the world, as clearly Ogede is not? What does one make of Achebe's novel if one does not believe that human history is necessarily headed toward progressive human freedom but fears that it is headed instead toward ecological disaster, unprecedented scales of suffering, and ever more powerful forms of tyranny? For certainly it is possible at the present moment to doubt that history has offered people outside the center of empire greater freedom or improved their capacity to make it in the world. Even if one accepts, as I think one must, that the spread of a secular, liberal ethos is a good, it is not self-evident that it required empire, the slave trade, and the reduction of half the globe to misery in order to be realized.[2] It is just as possible that the march of liberal progress has been and continues to be shadowed and often overwhelmed by deplorable forces in the form of racism and exploitation. The extermination of cultures valuable for their difference, and even for their superiority, as ways of promoting human welfare does not necessarily serve an increased awareness of a common humanity, as Moses trusts it does, but may merely facilitate the exploitation of the many by the few.

All who are skeptical about the direction of the world and who deplore the actual state of affairs must be suspicious of tragedy. Raymond Williams points out that "The most infiuential kinds of explicitly social thinking have often rejected tragedy as in itself defeatist. Against what they have known as the idea of tragedy, they have stressed man's powers to change his condition and to end a major part of the suffering which the tragic ideology seems to ratify."[3] Wole Soyinka, in his prison memoirs, urges, "Destroy the tragic lure!" for "Tragedy is possible solely because of the limitations of the human spirit," and he denounces "the historic conspiracy, the literal brainwashing that elevates tragedy far and above a regenerative continuance of the promethean struggle."[4]

---

2. Charles Mills, who, like Moses, presumes a common trajectory for human development, plausibly argues that imperialism frustrated that goal: "It was far from the case that Europe was specially destined to assume economic hegemony; there were a number of centers in Asia and Africa of a comparable level of development which could potentially have evolved in the same way. But the European ascent closed off this development path for others because it forcibly inserted them into a colonial network whose exploitative relations and extractive mechanisms prevented autonomous growth." Mills, *The Racial Contract* (Ithaca: Cornell University Press, 1997), 35. Henceforth cited as *RC*.
3. Raymond Williams, *Modern Tragedy* (London: Hogarth Press, 1992), 63. Henceforth cited as *MT*.
4. Wole Soyinka, *The Man Died* (Harmondsworth, Great Britain: Penguin, 1975), 89.

About the world I am less persuaded by Moses than by Reiss, but I am unwilling to follow Ogede in his condemnation of Achebe. I note a seeming contradiction in Reiss's argument. When Europeans are the heroes, tragedy is the source of their great predatory power, but when Africans and Native Americans are depicted as tragic, they are condemned to isolation and impotence. The tragic severing of self from the world that accounts for the virulence of the West also somehow cripples the non-West. Reiss resolves the contradiction by arguing that tragedy has always been the particular mark of the West and that it can therefore only serve the West and will harm anyone else who takes it up. By this analysis, modern African tragedy stands twice condemned: because it participates in a debilitating narrative that justifies the devastation of culture as historical inevitability and because it mimics a non-African form. Reiss goes further—he regards modern African tragedy as an oxymoron: if it is tragedy it cannot be truly African. Reiss does not discuss Achebe, but he would presumably judge him as he does the plays of John Pepper Clark, in which he finds a "very western incomprehension and rupture" (*AA*, 140). If we followed Reiss's argument (and it is close to Ogede's), we would find that the author of *Things Fall Apart* both imitates European forms and confirms European notions of Africa, that is, Achebe is guilty of mimicry and othering at the same time.

Reiss argues that African audiences laugh in incomprehension when they see tragedy on stage. But, while it may be possible, as Ogede also argues, that African tragedy is a mistake, it is not true that Africans do not write tragedy. Achebe has. The effect of Reiss's argument is to condemn what African writers actually write. To insist that tragedy is necessarily and forever foreign to Africa leads up the same path as the insistence that the English language, historical consciousness, the novel as a genre, or literacy are foreign to Africa. We must be skeptical of such notions of deep culture as Reiss's. Williams reminds us that if we think of tragic theory as "about a single and permanent kind of fact, we can end only with the metaphysical conclusions that are built into any such assumption" (*MT*, 45). If tragedy is a cultural instrument, as Reiss argues, then manifestly it is one that African writers, including Clark, Achebe, and even Soyinka, author of *Death and the King's Horseman,* have put to use (albeit to different uses). I do not mean that cultural instruments are neutral and fully in the control of those who wield them. It is indeed all too likely that writers are remade by the instruments they seek to manipulate. But I also assume that tragedy is not limited to a single meaning but can serve different purposes in different contexts.

What happens if we take Reiss's strictures against tragedy seriously, yet admit that the most influential novel to come out of Africa is a tragedy on classical lines? My interest is not primarily in defending

Achebe (though I do so), but in understanding him. Instead of asking the meaning of tragedy always and everywhere, we must ask of each manifestation of tragedy. Why now? Why here? When we ask why Achebe writes tragedy, we should keep in mind Williams's defense of modern tragedy against those who see it as anti-revolutionary: "tragic experience, because of its central importance, commonly attracts the fundamental beliefs and tensions of a period, and tragic theory is interesting mainly in this sense, that through it the shape and set of a particular culture is often deeply realized" (*MT*, 45).

Reiss, who believes that tragedy is central to what it means to be Western and is a mode unknown outside the West, also argues that tragedy has only made its appearance at particular moments in history, "at times of reorganization of the political and social order" (*AA*, 116). Williams comes to similar conclusions: "Important tragedy seems to occur, neither in periods of real stability, nor in periods of open and decisive conflict. Its most common historical setting is the period preceding the substantial breakdown and transformation of an important culture" (*MT*, 54). It seems likely that the historical conjunctures that call forth tragedy from wherever it is supposed to reside in the Western psyche may occur in Africa as well. If so, such a moment would be the one in which Achebe wrote: the fifties and sixties of the last century, when in Africa things had fallen apart, leaving people no longer at ease, while the beautiful ones were not yet born or, more prosaically, on the eve and morrow of political independence.

Nigeria's independence in 1960 did not just mark the triumph of anti-colonial resistance, but also a moment of deep uncertainty and ambivalence. As Philip Zachernuk reminds us, "No sooner had the nationalists' demands been granted, it seems, than Nigerians became unsure of the way forward."[5] Zachernuk quotes F. O. Onipede, writing in 1956, the year before the publication of *Things Fall Apart*: "Today, as never before in the history of west African nationalism, there is a marked feeling of doubt about the objectives of nationalism" (*CS*, 167). This persistent doubt explains "the notable lack of festivity in Lagos streets on Independence Day" (*CS*, 179).

Why write tragedy in Nigeria on the eve of independence? Because, as Peter Euben has argued with regard to classical Greece, tragedy is a way of meditating on political questions, in particular on justice and identity.[6] Jean-Pierre Vernant agrees: "Tragedy is contemporaneous with the City and with its legal system. In this sense

---

5. Philip S. Zachernuk, *Colonial Subjects: An African Intelligentsia and Atlantic Ideas* (Charlottesville: University Press of Virginia, 2000), 167. Henceforth cited as *CS*.
6. Peter Euben, *The Tragedy of Political Theory* (Princeton: Princeton University Press, 1990).

one can say that what tragedy is talking about is itself and the problems of law it is encountering": "the true subject matter of tragedy is social thought and most especially juridical thought in the very process of elaboration."[7]

Nigeria, a colonial territory that did not correspond to any precolonial political entity but that was created within living memory by brute force so absolute that it could style itself as peace-making,[8] was about to be reestablished as a modern sovereign and democratic state requiring the consent of all who live within its borders. The would-be citizens of the new state needed a narrative that would account for the future in terms of the past. But they knew two pasts, the precolonial and the colonial, pointing to different futures. One available narrative was of the passing of tradition and the coming of modernity. According to this narrative, colonization was but a catalyst of progress. Another narrative, however, was of the restoration of African self-rule after the lost years of colonial subjection. Was what happened under colonialism enforced modernization or a loss of self? The possibility of two narratives creates tremendous ambivalence: not just a conflict between rival goods, as Moses would have it, but a contest between rival narratives.[9]

According to Moses, the crux of tragedy as a genre is the transition from tradition to modernity. He sees in the heroic warrior ethos of Achebe's novel a "noble" or "aristocratic" order analogous to European feudalism, and he compares Okonkwo to Achilles (*NGC*, 123). Vernant explains that tragedy arose at the particular moment in history when the heroic age of kings, the age of Homer, gave way to the democratic city-state, of which Athens is the exemplar:

> The drama brings to the stage an ancient heroic legend. For the city this legendary world constitutes the past—a past sufficiently distant for the contrasts between the mythical traditions that it embodies and the new forms of legal and political thought to be clearly visible; yet a past still close enough for the clash of values still to be a painful one and for this clash still to be currently taking place. As Walter Nestle correctly points out, tragedy is born when myth starts to be considered from the point of view of a citizen.[1]

---

7. Jean-Pierre Vernant, "Greek Tragedy: Problems of Interpretation," in *The Languages of Criticism and the Sciences of Man,* ed. Richard Macksey and Eugenio Donato (Baltimore: Johns Hopkins University Press, 1970), 278–9. Henceforth cited as *GT.*
8. The District Commissioner in *Things Fall Apart* is writing an ethnographic account of his experience to be called *The Pacification of the Primitive Tribes of the Lower Niger.*
9. I agree with Richard Begam ("Achebe's Sense of an Ending: History and Tragedy in *Things Fall Apart,*" *Studies in the Novel* vol. 29, no. 3: 396–411) that *Things Fall Apart* demands "a palimpsestic reading," though I think he simplifies the multiple narratives the novel offers.
1. Jean-Pierre Vernant, "Tensions and Ambiguities in Greek Tragedy," in Jean-Pierre Vernant and Pierre Vidal-Naquet, *Tragedy and Myth in Ancient Greece,* trans. Janet Lloyd (Sussex: Harvester, 1981), 9. Henceforth cited as *TAGT.*

Arguably, Achebe's own generation, like the citizens of fifth-century Athens, "became aware of the need to choose between the values of an archaic tribal past preserved in mythic form and the new political and juridical reality of the emerging city-state."[2]

The cultural and temporal distance between the mythic age of the story—Okonkwo's wrestling match with Amalinze the Cat is the stuff of legend, echoing the seven-day battle between the founder of Umuofia and "a spirit of the wild" (*TFA*, 3)—and the self-conscious modernity of author and readers is dramatically figured within the narrative by the division of the action between hero and chorus. Vernant explains that in Greek tragedy the chorus, "the collective and anonymous presence embodied by an official college of citizens," expresses "through its fears, hopes, questions and judgements, the feelings of the spectators who make up the civic community" (*TAGT*, 10). In *Things Fall Apart*, the elders of Umuofia, like the Argive elders in Aeschylus's *Oresteia*, take turns functioning as the chorus: their unheeded advice and proverb-laden commentary provide a counterpoint to the spectacle of the rise and fall of the House of Okonkwo. Often they are critical of Okonkwo's pride: one elder says, "Looking at a king's mouth . . . one would think he never sucked at his mother's breast"; another says, "those whose palm-kernels were cracked for them by a benevolent spirit should not forget to be humble" (*TFA*, 19). At the end of Part One, Obierika, Okonkwo's friend, voices the questions also asked by the reader—e.g., "Why should a man suffer so grievously for an offence he had committed inadvertently?" (*TFA*, 87)—and at the end of the novel, he summarizes the peripety, the cruel reversal of fortune that is at the heart of the tragedy: "That man was one of the greatest men in Umuofia. You drove him to kill himself; and now he will be buried like a dog . . ." (*TFA*, 147). The chorus representing the community is a counterpoint to the solitude of the tragic hero: beside Obierika with his doubts and reasoning, Okonkwo, like the central figure in a classical tragedy, "appears as a hero from an age gone by, always more or less estranged from the ordinary condition of the citizen" (*TAGT*, 10).

Let us compare Achebe's novel to Aeschylus's *Oresteia*, which Achebe may even have had in mind when he originally projected a trilogy, of which *Things Fall Apart* was to have been the first volume.[3] The tragedy of the *Oresteia* started ten years before the opening scene, when Agamemnon, king of Argos, preparing to lead the Greek armies against Troy, sacrificed his daughter Iphigenia in obedience to the injunction of an oracle in order to secure the favor of the gods.

2. Vernant as quoted in Euben (cited above at note 6), 100.
3. Rowell, "An Interview with Chinua Achebe," in *Conversations with Chinua Achebe* (cited above at note [3, p. 335]).

Because of that original act, "unholy, untasted, / working bitterness in the blood / and faith lost," the king's resentful wife, Clytemnestra, and her lover cut down the general upon his return in triumph from the war.[4] There are parallels with Achebe's novel: Okonkwo's disaster, like Agamemnon's, is his betrayal by his own family, a betrayal that has its origins in the ritual sacrifice of his foster son Ikemefuna (whose name bears an uncanny resemblance to Iphigenia's) at the behest of an oracle. As Calchas the seer predicts in *Agamemnon,* the first play of Aeschylus's trilogy, "For the terror returns like sickness to lurk in the house; / the secret anger remembers the child that shall be avenged" (*O:A,* 11. 153–5).

In the second play of the trilogy, Orestes, Agamemnon's son, kills his mother in revenge for his father, and in the third, he is pursued by the Furies, angry female spirits associated with the Earth and the Night, intent on punishing him. Richard Lattimore characterizes the Furies as follows: "in a Greek world they stand for the childhood of the race before it won Hellenic culture, the barbarian phase of pre-Hellenism, the dark of the race and of the world; they have archaic uprightness and strictness in action, with its attendant cruelty; they insist on the fact against the idea."[5] Orestes, on the other hand, has the support of Apollo, representative of a younger generation of gods, who "stands for everything which the Furies are not: Hellenism, civilization, intellect, and enlightenment": "He is male and young. He despises cruelty for the fun of cruelty, and the thirst for blood, but he is as ruthless as the Furies" (*Intro,* 30). The goddess Athena has to intervene to reconcile the spirit forces old and new. She brings to an end the blood feud inherited by each generation of the House of Atreus by a judicial process which is able to reconcile the combatants and transform the Furies into the Eumenides, the "Kindly Ones." Lattimore calls the *Oresteia* "a grand parable of progress"; readers of Achebe, however, might prefer to give Aeschylus's trilogy the subtitle, "The Pacification of the Primitive Tribes of the Lower Peloponnesus."

In *Things Fall Apart,* as in Aeschylus, a world characterized by blood sacrifice gives way to the modern rule of law. At the end of Achebe's novel, the old gods have been grievously wounded by the violent unmasking of one of the *egwugwu* masquerades: "That night the Mother of the Spirits walked the length and breadth of the clan, weeping for her murdered son. It was a terrible night. Not even the oldest man in Umuofia had ever heard such a strange and fearful sound, and it was never to be heard again. It seemed as if the very

---

4. *Agamemnon,* in Aeschylus, *Oresteia,* trans. Richard Lattimore (Chicago: University of Chicago Press, 1953), 11. 151–3. Henceforth cited as *O:A.*
5. Richard Lattimore, "Introduction," in Aeschylus, *Oresteia* (Chicago: University of Chicago Press, 1953), 30. Henceforth cited as *Intro.*

soul of the tribe wept for a great evil that was coming—its own death" (*TFA*, 132). If the goddess's lament were given words, it might sound like that of the Furies, her sisters in grief: "That they could treat me so! / I, the mind of the past, to be driven under the ground out cast, like dirt!"[6] The Furies warn of the falling apart of a social order— "Gods of the younger generation, you have ridden down / the laws of the elder time, torn them out of my hands" (*O:TE*, 11. 778–9)—and denounce the injustice of their overthrow: "Such are the actions of the younger gods. These hold / by unconditional force, beyond all right, a throne / that runs reeking blood, / blood at the feet, blood at the head" (*O:TE*, 11. 162–5).

The comparison with Aeschylus makes clear, however, how much *Things Fall Apart* ironizes the new age of law inaugurated by British colonial rule. The *Oresteia* ends with the establishment of a new court of justice, as Athena proclaims, "I shall select judges of manslaughter, and swear / them in, establish a court into all time to come" (*O:TE*, 11. 483–4). The son is forgiven and restored, the dead father honored. Athena even brings the Furies onside, assuaging their anger and finding a role for them in the new dispensation. At the end of *Things Fall Apart,* the District Commissioner, like some modern Athena, believes that he is bringing peace and justice to a primitive world. After the destruction of the mission church by the *egwugwu*, the District Commissioner invites six leaders of Umuofia, including Okonkwo, for a palaver: "I have been told a few things but I cannot believe them until I have heard your own side" (*TFA*, 137). The new rule of law presents itself as rational: it listens to both sides; it protects all equally against ill-treatment; it presumes that all will give their consent to its manifest wisdom. "Let us talk about it like friends and find a way of ensuring that it does not happen again," says the District Commissioner: "We have brought a peaceful administration to you and your people so that you may be happy. If a man ill-treats you we shall come to your rescue. But we will not allow you to ill-treat others. We have a court of law where we judge cases and administer justice just as it is done in my own country under a great queen" (*TFA*, 137). However, the elders who listen to the District Commissioner's lines about the magnanimous impartiality of the justice that he upholds have been forcibly seized and sit in handcuffs. The new law, which derives its claim to legitimacy from the consent of the governed, the impartiality of its judgments, and the manifest reasonableness of its decisions, does not actually need the consent of the elders, whom it regards as irrational and in need of coercion until they comply with reason.

6. *The Eumenides,* in Aeschylus, *Oresteia,* trans. Richard Lattimore (Chicago: University of Chicago Press, 1953), 11. 837–9. Henceforth cited as *O:TE*

Pacification by the British meant everyone was treated equally and rationally, *except* those the empire deemed primitive and irrational, which is to say, the colonized. The new administration thus hides from itself how much it is based on violence and on arbitrariness: the administration gives unequal access to power to those who learn English and rejects as irrational those who do not comply. As Timothy Mitchell writes of colonialism, "Law was presented as the opposite of violence, exception, arbitrariness, and injustice, yet somehow these features were all incorporated within it. How could law be both order and violence, justice and injustice, universal and exceptional?"[7] There is a contradiction at the heart of imperialism, which is also the contradiction Mehta finds at the heart of British liberalism. On the one hand, the imperial nations consider themselves more civilized than others because they are democratic and respect rights and freedoms. On the other hand, they will employ force if necessary in order to implement their program to better the world. At home, a concern for rights and individual freedom balances the impulse to reform, but in the field of empire, subject peoples can be denied rights and freedoms because they are cast as uncivilized and located back in time, at an earlier stage in human progress (*LE*, 80).

Where traditional Umuofia located its other outside itself, in the Evil Eorest, modernity locates its own other not just elsewhere in space but also back in time, and relegates tradition to the past. Zygmunt Bauman explains that

> Modernity was open-ended, and inevitably so; indeed, the open-endedness was seen as the paramount, perhaps defining, attribute of modernity. Against the intrinsic mobility of modernity, the pre-modern forms appeared stagnant, organized around the mechanism of equilibration and stability, almost devoid of history. This optical effect resulted from choosing modernity as the vantage point from which to contemplate features of alternative societies; and choosing to consider modernity as the historically, or logically, later form. This choice enclosed and objectified other social forms, and prompted them to be perceived as finished, complete objects—a perception which had been articulated as their intrinsic timelessness.[8]

The assumption of those who believe in the "end of history" (the end both in the sense of arrival and of goal) is that non-Europeans are somehow located back in time, further from the end as defined by Europe. As Charles Mills writes, "The establishment of society thus

7. Timothy Mitchell, *Rule of Experts: Egypt, Techno-politics, Modernity* (Berkeley: University of California Press, 2002), 77–8.
8. Zygmunt Bauman, *Legislators and Interpreters: On Modernity, Post-Modernity and Intellectuals* (Ithaca: Cornell University Press, 1987), 116.

implies the denial that a society already existed; the creation of society *requires* the intervention of white men, who are thereby positioned as *already* socio-political beings" (*RC*, 13).

In Moses' account of history, ancient, class-ridden society supposedly makes way for modern egalitarian society, but modern society itself, for all its much vaunted openness, is also based on exclusion: it requires the exclusion of what it deems the primitive. If sacrifice, the death of the innocent individual in the supposed interest of the community, represents the kind of primitive thinking that must give way to modernity, we should note that modernity still presumes sacrifice. Moses reads the tragedy of Okonkwo as the sacrifice of the primitive on the altar of modernity, the death of the individual in the greater interest of the collective, exactly the kind of sacrificial logic modernity is supposed to overcome. In other words, modernity is predicated on the sacrifice of the sacrificer, and needs sacrifice just as much as so-called primitive society does.

What happened in history, as Achebe tells it, was not, however, the triumph of universal reason but the defeat of small-scale finite worlds by a distant empire with universal pretensions. Achebe explains to Jonathan Cott:

> My world—the one that interests me more than any other—is the world of the village. It is one, not the only, reality, but it's the one that the Igbo people, who are my people, have preferred to all others. It was as if they had a choice of creating empire or cities or large communities and they looked at them and said, "No, we think that what is safest and best is a system in which everybody knows everybody else." In other words, a village. So you'll find that, politically, the Igbos preferred the small community; they had nothing to do—until recently—with kings and kingdoms. Now I'm quite convinced that this was a conscious choice. Some people look at the Igbos and assert that they didn't evolve to the stage of having kings and kingdoms. But this isn't true—the Igbos have a name for "king," they have names for all the paraphernalia of kingship—it isn't as if they didn't know about kings. I think it's simply that, looking at the way the world operates, they seemed to have said to themselves, "Of all the possible political systems, we shall insist on the one where there are only so many people."[9]

Achebe speaks here of "conscious choice" and of people having several political systems to choose among, in other words, of a social contract. According to this narrative, colonization did not represent the institution of a new social contract to replace a state of nature

---

9. Jonathan Cott, "Chinua Achebe: At the Crossroads," in *Conversations with Chinua Achebe*, cited above at note 2, 77.

but, rather, itself violated an original social contract. Umuofia, usually called a clan, but also called a "town" (*TFA*, 3), originally exists in a world of small-scale communities with no larger sovereignty to mediate among them. There are slaves (the *osu*), as there were in Athens, but there is no division into nobles and plebeians. As in the Greek city-states, power lies with assemblies of all free adult males. Questions of public policy, such as going to war (as opposed to personal matters, which are judged by the *egwugwu*), are debated in public, and disputes are won by rhetoric and reason. If we think of Umuofia as already a democracy, then the coming of the British does not bring justice: rather, it is as though the Persians had succeeded in conquering the Greek city-states. Instead of Athenian democracy replacing an aristocracy, as Moses supposes, the reverse took place and an Athenian-style democracy found itself overthrown.

Achebe says the village is a world "in which everybody knows everybody else": it does not have to be "imagined" in the sense in which Benedict Anderson says the nation-state must be.[1] Does the village world of Umuofia represent the natural and human scale of things that gives way to something transhuman and more abstract and sinister, or does it represent instead a primitive world ruled by blood, in the sense both of kinship and of sacrifice, that inevitably gives way to more abstract but also more rational and more modern forms of social organization? To some extent the question is moot. Igbos may prefer the village as the unit of society, and the village may even be inherently preferable, but Igbos now find themselves citizens of Nigeria. On the eve of independence, it is not enough for Achebe to show that things have fallen apart, for a return to the small-scale communities whose virtue he praises is no longer possible. The law and its attendant reason that the District Commissioner is so proud of will be the basis of the new state of Nigeria. What is needed at this historical juncture is a new social contract narrative. *Things Fall Apart* must ask the questions that, according to Vernant, tragedy also asks:

> What is authority, the authority of the man over the woman, of husband over wife, of the head of the State over all his fellow-citizens, of the city over the foreigner and the metic, of the gods over mortal men? Does it depend on right, that is to say mutual agreement, gentle persuasion, *peitho*? Or, on the contrary, upon domination, pure force, brute violence, *bt'a* (*TAGT*, 15)?

Things Fall Apart is a social contract narrative like the narratives of Hobbes, Locke, Rousseau, and Freud, or like the *Oresteia*. In her analysis of the bourgeois liberal social contract as imagined by Locke,

1. Benedict Anderson, *Imagined Communities* (London: Verso, 1991).

Carol Pateman explains that, under the old, kinship-based dispensation, the "patriarchal father enjoys the absolute power of the *patria potestas* who, under Roman law, had power of life and death over his sons."[2] This is the power that Okonkwo wields over his wives and especially his sons, and is most conspicuous when he brings his "matchet" down on Ikemefuna. Pateman explains that "Classic contract theory" derives "from a revolutionary claim": "that individuals are naturally free and equal to each other, or that individuals are born free and born equal" (*SC*, 39). The "doctrine of natural individual freedom and equality" swept away "in one fell swoop, all the grounds through which the subordination of some individuals, groups or categories of people to others had been justified" (*SC*, 39). Okonkwo's son Nwoye no longer identifies with the community's acts of sacrifice, as his father so tragically does, but, rather, with the victim and with all victims. The horror that the people of Umuofia feel at the birth of twins (presumably because twins challenge the category of the human and represent a terrifying lack of differentiation), Nwoye feels instead for the twins' death. This horror brings him to the Church of the missionaries: "The hymn about brothers who sat in darkness and in fear seemed to answer a vague and persistent question that haunted his young soul—the question of the twins crying in the bush and the question of Ikemefuna who was killed" (*TFA*, 104).

Upon his conversion to Christianity, Nwoye renames himself Isaac. He thereby recasts his relation to his father in terms of the Biblical Abraham's sacrifice of his son and heir Isaac. The choice of name marks his identification with his foster brother, Ikemefuna, and reflects his new understanding that the Old Testament God of Wrath, who demands sacrifice, has been replaced by a New Testament God of Mercy, whose sacrifice of his own son obviates the need for any further sacrifice. The missionaries to Africa frequently cast the societies they met in the role of Old Testament tribes to whom they were bringing the Good News.[3] Nwoye's "callow mind" regards colonization as a new dispensation that both completes and does away with the old (*TFA*, 104). Michael Valdez Moses, the modern Hegelian, argues that the Christian missions are themselves but another ruse of reason: although they are as "misguided in their religious beliefs as are the oracles, *dibia*, elders, and priests of the Igbo, these Protestant

---

2. Carol Pateman, *The Sexual Contract* (Cambridge: Polity Press, 1988), 26. Henceforth cited as *SC*.

3. In order to explain the rapid rate of conversion among them, Igbos even today sometimes emphasize the parallels between themselves and the Jews: I have heard the word "Igbo" etymologically derived from "Hebrew." The Reverend Samuel Johnson's history of the Yoruba also emphasizes Middle Eastern origins "in order to link the Yoruba to the great literate cultures and world religions that originated from the Middle East, namely, Islam and Judeo-Christianity" (Oiakunle George, *Relocating Agency: Modernity and African Letters* [Albany: State University of New York Press, 2003], 130). Henceforth cited as *RA*.

evangelicals nevertheless unwittingly serve to advance the ration-
alization and modernization of life" in Igboland (*NGC*, 131). That is
one way of looking at it. Another way would be to see that Hegel and
the reason of history are themselves but a secular manifestation of
the teleology originally found in Christianity.

Achebe's novel has some sympathy for Nwoye's narrative. Events
are given to us from Nwoye's perspective on seven different occasions: only Okonkwo and his favourite wife, Ekwefi, have more pages
dedicated to their thoughts.[4] The narrative presents several thematic
touchstones through Nwoye's imagination and memory: the child's
love of words and story, the psychological impact of Ikemefuna's
death, and the appeal of Christianity for Igbos. The only direct references to a time after the events of the story—we are told that Ikemefuna's "sad story is still told in Umuofia unto this day" (*TFA*, 9)
and that Nwoye remembered the three years he lived with Ikemefuna
"very vividly till the end of his life" (*TFA*, 25)—suggest the closeness
of Nwoye's personal memory to the collective memory of Umuofia.
After all, Nwoye's version of events, the Christian version, is what
Achebe inherited from his own father and what he grew up with. It
would have filled the world he knew. The important thing to notice,
however, is how careful Achebe is to distance himself from Nwoye's
version of events. Instead of fitting Igbo history into Biblical patterns,
Achebe uses Biblical patterns as an ironic comment on Igbo history.
We should remember that *Things Fall Apart* is written by a young man
who has grown up in a Christian household but who now describes
himself as "an ancestor worshipper."[5] In other words, the precolonial
world of *Things Fall Apart* that is displaced by Christianity in the
course of the narrarive itself displaces Christianity in the experience
of the young Nigerian author.

Pateman summarizes the story of the modern social contract as
developed in Europe thusly: "the father is (metaphorically) killed by
his sons, who transform (the paternal dimension of) the father's
patriarchal right into civil government. The sons alienate this aspect
of political power into the hands of representatives, the state" (*SC*,
32). Olakunle George expresses this as the contradiction of modernity: "society opens up to the subject the promise of unhindered self-
realization, even as a crucial condition of that realization is the
subject's subjection to the order of civil society" (*RA*, 125). This paradox of modernity, that, in the name of escaping a cruel regime based
on sacrifice, the subject is himself sacrificed, is, of course, felt most

---

4. Nwoye's thoughts are presented on pages 25, 37, 38, 43, 104, 106, and 108. Okonkwo's
   thoughts are presented on twenty different pages, Ekwefi's on nine.
5. Lewis Nkosi and Wole Soyinka, "Conversation with Chinua Achebe," in *Conversations with
   Chinua Achebe* (cited above at note 2),14.

acutely in the colony, where the social contract was drawn up by others elsewhere and never received the consent of the governed.

Moses assumes that the tragedy in *Things Fall Apart* presents not just what actually happened in history but also what, if people could see it from the external perspective afforded by what Hegel calls the end of history or what John Rawls calls the "veil of ignorance," they would choose to have happen.[6] The modern social contract as Achebe depicts it is not, however, the ideal. He offers merely a naturalistic model, as Pateman also offers, of what actually did happen in history. His social contract narrative resembles what Mills calls the "racial contract": the story of the establishment of global white supremacy. The hero of Achebe's tragedy is a patriarch and a filicide who drives his son into the arms of the future. Achebe must tell the story of the modern social contract as a tragedy—the sacrifice of the upholder of tradition explains what happened—but he also suggests that what happened did not have to happen as it did. The novel makes clear that Okonkwo did not have to join the sacrificial party that killed Ikemefuna. Even at the time there was another course of action possible.

Four chapters after the death of Ikemefuna, Achebe's novel sets up a contrast to Okonkwo's behavior meant to comment on the road not taken. The Oracle again asks for one of Okonkwo's children. This time, speaking through Chielo, his priestess, the voice of Agbala asks for Okonkwo's favorite daughter, Ezinma. When Chielo carries off the girl, to her mother's consternation, Okonkwo asks Ekwefi, "Why do you stand there as though she has been kidnapped?" (*TFA*, 72). He means to reassure her—Ezinma has not been kidnapped—but Ekwefi has seen what already happened to another child taken from the compound in the name of the Oracle, and she refuses the consolation. She rushes in pursuit of Chielo. The desperate mother follows Chielo and her daughter through the night to the cave of the Oracle, disobeying the latter's explicit instructions not to come before him of her own accord and risking his blazing anger (*TFA*, 71). Eor Ezinma's sake, Ekwefi is willing to challenge the gods and, just as terrifying, the darkness. The contrast with Okonkwo's previous failure as a parent could not be greater.

Once again, just as he had done with Ikemefuna, Okonkwo follows, matchet in hand, the one who takes away his child at the behest of the Oracle, but this time he shadows Ekwefi in her lonely vigil outside the Oracle's cave. The procession—Chielo carrying Ezinma followed by Ekwefi, tracked by Okonkwo—recalls the earlier procession that led Ikemefuna to his death. That earlier procession took place in sunlight and involved men, but it also brought a child in obedience

6. John Rawls, *A Theory of Justice* (Oxford: Clarendon Press, 1972).

to the summons of the Oracle, and Okonkwo brought up the rear then, too. The repetition serves to underline the difference: in the first case, Okonkwo did not behave as a loving parent but participated in the killing; in the second case, the two parents, motivated by love, are directly disobeying the Oracle's instructions not to follow.

Since long before Kierkegaard made it the centerpiece of *Fear and Trembling,* the story of Abraham and Isaac has represented the paradigm of religious faith in Judeo-Christian theology, and that is how Achebe, growing up in a Christian family, would have learned to think of it.[7] Abraham had been promised that, in spite of the advanced age of his childless wife, Sarah, his progeny would number as the stars in heaven. Yet, after the birth of a son, Isaac, fulfills that promise, God commands that Abraham sacrifice his son to prove his love for Him. Abraham, the epitome of the man of faith, prepares to obey. St. Paul writes to the Romans: "Abraham believed and hoped, even when there was no reason for hoping, and so became 'the father of many nations.'"[8] At the last moment, an angel intervenes and rescues Isaac. In *Things Fall Apart,* as in the Biblical story, the sacrifice of a son highlights the nature of a father's relation to the transhuman. Okonkwo ostentatiously carries out the will of the Oracle, even though it means killing the foster son he has learned to care for, and even though such an act offends the earth. He casts himself as the upholder of a divine law that is superior to, and can even contravene, natural moral law. He welcomes the sacrifice as a way of proving his faith. "Faith," of course, is a word borrowed from the Christians and not usually applied to traditional spirituality. Robert Wren, for instance, assumes that precolonial Africans did not need faith: "The priest of Ani in 'Dead Man's Path' [an early Achebe story] . . . needs to prove nothing, to argue nothing, because he knows something beyond proof. And Achebe had become aware that he himself, mission schoolboy, university educated, had lost that same ancestral knowledge."[9] Precolonial Africans, Wren assumes, did not have to believe; they simply lived. "Faith," however, is the right word in the case of Okonkwo, who obeys the Oracle. His concern with fulfilling the divine will at all costs, without room for qualification, is the behavior of someone afraid of doubting. His obedience to the Oracle is the opposite of, *and the corollary of,* doubt. Okonkwo accompanies the sacrificial party and even brings his own matchet down on the boy because "he was afraid of being thought weak" (*TFA,* 43). What the chorus says of Agamemnon can be said of Okonkwo as well, that he

7. Soren Kierkegaard, *Fear and Trembling,* trans. Walter Lowrie (Princeton: Princeton University Press, 1941).
8. Romans 4:5.
9. Robert M. Wren, *Achebe's World: The Historical and Cultural Context of the Novels of Chinua Achebe* (Washington: Three Continents Press, 1980), 16.

"made himself the accomplice of a capricious destiny rather than criticise a diviner."[1] Okonkwo lays claim to a relation to the sacred greater than that of his fellows: while others resign themselves to the inscrutable will of the infinite, he is determined to serve that will. His role in the sacrifice of Ikemefuna fulfills an image of himself in his own and others' eyes as the man who does whatever the Oracle commands, unafraid of blood and indifferent to emotion. He may be "afraid of being thought weak" but not, it seems, of being thought disrespectful or irrational. His is a stiff-necked, unreasoning faith that mistrusts itself. It is this that makes him tragic.

True faith, however, as Ekwefi's example proves, does not mean acquiescing in the will of the gods; true faith challenges the will of the gods and is close to blasphemy. Like Sarah, the wife of the Biblical Abraham, Ekwefi had been given a child long after she had given up hope of having one who will remain. Ezinma is an *ogbanje,* a child who punishes its parents by repeatedly dying young then being reborn. Ekwefi believes that this time the *ogbanje* will stay among the living because "it was that faith alone that gave her own life any kind of meaning" (*TFA,* 56). "Faith" is clearly a key word in this context: Ekwefi's faith in the future leads her to defy the gods. Ekwefi stands before the cave of the Oracle and "swore within her that if she heard Ezinma cry she would rush into the cave to defend her against all the gods in the world. She would die with her" (*TFA,* 76). Ekwefi does not deny the gods: she is genuinely afraid. But neither does she acquiesce in the will of the gods and make it her own. Okonkwo's sacrifice of Ikemefuna was a self-affirmation: it made the killer into the one who upholds the law and it was done to confirm the self in the eyes of others. The night vigil before Agbala's cave represents the converse: Okonkwo and Ekwefi act entirely outside the knowledge of others, indifferent to how they might appear. They do not act to confirm the self but put the self at risk in order to rescue a beloved other. Ekwefi's challenge to the gods at the risk of death and self-obliteration is a confrontation with the Lacanian Real, what Slavoj Zizek calls an "act."[2] We can say of Ekwefi what Zizek says of Antigone, the eponymous heroine of Sophocles' play: "her act is literally suicidal, she excludes herself from the community, whereby she offers nothing new, no positive program—she just insists on her unconditional demand" (*EYS,* 46). Yet such an act, representing a rupture with all that has come before and a wager on an unknown future, is closer to the direction of history and to the potential redirection of history

1. Jean-Pierre Vernant's translation in "Intimations of the Will in Greek tragedy" in Jean-Pierre Vernant and Pierre Vidal-Naquet, *Tragedy and Myth in Ancient Greece* (cited above at note 1), 49.
2. Slavoj Zizek, *Enjoy Your Symptom* (New York: Routledge, 2001). Henceforth cited as *EYS.*

than is a teleology based on the privileged backward gaze of the philosopher and the liberal historian:

> With an act, *stricto sensu,* we can therefore never fully foresee its consequences, i.e., the way it will transform the existing symbolic space: the act is a rupture after which "nothing remains the same." Which is why, although History can always be explained, accounted for, afterward, we can never, as its agents, caught in its flow, foresee its course in advance: we cannot do it insofar as it is not an "objective process" (but a process continuously interrupted by the scansion of acts) (*EYS*, 45–6).

Zizek writes that the "paradigmatic case" of an "act," a rupture with the symbolic order, is "feminine" (*EYS*, 46). According to Hegel, the public sphere, "called variably the community, government, and the state," only acquires its existence through interfering with the happiness of the family; thus, it creates for itself "an internal enemy—womankind in general. Womankind—the everlasting irony [in the life] of the community."[3] Okonkwo the father-sacrificer and Ekwefi the mother-rescuer stand in relation to each other much as Creon, ruler of Thebes, to Antigone.[4] Okonkwo the killer of Ikemefuna, like Creon, upholds the rule of law, which he knows to be arbitrary, but which he believes holds society together and on which he relies as the source of his own authority. As Zizek explains, "*Sacrifice is a guarantee that 'the Other exists'*: that there is an Other who can be appeased by means of the sacrifice" (*EYS*, 56). For that same reason, however, Ekwefi, like Antigone who says "No!" to Creon's state power, takes a stand for a realm conceived to be before or outside the law.

If, as Hegel argued, Sophocles' *Antigone* represents the transition from kinship to law, then it is significant that Achebe depicts a similar transition as occurring *before* the colonizers appear. Colonial modernity, as we have seen, requires the sacrifice of the sacrificer: Moses believes Achebe is prepared to countenance the sacrifice of Okonkwo, the upholder of tradition, for the greater good. But in the vigil at the cave of Agbala, Achebe depicts Okonkwo as himself capable of renouncing "the symbolic alliance which defines the very kernel" of his being (*EYS*, 167), that is, of renouncing sacrifice itself. Traditional Igbo society had a potential to modernize itself, that is, to abandon sacrifice, that would not have involved the sacrifice of the sacrificer.

Achebe tells Kalu Ogbaa that it is not possible and not desirable to return to precolonial society.[5] What he regrets, however, is not the

3. Hegel is quoted by Judith Butler, *Antigone's Claim: Kinship Between Life and Death* (New York: Columbia University Press, 2000), 35.
4. Sophocles, *Antigone,* trans. Elizabeth Wyckoff, in *Sophocles I* (Chicago: University of Chicago Press, 1954).
5. Kalu Ogbaa, "An Interview with Chinua Achebe," in *Conversations with Chinua Achebe* (cited above at note 2), 64–75.

precolonial world, as if that had been a single monolithic entity and doomed to be displaced, but the pre-colonial world's potential, all that it might have become. *Things Fall Apart* reminds us that more than one lifeworld existed at the same moment. Moreover, all these contemporary lifeworlds represented potential futures. While it is true that only one future was realized, the unrealized futures are just as important as what actually happened, and they are crucial for understanding it.

Moses assumes a vision of progress whereby some life forms exist fully in the present because they will be the future, while others, although contemporaneous, do not exist in the present because they will be superseded and therefore represent the past. Mehta criticizes this kind of liberalism because it "cannot admit the present as present" and "moreover, cannot see in the present an agentiality, a will, a life form that tenaciously exists against the insistence of a theory that has it designated as dead" (*LE*, 108). Redeeming the past does not involve celebrating it or seeking to return to it; it does involve recognizing that it had potential that went unrealized and remembering that potential. There have been other ways of life and, just as importantly, other potential futures that liberal empire and its heir, globalization, have ignored and stifled.

MALA PANDURANG

Chinua Achebe and the "African Experience": A Socio-Literary Perspective†

I

Albert Chinualumogu Achebe was born on the 16th of November 1930 at Ogidi, east of Onitsha, in the eastern region of Nigeria. The young Achebe spent his formative years under the care of his brother Reverend John Chukwuemeka Achebe, and attended the Nekede

---

† From *Chinua Achebe: An Anthology of Recent Criticism*. Ed. Mala Pandurang (Delhi: Pencraft International, 2006), 13–25. Reprinted by permission of the author.
[The term 'African' is used here as a referent to a specific area of shared cultural and socio-political experience and does not suggest a homogenous African identity. If the label of 'African' was employed by European colonizers to construct a monolithic entity out of a continent of diverse peoples, languages, religions and socio-cultural practices, then within categories of anti-colonial responses and decolonizing narratives, the word 'African' becomes a term of reference as in opposition to colonial and neo-colonial operations. Abiola Irele prefers a more flexible term, "the African Imagination", to refer to a "certain conjunction of impulses which can said to have been given a unified expression in a body of literary texts". He explains that it is from these impulses "grounded in both a common experience and common cultural references that these literary texts assume a particular significance."]

Central School until standard six. He then gained entrance to the University College at Ibadan in 1948 with a major scholarship, and subsequently switched his field from the study of medicine to that of arts. In 1952, as a university student, Achebe encountered Joyce Cary's much-praised *Mister Johnson* (1939). Achebe's anger at Cary's racist-colonialist representation of Africa, and the African, is a much-cited incident but cannot be glossed over, for it compelled a frustrated Achebe to write his first novel *Things Fall Apart*. As Achebe asserts, the story of Africa was something that ". . . could not be told for us by anyone else, no matter how gifted or well-intentioned" (1975, 123). *Things Fall Apart* is recognized today as one of the most significant counter-narratives of the twentieth century. Ineed, "the transformative nature of *Things Fall Apart* is undisputed" (Gikandi 2004, iii).

Alan Hill, who was the then educational books director of Heinemann, recalls the background to the publication of this remarkable narrative. Achebe, he relates, "just parceled the one handwritten copy in brown paper and sent it by ordinary mail to London, in response to an advertisement in *The Spectator*: 'Author's manuscripts typed'." A year later, he received a typed copy. Shortly afterwards Achebe was in London for a course at the BBC and showed it to his course officer, who then sent it to Heinemann. After initial hesitation, Heinemann published an initial run of just 2000 copies of the novel on June 17th 1958 (in Peterson and Rutherford, 149–150).

It was not long before *Things Fall Apart* was identified as a pathbreaking novel. Consequently, there have been sales in excess of eight million copies worldwide and this remarkable book has been translated into fifty-five different languages (figures cited in Emenyonu 2004, 1). The tremendous reception of Achebe's first novel should not however be detrimental to our appreciation of the rest of Achebe's literary oeuvre, which comprises four more works of longer fiction, collections of short stories and of poetry, children's fiction, and incisive critical and political commentaries.

African writing in English evolved primarily as a result of the Euro-African colonial encounter and its aftermath, and each of Achebe's novels marks a significant moment in the growth of this relatively young body of literature. This introductory chapter will locate Achebe's literary production within the framework of a larger socio-historical process of colonial domination, and subsequent movement for decolonization. As Simon Gikandi puts it:

> It is crucial to understand how Achebe occupies a crucial diachronic role in the history of an African literature almost always driven by the desire to imaginatively capture the key moments of African history from the beginning of colonialism to what has come to be known as postcoloniality. (xii)

Alistar Niven rightly suggests that we read Achebe's work in the chronological order of African, and Nigerian history, from the 1890s to the present day. He points out that Achebe's fiction chronicles different phases in the development of modern Africa: "Each work is wholly different in character from the other, but together they legitimately can be seen as aspects of one gathering sequence of human imperfection" (49). Achebe's fiction can be divided into two categories. *Things Fall Apart* (1958) and *Arrow of God* (1964) represent a pre-colonial Igbo culture struggling against all odds to retain its integrity against the loss of autonomy. *No Longer at Ease* (1960), *A Man of the People* (1966), and *Anthills of the Savannah* (1987) are primarily preoccupied with the crisis of neo-colonialism and decolonisation. "Achebe's fiction and literary criticism," explains Naheem Yousaf, "comprise an important literary archive for Nigeria-in-the making" (15).

There were African writers who had published in English prior to Achebe's first novel—Sol Platje, Amos Tutuola and Cyprian Ekwensi among others. *Things Fall Apart* has, however, been credited as the "originating voice in African fiction" (Yousaf, 1), and as occupying "the inaugural moment of African literary history" (Gikandi, ix), for a number of reasons. In order to contextualize the lead role played by Chinua Achebe in initiating a movement towards the articulation of a strong counter-hegemonic discourse of resistance, it is necessary to chart a historical review of the trajectory of modern African fiction in English as a genre generated by the intense historical experience of colonization, decolonisation and neo-colonisation. This approach will be combined with biographical inputs on the various circumstances, which have shaped the relationship between writer, text and his environment.

II

European colonial expansion on the African continent in the nineteenth century, as in other parts of the world, was initiated primarily for the purpose of economic exploitation. It was impossible for European imperial powers to physically control such a vast continent and the great imperial project had to be sustained through ideological mechanisms, the operation of which has been discussed in much detail in postcolonial theorizing. Ideological imposition in the African context was of a much harsher nature than in the Asian colonies because of the predominance of traditions of oral communication in most indigenous African cultures. The absence of a written tradition allowed for the imposition of the colonizer's language through the mechanisms of education in English, and this consequently led to the control of one form of communication over the other, that of writing over orality. Taking overt advantage of the absence of a documented past, people south of the Sahara were denied an existence in the writing of the Western master narrative of colonial history. With the established control of the Church over education, the power to block out indigenous narratives passed into the hands of the various colonial authorities. One of the most effective tools of colonial hegemonic control became the negation of identity through the denial of a collective history. Kenyan novelist and radical critic Ngugi wa Thiong'o summarizes the complicity of religion, language and education over the dissemination of knowledge: "the missionary carried the Bible, the soldier carried the gun, the administrator and the settler carried the coin. Christ, commerce, civilization, the Bible, the coin, the gun" (*Petals of Blood*, 88).

The history of the African novel, as D. Ivezbaye explains in *Issues in the Reassessment of the African Novel*, has been "essentially a history of an evolving racial consciousness" (28). What is unique about the growth of the modern African novel is that it has been coeval to a collective intellectual hijacking of Africa by the Western colonial enterprise. However, the awakening of creative responses to counter the undervaluing of indigenous systems of thought and communication was not a sudden coming into consciousness. Es'kia Mphahlele points out in *African Literature and the Social Experience in Process* (1983) that the arrival of Edmund Blyden in Liberia in 1851 marked a crucial stage in the development of modern African thought. Blyden's most important contribution was his promulgation of the theory of the 'African Personality' formulated as one possible means of regaining the African's 'disinherited self'. Consequently, Afro-American literary movements of the early twentieth century played an influential role in the gradual assertion of pride in being black. The movement towards establishing a common Negro identity gained further momentum in the 1920s when under the influence of the ideology of the Black nationalism of Marcus Garvey and the Pan-Africanism of Du Bois, the Negritude movement was born. The preoccupation with a 'black affirmation' dominated the literary expression of Francophone poets and intellectuals of the 1940s like Aime Césaire, David Diop and Léopold Senghor. While there have been several debates on the aesthetic principles of Negritude, it has been generally accepted that the movement served as a springboard for the articulation, and hence growth, of a black consciousness among Anglophone African writers. Writing began to be marked by a convergence of political and nationalistic thinking and set the stage for a literature of nation-building.

By the 1950s, the struggle for independence in former British colonies of Ghana, Nigeria and Kenya had begun to grow in strength. Conversely, the literature of the period was marked by a convergence of anti-colonial indignation and nationalist thinking. The first stage of writing of cultural nationalism and racial assertion was governed by the ideological intention of awakening the African consciousness, and a performing of the therapeutic role of healing the wounds and humiliation inflicted by the colonising process. As Fanon points out in *The Wretched of the Earth*, "the birth of national consciousness in Africa has a strictly contemporaneous connection with the African consciousness" (199). Cultural nationalist fiction tended to be dominated by a forward-looking optimism. Promises of an egalitarian and classless society had been an integral part of the socialist manifestos of nationalist leaders, and a general sanguinity about the potential of indigenous cultures is reflected in the literary output of the first-generation fiction.

Most first-generation African novelists who were writing in English found themselves in a double-bind situation. As products of a colonial system of mission education in English, they had to re-assert their own unique African sensibility in a borrowed tongue. Paradoxically, they appropriated the English language as a counter-weapon to perform a psychologically affirmative function and to inscribe new meanings. There are innumerable and exciting examples of the creative breaking and re-making of the English language, largely through retention of the stamp of orality. In 1953, Amos Tutuola's *The Palm-Wine Drinkard* was the first Nigerian novel to be published by a reputed British company. Tutuola became a controversial figure in the critical reception of the novel in English for the 'strangeness' of his style, and the use of what Dylan Thomas referred to as 'young English'. In this magic-realistic narrative, Tutuola incorporates Yoruba myth and folklore, and human beings mix freely with the beings from the spiritual world.

However, the novel that received widespread international acclaim was Chinua Achebe's *Things Fall Apart*. This novel inspired an entire first generation of African novelists to appropriate the English language by incorporating techniques of oral storytelling for a political purpose. Achebe demonstrated his masterly ability to 'Africanize' the English language through the introduction of Igbo words and proverbs into the flow of the text in *Things Fall Apart*. The roots of this writing was grounded in an urgency for self-assertion and the recovery of an 'African' identity in view of the severe colonial negation of the psyche of the black African.

Things Fall Apart portrays the history of Igboland between 1875 and 1904. Clement Okafor positions Igboland in the territory of southeastern Nigeria, located on both banks of the River Niger. While the main narrative is that of the protagonist Okonkwo and his tragic inability to deal with the new colonial dispensation, there is also the larger story of the encounter between the colonial intruders and the Igbo village of Umuofia. Igbo society, Okafor explains, is "historically egalitarian and democratic in the sense that the people never had rulers with anything approaching autocratic powers" (87). Achebe consciously set out to contest imperial stereotypes of Africa in *Things Fall Apart* and successfully compels an acknowledgment of the existence of other non-Eurocentric 'cultures' and 'histories' as against the Western master narrative. In "African Literature as Celebration", Achebe cites examples of Western literary classics that reinforced the severe cultural negation of the African. For instance, he reacts angrily to the stereotyping that takes place in the work of Joseph Conrad:

> Conrad's famous novel *Heart of Darkness* portrays Africa as a place where the wandering European may discover that the dark impulses and unspeakable appetite he has suppressed and forgotten through ages of civilization may spring into life again in anger to Africa's free and triumphant savagery. (1990, 5–6)

Biodun Jeyifo suggests that *Things Fall Apart* can be read at two levels. First, as a grand narrative of the colonial encounter, and secondly, as counter narratives and fragmentary stories of decentered identities of subaltern groups (65). Those who are first converted in the village of Umuofia to Christianity, and co-opted by the colonial administration as messengers and petty officials, are from the group of social outcasts (the osu) and marginalized 'others' who view the new economic and social order as liberating and privileging. However, Jeyifo explains, "Achebe's ironic vision extends as well to their liberation by colonialism" (65). Once co-opted into the new system they actively propagate corruption, are alienated, and become instruments of colonial brutality. To Achebe's credit, he does not compel the reader to choose between two value systems. Rather he presents the colonial encounter as a paradoxical process of induction of the old into a new, complex social order.

In the brilliant and ironic ending of *Things Fall Apart* is the crux of the politics of representation, central to postcolonial debates on identity. The reader is witness to an act wherein the indigenous oral account of Okonkwo will be usurped by the written 'official account' of the white District Officer for his intended book on the *Pacification of the Primitive Tribes of the Lower Niger*. The District Officer thus emerges, as Jeyifo points out, "a figure not merely of political, administrative power but also of narrative, discursive, epistemic authority" (55).

Several of the seminal issues introduced in *Things Fall Apart* recur in Achebe's later work. These include: the colonial encounter and the fragmentation of the Igbo community; the loss of its self-regulatory power and moral base; the politics of identity and the problematics of representation; and the question of leadership, responsibility and consequences of the growing schism between the political elite and the community.

In 1960 Achebe became the commissioning editor of Heinemann's *African Writers Series*. This gave him the opportunity to shape the direction of modern African writing in English. He was responsible for the 'discovery' of new writers like Ngugi wa Thiong'o (then James Ngugi), and added Ngugi's first two novels (*The River Between* and *Weep Not, Child*) to the Heinemann list. Achebe's association with Heinemann ended with the publication of the hundredth title, his own collection of short stories, *Girls at War* (1972).

In 1964, Achebe published *Arrow of God*. In the preface to the revised edition of the novel, Achebe admits that of all his work, it is this structurally complex novel that he is ". . . most likely to be caught sitting down to read again". Achebe returns to the period of the intrusion of the colonizer, and the theme of the collapse of the traditional Igbo social order. The narrative focuses on the socio-historic-political engagement between the priest of Ulu (Ezeulu), the villages of Umuaro, and the new colonial administration, and particularly explores the relationship between religion and the social order. The cultural paradigm here, as in Ngugi's early novels, is dominated by "a conscious desire to reject the claims of the Centre for exclusivity" (Soyinka, xi). Margaret Turner argues that the central issue here is more of conflict over the acquisition of power. She points out that there is "no return to the order of morality at the end of the novel, only to an order of power" (35).

Turner offers an important observation in her reading of the element of personal and cultural tragedy in Achebe's work. She points out that "rather than catharsis, a cleansing of the emotions through the re-establishment of a moral order, a vague uneasiness and dissatisfaction remain after each novel" (33). This element of unease becomes increasingly predominant in Achebe's *No Longer at Ease* (1960), the third novel in the chronology, though published two years prior to *Arrow of God*.

Set in the 1950s, *No Longer at Ease* marks the end of the colonial rule in Nigeria, and describes a society on the eve of self-rule. Obi Okonkwo, the grandson of the protagonist of *Things Fall Apart*, returns home from England, and finds himself caught between the older 'traditional' and the new 'modern' value systems. Obi's predicament mirrors the ambivalence experienced by young university graduates, once removed from their traditional locales, and yet indebted to their communities for the opportunity for higher education. This theme of the alienation of the 'been-to' was taken up by other novelists through the 1960s, and has been explored very poignantly in Armah's *Fragments* (1970). Obi, we are informed, is the first son of

Umuofia to be sent abroad. Despite his initial resistance, Obi is unable to cope with the "practical expectations of the Umuofians" now residing in Lagos (Colmer, 89), or to assert his moral stance viz. his relationship with his girlfriend Clara who is an osu, and therefore forbidden to marry a non-osu. *No Longer at Ease* indicates how western capitalism and consumerism has already set the framework for cultural paralysis in post-independence African society, and Obi soon succumbs to the rapidly prevailing culture of corruption. There are also starting signs of the alienation of the intellectual from the political class: "In Nigeria, the government was 'they'. It had nothing to do with you or me" (NLE, 29–30).

In a detailed discussion on *Post Independence Disillusionment in Three African novels*, Emmanuel Obiechina points out that "between 1960 and 1968 there were 25 unconstitutional changes of government, of which 18 were military coups and others were military inspired" (110). Although almost all the former Anglophone colonies had attained their political independence from the British by the 1970s, the post-independence experience of the new nation-states came to be structured by what Neil Lazarus describes as "the deadly sinuosity of neo-colonialism" (17). It took less than a decade for sub-Saharan Africa to slide into a condition of profound economic and political crises. A legacy of colonialism, the term neo-colonialism is usually used to describe the high degree of economic control over a former colony's affairs by western business interests. Although the political relationship between the imperial power and the African colonies had theoretically altered through *flag independence*, western hegemonic control continued to exercise considerable influence with both political and psychological consequences. The complex extension of western dominance was achieved with the complicity of the neo-colonial elite. Archie Mafege points out in *Neo-colonialism, State Capitalism or Revolution* that while colonialism was "an unmitigated imposition", neo-colonialism is a "contractual relationship" (31). Infamous megalomaniac rulers like Idi Amin of Uganda and 'Emperor' Jean Bedel Bokassa of the Central African Republic were tragically propped by Western vested interests. Progressive socialist experiments, which had once promised so much change, also collapsed. The founding fathers of African nationalism Kwame Nkrumah of Ghana, Kenneth Kaunda of Zambia and Jomo Kenyatta of Kenya not only failed to deliver their pre-independence promises, but had also turned into one-party, semi-dictatorial leaders. Nigeria too suffered a spate of not less than six military coups between 1950 and 1980.

The African intellectual-artist had attached enormous importance to the promises of nationhood in the early years of independence, and therefore bitter disappointment, anger and blame replaced what could have been "the third world's springtime of nationalist idealism" with a "nationalism of mourning" (Brennan, 3). The political elite were now regarded as having sold out, and could no longer be regarded as the legitimate representatives of the people. "The new tribalism of African society", laments Ngugi, "was that of haves and have nots" (1972, xvii). As a consequence of the increasing disassociation between the dissident post-colonial intellectual and the governing elite, creative writing now enters a new phase antithetical to the pre-immediate independence mood of affirmation. There is a shift, for instance, from hope-filled descriptions of the future in Ngugi's first novel *The River Between* (1965) to a caustic critique of Kenyan government's humiliating reliance on international financial institutions in his fourth novel *Petals of Blood* (1977), which is militant in its indignation and radically leftist in content. A similar mood of weary cynicism recurs in Achebe's *No Longer at Ease* (1960), in Wole Soyinka's *The Interpreters* (1965) and *Season of Anomy* (1972), Kofi Awoonoor's *This Earth My Brother* (1966), and Ayi Kwei Armah's *The Beautyful Ones Are Not Yet Born* (1968) and *Fragments* (1970).

The bitter political and social realities of the new nation-states necessitated moving away from simplistic Manichean oppositions of black/white, colonized/coloniser. The writer was compelled to address pressing issues on the nature and purpose of their art, and the responsibilities of the artist towards the population at large. New reinterpretations and interrogations of identity also compelled a rethinking of hierarchies of gender, class, religious and linguistic differences. One of Africa's most polemical writers Ayi Kwei Armah defines the process of decolonisation as "the search or research for positive African ideas, perspectives, values". "The enterprise", he adds, "is tautologically centered on Africa" (64). Decolonization, according to Armah, involves a parallel process of 're-Africanization' or a discursive formulation wherein the artist reconstructs an identity s/he has hitherto been denied or deprived of. The very act of writing thereby becomes a means of self-realization.

As early as 1966, with the publication of his fourth novel, *A Man of the People*, Achebe forewarns of the peculiar situation of neo-colonialization. Emmanuel Ngara describes the book as "the first major novel of disillusionment" (114). The novel offers a severe critique of the neo-elite/political class and the serious consequences of intellectual and cultural dependency. In *The Wretched of the Earth*, Fanon had caustically referred to this class of people as 'pimps of the western world', unproductive, parasitic and determined to maintain inherited privileges. *A Man of the People* is particularly scathing in its attack on corrupt and irresponsible leadership. The political figure of Chief, the Honourable Dr Micah A Nanga M.P., L.L.D, like that of Koomson in Armah's *The Beautyful Ones*, Chimba in Mphahlele's

Chirundu, and Nderi in Ngugi's *Petals of Blood*, is a prototype of the leader who compromises idealism for the privileges of power that neo-colonial politics offered. Young idealistic Odili Samulu, who is the narrator of the novel, challenges Nanga for a seat in Parliament but fails because he is alienated from the traditions of the people, and is out of touch with the common man. Rosemary Colmer explains: "*A Man of the People* looks at the possibilities of right government and finds a dearth of right-minded men to make up such a government" (90).

Co-incidentally, *A Man of the People* was published just nine days after the 1966 military coup wherein a group of Igbo military officers led by Major General John T.Y. Aguiyi-Ironsi took charge. Bernth Lindfors suggests that to interpret the military coup in *A Man of the People as* 'a prophecy' is to suggest that Achebe meant the novel to relate only to Nigeria. On the other hand, Lindfors chooses to read the coup as "an African parable, not a Nigerian prophecy":

> By ending with a coup, an event anticipated yet still unknown in Nigeria but familiar elsewhere in Africa, Achebe added a dimension of universality to his story. It was no longer merely a satire on Nigeria but a satire on the rest of independent Africa as well. If the coup had a special meaning for Nigeria in the mid-sixties, it also contained a relevant moral for other emerging African nations, wracked by internal upheavals." (282)

The 1966 coup was soon followed by a counter-coup led by Hausa officers that established Lieutenant Colonel Yakubu Gowan as head of state. The killing of Ironsi and massacres of Igbo in the north, followed by a series of ethnic and political conflicts, led to a declaration of the secession of the eastern region from the rest of Nigeria. The Biafra civil war of 1967–70 followed. Achebe left Nigeria for the United States for four years and is said to have acted as the unofficial Biafran fund-raising ambassador. Achebe articulates his support for Biafra in the essay "The African Writer and the Biafran Cause", and calls upon the artist-writer to point out, at all times, the "faintest nuances of injustices" (1968, rpt in *Morning Yet on Creation Day*, 1975). In 1970, Biafra surrendered and rejoined the Nigerian state. In 1976, Achebe returned as Professor at the University of Nsukka, though he still continues to spend considerable time teaching in universities in the United States, to date.

Although Achebe did not produce another long work of fiction for almost twenty years, he wrote poetry, short stories, and lectured intensively. The context for Achebe's collection of poems in *Beware Soul Brother* (1971) is the trauma of the war years. *Girls at War* (1972) is a compilation of stories written between 1952 and 1971. Achebe also contributed four books to African Children's literature—

Chike and the River (1966), *How the Leopard got His Claws* (1972), *The Flute* (1977) and *The Drum* (1977). The latter three books are animal tales "in which Achebe recreates traditional tales and myths, giving them new meanings to suit modern events and situations" (Emenyonu 1998, 7). Achebe also put together a collection of incisive essays on issues such as the language debate, appropriate critical standards, the aesthetic and functionalist concept of art, and the social responsibility of the writer in *Morning Yet on Creation Day. Essays* (1975) and *Hopes and Impediments. Selected Essays, 1965–87* (1988).

Achebe voiced his frustration against the failure of post-colonial political elite to assume responsibility in *The Trouble with Nigeria*, a pre-election pamphlet produced in 1983. He categorically states: "The trouble with Nigeria is simply and squarely a failure of leadership" (1). This scathing attack on graft in high places sets the tone for Achebe's fifth novel, *Anthills of the Savannah*, published in 1987, almost twenty years after *A Man of the People*. Shortlisted for the Booker prize, the novel received critical attention for its skilful combination of sophisticated literary devices and oral narrative traditions. Achebe once again displays his supremacy in the use of proverbs and storytelling techniques. The novel's complex plot deals with a coup in the imaginary state of the Republic of Kangan, closely identifiable with Nigeria of the 1980s. The narrative is presented from the point of view of the three characters in the novel—Chris Oriko, the Commissioner for Information; Ikem Osodi, editor of the *National Gazette*; and Beatrice Okoh, Chris' girlfriend and a senior secretary in the Ministry of Finance. While the novel is a critique of the functioning of the modern African nation-state, and the failure of the democratic model, it also touches upon issues of sub-nationalism such as tribalism and ethnic politics. Achebe makes a conscious attempt to address the alienation of the elite from the masses. Importantly, as Elleke Boehmer points out, Achebe is more attuned to issues of gender and the novel's format of "a new life-affirming sisterhood" signifies "a new concept of rulership and a new moment in Achebe's work" (103).

Over the last two decades, the failure of political promises, debt-traps the making of the IMF and the World Bank, and ethnic clashes have compelled the African intellectual-writer to assert the responsibilities of the artist, to cite Fanon, as an "awakener of the people". Creative writers who have taken this role seriously have paid the price for their outspoken criticism against authoritarian governments. Ngugi wa Thiong'o and the Somalian novelist Nuruddin Farah have spent considerable years in political exile from their homeland. A pacifist and environmentalist, Saro Wiwa had accused the Nigerian military regime of Sani Abacha of environmental terror against Ogoniland, where a significant portion of the country's oil is located. He was executed on trumped-up charges in November 1995 by the Nigerian government despite international protests. Josaphat Kubayanda categories this emerging body of voices as the 'anti-dictatorial literature' of post-independence Africa. In this context, questions have been raised on the trajectory of Achebe's own ideological perspective. Ngara debates whether Achebe's authorial stance has sufficiently developed "from nationalist politics to revolutionary politics", as in the case of Ngugi (118). Maughan-Brown suggests that unlike Ngugi, the key thrust of Achebe's novel is on the ideology of leadership and reform, rather than revolution. With reference to *Anthills of the Savannah*, he adds:

> We find an assertion that the world belongs to the people of the world, but no suggestion as to how those people can become involved in the government of their world. Instead, we are presented with a view of people sufficiently unflattering for us not to be particularly enthusiastic about encouraging their involvement in government. (147)

On his part, Achebe has reasserted on a number of occasions his firm belief that political rhetoric is not enough. Reform will come about only if there is change at the level of the individual's consciousness and the duty of the writer is not to give answers but to pose the appropriate questions. Achebe uses Ikem in *Anthills of the Savannah* to articulate his stance:

> No I cannot give you the answer you are clamouring for. Go home and think! I cannot decree your pet, textbook revolution. I want instead to excite general enlightenment by forcing all the people to examine the condition of their lives, because as the saying goes, the unexamined life is not worth living . . . As a writer I aspire only to widen the scope of that self-examination. (158)

In 1990 Achebe was injured in a car accident on his way to Lagos, and was paralysed from his waist down. The 1990s also witnessed a spate of books and tributes to the veteran writer, which included three fascinating biographies (Ezenwa-Ohaeto 1997, Sallah 2003, and Phanuel Akubueze Egejuru 2003), as well as an encyclopaedia devoted to the writer (Booker 2003). Achebe has not written another longer novel after *Anthills*, but has been active in the arena of nonfiction. He dissects the West's commonly held stereotypes of Africa in *Another Africa* (1998). The text of three lectures delivered at Harvard University in 1998 have been published in *Home and Exile* (2000), wherein Achebe offers his views on the current trend of 'fashionable cosmopolitanism', and expresses his unhappiness at the privileging of the exile motif by writers like Salman Rushdie. Achebe has also issued a revised collection of his earlier poetry with a few additions in *Collected Poems* (2004). His forthcoming publication *Africa: A Short History* is eagerly awaited.

Works Cited

PRIMARY TEXTS BY CHINUA ACHEBE

Things Fall Apart. London: William Heinemann, 1958; New York: Astor Honor, 1959; London: Heinemann Educational Books, 1962.

The Sacrificial Egg and Other Short Stories. Onitsha: Etudo, 1962.

No Longer at Ease. London: William Heinemann, 1960; New York: Obolensky, 1961; Heinemann Educational Books, 1963; New York: Anchor-Doubleday, 1994.

Arrow of God. London: William Heinemann, 1964; New York: John Day, 1967; London: Heinemann Educational Books, 1965: revised edition, London: Heinemann Educational Books, 1974; New York: Anchor-Doubleday, 1989.

A Man of the People. London: William Heinemann, 1966; New York: John Day, 1966; London: Heinemann Educational Books, 1966; New York: Anchor-Doubleday, 1987.

Chike and the River. Cambridge: Cambridge UP, 1966. Rpt. Nairobi: Heinemann, 1990.

Beware, Soul Brother and Other Poems. Enugu: Nwankwo-Ifejika, 1971; revised and enlarged edition, London: Heinemann Educational Books, 1972; Reprinted as *Christmas in Biafra and Other Poems.* Garden City, NY: Anchor-Doubleday, 1973.

Girls at War and Other Stories. London: Heinemann Educational Books, 1972; Garden City NY: Anchor-Doubleday, 1973. (Includes in revised versions the stories in *The Sacrificial Egg and Other Stories.*)

With John Iroaganachi. *How the Leopard Got His Claws.* Enugu: Nwamife, 1972; New York: The Third Press, 1973.

The Drum. Enugu: Fourth Dimension, 1977.

The Flute. Enugu: Fourth Dimension, 1977.

Anthills of the Savannah. London: William Heinemann, 1987; New York: Doubleday, 1988.

Collected Poems. Anchor Books, 2004.

Morning Yet on Creation Day. Essays. London: Heinemann Educational Books, 1975.

The Trouble With Nigeria. Enugu: Fourth Dimension Publishers, 1983; Oxford: London: Heinemann, 1984.

"African Literature as Restoration of Celebration." Peterson and

Rutherford. *Special Issue in Celebration of Chinua Achebe*, 1990: 1–10.

Another Africa. USA: Anchor Books, 1998.

Home and Exile. Oxford: Oxford University Press, 2000.

SECONDARY READING

Armah, Ayi Kwei. "Masks and Marx. The Marxist Ethos vis-à-vis African Revolutionary Theory and Praxis." *Presence African* (1984), 131: 35–65.

Booker, Keith M. *The Chinua Achebe Encyclopedia*. Westport, CT; London, 2003.

Brennan, Timothy. *Salman Rushdie and the Third World Myths of the Nation*. The Macmillan Press Ltd, 1989.

Elleke Boehmer. "Of Goddesses and Stories: Gender and a New Politics in Achebe's *Anthills of the Savannah*." Peterson and Rutherford. *Special Issue in Celebration of Chinua Achebe*: 102–112.

Colmer, Rosemary. "*Quis Custodies Custodiet?* The Development of Moral Values in *A Man of the People*." Peterson and Anna Rutherford. *Special Issue in Celebration of Chinua Achebe*: 88–101.

Desai, Gaurav. "English as an African Language." Cambridge University Press: *English Today* 34, Vol. 9, No 2 (April 1993).

Egejuru, Phanuel Akubueze. *Chinua Achebe: Pure and Simple An Oral Biography*. Lagos: Malthouse, 2003.

Emenyonu, Ernest N. "Chinua Achebe's *Things Fall Apart*: A Classic Study in Diplomatic Tactlessness." Peterson and Rutherford. *Chinua Achebe*: 83–88.

———. "(Re-inventing) the Past for the Present. Symbolism in Achebe's *How the Leopard got its Claws*." *Bookbird*, Vol. 36, No 1 (Spring 1998): 6–11.

———. *Emerging Perspectives on Chinua Achebe. Vol. 1. Omenka the Master Artist. Critical Perspectives on Achebe's fiction*. Trenton NJ: Africa World Press, 2004.

Fanon, Frantz. *The Wretched of the Earth*. 1961. Rpt. Penguin, 1973.

Gikandi, Simon. "Foreword. Chinua Achebe and the Institution of African Literature." Booker, Keith M. *The Chinua Achebe Encyclopedia*. Westport, CT; London, 2003: vii–xv.

Innes, C.L. "Conspicuous Consumption." ed. Abdulrazak Gurnah. *Essays in African Writing, II. A Revaluation*. Heinemann Books, 1995.

Irele, Abiola. "The African Imagination." Research in African Literatures 21.1 (1990): 40–67.

Ivezbaye, Dan. "Issues in the Reassessment of the African Novel." *African Literature Today. 10*, 1979.

Jeyifo, Biodun. "For Chinua Achebe: The Resilience and the Predicament of Obierika." Peterson and Rutherford. *Special Issue in Celebration of Chinua Achebe*: 51–70.

Kubayanda, Josaphat B. "Dictatorship, Oppression and New Realism." *Research in African Literatures*. Summer, 21. 2 (1990).

Lazarus, Neil. *Resistance in Post-colonial African Fiction*. New Haven: Yale University Press, 1990.

Lindfors, Bernth. "Achebe's African Parable." Ernest Emenyonu. *Emerging Perspectives on Chinua Achebe*: 85–95.

Mafege, Archie. "Neo-colonialism, State Capitalism or Revolution?" *African Social Studies: A Radical Reader*. eds. Gutkind and Waterman. London: Heinemann Educational Books, 1978.

Maughan-Brown, David A. "*Anthills of the Savannah* and the Ideology of Leadership." Peterson and Rutherford. *Special Issue in Celebration of Chinua Achebe*: 139–48.

Mphahlele, Es'kia. *African Literature and the Social Experience in Progress*. Typescript of Inaugural Lecture delivered at the University of Witwatersrand. 25th October 1983.

Ngara, Emmanuel. "Achebe as Artist: The Place and Significance of *Anthills of the Savannah*." Peterson and Rutherford. *Special Issue in Celebration of Chinua Achebe*: 113–29.

Ngugi wa Thiong'o. *Homecoming: Essays on African and Caribbean Literature, Culture and Politics*. London: Heinemann, 1972.

———. *Petals of Blood*. Harare: Zimbabwe Publishing House, 1977.

Niven, Alistar. "Chinua Achebe and the Possibility of Modern Tragedy." Peterson and Rutherford. *Special Issue in Celebration of Chinua Achebe*: 41–50.

Obiechina, Emmanuel. "*Post Independence Disillusionment in Three African novels*." ed. Lindfors and Ulla Schild. *Essays in memory of Jahnheinz Jahn*. Weisbaden: Heymann, 1976.

Okafor, Clement. "Igbo Cosmology and the Parameters of Individual Accomplishment in *Things Fall Apart*." Ernest Emenyonu. *Emerging Perspectives on Chinua Achebe*: 85–95.

Okara, Gabriel. "Towards the Evolution of an African Language for African Literature." Peterson and Rutherford. *Special Issue in Celebration of Chinua Achebe*: 11–18.

Pandurang, Mala. *Post-Colonial African Fiction. The Crisis of Consciousness*. New Delhi: Pencraft International, 1997.

Peterson, Kirsten Holst, and Anna Rutherford, ed. *Special Issue in Celebration of Chinua Achebe. Kunapipi*, 12, 2 (1990).

Peterson, Kirsten Holst, and Anna Rutherford. "Working with Chinua Achebe: The African Writers Series; James Currey, Alan Hill and Keith Sambrook in conversation with Kirsten Holst Petersen." Peterson and Rutherford. *Special Issue in Celebration of Chinua Achebe*: 149–159.

Soyinka, Wole. *Myth, Literature and the African World.* New York: Cambridge University Press, 1976.

Turner, Margaret, E. "Achebe, Hegel, and the New Colonialism." Peterson and Rutherford. *Special Issue in Celebration of Chinua Achebe*: 31–40.

Yousaf, Nahem. *Chinua Achebe*. Tavistock, Devon: Northcote House in association with the British Council, 2003.

Essays on *Things Fall Apart*

OLADELE TAIWO

Things Fall Apart[†]

Things Fall Apart presents the breakdown in communication at two levels: the personal level, between Okonkwo and Umuofia society, and the group level, between Umuofia society on one hand and Christianity and the British Administration on the other. The hero Okonkwo embodies in a magnified form the strengths and weaknesses of his society, and because of the skill with which Achebe handles his material Okonkwo's importance emerges quite naturally and unobtrusively out of the living situation of the novel. Right from the first page we are told one of the incidents to which he owes his position in society.

> The drums beat and the flutes sang and the spectators held their breath. Amalinze was a wily craftsman, but Okonkwo was as slippery as a fish in water. Every nerve and every muscle stood out on their arms, on their backs and their thighs, and one almost heard them stretching to breaking point. In the end Okonkwo threw the cat. (*page 3*)

This is Achebe's description of how Okonkwo throws the great wrestler, Amalinze the Cat. In this short passage the author, by apt comparisons and economy of style, builds the two opponents to almost equal strength in order to bring out clearly the importance of Okonkwo's victory.

But although Okonkwo is undoubtedly an important member of Umuofian society, he is hardly a typical representative of that society. True enough, he shares the ideals of the society with his fellow-clansmen and partakes of its corporate life in peace and war. Achebe puts Okonkwo in many social contexts—as a wrestler, a spectator at the 'ilo,' an emissary for his tribe, a father, a head of his household and a village elder—in order to emphasise the fact that he has his

† From *Culture and the Nigerian Novel* (New York: St. Martin's Press, 1976), 114–25.

roots firmly on Umuofian soil. His personal achievements are such
as the tribe admires—three wives, two titles, large barns full of yams.
He works so hard that, even as a young man, he is already one of the
greatest men of his time. 'Age was respected among his people, but
achievement was revered.' (*page* 8) The first part of the novel is
devoted to the evocation of Umuofia society, and Achebe's method of
exposition is to integrate Okonkwo fully into the society so that the
reader may appreciate the background from which he is later to be
alienated.

It is usually through the detailed narration of certain important
events that Achebe shows Okonkwo's place in society and the hero's
concern for the customs and traditions of his ancestors. Consider, for
example, Achebe's description of the wrestling contest at the village
arena.

> The whole village turned out on the *ilo*, men, women and chil-
> dren. They stood round in a huge circle leaving the centre of the
> playground free. The elders and grandees of the village sat on
> their own stools brought there by their young sons or slaves.
> Okonkwo was among them. All others stood except those who
> came early enough to secure places on the few stands which had
> been built by placing smooth logs on forked pillars.
> The wrestlers were not there yet and the drummers held the
> field. They too sat just in front of the huge circle of spectators,
> facing the elders. Behind them was the big and ancient silk-
> cotton tree which was sacred. Spirits of good children lived in
> that tree waiting to be born. On ordinary days young women who
> desired children came to sit under its shade.
> There were seven drums and they were arranged according to
> their sizes in a long wooden basket. Three men beat them with
> sticks, working feverishly from one drum to another. They were
> possessed by the spirit of the drums. (*page* 42)

A passage like this helps to evoke the feel of life in Umuofia before
the advent of Christianity and the British Administration. The reader
can feel the excitement of the people and the very rhythms of life as
reflected by the beating of the drums and the resilience of Achebe's
prose. Achebe's description conveys an impression of an orderly hierarchical society in which both age and status matter a great deal. Not
only does he show an eye for detail, visualisation is also sharp. Everybody in the crowded 'ilo' takes his rightful place and contributes in
some way, whether as actor or spectator, to the success of the festive
occasion. So we find that the spectators 'stood round in a huge circle leaving the centre of the playground free' for the drummers and
wrestlers and that 'except those who came early enough to secure
places on the few stands . . .' others are content to stand. The young

ones and slaves carry the stools on which elders sit. Before the wrestlers were ready 'the drummers held the field'. The seven drums are arranged 'according to their sizes in a long wooden basket'. Such realistic descriptions are possible only because of Achebe's power of observation and his firm control of English. In this passage, for example, the novelist's prose becomes less dispassionate as one reads from paragraph one to paragraph three. In paragraph three the 'spirit of the drums' is reflected in the increased speed of narration, especially in the use of expressions like 'working feverishly', 'possessed'.

It is through such descriptions that Achebe gives Umuofia what William Walsh has called 'a coherent anatomy of standards and beliefs and a solid convincing body.' But even where, as in this passage, Achebe appears to be showing a nostalgia for the past, there is always a sustained balance between his own nostalgia and the need for artistic objectivity. This, as will be continually stressed, * * * gives his works their complexity. It is a mark of Achebe's intelligent objectivity that in a description of a successful sporting event we are given an indication of the fear of capricious gods and magic and the adherence to superstition which are a feature of life at Umuofia. The 'ancient silk-cotton tree which was *sacred*', referred to in the second paragraph of the passage, is a case in point. 'Spirits of good children', we are told, 'lived in that tree waiting to be born. On ordinary days young women who desired children came to sit under its shade.' The 'young women' are no doubt convinced of the usefulness of their action. But the way the information about the 'sacred' tree is given— so casually—in this passage reveals a slightly sardonic intent on the part of the novelist. 'Good children' is used here in ironic contrast to twins, 'ogbanje' and 'osu' which traditionally are regarded as a threat to the collective security of Umuofia.

Nothing demonstrates more clearly Okonkwo's importance in society than the scene in which, as an 'egwugwu', he appears with 'nine of the greatest masked spirits in the clan' (*page 81*). The 'egwugwu' is 'the most powerful and the most secret cult in the clan' (*page 80*), and, by devoting the whole of chapter ten of the novel to it, Achebe intends to emphasise its unique place in Igbo culture. The performance takes the form of a trial in which the 'masked spirits' settle a marital dispute, but the reader's interest is aroused by the way Achebe includes elements of both the grotesque and the deeply impressive. Evil Forest, the leading 'egwugwu', strikes one as an object of terror not so much because 'smoke poured out of his head' but mainly because of the dreadful responsibility of his office.

'*Umuofia kwenu!*' shouted the leading *egwugwu*, pushing the air with his raffia arms. The elders of the clan replied, '*Yaa!*'
'*Umuofia kwenu!*'

'Yaa!'
'Umuofia kwenu!'
'Yaa!'
Evil Forest then thrust the pointed end of his rattling staff into
the earth. And it began to shake and rattle, like something agitating with a metallic life. He took the first of the empty stools
and the eight other egwugwu began to sit in order of seniority
after him. (page 81)

In the whole of this scene Achebe has had to rely heavily on the
resources of Igbo language and culture to dramatise the interrelation
between environment and character, between Evil Forest acting in
the name of the elders on one hand and the litigants and audience
on the other. For it is only on the assumption that the egwugwu's
authority is unassailable and will be readily accepted by the people
that a scene like this can succeed—and does succeed. The word 'rattling' is significant. Throughout the scene the symbol of metal, usually associated with the egwugwu, is used to integrate Okonkwo with
his cultural environment. Expressions like 'an iron gong sounded'
(page 80), 'the metal gong beat continuously' (page 80), 'the sound of
the many tiny bells and rattles' (page 82), found elsewhere in the narrative, help to reinforce this symbol. Metal denotes strength and
durability, and might have been used here as a symbolic reminder of
what, up to now, has been an essential quality of Igbo culture—its
conservatism and inflexibility. There is, however, the suggestion that
this situation cannot remain unchanged for much longer. Forces are
already at work which will finally disrupt the present apparently
smooth surface of communal life and dislodge institutions like the
egwugwu from their positions of strength. All this is symbolically suggested by the behaviour of Evil Forest's staff which 'began to shake
and rattle, like something agitating with a metallic life.' The word 'agitating' symbolises the state of restlessness, the imperceptible change
of which Umuofia society is as yet blissfully ignorant.

Meanwhile, Evil Forest, as the leading egwugwu, brings the trial
scene to an impressive end after each party to the dispute has stated
his case.

'Uzowulu's body, I salute you,' he said.
'Our father, my hand has touched the ground,' replied
Uzowulu, touching the earth.
'Uzowulu's body, do you know me?'
'How can I know you, father? You are beyond our knowledge,'
Uzowulu replied.
'I am Evil Forest. I kill a man on the day that his life is sweet-
est to him.'
'That is true,' replied Uzowulu.

'Go to your in-laws with a pot of wine and beg your wife to return to you. It is not bravery when a man fights with a woman.' He turned to Odukwe, and allowed a brief pause.

'Odukwe's body, I greet you,' he said.

'My hand is on the ground,' replied Odukwe.

'Do you know me?'

'No man can know you,' replied Odukwe.

'I am Evil Forest, I am Dry-meat-that-fills-the-mouth, I am Fire-that-burns-without-faggots. If your in-law brings wine to you, let your sister go with him. I salute you.' He pulled his staff from the hard earth and thrust it back.

'*Umuofia kwenu!*' he roared, and the crowd answered. (*pages 84–5*)

It is the dignity of the scene which impresses the reader most. This dignity is evoked by details such as the formality of address, the repetition of certain conventional statements and answers, the willing performance of ritualistic acts like touching the ground as a sign of total submission to the egwugwu and the orderliness of the whole procedure. However, the scene is not without some sombre aspects. Evil Forest endows himself with terrible attributes and gives himself grotesque cognomens: 'I am Dry-meat-that-fills-the-mouth, I am Fire-that-burns-without-faggots'. Do these aspects add to the dignity of the scene or detract from it? Is there any ironic intention on the part of the novelist here? Is it being suggested, for instance, that Evil Forest's authority rests on his capacity to do evil? Do the cognomens have the same devastating effect as the praise-names which the elders give themselves in Okara's *The Voice*? Achebe's attitude is not altogether clear. But since these cognomens are presented as direct translations from the Igbo original, his intention may be to show how rooted in Igbo tradition the scene is in content and language. After all, quite rightly, in the whole passage he has had to rely heavily on the linguistic characteristics of Igbo and Igbo speech rhythm in order that the various statements and responses may be 'in character'. For example, when the egwugwu says 'It is not bravery when a man fights with a woman' he is expressing in direct straightforward English what every Igbo recognises in his language as an idiom. It is through such devices as we find in the egwugwu scene that Achebe demonstrates Okonkwo's importance in society and the conservative nature of Igbo culture.

Okonkwo's tragedy arises from the fact that he wants the old order retained. Anything which disturbs this order he regards as a personal threat to himself. Of the events which lead to the alienation of Okonkwo from the people of Umuofia and his son Nwoye, the death of Ikemefuna is probably the most important. In his presentation of this incident Achebe dramatises the ambiguity in the relationship between man and his gods in Umofia society.

'I cannot understand why you refused to come with us to kill
that boy,' he asked Obierika.
'Because I did not want to,' Obierika replied sharply. 'I had
something better to do.'
'You sound as if you question the authority and the decision
of the Oracle, who said he should die.'
'I do not. Why should I? But the Oracle did not ask me to carry
out its decision.'
'But someone had to do it. If we were all afraid of blood, it
would not be done. And what do you think the Oracle would do
then?'
'You know very well, Okonkwo, that I am not afraid of
blood; and if anyone tells you that I am, he is telling a lie. And
let me tell you one thing, my friend. If I were you I would have
stayed at home. What you have done will not please the Earth.
It is the kind of action for which the goddess wipes out whole
families.'
'The Earth cannot punish me for obeying her messenger,'
Okonkwo said, A child's fingers are not scalded by a piece of hot
yam which its mother puts into its palm.' (*pages 60–61*)

By the juxtaposition of two different points of view—those of Okonkwo
and Obierika—Achebe successfully dramatises the complexity of the
situation. A situation like this does not admit of any easy judgement or
conclusion. It reminds one of some of Tutuola's dilemma tales in which
any particular solution to a given situation is applicable only in a limited way. The argument of both parties appears sound. But when one
considers the trend of events, and it turns out later that it is at the
funeral ceremony of Ezeudu (who had warned Okonkwo to have no
part in Ikemefuna's death) that Okonkwo is involved in an accidental
killing that exiles him from Umuofia, one begins to wonder whether
Obierika's has not been the voice of reason; whether in fact, Okonkwo
has not misinterpreted the will of the gods. For such is the ambiguous
relationship between man and god in Achebe's novels that man's survival usually depends on his ability to carry out correctly the wishes of
the gods. We are confronted here with an ironic situation in which
Okonkwo, in his attempt to uphold 'the authority and the decision of
the Oracle' displeases the earth goddess.

The situation is made even more complex by Okonkwo's personal
reaction to Ikemefuna's death.

Okonkwo did not taste any food for two days after the death
of Ikemefuna. He drank palm-wine from morning till night, and
his eyes were red and fierce like the eyes of a rat when it was
caught by the tail and dashed against the floor. He called his son,
Nwoye, to sit with him in his *obi*. But the boy was afraid of him
and slipped out of the hut as soon as he noticed him dozing.

He did not sleep at night. He tried not to think about Ikeme-funa, but the more he tried the more he thought about him. Once he got up from bed and walked about his compound. But he was so weak that his legs could hardly carry him. He felt like a drunken giant walking with the limbs of a mosquito. (*page* 57)

Okonkwo is overcome by grief after the death of Ikemefuna. He feels deserted and lonely, and therefore calls his son 'to sit with him in his *obi*'. He cannot eat or sleep and unsuccessfully seeks to drown his sorrow in palm-wine. Achebe dramatises this grief and brings it vividly before the reader in the verbal picture he draws of Okonkwo's eyes which 'were red and fierce like the eyes of a rat when it was caught by the tail and dashed against the floor.' Why does a man who is anxious not to be considered weak and who seems certain that what he has done has the approval of the gods become inconsolable at the death of a boy? Given this situation, what justification does the novel provide for Okonkwo's brutal treatment of his wives and children? We are told in the last sentence of the passage that Okonkwo feels 'like a drunken giant walking with the limbs of a mosquito'. Bearing in mind this contrast between the giant and the mosquito, and the complexity with which Okonkwo's character is drawn, it seems likely that the author's intention is to suggest that, despite Okonkwo's preoccupation with masculinity and contempt for the display of all gentle emotions, he is not completely devoid of humanity. In fact, evidence abounds in the novel that he has not always been harsh and brutal. We have the testimony of Ekwefi to the fact that in early life he was gentle and kind. We see how relieved he is that his wife is unharmed after the gun-fire incident and how distressed he is now at the death of Ikemefuna. In order to comfort Ekwefi, he goes looking for her at the entrance of the cave where she is waiting to receive Ezinma back from Chielo, the priestess of Agbala. However, in spite of this occasional display of kindness, it is Okonkwo's brutalities which influence the course of events in the novel and finally alienate him from his people. It is, for example, because of his harsh treatment of Nwoye and his part in the killing of Ikemefuna that tension develops between Okonkwo and his son, leading to a complete breakdown in communication between the two. As we are told in the passage, Nwoye 'was afraid of him [Okonkwo] and slipped out of the hut as soon as he noticed him dozing.' This is the beginning of the estrangement between father and son which reaches its climax with Nwoye becoming a Christian.

But all this leaves a basic problem only partially resolved. Why does Okonkwo appear to have purged himself of all gentle emotions, so as completely to ignore the softer dimensions of tribal life? Nothing in Umuofian code of ethics prevents a man from being strong and successful but gentle at the same time. Can it be that Okonkwo shows

kindness only as a matter of necessity? Is he doing violence to his true
nature when he tries to damp down all outside manifestations of gentleness? Or is it just a matter of putting public virtue in a conformist
sense over and above his private feelings? What, for example, prevents
Okonkwo from adopting, like his father, the liberal tradition within Igbo
culture? The novel does not provide entirely satisfactory answers to
these questions even though Achebe gives clear insights into Okonkwo's
two important motivations for action by linking his present temperament first with the values of his society and secondly with the need to
live down what he considers the disgrace of his father's life. Achebe
accounts successfully in the novel for the social and psychological factors arising from the first motivation. These, as has been pointed
out, show Okonkwo as an embodiment, in a magnified form, of the
strengths and weaknesses of his society. Achebe does less well with the
second which, at best, provides only a negative reason for his hero's
actions. The reader would require much more information about
Unoka to be convinced that his memory can influence Okonkwo to the
extent the novel claims. The little information we have shows Unoka as
a lover of music and the arts and as one endowed with those human
qualities which Okonkwo would have been the better for possessing.

> He was very good on his flute, and his happiest moments were
> the two or three moons after the harvest when the village musi-
> cians brought down their instruments, hung above the fireplace.
> Unoka would play with them, his face beaming with blessedness
> and peace. Sometimes another village would ask Unoka's band
> and their dancing *egwugwu* to come and stay with them and
> teach them their tunes. They would go to such hosts for as long
> as three or four markets, making music and feasting. Unoka
> loved the good fare and the good fellowship, and he loved this
> season of the year, when the rains had stopped and the sun rose
> every morning with dazzling beauty. (*page 4*)

Unoka is not the worthless man that his son makes him out to be. He
is an accomplished artist whose expertise is much sought after by other
villages. The picture of him which comes through from the pages of
the novel is one of almost unqualified approval. Given this situation,
the critic is entitled to wonder why the only use made of Unoka in the
novel is the negative motivation he provides for Okonkwo.

Whatever the part played by the gods, social and psychological factors contribute to Okonkwo's alienation from his people. The spiritual isolation which starts among his own people at Umuofia
becomes more intense during his period of exile at Mbanta. When he
finally returns, he never really captures the prevailing mood of the
times and proves completely incapable of adjusting himself to the
new situation created by the presence of the Christian missionaries.

The conflict in this novel arises more from a particular than from a general failure. It results mainly from Okonkwo's unpreparedness to face reality and accept the fact that the unity of the tribe has been considerably weakened by those aspects of tribal life which many begin not to understand or appreciate. He forgets that he can no longer act as a spokesman for Umuofia, that as Achebe says,

> Seven years was a long time to be away from one's clan. A man's place was not always there, waiting for him. As soon as he left, someone else rose and filled it. The clan was like a lizard; if it lost its tail it soon grew another. (*page 155*)

Okonkwo is too mentally isolated from his community to appreciate the significance of the proverb in the quotation since this in itself is part of the function of the society from which he is now estranged. It is this isolation which prevents him from realising earlier that the solution to the problems of Umuofia lies in a concerted, not a unilateral, action. When he finally acts on his own initiative and kills the court messenger, he realises for the first time—what he ought to have known a long time before—that he is alone. It is the thought that the unity of the tribe is gone for ever and that there is no hope of reviving the old martial spirit that drives him to commit suicide. Such a tremendous sacrifice and display of heroism might not have been necessary if Okonkwo had remained all along in spirit and action an integral member of the Umuofian community and had been more inclined to accept an accurate assessment of the situation by his reasonable and trusted friend, Obierika.

> The white man is very clever. He came quietly and peaceably with his religion. We were amused at his foolishness and allowed him to stay. Now he has won our brothers, and our clan can no longer act like one. He has put a knife on the things that held us together and we have fallen apart. (*page 160*)

Okonkwo provides a good example of a man who 'falls alone'. But with him safely out of the way, and given the moderate position of some important Umuofian citizens like Obierika, is there any possibility of reconciling the two systems, of establishing a bridge of understanding between Umuofia on the one hand and the British Administration and Christianity on the other? All the evidence in the book points to the fact that a policy of accommodation is not contemplated by either side and, in fact, has very little chance of succeeding. Nothing reveals this more clearly than the attitude of the District Commissioner at the end of the novel. He seems to be just as out of touch with the true feelings of Umuofia as Okonkwo, and he is hardly the type of administrator needed at this crucial time to bring home to Umuofians the advantages to be derived from British

Administration. First, through a combination of treachery and naked show of power he arrests the six leaders of the people, offers them no opportunity to defend themselves and then proceeds to harangue them in a speech which reminds one of some of the speeches of Sanders in *Sanders of the River*. The District Commissioner misses the whole significance of the death of Okonkwo—Obierika's explanation leaves no impression on him. To him the dangling body of Okonkwo constitutes 'undignified details', only good enough to be relegated to a paragraph in a book he is planning to write.

> The story of this man who had killed a messenger and hanged himself would make interesting reading. One could almost write a whole chapter on him. Perhaps not a whole chapter but a reasonable paragraph, at any rate. There was so much else to include, and one must be firm in cutting out details. (*page 187*)

There is a lack of rapport between the two groups and therefore very little hope of a peaceful co-existence between the two. What finally brings the two sides into tragic conflict is the uncompromising attitude of the new leader of the Christian missionaries.

> Mr Brown's successor was the Reverend James Smith, and he was a different kind of man. He condemned openly Mr Brown's policy of *compromise and accommodation*. He saw things as black and white. And black was evil. He saw the world as a battlefield in which the children of light were locked in mortal conflict with the sons of darkness. He spoke in his sermons about sheep and goats and about wheat and tares. He believed in slaying the prophets of Baal. (my italics, *page 166*)

Brown has been willing to respect and accommodate traditional opinion to some extent and curb the activities of the overzealous members of his flock, such as one Enoch who is believed to have killed and eaten the sacred python. If he had remained in control of the mission, disaster might have been averted. But, as the passage shows, his successor adopts an entirely different attitude to his work and introduces a new element into the situation. 'He saw things as black and white. And black was evil.' He is a missionary in a fighting mood. He rules out any possibility of 'compromise and accommodation' by his rigid division of Christians and non-Christians into 'sheep and goats', 'wheat and tares'. His actions bring about a complete breakdown in communication between the two systems. It is the author's deliberate doing that any chance of reconciling the views and positions of both sides is irredeemably lost. One leaves the novels with a feeling that the people of Umuofia are at the beginning of a long and bitter struggle against the combined forces of British Administration and Christianity, which they have no chance of winning. It may well be that it is this feeling of tragic inevitability that Achebe wishes to arouse in the reader. For why, one is entitled to ask, is a man like Rev. Smith, who carries out his mandate with such iconoclastic zeal and shows no regard for the established customs and religious practices of the people, put in charge of the Mission at Umuofia at such a crucial period? Why is Mr Brown removed from the scene when his policy of reconciliation has started to bear fruit? Why is the Colonial Administration at this important point in history left in the hands of a District Commissioner who appears pathologically incapable of understanding the point of view of the villagers? One cannot help feeling that if the conditions had existed for the people of Umuofia to be fully exposed to the blessings of the British Administration they would have tried to reconcile their interests with those of the white man. By making such conditions unobtainable, the author, like Rev. Smith, rules out the possibility of 'compromise and accommodation'.

In the face of these facts, to argue as Robert Serumaga does, that the death of Okonkwo has no repercussion at all on Umuofia is to play down the communal nature of Umuofian culture and to ignore the wider issues raised in the novel. For, apart from other misinterpretations, this is the impression given by Serumaga's statement.

> Okonkwo hangs himself. He has been unable to maintain a particular faith, and he takes the easiest way out, which is the way of the coward. Chinua Achebe's society is not falling apart because a lot of people are coming in and bringing new ideas. In fact what happens in this book is that the character Okonkwo kills himself because he refuses to change and embody both experience. He is the one who hangs himself; the society goes on.[1]

It is true that society goes on. But it is also important to stress that it is not in the same way as before. A. G. Stock comes closer to the truth in this matter when she finds that 'Okonkwo's end was not only that of an obstinate hero running his head against a machine too big for him, it was the end of a way of life'.[2] This may be overstating the case slightly. But there is enough evidence in the book to show that Okonkwo's death signifies the beginning of the end. We have Obierika's word for it that in Umuofia 'if the clan did not exact punishment for an offence against the great goddess, her wrath was loosed on all the land and not just on the offender . . . if one finger brought oil it soiled the others.' (*page* 114) This is an important statement in the novel because it reveals the complex nature of the work. It brings out clearly the fact that here we are dealing with both the personal tragedy of Okonkwo and the collective tragedy of Umuofia.

1. Robert Serumaga, "A Mirror of Integration." In C. Pieterse and D. Munro, eds., *Protest and Conflict in African Literature* (London: Heinemann, 1969) 76.
2. A. G. Stock, "Yeats and Achebe," *Journal of Commonwealth Literature* 5 (1968): 110.

In the language of Obierika's statement the offender is Okonkwo, but it is on the whole clan that the wrath of the goddess 'was loosed'. The finger which brings oil is Okonkwo's, but there is no effective means of preventing the oil 'soiling' other members of the community. After all, Okonkwo is 'one of the greatest men in Umuofia', and his excesses and abnormality are derived from that society. So it is only reasonable to expect that, as in all great tragedies, his death, whatever the circumstances, will have a tragic effect on his community.

We must therefore conclude that the Umuofian society we see at the end of the novel is not strong enough to absorb the shock of Okonkwo's death, endure the disastrous effects of a foreign religion and British Administration and yet remain its old self. Although Okonkwo falls alone, his death brings general dismay and strikes terror into the hearts of already-confused Umuofians. In presenting these events, it is not unlikely that Achebe had in mind the confrontation which actually took place between traditional society and the Church at Aro-Ndizuogu in 1916.[3] This brought about widespread dislocation of tribal life in the same way that the events in *Things Fall Apart* mark the beginning of the eventual liquidation of an old way of life. To limit our interpretation of tragedy only to the fate of Okonkwo is, therefore, to ignore the profound human issues raised in the novel, unduly narrow its scope, misread its title (*Things* not *Something*) and undermine the achievement of the novelist in this impressive work.

SOLOMON O. IYASERE

Narrative Techniques in *Things Fall Apart*[†]

No West African fiction in English has received as much critical attention as *Things Fall Apart*, Chinua Achebe's first and most impressive novel. In defending its importance, most critics link its value solely to its theme, which they take to be the disintegration of an almost Edenic traditional society as a result of its contact and conflict with Western practices and beliefs. These enthusiastic critics, such as Gleason and Killam, are primarily interested in the socio-cultural features of the work, and stress the historical picture of a traditional Ibo village community without observing how this picture is delimited, how this material serves the end of art. This approach, which cannot

---

3. See Mbonu Ojike, *My Africa* (New York: John Day, 1946), Ch. 1.
† From *Critical Perspectives on Chinua Achebe*. Ed. C. L. Innes and Bernth Lindfors (Washington: Three Continents Press, 1978), 92–110.

withstand critical scrutiny, does great violence to the text and denies it the artistic vitality they so vigorously claim for it.

Overemphasizing the ways in which Okonkwo represents certain values fundamental to the Umuofia society, Killam turns Okonkwo into an embodiment of the values of this society, averring, "Okonkwo was one of the greatest men of his time, the embodiment of Ibo values, the man who better than most symbolizes his race" (*The Novels of Chinua Achebe, 17*). Eustace Palmer, a moralistic critic, presents a similar interpretation but extends Okonkwo's role from champion to victim:

> Okonkwo is what his society has made him, for his most conspicuous qualities are a response to the demands of his society. If he is plagued by fear of failure and of weakness it is because his society put such a premium on success. . . . Okonkwo is a personification of his society's values, and he is determined to succeed in this rat-race. (*An Introduction to the African Novel, 53*)

The inaccuracies of this view derive from disregarding the particularities of the rhetoric of Achebe's controlled presentation. Killam and Palmer take as authoritative Okonkwo's vision of himself as a great leader and savior of Umuofia and so fail to realize that this vision is based on a limited perception of the values of that society. Nowhere in the novel is Okonkwo presented as either the embodiment or the victim of Umuofia's traditional laws and customs. To urge that he is either, as do Killam and Palmer, is to reduce the work to a sentimental melodrama, rob Okonkwo of his tragic stature, and deny the reader's sympathy for him.

More responsive to the novel's simultaneous sympathy for and critical judgment of Okonkwo, David Carroll observes:

> As Okonkwo's life moves quickly to its tragic end, one is reminded forcibly of another impressive but wrongheaded hero, Henchard in *The Mayor of Casterbridge*. They share an obsessive need for success and status, they subordinate all their private relations to this end, and both have an inability to understand the tolerant, skeptical societies in which their novel single-mindedness succeeds. . . . Viewed in the perspective of the Wessex, rustic way of life, Henchard is crass, brutal, and dangerous; but when this way of life as a whole is threatened with imminent destruction, then his fierce resistance takes on a certain grandeur. The reader's sympathy describes a similar trajectory as it follows Okonkwo's career. By the values of Umuofia his inadequacies are very apparent; but when the alien religion begins to question and undermine these values, Okonkwo, untroubled by the heart-searching of the community, springs to its defense and acts. (*Chinua Achebe, 62–63*)

Carroll's comment is to the point in directing our attention to the crucial limitations Okonkwo places on his relationship to and acceptance of Umuofia's standards. But simply focusing attention on this matter is not sufficient; we must see how Achebe is able to achieve this control of sympathy for Okonkwo.

Things Fall Apart seems a simple novel, but it is deceptively so. On closer inspection, we see that it is provocatively complex, interweaving significant themes: love, compassion, colonialism, achievement, honor, and individualism. In treating these themes, Achebe employs a variety of devices, such as proverbs, folktales, rituals, and the juxtaposition of characters and episodes to provide a double view of the Ibo society of Umuofia and the central character, Okonkwo. The traditional Ibo society that emerges is a complex one: ritualistic and rigid yet in many ways surprisingly flexible. In this society, a child is valued more than any material acquisition, yet the innocent, loving child, Ikemefuna, is denied loved, denied life, by the rigid tribal laws and customs. Outwardly, Umuofia is a world of serenity, harmony, and communal activities but inwardly it is torn by the individual's personal doubts and fears. It is also a society in which "age was respected . . . but achievement was revered." It is this sustained view of the duality of the traditional Ibo society that the novel consistently presents in order to create and intensify the sense of tragedy and make the reader understand the dilemma that shapes and destroys the life of Okonkwo.

No episode reveals more dramatically the concomitant rigidity and flexibility of the society than the trial scene in which the domestic conflict between Uzowulu and his wife Mgbafo is settled. Uzowulu has beaten his wife so often and so severely that at last she has fled to her family for protection from him. While such conflicts are usually settled on a personal level, Uzowulu is the kind of man who will listen only to the judgement of the great *egwugwu*, the masked ancestor spirits of the clan. This ceremony proceeds with marked ritual (*TFA*, 85).

The ritualistic procedure of this event reflects the seriousness and formality with which the people of Umuofia deal with internal problems, even trivial ones, that undermine or threaten the peaceful coexistence of the clans. The stereotyped incantatory exchange of greeting, the ceremonious way in which the spirits appear, the ritual greeting, "Uzowulu's body, I salute you," and Uzowulu's response, "Our father, my hand has touched the ground," even the gestures of these masked spirits, define the formality of the society and dramatize the fact that the peace of the tribe as a whole takes precedence over personal considerations. The decrees of the gods are always carried out with dispatch, even if it means a ruthless violation of human impulses, as in the murder of Ikemefuna or the throwing away of twins. But this formality does not preclude dialogue, probing, and debate, aptly demonstrated in that the parties involved in the conflict are allowed to present their opposing, even hostile views. The way this domestic issue is resolved reveals the unqualified emphasis the people of Umuofia place on harmony and peaceful coexistence (*TFA*, 89).

The formality of this event, the firmness with which the society controls impending disorder, becomes even more apparent when contrasted with the spontaneous communal feasting that precedes it—the coming of the locust. This sudden occurrence aptly demonstrates the joy and vitality of the society when it is is not beleaguered by internal disharmony (*TFA*, 54–55).

The overabundance of locusts provides an equal measure of joy for Umuofia. While the people restrain themselves enough to heed the elders' instructions on how to catch the insects this control of happiness is momentary, and no one spares either time or effort in responding to this unexpected feast. For the moment, Umuofia is at peace; Okonkwo and his sons are united in sharing the joy which envelops the community. Against the joyfully harmonic rhythm of this event, the withdrawn, controlled formalism of the judgement of the *egwugwu* stands in sharp relief. By juxtaposing these events, Achebe orchestrates the modulating rhythms of Umuofia, the alternating patterns of spontaneous joy and solemn justice. This modulation of rhythms developed out of the juxtaposition contrasting events open as well within the framework of the same episode. The suddenness with which the locusts descend on the people, bringing joy, is matched by the suddenness with which that joy is taken away. The very moment that Okonkwo and his sons sit feasting, Ezeudu enters to tell Okonkwo of the decree of the Oracle of the Hills and Caves (*TFA*, 55–56).

Just as Okonkwo's response to the celebration of feasting is controlled by the almost simultaneous announcement of the doom of the innocent child, Ikemefuna, so the narrator modulates the reader's response to the contrasting values and customs of Umuofia. On the very day Ikemefuna sits happily with his "father," Ezeudu somberly states, "Yes, Umuofia has decided to kill him."

Similarly, in order to articulate and call attention to the rigidity of the Ibo code of values in requiring the exile of Okonkwo for the inadvertent killing of Ezeudu's son, Achebe skillfully orchestrates the circumstances of the boy's death. In presenting this scene, Achebe emphasizes the atmosphere, the action, and the situation without individualizing Okonkwo's role. Such deliberate attention to the circumstances that day intensifies the sense of accidental occurrence. The death of Ezeudu's son comes as a result of the situation, of the circumstances, not as any deliberate act on Okonkwo's part. With this sense of chance established, the scene makes more apparent the rigidity of the tribal laws in dealing with this accidental event:

The only course open for Okonkwo was to flee from the clan. It was a crime against the earth goddess to kill a clansman, and a man who committed it must flee from the land. The crime was of two kinds, male and female. Okonkwo had committed the female because it had been inadvertent. He could return to the clan after seven years. (*TFA, 117*)

In probing and evaluating this code whose rigidity negates circumstantial and human considerations, the thoughtful Obierika questions, "Why should a man suffer so grievously for an offense he had committed inadvertently?"

Obierika's thoughts reflect the submerged fears of the village elders, particularly Uchendu, Okonkwo's uncle, and Ezeudu, as well as the doubts and questions of Okonkwo's wives and even his son Nwoye. Indeed, he gives voice to the very question the reader himself asks.

The inflexibility of this tribal code and its application is revealed not only in the formal decrees of the Oracles and the judgments of the *egwugwu* but also in the small details of every day life. The simple act of a cow getting loose in the fields is met with a harsh penalty (*TFA, 108–109*). Since the preservation of crops is essential in an agricultural society, the imposition of a severe fine on those whose animals destroy the produce is understandable. But the crucial point the narrator stresses here is that the laws are applied with absolute rigidity, with no regard for mitigating circumstances. Even though the responsible party in this instance was only a small child being watched by his father, who does not usually watch the children, while the mother was busy helping another prepare a feast to ensure the proper observance of the marriage ceremonies, the same penalty is exacted. Just as Okonkwo is harshly punished for an inadvertent act which occurred while he was observing the proper funeral rites of the clan, so is Ezelagbo's husband punished for an offense his small child committed both unintentionally and unknowingly. In these subtle ways, Achebe succeeds in presenting the inflexibility of the code of values of Umuofia as it responds to any threat, no matter how small, to the overall stability of the clan.

Yet to insist that this code is entirely inflexible is to present only one-half of the picture. The people of Umuofia can adapt their code to accommodate the less successful, even effeminate men, like Okonkwo's father, Unoka, despite the fact that according to their standards of excellence, solid personal achievement and manly stature are given unqualified emphasis. This adaptability to changing or different situations is further demonstrated in Ogbeufi Ezeudu's comment on the punishment meted out to Okonkwo for his violation of the sacred Week of Peace.

"It has not always been so," he said. "My father told me that
he had been told that in the past a man who broke the peace was
dragged on the ground through the village until he died. But
after a while this custom was stopped because it spoiled the
peace which it was meant to preserve."

"Somebody told me yesterday," said one of the younger men,
"that in some clans it is an abomination for a man to die during
the Week of Peace."

"It is indeed true," said Ogbuefi Ezeudu. "They have that custom in Obadoani. If a man dies at this time he is not buried but
cast into the Evil Forest. It is a bad custom which these people
observe because they lack understanding. They throw away large
numbers of men and women without burial. And what is the
result? Their clan is full of evil spirits of these unburied dead,
hungry to do harm to the living." (*TFA*, 33)

It seems clear from this instance that in some ways the social code
of Umuofia is responsive to change; if the people find elements of the
code contradictory, they will alter them, provided such modification
does not conflict with the will of the gods. This receptivity to change
is coupled with a willingness to accept and accommodate even those
who do not perfectly conform to their ways, in accordance with the
proverbial wisdom, "Let the kite perch and let the eagle perch too. If
one says no to the other, let his wing break" (*TFA*, 21–22). Though
Unoka was the subject of jest, he was not cast out, and even the albinos, whom the Ibos of Umuofia consider aliens, were accepted members of the clan, for, as Uchendu indicates to Obierika, " 'There is no
story that is not true,' said Uchendu. 'The world has no end, and what
is good among one people is an abomination with others. We have
albinos among us. Do you not think that they came to our clan by
mistake, that they have strayed from their way to a land where everybody is like them?' " (*TFA*, 130). Throughout the novel, this complex,
dualistic nature of the customs and traditions of the Ibo society of
Umuofia is made clear. This duality is well presented through
Achebe's technique of skillfully juxtaposing contrasting events,
events which define and articulate the code of values of the tradition
oriented people. On the one hand, we see the villagers actively
engaged in a spontaneous communal activity, such as enjoying a marriage feast, or in gathering and sharing the locusts, while, on the
other hand, we see the rigid application of tribal laws and decrees of
the gods which often deny and violate human responses.

These elements are set in opposition to one another to give a complete, if self-contradictory, view of the society. To accept and emphasize only one aspect is to oversimplify and defend, as does Okonkwo,
a limited perception. It is against this balanced view of the proud traditional Ibo society that the novel invites us to evaluate the actions

and tragic life of the central character, Okonkwo. Only through such examination do the problems of Okonkwo's relationship to the culture of his people become clear.

As a careful reading of *Things Fall Apart* reveals, one of Achebe's great achievements is his ability to keep alive our sympathy for Okonkwo despite our moral revulsion from some of his violent, inhuman acts. With Obierika, we condemn him for participating in the killing of the innocent boy, Ikemefuna. We despise him for denying his son, Nwoye, love, understanding, and compassion. And we join the village elders in disapproving Okonkwo's uncompromisingly rigid attitude toward unsuccessful, effeminate men such as his father, Unoka, or Osugo. Yet we share with the narrator a sustained sympathy for him. We do not simply identify with him, nor defend his actions, nor admire him as an heroic individual. We do give him our innermost sympathies because we know from his reactions to his own violence that deep within him he is not a cruel man. It is this contrasting, dualistic view of Okonkwo that the narrator consistently presents. On the one hand, we see Okonkwo participating in the brutal killing of Ikemefuna, his "son," but on the other, we see him brooding over this violent deed for three full days. In another instance, we see him dispassionately castigating his fragile, loving daughter, Ezinma, and deeply regretting that she is not a boy, while on another occasion we see him struggling all night to save her from *iba* or returning again and again to the cave to protect her from harm at the hands of Chielo, priestess of *Agbala*.

Throughout the novel, Okonkwo is presented as a man whose life is ruled by one overriding passion: to become successful, powerful, rich, found a dynasty, and become one of the lords of the clan of Umuofia. And Okonkwo's unflagging commitment is not without cause, for

> . . . his whole life was dominated by fear, the fear of failure and of weakness. It was deeper and more intimate than the fear of evil and capricious gods and of magic, the fear of the forest, and of the forces of nature, malevolent, red in tooth and claw. Okonkwo's fear was greater than these. It was not external but lay deep within himself. It was the fear of himself, lest he should be found to resemble his father. And so Okonkwo was ruled by one passion—to hate everything that his father Unoka had loved. One of those things was gentleness and another was idleness. (*TFA, 16–17*)

Emphasis here is placed on Okonkwo's divided self, especially on his inner struggle to control and suppress his fears of failure which arise in reaction to his father's disastrous life and shameful death. In some respects, the reader's initial reaction is to identify with Okonkwo, to join with him in severe condemnation of his father, for "Unoka the grown up was a failure. He was poor and his wife and children had barely enough to eat. People laughed at him because he was a loafer, and they swore never to lend him any more money because he never paid back" (*TFA*, 9). In modulating this initial response, the narrator also makes it quite clear that among these same people, "a man was judged according to his worth and not according to the worth of his father," and that while achievement was revered, age was respected. In violently repudiating all that his father represented, Okonkwo repudiates not only his undignified irresponsibility, but also those positive qualities of love and compassion and sensitivity (*TFA*, 8, 10). Many of the qualities which to Okonkwo were marks of femininity and weakness are the same qualities which were respected by the society Okonkwo wished to champion. In a larger sense, Okonkwo's rigid repudiation of his father's "unmanliness" violates a necessary aspect of the society's code of values. We come to see that in suppressing his fears and those attributes which he considers a sign of weakness, Okonkwo denies as well those human responses of love and understanding which Umuofia recognizes as requisite for greatness.

This obsession with proving and preserving his manliness dominates Okonkwo's entire life, both public and private: "He ruled his household with a heavy hand. His wives, especially the youngest, lived in perpetual fear of his fiery temper, and so did his little children" (*TFA*, 16). Even in the informal, relaxed story-telling sessions, Okonkwo sees a threat to himself and his "dynasty," for these stories will make women of his sons, make them like their grandfather rather than like their father. So, at those times, "Okonkwo encouraged the boys to sit with him in his *obi*, and he told them stories of the land— masculine stories of violence and bloodshed" (*TFA*, 52).

No episode in the novel dramatizes Okonkwo's desire to assert his manliness more clearly than the killing of Ikemefuna whom Okonkwo loves as his own.

It is the closeness of this father-son relationship, reiterated in the feasting on the locusts, that Ezeudu interrupts to tell Okonkwo that Ikemefuna must die. But Ezeudu provides more than this stark message; as a respected elder of the clan he also advises Okonkwo on his conduct in heeding the decree, "Yes, Umuofia has decided to kill him. The Oracle of the Hills and Caves has pronounced it. They will take him outside Umuofia as is the custom, and kill him there. But I want you to have nothing to do with it. He calls you his father." Though his feeling for the boy comes through in his effort to cloak the grim reality from the youth's eyes—"later in the day he called Ikemefuna and told him that he was to be taken home the next day" (*TFA*, 56)—Okonkwo nevertheless disregards Ezeudu's advice and accompanies the men in their brutal task—"Okonkwo got ready quickly and the party set out with Ikemefuna carrying the pot of wine" (*TFA*, 56–57). This same mixture of feelings controls Okonkwo's actions on that mission. He walks behind the others and gradually draws to the rear as the moment of execution arrives; indeed, he looks away when one of the men raises his machete to strike the boy. But he is forced by his own dogged insistence on masculinity to deal the fatal blow. The child runs to Okonkwo for protection but finds instead the cold, hard steel of Okonkwo's machete: "As the man who had cleared his throat drew up and raised his machete, Okonkwo looked away. He heard the blow. The pot fell and broke in the sand. He heard Ikemefuna cry, 'My father, they have killed me!' as he ran towards him. Dazed with fear, Okonkwo drew his machete and cut him down" (*TFA*, 59). He does so, as the narrator affirms, because "he was afraid of being thought weak." So extreme is his desire that he might not appear weak, that he might not be like his father, that Okonkwo blinds himself to the wisdom of the advice of the elder Ezeudu, the wisdom Obierika reasserts, "'If I were you I would have stayed at home . . . if the Oracle said that my son should be killed I would neither dispute it nor be the one to do it'" (*TFA*, 64–65). So determined is his effort to be known for achievement, which his society reveres, that Okonkwo gives no heed to the wisdom of age, which his society respects. The way which both Ezeudu and Obierika espouse is the way of compromise, of blending the masculine and feminine, but this is a compromise of which Okonkwo is incapable.

For the most part, Okonkwo resorts to violence in order to maintain control of a situation and assert his manliness. Even in his relationship to his *chi*, or personal god, Okonkwo exerts force to mold his *chi* to his will. But in wrestling with his *chi*, in coercing it into submission to his will, Okonkwo violates the conventional, harmonious relationship one has with his personal god: "The Ibo people have a proverb that when a man says yes, his *chi* says yes also. Okonkwo said yes very strongly, so his *chi* agreed. And not only his *chi*, his clan, too" (*TFA*, 29). On all levels, then, Okonkwo must dominate and control events; by sheer force and, if necessary, brutality, Okonkwo bends to his will his *chi*, his family, and his clan. If "things fall apart," it is because "the center cannot hold"—because Okonkwo cannot maintain the precarious tension which forcefully holds in place *chi*, family, and clan.

Yet Okonkwo is not wholly a brute force. Even at the very moment of his violence against Ikemefuna we glimpse the humanity locked inside: "As the man who had cleared his throat drew up and raised his machete, Okonkwo looked away." Okonkwo looks away not because he is a coward, nor because, like his father, he could not stand the sight of blood; after all, "in Umuofia's latest war he was the first to bring home a human head" (*TFA, 14*), his fifth. Okonkwo looks away because this brutal act is too much even for his eyes and his "buried humanity" struggles to express itself.

The narrator includes these subtle details which emphasize the submerged human responses of Okonkwo to explore Okonkwo's tragic dilemma and modulate our responses to him. Reemphasizing these positive human aspects which Okonkwo possesses but which he struggles to stifle lest he appear weak, the narrator sympathetically relates Okonkwo's reaction to his own violence, without approving the violent act itself:

> Okonkwo did not taste any food for two days after the death of Ikemefuna. He drank palm-wine from morning till night, and his eyes were red and fierce like the eyes of a rat when it is caught by the tail and dashed against the floor.
>
> He did not sleep at night. He tried not to think about Ikemefuna, but the more he tried the more he thought about him. Once he got up from his bed and walked about his compound. But he was so weak that his legs could scarcely carry him. He felt like a drunken giant walking with the limbs of a mosquito. Now and then a cold shiver descended on his head and spread down his body.

In private, unguarded moments like this, Okonkwo cannot but allow his "buried humanity" to express itself. But he does not allow his reaction to Ikemefuna's death to lead to self-pity and, in so doing, does not allow our sympathy for him to degenerate into pity. In his rigid view, any brooding, introspection, or questioning is a sign of weakness: "Okonkwo was not a man of thought but of action" (*TFA, 66*). For this reason, on the morning of the third day of brooding over Ikemefuna, Okonkwo calls for food and answers his brooding with action. His attitude these three days brings him to question himself, but these questions do not investigate motive nor justify his deed; instead, they chastise him for his weakness in responding so to the death of his "son." "He sprang to his feet, hung his goatskin bag on his shoulder and went to visit his friend, Obierika" (*TFA, 63*). It is now daytime and no one must see Okonkwo submit to the human feeling of grief.

Publicly, especially among the members of his own clan, Okonkwo struggles to maintain the image of an unusually calm and stalwart individual, a man worthy to be a lord of the clan. It is only in private— and often in the dark—that Okonkwo spontaneously reveals the love and warmth he feels for his family. In the dark, he rushes to protect his daughter from harm by Chielo; without thought, he rushes to save her from *iba*. Ironically, it is with the same quickness that

Okonkwo prepared for the killing of Ikemefuna that he attends to the dying Ezinma (*TFA*, 72–73).

For Okonkwo, the conflict between private self and public man is the conflict between the feminine and masculine principles. His inability to comprehend the fact that those feminine attributes he vigorously suppresses in himself are necessary for greatness is revealed in his naive comments on the deaths of Ogbuefi Ndulue and his eldest wife, Ozoemena (*TFA*, 65–66).

The sudden, willed death of Ozoemena is strange, as Ofoedu, Obierika, and Okonkwo agree. Yet, as is characteristic of Okonkwo, he can perceive and respond only to the obvious and well-defined. What Okonkwo cannot understand in this episode, despite Obierika's explanation, is the full significance of Ozoemena's death, especially as it is a willed response to her husband's death. The union in life and in death of Ndulue and Ozoemena is a symbolic dramatization of the union of the masculine and feminine attributes essential in a great man. Ndulue was a great warrior and a great man, the respected elder of his village, because he was able to find that balance of strength and sensitivity, of masculine and feminine principles. And it is this union men as Ndulue and Ezeudu are able to achieve and which Umuofia respects and seeks in its leaders. For Okonkwo, one is either a man or a woman; there can be no compromise, no composite. He is baffled by Ndulue's relationship to Ozoemena, for to him a strong man would in no way depend on a woman. This one-sided concept of what it takes to be a man determines Okonkwo's actions and attitudes, and can be seen clearly in his thoughts about his children. To him, Ezinma should have been a boy and Nwoye has "too much of his mother in him" (*TFA*, 64).

Okonkwo has held this monochromatic view of what people should be, with men and women performing sexually-defined tasks and exhibiting equally well-defined characteristics, since his youth. Traumatized by his father's failure as owing to his gentleness and idleness, Okonkwo determines to be all that his father was not—firm and active. But in living up to this design, Okonkwo becomes inflexible and his action allows no room for reflection. Throughout his life he clings to this pattern steadfastly and without question. Such a rigid commitment to a code of behavior and design for action thwarts Okonkwo's personal development. He does not grow and change with age and experience; as a man he is dedicated to the same stereotypes he formed in his youth. Even after his code fails him and necessitates his exile, Okonkwo cannot see the limitations of that code in its denial of the "feminine" principles. While in exile in his mother's land, Mbanta, Okonkwo is lectured on the importance of these feminine principles by the elder Uchendu, but still Okonkwo cannot see:

"Can you tell me, Okonkwo, why it is that one of the commonest names we give our children is Nneka, or 'Mother is Supreme'? We all know that a man is the head of the family and his wives do his bidding. A child belongs to its father and his family and not to its mother and her family. A man belongs to his fatherland and not to his motherland. And yet we say Nneka— 'Mother is Supreme.' Why is that?"

There was silence. "I want Okonkwo to answer me," said Uchendu.

"I do not know the answer," Okonkwo replied.

Through probing questions, Uchendu deliberately attempts to lead Okonkwo to an understanding of the importance of the feminine qualities which Okonkwo seeks to deny: he reminds Okonkwo that the consequence of this denial which has already resulted in Okonkwo's alienation from his clan, his family, and himself, is doom. But Okonkwo is not the type of man who does things half way, "not even for fear of a goddess." He is too "manly," too single-minded to deal with subtleties which do not fit easily into his well-defined code of action. For this reason, he cannot respond to Uchendu's questions, for they directly threaten his rigid philosophy of life.

Uchendu, like Ndulue and Ezeudu, represents the traditional way of life which allows for flexibility and compromise within its exacting system. And in rejecting compromise and flexibility, Okonkwo rejects the values of the society he determines to champion. In contrasting these two antithetical modes of perception and patterns of action, the narrator illustrates the extent to which Okonkwo has alienated himself from his society. The contrasting modes of action determine the different reactions of Uchendu and Okonkwo to Obierika's tales of the killing of the white man on the iron horse, in Abame, which in turn led to the death of a large number of villagers. Hearing this tale of disaster and death, Uchendu ground his teeth together audibly and then burst out, "Never kill a man who says nothing. Those men of Abame were fools. What did they know about the man?" (*TFA, 129*). As is characteristic of a wise and prudent man, Uchendu blames the people of Abame for not being cautious and for fighting a "war of blame" which the society condemns. But Okonkwo sees the whole situation as supporting his method of turning to violence for a solution to all problems. Instead of questioning and seeking a compromise between conflicting views, Okonkwo demands a violent action, "'They were fools,' said Okonkwo after a pause. 'They had been warned that danger was ahead. They should have armed themselves with their guns and their machetes even when they went to market'" (*TFA, 130*).

Throughout his life then, Okonkwo is bound to violence. He rigidly commits himself to a code of values which negates human response and severs him from his traditional roots. Even at crucial moments when all indications point to the limitation and inadequacy of his rigid system, Okonkwo still holds firmly to these values, even to his death. The failure of his code is clear in his attitude toward Nwoye and in his son's subsequent rejection of him. The feelings of tenderness and affection Okonkwo has so long suppressed erupt as violence. When he is confronted by the limitation of his values in responding to human needs, especially manifest in Nwoye's turning to Christianity for an answer to these needs, Okonkwo's recourse to violence is even more extreme:

> It was late afternoon before Nwoye returned. He went into the *obi* and saluted his father, but he did not answer. Nwoye turned round to walk into the inner compound when his father, suddenly overcome with fury, sprang to his feet and gripped him by the neck.
> "Where have you been?" he stammered.
> Nwoye struggled to free himself from the choking grip.
> "Answer me," roared Okonkwo, "before I kill you!" He seized a heavy stick that lay on the dwarf wall and hit him two or three savage blows.
> "Answer me!" he roared again. Nwoye stood looking at him and did not say a word. The women were screaming outside, afraid to go in.
> "Leave that boy at once!" said a voice in the outer compound. It was Okonkwo's uncle, Uchendu. "Are you mad?"
> Okonkwo did not answer. But he left hold of Nwoye, who walked away and never returned. (*TFA, 141*)

The bondage in which Okonkwo has kept his "feminine" qualities is the bondage in which he has tried to keep Nwoye. Coercing, cajoling, threatening, and even beating his son into conforming to his ways, Okonkwo alienates the "dynasty" his actions sought to insure. For Nwoye will not be kept enslaved to Okonkwo's ways; he seeks release from bondage in the new religion of the white man.

Okonkwo's tragedy is not merely that he fails to understand the needs of his son Nwoye but that he also cannot comprehend certain of the society's values. Unable to change himself, he will not accept change in others, in the world around him, in the people of Umuofia. When he returns from exile, Okonkwo faces an altered society, a society that in its flexibility has allowed a place for the white Christian missionaries. Like the recalcitrant Rev. Smith, Okonkwo views the situation in terms of absolute, irreconcilable antipodes.

When the entire clan gathers to decide how to deal with the inroads established by the missionaries, Okonkwo's response is predictable. He will brook no compromise and demands a violent repulsion of the new religion. But this recourse to violence is not the view of this society any more now than it was in the past. Indeed, Okonkwo's views set him apart from his clan at this moment as earlier in his exile: but it is too late for Okonkwo to change now. If the society will not violently repel this threat, Okonkwo will. Compelled by his own uncompromising attitudes as they confront and clash with the equally adamant positions of Rev. Smith, Okonkwo turns to the only means he knows—violence—to solve the problem:

> In a flash Okonkwo drew his machete. The messenger crouched to avoid the blow. It was useless. Okonkwo's machete descended twice and the man's head lay beside his uniformed body.
>
> The waiting backcloth jumped into tumultuous life and the meeting was stopped. Okonkwo stood looking at the dead man. He knew that Umuofia would not go to war. He knew because they had let the other messengers escape. They had broken into tumult instead of action. He discerned fright in that tumult. He heard voices asking, "Why did he do it?"
>
> He wiped his machete on the sand and went away. (*TFA*, 187–188)

When the society does not respond as he does, Okonkwo comes to the sudden, belated realization that he is all alone, set apart from his clan by the values he holds. This most recent act of violence severs finally the precarious link between Okonkwo and his people. And, as before with the killing of Ikemefuna and the beating of Nwoye, Okonkwo's brutal force creates for him an even greater dilemma than the one he resorted to violence to solve. If at the edge of Umuofia before this last violent act, Okonkwo is now pushed outside his society. He cannot return. He cannot begin again. Having no place in this new Umuofia, driven out by his own inability to bend and change, Okonkwo ends his life as he lived it—by violence.

This act of violence against himself ironically fulfills Obierika's "request" of several years ago:

> "I do not know how to thank you."
> "I can tell you," said Obierika. "Kill one of your sons for me."
> "That will not be enough," said Okonkwo.
> "Then kill yourself," said Obierika.
> "Forgive me," said Okonkwo, smiling. "I shall not talk about thanking you any more." (*TFA*, 131–132)

Okonkwo's suicide is, as Obierika explains (*TFA*, 190–191), an offense against the earth, an abomination. Okonkwo's clansmen cannot touch him, cannot bury him, cannot consider him one of their own. In death, as in life, Okonkwo's commitment to achievement through violence ostracizes him from the very society he sought so desperately to champion and honor.

On the other hand, we do not justify Okonkwo's killing of the messenger in an effort to save the doomed way of life of his beleaguered
clan, a way of life whose subtle codes Okonkwo does not understand.
Nor do we approve his unflagging commitment to his own code which
does not provide for life. Yet we sympathize with him, even in his
death, though perhaps not so emotionally as Obierika who, at this
moment, loses all sense of objectivity. Temporarily blind to Okonkwo's
limitations, Obierika seems to make Okonkwo the innocent victim of
the brutal laws of the white missionaries. Prior to this dramatic confrontation with the white missionaries, the narrator has made it
inevitable that Okonkwo's violent actions will lead him to his doom.
At the same time, this knowledge does not deny him our innermost
sympathies, especially when we evaluate his actions as juxtaposed
against the actions of the "purist," Rev. Smith, who "saw things as
black and white. And black was evil. He saw the world as a battlefield
in which the children of light were locked in mortal combat with the
sons of darkness. He spoke in his sermons about sheep and goats and
about wheat and tares. He believed in slaying the prophet of Baal"
(*TFA, 169*). Rev. Smith's approach was, in all respects, antithetical to
that of his predecessor, Rev. Brown, and Achebe shows Rev. Smith to
be a far more vicious, brutal, and violent man than Okonkwo.

> There was a saying in Umuofia that as a man danced so the
> drums were beaten for him. Mr. Smith danced a furious step and
> so the drums went mad. The over-zealous converts who had
> smarted under Mr. Brown's restraining hand now flourished in
> full favor.

Following Rev. Smith's cue, an over-zealous convert, Enoch, likewise
resorts to extreme actions and goes so far as to unmask an *egwugwu*,
throwing Umuofia into confusion (*TFA, 170*). In retaliation, the
egwugwu swarm into the church and level it: "Mr. Smith stood his
ground. But he could not save his church. When the *egwugwu* went
away the red-earth church which Mr. Brown had built was a pile of
ashes. And for the moment the spirit of the clan was satisfied" (*TFA,
175*). Replacing Rev. Brown's law of peace and love with his own code
of aggression and hatred, Rev. Smith undoes the good Rev. Brown
had accomplished. Rather than convert the heathen ways to Christian purpose, Rev. Smith determines to destroy the traditional practices. He will force the villagers to accept his ways and humiliate or
eliminate those who don't.

Working through the District Commissioner, the new law of the
land, Rev. Smith has the *egwugwu*, including Okonkwo, disgraced
and humiliated, their heads shaved in testimony to their dishonor.
Rev. Smith's malice goes far beyond Okonkwo's rigidity in ruthlessly
dishonoring the customs of the Umuofia people and instigating an

unprovoked attack on their religion. We are invited to condemn Rev. Smith's ruthless methods in converting these supposed heathens to his religion. Because we see Rev. Smith in such a negative light, we almost come to see his religion in the same terms. For these reasons, we sympathize with Okonkwo while we see the pointlessness of his violent action in killing the messenger and taking his own life.

Though Rev. Smith's actions tend to obfuscate the positive aspects of Christianity, we can still recall its essentially valuable tenets as lived and spread by Rev. Brown. This religion, with its emphasis on individual salvation and love responded to a need deeply felt by certain people in Umuofia, such as Obierika and Nwoye, but never openly expressed. Christianity answered these private fears and doubts over the arbitrariness of the gods' decrees, decrees which deny personal or human considerations in their application. Christianity is then the catalyst but not the primary cause of things falling apart. Umuofia was already disintegrating and re-forming, for Christianity would not have spread if it did not fill a pre-existing need. This new religion takes root and flourishes in the very place where the twins are thrown away and Ikemefuna was killed, the Evil Forest outside Umuofia.

From Achebe's juxtaposition of conflicting values and actions emerge the paradoxes and ironies of *Things Fall Apart*. The flexibility of Umuofia allows room for Christianity which in turn contributes to the passing of the traditional ways in fulfilling the needs the inflexibility of Umuofia left unanswered. For a time the traditional and the Christian can exist side by side in peace, before the coming of Rev. Smith and the return from exile of Okonkwo. Each man believes himself to be the champion of his society's religion and customs but each, in his extremism, distorts that religion and those customs so that ultimately—and paradoxically—he negates the very values he seeks to defend. This technique of juxtaposition works well in articulating the complexities and contradictions of Umuofia, of Okonkwo, and of the dilemma which arises when they confront Christianity.

DAVID CARROLL

Things Fall Apart[†]

The Village

The most impressive achievement of *Things Fall Apart* (1958), Achebe's first novel, is the vivid picture it provides of Igbo society at

† From *Chinua Achebe: Novelist, Poet, Critic* (Basingstoke: Macmillan, 1990), 32–61. By permission of Palgrave Macmillan.

the end of the nineteenth century. To the reader nurtured on the attenuated diet of individual self-consciousness and introspection, the impact of the life of this West African people is considerable. Here is a clan in the full vigour of its traditional way of life, unperplexed by the present and without nostalgia for the past. Through its rituals the life of the community and the life of the individual are merged into significance and order. This is most apparent in the village meetings which, interspersed through the action, give the novel so much of its special character.

The arrival of the ancestral spirit or *egwugwu* in the following scene is a typical example of this communal drama in which the fears and hopes of the villagers are both expressed and contained by their rituals.

> And then the *egwugwu* appeared. The women and children set up a great shout and took to their heels. It was instinctive. A woman fled as soon as an *egwugwu* came in sight. And when, as on that day, nine of the greatest masked spirits in the clan came out together it was a terrifying spectacle. Even Mgbago took to her heels and had to be restrained by her brothers.
>
> Each of the nine *egwugwu* represented a village of the clan. Their leader was called Evil Forest. Smoke poured out of his head.
>
> The nine villages of Umuofia had grown out of the nine sons of the first father of the clan. Evil Forest represented the village of Umueru, or the children of Eru, who was the eldest of the nine sons.
>
> 'Umuofia kwenu!' shouted the leading *egwugwu*, pushing the air with his raffia arms. The elders of the clan replied, 'Yaa!'
>
> 'Umuofia kwenu!'
>
> 'Yaa!'
>
> 'Umuofia kwenu!'
>
> 'Yaa!'
>
> Evil Forest then thrust the pointed end of his rattling staff into the earth. And it began to shake and rattle, like something agitating with a metallic life. He took the first of the empty stools and the eight other *egwugwu* began to sit in order of seniority after him.

The gestures, the ritual, the formal greetings are in no sense merely part of the African local colour. We approach these meetings of the clan from the inside, from the point of view of the major characters. Then in the debates which follow we witness their private fears and hopes becoming formalised in the communal decisions.

The success of these scenes is due in large part to Achebe's sensitive control of the narrative voice. The novel is narrated in the third person, but there is no suggestion of an ominiscient observer scrutinising and analysing the customs and habits of this Igbo community. The voice is that of a wise and sympathetic elder of the tribe who has witnessed time and time again the cycle of the seasons and the accompanying rituals in the villages. This measured tone of voice implants in the reader's mind the sense of order, perspective and harmony whose later destruction is most poignant.

The coming of the locusts early in the novel exemplifies this vital but unobtrusive function of the narrative voice. First, the narrator presents the arrival of the locusts in traditional terms, offering the reader the tribal myth without comment:

> In this way the moons and the seasons passed. And then the locusts came. It had not happened for many a long year. The elders said locusts came once in a generation, reappeared every year for seven years and then disappeared for another lifetime. They went back to their caves in a distant land, where they were guarded by a race of stunted men. And then after another lifetime these men opened the caves again and the locusts came to Umuofia.
>
> They came in the cold harmattan season after the harvests had been gathered, and ate up all the wild grass in the fields.

The narrator then moves from this larger rhythm of the generations to the rhythm of the seasons, to Okonkwo and his sons repairing the walls of their compound. Although this is a particular activity described in detail, the larger perspective gives it a strong sense of typicality. The feeling of calm and ritual recurrence is strengthened by the silence in which the men work: 'the harmattan was in the air and seemed to distil a hazy feeling of sleep on the world. Okonkwo and the boys worked in complete silence, which was only broken when a new palm frond was lifted onto the wall or when a busy hen moved dry leaves in her ceaseless search for food.'

The cycles, the human and the seasonal, have been established. Now they interact in the particular scene as the locusts arrive:

> And then quite suddenly a shadow fell on the world, and the sun seemed hidden behind a thick cloud. Okonkwo looked up from his work and wondered if it was going to rain at such an unlikely time of the year. But almost immediately a shout of joy broke out in all directions, and Umuofia, which had dozed in the noon-day haze, broke into life and activity.
>
> 'Locusts are descending,' was joyfully chanted everywhere, and men, women and children left their work or their play and ran into the open to see the unfamiliar sight. The locusts had not come for many, many years, and only the old people had seen them before.
>
> At first, a fairly small swarm came. They were the harbingers sent to survey the land. And then appeared on the horizon a slowly-moving mass like a boundless sheet of black cloud drifting

> towards Umuofia. Soon it covered half the sky, and the solid
> mass was now broken by tiny eyes of light like shining star-dust.
> It was a tremendous sight, full of power and beauty.

The routines of the soporific harmattan season are disturbed but
without any sense of disorder; the people move joyfully into the larger
rhythm of the locusts' visit, the knowledge of which has been handed
down in myth and legend. The narrative voice, it will be noticed,
abandons some of its detachments and participates in the common
rejoicing:

> Everyone was now about, talking excitedly and praying that the
> locusts should camp in Umuofia for the night. For although
> locusts had not visited Umuofia for many years, everybody knew
> by instinct that they were very good to eat. And at last the locusts
> did descend. They settled on every tree and on every blade of
> grass; they settled on the roofs and covered the bare ground.
> Mighty tree branches broke away under them, and the whole
> country became the brown-earth colour of the vast hungry
> swarm.
>   Many people went out with baskets trying to catch them, but
> the elders counselled patience till nightfall. And they were right.
> The locusts settled in the bushes for the night and their wings
> became wet with dew. Then all Umuofia turned out in spite of
> the cold harmattan, and everyone filled his bags and pots with
> locusts. The next morning they were roasted in clay pots and
> then spread in the sun until they became dry and brittle. And for
> many days this rare food was eaten with solid palm-oil.

Episodes of this kind are crucial to the success of the novel. In particular, they create a depth of perspective through which we witness
the actions of the protagonists. The next sentence brings us back to
these actions: 'Okonkwo sat in his *obi* crunching happily with Ikemefuna and Nwoye, and drinking palm-wine copiously, when
Ogbuefi Ezeudu came in.' We now sense intuitively how the subtle
rhythms of village life condition the characters' response to the
events of the novel which are about to unfold. The detached yet tolerant tone of the narrator creates this perspective, and acts as a most
effective mediator between the individual and the community,
between the present and the past.
   To the reader accustomed to European fiction, the modulation
from the communal life of the village to the individual consciousness
and back again is unexpectedly powerful. No longer is individual
introspection the fictional norm as in the European novels of the
nineteenth and twentieth centuries. It now appears foreign and
unnatural, so that when the narrator begins to delve into the single
mind we anticipate with foreboding an unpleasant turn of events.

The individual seems vulnerable in his solitude and introspection; it is with relief that we see him reabsorbed into the life of the community. There, his doubts and fears can be exorcised publicly and ritualistically. This is the dimension of the novel to which previous fiction has not accustomed us—the direct translation of problems, moral, political and religious, into public debate and action. In the episode at the beginning of this chapter, the arrival of the *egwugwu* or masked spirits suddenly transforms the workaday tempo of village life into the dramatic ritual of the public meeting. Some kind of crisis is at hand and the village needs to debate it with itself; the ritual formula is enacted, the incantatory greeting recited, and the community abandons its local differences and becomes one. Then, when a decision has been reached, the control of the ritual is relaxed, the collective intensity dissipated, and the novel modulates back to the more relaxed rhythm of the seasons and the permissive variety of village life. The manipulation of this social perspective gives an unexpected depth of implication to the events of this relatively short work. Achebe's advantage is that he is able to use with economy and confidence rituals and conventions each of which symbolises the society he is describing. The novel in Europe, on the other hand, has its origin in the breakdown of such conventions, so that the perspective Achebe creates so effortlessly has to be reconstructed there far more self-consciously.

It would be quite wrong, however, to give the impression that the tribal society of *Things Fall Apart* is formidably monolithic. This is far from Achebe's intention. He is anxious to display the flexibility of the social structure, for only by understanding this can we understand the life and death of the central character, Okonkwo. What at first sight appear to be rigid conventions invariably turn out to be the ritual framework within which debate and questioning can be carried on. The stylised exchange between the *egwugwu*, for example, introduces a law case in which the masked spirits are asked to judge a marriage dispute. Two radically different accounts of the dispute are presented by the husband and by the wife's brother. The husband blames the interference of the wife's family; the brother blames the husband's cruelty. This is the dialectic we see in action again and again within the tribe, and the way it is resolved is significant:

> The nine *egwugwu* then went away to consult together in their house. They were silent for a long time. Then the metal gong sounded and the flute was blown. The *egwugwu* had emerged once again from their underground home. They saluted one another and then reappeared on the *ilo*.
> '*Umuofia kwenu!*' roared Evil Forest, facing the elders and grandees of the clan.

'*Yaa!*' replied the thunderous crowd; then silence descended from the sky and swallowed the noise.

Evil Forest began to speak and all the while he spoke everyone was silent. The eight other *egwugwu* were as still as statues.

'We have heard both sides of the case,' said Evil Forest. 'Our duty is not to blame this man or to praise that, but to settle the dispute.' He turned to Uzowulu's group and allowed a short pause.

'Uzowulu's body, I salute you,' he said.

'Our father, my hand has touched the ground,' replied Uzowulu, touching the earth.

'Uzowulu's body, do you know me?'

'How can I know you, father? You are beyond our knowledge,' Uzowulu replied.

'I am Evil Forest. I kill a man on the day that his life is sweetest to him.'

'That is true,' replied Uzowulu.

'Go to your in-laws with a pot of wine and beg your wife to return to you. It is not bravery when a man fights with a woman.' He turned to Odukwe, and allowed a brief pause.

'Odukwe's body, I greet you,' he said.

'My hand is on the ground,' replied Odukwe.

'Do you know me?'

'No man can know you,' replied Odukwe.

'I am Evil Forest, I am Dry-meat-that-fills-the-mouth, I am Fire-that-burns-without-faggots. If your in-law brings wine to you, let your sister go with him. I salute you.' He pulled his staff from the hard earth and thrust it back.

'*Umuofia kwenu!*' he roared, and the crowd answered.

Despite the ancient formulae, the ritual exchanges, the apparently inflexible ceremony, this is a very fluid system of negotiation. No attempt is made to extract a true version from the conflicting accounts; no principles of traditional law are invoked to apportion blame. Opposing claims are juxtaposed, and then Evil Forest uses his authority to reconcile the disputants as painlessly as possible. The peace and continuance of the tribe are the only criteria and these allow considerable freedom in dealing with internal dissension. The refusal to rely upon absolute principles of law reflects the widespread scepticism of the people of Umuofia toward authority and custom. The incident we have just examined contains an ironic footnote which underlines this:

'I don't know why such a trifle should come before the *egwugwu*,' said one elder to another.

'Don't you know what kind of man Uzowulu is? He will not listen to any other decision,' replied the other.

As they spoke two other groups of people had replaced the first before the *egwugwu*, and a great land case began.

Far from being the embodiment of unchanging laws, the impressive ritual is at the service of the personal idiosyncrasies of the villages. Such scrutiny of law and custom is one of the perennial activities of Umuofia. The villagers probe into the logic of their traditional rites to test their usefulness; they compare them with the customs of neighbouring villages; and the elders recall the evolution of the present traditions from the past. We see this process in action early in the novel when Okonkwo breaks the Week of Peace:

> Ogbuefi Ezedu, who was the oldest man in the village, was telling two other men who came to visit him that the punishment for breaking the Peace of Ani had become very mild in their clan.
>
> 'It has not always been so,' he said. 'My father told me that he had been told that in the past a man who broke the peace was dragged on the ground through the village until he died. But after a while this custom was stopped because it spoilt the peace which it was meant to preserve.'

Contradictions such as this must be prevented by allowing the discussion of opposing claims plenty of freedom in which to operate. And in Umuofia it operates constantly in casual conversation, sceptical asides and formal debate. This activity is a vital part of the social texture of the community, and it is symptomatic of their openness to new ideas, their irony and their self-consciousness.

'What is good in one place,' they remind each other, 'is bad in another.' And they enjoy testing each other's credulity to the utmost. On one occasion, Okonkwo's curious item of kinship lore ('in some tribes a man's children belong to his wife and her family') is too much for his friend who tries to outbid him. 'You might as well say that the woman lies on top of the man when they are making children.' The final exaggeration to which this leads suddenly introduces more disturbing implications:

> 'It is like the story of white men who, they say, are white like this piece of chalk,' said Obierika. He held up a piece of chalk, which every man kept in his *obi* and with which his guests drew lines on the floor before they ate kola nuts. 'And these white men, they say, have no toes.'
>
> 'And have you never seen them?' asked Machi.
>
> 'Have you?' asked Obierika.
>
> 'One of them passes here frequently,' said Machi. 'His name is Amadi.'
>
> Those who knew Amadi laughed. He was a leper, and the polite name for leprosy was 'the white skin'.

The joke brings the conversation safely back home after its survey of alien customs, but before it does so Achebe has suggested with skill the curiosity and open-mindedness of the villagers, and the way in which they prepare themselves for change by exploring and assessing their neighbours' way of life. More ominously, the author has introduced the aliens, white with no toes, who will before the end of the novel exploit this openness by introducing changes which the tribal structure will not be able to withstand. But, for the moment, the society is secure, stabilised by the questioning, modification, and adaptation which are part of the Igbo way of life.

This flexibility is seen not only in the absence of a central authority, the rejection of absolute laws, and the fluidity of village groupings. It is manifest in all areas of Igbo life. At the other end of the spectrum from the organisation of society is the life of the self, and here too the reciprocal bargaining between competing claims is apparent. The Umuofians believe that each person possesses a *chi* or personal god which plays an important role in his destiny—but not to the exclusion of all other factors. As the Oracle of Agbala says on one occasion: 'When a man is at peace with his gods and ancestors, his harvest will be good or bad according to the strength of his arm.' This suggests that when all other claims and duties are in equilibrium, the individual is in a position to act decisively. Therefore, one is in limited control of one's destiny: 'The Ibo have a proverb that when a man says yes his *chi* says yes also. But anyone who oversteps the limits of this freedom is reminded of 'the little bird *nza* who so far forgot himself after a heavy meal that he callenged his *chi*'. In this way, the respective claims of free will and necessity are characteristically juxtaposed without a final resolution, so that the complex interaction of inner self and external reality will not be vulgarised.

This kind of flexibility and pluralism in all areas of organisation and belief clearly encourages a tolerant scepticism toward authority and custom. At the same time, it should be added, such a system precludes the directness, the unanimity and the security which a more static, centralised system would provide. This is the society in which Achebe traces the career of his hero, Obi Okonkwo.

Okonkwo

From the first, Okonkwo is in the grip of his father's failure. Unoka has not achieved any kind of status in the tribe by the usual means of wealth or titles. He is a gentle, improvident man, most happy when playing his flute, relaxing with the villagers, and recalling his happy boyhood. He is ill at ease when the conversation turns to warfare or to any of the other more aggressive features of village life; then he finds an escape in his flute playing.

Such a father need not have been a hindrance to Okonkwo's ambitions. The tolerance and openness of Igbo society enable the individual with drive and ability to succeed: 'Fortunately, among these people a man was judged according to his worth and not according to the worth of his father.' But Okonkwo does not see it in this way. He feels that he must succeed in everything his father failed at and so wipe out his memory. This is the hidden motive behind his impressive achievements, and Achebe describes it in one of his few passages of extended analysis:

> Okonkwo ruled his household with a heavy hand. His wives, especially the youngest, lived in perpetual fear of his fiery temper, and so did his little children. Perhaps down in his heart Okonkwo was not a cruel man. But his whole life was dominated by fear, the fear of failure and of weakness. It was deeper and more intimate than the fear of evil and capricious gods and of magic, the fear of the forest, and of the forces of nature, malevolent, red in tooth and claw. Okonkwo's fear was greater than these. It was not external but lay deep within himself. It was the fear of himself, lest he should be found to resemble his father. Even as a little boy he had resented his father's failure and weakness . . . And so Okonkwo was ruled by one passion—to hate everything that his father Unoka had loved. One of those things was gentleness and another was idleness.

Driven by this private obsession, Okonkwo has only one aim in life—to succeed, and to succeed in terms of warfare, wrestling, wealth and status. At first, his achievements are remarkable. Despite unimaginable difficulties he survives a general farming catastrophe, and this, like other successes, reinforces his inner driving force: ' "Since I survived that year," he always said, "I shall survive anything." He put it down to his inflexible will.' And Umuofia is impressed. Although the villagers do not fall into the error of believing a man is in complete control of his destiny, they are prepared to acknowledge his achievements:

> If ever a man deserved his success, that man was Okonkwo. At an early age he had achieved fame as the greatest wrestler in all the land. That was not luck. At the most one could say that his *chi* or personal god was good. But the Ibo people have a proverb that when a man says yes his *chi* says yes also. Okonkwo said yes very strongly; so his *chi* agreed. And not only his *chi* but his clan too, because it judged a man by the work of his hands.

As Achebe presents this growing success, he insinuates the cause of future conflict: Okonkwo's inflexible will is bringing him success in a society remarkable for its flexibility. At first, the impetus of his fanatical ambition brings quick results; only later does the rigidity of his aims begin to upset the equilibrium of a system developed in conformity with a far less aggressive concept of character. This danger first makes its appearance within the family. The traditional balance here, as Achebe depicts it, is between the masculine and feminine virtues. But Okonkwo, reacting against his father's effeminacy, simplifies this pattern and insists that his sons share his thoroughly masculine aggression and virility. 'So Okonkwo encouraged the boys to sit with him in his *obi*, and he told them stories of the land—masculine stories of violence and bloodshed. Nwoye knew it was right to be masculine and to be violent, but somehow he still preferred the stories that his mother used to tell . . .' Okonkwo has created a false contradiction between strength and gentleness, and the consequences of this oversimplification are evident not only in his own tragedy but also in the life of his son Nwoye.

As Okonkwo's status and wealth increase so does his self-assertion. We sense a growing alienation between him and his easy-going clansmen as he enforces his will more and more emphatically upon his family. The incident which first dramatises this growing estrangement is the breaking of the Week of Peace. Furious with his youngest wife for neglecting her duties, Okonkwo beats her severely: 'In his anger he had forgotten that it was the Week of Peace. His first two wives ran out in great alarm pleading with him that it was the sacred week. But Okonkwo was not the man to stop beating somebody halfway through, not even for fear of a goddess.' His aggressive individualism must be punished and the balance of forces re-established. Ezeani, the priest of the earth goddess, defines his crime and imposes the fine:

> 'You know as well as I do that our forefathers ordained that before we plant any crops in the earth we should observe a week in which a man does not say a harsh word to his neighbour. We live in peace with our fellows to honour our great goddess of the earth without whose blessing our crops will not grow. You have committed a great evil.' He brought down his staff heavily on the floor. 'Your wife was at fault, but even if you came into your *obi* and found her lover on top of her, you would still have committed a great evil to beat her.' His staff came down again. 'The evil you have done can ruin the whole clan. The earth goddess whom you have insulted may refuse to give us her increase, and we shall all perish.' His tone now changed from anger to command. 'You will bring to the shrine of Ani tomorrow one she-goat, one hen, a length of cloth and a hundred cowries.' He rose and left the hut.

Okonkwo's self-assertion has broken the organic links between the individual, the family and the village, and obscured the larger perspective in which duties must be defined. (In this, he is the reverse of his father who neglected his personal responsibilities in order to abandon himself to the village festivals and celebrations.) Although he is repentant, Okonkwo will not admit his error, and so opinion turns against him. He has not only challenged his *chi*, say the villagers; he has shown disrespect to the gods of the clan.

The violation of the Week of Peace prepares us for the more extended incident of the death of Ikemefuna. This has been intruded subtly but with increasing insistence from the beginning of the novel. As the hero's early achievements are described, the narrative circles back repeatedly to the hostage Ikemefuna. The first chapter ends its list of Okonkwo's successes in this way: 'And that was how he came to look after the doomed lad who was sacrificed to the village of Umuofia by their neighbours to avoid war and bloodshed. The ill-fated lad was called Ikemefuna.' Okonkwo is chosen as guardian because of his status, yet the compassionate narrative voice seems to be establishing another rhythm, contrapuntal to Okonkwo's success. When we circle back again a few pages later and witness the hero, the impressive representative of his clan, making his demands to the enemy, we experience again the same ambiguity: 'And so when Okonkwo of Umuofia arrived at Mbaino as the proud and imperious emissary of war, he was treated with great honour and respect, and two days later he returned home with a lad of fifteen and a young virgin. The lad's name was Ikemefuna, whose sad story is still told in Umuofia unto this day.' The feeling of foreboding is created by the double time perspective. The final sentence represents the mature, resigned perspective of tribal history which questions the more limited perspective of Okonkwo's moment of grandeur.

Ikemefuna lives in Okonkwo's family for three years and becomes a popular member of the household, especially with the eldest son Nwoye. 'Even Okonkwo himself became very fond of the boy— inwardly, of course. Okonkwo never showed any emotion openly, unless it be the emotion of anger.' Ikemefuna eventually feels himself one of the family. Then one day they receive a visit from the great warrier, the aged Ezeudu, who announces abruptly to Okonkwo: 'That boy calls you father. Do not bear a hand in his death . . . Yes, Umuofia has decided to kill him. The Oracle of the Hills and Caves has pronounced it. They will take him outside Umuofia as is the custom, and kill him there. But I want you to have nothing to do with it. He calls you his father.' This is the dilemma the counter-movement of the novel has been preparing. Loyalty to the public Oracle of the tribe is in conflict with the private loyalties of the home, and there is no chance of reconciliation. Ezeudu proposes the most humane solution—neither defy the gods by resisting, nor offend one's conscience by assisting in the death. But Okonkwo will not accept this casuistical balancing of claims. Having mastered his anguish, he insists not only on going on the journey of death through the forest but also on participating in the execution: 'He heard Ikemefuna cry,

"My father, they have killed me!" as he ran toward him. Dazed with fear, Okonkwo drew his matchet and cut him down. He was afraid of being thought weak.'

His inner fear renders him incapable of accommodating competing claims. He needs a clearly defined standard of conduct against which to measure his will and achievements; when he cannot find this in Umuofia, he radically oversimplifies the tribal ethic. Obierika expresses the tribe's disapproval of this literal interpretation of the Oracle when he is questioned about his absence by Okonkwo:

> 'Because I did not want to,' Obierika replied sharply. 'I had something better to do.'
>
> 'You sound as if you question the authority and the decision of the Oracle, who said he should die.'
>
> 'I do not. Why should I? But the Oracle did not ask me to carry out its decision.'
>
> 'But someone had to do it. If we were all afraid of blood, it would not be done. And what do you think the Oracle would do then?'
>
> 'You know very well, Okonkwo, that I am not afraid of blood; and if anyone tells you that I am, he is telling a lie. And let me tell you one thing, my friend. If I were you I would have stayed at home. What you have done will not please the Earth. It is the kind of action for which the goddess wipes out whole families.'
>
> 'The Earth cannot punish me for obeying her messenger,' Okonkwo said. 'A child's fingers are not scalded by a piece of hot yam which its mother puts into its palm.'
>
> 'That is true,' Obierika agreed. 'But if the Oracle said that my son should be killed I would neither dispute it nor be the one to do it.'

Obierika seeks a reconciliation, or at least a compromise, between conflicting loyalties. Okonkwo, on the other hand, simply wants to fulfil his duties as scrupulously as possible, and his answer to Obierika's warning is irrefutable: 'The Earth cannot punish me for obeying her messenger.' But Obierika is groping for a way out of this cul de sac, a more positive synthesis of the dialectical claims than the passive compromise he recommends to Okonkwo. The tribal ethic, however, for all its flexibility cannot provide the answer.

The death of Ikemefuna is a turning point in the novel. The guardianship of the boy was a mark of Okonkwo's hard-won status and the highest point of his rise to power. The execution of Ikemefuna is the beginning of Okonkwo's decline, for it initiates the series of catastrophes which end with his death. But this event is not only a milestone in the career of the hero. The sympathetic rendering of Ikemefuna's emotions as he is being marched through the forest to his death has wider implications. At first, the narrative is detached and matter-of-fact:

The sun rose slowly to the centre of the sky, and the dry, sandy footway began to throw up the heat that lay buried in it. Some birds chirruped in the forests around. The men trod dry leaves on the sand. All else was silent. Then from the distance came the faint beating of the *ekwe*. It rose and faded with the wind—a peaceful dance from a distant clan.

The touch of regret in the final phase prepares us for the increasing tension. Then the narrative modulates into the consciousness of Ike-mefuna and the unsuspecting innocence of the victim of tribal laws is vividly portrayed. Only he believes that he is being taken back to his own people.

> Thus the men of Umuofia pursued their way, armed with sheathed matchets, and Ikemefuna, carrying a pot of palm-wine on his head, walked in their midst. Although he had felt uneasy at first, he was not afraid now. Okonkwo walked behind him. He could hardly imagine that Okonkwo was not his real father. He had never been fond of his real father, and at the end of three years he had become very distant indeed. But his mother and his three-year-old-sister . . . She would want to hear everything that had happened to him in all these years. Could he remember them all? He would tell her about Nwoye and his mother, and about the locusts . . . Then quite suddenly a thought came upon him. His mother might be dead. He tried in vain to force the thought out of his mind.

Worrying about his mother, he is finally cut down.

This incident is not only a comment on Okonkwo's heartlessness. It criticises implicitly the laws he is too literally implementing, for, as we have seen, even the compassionate Obierika is unable to reconcile the claims of the gods and those of personal affection into any satisfactory compromise. Ikemefuna has got to die. As we watch him being taken unsuspectingly on this apparently innocent journey, the whole tribe and its values is being judged and found wanting. For the first time in the novel we occupy the point of view of an outsider, a victim, and from this position the community appears cruel. Yet, the flexibility of the clan is such that we feel the antinomies, in this case, the commands of the Oracle and the inner world of the suffering hostage, might eventually be resolved. Unfortunately, there isn't time. External forces are already approaching to threaten the precarious balance even now disturbed by Okonkwo's rectitude. Then the unresolved contradictions in Umuofia will be used in its downfall. There is already a hint of this in Nwoye's reaction to the death of his friend. Obscurely he sees that cruelty is a recurrent feature of life in Umuofia:

> As soon as his father walked in, that night, Nwoye knew that Ike-mefuna had been killed, and something seemed to give way

inside him, like the snapping of a tightened bow. He did not cry.
He just hung limp. He had had the same kind of feeling not long
ago during the last harvest season . . . They were returning home
with baskets of yams from a distant farm across the stream when
they had heard the voice of an infant crying in the thick forest.
A sudden hush had fallen on the women, who had been talking,
and they had quickened their steps. Nwoye had heard that twins
were put in earthenware pots and thrown away in the forest, but
he had never yet come across them. A vague chill had descended
on him and his head had seemed to swell, like a solitary walker
at night who passes an evil spirit on the way. Then something
had given way inside him. It descended on him again, this feeling, when his father walked in, that night after killing Ikemefuna.

The force of this depends upon the first-person point of view from
which it is described. Coming so soon after the rendering of Ikemefuna's frightened inner world, this second relapse from the communal to the private indicates a feature of life which the tribal narrative
voice is not equipped to delineate.

The death of Ikemefuna has no immediate repercussions within
Umuofia. Okonkwo recovers his equanimity, and the customs of the
tribe regain their unquestioned sway. The narrative, moving continuously between the daily events of Okonkwo's household and the
more public affairs of the clan, integrates effortlessly the daily routine and the ceremonial by which it is articulated. We see the characters in the two perspectives of the family and the clan experiencing
no discrepancy between the roles they are called upon to play. But the
harmony is not complete. Achebe brings out increasingly the tensions
(which the death of Ikemefuna has crystallised) between the family
and the larger community. A typical example of this persistent feature
of life occurs when the priestess of Agbala comes to the village to take
Ezinma, the daugher of Okonkwo and Ekwefi, to pay homage to her
god. The parents' protestations are useless, and the weeping girl is
carried off to the Oracle of the Hills and Caves. Significantly, we witness the event from within Okonkwo's household. We see the domestic calm destroyed by the arrival of the priestess, and we share the
mother's distracted fear: 'Ekwefi stood rooted to the spot. One mind
said to her: "Woman, go home before Agbala does you harm!" But she
could not. She stood until Chielo had increased the distance between
them and she began to follow again.' And on the next day, after
Ezinma has been returned home safely, we learn with surprise that
Okonkwo has also been troubled by these conflicting loyalties. These
tensions, endemic to Umuofia, prepare us for the climax to the first
part of the novel where Okonkwo becomes a victim of the harsh laws
he had previously defended and administered.

The episode is introduced by the cannon and drum announcing the death of Ezeudu. 'A cold shiver ran down Okonkwo's back as he remembered the last time the old man had visited him. "That boy calls you father," he had said. "Bear no hand in his death".' Ezeudu is now about to join his ancestors and Okonkwo fears the displeasure of an *egwugwu* much more than that of the living Ezeudu. His forebodings are quickly justified. While the traditional farewell is being celebrated, Okonkwo's gun explodes accidentally and kills the dead man's son. By killing a clansman, Okonkwo has committed a crime against the earth goddess, and so he must flee to the home of his mother. His friends console him and then must act as the agents of the enraged goddess:

> As soon as the day broke, a large crowd of men from Ezeudu's quarter stormed Okonkwo's compound, dressed in garbs of war. They set fire to his houses, demolished his red walls, killed his animals and destroyed his barn. It was the justice of the earth goddess, and they were merely her messengers. They had no hatred in their hearts against Okonkwo. His greatest friend, Obierika, was among them. They were merely cleansing the land which Okonkwo had polluted with the blood of a clansman.

Okonkwo goes into exile, and the events of part one of the novel end. For a final comment, Obierika recapitulates the painful tensions within the tribe in a way which proves in the long run to be more ominous than the temporary eclipse of the hero. Mourning his friend's calamity, he questions the dictates of the inscrutable tribal gods: 'Why should a man suffer so grievously for an offence he had committed inadvertently?' The traditional answer no longer satisfies him. Obierika is rebelling against a system in which two sets of values, the tribal and the personal, are juxtaposed but remain quite distinct. An individual is punished and the tribe is safe again, but there is no organic connection between the public event and the private:

> He remembered his wife's twin children, whom he had thrown away. What crime had they committed? The Earth had decreed that they were an offence on the land and must be destroyed. And if the clan did not exact punishment for an offence against the great goddess, her wrath was loosed on all the land and not just on the offender. As the elders said, if one finger brought oil it soiled the others.

The dilemma is additionally painful because one person is frequently required to act both the roles demanded by these double responsibilities. Obierika first consoles his friend and then destroys his compound; the father of twins must become the goddess's agent and destroy them. At the beginning of the novel, this duality of roles was presented simply as a characteristic of tribal life which the villagers accept unquestioningly. It is a habit of mind which allows different orders of experience, particularly the human and divine, to be juxtaposed conveniently. No good is done by confusing the two: 'Okonkwo's wives, and perhaps other women as well, might have noticed that the second *egwugwu* had the springy walk of Okonkwo. And they might also have noticed that Okonkwo was not among the titled men and elders who sat behind the row of *egwugwu*. But if they thought these things they kept them within themselves. The *egwugwu* with the springy walk was one of the dead fathers of the clan.' This involuntary mental lacuna controls the disposition of the two adjacent worlds upon which the functioning of tribal life depends.

One can perhaps see in this another example of the balancing of claims and values against each other which we noticed earlier. The main purpose of such balancing was not to create a synthesis, a unitary system which would finally reconcile all into a consistent whole, but to accommodate in terms of an equilibrium. The author keeps leading us back to this mode of thought until we come to accept it as the most pervasive feature of life in Umuofia. And certainly in terms of debate and social flexibility its benefits are indisputable. But the cost to the individuals who make the mental accommodation has not been examined. The narrator seems unwilling to scrutinise the nature of this inner adjustment. ('But if they thought these things they kept them within themselves.') Gradually what seems an admirably flexible and open attitude to experience changes its nature under Achebe's scrutiny. He draws out the inner conflict and suffering which such accommodation exacts from the villagers. The equilibrium and adjustments of Umuofia conceal at their centre a radical contradiction between human and divine values, and the contradiction is institutionalised in the role playing of the tribal officials. The antinomies of any possible dialectic are, in other words, frozen into a static equilibrium which admits of no synthesis. The first part of the novel ends with Obierika's baffled comment on this painful deadlock, of which the hero himself is now a victim.

The Missionaries

The muted but finely managed second part of the novel describes Okonkwo's seven-year exile in Mbanta with his mother's kinsmen. He remains the focus of attention and yet, since he is a stranger in this new clan, he is no longer the centre of the stage. Impotently he watches and criticises the turn of events both here and at home in Umuofia. The two threads of narrative are kept parallel by the annual visits of Obierika.

The significance of this central section of the novel is suggested by the two formal speeches which open and close it. First, Uchendu, the brother of Okonkwo's mother, reprimands Okonkwo for being so resigned and gloomy and his explusion. He questions him on the role of the mother in the clan. Why is a woman taken home to be buried with her kinsmen? Why is Okonkwo exiled to his mother's village after being expelled from his own? These questions, which Okonkwo is unable to answer, stress the importance of the mother in the family, the village and the clan—and even beyond to the web of relations which links clan to clan. Uchendu is developing an attack upon Okonkwo's dangerous oversimplification of the tribal ethic. He sees that his nephew's despair is the result of the obsessive and narrow-minded pursuit of status; when this has been thwarted by factors outside his control, he has nothing else to live for. Uchendu seeks to redress the balance by reminding him of the maternal virtues within the family which are as essential as the aggressive, male values by which Okonkwo lives:

> It's true that a child belongs to its father. But when a father beats his child, it seeks sympathy in its mother's hut. A man belongs to his fatherland when things are good and life is sweet. But when there is sorrow and bitterness he finds refuge in his motherland. Your mother is there to protect you. She is buried there. And that is why we say that mother is supreme. Is it right that you, Okonkwo, should bring to your mother a heavy face and refuse to be comforted? Be careful or you may displease the dead. Your duty is to comfort your wives and children and take them back to your fatherland after seven years. But if you allow sorrow to weigh you down and kill you, they will all die in exile . . . If you think you are the greatest sufferer in the world ask my daughter, Akueni, how many twins she had borne and thrown away. Have you not heard the song they sing when a woman dies?
>
> > 'For whom is it well, for whom is it well?
> > There is no one for whom it is well.'
>
> I have no more to say to you.

Uchendu's reprimand shows the limitations of the pursuit of success and status. Suffering and sorrow are an integral part of life, however meticulously one obeys the dictates of the gods. Therefore, it is the height of folly to ignore the female, maternal side of the tribal ethic, for this provides the comfort and sympathy which alleviate the suffering caused by the contradictions and injustices of life. In this way a characteristic equilibrium can be maintained.

The second speech, which brings to an end this section of the novel, is very different in tone. One of the elders of Mbanta thanks

Okonkwo formally for the feast he has given to celebrate the end of his exile: 'It is good in these days when the younger generation consider themselves wiser than their sires to see a man doing things in a grand, old way.' It seems that Okonkwo has come to terms with his exile and that once again, here among his mother's kinsmen, he is fulfilling all his duties punctiliously. But there is another more disturbing reason for the change of attitude toward Okonkwo in Mbanta:

> 'You may ask why I am saying all this. I say it because I fear for the younger generation, for you people.' He waved his arm where most of the young men sat. 'As for me, I have only a short while to live, and so have Uchendu and Unachukwu and Emefo. But I fear for you young people because you do not understand how strong is the bond of kinship. You do not know what it is to speak with one voice. And what is the result? An abominable religion has settled among you. A man can now leave his father and his brothers. He can curse the gods of his fathers and ancestors, like a hunter's dog that suddenly goes mad and turns on his master. I fear for you; I fear for the clan.' He turned again to Okonkwo and said, 'Thank you for calling us together.'

This is the real reason for the change of tone. Between these two speeches, a new religion has come to Mbanta and begun to destroy the traditional culture. Now the elders are not concerned merely with the balancing of values within the tribe, for their whole way of life is threatened. In this crisis, Okonkwo's inflexible adherence to the letter of the law makes him an inevitable defender of the beleagured clan. He replies to neither of the speeches; as the reprimand turns to eulogy one imagines that his silence is that of self-justification.

The arrival of Christianity in this part of Africa is managed by Achebe with subtlety and detachment. There is no dramatic confrontation, no sudden conversion. Obierika brings news of the murder of a missionary in Abame and the subsequent punishment of the clan. The startling piece of information is discussed and analysed. For some, Abame acted wrongly in killing the missionary; in Okonkwo's opinion they were foolish not to prepare themselves for reprisals; others can hardly believe the events are true. Perhaps Uchendu represents best the point of view we have come to associate with traditional Igbo society: 'There is no story that is not true . . . The world has no end, and what is good among one people is an abomination with others. We have albinos among us. Do you not think that they came to our clan by mistake, that they have strayed from their way to a land where everybody is like them?' This fatal ability to acknowledge alien forms of life prevents any clear-cut conflict. It is this which makes the tribe so vulnerable. By the time of Obierika's next visit to Mbanta, the missionaries have penetrated to

Umuofia and are using it as a centre of their religion. But again there is no sense of urgency, for the early converts are merely the despised and worthless members of the village. 'Chielo, the priestess of Agbala, called the converts the excrement of the clan, and the new faith was a mad dog that had come to eat it up.' The only disturbing piece of news is that Nwoye has joined the converts.

The first white missionary to come to Mbanta is greeted with ironical good humour by the villagers. They are amused by the strange Igbo dialect spoken by his interpreter and, as they weave jokes around his oddities of speech, they seem unaware of the uncompromising doctrine that is being preached: 'He told them that the true God lived on high and that all men when they died went before Him for judgement. Evil men and all the heathen who in their blindness bowed to wood and stone were thrown into a fire that burned like palm-oil.' They laugh derisively at the missionary's dismissal of their most powerful gods; this is not the subtle dialectic they are accustomed to. But the biggest joke of all is provided by the doctrine of the Trinity, and even Okonkwo joins in the debate at this point: 'You told us with your own mouth that there was only one god. Now you talk about his son. He must have a wife, then.' As he goes off to tap his afternoon's palm-wine he is convinced the missionary is mad. The Umuofians, we feel, are justifiably sceptical toward the new religion which is being imported in this gauche and complacent manner into the midst of their self-conscious society.

But not everything is greeted with laughter and incredulity. There is one point in this meeting of religions when the missionaries cease their blunt attacks and, relying upon the emotional appeal of their message, sing a hymn:

> Then the missionaries burst into song. It was one of those gay and rollicking tunes of evangelism which had the power of plucking at silent and dusty chords in the heart of an Ibo man. The interpreter explained each verse to the audience, some of whom now stood enthralled. It was a story of brothers who lived in darkness and in fear, ignorant of the love of God. It told of one sheep out on the hills, away from the gates of God and from the tender shepherd's care.

The Christian god cannot rival the great Chukwu in power, but in his loving, personal care for the individual he appeals to all the unresolved fears of Umuofia. He can break the deadlock between divine law and personal affection which has caused so much anguish in the clan. This is the god who has captivated Nwoye still in rebellion against his father's harsh and rigid literalism:

> It was not the mad logic of the Trinity that captivated him. He did not understand it. It was the poetry of the new religion,

> something felt in the marrow. The hymn about brothers who sat
> in darkness and in fear seemed to answer a vague and persistent
> question that haunted his young soul—the question of the twins
> crying in the bush and the question of Ikemefuna who was
> killed. He felt a relief within as the hymn poured into his
> parched soul. The words of the hymn were like the drops of
> frozen rain melting on the dry palate of the panting earth,
> Nwoye's callow mind was greatly puzzled.

This is how Christianity makes its inroads in the novel. Not by a
frontal attack, backed by the colonising forces, but by responding
clearly to a need so deeply felt that it has not been clearly formulated.
Then, upon this appeal it extends its power by a logical yet almost
indiscernible process of erosion.

First, as a macabre joke, the eager missionaries are allowed to build
a church in the 'evil forest', the 'dumping-ground for the potent
fetishes of great medicine-men when they died.' When they have not
been killed in the expected four days by the forces of darkness, the
Christians have won their first victory. Then the outcasts or *osu*, the
tabooed slaves dedicated to the various deities, shave off their long,
tangled hair, and go over to the new religion. When the missionaries
accept them into full membership of the church, Igbo egalitarianism
has been challenged and surpassed. Finally, the new converts, becoming more aggressive as their numbers increase, are rumoured to have
killed Mbanta's sacred python. In the debate which follows, the
dilemma of the tribe becomes apparent. Should Umuofia punish the
converts on behalf of its gods? 'If we put ourselves between the god
and his victim we may receive blows intended for the offender.' And
the white man, they are aware, has brought not only a religion but a
government to protect the converts. But most perplexing of all is the
deep-seated conviction that the converts are still members of the
tribe: 'No one could kill them without having to flee from the clan,
for in spite of their worthlessness they still belonged to the clan'.
Okonkwo wants to solve Mbanta's dilemma in his usual way—whip
the Christians out of the village. But the elders, troubled by the implications of such a course of action, finally compromise and decide to
ostracise the converts. Umuofia is baffled because it is being challenged by a religion quite different from its own. The villagers' religion
is inseparable from the tribe which stretches back through countless
generations of ancestors; for them, rival religions are not possible and
conversion is meaningless. Now they are confronted by a religion with
the opposite premise: they are all, like the white man, sons of God
and equal in his sight. Priority has shifted from the tribe and its continuance to the salvation of the individual and, as Okonkwo muses
bitterly over his son's defection, we catch a glimpse of the terrible
consequences of this to Umuofia:

Now that he had time to think of it, his son's crime stood out in its stark enormity. To abandon the gods of one's father and go about with a lot of effeminate men clucking like old hens was the very depth of abomination. Suppose when he died all his male children decided to follow Nwoye's steps and abandon their ancestors? Okonkwo felt a cold shudder run through him at the terrible prospect, like the prospect of annihilation. He saw himself and his fathers crowding round their ancestral shrine waiting in vain for worship and sacrifice and finding nothing but ashes of bygone days, and his children the while praying to the white man's god.

Such neglect is a tribal vision of hell, and it underlines the vulnerability of Umuofia. As soon as one link in the elaborate network of tribal affiliations or in the carefully preserved chain of ancestors is broken, then confusion and annihilation quickly follow. As Obierika says, with clear hindsight: 'The white man is very clever. He came quietly and peaceably with his religion. We were amused at his foolishness and allowed him to stay. Now he has won our brothers, and our clan can no longer act like one. He has but knife on things that held us together and we have fallen apart.'

The rapid changes which have taken place in Umuofia destroy the triumph of Okonkwo's return from exile in part three of the novel. Not only has the new religion grown in strength, the Europeans have also brought their own form of government, and increased trade in the area. 'The white man had indeed brought a lunatic religion, but he had also built a trading store and for the first time palm-oil and kernel became things of great price, and much money flowed into Umuofia.' Matters of principle can, if necessary, be sacrificed to this obvious good, especially if the missionaries are prepared to proselytise inoffensively. Mr Brown, the white missionary, accepts this truce and 'came to be respected even by the clan, because he trod softly on its faith'. His acute discussions with the elder Akunna clearly define the crucial differences between these rival religions and make Brown realise that he cannot win by a frontal attack. He goes to work by building a school and hospital in Umuofia and by convincing them that: 'If Umuofia failed to send her children to the school, strangers would come from other places to rule them.'

Unfortunately, Brown falls ill and his successor rejects the policy of mutual accommodation. He is a literalist, as adamant an authoritarian in his beliefs as Okonkwo. The Reverend James Smith translates the complex situation he inherits from his predecessor into the extreme and inapplicable imagery of the Bible: 'He saw things as black and white. And black was evil. He saw the world as a battlefield in which the children of light were locked in mortal conflict with the sons of darkness. He spoke in his sermons about sheep and goats and

about wheat and tares. He believed in slaying the prophets of Baal.'
Now, there is no negotiation between rival myths. Smith is an Old
Testament prophet, dealing in clear-cut antitheses, who divides the
tribe with its elaborate affiliations into the simple categories of his
creed. Unlike Brown, he stresses the exclusiveness of Christianity to
the baffled villagers: 'Our Lord Himself stressed the importance of
fewness. Narrow is the way and few the number.' This aggressive
challenge to the community draws the lines of battle and only the
occasion for conflict is needed. This is provided by Enoch, the son of
the snake-priest and a recent convert, who unmasks in public one of
the *egwugwu* and so strikes at the heart of the clan. The mask of the
egwugwu epitomises, as we have seen, the duality of roles by which
the inscrutable world of the gods and the human world are uneasily
accommodated. Enoch's action challenges this strategy. 'Enoch had
killed an ancestral spirit, and Umuofia was thrown into confusion.'

Achebe achieves a fine equilibrium of approval and regret at this
turning point in the novel. We have witnessed the cruelty and suffering which is part of the life of Umuofia, and yet we share their
sense of outrage at this unprovoked attack upon their traditional values. This is the last of the communal scenes which have been such
an impressive feature of the novel. With the encroachments of Christianity they have become less frequent and unanimous. The tribal
narrative voice which spoke with sympathy and authority in the earlier days of Umuofia has gradually become less confident and inclusive, merely reporting the different points of view of the rival groups.
But now it seeks to recapture its old tone of voice:

> That night the Mother of the Spirits walked the length and
> breadth of the clan, weeping for her murdered son. It was a ter-
> rible night. Not even the oldest man in Umuofia had ever heard
> such a strange and fearful sound, and it was never to be heard
> again. It seemed as if the very soul of the tribe wept for a great
> evil that was coming—its own death.
>
> On the next day all the masked *egwugwu* of Umuofia assem-
> bled in the market-place. They came from all the quarters of the
> clan and even from neighbouring villages. The dreaded Otakagu
> came from Imo, and Ekwensu, dangling a white cock, arrived
> from Uli. It was a terrible gathering. The eerie voices of count-
> less spirits, the bells that clattered behind some of them, and the
> clash of matchets as they ran forwards and backwards and
> saluted one another, sent tremors of fear into every heart. For
> the first time in living memory the sacred bull-roarer was heard
> in broad daylight.

The tribe has rallied only to celebrate its own demise. The narrative
voice falters as it describes the unique act of rebellion, and then

assumes a new and impersonal perspective ('and it was never to be heard again') in which the clan has no existence. But punishment is inflicted upon the Christians. The *egwugwu* destroy both Enoch's compound and the church, and Umuofia is placated.

When the district commissioner returns to Umuofia, however, the six elders of Umuofia are imprisoned by a trick. After being ridiculed by the court messengers, they are set free on the payment of a fine and return home in disgrace to a subdued clan. Okonkwo is infuriated by the treatment he has received and yet in a curious way he is elated. 'Before he had gone to bed he had brought down his war dress, which he had not touched since his return from exile. He had shaken out his smoked raffia skirt and examined his full feather headgear and his shield.' This is the moment he has been waiting for, a chance to redress the mysterious setbacks to his career, the frustration of the years of exile, the innumerable compromises. Now that his fears have been justified, the tribe must act. Looking back to his earlier successes, like the quarrel with Mbaino which opened the novel, Okonkwo hopes to recover his past authority by solving these new problems in the old way. But the old ways are no longer applicable, for the tribe is divided. Okonkwo and his friends seek to act with the old vigour and decision in this new situation:

> 'If we fight the stranger we shall hit our brothers and perhaps shed the blood of a clansman. But we must do it. Our fathers never dreamt of such a thing, they never killed their brothers. But a white man never came to them. So we must do what our fathers would never have done . . . We must root out this evil. And if our brothers take the side of evil we must root them out too.'

In their anxiety to force Umuofia into open conflict, Okonkwo's party use the extreme categories of their enemies. But Umuofia is not ready, and, as the court messengers appear, Okonkwo finds that the conflict is his alone. 'In that brief moment the world seemed to stand still, waiting. There was utter silence. The men of Umuofia were merged into the mute backcloth of trees and giant creepers, waiting.' The head messenger orders the meeting to stop in the name of the white man. With two blows of his matchet Okonkwo beheads the man and knows immediately that the tribe will not support his action. 'He knew that Umuofia would not go to war. He knew because they had let the other messenger escape. They had broken into tumult instead of action. He discerned fright in that tumult. He heard voices asking: "Why did he do it?"'

He wipes his matchet on the sand and goes away to kill himself, thereby committing the final abomination, 'an offence against the Earth, and a man who commits it will not be buried by his clansmen.

His body is evil, and only strangers may touch it.' This is where Okonkwo's narrow rectitude has led him; the embodiment of traditional law has become the outcast of the tribe. The paradox prompts Obierika's final baffled cry to the DC: 'That man was one of the greatest men in Umuofia. You drove him to kill himself; and now he will be buried like a dog . . .' In his anguish, Obierika accuses the intruder of the death of his friend. But clearly, this is an oversimplification; the white man is the catalyst of a struggle which has been in progress since the beginning of the novel. At first, Okonkwo was dogmatically defending the letter of tribal law against the more humane members of the clan who insisted that this should be modified and controlled by its interplay with particular situations. With the arrival of the missionaries, Okonkwo's position became stronger; the flexibility and tolerance of Igbo society was shown to be the cause of its vulnerability. And so, just as at the beginning of the novel Okonkwo was successful in Umuofia because of his ignorance of its subtle dialectic, now he is its most stalwart defender because he is too obtuse to appreciate the attractions of the new religion. He himself has never been troubled by the discrepancy between the divine and human systems of value, and so a new rconcilation is of little interest. For a man who has consistently belittled sympathy and affection, a loving god is an irrelevance.

In his wrongheaded way he is correct in his resistance. Firm, decisive action at the outset might have repulsed the missionaries. As soon, however, as any kind of contact is permitted, then Achebe shows by the logic of his narrative that traditional tribal society is doomed. For this new religion questions radically all the basic tenets of Umuofia, and in providing answers to some of their dilemmas it undermines their other sanctities. Okonkwo acts as if he understands these dangers. He forces a clear-cut confrontation out of a complex process which has been going on for some time and seeks to involve against its will a society he does not understand in a war against the intruders. His isolation and suicide are inevitable, and they provide the final example of the dislocation between the human predicament and the divine decrees. Okonkwo will be buried like a dog in the 'evil forest', rejected by the tribe and the Earth Mother he has defended with such loyalty.

As Okonkwo's life moves quickly to its tragic end, one is reminded forcibly of another impressive but wrongheaded hero, Henchard in *The Mayor of Casterbridge*. They share an obsessive need for success and status, they subordinate all their private relations to this end, and both have an inability to understand the tolerant, sceptical societies in which their novel single-mindedness succeeds. But the similarity becomes more striking when their worlds, threatened from the outside by disruptive forces, begin to disintegrate. Then, paradoxically, these aggressive and fiery individuals who achieved power by simplifying and finally flouting traditional values become the fierce defenders of the status quo, and our sympathy shifts accordingly. Viewed in the perspective of the Wessex, rustic way of life, Henchard is crass, brutal and dangerous; but when this way of life as a whole is threatened with imminent destruction, then his fierce resistance takes on a certain grandeur. The reader's sympathy describes a similar trajectory as it follows Okonkwo's career. By the values of Umuofia his inadequacies are very apparent; but when the alien religion begins to question and undermine these values, Okonkwo, untroubled by the heart-searching of the community, springs to its defence and acts. But Umuofia, too disunited to follow his lead, capitulates to the forces which will destroy it. Both men end their lives as outcasts, and their death is the price of the destructive compromises which their communities are now forced to make. In this way, Henchard and Okonkwo become for the only time in their lives representative of a way of life which has been lost.

There is a final incident in the novel which reduces these complexities to ironically manageable proportions. Supported by his African soldiers who already speak colonial pidgin English, the DC arrives on the scene to arrest Okonkwo. He finds that he has hanged himelf, and the tribe will not touch his abominated body. As an amateur anthropologist his interest is immediately kindled by this strange custom. The famous last page of the novel is presented from his point of view.

> 'Take down the body,' the Commissioner ordered his chief messenger, 'and bring it and all these people to the court.'
>
> 'Yes, sah,' the messenger said, saluting.
>
> The Commissioner went away, taking three or four of the soldiers with him. In the many years in which he had toiled to bring civilisation to different parts of Africa he had learnt a number of things. One of them was that a District Commissioner must never attend to such undignified details as cutting down a hanged man from the tree. Such attention would give the natives a poor opinion of him. In the book which he planned to write he would stress that point. As he walked back to the court he thought about that book. Every day brought him some new material. The story of this man who had killed a messenger and hanged himself would make interesting reading. One could almost write a whole chapter on him. Perhaps not a whole chapter but a reasonable paragraph, at any rate. There was so much else to include, and one must be firm in cutting out details. He had already chosen the title of the book, after much thought: *The Pacification of the Primitive Tribes of the Lower Niger.*

This is clearly the most radical shift of point of view in the whole novel. Our immersion in the world of Umuofia has continued up to the last page, and then Achebe has suddenly detached us from this

sympathetically rendered world and asked us to share the point of view
of the British DC who, from the outside, sees Umuofia as the world of
primitive custom, the heart of darkness of the European imagination.
The DC is not an unfamiliar figure; he comes at the end of a long line
of explorers, missionaries and administrators whose preconceptions
have enabled them to find in Africa what they wished to find. Here he
asks us to revoke the conventions and assumptions of the tribal world
which Achebe has made us accept so effortlessly, and translate the
tragic culmination of Okonkwo's career into the terms of colonial pacification and primitive customs, with which we are more familiar.

This ironical shift of perspective from the inside to the outside of the
fictional world is a device whose function is clear. It reminds us that
the assumptions we have come to accept in the course of the novel are
not the only ones, indeed are not the usual ones, in that realm of experience we have been exploring. The device has been used frequently
and effectively in William Golding's novels, and the comparison is
instructive. One of his main purposes also is to reassess unexplored or
stereotyped areas of experience; at the end of *Lord of the Flies* (1954),
when he shifts suddenly to the point of view of the captain, he is
returning us to a conventional perspective whose familiar contours can
never be the same again. Similarly in *The Inheritors* (1955), the conventional is transformed into the alien, and the alien becomes the conventional. At the end of that novel, the neanderthal world whose reality
we have shared is dramatically disturbed by the arrival of the mysterious creature, *homo sapiens*, already equipped with a stereotyped vision
of his prehistoric predecessors. In each of these novels the author is
recovering an area of experience from its stereotype, and the final
ironic shift is to challenge the reader to apply the stereotype once more
if he dare. The author is putting his fictional world to the test. What is
undermined in *Things Fall Apart*, as in Golding's novels, is not the fictional world but the persistent, stubborn stereotype.

EUSTACE PALMER

Character and Society in Achebe's
Things Fall Apart[†]

The recent publication of a collection of essays on Chinua Achebe
edited by Bernth Lindfors and Catherine Innes and entitled *Critical
Perspectives on Achebe* clearly demonstrates two main points: the

† From *An Introduction to the African Novel* (London: Heinemann, 1991), 145–56. Copyright
© 2003 by Chelsea House Publishers, an imprint of Infobase Publishing. Reprinted with
permission of the publisher.

accomplished artistry of the author who now justifiably occupies a central position in African letters and the dominance of his first novel *Things Fall Apart* in the Achebe canon. The essays on *Things Fall Apart* in that volume are not only much better in quality than those on its nearest rival *Arrow of God*, but the authors also go to great lengths to demonstrate its complex artistry. If, however, there is now general agreement about the quality of that novel, opinion is much more divided about the status of its hero Okonkwo and about attitudes (including the author's) towards him. On the one hand are those critics like Killam and the present writer who regard Okonkwo as essentially the embodiment of the major values and norms of his society, essentially a product of his society in fact, while on the other hand there are those like Iyasere, Innes and Carroll who see Okonkwo as deviating from those norms and being essentially out of step with his society.

Solomon Iyasere is most typical of this latter view. In his essay he suggests that the present writer in presenting Okonkwo as the embodiment of his society transforms him from champion to victim, and he goes on to suggest further that far from being an embodiment of the values of his society Okonkwo has only a very limited understanding of those values. Where his society is surprisingly flexible Okonkwo is utterly inflexible; where his society is able to accommodate the lazy and unsuccessful Okonkwo has no patience with them; where his society respects age Okonkwo shows scant regard for age; where his society is noted for its discreet blending of the masculine and feminine principles Okonkwo is openly contemptuous of all things feminine. Iyasere unwittingly transforms Okonkwo into a villain with few redeeming features, instead of the truly tragic hero with a blend of attractive and unattractive qualities that most readers know. The essence of great tragedy, surely, is that the hero possesses certain excellent qualities which arouse the reader's admiration, but he simultaneously possesses certain weaknesses which render him incapable of dealing successfully with the forces and circumstances he is confronted with. It is these which lead to his downfall, but the reader's sympathy is never totally alienated from him because he continues to be aware of those excellent qualities. The tragic hero is never completely villain nor completely victim and his tragedy is always brought about by a combination of his own personal inadequacies and external circumstances. Okonkwo is precisely such a tragic hero.

Like the good critic he is Iyasere senses that that the reader's sympathy is never totally alienated from Okonkwo but the position he has adopted at the start of his essay prevents him from pursuing this hunch to its logical conclusion and realising, firstly that Okonkwo has many more admirable qualities than merely not being at heart a violent man (which is the reason he gives for the retention of the

reader's sympathy), and secondly that the very predisposition to violence which he so copiously demonstrates has been conditioned in
Okonkwo partly by the need to conform to his society's norms. In his
attempt to demonstrate the extent to which Okonkwo deviates from
his society Iyasere over-idealises Umuofia society and blinds himself
to its harshness. He also has a very narrow interpretation of the term
"embodiment." Surely, when one says that Okonkwo is the embodiment of his society's values one does not mean that every single
aspect of Okonkwo's character has been conditioned by his society;
one means that his public attitudes and ideas like attitudes towards
women, customs, children or wealth would have been largely determined by his society's norms, but at the same time he would himself
possess certain personal idiosyncracies like impulsiveness, ill-temper
or nervousness which might themselves contribute towards his
downfall, but which still do not mean that he is not the embodiment
of his society's values. When talking about the interrelationship
between character and society one must be careful to make the distinction between public attitudes, ideas and beliefs which have been
adopted in conformity with the society's norms, and more personal
qualities. It is possible to be the embodiment of one's society and yet
possess certain personal individual human qualities. This is the case
with Okonkwo. It is the purpose of this paper to demonstrate that
Okonkwo's virtues are largely the virtues of his society, just as his
weaknesses are largely the weaknesses of his society. In this sense, his
tragedy is similar to that of his society, for these weaknesses largely
contribute to his downfall, just as they surely lead to the capitulation
of his society to an alien force. But of course Okonkwo's own personal qualities, such as his impulsiveness, also play a contributory
role, but they do not necessarily suggest that he is a deviant from his
society.

It is clear that Okonkwo's admirable qualities, such as courage,
fearlessness, determination, industry, energy, perseverance, resilience
and tribal pride are either qualities he shares with his society or have
been produced in him by the need to respond to the demands of that
society. Okonkwo accepts most of his society's major attitudes such
as its concern for rank and prestige, its reverence for courage, bravery and success in war or wrestling, and its premium on material and
social prosperity. In discussion with Obierika about the law which
forbids men of title to climb palm trees Okonkwo can say quite categorically that "the law of the land must be obeyed" and all his
actions are determined by this conviction. Even when he breaks the
week of peace and unwittingly infringes the law, he accepts that he
is wrong and that the law is right, and he submits to his punishment.
Okonkwo does not deviate from his society's norms and it is inaccurate to say that he has only a limited understanding of them; rather

it is the intelligent Obierika who constantly questions his society's values; it is he who suggests that the law forbidding men of title to climb palm trees is a bad law; it is he who questions the throwing of twins into the evil forest and the banishing of a man for seven years from his fatherland for accidentally killing a kinsman. Okonkwo never does; and yet no one has accused Obierika of deviating from his society's norms.

Very early in the novel there is an episode demonstrating that even in his youth Okonkwo is determined to be the personification of those values that his society holds sacred. He goes to Nwakibie to ask for seed yams and says: "I know what it is to ask a man to trust another with his yams, especially these days when young men are afraid of hard work. I am not afraid of work." Critics like Innes and Iyasere might see this as the most towering conceit on Okonkwo's part, but in reality it shows his confidence in himself and his determination to be different from other young men and conform to his society's aspirations. And Nwakibie who is very much in line with his society's norms and is a pillar of that society, agrees with Okonkwo and confirms the truth of what he has just said: "It pleases me to see a young man like you these days when our youth have gone soft. Many young men have come to me to ask for yams but I have refused because I knew they would just dump them in the earth and leave them to be choked by weeds." To Nwakibie, Okonkwo stands for everything that he is looking for in a deserving young man. Later in Mbanta we see an elder identifying Okonkwo with the traditional ways of doing things while castigating the younger generation for deviating from the tribe's paths: "It is good in these days when the younger generation consider themselves wiser than their sires to see a man doing things in the grand old way." The society's recognition that Okonkwo is an embodiment of their values is illustrated in their choice of him as the emissary to Mbaino and the guardian of Ikemefuna. He is also the representative of his village among the nine masked egwugwu of Umuofia. If anything Okonkwo's tragedy is caused not by his deviation from the norms of his society, but because he tries to adhere to those norms too completely.

No other issue illustrates Okonkwo's oneness with his society more than his regard for the concept of manliness. Iyasere and Innes would have us believe that Umuofia society, while adhering to the concept of manliness, holds the female principle in very high regard, and its world view is based on a subtle blend of the masculine and feminine principles, a subtlety which Okonkwo is incapable of understanding. Iyasere cites the aged Uchendu's words of caution to the exiled Okonkwo when the former tries to explain the meaning of the adage "mother is supreme", illustrating that the mother, and therefore the female principle, stands for sympathy and compassion. Furthermore

the importance of the female principle in Umuofia society is illustrated by the fact that the powerful earth deity Ani is feminine, and
the no less powerful Oracle Agbala is represented as female, as is her
mouthpiece—the Priestess of Agbala. It is true that Umuofia society
gives some regard to the female principle, but there is little doubt that
in the novel itself much greater importance is attached to the masculine principle and the concept of manliness. Okonkwo's regard for
manliness is no more and no less than his society's regard for it. This
is particularly demonstrated in the symbolic importance of the yam.
We are told quite early in the novel: "His mother and his sisters
worked hard enough, but they grew women's crops, like coco-yams,
beans and cassava. Yam, the king of crops, was a man's crop." And
Achebe's rhetorical guidance suggests that this is the view, not just of
Okonkwo, but of his entire society. This is even more obvious in "Yam
stood for manliness, and he who could feed his family on yams from
one harvest to another was a very great man indeed." The almost
proverbial ring in "he who could feed his family" suggests that this is
the point of view of the entire society; it is part of the tribal wisdom.
The New Yam Festival is linked with manly men: "The New Yam Festival was thus an occasion for joy throughout Umuofia. And every
man whose arm was strong, as the Ibo people say, was expected to
invite large numbers of guests from far and wide." If Okonkwo exalts
the concept of manliness into a kind of shibboleth, it is precisely
because his society reveres men whose arms were strong and who in
moments of crisis did not behave like shivering old women. On their
way to kill the ill-fated Ikemefuna the men of Umuofia pour ridicule
on those "effeminate" men who had refused to come with them. It
would probably have been more human for Okonkwo to have stayed
away as the aged Ezeudu advised him to do, and as Obierika himself
did; but there is little doubt that the majority of masculine opinion in
Umuofia would have considered him a coward. When at the
betrothal of Obierika's daughter's the suitor's family's pots of wine
begin to number more than thirty "the hosts nodded in approval and
seemed to say 'now they are behaving like men.'" The concept of
manliness is paramount. If Okonkwo rules his family with a heavy
hand, it is because basically his society believes that women and children must be kept in check: "No matter how prosperous a man was,
if he was unable to rule his women and his children (and especially
his women) he was not really a man. He was like the man in the song
who had ten and one wives and not enough soup for his foofoo."
Once more Achebe's rhetorical guidance suggests that this is the
point of view, not just of Okonkwo, but of his entire society. The
proverbial saying in the song from the oral tradition gives it the
weight of tribal wisdom. When Okonkwo encourages his boys to sit
with him in his Obi and listen to stories of war and bloodshed it is

because his society reveres masculine prowess in war and he feels the boys have reached the stage when they should hear such stories. And the young and rather feminine Nwoye knows what his society believes; he knows it is right to be masculine, even though deep down he prefers his mother's stories. Conclusive proof that this is a male oriented society whose views are very much like Okonkwo's is provided by the discussion during the betrothal proceedings:

> "The world is large", said Okonkwo. "I have even heard that in some tribes a man's children belong to his wife and her family."
> "That cannot be", said Machi. "You might as well say that the woman lies on top of the man when they are making the children."

As in most things he does, Okonkwo probably carries this regard for manliness too far, but it is basically a central tenet of his society's beliefs and in adhering to it one cannot say that he deviates from his society's norms, the subtle discriminations of which he is incapable of understanding. Moreover, the female principle which is supposed to be subtly blended with the masculine and to represent compassion and sympathy, does not, in practice, suggest anything of the kind, does not make for flexibility. The Earth Goddess Ani is a harsh unrelenting deity who is dreaded by the people. It is in obedience to her dictates that twins, suicides and those who die of the swelling sickness are cast off into the evil forest and a man is exiled for seven years for the accidental slaying of a kinsman. Some of the most repulsive and most cruel practices of this society are caused by its adherence to the will of the Earth Goddess, and her will is totally inflexible. The Oracle of Agbala is not much better. If it directs that a young child must be carried away from its mother into the depths of the forest in the dead of night, or that a young and innocent hostage must be killed, then its will must be unquestioningly obeyed. And the Oracle has no more compassion for the lazy Unoka than his male-oriented society. If anything the female principle induces terror. We must never forget that the most active ingredient in Umuofia's war medicine which is the terror of its neighbours is an old woman hopping on one leg. It is inaccurate to suggest that the female principle, representing compassion and sympathy, modifies the masculine and that the two are subtly blended and that Okonkwo is blind to this subtle blending. If anything the female principle merely reinforces the male with its harshness.

One of the mainsprings of Okonkwo's actions is his rather negative revulsion against everything his father had stood for. Humiliated by his father's shameful life and even more shameful death Okonkwo is determined to be everything his father was not. He must be brave and materially successful, he must take the highest titles, he must provide for and rule his womenfolk and children and he must never be thought weak or a coward. In the process he becomes dehumanised, but Okonkwo's determination is conditioned by his society's attitudes and beliefs. If he reacts violently against everything his father stood for, it is because his society despised his father. It is surely inaccurate to suggest, as Iyasere does, that Umuofia society adapts its code to accommodate less successful men. It does not banish them, of course, since they are still members of the clan, but all the evidence suggests that it regards them with the greatest contempt. For instance, all the men are amused by Obiaka's retort when informed that his dead lazy father wants him to sacrifice a goat to him. "Ask my father if he ever had a fowl when he was alive." When Okonkwo hints that his son Nwoye has too much of his mother in him Obierika says inwardly that the young man has too much of his grandfather in him. The priestess of Agbala lashes out at Unoka in the harshest terms when the latter goes to consult the Oracle on the question of his failure. Iyasere suggests that Okonkwo should have given his father the respect due to age in conformity with the norms of his society for "while achievement was revered, age was respected." But Iyasere unwittingly turns the text on its head for the text actually reads: "Age was respected among his people, but achievement was revered. As the elders said, if a child washed his hands he could eat with kings." The drift of the entire passage is the premium that these people place on achievement, rather than on age per se; "among these people a man was judged according to his worth and not according to the worth of his father." There is nothing to suggest that in secretly despising his father and repudiating all he stood for Okonkwo was violating a necessary aspect of the society's code of values. On the contrary, Okonkwo's attitude is completely shared by his society. Of course one would agree with Iyasere that in suppressing his fears and those attributes he considers a sign of weakness Okonkwo denies human responses of love and understanding; and, responding to Achebe's rhetorical guidance, we do realise that Unoka has very human qualities which Okonkwo would have been the better for possessing and that in repudiating him the latter was also repudiating positive qualities of love, compassion and sensitivity. But it is the reader who thinks so, not Okonkwo's society. Many of Okonkwo's weaknesses are also the weaknesses of his society.

There is very little sign of the tolerance and flexibility that critics like Innes and Iyasere see in Umuofia society. Okonkwo's own inflexibility, intolerance and conservatism are merely reflections of his society's. On essential questions of religion, justice and class Umuofia shows no flexibility. The penalties imposed by the gods and by custom must be adhered to. If a cow strays accidentally into somebody's field its owner must pay the full penalty even though no damage has been done and the real culprits are some negligent children who were put in charge of the cow. The question of the osus vividly illustrates the clan's intolerance on essential matters. Even the Christian converts, many of whom are themselves among the underprivileged in their society, refuse to have contact with the osus.

On one matter and one matter alone the clan seems to demonstrate some tolerance, and this is in its attitude towards the new religion. Initially they allow the new converts and their missionaries to practise their religion unmolested, but this is in line with the clan's general courtesy to strangers, and in any case the new converts are still regarded as members of the clan and cannot therefore be ostracised without infringing the clan's own rules. In fact, the clan harbours the most sovereign contempt towards the new converts who in their view are the *efulefu* or worthless excrement of the clan and therefore not worth bothering about. Initially Okonkwo's attitude towards the missionaries is exactly the same as the clan's; it is one of amused tolerance, for he, like the clan, thinks that the missionaries are mad. In reality the tolerance is only apparent, for at Mbanta the clan secretly hopes to bring about the death of the new missionaries. When the latter ask them for land to build their church, they offer them the evil forest in the hope that they will all die there. The clan will not modify its own beliefs and it will allow the new converts to practise their religion only for as long as its own position and religion are not threatened. When some over-zealous converts boast openly that they are prepared to defy the gods by burning all their shrines they are seized and beaten until they stream with blood. When another convert kills the sacred python Okonkwo suggests that the abominable gang should be chased out of the village with whips, but although many do not agree with him, he is certainly not isolated in his view for we are told that many of the elders spoke at great length and in fury. In the end those who suggest gentler measures prevail. And when Okonkwo expresses the view that such a thing would never happen in his own fatherland Umuofia, we must realise that he speaks with the authority of one who knows how his clan would have behaved on such an occasion. Mbanta is by all accounts a gentler clan than Umuofia; but even so the women who are sent for red earth to decorate the church are severely whipped and when they go to the stream for water they find themselves debarred, an unheard of thing. To suggest that the clan is flexible and that Okonkwo's inflexibility is due to a lack of understanding of the subtle variations within the code, is to misread the novel.

The killing of Ikemefuna illustrates the essential inflexibility and brutality not just of Okonkwo, but of the entire clan. It is difficult, in fact, to accept the charge of brutality that critics like Iyasere would bring against Okonkwo in the killing of Ikemefuna. It is the society

which is brutal for it is this society which has asked the men to perform a brutal task. On a personal level, perhaps it would have been
more human for Okonkwo to have heeded Ezeudu's advice not to
have a hand in Ikemefuna's death since the boy regarded him as his
father. It is a point we hold against Okonkwo, but we hold it against
his society as well, for if Okonkwo decides to accompany the men it
is because he knows that if he does not do so he would be considered
weak and womanish, and the comments of the men as they take Ikemefuna to his death reinforce this. Some critics feel that in disregarding the aged Ezeudu's advice Okonkwo shows scant regard for
age which his society reveres and is therefore going against the norms
of that society. But Ezeudu's advice is a personal one which does not
necessarily have the backing of his society, for otherwise he would
not have felt compelled to offer it. All the evidence suggests on the
contrary, that the majority of masculine opinion in Umuofia expects
Okonkwo to be a part of the delegation.

   In reality, Okonkwo never intended to bear a hand in Ikemefuna's
death. He had become extremely fond of the child whom he had
come to regard as his own son. Indeed, the relationship with Ikemefuna brings out in Okonkwo those human qualities which we have
hitherto missed. When it is announced that the boy must be killed
Okonkwo is thrown into the depths of despair and although he
accompanies the men on their mission of death he keeps to the rear
thus demonstrating that he has no intention of lifting his hand against
the boy. He fully intends, in his own way, to heed Ezeudu's advice.
When he hears the murderous blow he turns his head; he cannot
bear to see a boy whom he regards as his son struck down before his
eyes. If that first blow had done its work Okonkwo would never have
borne a hand in the killing of Ikemefuna; if Ikemefuna in his terror
had not run towards Okonkwo with his anguished cry "they have
killed me father" the former would never have cut him down. By making that cry Ikemefuna was invoking the help of Okonkwo as a father
and defender against those murderous men and all eyes must have
been on Okonkwo to see whether he would yield to what they must
consider sentimental ties rather than demonstrate loyalty to his clan
and obedience to the dictates of his gods; and for Okonkwo outward
displays of sentimentality are out of the question because he does not
want his clan to consider him weak; and loyalty to the clan and the
dictates of the gods are of over-riding importance. So he cuts Ikemefuna down.

   Even so Okonkwo is aware that he has done something which goes
against his best instincts and he is racked by internal torment for days
afterwards. We see human dimensions here in Okonkwo that we have
never suspected before. In his despair he even longs for companionship and sends for the now hostile Nwoye to sit with him in his obi.

A number of critics would have us believe that Nwoye's attitude towards his father hardens because he sees the latter as having killed Ikemefuna. This is an oversimplification of the actual position. We are told that the moment Okonkwo walked into the obi Nwoye knew that Ikemefuna had been killed and something seemed to give way inside him like a tightened bow. Nwoye does not, and cannot, accuse his father of having cut down Ikemefuna since he was not present at the killing and could not possibly know that Okonkwo had dealt the final blow. What he blames his father for is taking part in the general clan brutality. That this is so is demonstrated by the anecdote of the twins in the bush which was the first occasion when Nwoye had had the feeling of something giving way inside him. That anecdote also relates to the general brutality of this society and it is this which now impresses itself once more on Nwoye's mind when he has that same feeling. In deciding, in consequence, to join the Christians who are more compassionate and humane, Nwoye rejects not just his father, but his entire society.

The Ikemefuna episode copiously demonstrates that Okonkwo is not really an inhuman person. He does have warm, human feelings, even of compassion and love. If he appears dehumanised and inflexible it is because in order to please his society, conform to its norms and measure up to its demands on him, he is forced to smother his best instincts. This is one of the reasons why we continue to sympathise with him. Okonkwo might bully his boys in order to get them to be manly in line with his society's demands, but he knows inwardly that the boys are still too young to understand fully the difficult art of preparing yams. He might be pleased inwardly at his son's development but he knows he must keep his feelings tightly under control. Okonkwo is what his society has made him, and there is very little support in the text for the view that he is what he is because of a radical misunderstanding of the subtle shades of his society's codes.

Okonkwo, of course, possesses certain harsh personal qualities which are not the result of conditioning by his society. The most conspicuous of these is his uncontrollable temper which is related to his impulsiveness. It almost seems as though there is some irrational ungovernable force within Okonkwo propelling him to insane outbursts of anger and wildly impulsive actions which have increasingly disastrous consequences. In this sense he is rather like Hardy's Michael Henchard. Thus he terrorises the young Ikemefuna when the latter refuses to eat, viciously beats one wife thus breaking the week of peace and nearly murders another with his gun for making disparaging references to his ability as a hunter. We are meant to see the slaying of Ezeudu's son, though an accidental occurrence, as the culmination of a number of increasingly serious and senseless acts partly motivated by his impulsiveness and irrational temper. We are

also informed of his brusqueness and impatience with less successful men; he knew how to kill a man's spirit. There is also a basic restlessness in Okonkwo; he always seems to be charged with an
overabundance of nervous energy and is always yearning for action.
These are qualities, of course, which are related to his impulsiveness
and they contribute to his disastrous actions. But Okonkwo is always
full of regret for these acts when he comes to himself. His impulsiveness may lead him to forget the week of peace and break the law, but
he regrets immediately, accepts that he has been at fault and accepts
his punishment. When ever he transgresses against his society's laws,
he does so unwittingly or accidentally, never deliberately, and he is
quite willing to take full responsibility later. When he insults a clansman by calling him a woman, the people take sides with the man
against Okonkwo, and he decently apologises. Okonkwo's harsher personal qualities, therefore, might contribute to his eventual downfall,
but they do not suggest that he is a deviant from his society's norms.

A number of people in the novel make disparaging comments
about Okonkwo, but we must not necessarily assume that Achebe
endorses these; we must follow his rhetorical guidance in order to
ascertain his point of view. When Okonkwo insults the man at the
meeting for instance, the oldest man present says sternly that "those
whose palm-kernels were cracked for them by a benevolent spirit
should not forget to be humble." But Achebe's rhetorical guidance
suggests that the man's judgement is quite wrong, motivated in all
probability by envy at Okonkwo's achievements and sudden rise to
prominence though still a young man:

> But it was really not true that Okonkwo's palm-kernels had
> been cracked for him by a benevolent spirit. He had cracked
> them himself . . . If ever a man deserved his success, that man
> was Okonkwo . . . At the most one could say that his *chi* or per-
> sonal god was good. But the Ibo people have a proverb that when
> a man says yes his *chi* says yes also. Okonkwo said yes very
> strongly; so his *chi* agreed. And not only his *chi* but his clan too,
> because it judged a man by the work of his hands.

The old man fails to give due weight to Okonkwo's personal determination and industry. Similarly when Okonkwo breaks the week of
peace his enemies go around saying that he has no respect for the
gods of the clan and that his good fortune has gone to his head. But
Achebe guides us by openly terming these people 'enemies' and he
informs us in any case, that inwardly Okonkwo was repentant. It is
simply not true that he has no respect for the gods or that success has
gone to his head. Generally Achebe remains most sympathetic
towards Okonkwo, while recognising his faults, and he succeeds in
generating this sympathy in the reader as well.

Many critics have not been alive to the full significance of Okonkwo's absence for seven years from his fatherland at a time when the new religion is consolidating itself and making inroads into traditional society. That accidental slaying of Ezeudu's son was a shrewd masterstroke of the author's with an important bearing on the plot and on the development of the themes and Okonkwo's character. For during that absence the clan changes profoundly while Okonkwo does not; and it is only now that a gap appears between Okonkwo and his society. But it is not so much Okonkwo who deviates, as his society which is forced to shift from the old paths. Nor is the shift in the society's position due to its flexibility, to a willingness to welcome change. It simply recognises the presence of a militarily superior force, and it is cowed in spite of itself into submission. Furthermore it has been racked by internal disunity enhanced by its own rigidity and lack of compassion. The osus, the mothers of twins and all those who are outcasts from this society or who have something to dread from its harsh unrelenting laws flock to the new religion. There are those, of course, who welcome the new regime, because it has brought trade and prosperity, and we know that Umuofia society has always been materialistic. The downfall of the society is already in progress when Okonkwo returns, and it is brought about, in part, by those very qualities which will also contribute to Okonkwo's own disaster.

So far is Okonkwo from deviating from his society's norms that on his return he is one of the very few who still hold on to the old values—the belief in courage, tribal independence, and pride in the tribe's traditions. That these values have not entirely been lost sight of, that the tribe does not willingly submit to change and to the white man's rule and that Okonkwo's attitude is not such an aberration as commonly supposed, is authenticated by the discussion at the great meeting called to discuss the white man's humiliation of the clan's elders. Sensing the resurgence of the tribal spirit Okonkwo takes heart and gets down his war gear. At the meeting itself Okika the great orator speaks out powerfully for war, thus suggesting that Okonkwo is not entirely isolated in his championing of the old values.

The killing of the messenger is one of Okonkwo's impulsive and foolish acts which have disastrous consequences. This is why certain voices ask why he did it. He attempts to force his society's hand by an act which would almost certainly result in war, whereas his clan would have wanted to take the decision in a more rational way. But there is little doubt that the old Umuofia would have backed Okonkwo, for this would not have been a war of blame since the court messengers were not really messengers but haughty aggressors attempting to stop the meeting by force. But the present, much changed Umuofia would never go to war, as Okonkwo correctly realises; it is cowed by this manifestation of the white man's power into final submission. This is

the real death knell of traditional Umuofia society. It is his realisation
of this which leads to Obierika's impassioned outburst against the
uncomprehending District Commissioner: "That man was one of the
greatest men in Umuofia. You drove him to kill himself; and now he will
be buried like a dog . . ." Iyasere is surely wrong in suggesting that
Obierika at this point loses all sense of objectivity. Obierika has been
the sanest and the most sensible man throughout the novel and we can
be sure that at this stage he carries Achebe's endorsement. Okonkwo
has been one of the greatest men in Umuofia, endorsing all of his society's norms to the very last, even when others are cowed into submission. He is neither victim, nor villain, but a truly tragic hero, a man
with admirable qualities reflecting those of his society, and weaknesses
also reflecting those of his society; but in spite of these he never loses
the author's or the reader's sympathy. His tragedy resides partly in the
fact that the society which he has championed for so long is forced to
change, while he finds that he cannot.

B. EUGENE McCARTHY

Rhythm and Narrative Method in Achebe's
Things Fall Apart†

Before the publication of Chinua Achebe's *Things Fall Apart* in 1958
public awareness in the West of fiction from Africa was confined
chiefly to white writers such as Doris Lessing, Alan Paton, or Nadine
Gordimer. Thus Achebe's first novel, written in English, though he is
himself a Nigerian of the Igbo people, was a notable event. More
noteworthy was the fact that it was a very good novel and has become
over the years probably the most widely read and talked about African
novel, overshadowing the efforts of other West African novelists as
well as those of East and South Africa. Its reputation began high and
has remained so, stimulating critical analysis in hundreds of articles,
many books, and dissertations. Its story describes, whatever one may
expect from its Yeatsian title, the life of a traditional Igbo rural village
and the rise of one of its gifted leaders, Okonkwo, before colonization, and then observes the consequences for the village and the hero
as they confront the beginnings of the colonial process. Achebe's subsequent three novels, more or less related but not sequential, *No
Longer At Ease* (1960), *Arrow of God* (1964), and *Man of the People*
(1966), though all respected, have not matched its success. Achebe's
fiction established firmly that there is an African prose literature—

† From *Novel: A Forum on Fiction* 18.3 (Spring 1985): 243–56. Copyright Novel Corporation,
© 1985. Reprinted with permission.

poetry had probably been well known since Senghor in the 1940s—
even when written in English. Not that there has not been debate
over and criticism of *Things Fall Apart*, and from Achebe's standpoint
a good deal of misunderstanding through refusal of readers to take its
African character seriously; but as a recent study confirms he, continues to be "the most widely read of contemporary African writers."[1]
His first novel has been "as big a factor in the formation of a young
West African's picture of his past, and of his relation to it, as any of
the still rather distorted teachings of the pulpit and the primary
school,"[2] and of course he has influenced his fellow writers just as
significantly in finding their own subject matter and voice.

When beginning Chinua Achebe's novel *Things Fall Apart*, readers
are often struck by the simple mode of narration and equally simple
prose style, which critics have seen as Achebe's desire to achieve an
"English . . . colored to reflect the African verbal style [with] stresses
and emphases that would be eccentric and unexpected in British or
American speech."[3] He reshapes English in order to imitate the "linguistic patterns of his mother tongue," Igbo.[4] I would like, as a further means of understanding this special quality of Achebe's prose,
to propose a way of reading and of understanding the novel through
the concept of rhythm, within the oral tradition.

In the opening passage of the novel, the narrator's repetition of
words and phrases, both verbatim and synonymous, and his mode of
emphasis and patterning suggest a deliberateness and complexity
well beyond the surface simplicity:

> [A] Okonkwo *was* wel[a]l known *throughout the nine villages and*
> [A] [a] even beyond. His *fame rested on solid personal achievements. As*
> [A] *a young man of eighteen* he had brought hono[a]ur *to his village by*
> [B] [C] throwing Amalinze the Cat. Amalinze *was the great wrestler who*
> [D] *for seven years was unbeaten, from Umuofia to Mbaino. He was*
> [C] called the Cat *because his back would never touch the earth. It*
> [C] [A] [B] was this man *that* Okonkwo threw *in a fight which the old men*
> [E] agreed was one of the fiercest *since the founder of their town*
> [E] [D] engaged a spirit of the wild *for* seven days and seven nights.
>
> *The drums beat and the flutes sang and the spectators held*
> [C] [E] [A] their breath. Amalinze *was a* wily *craftsman, but* Okonkwo *was*

---

1. C. L. Innes and Bernth Lindfors, eds., *Critical Perspectives an Chinua Achebe* (Washington. D.C.: Three Continents Press, 1978), p. I.
2. Ibid., p. 5, quoting from *TLS* in 1965.
3. John Povey, "The English Language of the Contemporary African Novel," *Critique* XI, 3
(1969), 93.
4. Ihechukwu Madubuike, "Achebe's Ideas on African literature," *New Letters* 40, 4 (1974), 87.

> E   E
> *as* slippery *as a fish in water.* Every nerve and every muscle stood
> out *on their arms, on their backs and their thighs, and one almost*
>   E   A
> *heard them* stretching to breaking point. *In the end* Okonkwo
>   B   C
> threw the Cat.[5]

The narrator's repetitions in this passage are a technique of the traditional oral storyteller, sitting talking to a group of listeners (though he is not a *griot,* or oral historian).[6] For example, the subject "A" repeats four times, the modifier "a" repeats but varies to add meanings; other words, such as those about the intensity of the fight, likewise are repeated to emphasize their importance and to vary meanings. Walter Ong refines our understanding of oral thought and expression in prose by pointing out that the oral narrator's "thought must come into being in heavily rhythmic, balanced patterns, in repetitions and antitheses, in alliterations and assonances, in epithetic and other formulary expressions . . . ." Such primary devices for memory ("for rhythm aids recall") and communication simplify the story so that the listeners can grasp characters and events graphically and surely. More specifically, oral expression is "additive rather than subordinative," "aggregative rather than analytical," "redundant or 'copious,'" that is, "backlooping" by means of "redundancy, repetition of the just-said."[7] The additive and redundant elements are apparent in the above passage, when Achebe's narrator repeats a phrase, for example, "Amalinze the Cat," then carries it forward with new information. Once a name or event is introduced he proceeds by moving forward, then reaching back to repeat and expand, moving onward again, accumulating detail and elaborating: "well known" advances to "fame" and to "honour," just as "It was this man that Okonkwo threw" repeats what has gone before and underlines its importance. Karl H. Bottcher calls the narrator's method "afterthoughts,"[8] but Ong's "backlooping" conveys better the active methodology of the narrator.

The style is not "aggregative" for key epithets are not attached to characters, no doubt because the novel is written, not spoken. A more

---

5. Chinua Achebe, *Things Fall Apart* (London: Heinemann, 1958), p. 3. All subsequent quotations from the text are from this edition. Note: the word "men" above is written "man" in the text, which seems inconsistent with the referent "founder of *their* town."
6. Meki Nzewi, "Ancestral Polyphony," *African Arts 11,* 4 (1978), 94: "But Chinua does not see a link between the modern Igbo novelist and the traditional storyteller." According to Professor Chidi Ikonne of Harvard University the narrator is not a *griot* (from private conversation). Yet Kofi Awoonor, *The Breast of the Earth* (Garden City, N.Y.: Doubleday, 1976), p. 257, adds, there is a "straight-forward simplicity about the language . . . that recalls the raconteur's voice."
7. Walter J. Ong, S.J., *Orality and Literacy* (London: Methuen, 1982), pp. 34, 37–40. Ong says Achebe's *No Longer at Ease* "draws directly on Ibo oral tradition . . . [providing] instances of thought patterns in orally educated characters who move in these oral, mnemonically tooled grooves," p. 35.
8. Karl H. Bottcher, "The Narrative Technique in Achebe's Novels," New *African Literature and the Arts* 13/14 (1972), 7.

important departure from strict oral procedure is the narrator's distance from his characters and his reluctance to intrude his views, for as Ong tells us, empathy and participation are elements of orality, objectivity a consequence of writing.[9] For the most part the narrator reveals only what was done or said by others: "a fight which the *old men agreed* was one of the fiercest . . . ," "*it was said* that, when he slept . . . ," "he *seemed* to walk on springs, *as if*. . . ." We understand an apparent intrusion such as the following as reflecting not the narrator's bias but the way the people thought: "When Unoka died he had taken no title at all and he was heavily in debt. Any wonder then that his son Okonkwo was ashamed of him? Fortunately, among these people a man was judged according to his worth and not according to the worth of his father" (6).

The patterning and repetition in Achebe's novel are characteristics of the self-conscious artistry of oral narrative performance, where plot moves by repetition and predictability. Harold Scheub argues the "centrality of repetition in oral narratives as a means of establishing rhythm."[1] Such rhythmic textures establish the narrative method as imitative of the African oral rather than the English "literary" tradition. Indeed rhythm is a quality at the heart of African culture. Léopold Sédar Senghor has written: "Rhythm is the architecture of being, the inner dynamic that gives it form, the pure expression of the life force." The dramatic interest of a work is not sustained, he writes, by "avoiding repetition as in European narrative . . . , [but] is born of repetition: repetition of a fact, of a gesture, of words that form a *leitmotiv*. There is always the introduction of a new element, variation of the repetition, unity in diversity."[2] In the text where he quotes this statement, Jahnheinz Jahn illustrates prose rhythms with a passage from Nigerian writer Amos Tutuola's *Palm-Wine Drinkard*: "the rhythmical kind of narrative in which the repetition intensifies the dramatic quality of the action, makes Tutuola's story oral literature."[3]

9. Ong, pp. 45–46. See Bottcher on narrator's distance, pp. 1–5.
1. Unpublished essay as quoted by Ron Scollon, "Rhythmic Integration of Ordinary Talk," in *Analyzing Discourse: Text and Talk*, ed. Deborah Tannen (Georgetown: Georgetown University Press, 1982), p. 337. See also Emmanuel Obeichina, *Culture, Tradition and Society in the West African Novel* (Cambridge; Cambridge University Press, 1975), p. 174: "The main impulse in [Nigerian novelist Gabriel Okara's] *The Voice* obviously derives from the oral tradition . . . especially his deliberate repetitions, his metaphorical and hyperbolic elaborations and his colloquial rhythm."
2. Quoted in Jahnheinz Jahn, *Muntu* (New York: Grove Press, 1961), pp. 164–66. See original, Senghor, "L'Esthétique Négro-Africaine," *Liberté I, Néritude et Humanisme* (Paris: Editions du Seuil, 1964), pp. 211–12; and his premise: "*Image* et *rythme*, ce sont les deux traits fondamentaux du style négro–africain," p. 209. See also Obeichina: "The most striking feature of Okara's art is the repetition of single words, phrases, sentences, images or symbols, a feature highly developed in traditional narrative," p. 173; and Daniel P. Biebuyck, *Hero and Chief, Epic Literature from the Banyanga* (*Zaire Republic*) (Berkeley: University of California Press, 1978), p. 79: "Somewhat related to the formulaic system are the innumerable repetitions that add emphasis, effect, clarity and thus give fullness to the description [and] lend sonority, additional rhythm, and emphasis to the statements."
3. *Ibid.*, p. 168.

As Robert Kellogg tells us, there are many sorts of rhythm, "phonic, metrical, grammatical, metaphoric, imagistic, thematic";[4] and modern studies have argued that prose as well as verse has its rhythms, usually found first in syntax.[5] The repetitions of syntactic patterns of word and phrase underscore emphases (sometimes vocal) and stresses of meaning. Thus Roger Fowler describes in passages from David Storey the syntactic repetitions by which "syntax becomes rhythmical" and finds "sentence- and phrase-rhythms" there like "'thickening, deepening, then darkening'": "When syntax is repetitious, highlighting by reiteration a small number of patterns," he argues, "a palpable rhythm is established through the regularity of voice tunes."[6] Such repetition is the most obvious stylistic feature we notice in the passage from Achebe's novel. Syntactically, these repetitions stress key words, often polysyllables in contrast to the predominating one or two syllable words, chiefly subject nouns, object nouns, pronouns and modifiers of these nouns, and verbs, with occasional stress on time or place. Though emphasis may be difficult to assess uniformly—e.g., "through the NINE villages," or "through the NINE VILLAGES," or even possibly "through the nine VILLAGES"— there are some evident emphases on subjects, objects, or verbs; for example, "In the end Okonkwo threw the Cat" stresses all three. Parallelism enhances the repetitions and strengthens the rhythms: the parallel subject-verb sentence opening: "Okonkwo was" with "fame rested," or "Amalinze was" with "he was" with "It was." In the third (unquoted) paragraph, the parallel repetitions become insistent, as the verbs become increasingly active: "he was tall," "he breathed," "he slept," "he walked," "he seemed to walk," "He was going," "he did pounce," "he had," and finally, "He had no patience. . . ." Alliteration too accents these repetitions: "called" and "Cat"; "fight," "fiercest," and "founder"; "Spirit," "seven," and "seven." One may even discern a distinct metrical rhythm in some lines, such as, "The drums beat and the flutes sang and the spectators held their breath," which could

4. Robert Kellogg, "Literature, Nonliterature, and Oral Tradition," *New Literary History* 8 (Spring, 1977), 532. This issue of *NLH* has a valuable collection of essays on "Oral Cultures and Oral Performances."
5. Roger Fowler, *Linguistics and the Novel* (London: Methuen, 1977), p. 28: "the surface structure of a text (which is a sequence of sentences) has, like the surface structure of a sentence, qualities such as sequence, rhythm, spatial and temporal expressiveness." Raymond Chapman, *The Language of English Literature* (London: Edward Arnold, 1982), pp. 84–85: "We have seen that the traditional metres of English poetry have some connection with the rhythms of ordinary speech. . . . Rhythm of course is not confined to poetry . . . prose can have its distinctive cadences." Richard Ohmann, "Generative Grammars and the Concept or Literary Style," in *Linguistics and Literary Style*, ed. Donald Freeman (New York: Holt, Rinehart and Winston, 1970; previously published 1964), p. 260: "let me state this dogmatically—in prose, at least, rhythm as perceived is largely dependent upon syntax, and even upon content, not upon stress, intonation, and juncture alone."
6. Fowler, pp. 60, 63. See also Michael Riffaterre, "Criteria for Style Analysis," in *Essays on the Language of Literature*, eds. Seymour Chapman and Samuel Levin (Boston: Houghton Mifflin, 1967), pp. 420–29.

be marked, short, long, long; short, short, long, long, and so on. The third paragraph summarizes with a strongly trochaic, blues-like line: "That was many years ago, twenty years or more," but the near domination of metric regularity changes to "and during this time, Okonkwo's fame . . ." If there is such a thing as a dominant meter in prose (English is considered to be naturally iambic),[7] Achebe's prose would seem to be largely anapestic: "It was this/ man that Okon/kwo threw/ in a fight/ which the old/ men agreed/ was one/ of the fierc/est since the found/er of their town/ engaged a spir/it of the wild/ for sev/en days/ and sev/en nights," ending with a series of four iambs. Note another anapestic line: "Every nerve/ and every mus/cle stood out/ on their arms/ on their backs/ and their thighs." The point here is not to scan the lines but to show the rhythmical quality of the prose, more markedly rhythmical than traditional English prose, closer to an oral African quality.

I will explore now further levels of rhythm in the novel, moving from the stylistic to the structural, and then to the thematic, for not only the style but the entire narrative method can be considered rhythmical. Critics have mentioned the structuring of events in the novel in terms of rhythm. According to David Carroll, "the narrator then moves from this larger rhythm of the generations to the rhythm of the seasons, to Okonkwo and his sons repairing the walls; . . . yet the compassionate narrative voice seems to establish another rhythm, contrapuntal to Okonkwo's success."[8] S. O. Iyasere says, "Against the joyfully harmonic rhythm of this event [the locusts], the withdrawn, controlled formalism of the judgment of the *egwugwu* stands in sharp relief. By juxtaposing these events, Achebe orchestrates the modulating rhythms of Umoufia."[9] The structural tightness of the novel has been demonstrated by critics such as Robert Wren on the novel as a whole,[1] and Karl Bottcher on the narrator's voice and other stylistic techniques.[2] The narrative procedure that we see in the opening passages, involving a regular introduction of new materials, a little at a time, awaiting further amplification, is similar to African polymetric rhythms in which various meters are heard simultaneously, though not introduced at one time.[3] This is not a rhythm of percussive stress or beat, but an accentuation

7. Raymond Chapman, p. 43: "One of the most common metrical lines in English poetry is the iambic pentameter. . . . It follows very closely the pattern of everyday speech. . . . The iambic pentameter can be given many variations, but it remains close to what sounds 'natural' in English."
8. David Carroll, *Chinua Achebe* (New York: Twayne, 1970), pp. 37, 47.
9. Solomon O. Iyasere. "Narrative Techniques in Things Fall Apart,'" *New Letters* 40, 3 (1974), 76. See also Iyasere, "Oral Tradition in the Criticism of African Literature," *Journal of Modern African Studies* 13, 1 (1975), 111–14.
1. Robert Wren, *Achebe's World* (Washington, D.C: Three Continents Press, 1980), pp. 23 ff.
2. Bottcher, pp. 1–12.
3. Cf. Jahn, p. 165; and J. H. Kwabena Nketia, *The Music of Africa* (New York: Norton, 1974), p. 136: "the crucial point in polyrhythmic procedures . . . is the spacing or the placement of rhythmic patterns that are related to one another at different points in time so as to

by word, phrase or theme. As our awareness is sharpened to the introduction of new materials—the "additive" element of orality—we
become aware of the multiple rhythms at work: words that emulate the
"redundant" aspect of orality by early or late repetition (e.g. "breathe,"
"seven"), themes that are briefly expanded or developed later (e.g.
fierceness, wrestling), and those such as *masculine* and *feminine* that
evolve slowly but consistently. We thus become more conscious of the
process of development of words, phrases, and themes, and are less
likely to overemphasize one and miss another. We will also see that the
narrative makes increasingly evident a connection between these
rhythmic elements of style and form and the basic rhythm of clan life,
with the result that rhythm becomes significant thematically to
Okonkwo's response to clan life and to the ultimate breaking of that
life. I will sketch the pattern of the thirteen chapters of Part One to
show how the narrative is laid before us, like pieces of a complex puzzle
that slowly reveal coherence.

In Chapter One we meet Okonkwo as a man of great achievement
and greater potential, and we see the heritage of his father the failure,
a heritage Okonkwo wishes to flee. But as Okonkwo hastens to
achieve his goals he inadvertently becomes involved with the hostage,
the boy Ikemefuna whom the narrator refers to as "doomed" and "ill-
fated," though we are unsure why at this point. The pacing of Chapter Two is particularly suggestive of the narrative method used
thereafter in the novel. Set in three parts the chapter begins with
Okonkwo, about to go to bed, hearing "a clear overtone of tragedy in
the crier's voice." We drift briefly from that motif to hear lore of
the night before we continue the episode of Ikemefuna's arrival in
Umuofia into the care of Okonkwo. The second part turns abruptly to
the character of Okonkwo, "dominated by fear, the fear of failure and
of weakness," specifically of being thought an "agbala," a woman, or
a man with no titles, like his father. "And so Okonkwo was ruled by
one passion—to hate everything that his father Unoka had loved. One
of those things was gentleness and another was idleness" (10). When
in the third part the chapter returns to details of Ikemefuna's arrival—
as Bottcher says, "the point of departure is resumed almost word by
word"[4]—we have in a nutshell the whole novel: Okonkwo's passions,
hatred of weakness or womanliness, his success and strengths, his
connection with the hostage, and the overtones of tragedy.

---

produce the anticipated integrated structure." All of Chapter 12 is relevant here. Isaidore
Okpewho, *The Epic in Africa: Toward a Poetic of Oral Performance* (New York: Columbia
University Press, 1979), pp. 61–2, asks, "What is the nature of this musical element in
African heroic song?" and responds, "one fundamental aspect, its polyrhythmic nature, is
relevant here. . . . Polyrhythms . . . vary as one moves from east to west, with West Africa
as the region of greatest complexity."
4. Bottcher, p. 7.

The three parts of Chapter Two offer an episodic advancement of the plot, both adding to what has been mentioned and reflecting on the parts to which they are juxtaposed for commentary and contrast, as well as introducing new materials, all in the oral-rhythmic process of addition of new and amplification of old themes. Chapter Three, also of three parts (though the chapters vary generally from one to four parts), begins with Agbala, not the scornful title of "woman" but the Oracle whose priestess people visit "to discover what the future held . . . or to consult the spirits of their departed fathers" (12). Agbala had once told Unoka why he was a failure. Now, to overcome the disadvantages of a useless father, Okonkwo visits not Agbala but, more practically, a wealthy man for a loan of yams to start his own farm. Part Three then reverses the trend of the story thus far, for Okonkwo fails, and establishes the possibility of things going badly to the point of suicide. "The year had gone mad," and all his seed yams have been destroyed. One man hangs himself, but Okonkwo survives because of "his inflexible will."

Having established Okonkwo's direction, the narrator wishes to expand the context of the novel and offer several correctives, for the implications of the incident of Okonkwo's "survival" are not resolved until Chapter Four. "'Looking at a king's mouth,' said an old man, 'one would think he never sucked at his mother's breast.' He was talking about Okonkwo" (19), who had indeed forgotten his maternal life, and preferred "to kill a man's spirit" by calling him "woman." Okonkwo's fear of weakness is here qualified as specifically anti-feminine: "To show affection was a sign of weakness," so he beats his hostage, and in the next part beats one of his wives in violation of the Week of Peace dedicated to the Goddess Ani, an evil act that "'can ruin the whole clan. The earth goddess whom you have insulted may refuse to give us her increase, and we shall all perish'" (22).

The importance of the feminine element in the culture could be overlooked because of the emphasis Okonkwo places on masculine virtues and achievements for which he is justly celebrated. But the novel steadfastly points to the centrality of the feminine.[5] Okonkwo's masculine sensibility terrorizes his son Nwoye whom he wishes to be "a great farmer and a great man" (23), and enhances his affection for the already manly Ikemefuna, who significantly entertains such "womanly" traits as telling (24) and hearing (42) folk tales. Okonkwo's emphasis on "his inflexible will" as the cause of his survival is corrected here when the narrator explicitly states, "the personal

5. For discussions of the feminine, see Ernest Champion, "The Story of a Man and his People," *NAIF* 6 (1972), 274; G. D. Killam, *The Novels of Chinua Achebe* (New York: Africana, 1969), pp. 20 ff.; Iyasere, "Narrative . . . ," pp. 79 ff.; Wilfred Cartey, *Whispers from a Continent* (New York: Random House, 1949), Chapter 1, "Mother and Child." Awareness of the masculine/feminine element is now widely manifested by critics.

dynamism required to counter the forces of these extremes of weather would be far too great for the human frame" (24).

One new element is introduced in this chapter, the concern with customs. Since Okonkwo had violated the custom of the Week of Peace, the discussion is appropriate, but its importance here is in revealing that the clan's customs are not absolute: "the punishment for breaking the Peace of Ani had become very mild in their clan." The men mock those clans who do not alter customs as they see fit: "they lack understanding." If we think too much on change as things-falling-apart, we are apt to miss the ameliorative process of change which is inherent in the clan. Throughout the story several old men and some young men ponder the sanity of customs, such as the particularly agonizing one of killing twins, and we are conscious that eventually it too would be changed. Desire for change, founded in emotional distress, is what brings Nwoye to Christianity for solace.

Chapter Five returns to another feast of the Earth Goddess to elaborate her position. The "source of all fertility[,] Ani played a greater part in the life of the people than any other deity. She was the ultimate judge of morality and conduct" (26). During her feast, for which the local women inscribe themselves and their huts with detailed patterns, and to which visitors come from the motherland (and reportedly spoil the children!), the violence of Okonkwo once more erupts. He rages that a tree has been killed—"As a matter of fact the tree was very much alive"—and then shoots at his wife, the one who (as we later learn) had left her husband out of admiration for Okonkwo's excellence as a wrestler. The implications of this wild act of shooting eventually become clear for though there was no formal violation of the harvest festival, Okonkwo here mishandles a gun as he will later do in fatefully killing a boy.

The remainder of Chapter Five is filled with the wonderful power of the drums, like the rhythmic pulse of the heart of the clan, sounding insistently behind the action—"Just then the distant beating of drums began to reach them" (30), "The drums were still beating, persistent and unchanging" (31), "In the distance the drums continued to beat" (32). They are a pulse countered only by Okonkwo's roaring at his daughter Ezinma whom he wished were a boy. At this point rhythm takes on thematic dimensions as the narrator contrasts Okonkwo's eccentric or asymmetrical behavior with the rhythmic spirit of the clan. The significance of the drum beat is amplified in the following chapter (Six) where the chief entertainment of the clan, wrestling, takes place on the *ilo*, the village circle, a dramatic space where the central physical and cultural acts of the people occur (recall the spiritual "dark, endless *space* in the presence of Agbala," 12). Later (Chapter Ten) judgments are passed there on major legal cases, and finally (Chapter Twenty-three) when the clan is disrupted and the imagery is of coldness and ashes, no acts take place: "the village *ilo* where they had always gathered for a moon-play was empty" (139). Our attention is drawn inexorably to the *ilo* by the drums so that by the time the celebration begins, we watch the people drawn in every sense together by the drums, for the drummers are literally "possessed by the spirit of the drums" (33) and their "frantic rhythm was . . . the very heart-beat of the people" (35–36). Rhythm is central. We are to see this celebration as the focal dramatic act of the dramatic space which is the center of the people—harmonic life—as if we as visitors to the clan must see at least once what rhythm means in its fullest articulation, must be reminded what it was like when, as the novel opened, Okonkwo threw the Cat, and when now, in almost exact repetition for Okonkwo, for his wife, for the clan, "The muscles on their arms and their thighs and on their backs stood out and twitched, . . .

> *Has he thrown a hundred Cats?*
> *He has thrown four hundred Cats."* (36)

This is the cultural center of the novel—the *ilo* becomes a metaphor for the dramatic space of the novel, the cultural locus upon which Okonkwo performs, first as wrestler, then as tragic actor. In *Achebe's World* Robert Wren also emphasizes this chapter: the novel's twenty-five chapters "are upon closer analysis divided into four groups of six chapters each, with one pivotal chapter, XIII, where Okonkwo accidentally kills Ezeudo's son and must flee."[6] Wren goes on to note that Part One actually "has two six-chapter units plus the pivotal chapter." The stress then is on Chapter Six, the drum chapter, as a center of this Part (for with Seven we move to the killing of Ikemefuna), so there is an imbalance with Chapter Thirteen: the "alternating chapters show Okonkwo in crisis": VII, IX, XI and XIII.[7]

Hereafter in Chapter Seven as things begin to break down, we can view Okonkwo's eventual tragedy as a violation of this harmony. We notice how he stands obnoxious and restless against the festival of drums: "never . . . enthusiastic over feasts," he picks a quarrel over the "dead" tree, shoots at his wife, jealously sees Obierika's son become wrestling hero instead of his son (34). Playwright and critic Wole Soyinka tells us that a person must constantly attempt to bridge the gulf between the area of earthly existence and the existence of deities, ancestors and the unborn by "sacrifices, the rituals, the ceremonies of appeasement to those cosmic powers which lie guardian to the gulf . . . Tragedy, in Yoruba traditional drama, is the anguish of this severance, the fragmentation of essence from self."[8]

---

6. Wren, p. 23.
7. *Ibid.*, p. 24.
8. *Myth, Literature, and the African World* (Cambridge: Cambridge University Press, 1976), pp. 144–45.

Achebe's narrator underscores the same sense of cosmic responsibility in Chapter Thirteen: "A man's life from birth to death was a series of transition rites which brought him nearer and nearer to his ancestors" (85). Achebe's is not Yoruba fiction, but Soyinka's description gives, I think, an important clue to Okonkwo's tragedy: separation from what the clan adheres to as value, specifically here the rhythmic center of life.

In Chapter Seven the actions run together without division and there is a symbolic heightening of word and action as if we are continuing from the previous chapter with specially meaningful narrative. As Okonkwo told Nwoye and Ikemefuna "masculine stories of violence and bloodshed . . . they sat in darkness," a terrible symbolic image, especially in contrast to Nwoye's love of "stories his mother used to tell," folk tales of mercy and pity at which "he warmed himself" as Vulture did in the tale (38). (Note that Okonkwo almost inadvertently remembers in detail his mother's folk tale, 53.) Then the locusts came, destroyers later identified with "the white man" (97). Okonkwo is warned "to have nothing to do with" killing Ikemefuna, for "He calls you his father." But then—in the suddenly symbolic phrasing of the narrator, "in the narrow line in the heart of the forest," the narrow line between obedience to the Oracle or obedience to humanity and the advice of Obierika, a line which crossed either way would be destructive—"Dazed with fear, Okonkwo drew his matchet and cut him down. He was afraid of being thought weak" (43). And Nwoye, knowing what his father had done, felt "something . . . give way inside him," just as he did before when he "heard the voice of an infant crying in the thick forest," thrown there to die in a pot. "It descended on him again, this feeling, when his father walked in, that night after killing Ikemefuna" (43).

The rhythm of the narrative does not end here with the broken rhythm of Okonkwo's life. The style continues much as before; Wilfred Cartey observes Achebe's repetition of images in Part Two: "When the rain finally came, it was in large, solid drops of frozen water which the people called 'the nuts of the water of heaven'" (92); similarly, Nwoye feels Christianity "like the drops of frozen rain melting on the dry palate of the panting earth" (104).[9] In the first chapter of Part Two, Okonkwo is instructed through a kind of repetition or review of his life from childhood to manhood, for the purpose of renewing his way of seeing. The first truth he is taught is the role of the female; not only has Okonkwo committed a female crime of inadvertently killing a boy when his gun exploded, but his penalty is seven (the number we saw in the opening passage) years exile in his motherland:

9. Cartey, p. 100.

Can you tell me, Okonkwo, why it is that one of the commonest
names we give our children is Nneka, or 'Mother is Supreme'? We
^A
all know that a man is the head of the family and his wives do his
bidding. A child belongs to its father *and his family and* not to its
^B   ^C
mother *and her family.* A man belongs to his fatherland *and* not
^B
to his motherland. *And yet we say* Nneka . . .
^C   ^A

You do not know the answer? So you see that you are a child. . . .
Listen to me. . . . *It's true that* a child belongs to its father. *But*
^B
when a father beats his child, it seeks sympathy in its mother's
^D
hut. A man belongs to his fatherland *when things are good and*
^B
life is sweet. But when there is sorrow and bitterness he finds
refuge in his motherland. Your mother is there to protect you.
^D   ^D
She is buried there. And that is why we say that mother is supreme
^A
(94).

In spite of the additive qualities of the motherland (D) as sympathy,
refuge and protection, Okonkwo's course is clear cut: he will eschew
the feminine and, unchanged, act towards others as he acted before.
Though the rhythms of the clan are by no mean perfect, he refuses to
respond to their fulfillment and direction, and refers later to these
years as "wasted." "He cannot see the wise balance," Ravenscroft
writes, "in the tribal arrangement by which the female principle is felt
to be simultaneously weak and sustaining."[1] But the newly introduced
element of the white men will alter his course much further. As subtle as the colonists' entrance is the narrator's addition of a feature at
a time: at first an unknown, the white men become a joke, then formidable missionaries, then government, then place of judgment, then
"religion and trade and government" and prison (123).

For all the disruption wrought by the whites, Christianity is not
itself necessarily bad. The customs of the clan, which had been considered by some to be foolish or baneful and would in time be altered
as others had, are accelerated to change by Christianity. Nwoye
accepts the religion primarily because it answers a felt need. "It was
the poetry of the new religion, something felt in the marrow," like the
folk tales he loved earlier. "The hymn about brothers who sat in darkness and in fear seemed to answer a vague and persistent question
that haunted his young soul [just as he and Ikemefuna had sat in darkness listening to Okonkwo's tales of the past]—the question of the
twins crying in the bush and the question of Ikemefuna who was

1. Arthur Ravenscroft, *Chinua Achebe* (London: Longmans, Green, 1969), p. 13.

killed" (104). Christianity speaks directly to Nwoye's needs, not in rational or doctrinal terms but in mercy and comfort of spirit. Nor does it seem that his reaction is destructive of any of the prior values of the clan; certainly Ikemefuna was a richly responsive human, lacking neither masculine strength nor feminine mercy, and the only counter to Nwoye's inclinations was Okonkwo's insistence on masculinity. Christianity itself is greatly varied by its practitioners, the missionaries, for whereas Brown (midway between black and white) actually tried to understand African belief and respond with some sensitivity to the people (he is still obtuse: "a frontal attack . . . would not succeed," 128), another, with the nondescript name of Smith, "saw things as black and white. And black was evil" (130). Such dogmatic cruelty had not appeared in the novel until this missionary; and of course he succeeds because he is inflexible and tyrannical, while complex persons of compassion are overcome or bypassed.

> Seven years *was a long time* to be away *from one's* clan. *A man's* place *was not always there, waiting for him. As soon as he* left, *someone else rose and filled it. The* clan *was like a lizard; if it* lost *its tail it soon grew another.*
>
> *Okonkwo* knew *these things. He* knew *that he had* lost *his* place *among the nine masked spirits who administered justice in the* clan. *He* had lost *the chance to lead his warlike* clan *against the new religion, which, he was told, had gained ground. He* had lost *the years in which he might have taken the* highest titles *in the* clan. *But some of these* losses *were not irreparable. He was determined that his* return *should be marked by his people.* He would return *with a flourish, and regain the* seven *wasted years.*
>
> *Even in his first year of exile he had begun to plan for his* return. *The first thing he* would do *would be to* rebuild *his compound on a more magnificent scale. He* would build *a bigger barn than he had before and* he would build *huts for two new wives. Then he* would show *his wealth by initiating his sons in the 'ozo' society. Only the* really great men *in the* clan *were able to do this. Okonkwo* saw clearly the *high esteem in which he* would be held, *and* he saw *himself taking the* highest title *in the land.* (121)

The rhythms are clearly evident with the beat of key words and tenses and voices: "he knew" (twice), "he had lost" (three times), and so on to "he would return," "he would build," "he would show," "he would be held," and "he saw." One of the peculiar effects of this repetition is that "he" is doing all the acting and thinking so that the repetitions advance with very little return to the beginning for elaboration. The "redundancy" lacks the element of "addition." Okonkwo marches forward, dreaming, not reflecting, not in fact building upon the prior words and thoughts. His mind works from knowing in truth to seeing in fantasy, from knowledge of loss to determination to overcome and excel. The repetitions mirror the stress between Okonkwo's linear mentality and the clan's circular, rhythmic mode of repetition. For Okonkwo personally nothing has changed at home: he curses his son Nwoye from the family and wishes Ezinma were a boy, "She understood things so perfectly" (122). Socially, however, outside Okonkwo's mind, there is now the new religion, trade, government; and everyone knew the white man "'has put a knife on the things that held us together and we have fallen apart'" (124–25).

The rhythmic coherence of the novel is sustained through to the end, at least when the narrator is describing the actions of the clan. The words of the District Commissioner, however, or words describing his actions, appear to be syntactically and philosophically different. For instance, in the final chapter we read the complex sentence:

> *When the District Commissioner arrived at Okonkwo's compound at the head of an armed band of soldiers and court messengers he found a small crowd of men sitting wearily in the* obi. *He commanded them to come outside, and they obeyed without a murmur.* (146)

The sentences are "subordinative" and sequential in narration of facts—this happened and then that—not at all in the "additive" rhythmic manner of accumulation of detail by repetition.[2] We are confronted by the difference between his speech and the clan's speech when the Commissioner complains to himself, "One of the most infuriating habits of these people was their love of superfluous words," for redundancy or copiousness is indeed one of the marks of oral speech. Rhythmic language follows as Obierika and his fellows approach Okonkwo's body hanging from a tree:

> *There was a* small bush *behind Okonkwo's* compound. *The only opening into this* bush *from the* compound *was a little* round hole *in the red-earth* wall *through which fowls went in and out in their endless search for food. The* hole *would not let a man through. It was to this* bush *that Obierika led the Commissioner and his men. They skirted round the* compound, *keeping close to the* wall. *The only sound they made was with their feet as they crushed dry leaves.*

The passage features assonance of the "o" to depict the "round hole," the now-familiar parallelism, repetition, specificity of detail and images, and continual expansion of the scene by repetition and addition. The verb "to be" dominates the sentences—"There was," "the opening . . . was," "it was"—and the weight of meaning is carried by

---

2. Cf. Senghor, p. 214: "Il y a plus, la structure de la phrase négro-africaine est naturellement rythmée. Car, tandis que les langues indo-européennes usent d'une syntaxe Iogique de subordination, les langues négro-africaines recourent, plus volontiers, à une syntaxe intuitive de *coordination et de juxtaposition.*" See also Robert Kauffman, "African Rhythm: A Reassessment," *Ethnomusicology* 24, 3 (1980), 402, 406.

objects, "bush," "compound," "hole," as if one's actions are relatable chiefly to stable poles of identification in the village rather than to one's personal activities.[3] The monosyllabic detail of the words quoted above gives them a symbolic tone, as if that little hole were the impossible fissure through which Okonkwo had passed by suicide into nonexistence. The rhythmic phrasing stands sharply against the closing words of the Commissioner which are again logical and process-oriented, analytical, unsuperfluous, and non-African, with weight on verbs: he "arrived," "found," "commanded . . . and they obeyed." His arrogant dismissal of Okonkwo's story as deserving a bare paragraph in his book is mirrored in the straightforward, one-dimensional prose.

The style of the novel and its structure thus draw attention to the exquisite tension between traditional English prose and the unique African and/or Igbo quality Achebe has created; it is, as Lloyd Brown says, "a total cultural experience, . . . the embodiment of its civilization."[4] Achebe himself is keenly aware of this quality of African style, as he points out in a passage from a Fulani creation myth: "You notice . . . how in the second section . . . we have that phrase *became too proud* coming back again and again like the recurrence of a dominant beat in rhythmic music?"[5] In a discussion of his own prose, he illustrates "how I approach the use of English":

> *'I want one of my sons to join these people and be my eyes there. If there is nothing in it you will come back. But if there is something there you will bring home my share. The world is like a Mask, dancing. If you want to see it well you do not stand in one place. My spirit tells me that those who do not befriend the white man today will be saying* had we known *tomorrow.'*

> Now supposing I had put it another way. Like this for instance:

> *'I am sending you as my representative among these people— just to be on the safe side in case the new religion develops. One has to move with the times or else one is left behind. I have a hunch that those who fail to come to terms with the white man may well regret their lack of foresight.'*[6]

3. In the quotation from p. 123 the repetition of "he" and active verbs—"He knew," "he would do," "he would rebuild."—confirms our sense that Okonkwo is operating outside the cultural rhythms of the clan. Marjorie Winters in "An Objective Approach to Achebe's Style," *Research in African Literatures* 12, 1 (1981), 55–56, describes the length of the narrator's sentences, his spare use of adjectives and adverbs, the "unusual" number of "introductory demonstratives," the clarity achieved by his "redundancy of connective signposts" ('and so'), "as well as other repetitive elements." Her approach differs from mine but her results do not oppose conclusions drawn here.
4. Lloyd Brown, "Cultural Norms and Modes of Perception in Achebe's Fiction," *Critical Perspectives on Nigerian Literature*, ed. Bemth Undfors (Washington, D.C.: Three Continents Press, 1976), p. 133.
5. Chinua Achebe, "Language and the Destiny of Man," Morning *Yet on Creation Day* (New York: Doubleday, 1975), pp. 56–7.
6. Achebe, "The African Writer and the English Language," *Morning Yet on Creation Dag*, pp. 101–02.

Though Achebe does not spell out the differences between these passages, he seems fully conscious that the repetition of the "if" clauses creates that quality of rhythm which is missing in the "English" version, the metaphorical phrasing which, we should observe, is used in a colloquial rather than philosophical or proverbial sense. Rhythm, as Achebe seems well aware, thus can range from a stress within a phrase or sentence, to the structuring principle of a paragraph, to the form of an entire work. Through such a reading we may learn about the nature of rhythm and orality, and about the form of the novel, but especially we may better see the unique English Achebe has created and realize its African tone in order "to understand another whose language" one, as a non-African, "does not speak." [7]

C. L. INNES

"A Less Superficial Picture": *Things Fall Apart*[†]

Joyce Cary's *Mister Johnson* tells the story of a young Nigerian clerk who takes a bribe, loses his job, regains it, helps and encourages the young British colonial officer Rudbeck build a road, embezzles taxes to do so, murders a white storekeeper, and is subsequently tried and executed by Rudbeck. The novel seeks above all to celebrate the character of Johnson, who is portrayed as a Dionysian character, bursting with emotion, song, dance and spontaneity, and enamoured of European civilization. He is contrasted both with the self-interested and unimaginative pagan and Muslim Africans and with the British colonial officers, who are characteristically tight-lipped, constrained by reason and the letter of the law. Johnson provides Rudbeck with the inspiration and energy as well as the labour force and the money to build a road through his district. Cary's implication is that Johnson's qualities must be linked to and put to the service of Rudbeck's vision and technological knowledge, and that Rudbeck can become more humane and more creative by learning from Johnson, although Johnson's anarchic and destructive tendencies must be suppressed. At the end of the novel, Rudbeck follows the letter of the law in trying and condemning Johnson, but bends the law by agreeing to personally execute Johnson, who pleads with him to do so, reminding Rudbeck that he (Johnson) has always regarded him as 'his father and mother'.

Achebe originally planned his first novel as another version of *Mister Johnson*. However, the rewriting turned into two novels, *Things Fall Apart* and *No Longer at Ease*, and it is the second which seems at first

7. Achebe, "Where Angels Fear to Tread," *Morning Yet on Creation Day*, p. 79.
† From *Chinua Achebe* (Cambridge: Cambridge University Press, 1990), 21–41. Reprinted with permission of Oxford University Press, Inc.

glance to carry the burden of responding to Cary's story of a clerk who takes bribes while working for the British administration and is disgraced. But while the plots of *Mister Johnson* and *No Longer At Ease* are similar, thematically *Things Fall Apart* takes up the issues raised by Cary's novel. It is an attempt to give a less 'superficial' picture 'not only of the country—but even of the Nigerian character';[1] it also dramatizes the conflict between intuitive feeling and rigid social codes, between liberalism and conservatism, and between creativity and sterility. As Cary's novel opposes the spontaneous African man of feeling inspired by the romance of European civilization to the iron rule of native conservatism or of European law, so *Things Fall Apart* contrasts Okonkwo's rigidity and refusal to acknowledge feeling (a trait shared by the District Commissioner) with the intuitive knowledge and imaginative sympathy felt by Unoka and Nwoye, which the latter imagines to be a property of the western missionaries. Whereas in Cary's novel these opposing tendencies cluster around European and African respectively, in *Things Fall Apart* they become associated in Okonkwo's mind—and also in the reader's—with masculine and feminine principles.

The fact that the conflicts are located *in* the African community and then shadowed by the British characters makes an important difference, for at once the Africans become something more than symbols of qualities which, however important, are nevertheless subordinate elements in the total complex of the European psyche. Achebe's characters are complex individuals, types rather than archetypes, the resolution of whose conflicts is central to the plot. Okonkwo's role is not to save the British administrator and it is clear that Achebe's Europeans, even the more liberal ones like Mr. Brown, will never dream that they have anything to learn from Africans—who may be studied but never imitated. That is part of the tragedy for the Africans, who find it almost impossible to comprehend the depth and consequences of the white man's arrogance.

Part 1 of *Things Fall Apart* focuses on two things: the portrayal of Okonkwo and his psychology, and the portrayal of the social, political and religious life of Umuofia, the Igbo village to which Okonkwo belongs. On reading *Things Fall Apart* after *Mister Johnson* one becomes aware of a number of specific ways in which Achebe's version of African society contrasts with Cary's. One of the earliest scenes in *Mister Johnson* involves the bartering of Bamu, the young woman Johnson seeks to marry, by her 'pagan' family who equate her with a choice piece of horseflesh. Her family is motivated by sheer greed, and family loyalty is seen chiefly as the exercise of property rights. Bamu herself has no feeling other than contempt for Johnson, and stoically accepts her fate as a counter in the bargaining. She will

1. 'Chinua Achebe', *African Writers Talking*, p. 4.

stay with him only as long as the terms of the bargain are kept. One may contrast Achebe's depiction of the agreement and discussion over the marriage contract for Obierika's daughter, Akueke. First there is a long period of drinking and chatting before the business of settling the bridal dowry is brought up. As if to make the contrast quite explicit, one of the men compares their traditional method of using a bundle of sticks to settle the dowry with the customs of other clans such as Abame and Aninta: 'All their customs are upside down. They do not decide bride price as we do, with sticks. They haggle and bargain as if they were buying a goat or a cow in the market.'[2] Achebe does not let the point rest, for we are shown yet another part of a marriage ceremony in part 2, the consummation of the marriage of Uchendu's youngest son (pp. 92–3); in part 3 the question of the marriage of Okonkwo's daughters is discussed, and we learn of their willing agreement to await their return to Umuofia. We are also reminded several times of the special relationship between Okonkwo and Ekwefi.

Bamu regards her marriage to Mister Johnson as no more than a business proposition; she will cook and breed for him only as long as he can provide for her, and she prepares to leave him as soon as he is in trouble. There is never any question that Okonkwo's wives would desert him—especially when he is in trouble—despite his hasty and sometimes cruel treatment of them. Relationships between Igbo husbands and wives in *Things Fall Apart* are as complex and varied as the relationship between Rudbeck and his wife, Celia, in *Mister Johnson*. In the same chapter telling of Akueke's betrothal, there is the story of Ndulue, whose wife Ozoemena died immediately after she learned of his death. '"It was always said that Ndulue and Ozoemena had one mind." said Obierika. "I remember when I was a young boy there was a song about them. He could not do anything without telling her"' (pp. 47–8). Then there is the relationship between Ekwefi and Okonkwo, his gruff affection for her and his concern when she follows Chielo and her daughter, and the story of her coming to him when he had been too poor to marry her earlier. We are shown also the settlement by the elders of a marriage dispute—an attempt to bring about reconciliation in the best interests of the couple and the community—very different from the self-interested commands of Bamu's brother, Aliu, or of the Waziri who supposedly governs Fada, where Cary's novel is set.

The scene showing the deliberation and judgement of the elders, along with other such scenes in the novel, also contrasts Achebe's version of African government with Cary's. Whereas *Mister Johnson* shows only despotic and greedy native rulers with little concern for the welfare of the people they govern, *Things Fall Apart* portrays a group of elders who share decision making, who are trusted by the

2. *Things Fall Apart*, p. 51. Subsequent page references to this novel will be introduced in the text.

people, and whose primary concern is the maintenance of a peaceful, prosperous and respected community for all. Moreover, their decisions are neither arbitrary nor individualistic, as Cary's novel asserts, but grow out of a long tradition and a finely interwoven set of beliefs—religious, social and political.

Perhaps one of the most significant things about *Things Fall Apart* is the way in which it demonstrates the intricate relationship between a man's individual psychology and the social context in which he has grown up. And that is where the novel makes its firmest response to Cary. Mister Johnson is representative of the free and unfettered spirit; he is an earlier version of Gulley Jimson, the carefree artist in Cary's later and more successful novel, *The Horse's Mouth*. So in terms of the theme of the novel it is appropriate that he have no family, no background, no social context other than the vague suggestion of a mission education. He is a man without roots, belonging to romance rather than to historical narrative. The European reader, long accustomed to such figures in literature if not in life—wandering poets, Synge's tramps and playboys, bohemian artists—does not readily question Mister Johnson's rootlessness. But Mister Johnson is essentially a European creation. To the Nigerian reader, according to Achebe, such a figure is hard to imagine; no Southern Nigerian (as Johnson is supposed to be) in the early part of the twentieth century could be without a family or relatives to care for him and come to his assistance when he is in trouble.[3]

However, after encountering Chinua Achebe's novels even the European reader may be struck by the discontinuity between Mister Johnson's character and his origins. Cary's novel rests on an opposition between the archetypal force Johnson suggests—id, or feeling and instinct—and the Europeans—who are associated with superego, or moral and intellectual qualities—so matching closely the kind of colonialist psychology and projection described by Fanon and Zahar. Nowhere in *Mister Johnson* does Cary suggest that the African might have his own system of values, intelligently conceived and based on a long and evolving tradition, comprehending concern for others and the welfare of the community as a whole. The theme and project of *Mister Johnson* demand that the African possess not even a 'primitive' set of beliefs, for any action in terms of mind rather than feeling or sensual gratification would spoil the series of contrasts. It might also question the assumptions upon which colonial rule is based.

The Igbo community presented to us in *Things Fall Apart* is one which has established a balance, though sometimes an uneasy one, between the values clustered around individual achievement and those associated with community, or between materialism and spirituality. Those groups of values tend to be identified as masculine and

3. Conversation with Chinua Achebe and students included at the University of Massachusetts, Amherst, 1974.

feminine respectively and are epitomized in the two proverbs, 'Yam is King', and 'Mother is supreme', which dominate the first and second parts of the novel. Okonkwo prizes 'manliness' above all, and judges action and talk by that criterion, classifying everything he admires as 'manly' and everything he despises as 'womanly'. Fear of being called, like his father, an *agbala*, meaning both a man without a title and an old woman, is shown to be the motivating force in his life. He continually regrets that Ezinma, his favourite daughter, is a girl, laments that Nwoye 'has too much of his mother in him'; and it is fear of being thought effeminate that drives him to participate in the killing of Ikemefuna. In the use of these opposing categories of male and female, Okonkwo shares the thinking of his people, although he is less respectful than they are to the values embodied by the Earth Goddess, Ani, the priestess Chiclo, and the sympathy, comfort and solace offered by his motherland. But the reader never doubts that he is the product of his society's system, and from the very beginning we are told that he is one of the great men of the village. The texture of his mind is made up of the proverbs, the sayings, the imagery, the rituals, the language which embody that system. He is, as A. R. JanMohamed argues, a *type* of his society, and Achebe is careful to show us how he has come into being through a combination of social moulding and family circumstance.[4] In this abstract sense he is much closer to Cary's Rudbeck and Bulteel and Rackham than he is to Mister Johnson whose most consistent trait is his lack of any social or psychological roots.

There is in *Things Fall Apart* one character who bears some resemblance to Mister Johnson, and that is Unoka, Okonkwo's father. Like Johnson, he is a man who refuses to accept responsibility for his debts, who is childlike and charming and exasperating. Like Johnson he is essentially an artist:

> Unoka, for that was his father's name, had died ten years ago. In his day he was lazy and improvident and was quite incapable of thinking about tomorrow. If any money came his way, and it seldom did, he immediately bought gourds of palmwine, called round his neighbours and made merry. He always said that whenever he saw a dead man's mouth he saw the folly of not eating what one had in one's own lifetime. Unoka was, of course, a debtor, and he owed every neighbour some money, from a few cowries to quite substantial amounts. (p. 8)

Unlike Mister Johnson, Unoka *does* have a family which is obliged, though shamefacedly, to take care of him. And one of the themes in the novel deals with the importance of kin to the Igbo. Unoka is taken care of by his son and the community does not let him starve. In his

4. 'Chinua Achebe: The Generation of Realism', *Manichean Aesthetics*, pp. 151–84.

trouble Okonkwo is sustained materially and psychologically by his mother's relatives, and one of the bitterest things for Okonkwo to envision is the breaking up of clan and the family system through the influence of missionaries like Mr Kiaga who praise Nwoye for leaving his family: 'Blessed is he who leaves his father and his mother in my name', he quotes from the New Testament—a declaration which, we are told, 'Nwoye did not understand fully' (p. 142).

Unoka is also unlike Mister Johnson in that he is a conscious rather than an unconscious artist. His music does not just well instinctively from some primitive source, nor is Unoka unaware of the effect he is creating and the techniques which he is using. Whereas Mister Johnson is presented as a youth who creates in a kind of trance, whose consciousness is submerged in a Dionysian state of oneness with his audience, nature and the work of creation, Unoka is both creator and critic, he is a craftsman and teacher as well as a man of feeling. Although Unoka is a minor character, sketched in briefly in the passage above, he is given a context: a social and natural environment, memories of childhood, of past festivals and seasons, images of bright skies, hovering kites, snatches of folk tale, anecdote and everyday conversation about the weather and village affairs. And so Unoka emerges not as an archetypal character, but as a realistic one, not a rootless free spirit, but a believable human being, differing in degree rather than essence from the norms of his own and other communities.

But *Things Fall Apart* does continue Cary's identification of intuitive knowledge and feeling with music and poetry. As Mister Johnson in some sense embodies the feeling and imagination that Rudbeck often tries to suppress, so Unoka is identified with the tenderness and humanity with which the inarticulate Okonkwo wrestles. We are told that Okonkwo's whole life is dominated by the fear of being thought effeminate like his father, that he discourages his son from listening to 'womanly' folk tales and songs, and that the unspoken fear that Nwoye will turn out like Unoka haunts him. Both Okonkwo and Rudbeck are commanded to execute the boys who call them father, and both determine to participate in that execution in ways unacceptable to the elders in their communities. In both novels, this incident takes a crucial place and significance: in *Mister Johnson* it is the final act, approved wholeheartedly by Johnson and apparently intended to suggest new hope for Rudbeck who has allowed Johnson's 'inspiration' to supersede the exact letter of the law.

> Johnson, seeing his gloom and depression, exerts himself. 'Don' you mind, sah, about dis hanging. I don't care for it one lil bit. Why'—he laughs with an air of surprise and discovery—'I know fit nutting about it—he too quick. Only I like you do him yourself, sah. If you no fit to shoot me. I don' 'gree for dem sergeant

do it, too much. He no my frien'. But you my frien'. You my father and my mother. I tink you hang me youself' . . .

Johnson knows then that he won't have to get up again from his knees. He feels the relief like a reprieve, unexpected, and he thanks Rudbeck for it. He triumphs in the greatness, the goodness, and the daring inventiveness of Rudbeck. All the force of his spirit is concentrated in gratitude and triumphant devotion; he is calling at the world to admit that there is no god like his god. He burst out aloud 'Oh Lawd, I tank you for my frien' Miser Rudbeck—de bigges' heart in de worl'.'

Rudbeck leans through the door, aims the carbine at the back of the boy's head, and blows his brains out. Then he turns and hands it back to the sentry. 'Don't forget to pull it through.'

He is surprised at himself, but he doesn't feel any violent reaction. He is not overwhelmed with horror. On the contrary, he feels a peculiar relief and escape, like a man who, after a severe bilious attack, has just been sick.[5]

As a number of critics have argued, Cary wishes to indicate that Rudbeck, in the narrator's words at the end of the novel 'growing ever more free in the inspiration which seems already his own idea', has moved away from mechanical rationalism, signified by the weighing of Johnson and establishing of his equivalent in bags of money and goods, to acknowledging Johnson's humanity and Rudbeck's own sense of responsibility to the boy who calls him his 'father and mother'.

The boy who is executed in *Things Fall Apart* is Ikemefuna, to whose significance readers are alerted in the very first chapter of *Things Fall Apart* when we are told in the final sentence of that chapter that Okonkwo was asked to 'Look after the doomed lad who was sacrificed to the village of Umuofia by their neighbours to avoid war and bloodshed. The ill-fated lad was called Ikemefuna' (p. 6). We are reminded again in chapter 2 that Ikemefuna's story is a sad one, 'still told in Umuofia unto this day' (p. 9). Hence the reader watches Ikemefuna's appearance and developing relationship with Nwoye and Okonkwo with apprehension and alert attention. It becomes apparent that Ikemefuna, although an outsider, is the ideal type of the clan. As a skilful hunter *and* musician, sympathetic to the troubles of his adopted sister when she carelessly breaks her water pot, encouraging Nwoye to develop the 'manly' virtues that please Okonkwo, he succeeds in balancing masculine and feminine attributes. Hence the killing of Ikemefuna is not only a tragic destruction of a promising and guiltless individual, it connotes the murder of the clan's potential; Ikemefuna's sacrifice is both a symbol of what the clan lacks and a realistic dramatisation of the clan's inability to maintain a harmonious balance

5. *Mister Johnson* (Harmondsworth: Penguin, 1965), pp. 248–9.

between male and female principles, rather than an uneasy dialectic without synthesis. The image of tension between opposites, of a taut balance destroyed, is taken up and emphasized when we are told of Nwoye's reaction to the killing: 'Something seemed to give way inside him, like the snapping of a tightened bow' (p. 43). The sacrifice of Ikemefuna and his father's participation in it is the focal act which finally alienates Nwoye from the clan and Okonkwo and leads him to seek a more humane community among the Christians.[6]

Whereas Mister Johnson accepts his fate without question and is full of gratitude to Rudbeck for taking the execution into his own hands, an act which for Rudbeck is a courageous one, Ikemefuna instinctively turns to Okonkwo for salvation, and Okonkwo's intervention is portrayed as an act of cowardice: 'Dazed with fear, Okonkwo drew his matchet and cut him down. He was afraid of being thought weak' (p. 43). For Rudbeck, the shooting is cathartic: 'he feels a peculiar relief and escape, like a man who, after a severe bilious attack, has just been sick' (p. 249), and he returns to his house feeling hungry and ready for breakfast. The final lines of the novel indicate that he feels (and that the reader should approve) a certain pride in his action: 'But Rudbeck, growing ever more free in the inspiration which seems already his own idea, answers obstinately, "I couldn't let anyone else do it, could I?"' Okonkwo, on the other hand, is unable to eat for three days, drinks heavily to avoid self-condemnation, and the reader endorses Obierika's disapproval (p. 46). The contrasts between the two scenes subtly undermine stock European assumptions about the relative humanity of Africans and Europeans. (Cary's Aissa Saved and The African Witch dwell repeatedly on callous murders and tortures, including Aissa's death as she is eaten alive by ants.) Moreover, these contrasts subvert the closing scenes of Mister Johnson, which now seem overwritten, quite unconvincing in the portrayal of a young man's response to death and his executioner, and callous in their turning of the loss of one human life so quickly to another man's profit. This final point is also underlined in the ending of Things Fall Apart when the District Commissioner turns from the body of Okonkwo to meditate upon the usefulness of this death for his planned book for the edification of Europeans.

The novelist and his reader

Although Cary's reader is to be 'carried unreflecting on the stream of events' and to refrain from judging Johnson or from 'distinguishing

6. The name Nwoye takes when baptised, Isaac, suggests a parallel with the Old Testament story of Abraham, whose god commanded the sacrifice of his son and who, like Okonkwo, was willing to execute the lad himself. The parallel is an ironic reminder of and commentary on aspects of Christianity of which the 'callow' Nwoye is unaware, and suggests further comparisons with the Old Testament and Igbo traditions.

style from action or character', he is not expected to *identify with* Johnson. The narrative tone is generally one of slightly amused, sometimes bemused detachment, and the reader is rarely allowed to view the characters or the action from any other perspective. Indeed, the vision of Africa presented by Cary in his novels is not unlike the view Cary ascribes to Celia, Rudbeck's wife, in *Mister Johnson*:

> But to Celia Africa is simply a number of disconnected events which have no meaning for her at all. She gazes at the pot-maker without seeing that she has one leg shorter than the other, that she is in the first stages of leprosy, that her pot is bulging on one side. She doesn't really see either woman or pot, but only a scene in Africa. Even Mr. Wog [Mister Johnson] is to her a scene in Africa.[7]

For Johnson, on the other hand, 'Africa is simply perpetual experience, exciting, amusing, alarming or delightful, which he soaks into himself through all his five senses at once, and produces again in the form of reflections, comments, songs and jokes'.

The reader is placed somewhere between the position of Celia for whom 'Africa is simply a number of disconnected events', and Mister Johnson for whom 'Africa is simply perpetual experience . . . soaked in through the senses'; 'simply' so in both cases. The reader is given no space or provision for reflection, criticism or judgement. The pace of the narrative is breathless. Only at the end of the novel is there time to stop and ask about meaning, significance, connection, morality, with the result that the reader is left to ponder the significance of Rudbeck's action and encounter with Johnson, not the significance and morality of Johnson's actions.

For Achebe, the relationship between reader and subject, and hence the relationship between narrative voice and subject, as well as the pace of the story, must be very different. His narrative persona is characterized from the opening paragraphs of the novel:

> Okonkwo was well known throughout the nine villages and even beyond. His fame rested on solid personal achievements. As a young man of eighteen he had brought honour to his village by throwing Amalinze the Cat. Amalinze was the great wrestler who for seven years was unbeaten, from Umuofia to Mbaino. He was called the Cat because his back would never touch the earth. It was this man that Okonkwo threw in a fight which the old men agreed was one of the fiercest since the founder of their town engaged a spirit of the wild for seven days and seven nights.
>
> The drums beat and the flutes sang and the spectators held their breath. Amalinze was a wily craftsman, but Okonkwo was as slippery as a fish in water. Every nerve and every muscle stood

---

7. *Mister Johnson*, pp. 102–3.

out on their arms, on their backs and their thighs, and one almost heard them stretching to breaking point. In the end Okonkwo threw the Cat.

Not only does this passage introduce Okonkwo as a heroic figure and wrestler (who will be seen to wrestle with others, with his *chi*, his father's heritage, his own character, and with the white man), but it also reveals the primary characteristics of the narrative voice. His world is that of the nine villages, from Umuofia to Mbaino; areas outside of these boundaries have little significance as yet, belonging simply to that vague realm 'beyond'. His values are those of his society, recognizing 'solid personal achievements' and approving those who thus bring honour to their village, values which in turn emphasize the close tie between individual success and the welfare of the community. And he is the recorder of a legend which will link up with the legends (of other great heroes and wrestlers) remembered by the old men. As in other tales developed from oral sources, such as *The Iliad* or *Beowulf*, history, myth and legend are closely connected; poetry and history are intertwined. The narrative voice is primarily a recreation of the persona heard in tales, history, proverbs and poetry belonging to an oral tradition; it represents a collective voice through which the artist speaks *for* his society, not as an individual apart from it—he is the chorus rather than the hero. As such he embodies not only the values and assumptions of his community, but also its traditions, its history, its past; and the present must be seen as growing out of that past, a product of it, as Okonkwo is seen as a product of his community and its structures.

The opening paragraph also suggests a kinship between the speaker and his implicit audience, for instance in the assumption that values are shared in regard to what constitutes worthwhile achievements. A sharp awareness of the needs of the audience, its call upon the speaker, is implied in the very qualities which make both the opening paragraph and the work as a whole, with its numerous digressions and episodic structure, reminiscent of oral composition. Explanations like that concerning the identity of Amalinze and the source of his nickname are inserted as the speaker feels his fictive audience's need for them, not with regard to a preconceived structure and sense of proportion typical of the written work planned by the District Commissioner at the end of the novel.

The language used by the narrator is also closely related to the speech of the Igbo characters who are at the centre of the novel. Expressions and proverbs used by Okonkwo, Obierika and others are repeated or echoed by the narrator, and thus the identity of the narrator as spokesman for the Igbo community is emphasized. At the same time, the dialogue is seasoned with proverbs which give the conversation flavour (for 'proverbs are the palm-oil with which words are eaten') and at the same time characterize the speaker, his mood, and the values of the society he represents.

Cary's narrative voice is quite distinct from the voices of any of his characters. It is furthest in tone and style from Johnson's childlike babble; nowhere does it approximate his idiom or his accent. Likewise it avoids the sentiment and romanticism of Johnson's songs. In tone and idiom it is closer to the language of the British administrators, but it is also much more flexible, concrete and precise than the threadbare clichés Rudbeck, Bulteel and Celia use as conversational counters and as substitutes for thinking and seeing. But Cary's breathless pace almost allows him to obscure the question of language: How and in what languages do the characters in *Mister Johnson* communicate? Pagans such as Bamu and her family utter animal-like screeches and grunts; their speech, like their comprehension, is represented as extremely simple and limited. It is emphasized again and again that Johnson is an outsider from the south, yet he has no *linguistic* difficulty in communicating with the natives of Fada and the interior, whether Muslim or pagan. Most of his conversation is characterized by a dialect somewhere between southern Afro-American speech and West African pidgin, but it becomes clear that Bamu does not understand any form of English when Johnson introduces her to Celia, and all remarks have to be translated. Such explicit references to the fact that the people of Fada speak a different language are rare, however.

In contrast, Achebe rarely lets his reader forget the otherness of Igbo culture and the language which embodies it. His use of Igbo words is one means of insisting on this otherness, of bringing the reader up against the barriers of non-English sounds and concepts. In general, the Igbo words such as *ilo, obi, jigida, agbala* and *ndichie* are immediately translated or explained in the text itself. Their function is not to mystify the reader but to remind him that the Igbo possess a language of their own, and that their culture, ranging from everyday surroundings and artefacts (*obi, jigida*) to complex religious and philosophical concepts (*ndichie, agbala*) is expressed through it. Many critics have analysed one of the most striking aspects of *Things Fall Apart*: the use of idioms, imagery and proverbs which suggest a non-English and specifically Eastern Nigerian culture, and there is no need to go over such ground again.[8] What may be emphasized for the purposes of this discussion is Achebe's repeated reminder of the linguistic barriers to communication and understanding, in contrast with Cary's implication that the barriers are ones of civilization and

8. See, for example, B. Lindfors, 'The Palm-Oil with Which Achebe's Words are Eaten' and Gareth Griffiths, 'Language and Action in the Novels of Chinua Achebe', both reprinted in *Critical Perspectives on Chinua Achebe*. See also the relevant chapters in David Carroll's *Chinua Achebe* and E. Obiechina's *Culture, Tradition and Society in the West African Novel*.

intelligence rather than language. In *Things Fall Apart* almost every encounter with the white man or his emissaries involves some reference to the alien language or dialect: there is the white man who repeats something incomprehensible at Abame; the ludicrous confusion of 'himself' and 'his buttocks' by the missionary; Obierika's bitter reply to Okonkwo's question, 'Does the white man understand our custom about land?'—'How can he when he does not even understand our tongue?'; the difference in syntax and idiom between the speech of the District Commissioner and that of the Igbo. Like Obi, who felt it necessary to remind Londoners that Africans have languages of their own, Achebe reminds his readers that Igbo is the language of his community.[9]

Paradoxically, Achebe uses the written word brought by the colonizers in order to record and recreate the oral world obliterated or denied by them. This paradox is related to the irony that although Achebe shows the failure of language to enlarge understanding, to become a means of communication, and to break out of a self-enclosed system, nevertheless the novel itself *is* an attempt to reach, through self-conscious use of the language of one culture, the culture of another. The paradox is highlighted by direct reference to the western literary tradition which now belongs also to the author: the title, *Things Fall Apart*, from Yeats' 'The Second Coming', is not only a reminder of that tradition but is also appropriate to the novel's record of the destruction of a civilization; at the same time, one recalls that Yeats' theory of the cycles of history ignores African history, as does European thought generally. A further irony of course is that Yeats' poem foresees the end of the Christian era, while Achebe's novel records the end of the non-Christian era in Eastern Nigeria. Yet that non-Christian tradition, its religion and culture, is in part validated for the western or westernized reader by indirect parallels with biblical tales; for instance, the parallel between Okonkwo's sacrifice of Ikemefuna and the story of Abraham and Isaac is brought to the surface when Nwoye takes Isaac as his Christian name. Within the text itself, the occasional inclusion of phrases such as 'nature . . . red in tooth and claw' from Tennyson's *In Memoriam*, or of literary words such as 'valediction' in the otherwise non-British and non-literary idiom, serve to remind the reader of the contrasting worlds that have finally come together in the authorial consciousness. That consciousness is to be distinguished from the epic voice discussed earlier, and it is closer to the questioning and alienated vision of Nwoye than the unquestioning and integrated culture which Okonkwo fights desperately to preserve. (The Hungarian critic Georg Lukács maintains in his *Theory of the Novel* that such a conflict

---

9. For further discussion of language as a theme in *Things Fall Apart* see my article in *Critical Perspectives on Chinua Achebe*, pp. 111–25.

between the nostalgia for epic totality and the consciousness alienated from its society is the core of the novel form.)

The reference to the poetry of the British and Christian cultural tradition and Achebe's use of the novel form also suggest the importance of the poetic as a means of bridging the gap between languages, of going beyond the Logos—the authoritative, self-enclosed and self-validating discourse—of each culture.[1] *Things Fall Apart* is a commentary on the ways in which language can become rigid and incapable of communication, but at the same time demonstrates the creative possibilities of language. The very proverbs and phrases which have become clichés for their Igbo speakers, which no longer have a living relation to the things signified, are yet for the western reader creative of a world in which the tension between word and referent, the awareness of metaphor as such, is alive and vibrant. When Okonkwo says, 'Let the kite and the eagle perch together', we are made aware of the ritualistic nature of those words for him; but this same sentence helps to create a world and its value system for us, and gains significance as the novel proceeds.

For Cary the barriers to understanding between Africans and Europeans arise mainly in the gap between what he sees as a static, undeveloped group, and an advanced, civilized and changing society. His natives have neither a past nor a future; they live from moment to moment. Therefore, cause and effect, development and change, and concepts of time are alien to them. Cary's African characters exist only in the present tense, from one isolated event to the next. They react—passively, indifferently, or with excitement—to events and people, but they never learn from them. And like Mister Johnson, Cary's narrative charges headlong from episode to episode, with exuberance but without dignity, until it comes to a shocking halt. Here again, Achebe's opposing vision leads him to adopt an entirely different narrative style and technique. The qualities exhibited in the opening passages of *Things Fall Apart* serve as a model for the structure of the novel as a whole as it moves backward and forward in time. Okonkwo is introduced at the height of his fame, although the story is set in the past, and is in turn related to a more distant historical and mythical past. His fame as the story begins, when he was about forty, rests on his achievements, including the memorable wrestling

---

1. My use of the term 'Logos' in this context derives partly from its usage by Derrida, Paul de Man and other deconstructionist critics. Derrida argues that western culture, and uses of language in the west, are grounded on a belief in the primacy of spoken over written language, and in the possibility of grounding logically consistent or rational truth and meaning entirely in the spoken utterances of a particular linguistic system. Derrida seeks to prove such a belief illusory. Achebe's fiction also questions logocentrism, but from a perspective with which the deconstructionists, caught as *they* are within western culture, have not been concerned, since they have not discussed the problem in terms of a culture which is entirely oral.

match when he was eighteen. The third paragraph returns to the
forty-year-old Okonkwo of the beginning of the story, the fourth
moves back again to the death of his father ten years previously, the
fifth to Unoka's childhood, the sixth to his irresponsible adulthood at
a time parallel to Okonkwo's present, and the final paragraph of the
chapter returns to Unoka's death, to Okonkwo's achievement, and
looks forward to the fate of Ikemefuna. Chapter 2 takes up the story
of Okonkwo in his prime when he is responsible for Ikemefuna, but
chapter 3 moves back again in time to Okonkwo's boyhood and difficult struggle as a young man. Such narrative movement is characteristic of Achebe's novels. All five begin at one moment in time and
then move further back before moving forward, frequently returning
to more or less distant pasts as the story proceeds. There is an irony
in this, since most of his protagonists seek to break free of their pasts
and create themselves anew. (In *Arrow of God*, however, Ezeulu seeks
to preserve the past and contain the future.)

The effect of this temporal movement of the narrative is on the one
hand to prevent the reader from being 'carried unreflecting on the
stream of events', and on the other to insist on reflections about cause
and effect, with particular regard to Okonkwo's success and failure in
his attempt to control his future. For Joyce Cary one of the fundamental constants facing all human beings, and of intense concern to
novelists, is the conflict between human nature and material facts,
between freedom and necessity, so that 'we have a reality consisting of
permanent and highly obstinate facts, and permanent and highly obstinate human nature'.[2] One might see that conflict voiced differently in
the recurring reference in *Things Fall Apart* to the relationship between
a man and his *chi* and the contrasting sayings concerning it: 'When a
man says yes, his *chi* says yes also' (p. 19) and 'A man could not rise
beyond the destiny of his *chi*' (p. 92) or 'He had a bad *chi*' (p. 13). Cary
turns Johnson's attempt to create and control his destiny into a comedy or farce whose outcome affects only Johnson and Rudbeck;
Okonkwo's attempt and failure is turned into tragedy which involves
the fate not just of an individual but of a whole community. Historical
awareness of the ultimate fate of Okonkwo's proudly self-contained
community combined with respect for Okonkwo's determination to
preserve all that he values in that community, nudges the reader into
frequent reflection on the question of what values and events will
either allow that community to survive or contribute to its distintegra-
tion. Such reflection is directed also by prophecies of doom, such as
that of the oracle of Abame about the coming of the whites, and
Uchendu's lamentation about the consequences of that visitation:

2. Joyce Cary, *Art and Reality: Ways of the Creative Process*, New York: Harper and Bros., 1958,
   p. 6.

'But I fear for you young people because you do not understand
how strong is the bond of kinship. You do not know what it is to
speak with one voice. And what is the result? An abominable religion has settled among you. A man can now leave his father and
his brothers. He can curse the gods of his fathers and his ancestors, like a hunter's dog that suddenly goes mad and turns on his
master. I fear for you; I fear for the clan.' He turned again to
Okonkwo and said, 'Thank you for calling us together.'

(p. 118)

Uchendu's lamentation ends part 2 of the novel and acts as a summary of the events dramatized in that section, where we have seen both
the value of kinship in the material and spiritual assistance given the
banished Okonkwo, and the inroads made by the new religion with its
blessing on those 'who leave their father and mother' for Christ's sake.
In these lines, the reader is asked to consider the wider significance of
Okonkwo's story and of Nwoye's choice. Similarly, part 1 ends with a
reflection and a series of questions:

Obierika was a man who thought about things. When the will of
the goddess had been done, he sat down in his *obi* and mourned
his friend's calamity. Why should a man suffer so grievously for
an offence he had committed inadvertently? But although he
thought for a long time he found no answer. He was merely led
into greater complexities. He remembered his wife's twin children, whom he had thrown away. What crime had they committed? The Earth had decreed that they were an offence on the
land and must be destroyed. And if the clan did not exact punishment for an offence against the great goddess, her wrath was
loosed on all the land and not just on the offender. As the elders
said, if one finger brought oil it soiled the others. (p. 87)

Obierika's reflection prods the reader to ask similar questions—not
only about the injustice of Okonkwo's banishment and the suffering
of innocent twins and their mothers, but also about the inadequacy
of Obierika's recourse to the formulas of the clan. One becomes
aware here of a way in which language can become an evasion of
intuitive understanding. The proverbs which so potently create for
the European reader another world and culture can prevent creative
change. Obierika feels that the twins and Okonkwo have committed
no crime; inner feeling, however, is soon suppressed by the prefabri-
cated declaration: 'The earth had decreed . . .' And the final proverb
closes off all further questions for Obierika, but not for the reader.

The questions of Nwoye and of the women who have lost their twins
are less easily silenced by the formulas of the elders. They are searching for a new language which will close the gap between their inner
feeling of what should be and the language the culture has developed

to justify what is. And above all it is 'the poetry of the new religion' which appeals to Nwoye when the Christians first bring their message:

> But there was a young lad who had been captivated. His name was Nwoye, Okonkwo's first son. It was not the mad logic of the Trinity which captivated him. He did not understand it. It was the poetry of the new religion, something felt in the marrow. The hymn about brothers who sat in darkness and in fear seemed to answer a vague and persistent question that haunted his young soul—the question of the twins crying in the bush and the question of Ikemefuna who was killed. He felt a relief within as the hymn poured into his parched soul. The words of the hymn were like drops of frozen rain melting on the dry palate of the panting earth. Nwoye's callow mind was greatly puzzled. (pp. 103–4)

The simile of words like drops of rain on the dry palate of the parched earth recalls 'the kind of story Nwoye loved' as a child, the story of how Earth and Sky quarrelled and Sky withheld rain for seven years. Vulture was sent to soften Sky with a song 'of the suffering of the sons of men. Whenever Nwoye's mother sang that song he felt carried away to the distant scene of the sky where Vulture, Earth's emissary, sang for mercy. At last Sky was moved to pity, and he gave to Vulture rain wrapped in leaves of cocoyam. But as he flew home his long talon pierced the leaves and the rain fell as it had never fallen before' (p. 38). Okonkwo has taught Nwoye that such stories are for 'foolish women and children', and to please his father Nwoye pretends to despise 'women's stories', listening instead to his father's accounts of tribal wars and his exploits as a warrior. Thus the deliberate link between these two scenes suggests that it is not specifically the words of the new religion that stir Nwoye, but the songs of suffering and poetry in general. In denying the fictional tales as womanish and insisting on stories which are factual and historical, Okonkwo has denied the poetic world, which in both contexts quoted is closely related to the world of myth. His rejection of the poetic is also related to his suppression of what he 'inwardly knows', or intuition, and for Nwoye poetry is equivalent to 'something felt in the marrow'. For Nwoye, then, the appeal of the new religion is its seeming recognition of that inner, unverbalized world, where the vague and persistent questions are felt in terms of situations, not understood on a verbal level. The 'poetry of the new religion' is at its most powerful for Nwoye and other Igbo when received through imagery and music: we are told that the rollicking hymn tunes pluck 'at silent and dusty chords in the heart' (p. 103), and that Nwoye is affected by the image of 'brothers who sat in darkness' and the image of the lost sheep. The 'dusty chords' again pick up the connection between the songs of suffering and the rain and the parched earth and are a subtle reminder of Unoka, who was a musician, an expert with the flute and a man of great feeling, constantly vacillating between extremes of joy and grief. He is called *agbala*. But the Oracle is also called Agbala, and symbolizes the power of the word at its highest level, and the word which is mysterious and enigmatic. Poetry, myth and fiction are all associated with the spiritual, the sacred, the feminine and, paradoxically, with the inner, unspoken word. All are linked with the powerful figures of Chielo, priestess of the Oracle, whose voice when possessed is described as unearthly. When Okonkwo pleads with her not to carry off Ezinma, she responds, 'Beware Okonkwo! . . . Beware of exchanging words with Agbala. Does a man speak when a god speaks? Beware!' (p. 71)

In the series of lectures published as *Art and Reality*, Joyce Cary discusses the gap between intuition and expression: 'A cold thought has to deal with a warm feeling. I said that intuitions are evanescent. Wordsworth's intuitions die not only for the man, they fade very quickly for the child. But the conceptual thought cannot only destroy them, it can bar them out.'[3] The conflict between cold thought and warm feeling is dramatized in *Mister Johnson*. But although Cary stresses in his essays the need for both artists and political thinkers to resolve that conflict, there is no coherent resolution in his African novels. For Achebe, the problem of artistic expression and the problem of social change are inextricable, for language is central to both. The reader's task is to be aware of the limits of language, to be alert to the ways in which words, formulas and rhetoric can obscure understanding. He is not allowed to separate feeling and judgement, to swim unreflecting before emerging on the shore to look back and criticize, but must continually combine criticism and sympathy. The concern with the problem of language and the demand that the reader learn to examine language critically take different forms in Achebe's later novels, but remain crucial to all of them.

F. ABIOLA IRELE

The Crisis of Cultural Memory in Chinua Achebe's *Things Fall Apart*[†]

If there is any single work that can be considered central to the evolving canon of modern African literature, it is, without question, Chinua Achebe's *Things Fall Apart*. The novel owes this distinction to the innovative significance it assumed as soon as it was published,

3. *Ibid.*, pp. 30–1.
† From *The African Imagination: Literature in Africa and the Black Diaspora* (New York: Oxford University Press, 2001), 115–53. Reprinted by permission of Oxford University Press, Inc.

a significance that was manifested in at least two respects. In the first place, the novel provided an image of an African society reconstituted as a living entity and in its historic circumstance, an image of a coherent social structure forming the institutional fabric of a universe of meanings and values. Because this image of Africa was quite unprecedented in literature, it also carried considerable ideological weight in the specific context of the novel's writing and reception. For it cannot be doubted that the comprehensive scope of Achebe's depiction of a particularized African community engaged in its own social processes, carried out entirely on its own terms, with all the internal tensions this entailed, challenged the simplified representation that the West offered of Africa as a formless area of life, "an area of darkness" devoid of human significance.[1] Thus, beyond what might be considered its ethnographic interest, which lent the work an immediate and ambiguous appeal—a point to which we shall return—Achebe's novel articulated a new vision of the African world and gave expression to a new sense of the African experience that was more penetrating than what had been available before its appearance.

The second factor making for the esteem in which Achebe's novel is held has to do with the quality of his manner of presentation, in which the cultural reference governs not merely the constitution of the novel's fictional universe but also the expressive means by which the collective existence, the human experience framed within this universe, is conveyed. The novel testifies to an aesthetic project that consists of fashioning a new language appropriate to its setting, which serves therefore to give life and substance to the narrative content and thus to enforce the novelist's initial gesture of cultural reclamation. As a consequence, the manner of presentation became integral to the narrative development to a degree that must be considered unusual in novelistic writing. As Emmanuel Obiechina remarked, "the integrative technique in which background and atmosphere are interlaced with the action of the narrative must be regarded as Achebe's greatest achievement" (Obiechina, 1975, 142). It is especially with regard to this close imbrication of language and theme that *Things Fall Apart* can be said to have defined a new mode of African imaginative expression, hence Kwame Appiah's description of the work as "the archetypal modern African novel in English" (Appiah, 1992, ix).[2]

1. The phrase is of course an echo of V. S. Naipaul's title for the first of his three books on India. For a comprehensive discussion of the image of Africa in the Western imagination, see Fanoudh-Siefer (1968) and Hammond and Jablow (1992).
2. Achebe's example spawned a cluster of novels in Anglophone Africa focused on the theme of revaluation and cultural conflict. This is especially the case in the work of a group of Igbo writers who may be said to constitute a school deriving its inspiration and method from his work. Among these may be cited, as the most prominent, Flora Nwapa, John Munonye, Onuora Nzekwu, and Elechi Amadi; Buchi Emecheta's work bears an indirect

The work has acquired the status of a classic, then, by reason of its character as a counterfiction of Africa in specific contradiction to the discourse of Western colonial domination and its creative deployment of the language of the *imperium;* it has on this account been celebrated as the prototype of what Barbara Harlow has called "resistance literature" (Harlow, 1987).[3] The ideological project involved in its writing comes fully to the fore in the ironic ending in which we see the colonial officer, after the suicide of the main character, Okonkwo, contemplating a monograph on the "pacification" of the Lower Niger. Okonkwo, we are told, will get the briefest of mentions in the monograph, but we know as readers that the novel to which this episode serves as conclusion has centered all along upon this character who, as the figure of the historical African, the work endeavors to reendow with a voice and a visage, which allows him to emerge in his full historicity, tragic though this turns out to be in the circumstances.

Despite the novel's contestation of the colonial enterprise, clearly formulated in the closing chapters and highlighted by its ironic ending,

---

relation to this "school" (see Emenyonu, 1974). The long shadow cast by Achebe over these writers is best illustrated by the insufficient and even scant attention that has been paid to Elechi Amadi's powerful novel, *The Great Ponds*, in my view one of the masterpieces of modern African literature. Further afield, we may cite the case of Ngugi wa Thiong'o, who has acknowledged his debt to Achebe. To recognize the innovative significance of *Things Fall Apart* is, however, far from stating that Achebe "invented" African literature, as Gikandi claims in his 1991 study of Achebe, and repeats in his introduction to the annotated edition published in 1996. Unless the Anglophone area is to be taken as representing the whole field and the novel as the privileged medium, African literature cannot be said to have begun with the publication of Achebe's novel in 1958. That would discount the whole area of African literature in the indigenous languages, beginning with the oral tradition itself and extending to the written literature in the vernaculars, with the work of Thomas Mfolo and D. O. Fagunwa, for example, as major landmarks. Moreover, as regards African literature in the European languages, even if we set aside the work of African writers of European extraction (considered in my 1990 essay "The African Imagination"), the Francophone writers had established a new tradition of African literary expression before the publication of Achebe's novel in English. It is of course possible to consider such figures as René Maran and Paul Hazoumé as precursors but not Léopold Sédar Senghor, whose first volume of poems, *Chants d'ombre*, was published in 1945. The volume itself testifies to a conscious project of African literature, explicitly stated in the poem "Lettre à un Poète" dedicated to Aimé Césaire, a poem that presents itself as a veritable manifesto for the creation of a new literature expressive of the African environment. Later, Senghor elaborates this point in the essay "Comme les Lamantins vont boire à la source," which serves as postscript to his 1960 volume, *Ethiopiques*. Indeed, if we seek a precise reference for the "invention" of African literature, this can only be the historic *Anthologie de la nouvelle poésie nègre et malgache*, compiled by Senghor and published in 1948. The point is that African literature in the European languages was a distinct area of modern African expression well before Achebe came on the scene.

3. Achebe himself has sought to clarify this ideological project by presenting it as a vindication, in the face of persistent Western denigration, of the African claim to human achievement. According to him, the novel was motivated by the desire to demonstrate that the precolonial order in Africa was not "one long night of savagery" ("The Novelist as Teacher," *Hopes and Impediments*, 45). Furthermore, he has indicated that, in its elaboration as a work of fiction, *Things Fall Apart* represents his corrective response to the portrayal of Africa in Joyce Cary's *Mister Johnson* and Joseph Conrad's *Heart of Darkness* ("Named for Victoria, Queen of England" and "An Image of Africa," in the same volume, and Achebe's preface to *The African Trilogy*). To these writers must be added H. Rider Haggard, Edgar Wallace, and John Buchan, whose works were staples of the colonial literature in Nigeria and other African territories in the former British empire.

readers have always been struck by the veil of moral ambiguity with
which Achebe surrounds his principal character and by the disso-
nances that this sets up in the narrative development. As Obiechina
remarked in an oral presentation I had the privilege of attending, the
novel is constituted by "a tangle of ironies." For it soon becomes apparent that Achebe's work is not by any means an unequivocal celebration
of tribal culture; indeed, the specific human world depicted in this
novel is far from representing a universe of pure perfection. We are
presented rather with a corner of human endeavor that is marked by
the web of contradictions within which individual and collective des-
tinies have everywhere and at all times been enmeshed. A crucial factor, therefore, in any reading of Achebe's novel, given the particular
circumstances of its composition, is its deeply reflective engagement
with the particular order of life that provides a reference for its narrative scheme and development. In this respect, one cannot fail to discern a thematic undercurrent, which produces a disjunction in the
novel between its overt ideological statement, its contradiction of the
discourse of the colonial ideology, on one hand, and on the other, its
dispassionate and even uncompromising focus on an African community in its moment of historical crisis.

I will examine here the nature of this disjunction not only as it
emerges from the novel's thematic development but also as it is
inscribed, quite literally, within the formal structures of the work, in
the belief that it is by undertaking a closer examination of these two
dimensions of the work and relating them to each other that we are
enabled to fully discern its purpose. For the moral significance of the
work seems to me to outweigh the ideological burden that has so
often been laid upon it. I believe the implications of the novel extend
much further than the anticolonial stance that, admittedly, provides
its point of departure but which, as we shall see, eventually yields to
issues of far greater import concerning the African becoming.

We begin this examination with an observation that situates
Achebe's work in the general perspective of literary creation and cultural production in contemporary Africa. The most significant effect
of modern African literature in the European languages is perhaps the
sense it registers of the immediacy of history as a sphere of existence,
as a felt dimension of being and consciousness. Achebe's work is
exemplary in this regard, in the way he captures in his fiction the inner
movement of transition on the continent from an antecedent order of
life to a new and problematic collective existence, this new existence
contemplated as the outcome of an implacable historical development. Beginning with *Things Fall Apart*, his entire production seeks
to take a measure, in its full range and import for Africa, of what Molly
Mahood has called, in her study of the same title, "the colonial
encounter" (Mahood, 1977). Achebe's explicit concern with the

cultural dislocations provoked by the harsh circumstances of this encounter and their far-reaching consequences in human terms suggests at first a limited point of view, which appears to emphasize the primacy of an original identity owed to cultural and ethnic affiliations.

However, we cannot but observe that, as a writer, Achebe is in fact situated at the point of intersection between two world orders, the precolonial African and the Western or, more specifically, Euro-Christian, which impinge upon his creative consciousness. It is important to recall this defining factor of the total cultural situation by which Achebe's inspiration is conditioned and to stress the directing influence of his Western education and the sensibility associated with this education upon his fictional reconstruction of the collective traumas enacted by his novels and the comprehensive process of self-reflection they imply. Thus, an attention to its various inflections indicates that the narrative voice adopted by Achebe in his first novel has to be imputed in large part to his status as a Westernized African, the product of Christian education. This is a voice that speaks often, perhaps even primarily, from the margins of the traditional culture, as is evident in this passage from early in the novel:

> The night was very quiet. It was always quiet except on moonlight nights. Darkness held a vague terror for these people, even the bravest among them. Children were warned not to whistle at night for fear of evil spirits . . . And so on this particular night as the crier's voice was gradually swallowed up in the distance, silence returned to the world, a vibrant silence made more intense by the universal trill of a million forest insects. (7)[4]

The passage suggests that the perspective from which Achebe looks at the traditional world is that of an external observer, a perspective that implies a cultural distance from the background of life—of thought and manners—that provides the concrete reference of his fiction. We encounter the same stance in another passage where the narrator observes of the community to which the work relates: "Fortunately among these people a man was judged according to his worth and not according to the worth of his father" (6). Of these and similar passages, Nigerian scholar David Ker has commented: "Umuofia is simultaneously 'they' and 'we' and this subtle combination of detachment and participation helps Achebe to manipulate point of view" (Ker, 1997, 136). This is a plausible reading, which brings the novel's content into functional relation with its narrative codes, except that the personal testimony Achebe provides of his own education in a Christian household indicates clearly that his identification with the indigenous heritage was a later and conscious

---

4. *Things Fall Apart*, 1962. All further page references will be indicated in the text.

development. In other words, Achebe can be said to have undertaken the writing of *Things Fall Apart* out of an awareness of a primary disconnection from the indigenous background that he seeks to recover and to explore in the novel.

The point can be made from another perspective by observing that, as a modern African novelist, Achebe is hardly in the same position as the traditional storyteller, creating his stories un-self-consciously out of a full sense of coincidence with the culture within which he practices his art and that provides objective support for his imaginative projections. Moreover, Achebe is obliged to employ a newly acquired tongue, one that is at a considerable structural and expressive remove from the speech modes, habits of thought, and cultural codes of the historical community whose experience he undertakes to record in his fiction. Contrary to the claim by Romanus Egudu that Achebe's art in the novel is continuous with an Igbo narrative tradition (Egudu, 1981), the whole imaginative effort manifested in *Things Fall Apart* was called into play and given direction by a willed movement back to what the novelist regards as the sources of the collective self, which he has had to reconstitute both as a function of the ideological objectives of his novel and also, and much more important, as an imperative of the narrative process itself, a point to which we shall return.

We might observe, then, that the impression of the writer's familiarity with his material and the quality of authentic life registered by his language are in fact effects of this reinvestment of the self on Achebe's part, thrown into relief by the consummate art of the novelist. It is well to bear in mind these factors, which are attendant upon the process of creation from which Achebe's novel proceeds, for they are not without important consequences for its narrative development and, ultimately, for its aesthetic and moral significance. These are not merely entailed by the ostensible content of the work, its "propositional" ground, to echo Gerald Graff (1980), but also are inherent in its formal organization and language. It is to the relation among these various aspects of the work that we now turn.

Commenting upon his own work nearly forty years after its appearance, Achebe declared, "The story of Okonkwo is almost inevitable; if I hadn't written about him, certainly someone else would have, because it really is the beginning of our story" (Achebe, 1991).[5] Achebe's observation concerning his fictional creation draws attention to the allegorical significance that Okonkwo has assumed for the African imagination; he is not merely a character in a novel but the representative figure of African historicity. A determining element of the novel's structure and development is thus the way in which his

5. We might note that Achebe's observation about Okonkwo applies equally to Ezeulu, the focus of his third novel, *Arrow of God*; both function as characters in what Biodun Jeyifo (1993) has described as "fictional genealogies of colonialism" in Africa.

story is embedded within an elaborate reconstruction of forms of life in the traditional, precolonial culture, specifically, that of Achebe's own people, the Igbo of southeastern Nigeria. The tenor and warmth of Achebe's presentation of the traditional world, especially in the thirteen chapters that form the first part of the novel, with their elaborate representation of setting and involving in the process an insistence in positive terms upon the cultural context within which his fictional characters have their being, leaves us in no doubt that a polemical intent informs his reconstruction. The Igbo tribal world emerges here in all of its specificity, its daily routines and seasonal rituals attuned to the natural rhythms of its living environment. The language of daily intercourse that Achebe lends his characters endows with a special force the mobilization of minds and sensibilities within the society and animates with its poetic resonance its modes of social organization and cultural expression. The even cadence that marks the collective life in its normal course is summed up at one point in a simple but telling way with "In this way, the moons and the seasons passed" (39). The elaborate account of the New Yam Festival that opens chapter 5 (26) takes on added weight of meaning in the light of this declaration of a natural order of the communal existence. We are made to understand that the extraordinary coherence that the organic rooting of the tribe guarantees to the social order in its natural environment is an immediate function of an established system of values by which the collective life is regulated. What is more, Achebe's depiction of the prescribed pattern of social gestures and modes of comportment creates an overwhelming impression of a collective existence that unfolds in ceremonial terms, punctuated as it is by a train of activities that enhance the ordinary course of life and serve therefore as privileged moments in a more or less unending celebration of a social compact that is remarkably potent and is in any case fully functional on its own terms.

It is this intense quality of life that is conveyed symbolically by the drum, which functions so obviously as a leitmotif in the novel that it generates a singular connotative stream within the narrative. The omnipresence of the drum in Achebe's image of Igbo tribal life seems at times on the verge of betraying him into the kind of unmediated stereotyping of the African by Western writers to which he himself has vehemently objected. The intrusion into his own writing of the demeaning idiom of colonial discourse is recognizable: "Drums beat violently, and men leaped up and down in a frenzy" (86). But such a drop in narrative tone serves ultimately to enforce the larger vision he offers of the community he is presenting, for we soon come to grasp the true significance of the drum as manifesting a vitalism inherent in and interwoven with the community's organic mode of existence: "The drums were still beating, persistent and unchanging.

Their sound was no longer a separate thing from the living village. It was like the pulse of its heart. It throbbed in the air, in the sunshine, and even in the trees, and filled the village with excitement" (31).

Achebe presents us, then, with a dynamic framework of social interactions and interpersonal relations, which lay the affective foundation for what, in the language of Durkheim, we might call a collective consciousness, one that is properly commensurate with a sphere of existence and an order of experience that, by the fact of their being rigorously circumscribed, conduce to its institutional strength. It is instructive in this respect to remark upon the narrow range of the physical setting reproduced in Achebe's novel. This is established in what seems a deliberate manner in the novel's opening sentence and is associated by implication with the destiny of the central character who makes his appearance at the outset of the narrative devoted to him: "Okonkwo was well known throughout the nine villages, and even beyond" (3). The vagueness with which the narrator indicates the outer limits of Okonkwo's fame reflects the tribe's limited awareness of its location in space, of its specific place in the world. This accords with the curious vagueness of its name, Umuofia, or "people of the forest," a name that also doubles as the novel's locale and designates a community firmly situated within the natural world. The reduced spatial dimension of the tribe's sphere of existence enables a narrative focus on a world whose intimacy appears at first sight as a source of strength, the operative factor of an intensity of social experience that underlies an achieved state of equilibrium.

It should be noted that the contraction of the tribe's apprehension of space is closely associated with its bounded experience of time. The same opening paragraph of the novel in which we are introduced to Okonkwo provides us with a passing view of the tribe's myth of origin. It is not without interest to observe that this myth, in its evocation of a wrestling contest between the eponymous founder of the town and "a spirit of the wild," parallels the Old Testament story of Jacob wrestling with the angel, an encounter that, we are told, leaves him forever lame. The parallel suggests the way Achebe's mind is working through elements of his double cultural experience toward a unified conception of human destiny.

The tribe's myth of origin sets the tone for its entire mode of self-apprehension and structure of knowledge, what Gikandi has called "the Igbo epistemology" (Gikandi, 1991, 31–38; see also Nwoga, 1981). The prominence assumed by rituals of life in the culture, the tribe's periodic enactments of the various facets of its collective imagination, and its constant recall of foundations all ensure that time is experienced not as a static category but lived continuously and intensely, in the mode of duration. This consciousness of time permeates the collective life, so that the world view involves a ceaseless procession of a principle of life in an interpenetration of time and space that is ensured by the eternal presence of the ancestors:

> The land of the living was not far removed from the domain of the ancestors. There was coming and going between them, especially when an old man died, because an old man was very close to the ancestors. A man's life from birth to death was a series of transition rites which brought him nearer and nearer to his ancestors. (86)

The culture of Umuofia as depicted by Achebe functions through the immanence of its foundational myth in the collective life and consciousness. The immediate and practical implications of this myth and the system of belief derived from it are experienced at every level of the collective existence, for the mythic time of the ancestors serves as the measure of social control, as demonstrated by the role of the *egwugwu*, incarnations of the ancestors, in the administration of justice, a role that endows the laws and customs of the land with a sacred sanction. At the same time, the dialogue in which elders such as Ezeudu, Ezenwa, and Obierika engage with their own culture throughout the novel points to the process by which the principles governing the world concept and value system of the tribe are constantly debated, reexamined, and in this way, retrospectively rationalized. Thus, as represented by Chinua Achebe and contrary to the discourse of colonial anthropology, Umuofia, the primordial Igbo village, emerges as a locus of reflective civility.[6]

Achebe's attentive recreation of the processes of everyday living in the tribal society that he depicts in *Things Fall Apart* has led to the work being labeled an "ethnographic novel." The term may be taken as appropriate but only in the limited sense in which it serves to indicate a conscious effort of demonstration, aimed at presenting a particular society and its culture to an audience unfamiliar with its ways of doing and feeling, its beliefs about the world, and its strategies of response to the imperatives of human existence. The novel endeavors in this sense to create what Hochbruck (1996) has called the illusion of "cultural proximity" for the non-Igbo reader, who is confronted by the otherness, so to speak, of the human world that its cultural references are intended to designate or, at the very least, evoke.

We need to attend carefully to Achebe's handling of the ethnographic element of his novel in order to distinguish the varying modes of its integration into the narrative, for while several instances of

---

6. For an extensive discussion of the relation between Achebe's recreation of Igbo culture in his novels and the ethnographic literature on the Igbo by Western anthropologists (George Basden, P. Amaury Talbot, Charles Kingsley, Meek, and others), see Wren, 1980. Basden's *Among the Ibos of Nigeria* has long been considered the standard work on the subject.

authorial intervention intended to enlighten the reader on matters of cultural interest seem merely to provide orchestration for the bare outline of the plot and thus to lend it the richness of detail, others are indispensable for a proper comprehension of the narrative development itself and thus form an integral element of the novel's thematic unfolding. This is notably the case with the banishment of Okonkwo after his accidental killing of a clansman. The narrator points us deliberately to an understanding of the cultural implications of this episode: "The only course open to Okonkwo was to flee from the clan. It was a crime against the earth goddess to kill a clansman, and a man who committed it must flee from the land" (88). Further along, describing the organized destruction of Okonkwo's compound by the villagers after his departure, the narrator provides this insight into the mores of the land: "They had no hatred in their hearts against Okonkwo. His greatest friend Obierika was among them. They were merely cleansing the land which Okonkwo had polluted with the blood of a clansman" (88).

This last quotation illustrates the function that the novel's ethnographic content has usually been held to perform, its project of revaluation consisting of a comprehensive readjustment of viewpoint on a culture that had previously served as an object of Western deprecation. Achebe's conscious effort to project a new light upon the precolonial Igbo world is evident at many points in the novel; there is clearly at work here a resolve to promote an alternative image to its earlier representations in Western discourse, one that affords an inside view not merely of its uncoordinated details as lived in the immediacy of everyday experience but also of its overall, functional coherence. Thus, the narrative process amounts to a reformulation in the mode of fiction of the "scientific" discourse of the ethnographic literature on the Igbo, a process by which Achebe seeks to reclaim a preexisting Western discourse on his personal background for a new and different ideological purpose.

But we must go beyond the documentary aspect of Achebe's novel to consider the relation it bears to a serious artistic purpose. We need to observe the way in which the language of the novel, the whole bent of its narrative development, gives expression to an imaginative impulse that functions in its shaping beyond the explicit revisionist intent, which we may suppose to spring from its ideological conditioning. It needs to be emphasized that this impulse derives in the first place from the formal requirements that Achebe as a writer knew he had to satisfy, those conducive to the quality of verisimilitude that have come to be associated with the rise and development of the conventional Western novel. In other words, Achebe's fictional reproduction of Igbo life must be seen in its immediate relation to the diegetic purpose and mimetic function of the novel as a genre.[7] The necessity to reproduce in his novel the context of life appropriate to its theme and external reference comes to govern the process of cultural reclamation to which his work bears witness. We can thus restate the connection between the two impulses at work in the novel by observing that it develops as a redirection—inward—of Western anthropological discourse, toward the true springs of life and expression in the African world, which have been obliterated by this discourse.

But it is evidently the primacy of art that predominates in Achebe's construction of his novel; this has a consequence for grasping its moral import, which we shall come to presently. For the moment, we may note that Achebe's novel is distinguished by an economy of style and a marvelous restraint in the presentation that endow it with a certain austerity. The novel's ethnographic freight is never allowed to weigh down its human interest nor to obscure its aesthetic significance. Every scene is vividly imagined and realized, and the more expansive moments of the narration offer us powerful descriptions, including the entrance of the egwugwus, or masked spirits, at the trial and the subsequent proceedings (62–66), which give the novel dramatic lift at strategic moments. It is this process by which Achebe "naturalizes" his subject matter, to borrow Jonathan Culler's term (Culler, 1975), that also enables him to situate the narrative development and especially the cruel turn taken by Okonkwo's fate wholly and convincingly within the framework of the Igbo system of belief:

> His life had been ruled by a great passion—to become one of the lords of the clan. That had been his life-spring. And he had all but achieved it. Then everything had been broken. He had been cast

7. I have in mind here Ian Watt's thesis concerning the association between a realistic convention and the modern novel in its genesis, this convention arising from the diversified forms of experience ushered in by the change from an agrarian to an industrial mode of production (Watt, 1957). According to Watt, this made it imperative for the novelist to provide the reader with background information (down to the baking of bread) related to the context of the narrative. The example he cites of the buildup of detail in *Robinson Crusoe* is especially illuminating, insofar as the economic rationale for realism is disguised in this tale of a fantastic, exotic appearance. The same propensity toward realism is evident in the novels of Jane Austen, in which it serves a critical purpose. Despite a homogeneous public (or because of it?) the reproduction of everyday life and manners as part of the fabric of social experience in her time fostered immediate recognition by the reader, a response conducive to the creation by the novelist of the ironic distance necessary for her critical reflection on her characters and situations. The apogee of this realism was attained in the nineteenth-century French novel, which combined the same ironic function with a "documentary" character. For, despite the scorn poured by Roland Barthes in *Le degré zéro de l'écriture* upon the French realistic novel, its immediate connection to history and to the social transformations of the age created a powerful channel of social criticism that provided, according to Richard Terdiman, a challenge to the repressive institutions of an ascendant bourgeoisie (Terdiman, 1985). As a genre, the novel has of course moved beyond this convention of formal realism toward the modernist reflexive model in which we witness a reciprocal relationship between its narrative content and critical reflection on the art through which it is constituted (Boyd, 1983).

out of his clan like a fish onto a dry, sandy beach, panting. Clearly his personal god or *chi* was not made for great things. A man could not rise beyond the destiny of his *chi*. The saying of the elders was not true—that if a man said yea, his *chi* also affirmed. Here was a man whose *chi* said nay despite his own affirmation. (92)

The passage hardly serves to inform us about the nature of the *chi*, a task that Achebe undertakes in a famous essay (Achebe, 1975); rather, it illuminates the ambiguous relationship of Okonkwo to his personal god, a relationship that exemplifies, in the specific terms of Igbo apprehension of the world, the grounded insecurity of the human condition that is the mainspring of what Unamuno has called "the tragic sense of life." The novel's imaginative scope thus extends beyond mere documentation to convey, through the careful reproduction of its marking details, the distinctive character of Igbo tribal life as experienced by its subjects, the felt texture from which it derives its universal significance. It is this that gives *Things Fall Apart* its power of conviction and validates the project of cultural memory attested by the novel.

But the effort of recall and recreation, linked as it is to the diegetic purpose of the novelist's deployment of form, also involves as a necessary implication of the fictional process a critical engagement with the internal dynamics and value system of the world that he presents; one that, in the event, goes beyond its placid exterior to focus directly upon its deeper tensions, to explore its cleavages, and uncover its fault lines. It is at this level of enunciation that the novel enacts what seems to me a veritable crisis of cultural memory.

We are alerted to this crisis primarily by the correlation that the novel suggests between the conditions of existence in the tribal society and the mental universe that prevails within it. Despite its admirable qualities in some important areas of human experience, the world that Achebe presents is one that is closed in upon itself, limited in its capacities, and hobbled in certain crucial respects by its vision of the world. We have already remarked upon the way in which Achebe's Western education and Christian background determine a narrative point of view marked by a certain detachment, so that his narrator stands back sufficiently to indicate an external regard upon this world, for it is not seldom that he adopts an angle of vision that lifts a veil upon the grave disabilities with which tribal life is afflicted. For the image that Chinua Achebe presents in his novel is that of a primary society, one whose low level of technicity leaves it with few resources beyond the purely muscular for dealing with the exigencies of the natural world. Because it is confronted with what is nothing less than a precarious material situation, it has perforce to accord primacy to manliness as a manifestation of being at its most physical, elevated into a norm of personal worth and social value. The valuation of physical prowess, in play as in war, the emphasis on individual achievement, considered as instrumental to social solidarity, appear then as strategies intended to ensure the security and permanence of the group. For, like most early societies, this is a civilization that is dominated by a passion for survival. On this point, Umuofia closely resembles these earlier societies, alike in their cultivation of the heroic ideal based on physical prowess, an ideal necessitated by their dependence on outstanding individuals for group survival.[8]

This defining feature of the tribe is highlighted by the centrality of the yam to the culture and the symbolic value with which it is invested, over and above its utility as a source of nourishment, a feature that provides a graphic illustration of the continuum from material existence to collective vision and ethos. Because of the intense muscular effort required for its cultivation, the yam crop comes to represent an annual triumph wrested from nature, the sign of the rigorous dialectic between the human world and the natural environment, which governs the communal life and conditions what one might call the social aesthetic—the festivals, rituals, and other forms of public ceremony—that infuses the tribe's collective representations with feeling and endows them with meaning for each consciousness within the community. Thus, the image of the yam gathers up the force fields of the culture and functions as a metonymic representation of the tribe's mode of relation to the world (Echeruo, 1979). The organicism that we have observed as a fundamental feature of the tribal community is thus related to the fact that it has its being essentially within the realm of necessity.

If then, from a certain idealizing point of view, we come to appreciate the values of intimacy and intensity of living denoted by the closed universe of the novel, such as Gérard Genette postulates for the Cambrai of Marcel Proust (Genette, 1972), the critical current that runs through the narrative soon reveals this universe as one marked by a profound contradiction between the powerful constraints of the social ideal, which privileges the interests of the group, and the truths of individual human yearnings and desires as embraced by a modern sensibility. It is on this basis that Achebe develops the theme of Okonkwo's struggle for recognition and the larger existential implications of this theme in its evocation of the universal human predicament. This theme, we ought to note, is framed by the triadic structure of the novel: Okonkwo's rise to prominence at Umuofia, which is interrupted by his banishment and life in

8. Arnold Toynbee's observations regarding what he calls "military virtues" are relevant to a consideration of Achebe's world: "If we wish to understand either the value of the military virtues or the sincerity of the admiration which they win, we must take care to look at them in their native social setting. . . . The military virtues are cultivated and admired in a milieu in which social forces are not sharply distinguished in people's minds from the non-human natural forces, and in which it is at the same time taken for granted that natural forces are not amenable to human control" (Toynbee, 1950, 15).

exile at his maternal village, Mbanta, and his disastrous return to the scene of his early triumphs. The parallel between the story of Okonkwo and that of his society is thus made central to the narrative development, predicated as this is upon the interrelation between the rise and fall of Okonkwo, and the fortunes of the society and way of life he represents, and its unraveling by the forces of history.

It is useful at this point to consider the salient details of Okonkwo's story as recounted by Achebe and its bearing on the underlying theme of his novel. This story really begins with Okonkwo's father, Unoka; indeed, the elements of the singular dialectic that links Okonkwo with Unoka, on one hand, and with his own son, Nwoye, on the other, determine the temporal axis of the novel and indicate the succession of generations concerned by the action. This dialectic relates in a fundamental way to the structure of images and moral propositions contained by the novel. Unoka plays a double role here; not only does his fate and its effect upon his son provide the key to the latter's psychology, he also embodies the countervalues that stand in opposition to the inflexible social ideal of the tribe. For there is a real sense in which Unoka can be considered a rebel against the rigidities of tribal society. His unorthodox style of living is a conscious subversion of the manly ideal, to which he opposes the values of art along with a playful irony and an amorality that accords with his relaxed disposition to the world. It is true that his improvidence turns him into an object of general contempt and that he comes to a particularly disagreeable end, which seems at first sight to vindicate the severe reprobation of the tribe. But even his end in the Evil Forest constitutes a triumph of sorts, a form of defiance that the narrator emphasizes with this significant detail: "When they carried him away, he took with him his flute" (13). In the end, he attracts the reader's sympathy by his unprepossessing attitude and by a certain humane simplicity, which is associated with his type, for the portrait we have of Unoka is that of a folk hero, whose insouciance stands as a constant rebuke to the vanities of the great and powerful of his world.[9]

In the immediate context of the novel, Unoka's refusal to conform to the prevailing ethos of the tribe is of course considered in wholly negative terms. More important, its subversive significance is forcefully repudiated by his son, Okonkwo, who wills himself into becoming the antithesis of all that Unoka represents, so that he comes to assume what can only be judged a fearful aspect:

> He was a man of action, a man of war. Unlike his father he could stand the look of blood. In Umuofia's war he was the first to bring

9. The type as represented in Igbo culture reappears in the character of Danda in Nkem Nwakwo's novel of that name; the closest parallel in Western literature would be perhaps the good soldier Svejk, in Jaroslav Hasek's famous antiwar novel.

home a human head. That was his fifth head, and he was not an old man yet. On great occasions, such as the funeral of a village celebrity he drank his palm-wine from his first human head. (8)

It is this portrayal of Okonkwo that prompted Thomas Melone to propose, in his pioneering study devoted to the first four novels of Chinua Achebe, an evaluation that both captures the essence of the character and exaggerates its import; he describes him as a "complex and unsettling personality" (*une multiple et déroutante personnalité* (Melone, 1973, 64). Unsettling Okonkwo certainly is, but not exactly complex; given his delineation in *Things Fall Apart*, one would be inclined rather to consider him as a "flat" character, to use E. M. Forster's term. It is true that, in the particular context in which we encounter the character, the novelist nudges us to the edge of what could have been a powerful psychological portrait; considering his problematic relation to his father, who throws a long shadow over his life, Okonkwo's inordinate obsession with self has all the makings of a deep neurosis generated by a tenacious and consuming existential project, self-realization. *Things Fall Apart* can be summed up as largely the narrative of the process of self-fashioning by which Okonkwo is transformed into the somber inversion of his father. But the mental condition into which he falls as a result is not really explored, so that we are not led into the inner workings of his mind as a fully realized individual. Even at his moment of greatest mental turmoil (in the immediate aftermath of his killing of Ikemefuna) we are provided with hardly any insight into the happenings within his troubled soul. The point here is that, despite the occasional glimpses the narrative affords into states of mind, which are also occasions for introspection on the part of the character, the narrative narrows our gaze to focus upon what is presented as essential to his makeup: "Okonkwo was a man of action, not of thought" (48).

It is not therefore the pyschological depth of his portrayal that lends Okonkwo his power to fascinate but rather his physicality, all projected outward ("he was tall and huge," the narrator informs us [3]) in such a way as to constitute him as the incarnation of his society's ideal of manhood. This is the ideal that Okonkwo translates in his attitude and manners into an overbearing masculinity. Even then, we cannot but respond, at least in the beginning, to what we perceive as his immense vitality,[1] made all the more intriguing by its sexual undercurrent, an element of his total personality clearly indicated through the seductive power this exerts upon Ekwefi.

---

1. François Mauriac has remarked upon the procedure he terms *hypertrophie* by which novelists and dramatists tend to exaggerate specific moral or psychological traits in their characters at the expense of others, so that each one of these characters (e.g., Iago, Goriot, or Raskolnikov) strikes us as representative of a singular aspect of life or experience. We observe a similar process in the creation by Achebe of Okonkwo as an outsized character.

The allusion to Okonkwo's sexuality raises the issue of gender and its narrative implications for it is this element that seems to have inspired the most inattentive reading of Achebe's novel, especially by some feminists, who object to what they perceive as the work's undue focus on the masculine principle and a corresponding depreciation of the feminine. The feminist view is exemplified by Florence Stratton's negative interpretation of what she calls the novel's focus on "gender ideology" (Stratton, 1994, 164–70). More pertinent is the critique by Susan Z. Andrade, who remarks upon "the category of the masculine" in Achebe's novel, which, she says, "attempts to avoid the representation of colonial relations in gendered terms by inscribing an excessively masculine Igbo man." She goes on to observe:

> In the Manichean allegory of anti-colonial struggle . . . the colonial/European side is characterized as masculine, while the weak and disorderly native/African is necessarily feminine. . . . Paradoxically, Achebe's preoccupation with the implicitly gendered pattern of colonial relations means that he can only imagine a negative masculinity; he has no room for a celebratory feminism. (Andrade, 1996, 255–56)

It is plain that these readings and others of the same stripe ignore the evidence of the novel itself, which foregrounds the distortion of the communal ideal by Okonkwo in such a way as to suggest a narrative commentary upon the social and moral implications of this ideal. Far from endorsing what might be termed a cult of Igbo masculinity, Achebe's novel offers ample evidence of a narrative preoccupation with the less than reassuring features of what may be considered a "basic personality type,"[2] which is fostered presumably by the work's reference culture and exemplified so forcefully by the character of Okonkwo. We are more than once alerted to the fact that Okonkwo's adoption of the manly ideal is excessive and even wrongheaded, as when Obierika emphatically expresses to Okonkwo himself his lack of enthusiasm for the prowess in wrestling demonstrated by his own son, Maduka. Obierika seems to have been conceived as a foil to Okonkwo, serving as a kind of Menenius Agrippa to Okonkwo's Coriolanus, so that his attitude indicates the possibility of an alternative stance. This opposition enables us to discern a disavowal of Okonkwo at the level of the novel's system of connotations, a level at which we sense the imaginative direction of Achebe's novel and the moral sense it carries as it works toward a confounding of Okonkwo's exaggerated sense of self.

This critical focus is gathered up in the folktale that functions both as an interlude and as a narrative commentary upon Okonkwo's ego-

---

2. The expression served as methodological focus for the investigations in social psychology undertaken by Kardiner and Ovesey (Kardiner, 1945; see also Dufrenne, 1953).

ism, a device that is fully in line with the convention of storytelling in the African oral tradition. In this sense, it serves Achebe in formal terms as an intertextual resource in the construction of his novel within which it is deployed, through a process of *mise en abîme*, both as a supplement to its ludic function and as metafiction, in a redoubling of its narrative code (Obiechina, 1993). As a direct comment upon Okonkwo's hubris, it points beyond the immediate action to the moral problem involved in the tense dialectic between collective and individual. We must recall in this connection the function of the imagination as what may be termed the preconceptual foundation of the "life world" in traditional society, a function that gave to the art of storytelling its significance in the deepest sense—as a mode of critical reflection upon the vicissitudes of human existence (Towa, 1980).

The relevance of the folktale interlude to the imaginative discourse elaborated by the novel is that it affords a clear pointer to a critical preoccupation manifested explicitly as a distinct thematic cluster centered upon the issue of gender in the novel. As Solomon Iyasere has pointed out, Okonkwo is confronted at every turn by the female principle as it informs the organization of collective life and the communal consciousness of Umuofia (Iyasere, 1978). The female principle functions indeed as a major trope in *Things Fall Apart* and constitutes a significant dimension of its system of ironies. A striking instance of this is provided by one of the most dramatic episodes in the novel, the abduction of Okonkwo's daughter, Ezinma, by Chielo, the priestess of the Earth goddess, Agbala (70–77). Chielo detains the girl an entire night in her cave, while the great warrior Okonkwo is obliged to wait outside, unable to intervene to recover his daughter until the priestess is ready to return her to him in the morning. When we consider Okonkwo's affective investment in Ezinma, in whom he discerns the male qualities whose absence he bemoans in his son, Nwoye, Chielo's act, in its challenge to Okonkwo's manhood ("Beware Okonkwo! Beware of exchanging words with Agbala. Does a man speak when a god speaks?" [71]), presents itself as a pointed recall to his attention of the gender category to which Ezinma properly belongs and the possible calls upon her that the distribution of gender roles determines within the culture. More concretely, it is Chielo's way of designating Ezinma as her successor, of reclaiming the girl and restoring her to a realm of feminine mysticism from which she is beginning to be separated by Okonkwo's projection upon her of a male essence.

The reaffirmation of the female principle signified by the Chielo episode is reinforced by other indications that suggest a consistent undermining in symbolic terms of Okonkwo's masculinity throughout the novel. As Carole Boyce Davis has rightly observed:

The Chielo-Ezinma episode is an important sub-plot of the
novel and actually reads like a suppressed larger story circumscribed by the exploration of Okonkwo's/man's struggle with and
for his people. In the troubled world of *Things Fall Apart*, motherhood and femininity are the unifying mitigating principles.
(Davis, 1986, 245; see also Jeyifo, 1993b)

The second part of the novel, devoted entirely to Okonkwo's life
in exile in his mother's village after his accidental killing of his clansman, can be read as an extended development of this secondary
theme, which subtends the narrative at its primary level of development. For Okonkwo's refusal to reconcile himself to the turn of
events that leads to his exile provides an occasion for another
reminder of the significance of the female principle when he is
instructed by Uchendu, his maternal uncle, in the culture's veneration of the mother as source of life, its association of femininity with
the vital principle, which is enunciated in resolute terms in the dic-
tum *Nneka* (Mother is supreme). Okonkwo's glum acquiescence
contrasts with the enthusiasm that accompanies his return to
Umuofia, where his loss of social standing soon reveals itself as
irreparable, and a tragic fate awaits him. The irony that attends
Okonkwo's embodiment of manhood is that, pursued by the feminine principle as if by the Furies, he is finally vanquished by a destiny that culminates in his committing what we are pointedly
informed is a "female" fault, which leads first to his exile and finally
to his downfall.

In its deconstruction of Okonkwo's masculinity, the novel also
draws directly upon a significant feature of its reference culture for
validation. For while it reflects, in its account of individual behavior
and group attitudes within its fictional world, the reality of male
dominance as an empirical fact of the social system—the order of
precedence denoted by the seating arrangement at the trial scene
provides a graphic visual demonstration—the novel also directs our
attention to the ways in which this fact is controverted in other
spheres of the collective life and imagination, especially at the level
of religious belief and experience. Although the society upholds the
notion of manliness as a fundamental social norm, it is also compelled to recognize the controlling effect of biology upon its life processes and the obvious bearing of this factor upon group survival. If
the social dominance of the men is unequivocally asserted, the parallel valorization of women in the symbolic sphere, demonstrated by
the cult of Ala, emerges as a presiding topos of "the social imaginary," one that sets up a countervailing cultural and moral force to
the massive investment of the social sphere by the men. The male-
female dialectic thus serves to maintain an affective and ideological
balance in the group; in this, it corresponds to a certain primary per-

ception of a felt duality of the cosmic order as a principle of the universal imagination.[3]

This conceptual scheme is crucial for an understanding of Okonkwo's psychology as depicted in Achebe's novel, for it is against the feminine term of the gender dialectic, as understood and expressed in the culture—the nurturing instinct as opposed to the destructive, the tender as opposed to the violent, the aesthetic as opposed to the practical, in a word, the diurnal as opposed to the nocturnal—that Okonkwo has resolutely turned his face. The terms in which his cutting down of Ikemefuna is narrated suggest that behind the gesture of confident affirmation of male resolve, which he intends his act to represent, lies a profound discomfort in the presence of femininity. We are told that he is "dazed" with fear at the moment of the boy's appeal to him, but it is a fear that has been bred in his unreflecting mind by the image of his father, fear of having to reckon with the nuanced reformulation of established social meanings by the symbolic values associated with the female principle. Indeed, for Okonkwo to be reminded anew of his father's image by Ikemefuna's artistic endowments and lively temperament is to be impelled toward a violent act of repression.

As Keith Booker has remarked, the killing of Ikemefuna represents a pivotal episode in the novel (Booker, 1998, 70) not only as a reflection of Okonkwo's disturbed mental state but in its reverberation throughout the novel as a result of its effect upon his son, Nwoye. It marks the beginning of the boy's disaffection toward his father and ultimately his alienation from the community that Okonkwo has come to represent for him. We hardly need to ponder the cleavage between father and son to realize that it provides the most potent sign of the disintegration of Umuofia society, provoked by the introduction within it of the Christian religion. Over the three years of their companionship in Okonkwo's household, Ikemefuna has come to embody for Nwoye the poetry of the tribal society, which is erased for him forever by the young boy's ritual killing, an act against nature in which his father participates. The fate of Ikemefuna, its stark revelation of the grim underside of the tribal ethos, engenders the emptiness in his heart that predisposes Nwoye to Christian conversion. The terms in which his conversion is described make clear the conjunction between social and moral issues as the determining factor. It is not without significance that the conversion itself is presented as an inner drama of sensibility in which a new poetry takes the place

---

3. It is in this light that Lévi-Strauss has interpreted "The Story of Asdiwal" as a dramatization of the tension between the masculine and the feminine principles; the myth thus reflects, according to him, a perception of the dualism of the natural order and its resonances within the imagination (Lévi-Strauss, 1977). The contradiction between the symbolic representation of women and their social position is of course a feature of most traditional cultures; for a discussion as this applies to India, see Kumari, 2000.

of the ancient, fills a spiritual and affective void, and thus comes to satisfy a need to which the traditional order is no longer capable of responding:

> It was not the mad logic of the Trinity that captivated him. He did not understand it. It was the poetry of the new religion, something felt in the marrow. The hymn about brothers who sat in darkness and in fear seemed to answer a vague persistent question that haunted his young soul—the question of the twins crying in the bush and the question of Ikemefuna who was killed. He felt a relief within as the hymn poured into his parched soul. The words of the hymn were like the drops of frozen rain melting on the dry plate of the panting earth. Nwoye's callow mind was greatly puzzled. (104)

The purple prose is integral to the language of Christian evangelism that Achebe adopts in the passage, setting in relief the last sentence, which arrests its lyrical flight with the abrupt reference to Nwoye's "callow mind." The effect of the juxtaposition verges on bathos, but its purport is unmistakable, for we are left in no doubt that this phrase describes a condition for which Nwoye's tribal background is responsible. His conversion thus represents the prelude to the refinement of mind and sensibility that the new religion promises.

Nwoye's adoption of a new name, with the significance it carries of a rebirth, consolidates his sense of allegiance to the new religion. But the particular name he takes suggests an import beyond its immediate meaning of individual salvation, for the name Isaac recalls the biblical story of the patriarch Abraham and his substitution of an animal for the sacrifice of his son, an act that inaugurates a new dispensation in which we are made to understand that fathers are no longer required to sacrifice their sons to a demanding and vengeful deity. Nwoye's adoption of this name in effect enacts a symbolic reversal of the killing of Ikemefuna and gives its full meaning to his conversion as primarily the sign of his release from the constraints of the ancestral universe.

Nwoye's story closes a family history that revolves around the troubled relationships between fathers and sons.[4] Centered as it is on the personality and tragic fate of Okonkwo, this family history comprises

---

4. As a matter of comparative interest, we might note the parallel between Achebe's treatment of the father-son conflict in *Things Fall Apart* and Samuel Butler's treatment of the same theme in *The Way of All Flesh*. The family story in *Things Fall Apart* is taken up again in the sequel, *No Longer at Ease*. We now know that Achebe's original plan was to write a trilogy based upon a family saga, a plan that he abandoned with the writing of *Arrow of God*, the work that is, without question, his masterpiece. The irony of history is explored more fully in this work in a fictional register that incorporates a religious element and is focused on a hero, Ezeulu, who assumes the dimension of a world historical figure and whose tragic stature is underlined by the intertextual resonance of his bitter return, like Shakespeare's Lear, in a raging storm, accompanied by a character who functions as his shadow.

the novel's narrative framework and functions as an allegory of the destiny of the society they inhabit and to which they relate in diverse ways. What this allegory signifies, in the particular historical and cultural context of Achebe's novel, is the state of internal crisis into which this society is plunged, a crisis that we have come to appreciate as intrinsic to its presiding ethos. This crisis is rendered especially acute by the arrival of the white man, so that a major irony of the novel is that this historic event provides a resolution, an outcome that we sense as highly ambiguous insofar as it marks the harsh intrusion of the outer world upon the tribal universe, leading to the loss of its autonomy as a sphere of existence and expression.

Achebe's understanding of the epochal significance of this turn of events represents the conceptual foundation of the novel's narrative development. Its burden of historical truth derives from its external reference, the large correspondence of the events it narrates to the internal history of the society and culture with which it deals, and the profound upheaval in the Igbo world and indeed the entire region of what is now southeastern Nigeria, which culminated in the imposition of British colonial rule.[5] The formal working out of this understanding consists of the way it determines a double perspective of point of view, which is reflected in the narrative devices through which the drama of events unfolds in the novel and by which its moral import is clarified. This is evident in what we have called the novel's diegetic function, which relates to the explicit realism associated with the genre, the imperative of representation to which it responds. On one hand, it enables a positive image of tribal society to emerge, with its coherence and especially the distinctive poetry of its forms of life. On the other hand, we are made aware that this coherence is a precarious and even factitious one, deriving from an inflexibility of social norms that places an enormous psychological and moral burden on individuals caught within its institutional constraints, imprisoned by its logic of social organization, and inhibited by its structure of social conformities. The split that this occasions within the writer's creative consciousness makes for a profound ambivalence, which translates as a productive tension in the novel's connotative substratum.

We come to some idea of this deeper layer of meaning in the novel by considering the complex of images through which it develops.[6] At the risk of a certain reductionism, it can be observed that the structure of images in the novel revolves around the theme of contradiction, which functions as its organizing principle, amplified through the structure of ironic reversals by which the narrative is propelled.

5. For this historical background (not directly considered in Achebe's novel) see Diké, 1956; also Wren, 1980.
6. For a preliminary approach to an explication of the structure of imagery in *Things Fall Apart*, suggestive of the possibility of a Bachelardian analysis, see Muoneke, 1994, 101–2.

This feature is well illustrated by the contradictory meanings assumed by the image of the locusts on the two occasions it occurs in the text. The first, which recounts an actual invasion of the village by locusts, provides what may be considered the high point of the novel; contrary to expectations, the normal association of this pest with agricultural disaster is reversed as the entire population goes into a festive mood, collecting locusts and feasting on them. The irony of this episode is deepened by the fact that it immediately precedes the account of the consultations among the elders regarding the disposal of Ikemefuna and the narration of his ritual killing. It is not without significance for the narrative scheme that Okonkwo's participation in this ritual marks the precise moment at which his fortunes commence their downward spiral. The connection is directly established between his reverses and the fall of the clan in the second occurrence of the image of the locust, which reinforces the dark irony intimated by this narrative scheme by returning us to the conventional meaning of the image of the locusts in Obierika's designation of the white men, whose appearance on the scene he interprets as the ominous event it turns out to be: "I forgot to tell you another thing which the Oracle said. It said that other white men were on their way. They were locusts, it said, and the first man was their harbinger sent to explore the terrain" (97–98).[7] Within this scheme, the progression of events in the novel is organized around a system of dichotomies and their transformations. We move in particular from the preestablished hierarchy of values implied in the opposition between the village of Umuofia and the Evil Forest to a dramatic reversal of this hierarchy.[8] The binarisms by which the unfolding of events is plotted in the novel and the ironies entailed by the process are especially marked here, for it is in the Evil Forest, which starts out as the negative marker of social space in the community depicted by the novel, that the Christians establish their new religion, which is destined to triumph over the ancestral religion. It is here that they succeed in creating a new community cemented as much by the enthusiasm called forth in them by the new faith as by its rhetoric of liberation (112). It is pertinent to remark here that the pattern of reversals itself draws upon an eminently Christian trope, encapsulated in the biblical sayings about the last coming to be first and the meek inheriting the earth, a trope that, we may recall, prompted Nietzsche's repudiation of Christianity as the religion of the weak and powerless in the world.

7. The first title of the Italian translation (1962) is based on the imagery in this passage: *Le locuste bianche*. The title has since been changed in a more recent translation to *Il crollo* (1994).
8. The notion of "Evil Forest" is not unknown in English, in which the equivalent is "Devil's Dyke."

With these reversals as they occur in *Things Fall Apart*, the Evil Forest gradually becomes invested with moral authority and thus acquires a new and positive significance. Furthermore, the historical connection between the Christian mission and the incipient colonial administration and their collaboration in the overthrow of the tribal system constitutes this new space as the domain within which a new social order is to be elaborated. The account of this connection in the latter part of *Things Fall Apart* propels the Evil Forest to a position of centrality in the novel's system of meanings, so that, in its association with Christianity, it comes to represent the source of new humanizing values and, in this sense, simultaneously becomes an image of a transformation that prefigures a new future. In short, the Evil Forest comes to signify a new and developing realm of being.

The future to which this transformation is projected is clearly intimated in Mr. Brown's exhortations to his wards, exhortations that provide a temporal complement to the spiritual justification of his missionary activity: "Mr. Brown begged and argued and prophesied. He said that the leaders of the land in the future would be men and women who had learnt to read and write" (128). The remarkable prescience ascribed here to Mr. Brown is of course the product of narrative hindsight, propounded *ex post facto* and thus anticipating the historical moment of the events depicted in the novel. It is an imaginative prediction of the modernity that rises on the horizon, which is determined by the nexus between literacy and the new cash economy and which is destined to flow out of the process of social reconstruction set in motion by the advent and diffusion of Christianity:

> Mr. Brown's school produced quick results. A few months in it were enough to make one a court messenger or even a court clerk. Those who stayed longer became teachers; and from Umuofia, labourers went forth into the Lord's vineyard. New churches were established in the surrounding villages and a few schools with them. From the very beginning religion and education went hand in hand. (128)

Achebe's novel looks forward self-consciously here to the formation of a new Westernized elite and the emergence of a new national identity enabled by literacy and predicated on an ideology of modernization. The nationalist project that in the general consensus would devolve upon the Westernized elite finds a discreet echo here within Achebe's novel and gives it a thematic resonance that, as we shall see, extends its range into the field of utopia.[9]

Thus, by a strange and unpredictable turn of events, the Evil Forest

9. The implications of the historic connection between Christianity and education form the subject of J. F. Ade Ajayi's study, *Christian Missions in Nigeria, 1841–1891: The Making of a New Elite* (1965). As indicated by its subtitle, the study is not merely a historical account of the Christian evangelical effort in Nigeria but also a sociological analysis of its major

comes to gather to itself these various intimations, so that it functions as the marker of the historical consciousness that underlies the narrative development of the novel. The peculiar overlap of theme and imagery here enlarges the novel's field of reference and suggestion in such a way as to point up the deep intuition it expresses of the compelling force of history.

But it is especially at the level of language that the double movement of Achebe's imagination in *Things Fall Apart* is fully manifested. It is revealing of the novel's thematic direction to observe and follow the course charted by the language, which proceeds from the vigorous rhetoric of traditional life, which infuses its early chapters with their peculiar energy, to the bare discursiveness that predominates in the later chapters. It is primarily the language of the early chapters that endows Achebe's novel with an epic resonance. The impulse to a revaluation of Igbo culture is clearly discernible here, for we are left in no doubt that the language of Achebe's characters is one that is constitutive of the culture and woven into the fabric of social experience. This language, in which social life is "objectified," becomes expressive of its seamless whole, of its tensions as well as strategies for their resolution, a language that may be said to found a whole register of the collective being. It is to this interrelation of speech mode and communal life that Bernth Lindfors draws attention when he describes the language of Achebe's world as "a grammar of values" (Lindfors, 1968, 77).

We sense then, behind Achebe's handling of language, an ideological *parti-pris*, which is not without its aesthetic payoff. There is an obvious delectation in language in the early chapters, which betrays a large measure of complicity with his subject matter on the part of the novelist. This conditions the felicity of style that has so often been remarked upon as a distinctive quality of Achebe's writing.[1] And it is indeed this aesthetic dimension—as distinct from the novel's documentary or ethnographic interest—that qualifies it as creative endeavor, as a notable instance of *poiesis*.

But alongside what one might call the performative style reflective of oral discourse and as counterpoint to its expressivity, Achebe

---

consequence, the formation of a new Westernized elite in the country. A concrete testimony of this connection is provided by Wole Soyinka's biography of his father in *Isarà* As with similar elites in other parts of the world, it is to this social group that we owe the national idea in Nigeria. It should be noted that, for this group, an ideology of modernity is inseparable from its anticolonial stance (Geertz, ed, 1963), the tension between this stance and the movement for cultural revival is discussed in my "Dimensions of African Discourse" (Irele, 2001: 67–81). Despite the particular circumstances of its rise in the context of British colonial rule and within a multiethnic framework, Nigerian nationalism illustrates the determining influence highlighted by Gellner (1983) and Anderson (1983) of literacy and the role of intellectuals in the emergence of ideas of national identity. (For Nigeria in particular, see Coleman, 1958; Echeruo, 1977; Zachernuk, 2000.)

1. For an extended analysis of Achebe's style and its effect upon the organization of the novel, see Cook, 1977, 75–79. Kwame Appiah, for his part, remarks on Achebe's "mastery of form and language" (1992, ix), while Margaret Lawrence comments in these terms: "a prose plain and spare, informed by his keen sense of irony" (Lawrence, 1968, 107).

adopts the tone of objective narrative, a tone derived from the Western convention of literate discourse, whose impassibility reflects the distance that he is obliged to retain with regard to his subject. This tone is evident in the direct accounts of customs and beliefs and other notations related to the tribal way of life, passages in which the skepticism natural to the rational viewpoint is barely held in check and is masked only by the neutral tone of the narrative voice. We sense the way in which this skepticism is held back in the long description of the search for Ezinma's *iyi-nwa* (53–61), but it is reaffirmed in the matter-of-fact account of Okonkwo going into the bush to collect herbs that he will administer to Ezinma to combat her fever. This report of an eminently pragmatic behavior serves as a coda to the exuberance of the story of Ezinma's stone, dispelling the air of verisimilitude that seems to attach to this story with a sober notation of fact. Similarly, Ekwefi's reminiscence of her encounter with an evil spirit is juxtaposed with a realistic, almost banal explanation of her visions: "She had prayed for the moon to rise. But now she found the half light of the incipient moon more terrifying than the darkness. The world was now peopled with vague fantastic figures that dissolved under her steady gaze and then formed again in new shapes" (75).

These juxtapositions reflect the workings of the novelist's mind as it hovers between fascination and unbelief, between an impulse toward an embrace of the cultural values suggested by his imaginative exploration of setting and narrative elaboration of context and a positivist outlook inseparable from a liberated consciousness. We have no better evidence of this ambiguous subtext than the wry report of the *egwugwu* who is rooted to the spot for two days for daring to cross the path of the one-handed masquerade (86). And Obierika's expression of awe at the potency of a neighboring village's "medicine" indicates that even the intelligence of a wise elder like him can be preyed upon by the superstitions of the tribe. Thus, while it is evident that the passages in which Achebe reports these beliefs and the practices associated with them imply a certain measure of understanding of their ways, it would be clearly absurd to suggest that he identifies with them at any level of his intellectual makeup.

It is especially instructive in this regard to note the way in which the bewilderment of the villagers at the survival of the Christians in the Evil Forest affords Achebe scope for an indulgent satire upon their conceptual naiveté, as determined by the collective belief system. This naiveté takes on a more ominous character in Obierika's account of the killing of the white man by the people of Abame, who tie up his "iron horse" to prevent it from running away to call his friends (97). It is significant that later in the novel, as a demonstration of the inadequacy of the traditional world view, we are informed of the test of efficacy passed by the new medicine introduced by the missionaries: "And it was not long before the people began to say that the white man's medicine was quick in working" (128). The term *medicine* is now employed in the sense of a technology of healing grounded in verifiable science, in other words in association with an objectifying, instrumental rationality.[2]

The insistence of the narrative voice on the fundamental weaknesses of the traditional cognitive system is thus unmistakable, and it raises the issue of the skeptical distance that, as novelist, Achebe is obliged to maintain from this system and indeed the intellectual detachment from the world he presents, despite his deep sense of cultural involvement in and affective engagement with his material. The shifting perspectives we encounter in the novel and the varied tones of the narrative voice afford pointers to the fact that *Things Fall Apart* is written out of a consciousness that is no longer at one with the indigenous order of apprehension. We are constantly made aware that the traditional background functions for Achebe not as a reference for an objective structure of knowledge but rather for the novelist's narrative construction and imaginative purpose, as a touchstone of his aesthetic, as a stock of imaginative symbols endowed with an affective value that does not depend on belief nor devotional commitment for their force of appeal. The relationship of Achebe to his material is thus comparable in some important respects to that of the Western writer to pagan mythology and even to aspects of Christian belief that are no longer capable of commanding the writer's intellectual assent or even emotional identification.

The fact that Achebe's second, objective style is often marked by irony does not detract from its value as the instrument appropriate to the function of chronicler that, as novelist, he assumes in those passages when he turns to this style, moments when he is concerned above all with registering the facts as they present themselves to him as a dispassionate observer of history. The interaction between the evocative parts of his novel and the realistic mode of its thematic progression is thus expressive of the interface between the oral and the written, which is central to his double cultural awareness. In formal terms, this interaction marks the transition from the epic to the novel to which Bakhtin has drawn attention as distinctive of the evolution of narrative (Bakhtin, 1981; see also Ong, 1982; Goody, 1987). The significant point about this interaction is the tension produced in the novel between what one

2. The logic that underlies the reference here to the potency of the white man's medicine is of a piece with the argument of efficacy advanced by Charles Taylor (1982) and others in favor of the superior epistemological status of Western rationality. See also Wilson, 1970; the three essays in Lukes, 1977, pt. 2, "Rationality and Relativism," 121–74; and especially the comprehensive review of the question by Jürgen Habermas (1984, 8–75).
3. Marjorie Winters's analysis (1981), in which she discerns an evolution of Achebe's style toward the dry prose of official documents, calls to mind Max Weber's observation on the development of institutional bureaucracy and its impersonal character as a sign of the "disenchanted world" of modern society.

might call a Romanticism of its oral style, which derives from a personal attachment of the writer to his African antecedents, and the realism of the Western style, which corresponds to his awareness of their supersession in a new dispensation. The deep mechanisms at work in the novel thus come to the surface in the language, which enables us to grasp the full connotative weight and rhetorical direction of the narrative. This is a story that begins in the register of myth and ends on a note of chronicle, a transformation that is reflected in its narrative style, which becomes progressively "de-poetized," as Thomas Melone has rightly pointed out (Melone, 1973, 65).[3]

The "downward" progression of Achebe's expression thus charts the course of the depletion of language brought on by events in the community to which the novel refers, a process that is registered within the work by the transition from a textualized orality through which the characters and the world of the novel are not so much represented as evoked, called forth into being, to the passive record of events imposed by the conventions of literate discourse. For the interaction between styles, the play of language on which the narrative development turns, forms part of the movement of history traced in the novel. As the story advances, we witness a linguistic process that culminates in the triumph of the culture of literacy, a process that also signals the engulfing of the indigenous voice, which was carried exclusively through the oral medium, by the discourse of colonialism.

It is this latter discourse that finally calls attention to itself, at the end of the novel, in the total identification of the linguistic vehicle of the text with the actual language in which the thoughts of the colonial officer are formulated. The passage is remarkable in many respects, not least for the way it draws attention to the differentiated use in Achebe's novel of the device of indirect speech. For in its bare matter-of-factness, it stands in marked contrast to the remarkable stream of interior monologue through which, as he is led to his death, Ikemefuna's forebodings are translated—in a dramatic counterpoint between an immediate sense of personal danger, which is rendered through indirect speech, and the reassuring formulations of communal lore. The loss of the vivid quality of Ikemefuna's monologue in the colonial officer's reported speech indicates that we now have to do with the disembodied voice of history manifested through this faceless, nondescript character. The historic turning signified by the end of Okonkwo's personal story is thus registered at the specific level of language; from being subjects of their own discourse, Okonkwo and his people have now become the objects of the discourse of another, elaborated in a language foreign to them.

There is a sense, then, in which the advent of the imperial moment is developed in Achebe's novel as a linguistic experience, as more or less a misadventure of language, which unfolds through the discursive modes of its narration. In line with this development, the temporal scheme of the novel appropriately shifts from the cyclic plane, associated with a rich organicism and intense vitalism, to the strictly linear; the precipitation of events in the third part of the novel contrasts markedly with the unhurried pace of the telling in the earlier parts. At the same time, the spatial scheme itself becomes transformed, enlarged, and in the process impoverished: from the affectively charged compactness of the nine villages to the impersonal perspectives of the Lower Niger, evoked in the ruminations of the colonial officer that bring the narrative to its close.

Things Fall Apart displays in its own peculiar way what Frank Kermode has called "the ambiguous innocence of the classic text" (Kermode, 1983, 74). Kermode's phrase itself is a suggestive one, for we might conceive of the classic text in terms of its centrality to a tradition, either one that is fully established but must still accommodate new works for its reinvigoration—the sense of T. S. Eliot's celebrated essay "Tradition and the Individual Talent"—or one that is emerging, advertising itself by its novelty, as is generally held to be the case with modern African literature in the European languages. The poetics of *Things Fall Apart* seem in a curious way to unite both of these senses of the classic text. On one hand, its economy of style derives from what seems like a complete adherence to the norms of the conventional novel, exemplified by its strictly linear structure with a beginning, a middle, and an end, which leads inexorably to the final catastrophe, the progression clearly marked by the novel's three-part structure. Moreover, it achieves its effects by means that refuse to call attention to themselves. This makes for an austerity that places it alongside that other classic of the African canon, Cheikh Hamidou Kane's *Ambiguous Adventure*. At the same time, it has claims to a uniqueness that derives from its departure from the Western model in fundamental ways. As the discussion above indicates, a tension exists between the surface fluency that distinguishes Achebe's text and the resonances set up within it by its hidden places of signification. Although *Things Fall Apart* presents itself at first sight as what Roland Barthes has called a "readerly" rather than a "writerly" text (Barthes, 1970), the key elements of its internal features indicate that there is more to its transparent texture than is at first perceptible. These deeper promptings of the text indicate that its apparent simplicity is belied by the complexities of reference and suggestion that lie beneath its directness of enunciation.[4]

4. Barthes associates the "readerly" text expressly with the established classic, which requires hardly any strenuous engagement on the part of the reader, whereas Kermode's phrase draws attention to the inherent complexity of such texts. The recourse to orality gives Achebe's novel what, following Gates, one might call a "speakerly" quality (Gates, 1989).

The tension that these complexities generate in the text proceeds largely from the relationship that obtains between theme and form, which reflects an ambivalence that informs the fictional inspiration and therefore structures its formal expression. Simon Gikandi has endeavored to address this issue by claiming that this feature of the work derives from the writer's cultural background, which recognizes a plurality of discourses and admits different points of view, varying formulations of the truth of experience or reality (Gikandi, 1991, 44–50). But the ambivalence in the novel is so profound as to carry much more weight than Gikandi seems willing to allow. Rather than a function of cultural habit, it seems to me that this ambivalence stems from the critical consciousness inherent in Achebe's recourse to the novel as a narrative genre. The point can be made directly by observing that Achebe presents Igbo society "steadily and whole," to borrow Matthew Arnold's expression. For while this society is indeed marked by an internal coherence of its organization and a poetry of its expressive modes, it also betrays profound inadequacies and grave internal contradictions, which account for the disintegration that the novel records. Thus, *Things Fall Apart* does not merely embody a willed recall of cultural memory but develops also as an exploration of the specificities of life within the universe of experience it unveils, an exploration that amounts ultimately to a reassessment of its nature and presiding ethos. In other words, Achebe brings to his task of historical recollection a critical and moral intelligence.

The moral issue in *Things Fall Apart* seems to hinge upon how far Okonkwo can be considered representative of his society, how far he can be held to be its embodiment. For William Walsh, the centrality of Okonkwo to the issue is clear, as he says, "because of the way in which the fundamental predicament of the society is lived through his life" (Walsh, 1970, 52). But any categorical answer one way or the other skirts the question, since in fact, in real societies, individuals only partially embody the values of the community even when these are presumed to have been fully internalized, for in the process of acting out these values, they can also be found to strain against them. It is this dialectic between the individual and the society, inherent in what Durkheim terms "social constraint" (*la contrainte sociale*) that is so well mirrored in Achebe's novel in its depiction of Okonkwo's relation to his society.

This is a dialectic that is of course very much within the province of the novel. Indeed, as Sunday Anozie has pointed out, Okonkwo as a character corresponds in some respects to Lucien Goldmann's concept of the "problematic hero"; in Anozie's reading, Okonkwo emerges as something of a romantic hero, the bearer of a cult of the self (Anozie, 1970, 41–54, 120–141). It is easy to see how this attribute can constitute a menace to the kind of society that Achebe constructs, a potential factor of disaggregation in a tribal community. For the assiduous cultivation of individual self can only disturb the system of obligations and solidarities on which the sense of community is founded. Okonkwo's personal attitude and social conduct amount in fact to an idiosyncratic interpretation of social rules and lead irresistibly to a state of moral irresponsibility, despite his apparent conformity to norms. His self-absorption is of such magnitude as to test the limits of the dominant ideology and thus to reveal its points of weakness. It is this paradox of his situation that is dramatized by his exile, which can be read as a symbolic expression of the necessity to rein in his passionate individuality by its exclusion from the social sphere. This aspect of his character is presented as directly related to the simplified and totally unreflective approach to the world by which he lives and acts, in striking contrast to his friend Obierika. The same unreflective commitment to the communal ethos in his killing of Ikemefuna is manifested in his cutting down of the court messenger. Okonkwo's blinding passion leads him to a final act of egoism, which marks him with a tragic solitude, rendered tersely in the line in which we last glimpse him: "He wiped his matchet on the sand and went away" (145).

Contrary, then, to Gikandi's contention, the ambivalence by which the novel is governed inheres in the text itself and emerges clearly in the portrayal of Okonkwo. We must go further to observe that the largely negative thrust of this portrayal comes close to undermining the polemical intent of the novel. For if Okonkwo's tragic fate marks him as a symbol of the passion of the African in modern times, the ironic devaluation of the character and the ethos he embodies suggests a profound sense of unease on the part of his creator regarding many issues of moral import raised by the habits of mind and social practices that define the traditional universe of life and expression. There is thus a sense in which the sustained imaginative reflection upon Igbo society in Achebe's novel begins to tend toward a subversion of its ideological premises. It is as if Achebe's intellect, sensibility, and sense of artistic integrity had entered into contention with his primary affections for his cultural antecedents, thus bringing into peril his conscious project of bearing witness to the poetic quality of the universe in which they are rooted. Although it would be extreme to read Achebe's novel as the expression of a repudiation of the tribal ethos, as a form of recoil from the tribal universe, to consider the text in the light of its ambivalence is to recognize it for what it is: nothing less than an uncompromising reappraisal of the tribal world.[5]

5. It is well to place Achebe's appraisal of his own society's less flattering aspects against his now-celebrated critique of Joseph Conrad's *Heart of Darkness* in his essay "An Image of Africa" (*Hopes and Impediments,* 1–20). Achebe assails Conrad's work as a "racist novel" though he is far from calling for its elimination from the Western canon, as David Denby asserts in his 1995 article, "Jungle Fever." While Achebe does not altogether ignore the anti-

It is important to stress that this revaluation has nothing to do with the diminished conception of African humanity and capacities constitutive of colonial ideology but arises as an immediate factor of the historical process represented in the novel. We appreciate the intense feeling of insecurity of the Umuofia elders as they sense the world with which they are familiar going out from under them. We sympathize therefore with the claim to cultural integrity defended by Okonkwo and others, more so as the novel establishes a parallel between their attitude and that of Mr. Smith, whose intransigence on behalf of the Christian cause mirrors that of Okonkwo on behalf of the traditional world. They are the true protagonists, embodying each in his own way the logic of the cultural conflict enacted in the novel, the logic involved in the drama of the colonial encounter. Moreover, this conflict is situated within the perspective of a cultural pluralism that is at first rehearsed in a good-humored way in the theological disputations between the Umuofians and Mr. Brown, but which soon assumes an agonistic character in the confrontation with his successor, Mr. Smith; it is this later development that is voiced by one of the elders, Ajofia: "We cannot leave the matter in his hands because he does not understand our customs, just as we do not understand his. We say he is foolish, because he does not know our ways, and perhaps he says we are foolish because we do not know his" (134–35). But this balanced view of cultural relativism hardly represents the lever of the novel's groundwork of ideas nor the resting place of its ideological or narrative progression. *Things Fall Apart* complicates singularly the issues so often raised in the context of the debate within which it is usually situated: the tradition/modernity framework. It goes beyond the series of dichotomies so regularly invoked in this debate as to have become platitudes: established custom versus change; cultural loss versus reproduction; accommodation versus revolt; and acculturation versus cultural nationalism. These issues are obviously implicated in the total discursive range of the novel's narrative development, but they do not in the end, it seems to me, constitute the real heart of the matter. It is not enough to see *Things Fall Apart* as simply a statement of cultural and racial retrieval, as a novel that embodies a discourse of nativism. Rather than a unilateral revaluation of the past, the central preoccupation of this novel, as indeed of Achebe's entire production, revolves around the deeply problematic nature of the relationship of

---

imperialist thesis of the novella, he seems to equate Conrad's compassion for the Africans to the kind promoted by the ASPCA on behalf of domestic animals. This seems hardly fair to Conrad, but Achebe is not alone in missing the serious moral import of the novella as registered in the epigraph to the first edition ("But the dwarf answered: 'No; something human is dearer to me than the wealth of all the world'—*Grimm's Tales*"). It is regrettable that this epigraph is not always reproduced in current editions of the work, the notable exception being the Norton edition edited by Robert Kimbrough, which also contains Achebe's essay as well as responses to it. On this question, see Hamner, 1990. See also Watts's introduction to the Oxford edition of *Heart of Darkness* and, more recently, Firchow, 2000.

past to present in Africa. What is at issue here, in the most fundamental way, is the bearing of that past upon the present, fraught as
this is with implications for the future prospects of the continent.

Kwame Anthony Appiah's summing up of the novel is pertinent to
this question when he remarks, "Achebe's accounting includes
columns both for profit and loss" (Appiah, 1992, xii). Given what we
have seen as its ironic stances and the key of ambivalence on which
the narrative is rung, it seems to me that if the novel translates a sense
of loss, this cannot be overwhelming. *Things Fall Apart* can hardly be
read as a wistful lingering over an elusive past; nostalgia is not a determining nor even constitutive element of its atmosphere. The intellectual disposition of the writer, if not his imaginative consciousness,
operating at a level deeper than any ideological conception of his function, seems here to apprehend a decided lack of congruence between
the past of the novel's reconstruction, reanimated as a function of cultural memory, and the imperatives of the present, even as the claims
of that past to aesthetic significance are upheld, and its psychological
value in countering the debilitation of the colonial situation is acti-
vated. We are made aware of the inadequacy of the overarching ethos
by which the past was regulated, its limitations as embodied in historical forms, the inadequacy of this ethos and of these forms arising precisely from their mode of insertion in the world. Moreover, as Pierre
Nora has pointed out, the phenomenon of memory exceeds the
purview of history (Nora, 1989). In this particular context perhaps
more than any other, the dynamics of cultural memory involve much
more than reaching into a past; they also engage the present, insofar
as the traditional culture upon which they are focused remains a
vibrant contemporary reality. But while it continues to exert its force
upon minds, the question remains how far the past can be invoked to
legitimize the present, how far it is capable of functioning as a practical reference in the contemporary circumstances of African endeavor.

These, then, are some of the issues raised by Achebe's work. The
point is that the novel genre serves Achebe as a mode of reflection
upon the nature and significance of the African past and its relevance
to the African present. In *Things Fall Apart*, this reflective tone is
made evident in the conversations and dialogues he attributes to the
elders of the tribe, who are thereby presented through the course of
the narrative as minds engaged in a sustained deliberative process.
The novel takes on a discursive character as it stages a running
debate on customs and practices, on institutions and values, on systems of belief. This debate is in reality conducted as an interrogation
of the human possibilities offered by the material world and mental
landscape that together comprise the tribal culture and stamp it with
a distinctive quality. Although this interrogation is presented as internal, it amounts ultimately to an objective scrutiny in the light of an

alternative set of values that, in the nature of things, were not available to the subjects themselves. This scrutiny forms part of the implicit ideology of the novel, of the system of ideas presiding upon its organization, for which the Euro-Christian system of values begins to function as touchstone and measure. This is not to imply that the emphasis on Christianity as a factor of liberation authorizes us to read the work as a justification of the new religion, much less of colonial imposition, but rather we should view it as a mirror held up to African society, enabling a process of self-apprehension. In other words, a new African consciousness emerges through the mediation of the Christian/Western vision of the world.

The tension generated by the fundamental ambivalence of the novel's propositional content can be grasped most intensely at this level, for the process of self-reflection manifested in the novel is traversed by what one might call a deep cultural anxiety. This is nothing like the self-contempt displayed in Ouologuem's *Bound to Violence*, but it testifies to the way in which the need to validate the tribal culture in some emotionally satisfactory way runs up against the question of value, a question that is central to the order of meaning proposed by the novel. It is in this light that Obierika, who stands as the manifest antithesis of Okonkwo, can be said to function as the moral center of the novel. He comes closest among the novel's characters to a representation of what Michael Valdez Moses has called a "modern sensibility" (Moses, 1995, 113).[6] It is perhaps not farfetched to suggest that we have in Obierika not merely the one character with which, as Jeyifo points out, the novelist seems to identify but rather a subtle projection of the critical consciousness that Achebe himself brings to the imaginative conception of the novel (Jeyifo, 1991). The evidence of the novel lends enough weight to this view as to make it a matter of more than mere speculation.

Whatever the case, the debate enacted within the novel gives the work an analytical bent to which its initial ideological inspiration is

---

6. It is instructive in this regard to consider the comparison suggested by Michael Valdez Moses between the world depicted in Achebe's novel and the image of early Greek society that emerges from the great classical epics of the Western literary tradition. Moses speaks of the "strikingly Homeric quality of *Things Fall Apart*" and discerns "certain similarities between particular Greek and African civilizations in a way that breaks down the Manichean dualism of the West and its Other." He adds: "In fact, the differences between the ethos of Homer's Mycenaean heroes and that of their Igbo counterparts in Achebe's novels are far less striking than those between either of them and the moral standards and political norms that prevail among contemporary European, American and African intellectuals" (Moses, 1995, 113). Moses might have added that, in both Homer's *Iliad* and Achebe's *Things Fall Apart*, we witness a distancing of the narrator from the hero, which amounts to a questioning of the dominant ethos. In both, we sense a marked distaste for the violence accepted in earlier societies and reflected in epic narratives, which was carried to remarkable heights in the wanton violence and atrocities of the Norse sagas. This narrative distance in the *Iliad* reduces somewhat the analytical value of the distinction so often proposed between epic and novel in terms of the degree of the narrator's investment not only in the action and atmosphere of the narrative but in the moral values of the world it represents.

ultimately subordinated, for *Things Fall Apart* testifies to a clear recognition of a decisive break in the African experience of history occasioned by the colonial fact. It hardly needs to be stressed that this recognition is far from committing Achebe to an acquiescence in the methods of subjugation employed by colonial agents, whether white or black, exemplified by the deception and humiliation described in the latter pages of the novel in which the historical grievance of Africa is vividly represented and dramatized in the martyrdom of Okonkwo and the Umuofia elders. The pathos of their situation resonates through the entire society, takes on wider meaning as nothing less than the suspension of the entire culture, the arrest of those activities that gave both energy and poetry to everyday life in Umuofia. All of this portends the stifling of the tribe's spirit by a collective trauma: "Umuofia was like a startled animal with ears erect, sniffing the silent, ominous air, and not knowing which way to run" (139).

The anticolonial thrust of the novel is unmistakable here, but it becomes evident as we reflect upon the novel as a whole that this is not all there is to the story of Okonkwo and of Umuofia. The novel ends with the hero's suicide, but there is no real closure, for the white colonial officer's musings intimate a new and unpredictable future for the Umuofians and for the continent of which they form an integral and representative part. The import of the novel arises from this intimation, for what *Things Fall Apart* registers ultimately is an acute consciousness of the historical and cultural discontinuity occasioned by the colonial encounter in Africa and of its ontological implications—the necessity for a new mode of being, of relating to the world.

It is one of the of the novel's peculiar traits that the historical realism that directs the narrative progression harmonizes readily with the elegiac mood that serves as its groundbase, a conjunction that is registered in one of the most remarkable passages in the novel:

> That night the mother of the spirits walked the length and breadth of the clan, weeping for her murdered son. It was a terrible night. Not even the oldest man in Umuofia had ever heard such a strange and fearful sound, and it was never to be heard again. It seemed as if the very soul of the tribe wept for a great evil that was coming—its own death. (132)

The epochal significance of the passage is intensified and assumes cosmic resonance in the lament that pours out of one of the characters, Okika, at the final meeting of the clan: "All our gods are weeping. Idemili is weeping. Ogwugwu is weeping. Agbala is weeping, and all the others" (143). Okika's lament directs us to the heart of Achebe's novel: it is as an elegy that incorporates a tragic vision of history that *Things Fall Apart* elicits the strongest and deepest response.

Things Fall Apart inaugurates the imaginative reliving in Achebe's work of those significant moments of the African experience, which he has traced in his five novels to date. Given the comprehensive perspective of inspiration and reference within which they are situated, these novels compose a historical vision. Consequently, they pose the general theoretical question of the formal relation of the novel as a genre to the substantive fact of history, a relation within which the purpose of Achebe's work can be said to inhere. Because of its unique place in Achebe's corpus and in the African canon, *Things Fall Apart* presents itself as the indispensable point of departure for an examination of this question.

The transition of Achebe's style from an epic mode to one associated with the novel provides an indication of the changing modes of this relationship. This stylistic evolution of the novel may be interpreted as the scriptural sign of a corresponding adjustment of the writer's vision, reflecting his sense, as the narrative develops, of the pressure of history as it begins to exert itself upon the community that is the subject of the novel. This seems to accord with a Hegelian conception of history as the unfolding saga of modernity, with the modern novel as its imaginative equivalent. The received opinion stemming from these sources has tended to understand modernity as a historical phenomenon arising primarily from the Western experience and as the paradigm that commands the writing of scientific history and, as a consequence, the emergence of the novel, the literary genre that is thought to be most closely associated with modern culture. In this view, the novel as a specific modern genre affords a new medium for the construction in aesthetic and moral terms of a vision of a totality no longer immediately available to consciousness in the fragmented, reified world of modern civilization (Lukács, 1977).[7]

For the conception of history that underwrites the status of the novel alluded to above, the society depicted in Achebe's novel along with the culture it sustains appears as prehistoric, subsisting, as far as the record of its existence is concerned, on mythical narratives orally transmitted and therefore unworthy of the attention of serious historical scholarship. Consequently, it seems hardly appropriate as the subject of a novel in the normal acceptance of the term.[8] *Things*

---

7. Fredric Jameson has sought to get beyond this privileging of the novel on the part of Georg Lukács by recovering for critical practice a sense of wholeness for all forms of literary expression: "Indeed, no working model of the functioning of language, the nature of communication or of the speech act, and the dynamics of formal and stylistic change is conceivable which does not imply a whole philosophy of history" (Jameson, 1981, 59).

8. This conforms with Hegel's contemptuous dismissal of the literature of earlier societies as creditable historical material, a view given expression at the outset of his philosophy of history: "The historian binds together the fleeting rush of events and deposits it in the temple of Mnemosyne. Myths, folk songs, traditions are not part of original history; they are still obscure modes and peculiar to obscure peoples. Observed and observable reality is a more solid foundation for history than the transience of myths and epics. Once a people has reached firm individuality, such forms cease to be its historical essence" (Hegel, 1953, 3–4).

Fall Apart challenges this conception, for the whole purpose of Achebe's novel is to bring the existence of this culture into view as a historical reality, one that bears witness to the human world realized within it. The narrative mode, in both its epic aspect and at the novelistic level of articulation, affords Achebe the means of restating the grounded historicity of the African experience in a creative reconstruction of the stages of collective being.

It is of course true that the sequence of events narrated and the society and culture represented are products of an individual imagination, detached from any function of pure predication; the narrative unfolding of events conducted along a definite plot line is thus sustained by an aesthetic faculty that is fully engaged in Achebe's reconstruction. It is evident therefore that, despite their historical focus, *Things Fall Apart* and *Arrow of God*—the two novels need to be considered together on this point—are not only *not* histories in any ordinary sense of the word, they cannot be considered historical novels either, in the conventional or narrow sense of their dealing with real events in the past and featuring real historical personalities as characters.[9] But this sense is hardly satisfactory for an understanding of the narrative function, hence the need for a more inclusive conception, such as the one propounded by Hayden White, who posits a fundamental relationship between fiction and history as modalities of the narrative activity and process. The point is well clarified in the following observation regarding the significance of narrative as a universal phenomenon: "The affiliation of narrative historiography with literature and myth should provide no reason for embarrassment, . . . because the systems of meaning production shared by all three are distillates of the historical experience of a people, a group, a culture" (White, 1987, 44–45).[1] This suggests that the assimilation of fiction to history is authorized not merely in formal terms—what White calls "emplotment"—but also in content, insofar as in both cases, the real world of concrete experience features as a referent of the narrative. But here, we work with a special notion of referentiality peculiar to fiction, deriving from its enhanced value as symbolic representation of experience. To quote White again: "Thus envisaged, the narrative figurates the body of events that serves as its primary referent and transforms these events into intimations of patterns of meaning that any literal representation of them as facts could never produce" (45).

These remarks bear directly on Achebe's two novels, for they present themselves as acts of remembrance that entail an intense engage-

---

9. The conception of the historical novel summarized here is that of David Daiches (1956).
1. The point is made even more succinctly and more pointedly by Michel Zéraffa with regard to the novel: "Sont en cause, dans le roman, notre historicité et son sens" (At stake in the novel is our historicity as well as its meaning) (Zéraffa, 1971, 15).

ment of mind and sensibility upon a collective experience and thus move toward what White calls "an order of meaning." In specific terms, the two novels manifest an understanding of the essence of history as being bound up with momentous events that alter the collective destiny in ways that are unpredictable but prove ultimately definitive. These novels are informed by a profound sense of the radical contingency of history.

It is this deep intuition of history that, it seems to me, distinguishes Achebe's work from that of every other African writer. This distinction emerges clearly when we contrast the tone of *Things Fall Apart* with that of Francophone African writings roughly contemporaneous with it, especially the works of Camara Laye, Léopold Senghor, and Cheikh Hamidou Kane, all of whom have created in obedience to a paradigm of the self that privileges the ideal of wholeness. This accounts for the nostalgia for the past that pervades their work, an impossible longing for an earlier state of being denoted by Senghor's *le royaume de l'enfance*, a nostalgia further deepened by the religious/theological dimension it assumes in Kane's *Ambiguous Adventure*. It is not without interest to observe that a similar aspiration for an enhanced quality of being animates Soyinka's mythical evocations of origins (David, 1995).

Achebe's work registers a severe recognition of the compulsion upon the human estate of the historical process itself—what he has called "the power of events"—a compulsion that admits of only narrow margins for the play of human agency. It is this that I have called elsewhere "humane pessimism," which I believe Achebe shares with Joseph Conrad (Irele, 1987).[2] It must be understood, however, that this pessimism is not by any means a disabling one, for it does not imply a resignation born out of a passive suffering of events. It calls rather for a purposeful adjustment to those great shifts in the structure of the world that destabilize established constellations of thought, initiate a new historical process, and enforce therefore a new adventure of mind.

This seems to me the direction of meaning in Achebe's fiction, which, in its immediate reference, represents an imaginative remapping of the African experience within the space of history, the literary mode deployed as a means of shaping consciousness for the confrontation of the new realities on the horizon of African being. The ironies and the ambivalence that underscore the drama of cultural memory in his first novel emerge in a new light from this perspective, attesting to a somber consciousness but one resolutely oriented toward a future envisioned as pregnant with new possibilities.

---

2. For a discussion of the mental landscape that forms the background to Conrad's pessimism, see Jameson, 1981, 251ff.

In other words, a utopian component underlies the expressive modalities and encompassing vision in *Things Fall Apart*.

In a limited sense, the utopianism of the novel is inseparable from the nationalist vein that, as I have suggested, informs the narrative and the project of modernity that is its concomitant. This is not to imply that Achebe's nationalism in this or other works advertises itself as a programmatic fixation upon an ideal future. However, the understanding of history that underlies his system of ideas implies, as its necessary complement, a vision of African renewal. Thus, a tacit correlation exists between Achebe's imaginative discourse in its utopian implications and what Arjun Appadurai has called "the megarhetoric of developmental modernization" of African and Asian anticolonial nationalism (Appadurai, 1996, 22). It is well to remember that Achebe continues to sustain in his fiction right up to the present moment this vision of new beginnings in Africa, as demonstrated by the conclusion of *Anthills of the Savannah*.[3]

But the utopianism of Achebe's fiction, as it begins to declare itself in *Things Fall Apart*, has a broader scope than is suggested by the materialist and utilitarian preoccupations of nationalism. It involves what the Manuels have called "an idealizing capacity" as a defining property of the utopian imagination (Manuel and Manuel, 1979, 5). In this respect, it accords fully with the universalist interpretation of the utopian function of literature propounded by Fredric Jameson, whose reformulation of Lukács's categories of *conservative* and *progressive* expands their meaning in a new dichotomy between *ideology* and *utopia*. In this reformulation, intended to refurbish the terms earlier proposed by Karl Mannheim for historical and sociological understanding, the term *utopian* comes to designate the way in which literature, as a socially symbolic act, envisions the realm of freedom as a human possibility (Jameson, 1981).[4]

I will conclude then with the observation that what cultural memory delivers in Achebe's first novel is not so much a revalued past,

3. It is always hazardous to move from reading fiction to speculating about the author's opinions in the real world. However, Achebe's non-fictional works confirm his embrace of modernity as a necessary dimension of African renewal. But as his two novels relating to the postindependence period demonstrate—*A Man of the People* and *Anthills of the Savannah*—he takes full cognizance of the problems and dilemmas involved in the process of Africa's accession to modernity. Nevertheless, his commitment has remained firm, despite the frustrations and disappointments that seem indeed to have given him an even sharper edge. The title of his 1988 collection of essays, *Hopes and Impediments*, is sufficiently eloquent to indicate this direction of his sentiments. It seems therefore safe to say that, for Achebe, the African personality is not incompatible with a modern scientific culture. Thus he asks rhetorically, "Why should I start waging war as a Nigerian newspaper editor was doing the other day against 'the soulless efficiency' of Europe's industrial and technological civilization when the very thing my society needs may well be a little technical efficiency" ("The Novelist as Teacher," *Hopes and Impediments*, 43). Add to this the lament at the end of *The Trouble with Nigeria*, that Nigeria has lost the twentieth century and is running the risk of losing the twenty-first as well.

4. In a fine passage written shortly before his death, Irving Howe expanded on Jameson's notion when he defined utopianism as "a necessity of the moral imagination." He contin-

recollected in a spirit of untroubled celebration, as, ultimately, the opening of the African consciousness to the possibility of its transcendence, to the historic chance of a new collective being and existential project. The sense of the tragic clings nonetheless to this consciousness, for Achebe is aware that this historic chance, if real, is at best limited and fragile. His vision is probably best expressed by the voice of the Oracle in his poem "Dereliction" (in the volume *Beware Soul Brother*) who invites his questing worshipers to a form of action, perhaps a collective affirmation, in the precarious space constituted by the strip of dry land between sea and shore at the ebbing of the tide:

> Let them try the land
> Where the sea retreats
> Let them try the land
> Where the sea retreats

Achebe's tragic vision of history is presented in these lines in tension with his utopianism. But to invoke the tragic dimension of Achebe's first novel is not merely to seek to uncover the full scope of its statement of the colonial encounter in Africa but also to reach for its contemplative character, the sense it contains of the general human condition.[5] It is this sense that is conveyed by Barthes's summation of the tragedies of Racine as "the aesthetics of defeat" (*l'art de l'échec*) (Barthes, 1963, 61). The description applies equally to all of the great tragedies of world literature, among which *Things Fall Apart* must now be seen to occupy a distinctive place. Beyond its reference to the personal dilemmas of Racine's characters, Barthes's phrase points to the apprehension by the tragic imagination of the essential fragility of our human condition. The deep insight that tragedy provides into this condition may well shake our being with fear and trembling, but it is the illumination and psychic release it generates that enable humanity to keep going. As a necessary component of its exploration of the African experience, *Things Fall Apart* embodies this fundamental truth of the imaginative vision.

---

ued: "It doesn't necessarily entail a particular politics; it doesn't ensure wisdom in current affairs. What it does provide is a guiding principle, a belief or hope for the future, an understanding that nothing is more mistaken than the common notion that what exists today will continue to exist tomorrow. This kind of utopianism is really another way of appreciating the variety and surprise that history makes possible—possible, nothing more. It is a testimony to the resourcefulness that humanity now and then displays (together with other, far less attractive characteristics). It is a claim for the value of desire, the practicality of yearning—as against the deadliness of acquiescing in the given, simply because it is there" (Howe, 1993, 133).

5. The idea of *Things Fall Apart* as a tragedy in the classical sense was broached in an early essay of mine (Irele, 1965; see also Niven, 1990). Séverac discusses various responses to my classification of Achebe's novel as a tragedy (Séverac, 1997, 506–7).

BIODUN JEYIFO

For Chinua Achebe: The Resilience and the Predicament of Obierika[†]

> In one sense then [there is] a travelling away from its old self towards a cosmopolitan, modern identity while in another sense [there is] a journeying back to regain a threatened past and self-hood. To coax from it such unparalleled inventiveness requires the archaic energy, the perspective and temperament of creation myths and symbolism.
>
> Chinua Achebe

> So important have . . . stories been to mankind that they are not restricted to accounts of initial creation but will be found following human societies as they recreate themselves through vicissitudes of their history, validating their social organizations, their political systems, their moral attitudes and religious beliefs, even their prejudices. At . . . critical moments new versions of old stories or entirely fresh ones tend to be brought into being to mediate the changes and sometimes to consecrate opportunistic defections into more honourable rites of passage.
>
> Chinua Achebe

Antinomies of Post-coloniality

To write a critical tribute to any writer at the present time calls for a special kind of political criticism.[1] This is perhaps even more daunting when that writer happens to be Chinua Achebe who, beyond the fact of his being one of contemporary literature's most widely read and internationally prominent authors, has always figured as a complex, ambiguous presence in the post-colonial politics of identity and ideological affiliation. Perhaps nothing better expresses this ambiguity than the fact that much as Achebe's works have been invoked as powerful, exemplary texts of nationalist contestation of colonialist myths and distortions of Africa and Africans,[2] it is also the case that these texts have only been minimally concerned, at least at the thematic level, to depict or explore resistance to colonialism; rather, they have been particularly imbued with a melancholic sense of the falling

---

[†] From *Chinua Achebe: A Celebration.* Ed. Kristen Holst Petersen and Anna Rutherford (Portsmouth, NH: Heinemann, 1991), 51–70. Reprinted by permission of Pearson Education.

1. For apposite conceptions of 'political criticism' at the present time see Michael Ryan, 'Political Criticism' in G. Douglas Atkins and Laura Morrow, eds., *Contemporary Literary Theory* (Amherst: The University of Massachusetts Press, 1989) and Satya P. Mohanty, 'Us and Them: On the Philosophical Basis of Political Criticism', *Yale Journal of Criticism*, Volume 2 (Spring 1989), pp. 1–31.

2. See C. L. Innes and Bernth Lindfors, eds., *Critical Perspectives on Chinua Achebe* (Washington, D.C.: Three Continents Press, 1978), especially the essays, 'Politics and the African Writer' by Kolawole Ogunbesan and 'Chinua Achebe: A Man of the People' by Ngugi wa Thiong'o.

apart of things with the collapse of pre-colonial societies and cultures. Another distinct, but related expression of the ambiguous politics of Achebe's works pertains to his known identification with left-wing, anti-capitalist groups and intellectuals in his native Nigeria, and more broadly in Africa, at the same time that this identification has been fraught with problems and controversies.[3] Achebe is, in this sense, very much in the company of other post-colonial writers like Wole Soyinka, Gabriel García Márquez, Salman Rushdie, Nadine Gordimer and Carlos Fuentes whose left-identified politics sit very uneasily with the orthodox Left and its set revolutionary perspectives and objectives.

But this essay is not about 'literary fellow-travellers', a designation which always said as much about the Party's claims of privileged access to superior truths as it did about the writer's putative ambiguous, wavering political and moral affiliations.[4] What I wish to explore in this short critical tribute is how a profoundly but subtly emancipatory politics figures in Achebe's work, especially his first novel, *Things Fall Apart*,[5] as a sustained project of demythologization of pre-colonial, colonial and post-colonial myths of legitimation and delegitimation: legitimation of forces of reification and dehumanizing violence; delegitimation of oppositional constructions of community and ethical rationalism. Inevitably, this takes us to the over-determined space of post-coloniality. A few observations might serve both to illustrate this point and to contextualize its ramifications beyond Achebe's own work, the focus of this tribute.

Most of the recent books and essays in the field have argued persuasively that the post-colonial in literature and critical discourse essentially consists of the cultural representation of the destabilization of the fixities and bounded structures of the age of empire and colony under British and European world hegemony: the bounded colonial territory as an exclusive 'sphere of influence' of *one* metropolitan country under the regime of *nationally* administered capitalisms; the crystallized identity of the 'native' and the formation of subjectivities like the 'evolue' or 'assimile' within the generalized 'native' identity; the emergence of a nationalist anti-colonial challenge to foreign domination and external usurpation of sovereignty.

3. Achebe was closely associated with the left-of-centre People's Redemption Party (PRP) during the civilian Second Republic in Nigeria (1979–83). He was Deputy National President of the party and was even rumoured at one stage to being seriously considered as the party's Presidential candidate in the federal elections of 1983. Achebe's leftist, somewhat social-democratic political inclinations, with all their ambiguities, are clearly woven into his fourth and fifth novels, *A Man of the People* and *Anthills of the Savannah*.
4. The problem of so-called literary 'fellow travellers' in 20th century Communist and revolutionary politics is treated extensively, from the disillusioned writer's perspective, in R. H. S. Crossman, ed., *The God That Failed* (New York: Harper, 1950).
5. *Things Fall Apart* (Heinemann African Writers' Series, 1958). All page references are to this edition and are hereafter incorporated in brackets in the text of this essay.

If all this marks the world of coloniality, post-coloniality comes with
the epoch in which hegemonic American (and later Japanese) *multi-
national*, 'late' capitalism replaced the world domination of old-style
European imperialism. This is the age that one writer has characterized as 'imperialism without colonies'.[6] It is with respect to this dismantling of bounded enclaves and subjectivities that to be post-colonial
is to be more than merely and adventitiously 'ex-colonial'.

Within this general pattern two distinct antinomic conceptions
and articulations of post-coloniality have been forming, and are
being inscribed as textual practices and discursive, rhetorical strategies. It is pertinent to our purposes in this essay to briefly indicate the
broad outlines of these divergent, conflicting articulations of the
post-colonial.

There is, first, the post-coloniality of what I would call normativity
and proleptic designation in which the writer or critic speaks to, or
for, or in the name of the post-independence nation-state, the
regional or continental community, the pan-ethnic, racial or cultural
agglomeration of homelands and diasporas. In this post-coloniality of
the nation, of the regional community, or of a far-flung 'Black World',
'Arab World' or 'Latin America', one finds a Ngugi writing to and for
a Kenya that *is* and the Kenya that is to come; one finds Mahfouz
identifying himself as both an Egyptian writer and a voice from the
Arab World and its literary traditions; one finds also Octavio Paz, in
his appropriately titled book, *One Earth, Four or Five Worlds*,[7] enun-
ciating the dynamics of Latin American modernity by assailing what
he identifies as 'anti-modern' currents in the culture of the South
American regional community. If normativity in this conception of
the post-colonial usually entails what Cabral has called 'return to the
source', a reassertion or reinvention of traditions which colonialism,
not without considerable success, had sought to destroy or devalue,
there are also varying degrees of critical vigilance against the inscription of cultural norms and traditions as comforting but enervating
myths of pure origins, and as uncontaminated matrices of the self.[8]

This is the dominant, more pervasive literary and theoretical elaboration of post-coloniality. It is by no means a monolithic or homogeneous formation and this is perceptible if one compares the
positions and perspectives of its most influential theorists and pun-

6. See Harry Magdoff, 'Imperialism without colonies' in Roger Owen and Bob Sutcliffe, eds.,
   Studies in the Theories of Imperialism (New York: *Monthly Review Press*, 1972). The terms
   'post-coloniality' and 'coloniality' in the context of this essay refer to writings dealing with
   these historical and cultural phenomena considered as disciplinary formations, that is as
   objects of study.
7. Octavio Paz, *One Earth, Four or Five Worlds* (New York: Harcourt Brace Jovanovich, 1985).
8. For extensive debates centring on a critique of self-essentialization in the politics of identity
   within the Negritude movement, see accounts of the 'Negro Writers and Artists Conferences' of Paris, 1956 and Rome, 1959 published in *Présence Africaine*, Nos. 8–9–10
   June–November 1956 and Nos. 24–25, February–May 1959, English editions.

dits like Fernandez Retamar of Cuba,[9] Paik Nak-Chung of South Korea,[1] Ngugi wa Thiong'o of Kenya[2] and Andre Brink of South Africa.[3] This is also the tradition of post-coloniality within which Achebe has elaborated the powerful novelistic and essayistic project of demythologization which is the subject of this essay.

It is no easy task to take a measure of the other crystallized literary and theoretical formation of post-coloniality, a formation which, for want of a better term I shall call *interstitial* or *liminal*. The interstice or liminality here defines an ambivalent mode of self-fashioning of the writer or critic which is neither First World nor Third World, neither securely and smugly metropolitan, nor assertively and combatively Third Worldist. The very terms which express the orientation of *this* school of post-colonial self-representation are revealing: diasporic, exilic, hybrid, in-between, cosmopolitan.[4] Not only does the writer, theorist or critic refuse to speak on behalf of, or primarily to, the developing world, but more crucially, he typically calls into question the competing, polarized claims of centre and margin, metropole and periphery, Western and non-Western. It is perhaps on account of this dual movement that V. S. Naipaul does not belong in *this* post-coloniality of disavowal, even though he has made disavowals the abiding thematic centre of his work: the trajectory of this work bears the trace of a one-way path leading away from the island nation to 'an enigma of arrival' at the metropolitan suburbia.

Like the more dominant, more pervasive post-coloniality of reassertion and reinvention of identity and community of developing nations and their writers and critics, the post-coloniality of interstitiality and transnationality does not come as a monolith. This, neither in its literary expressions—as between its perhaps most paradigmatic figure, Salman Rushdie, and diverse other writers like Derek Walcott, J. M. Coetzee, and the late Dambudzo Marechera—nor in its theoretical, critical elaborations in such divergent texts as Trinth T. Minh-ha's *Woman, Native, Other*,[5] Homi Bhabha's *Nation and Narration*,[6] Gayatri Spivak's *The Post-colonial Critic*,[7] and Anthony Appiah's essay

9. Roberto Fernandez Retamar, *Caliban and Other Essays* (Minneapolis: University of Minnesota Press, 1989).
1. See, among other texts and documents, 'Program Notes of 1988 Seoul National Literature Festival' published by The Association of Writers for National Literature, Seoul, South Korea. See also Fredric Jameson's interview with Paik Nak-chung. English text, unpublished.
2. See Ngugi wa Thiong'o, *Writing Against Neocolonialism* (Wembley: Vita Books, 1986) and *Decolonizing the Mind: the Politics of Language in African Literature* (London: James Currey, 1986).
3. Andre Brink, *Writing in a State of Siege* (New York: Summit Books, 1983).
4. Timothy Brennan in *Salman Rushdie and the Third World* (London: Macmillan, 1989) has explored *this* expression of post-coloniality, especially with regard to Rushdie.
5. Trinh T. Min-ha, *Woman, Native Other* (Bloomington: Indiana University Press, 1988).
6. Homi Bhabha, ed., *Nation and Narration* (London and New York: Routledge, 1990).
7. Gayatri Chakravorty Spivak, *The Postcolonial Critic* (London and New York: Routledge, 1990).

'Out of Africa: Topologies of Nativism'.[8] For this reason, these conflicting, contradictory formations of post-colonial discourses and
representations will not be explored here. What needs to be done is,
I believe, to weave the salience of this categorical, antinomic divide
of post-coloniality into the elaboration of the subject of this essay:
Achebe's demythologizing literary aesthetics. The salience of this
divide can only be summatively presented here.

To my mind three essential points express the salience of this categorical antinomy. First, the writers and theorists of the second
formation—cosmopolitan, hybrid, exilic, diasporic, interstitial post-
coloniality—enjoy far greater visibility and acclaim in the acade-
mies, journals and media of the metropolitan First World countries
than the post-coloniality of the more nationalistic, counter-
hegemonic expression. This is due not only to the fact that most of
the writers and theorists of the former are physically and institu-
tionally located in the metropole, though this is indeed not without
its own significance. Rather, the visibility and acclaim derive from a
second salient point: the intersection of *this* post-coloniality with the
most 'advanced', fashionable artistic and intellectual currents of Europe and America, especially post-modernism and High Theory.
Thirdly, and this seems to me to be the most important issue, except
for a few prominent cases which we shall briefly explore hereafter,
these two formations of post-coloniality have had very little to say to
each other that is productive. The burden of this critical tribute to
Achebe is to argue that his work belongs to these few exemplary
cases.

The Representation of Imperialism, The Imperialism of Representation

The general celebration of *Things Fall Apart* as a work of great realistic fiction which more or less inaugurated the novelistic exploration by African authors of pre-colonial and colonial Africa has
often, quite appropriately, acknowledged the superb irony of the
novel's last page as a rhetorical trope, a narrative tactic of great

8. Anthony Appiah, 'Out of Africa: Topologies of Nativism', *The Yale Journal of Criticism*, Vol.
2, No. 1, Fall 1988, pp. 153–178. Given his well-known coolness toward deconstruction
and post-structuralism from the standpoint of analytic philosophy, it may seem out of place
to include Appiah's essay within this formation of a post-colonial discourse which is deeply
imbricated in post-structuralist theory. The inclusion is justified, I believe, in the fact that
if one conceptualises this expression of post-coloniality as one of 'disavowal', as I do here,
then Appiah is entirely at 'home' within this formation. Nothing so much expresses this as
the fact that if one is at first startled by Appiah's title—'Out of Africa'—which comes from
Isak Dinesen's text of that title, one looks in vain for any ironic deployment of the title in
Appiah's essay. All cultural-nationalists in Africa's post-colonial cultural politics are, it
seems to Appiah, little more than varieties, or 'topologies' of *nativism*, where nativism
means naive, uncritical self-essentialization in the politics of identity.

power and cogency.[9] This issue requires a closer, more nuanced scrutiny, with regard to some perspectives of contemporary critical theory and in relation to the subject of this critical tribute. For what is figured in this last page of *Things Fall Apart* in this short, narratological and rhetorical space, goes to the heart of the politics of representation as a central concern of post-colonial fiction and critical discourse.

The details can be quickly, summatively recalled. Obierika, leading the party of the colonial District Commissioner—a figure of great *political* authority in the colonial context—to the dangling body of Okonkwo who has hanged himself, asks the great man to have the corpse brought down by one of his men. Then we are told: 'The District Commissioner changed instantaneously. The resolute administrator in him gave way to the student of primitive customs' (p. 147). A dialogue then ensues in which the Commissioner, now become an inquiring cognitive subject, questions Okonkwo's people about the customs and ritual practices which forbade them to touch Okonkwo's body, thus requiring the assistance of strangers to do the simple, humane service. A few paragraphs later, the 'student of primitive customs' having received 'data' from his native informants, is transformed into a figure, not merely of political, administrative power, but also of *narrative, discursive, epistemic* authority, as the following ruminations from that much quoted, much admired final paragraph of *Things Fall Apart* reveal:

> The Commissioner went away, taking three or four of the soldiers with him. In the many years in which he had toiled to bring civilization to different parts of Africa he had learnt a number of things. One of them was that a District Commissioner must never attend to such undignified details as cutting down a hanged man from the tree. Such attention would give the natives a poor opinion of him. In the book he planned to write he would stress that point. As he walked back to the court he thought about that book. Every day brought him some new material. The story of this man who had killed a messenger and hanged himself would make interesting reading. One could almost write a whole chapter on him. Perhaps not a whole chapter but a reasonable paragraph, at any rate. There was so much else to include, and one must be firm in cutting out details. He had already chosen the title of the book, after much thought: *The Pacification of the Primitive Tribes of the Lower Niger.* (pp. 147–48)

Much critical commentary has been made on the ironic juxtaposition of the Commissioner's projected 'reasonable paragraph' on the

9. See, for examples of this, C. L. Innes, 'Language, Poetry and Doctrine in *Things Fall Apart*' in *Critical Perspectives on Chinua Achebe*, pp. 111–25, and Rhonda Cobham, 'Making Men and History: Achebe and the Politics of Revisionism in *Things Fall Apart*'. In Bernth Lindfors, ed., *Approaches to Teaching Achebe's* Things Fall Apart (New York: MLA, 1991) 91–100.

tragedy of Okonkwo with the *entire* narrative space of *Things Fall Apart* of which it is indeed a part: the last paragraph of a whole narrative sets itself up in an authoritarian fashion as *the* only significant detail in the narrative; far more tellingly, for the District Commissioner, the banished, excluded substantive narrative, as a version of the encounter of the colonizer and the colonized, simply doesn't exist. In other words, already in 1958 when *Things Fall Apart* was first published, Achebe had in this short, condensed narratological moment of the text, prefigured the post-modern scepticism toward the *grands récits* of the transcendent cognitive (European) subject, the grand, totalizing meta-narratives of the bourgeois-imperial imagination of European culture, especially in its encounter with 'native' peoples and cultures.[1] This is a point that Edward Said, among other contemporary critics and theorists, makes in relation to Conrad and *Heart of Darkness* which, according to him,

> works so effectively precisely because its aesthetics and politics . . . are imperialist; and that, by the time Conrad wrote, seemed an attitude that was inevitable and for which there could be no alternative. For if we cannot truly understand someone else's experience and if, as a result, we must depend simply upon the assertive authority of the sort of power Kurtz wields in the jungle or that Marlow possesses as narrator, there is no use looking for non-imperialist alternatives in a system that has simply eliminated, made unthinkable, all other alternatives to it. The circularity of the whole thing is unassailable.[2]

Achebe's famous, and must discussed (and much controverted) essay on Conrad and *Heart of Darkness* is thus only one further instance, one further elaboration of Achebe's novelistic and essayistic engagement not only of the representation of empire and imperialism—in the light of images, distortions, myths and stereotypes of 'native' peoples and cultures—but also, and perhaps more importantly, of *the imperialism of representation* which, in this historic case, excludes, or simply ignores (alter)-native versions and constructions 'from below'.[3] This battle over representation has continued as a central problematic of post-colonial

1. For two important books which, among others, deal with the triumphalism, the 'historical confidence' which accompanied European colonialist constructions of non-European, colonized peoples and cultures, see Talal Asad, ed., *Anthropology and the Colonial Encounter* (Atlantic Highlands, N.J.: Humanities Press, 1987) and Timothy Mitchell, *Colonizing Egypt* (Cambridge University Press, 1988). The *magnum opus* of the genre of course remains Edward Said's *Orientalism* (New York: Vintage Books, 1979).
2. Edward Said, 'Intellectuals in the Post-Colonial World', *Salmagundi*, No. 70–71, Spring-Summer 1986, p. 49.
3. For authoritative, useful collections of 'subaltern historiography' which give 'alternative versions' of the culture and history of colonialism 'from below' see, among others, Gary Y. Okihiro, ed., *In Resistance: Studies in African, Caribbean and Afro-American History* (Amherst: The University of Massachusetts Press, 1986) and Ranajit Guha, ed., *Subaltern Studies I* (Delhi: Oxford University Press, 1982).

discourse, as we shall see later in the concluding section of this essay. Meanwhile, it is important to note here that part of this battle over representation involves the trench war of *preferred versions:* A V. S. Naipaul being more preferred than say a Mahasweta Devi as a 'witness' to the agony and contradictions of post-colonial India, or an Isak Dinesen being more beloved than an Ngugi wa Thiong'o on Africans in East Africa caught in the dilemmas and antinomies of the cultural representation of the colonial encounter.[4]

Achebe looms large then in post-colonial discourse on account of the quality, wit and intelligence of his engagement of this war over representation which pits the post-coloniality of the developing world and its writers, theorists and critics against residual metropolitan colonialist preferences and predilections.[5] What is more important, however, is that this engagement goes much deeper, for his purview has also taken into account the same totalizing, exclusionary and reifying representational logic *within* the cultural and signifying ensembles of the colonized: Okonkwo, in the multiple ironic articulations of the narrative which constructs him, also prefigures the 'assertive sovereign inclusiveness' which Said identifies in Marlowe and Conrad,[6] and which we find so brilliantly encoded in the District Commissioner's projected 'reasonable paragraph' on our tragic protagonist. This is a perspective, a narratological 'alienation effect'[7] which we obtain through Obierika, Okonkwo's great friend and *alter ego.*

History, Doxa, Paradox(a), Dialectic

Concerning Obierika the character and his author, Chinua Achebe, the following excerpt from a long interview I once had with the author is an appropriate frame for the reflections in this critical tribute on the post-colonial politics of identity and (self)-representation:

---

4. For a vigorous discussion of this point see The Post-Colonial Intellectual: A Discussion with Conor Cruise O'Brien, Edward Said and John Lukacs' in *Salmagundi*, No. 70–11, Spring-Summer 1986, pp. 65–81.
5. The rash of nostalgic films about the British Raj in India, and films like 'Black and White in Color', 'Gorillas in the Mist' and 'Out of Africa', all projecting a yearning for the lost world of the colonials in East Africa, attest to the commodity value of this residual colonialist nostalgia in popular cultural production.
6. 'Intellectuals in the Postcolonial World', p. 49.
7. C. L. Innes in *Chinua Achebe* (Cambridge University Press, 1990) has related these aspects of Achebe's narrative style and technique to Brechtian and Bakhtinian perspectives. This is a novel, fruitful approach to Achebe's fictional art, especially since Innes stresses that Brechtian or Bakhtinian motifs in Achebe are not so much a matter of the direct influence of literary intertextuality as one of 'similarity of effects' based on the fact that all three 'learned those techniques and concepts of the relation between author/narrator and audience from a non-literary tradition', Achebe from an African one, Brecht and Bakhtin from European oral folk sources. What I have done here is to relate these aspects of Achebe's narrative art to post-modern, post-structuralist themes in post-colonial critical discourse, especially with the move away from the *grand récit* of European colonialist narrative and discursive traditions.

JEYIFO: If I may ask a question which I've always wanted to ask
you but which is . . . I know it's always a little too bold to see
a writer in terms of his fictional characters . . . However, I
have always wanted to ask if there is something of Achebe in
Obierika in *Things Fall Apart*?

ACHEBE: Yes, that is very bold indeed! Well, the answer is yes,
in the sense that at the crucial moment when things are happening, he represents this other alternative. This is a society
in *Things Fall Apart* that believes in strength and manliness
and the masculine ideals. Okonkwo accepts them in a rather
literal sense . . . [and] the culture 'betrays' him. He is 'betrayed'
because he's doing exactly what the culture preaches. But you
see, the culture is devious and flexible, because if it wasn't it
wouldn't survive. The culture says you must be strong, you
must be this and that, but when the moment comes for
absolute strength the culture says, no, hold it! The culture has
to be ambivalent, so it immediately raises the virtues of the
women, of love, of tenderness . . . and holds up abominations:
You cannot do this, even though the cultural norms say you
must do it . . . Obierika is therefore more subtle and more in
tune with the danger, the impending betrayal by the culture,
and he's not likely to be crushed because he holds something
in reserve.[8]

It is widely recognised that in Achebe's texts names and naming
convey layers of cultural codes and information. We need to stress
the analytic extensions of this principle, for it is within this that the
name Obierika achieves its tremendous resonance. Two sets of
terms are linked in the name: 'Obi', heart, soul or mind; and 'rika',
great, fulsome, capacious. There is also a sense in which 'obi', with
a proper tonal inflection, is the hut, or the *homestead*, in its more
social, affective connotation. From these aspects of the etymology of
the name we may project several linked or associative meanings:
great-heartedness, generosity of spirit; capacity for fellow-feeling;
the mind/soul/heart of an individual, a group, a people is infinite in
its potentialities.[9] It should be added that the name does imply in all
of these possible significations, an ethical, rationalist cast of mind
or disposition: 'greatness' here is not an ethically neutral capacious-
ness, even if it does not exclude an imaginative or reflective awareness of the 'banality of evil', in Hannah Arendt's famous words.

8. 'Literature and Conscientization: An Interview with Chinua Achebe' in Biodun Jeyifo, ed.,
   Contemporary Nigerian Literature (Lagos: Nigeria Magazine, 1988), pp. 12–13.
9. I must thank Don C. Ohadike of Africana Studies and Research Center, Cornell University, for help with my etymological analysis of the name Obierika. I should say, however,
   that I have taken the heuristic possibilities in the nomenclature way beyond Professor
   Ohadike's more exact, literal rendering; hence any errors or solecisms in this exertion
   remain mine.

Even the most cursory textual scrutiny of *Things Fall Apart* would reveal that Obierika 'lives his name', so to speak; in other words, the significations encoded in the name inhabit the character's experience of intersubjective sociality. He is astute in discerning the small, barely tangible but socially cementing velleities of personality and character; he is deeply humane and sensitive; he is imbued with a sagacious but unflaunted moral imagination. He is also of a generous, tolerant disposition and where his friend is a man of few or no words, much of the information about, and reflection on the realities and consequences of the invading colonial capitalism is given by Obierika. And he is not only Okonkwo's 'greatest friend', his is that loyalty in friendship that is deeply informed by a balanced sense of the friend's strengths, weaknesses and even neurotic susceptibilities.

While a moral and psychological portrait would find abundant textual details to cast Obierika as his friend's *alter ego*, the upshot of our interest here points away from such moralism and psychologism. For the crucial factor here is that Obierika is a *device* in the text of *Things Fall Apart*; he is a nexus of significations which allows us considerable purchase on a perception of culture as a necessary but expendable medium through which identity is negotiated between the self and others. It is this heuristic structure which subtends the textually pervasive inscription of both characters as fundamentally discrepant cultural avatars: Okonkwo as the culture hero who is doomed because of his rigid, superficial understanding—really misrecognition—of his culture; Obierika as a sceptical, dissenting and prescient observer of the culture's encounter with the self and the colonizing Other. The problem with most critical commentaries on these aspects of *Things Fall Apart* is to have almost completely missed out on the demythologization of identity and culture *within* the pre-colonial social order while fastening one-sidedly on the novel's ironic deflations of the binarisms and polarities of the encounter of the colonizer and the colonized.

Thus, it is Obierika who registers the falling apart of things; it is Obierika who records the collapse of the most vital identity-forming connections of the culture: kinship, community, ritual and ceremonial institutions. And it is significant that Obierika has to insist on this tragic insight—tragic because he is utterly helpless before its *historic*, and not merely metaphysical inevitability—against the wilful refusal of Okonkwo to see the cracks in the culture's fortifications:

> 'Perhaps I have been away too long,' Okonkwo said, almost to himself. 'But I cannot understand these things you tell me. What is it that has happened to our people? Why have they lost the power to fight?'
> 'Have you not heard how the white man wiped out Abame?' asked Obierika.

'I have heard,' said Okonkwo. 'But I have also heard that
Abame people were weak and foolish. Why did they not fight
back? Had they no guns and machetes? We would be cowards to
compare ourselves with the men of Abame. Their fathers had
never dared to stand before our ancestors. We must fight these
men and drive them from the land.'
      'It is already too late,' said Obierika sadly. 'Our own men and
our sons have joined the ranks of the stranger. They have joined
his religion and they help to uphold his government. If we
should try to drive out the white men in Umuofia we should find
it easy. There are only two of them. But what of our own people
who are following their way and have been given power? They
would go to Umuru and bring the soldiers, and we would be like
Abame.' He paused for a long time and then said: 'I told you on
my last visit to Mbanta how they hanged Aneto.'
      'What has happened to that piece of land in dispute?' asked
Okonkwo.
      'The white man's court has decided that it should belong to
Nnama's family, who had given much money to the white man's
messengers and interpreter.'
      'Does the white man understand our custom about land?'
      'How can he when he does not even speak our tongue? But he
says that our customs are bad; and our own brothers who have
taken up his religion also say that our customs are bad. How do
you think we can fight when our own brothers have turned
against us? The white man is very clever. He came quietly and
peaceably with his religion. We were amused at his foolishness
and allowed him to stay. Now he has won our brothers, and our
clan can no longer act like one. He has put a knife on the things
that held us together and we have fallen apart.' (pp. 124–25)

But Obierika's melancholy bears a janus face: he registers the
myths and distortions of the colonizer about the 'natives' which both
justify and inscribe the violent usurpation that is the regime of colonialism; at the same time his discomfited gaze had taken in the negat-
ing, destructive myths and hypostatizations in the central,
identity-giving institutions and practices of his culture. It is indeed
not over-extending the significations embedded in the text to read in
Obierika a divided, alienated subjectivity long before the avalanche
of colonizing reifications of the 'native' culture arrives on the scene
and initiates a new epoch. 'If the Oracle said that my son should be
killed,' Obierika had spat out his condemnation of Okonkwo's participation in the killing of the youth, Ikemefuna, 'I would neither dispute it nor be the one to do it.' This split is more poignantly and
powerfully rendered when Obierika *had* to, by the force of cultural
compulsion, enact, with others, the despoliation of his friend's homestead:

As soon as the day broke, a large crowd of men from Ezendu's quarter stormed Okonkwo's compound, dressed in garbs of war. They set fire to his houses, demolished his red walls, killed his animals and destroyed his barn. It was the justice of the earth goddess, and they were merely her messengers. They had no hatred in their hearts against Okonkwo. His greatest friend, Obierika, was among them. They were merely cleansing the land which Okonkwo had polluted with the blood of a clansman.

Obierika was a man who thought about these things. When the will of the goddess had been done, he sat down in his *obi* and mourned his friend's calamity. Why should a man suffer so grievously for an offence he had committed inadvertently? But although he thought for a long time he found no answer. He was merely led to greater complexities. He remembered his wife's twin children, whom he had thrown away. What crime had they committed? (p. 87)

It is important to recognize that Obierika's scepticism toward his culture achieves its tremendous force precisely because he bears deep, positive currents of values, predispositions, identity from the very same culture. A case in point is his notion of abomination which astutely plays upon, and somewhat secularizes its normative, sacral connotations.[1] Another affecting instantiation of this point comes across in the following exchange in which the discussion turns on customary prohibitions and exclusions of the titled 'ozo' holders from some mundane activities of the work-a-day world:

'Sometimes, I wish I had not taken the *ozo* title,' said Obierika. 'It wounds my heart to see these young men killing palm trees in the name of tapping.'

'It is so indeed,' Okonkwo agreed. 'But the law of the land must be obeyed.'

'I don't know how we got that law,' said Obierika. 'In many clans a man of title is not forbidden to climb the palm tree. Here we say he cannot climb the tall tree but he can tap the short ones standing on the ground. It is like Dimaragana, who would not lend his knife for cutting dogmeat because the dog was taboo to him, but offered to use his teeth.' (p. 48)

In the very idiom of his critical disquisitions on his culture, Obierika draws from the culture's common stock of imagery, rhetoric and humour.

There is thus at work in the mesh of significations in the construction of Obierika as a complex heuristic device a dialectic of, on

---

1. This pertains to his mythological but moral and philosophical interpretation of the 'abomination' of Okonkwo's participation in the killing of Ikemefuna, an action which, in his view, could bring ruin on whole families, as retribution from the earth goddess. Chapter 8, p. 46.

the one hand, cultural affirmation and on the other hand cultural critique and deflation. One pole, the pole of affirmation, may be said to
coalesce around *doxa*: belief, opinion, or custom perceived in terms
of elementary structures of ordered meanings, and centred, cohering
values. *Things Fall Apart* may be regarded in this respect as a vast doxological compendium of Igbo culture before the advent of colonialism. Indeed, it has been so critically examined by several scholars.[2]
At the opposite pole from *doxa* we have of course the pole of paradox(a), or irony and dialectic. This is the pole of cultural demystification of which *Things Fall Apart*, like Achebe's third novel, *Arrow of
God*, is also an exemplary textual articulation. If *Things Fall Apart*
bears a special significance for post-colonial discourse it is to the
extent that these two contradictory, dialectic poles of cultural affirmation and cultural demystification find balanced textual inscription
in the novel. For one pole is freighted with the discourse of the postcoloniality of nationalist assertion against colonial and imperial cultural subjugation, displacement or depersonalization; the other pole
is infused with the discourse of the critique of nationalism such as
we find, in different but apposite demythologizing registers, in
Cabral's notion of a necessarily *critical* 'return to the source',[3] or
Fanon's famous exhortations on the 'pitfalls of national consciousness'.[4] In moving to the concluding sections of this essay, I would like
to briefly explore the ideological assumptions and the narrative
machinery through, and by which Achebe is able to consummate this
double articulation.

To Leopold von Ranke is credited an expression which, I believe,
superbly captures the spirit of Achebe's narrativisation of nationalist
self-assertion in *Things Fall Apart*: all ages are equally immediate to
God. This bears a striking homology to a Yoruba proverbial expression: 'Ko si ede t'olorun Ko gbo'—there is no language or tongue that
is unintelligible to God. Both expressions seem to affirm the underlying premise of cultural relativism: each age or epoch, each culture
or society is an integrated, systematic, coherent whole or totality
which obeys its own laws and is comprehensible in terms of its own
reference points, no matter how imperfect these may be. This conception in turn accords, in almost all respects, with the following
statement of intent by Achebe relatively early in his novelistic and
essayistic career: 'I would be quite satisfied if my novels (especially
the ones I set in the past) did no more than teach my readers that

2. An example of this kind of scholarship on Achebe's works is Robert Wren, *Achebe's World:
   the Historical and Cultural Context of the Novels of Chinua Achebe* (Longman, 1980).
3. Amilcar Cabral, 'The Weapon of Theory' and 'National Liberation and Culture' in *Unity
   and Struggle* (Heinemann: African Writers Series, 1980).
4. Frantz Fanon, 'The Pitfalls of National Consciousness' in *The Wretched of the Earth* (New
   York: Grove Press, 1963).

their past—with all its imperfections—was not one long night of savagery from which the first Europeans acting on God's behalf delivered them.'[5]

Given the ideological and emotional charge of this statement of intent by Achebe, it is remarkable that it has not led to consummated grand narratives of emancipation, or for that matter, meta-narratives of retrieval of an absolutely originary past. It is also remarkable that this has not been adequately critically examined, given all the critical attention which Achebe has attracted to his work as a sustained response to the colonialist master narratives of European writers like Joseph Conrad, Rudyard Kipling, E. M. Forster, Graham Greene and Joyce Cary. In other words, why hasn't Achebe written a master narrative like *Heart of Darkness* or *A Passage to India*?

The answer to this question seems to be that since Achebe had, perforce, to write *reactive* counter-narratives to these meta-narratives of Western representations of the colonizing Self and the colonized Other he was thus structurally precluded from producing a master-narrative. But this seems too mechanistic an expression of something more complexly inscribed in the interstices of history, ideology and artistic discourse. One answer surely lies in the historic fact that the post-colonial writer is axiomatically and imaginatively excluded from the kind of intuitive, subjective access to the ideology of imperialism which makes the production of colonialist master-narratives possible.[6]

Speculations such as these somewhat occlude the specificity of Achebe's narrative art and, more pertinently, the fact that this narrative art involves a representational economy located at a juncture between the totalizing meta-narratives we now identify with a hegemonising imperialism of representation and the counter-narratives and fictions of de-totalizing, fragmenting discourses and inscriptions from the margins and from below. Thus the 'main' narrative logic of the text is linear, omniscient, centred around Okonkwo's 'inevitable' tragic destiny. For this, Achebe adopted the 'objectivity' and 'impersonality' which many scholars have remarked as the 'realistic' provenance of *Things Fall Apart*.[7] Some of the expressions of this 'objectivity' are quite exceptional in the tradition of African post-colonial fiction of the

5. Chinua Achebe, 'The Novelist as Teacher' in *Morning Yet on Creation Day* (London: Heinemann, 1975), p. 45.
6. This point is made with perspicacity by Timothy Mitchell in *Colonizing Egypt*, op. cit. See especially Chapters 1 and 2. See also, for the response of the colonized to this 'historical confidence', Bill Ashcroft et al., eds., *The Empire Writes Back: Theory and Practice in Post-colonial Literature* (London and New York: Routledge, 1989). One of the most theoretically sophisticated explorations of this subject, from the standpoint of modern intellectual and cultural history is Samir Amin, *Eurocentrism* (New York: Monthly Review Press, 1989).
7. See especially Emmanuel Ngara, *Art and Ideology in the African Novel* (London: Heinemann, 1985).

colonial past, both in their conception and execution. For instance, it is hard to find in this fictional tradition the kind of ethnographic self-distancing which allows Achebe's authorial voice such articulations as: 'Darkness held a vague terror for these people, even the bravest among them' (p. 7). Or: 'In Umuofia's latest war he [Okonkwo] was the first to bring home a human head. That was his fifth head, and he was not an old man yet. On great occasions such as the funeral of a village celebrity he drank the palm wine from his first human head' (p. 8). Moreover, this omniscient narrative logic presents both the pre-colonial social order and the new colonial presence, at least in their respective self-representations, as contending *totalities*. We are told that the 'new religion and government and trading stores' constituted an integral formation in the evolving consciousness of the historic encounter; and the representation of the pre-colonial order is itself all-encompassingly *systemic*: the democratic village assemblies and ritual-judicial institutions as political-administrative units; the inscription of conversational arts and a vast stock of proverbs, aphorisms, myths, legends, ceremonies as embodiment of an elaborate *superstructural* symbolic realm; farming, trading, warfare, recreation and the separate, parallel but hierarchically bounded orders of men's and women's lives and activities as the content of a mundane but primary sociality. Inside these totalities the logic of tragedy and 'inevitability' works itself out, propelled by the polarised agency of an Okonkwo among the colonized and among the colonizers by the manichean-minded missionary, Mr Smith who 'saw things as black and white' (p. 130).

Outside this omniscient totalizing meta-narrative, however, are the counter-narratives 'from below', the stories within stories, the fragments, episodic fictions, motifs and tropes which reveal a far more complex, dynamic, ambiguous and paradoxical world than that of the closed circuit of the 'main' narrative line, a world which in particular calls into question Okonkwo's rigid, authoritarian and masculinist identity. As I have argued elsewhere, the most central of these stories, motifs and tropes collectively inscribe a *topos* within the text of *Things Fall Apart* which explores the fundamentally *gendered* nature of Okonkwo's world (and not merely his personality or subjectivity, as most critics have tended to see it).[8] In this *topos*, there are 'men's stories' and 'women's stories', 'male' crops and 'female' crops, 'male' and

8. C. L. Innes explores this rather sharply in *Chinua Achebe*, op. cit., as does Carole Boyce Davis in 'Motherhood in the Works of Male and Female Igbo Writers: Achebe, Emecheta, Nwapa and Nzekwu', in Carole Boyce Davis and Anne Adams Graves, eds., *Ngambika: Studies of Women in African Literature* (Trenton: Africa World Press, 1986). My point here is that Achebe takes the question of gender beyond its neurotic, pathological expression in Okonkwo's masculinist, misogynist personality to the very division of knowledge and reality on gender terms. Consequently *Things Fall Apart* ought to be read as a critique, mostly implicit, of the dominant national-masculine tradition of post-colonial African fiction.

'female' crimes and abominations, as well as, more centrally, 'male' and 'female' deities. It is indeed significant that the 'female' deity Ani (by the way, 'the most important deity in the lives' of Okonkwo's people) has a *male* priest, Ezeani, while the 'male' deity of the Oracle of the Hills and the Caves has a *female* priestess, Chielo. But this is a point beyond Okonkwo's ken: he completely represses the 'female' principle and values in himself and his tragedy in fact largely derives from his remarkable success in this venture.

One cannot read the countless fragmentary stories around 'minor' characters like Unoka, Chielo, Ogbuefi Nbulue and his wife Ozoemena, Ikemefuna and Nwoye, Ekwefi and Ezinma, Okonkwo's uncle Uchendu, Akunna, Obiako and many others, without consciously or unconsciously feeling oneself in the presence of a narrative and discursive logic which admits of illogic and which makes *everything* negotiable, including the most sacrosanct values of the culture. Obiako's 'story' which confounds one of the supposedly most inviolable ritual and psychological injunctions of the culture—deference to the cult of the ancestors—is particularly trenchant in the way in which it as much questions Okonkwo's reified conception of the culture and the 'inevitability' of his fate:

> 'Obiako has always been a strange one,' said Nwakibie. 'I have heard that many years ago, when his father had not been dead very long, he had gone to consult the Oracle. The Oracle said to him, 'Your dead father wants you to sacrifice a goat to him.' Do you know what he told the Oracle? He said, "Ask my dead father if he ever had a fowl when he was alive".' Everybody laughed heartily except Okonkwo, who laughed uneasily because, as the saying goes, an old woman is always uneasy when dry bones are mentioned in a proverb. Okonkwo remembered his own father. (p. 15)

This story of Obiako, like many of the other fragmentary stories within the main linear, totalizing narrative of Okonkwo's tragedy and historic colonial 'pacification', has an emblematic significance within the double, fractured narrative scheme of the novel. The main totalizing narrative as it were deals with History capitalized, with the 'great' events and epochal shifts, all with a seeming inevitability, if not with a secret Hegelian telos. But the story fragments, the episodic fictions about the Obiakos deal with *histories*, with the interstices of the 'great' epochal movements. It is significant that these 'mini' narratives have to do with 'small people' in the community, not the 'lords of the land', the *male* 'ozo' title holders like Okonkwo who, it seems, always dominate discussions at the otherwise 'democratic', egalitarian village assemblies. Indeed, in the deeply *gendered* discourse of personality and identity in the novel, the other *name* for these small people,

where they are men, is *agbala*, which means 'woman'; collectively
both men and women within this subaltern group are named *efulefu*,
which means 'worthless'. Among many of the ironic twists and articulations of *Things Fall Apart* is the fact that while the main narrative
line about Okonkwo leads to tragedy and a general sense of social
malaise, the fragmentary stories and motifs of the *agbala* and the
efulefu move this social category to restitution at the end of the novel.
Almost all the first converts to the new religion, the first minor func-
tionaries of the colonial administration, the first teacher-pupils of the
new school, are drawn from this subaltern group. For this group,
things certainly did not fall apart! However, Achebe's ironic vision
extends as well to their 'liberation' by colonialism: already at the very
inception of their incorporation into a new social and economic
order, new forms of subjectivity are crystallizing as the corruptions
and alienation of a new social class are prefigured in the venality,
insensitivity and brutality of the messengers and petty officials of the
colonial administration and over-zealous Christian converts like
Enoch. Nonetheless, it is important to recognise Achebe's depiction
of the process of 'othering' within the pre-colonial social order, a process which creates a vast body of marginalised Others made up
mainly of the *osu* (slaves), social outcasts and, significantly, women.

Historical Confidence and Diffidence; Preferred Narratives and Discourses

Obiako in the short, fragmentary story we examined above takes on
the attributes of resilience and the salutary, worldly and human-
centred scepticism which we find brilliantly encoded in Obierika.
Obierika, on the other hand, leads us to the paradigmatic narrative
and discursive stance of his author, Chinua Achebe in many of his
novels and essays: stubborn hope, and an ethical rationalism marked
by a deeply ironic view of history and existence.[9] We are some three
decades into our post-independence disillusionment, and at this
stage of our neo-colonial history when things, again, seem to be
falling apart, we can learn much from this resilience. Historical
calamities like the many civil wars and the endless run of inter-
communal strife on the continent; political disasters like the regimes
of the likes of Idi Amin, Bokassa, Nguema, Mobutu; and the seeming historical impasse of arrested decolonization: all these contradictions and negations will not crush us. This resilience, though, is
not without its predicament: unlike Okonkwo, Obierika is not
crushed; but his survival, and the survival of the *agbala* and the

9. I have explored this aspect of Achebe's artistic vision in 'The glow-worm of consciousness:
   Achebe as a literary theorist' in Biodun Jeyifo, ed., *Contemporary Nigerian Literature*, op.
   cit.

efulefu of the neo-colonial present, is haunted by a sense of failure, of diffidence before these historical negations.

My reading of *Things Fall Apart* in this essay in terms of a narrative economy which both totalizes and detotalizes, which presents, on the one hand, a grand narrative of the colonial encounter as History capitalized and unified around great personages and events and, on the other hand, counter-narratives and fragmentary stories of decentred, overdetermined histories and identities of subaltern groups, might seem to indicate that Achebe's art and discourse are easily assimilable to post-modernist, post-structuralist or deconstructive perspectives. Nothing could be further from this, for Achebe has remained rather wary of modernist aesthetics, not to even talk of post-modernism and post-structuralism.[1] What I have tried to show in this critical tribute is that Achebe's particular brand of realist fiction and his profoundly ironic, demythologizing vision entail some of the problematics of cultural representation highlighted by post-modernism and post-structuralism. This is particularly true of the dangers and pitfalls of self-essentialization in the construction of community, identity or tradition by ex-colonised nations and peoples, and by minority, non-canonical or 'popular' cultural currents in the 'First World' context. I do not by this wish to imply that Achebe's texts are crying for post-structuralist, post-modern critical condescension and patronage. Rather, I wish to underscore the fact that post-colonial critics and theorists who think that these problematics of identity and representation are substantively or brilliantly articulated *only* in contemporary post-structuralist discourses may want to consider the case of Achebe, as elaborated here. It is important also to add that other texts of Achebe like *Arrow of God* and *Anthills of the Savannah* are also superb, engaging exemplifications or inscriptions of these issues. Indeed, on a much wider social and cultural terrain, the most important theorists and critics of post-colonial writings in the Third World are of this intellectual and ideological expression in their involvement in a vast project of demythologization of cultural production and cultural politics from the residue of colonialist myths and their more *neo-colonial* re-codings.

The potential contribution of post-modern, post-structuralist theoretical methods and perspectives to this project is incalculable, especially with regard to the thematization of language and signification as the very grounds of both self-essentialization and the possibility of its demystification. But the consummation of this potential contribution,

---

1. Achebe's reserve and coolness toward the aesthetic aspects of the works of writers like Armah and Soyinka comes largely, in my view, from this disdain for modernist aesthetics. See, for an example of his disdain, his remarks on Soyinka in 'Class Discussion' in Karen L. Morell, ed., *In Person: Achebe, Awoonor, and Soyinka* (Institute for Comparative and Foreign Area Studies, University of Washington, Seattle, 1975), pp. 50–51.

it seems, is conditional upon two factors, among others. First, it is conditional upon a salutary self-awareness of post-structuralism that the critique of essentialism did not start only in the last two decades. Secondly, there is also the need to recognise that post-structuralism breeds its own pieties, its own mythologies and reifications as well, some of these indeed assuming the paradoxical character of neo-colonial fetishism. An instance of this, which is pertinent to the subject of this essay, is the view that grand, totalizing discourses and narratives are exhausted and historically and culturally regressive.[2] For post-colonial writers and critics to accept this without qualification is to accept the delegitimation of *any* and *all* attempts to construct identity and community in the face of the continued ravages and displacements of neo-colonial barbarism, even of self-critical, politically sophisticated constructions of community and identity. Achebe is *not* post-modernist in his aesthetic sensibilities and predilections, at least in the contemporary theoretical understanding of the 'condition',[3] but the way in which he combines totalizing and detotalizing narratives and discourses, doxa and paradox(a), is a powerful critique of smug, fashionable pieties that an embrace of, or an interest in totalization is the ultimate in artistic and intellectual naivety.

RHONDA COBHAM

Problems of Gender and History in the Teaching of *Things Fall Apart*†

"This is a sexist novel!" the (female) (white) student declared. Her ethnic earrings jangled in angry assent as she stabbed the pages of her Heinemann paperback for emphasis. As if to distance itself from the offending object, her red checked imitation PLO scarf slipped backwards off her shoulders. It was clear that she spoke on behalf of all oppressed humanity.

In a voice tinged with longsuffering, her teacher (also white, but male) attempted to explain that not to write about wife beating in a

2. Fredric Jameson's most recent book, *Late Marxism: Adorno or the Persistence of the Dialectic* (London: Verso, 1990) is a powerful theoretical interrogation of this view whose most influential expression is perhaps to be found in Jean-François Lyotard, *The Postmodern Condition: A Report on Knowledge* (Minneapolis: University of Minnesota Press, 1989).
3. I have found the following very useful as sophisticated, but highly critical accounts of this 'condition': Fredric Jameson, 'Postmodernism, or the Cultural Logic of Late Capitalism' in *New Left Review*, 146, 1984; Philip Lewis, 'The Post-structuralist Condition' in *Diacritics*, Volume 12, Spring 1982; and Charles Newman, *The Postmodern Aura: the Act of Fiction in an Age of Inflation* (Evanston: Northwestern University Press, 1985).
† From *Chinua Achebe's* Things Fall Apart: *Modern Critical Interpretations*. Ed. Harold Bloom (Philadelphia: Chelsea House, 2001), 19–30. Reprinted by permission of Rodopi.

story about a society where it was practiced would be aesthetically inauthentic. He tried to shift the discussion back to an appreciation of the critical distance between the author and his main character before the jocks at the back of the class got wind of what was going on, but it was too late. Within seconds the high school class had degenerated into a slanging match between those who felt texts like *Things Fall Apart* should be expurgated from the syllabus and those who wanted to tell the censorship group what they would like Okonkwo to do to them if he were a member of the class. The teacher held his head in his hands and fantasized about reintroducing corporal punishment.

Change the bracketed terms of ascription and this in modified form becomes a scenario that all teachers of Achebe's novel must recognize. I encountered it in a more subtle, inverted form when a Nigerian university student (female) during a discussion of Buchi Emecheta's *Joys of Motherhood* suggested tentatively that though she could appreciate how Nnu Ego felt about her husband in the Emecheta novel, she thought that the writer was being polemical because "traditional Igbo women did not feel that way about these kinds of things," and it became apparent that her point of reference for the psychological responses appropriate for traditional Igbo women was the vision of early Igbo society presented in *Things Fall Apart*.

In an age where violence and the demand for women's rights are constant features of our public rhetoric, there may be something instructive about the way in which these representative student responses insist on conflating all kinds of textual and political issues. In the response of the wearer of ethnic earrings several issues have been conflated. In the first place, there is no concept of historical time in her reading of the novel. For all she probably knew, the Igbo society Achebe was describing was contemporaneous with both the author and herself. Achebe, through his pseudo autobiographical character, Okonkwo, was merely describing and rationalizing the attitude to women which he himself shared with the contemporary Igbo society. For her, this (mis)reading is borne out by Obierika's closing eulogy for his dishonoured friend which she reads simplistically as overt endorsement of all that Okonkwo stood for. Her sense of disease is compounded by the total identification of the most brutal elements within her own society with Okonkwo's attitudes and actions. PLO scarf notwithstanding, she cannot imagine what it must feel like for an entire culture to have its customs, values and idiosyncrasies not merely challenged but made totally irrelevant by a simple equation of moral authority with superior military strength.

Where Western student readers of *Things Fall Apart* complain that the novel is "sexist", meaning usually that they find Okonkwo misogynist, African student readers are more likely to praise Achebe and chastise a writer like Buchi Emecheta for not being as authentic as Achebe in portraying traditional Igbo women. Okonkwo's physical abuse of his wives is evaluated precisely within the novel on a scale of values that has at its highest point the devotion of the old couple Ndulue and Ozoemena who remain devoted to each other even in death, and at its lowest point the cruelty of wife batterer, Uzowulu, whom the Egwugwu themselves must discipline. But for the student reader in a Western culture, Okonkwo's petty viciousness remains a more vivid travesty of human rights than the action of the District Commissioner in the novel, when he enjoins the goalers to treat with dignity the elders whom he has just tricked, humiliated and imprisoned.

In the case of the African student reader, the issues that are conflated are somewhat different. Speaking from within modern Nigerian society, she cannot help but be aware of the differences between the world she inhabits and the one Achebe describes. She is a product of the Africanized Nigerian education system and has been taught to respect the world of tradition by her parents as well as by set books like *Things Fall Apart* on her school examination syllabus. She fully expects to be married in church as well as within some modified form of a traditional ceremony and to be the only legal wife of her modern educated husband. The polygamously married senior sisters of her father belong to a world to which she pays her respects but which she assumes is as remote to her reality as the Igbo village Achebe describes at the turn of the century—at least for the present. Because her interaction with traditional culture is indirect, and because she considers her emancipated notions of a woman's role a product of her westernized/nigerianized education, she cannot conceive of women in traditional Igbo society sharing her notions of selfhood. For her, the world that Achebe brings to life is a beautiful tableau that exists to reinforce her sense of belonging to a noble tradition. And this is true, whether her ethnic origins are Igbo, Yoruba or East African Kikuyu.

Both the readers of the novel described above imply by their conflation of lived and imagined realities that there is some truly objective, unbiased version of traditional life which it is the writer's duty to deliver to the reader in such a way that our sympathies are engaged for the "right" causes and our imaginations are stimulated in the "right" directions. Neither seems concerned that the imaginative point of departure for the writer could have incorporated different preoccupations and perspectives from the ones they bring to their reading of his work.

Achebe probably had an agenda in writing his novel quite different from either of these readers in studying it. As the son of a village catechist and a scholarship winner, first to secondary school and then to the newly established Ibadan College, Achebe was one of the first generation of African writers to be familiar from early childhood with Western and indigenous traditions. Both the eloquent oral traditions of the Igbo community and the compelling prose of the King James Bible would have imbued him with a love of beautiful language and an appreciation of the timing and perfect cadence of a well wrought sentence. The texts which formed his vision of Africa, however, were novels like Joyce Cary's *Mr. Johnson* and Conrad's *Heart of Darkness*, texts in relation to which Achebe has described himself as a resisting reader. Like his modern African readers, he would have been aware of the ways in which the values of his Christian family differed from or coincided with those of more traditional Igbo families. Like his Western readers, he must have been uncomfortably aware that many of the traditions which still influenced his life would have been considered brutal or misogynist from the perspective of the fictive author of *The Pacification of the Primitive Tribes of the Lower Niger.*

Unlike both groups of readers, however, and indeed, unlike either of the cultures to which they had access, Achebe's generation of African intellectuals had no readily available symbolic discourse through which they could represent and ascribe value simultaneously to the various cultural influences that had formed them. To be sure they could quote Yeats and Eliot at will to each other in one breath and spar with traditional proverbs in the next, but who besides them would "get" the joke? Who in their community who had come before them or was likely to come after them would understand and give full value to all aspects of their accomplishments and ways of seeing? Okonkwo voices a similar *angst* in a rare moment of filial solidarity with his father in *Things Fall Apart* as he contemplates the defection of his eldest son Nwoye to join the Christians:

> Suppose when he died all his male children decided to follow Nwoye's steps and abandon their ancestors? Okonkwo felt a cold shudder run through him at the terrible prospect, like the prospect of annihilation. He saw himself and his father crowding round their ancestral shrine waiting in vain for worship and sacrifice and finding nothing but ashes of bygone days and his children the while praying to the white man's god.

In the rhetoric of our age we would say that both Okonkwo and his creator are concerned with the construction of a personal, in this case masculine, identity through which to mediate their connections to past, present and future communities. Okonkwo's quest is easily charted. Deprived by his father's anomalous lifestyle of an inheritance of land, yam seed or junior wives, he has access to no material objects that can provide him with a reference for who he is or what he may become. In fact his most immediate point of male reference, his father, is described by the society as *agbala*, a word that "could . . . mean a man who had taken no title," but which also meant "woman." Like Shelley's monster in *Frankenstein*, Okonkwo must fabricate a social context for his identity and values rather than simply assuming a system of references in relation to which he can define himself. He does so by isolating and responding to specific symbols of masculinity within his culture as if they, in the abstract, could constitute all that a man needed to construct his social self.

The pivotal example of this process in the novel is Okonkwo's understanding of the concept of courage. At the outset it is the masculine attribute most immediately accessible to him, as it seems wholly contingent upon his performance as an individual. In the opening paragraphs of the novel Okonkwo is defined for us in terms of his courage when he throws Amalinze the Cat in wrestling. Later we discover that Okonkwo's courage on this occasion is immediately translated into affirmation of his social identity since it wins him the love of a woman whom, in terms of material wealth, he is not yet "man enough" to marry.

Such early instances of social recognition for his courage are compounded over the years as Okonkwo struggles manfully against bad weather and harvests to acquire his own yam seed and as he takes lives in battle. Gradually, for Okonkwo prestige and manliness become synonymous with the ability to do difficult, even distasteful jobs without flinching. Where the Oracle demands the life of his ward, Ikemefuna, Okonkwo finds himself without access to a system of values which would allow him to distance himself from the killing of the child who "calls [him] father" and remain a man. He strikes the blow that kills the child, offending the earth goddess, Ala and setting in motion a chain of events which ultimately lead to his downfall.

Okonkwo's limited personal understanding of physical ascendancy as courage and his equation of courage with masculinity are set against a much richer and more complex set of values available to his clan as a whole. In the novel Okonkwo's friend, Obierika, is the main spokesman for this greater tradition. His words are reinforced structurally by the narrative's juxtaposition of Okonkwo's actions and those of other members of the society in a way which invites us to consider the complexity of the clan's values. Thus Okonkwo sees tenderness as incompatible with masculinity, viewing marriage as yet another social situation in which a man's worth is measured by his ability to control others through superior physical strength. Yet the reader is made aware of the ways in which such notions of male prerogative are qualified by the community. Okonkwo's response to the almost simultaneous deaths of Ndulue and his wife Ozoemena dramatizes the gap between his personal code and that of the clan as a whole:

"It was always said that Ndulue and Ozoemena had one mind,"
said Obierika. "I remember when I was a young boy there was a
song about them. He could not do anything without telling her."
"I did not know that," said Okonkwo. "I thought he was a strong
man in his youth." "He was indeed," said Ofoedu. Okonkwo
shook his head doubtfully. "He led Umuofia to war in those
days," said Obierika.

Okonkwo himself is punished when he breaks the Week of Peace and
beats his wife, a judgement which reflects a symbolic recognition of
wifebeating a violence even though it may also be associated with
legitimate masculine privilege. Finally there is the unequivocal cen-
sure of the *egwugwu* who are called forth to reprimand the chronic
batterer, Uzowulu. Their judgement shows where the community
draws the line between physical prowess and bullying; courage and
cowardice.

Okonkwo's most complex conflation of brute force with the "masculine" virtue of courage occurs in the final pages of the story where
he cuts off the head of the court messenger and then hangs himself.
Here courage is dissociated from those other manly attributes: caution, diplomacy, and the ability to weigh both sides of an argument.
The irony is that none of these "higher" values in his society will have
any effect on the superior military might of the colonizers. Thus, in
a twisted sense, Okonkwo and the District Commissioner share the
same world view: that ultimately physical strength and the ability to
inflict one's will on another human being, be it one's wife, one's son
or one's natives are the only significant forms of social differentiation
in establishing a masculine identity.

The act of suicide marks symbolically the parting of the ways
between Okonkwo and his clan. Until now he has accepted the cen-
sure of his community for his unpremeditated acts of violence,
because at heart he accepts that their universe encompasses his.
Faced now with the whispered comment "why did he do it" after he
kills the messenger, Okonkwo finally decides that his clansmen no
longer share his values and that to be a man on their terms would be
a form of living death. His community reciprocates his final act of
distancing, to the extent that it denies him a man's burial. And yet,
ultimately, Okonkwo characteristically underestimates the flexibility
and comprehensiveness of the clan's values. When Obierika declares
"[t]hat man was one of the greatest men in Umuofia" he extends to
Okonkwo the same complex and qualified acceptance accorded to
Ndulue who was great and/but who could not do anything without
telling his wife. Thus the accolade of manhood is conferred on
Okonkwo even in default, both in the words of his friend and in the
act of narration which constitutes Achebe's novel.

Okonkwo's final solution brings us back full circle to the dilemma of his creator. Like Okonkwo, who attempts to carve out a relationship with his clan in the absence of an inherited sense of identity, Achebe must renegotiate a relationship to traditional Igbo society, which his education, religious training and internalized moral standards have made tenuous. Like Okonkwo he often proceeds by isolating specific aspects of the societies to which he has access, and allowing these to stand for many other possible readings of a given social situation. Achebe has described his mission in writing *Things Fall Apart* as being to teach other Africans that their past was neither so savage or benighted as the colonizers have represented it to be. Another way of stating this goal could conceivably be that Achebe needed to prove to himself that the best of the values he associated with his Christian upbringing were compatible with the values of traditional Igbo society.

There are many examples of selective incorporation of supposedly Western/Christian values into the celebration of the traditional way of life in *Things Fall Apart*. I would like to discuss briefly three: the killing of Ikemefuna, the presentation of marriage, and the selective elaboration of women's roles within traditional Igbo society.

In presenting Ikemefuna's death, Achebe, like Okonkwo, must find a way of synchronizing the qualities he wishes to represent with the values he has internalized. While sharing the mission school horror at the idea of human sacrifice that he attributes to the converts in *Things Fall Apart*, Achebe must find ways of addressing this issue while keeping the reader's sympathy for the community as a whole. He does so by structuring the story of Ikemefuna's death so that it parallels the biblical story of Abraham's near sacrifice of his son, Isaac. The journey out of the confines of the village, the boy's carrying of the vessels associated with the sacrifice and his last disarming words, "[m]y father, they have killed me" all resonate with the bible story. Isaac performs each of the roles attributed to Ikemefuna, including the utterance of a last disarming remark: "My father . . . behold the fire and the wood: but where is the lamb . . ." (Genesis 22: 7). The major difference, of course, is that no ram is provided to be a substitute for Ikemefuna. Yet we feel sure that, just as Abraham would have killed his son, had the ram not been caught in the thicket, Okonkwo would have spared his, had a ram materialized for him. Both fathers act in strict obedience to their Gods, and both contemplate the deed they must perform with horror as well as fortitude.

There are further parallels between Okonkwo's situation and the New Testament story about God's sacrifice of his son Jesus for the greater good of all humanity (itself a version of the Abraham/Isaac motif). What is important here, however, is that Achebe has picked the form of human sacrifice most compatible with Judaeo-Christian myth as the centerpiece of his examination of human sacrifice in Igbo culture. The more ubiquitous forms, such as the "throwing away" of twins in the bad bush or the killing of slaves on the death of their masters, are mentioned only in passing, as evils already under fire within traditional society, whose eradication is hastened by the coming of the missionaries. For the tragedy of Ikemefuna's death to be shared by his readers as a moment of pathos rather than one of revulsion, the parallel with Abraham must function as a shared archetype. The object of sacrifice must be a sentient individual, bound to the person who makes the sacrifice by bonds of affection. In this way the act of sacrifice becomes a symbol of devotion to a principle higher than earthly love, rather than the brute machinations of a culture incapable of elevated sentiments. Though Okonkwo's personal intervention in Ikemefuna's death remains tragically wrongheaded, the context in which he acts retains its dignity.

Achebe's technical manipulation of such parallels within his story are reinforced as thematic strategies in the conversations between the enlightened missionary Mr. Brown and the enlightened Igbo, Akunna. Their conversations may be read as a metaphor for Achebe's own search for a point of convergence between the two codes which have informed his ethics. Similarly, his description of what it is that attracts Nwoye to the Christians mirrors his own strategies with the reader in using biblical myth to reinforce Igbo values. As he points out: "It was not the mad logic of the Trinity that captivated [Nwoye]. He did not understand it. It was the poetry of the new religion, something felt in the marrow."

On the personal and political levels, Achebe's presentation of women within Igbo society can be seen to follow a similar pattern. Although we are told of Okonkwo's many wives and children, the male-female relationships in Okonkwo's family which Achebe isolates for our scrutiny are almost indistinguishable from those of monogamous couples within Western tradition. Okonkwo has three wives but we come to know only one: Ekwefi, the mother of Enzinma. She has married Okonkwo for love, having run away from her first husband. Her relationship with her husband, for better or worse, has all the passion, violence and shared trauma we associate with the Western romantic tradition. Achebe's point clearly is that all these emotions existed in traditional Igbo society but, as with his choice of situation in dealing with the issue of human sacrifice, the relationship he describes between Okonkwo and Ekwefi is by no means normative. We never really see the wives in Okonkwo's compound interacting with each other the way we are shown the men interacting among themselves or even Okonkwo interacting with his children. From a Western perspective the omission is hardly experienced as a loss, as the reader can identify effortlessly with the structure if not the content of the relationship described between Okonkwo and Ekwefi. Indeed, its similarity to versions of marriage with which Western students are familiar may help explain why empathy with Ekwefi's mistreatment is so spontaneous and a reading of the text as misogynist can take place so easily. By contrast students seem to have much more difficulty dealing with friendly alliances between senior and junior wives in the work of other African writers. Many of them reject outright the idea in Ama Ata Aidoo's *Anowa* that a wife could actively seek out a junior wife for her husband as a way of marking her own material consequence; of asserting her own identity. Such relationships are important in the constructing of female identity, and that is clearly not what Achebe's novel is about.

A similar selective process occurs in the presentation of women's public roles. Achebe names one of the two groupings within the clan which endowed women with specific political authority: the *umuada*, or daughters of the clan. Since Igbo marriage ties were usually exogamous a woman also belonged to another group in her husband's village consisting of the wives of the clan. Directly or indirectly, these groups controlled between them many aspects of civic and familial spheres of influence. In *Things Fall Apart* these range from the policing of stray animals to the solemnizing of certain stages within marriage and betrothal rituals and the preservation of a maternal line of land entitlement. Indeed, Okonkwo's survival in exile hinges on his right to exercise his entitlement to land in his mother's village via the connections vested in her as a wife in Okonkwo's father's clan and a daughter in her father's clan.

Achebe does not tell us, however, that the *umuada* also regulated the markets in each town and that their intervention or threatened intervention was crucial in civic as well as marital disputes. When Uzowulu is brought to judgement for chronic abuse of his wife, one of the elders asks why such a minor matter has been brought to the attention of the *egwugwu* and is told: "Don't you know what kind of man Uzowulu is? He will not listen to any other decision." It is clear that Achebe introduces the *egwugwu* here to underline for his audience in terms they can appreciate how seriously the community looks upon violence against women. But in fact it would seem from the anthropological accounts that a more likely scenario in a case such as this would have been the intervention of the wives of the clan, who would have enforced the judgement by "sitting" on the man in question: that is by so shaming him publicly through rude songs and obscene gestures that he would be forced to mend his ways. Alternatively, the female kinswomen of the battered women who had married into the clan of the offending male could have threatened to enforce a sexual strike if their husbands did not see to it that Uzowulu mended his ways.

Clearly Achebe would have been hard put to imbue such scenarios with the decorum expected of women within Western tradition. And indeed, he may have internalized a Western view of legal authority, defining male courts of law as the ultimate seat of power in any society, to such an extent that alternative ways of dramatizing Uzowulu's ostracism through female intervention may have seemed ineffective by comparison. In any event, their omission from the narrative leaves us with no example of female authority within the Igbo social structure that is not compatible with traditional Western ideals of femininity as nurturing, ornamental or in need of protection. Indeed, a truly jaundiced eye would have also to note that the women in the novel are described cooking, plaiting their hair, decorating their bodies, dancing, running from *egwugwu* and being given in marriage. We do not see them planting in their farms, bartering their goods in the market place, sitting in judgement on members of their community or taking action alongside or against their men. The only woman we see acting with any authority is the priestess of Chielo, and she is presented, in terms consistent with Western practice, as a witch—a force for good or evil separated from the regular run of womenfolk rather than part of a chain of ritual and social female authority.

Such omissions become all the more difficult to reconcile when one remembers that it was precisely the outbreak of the Women's War in Aba in 1929, organized by the wives and daughters of a number of clans that had delivered one of the most sweeping challenges to colonial authority in living memory among the Igbo at the time when Achebe was writing. In fact, it was this event which motivated the British government to give research grants to several "amateur" colonial anthropologists to study Igbo society specifically. These studies produced the spate of early anthropological accounts Achebe satirizes in his references to the District Commissioner's projected book on *The Pacification of the Primitive Tribes of the Lower Niger*.

One sees the consequence of this selective process in one situation in the novel which in my opinion would have been richer had Achebe paid closer attention to women's political structures within Igbo society. When Okonkwo is forced to flee to his motherland after committing the female crime of manslaughter he is given a lecture by his maternal uncle on the importance of the feminine principle in Igbo culture. Okonkwo, who can only define masculinity in relation to what his father was not, is understandably out of his depth when asked to accept a notion that his identity may also be formed by qualities represented by his mother. But because we as readers have no sense of the full range of qualities both protective and assertive that are associated with the feminine principle in Igbo society we are given as few options as Okonkwo in interpreting the scene. We know that he should be patient and dependent and grateful for the protection of his motherland. We also know that in spiritual terms the earth goddess Ala is the deity Okonkwo has most often offended and that she is responsible for his exile. However, we have no way of knowing that female power symbolized by Ala is represented in the clan by a system of legal codes and practices controlled by the women in Okonkwo's society . . . that in a sense Okonkwo's refusal to be comforted by his motherland is also a rejection of aspects of the very civic culture by which his access to the privileges of manhood is partially regulated. Much of this would seem to be implied in Achebe's presentation of this scene but there is none of the rich working out of all the implications that occurs elsewhere in the unfolding of masculine systems of values and authority.

Achebe's selective use of those aspects of Igbo traditional society which best coincide with Western/Christian social values, speak ably to his own need to establish a view of a world, both modern and traditional of which he can be a part. To call this treatment of the formation of a masculine sense of identity sexist is a facile and not very accurate reading of a gendered response to a specific cultural dilemma. That Achebe's narrative is indeed a selective, gendered one which partakes of both traditional and Judaeo-Christian patriarchal values only becomes a problem in the light of the history of *Things Fall Apart's* reception as the definitive, "objective" account of the Igbo, not to say African, traditional past. In expanding a hypothetical paragraph in a district commissioner's text into the saga of a lost civilization, Achebe was able to address imaginatively the nostalgia, social insecurity and nationalist sentiments of an entire continent. The problem is that he succeeded so well that his representation of the past has become a substitute for the reality which, inevitably, is far more complex than one novel could hope to make it. The result is that, like the institutions it helped debunk, Achebe's text has itself become the object of deconstructive exercises in the work of more recent Nigerian writers. In the work of Buchi Emecheta, Achebe's chapters (or perhaps extended paragraphs?) on the position of women in Igbo society have been revised to offer a complete alternative vision of the attitudes of traditional women to their status in the society. It is a partisan and revisionist picture, committed to challenging Igbo and Judaeo-Christian values from the perspective of an upwardly mobile fellow traveller in the women's movement. However it, too, must resist the temptation to limit the roles it ascribes to women in traditional society to those "invented" by Achebe. Indeed, for the modern woman writer in Africa, Achebe's authority must seem as compelling and as difficult to challenge as the district commissioner's voice must have been for Achebe in his time.

This irony serves to remind us that literature, like anthropology or history, is a form of selective representation, replete with its inherent assumptions about authenticity and "objectivity". For those of us who teach *Things Fall Apart* as an appendix to anthropological and socio-

logical documents, or as a way of bringing history to life, it is important to keep in mind that this particular fiction is a response to history which mimics the structure and claims to objectivity of "science"
without for a moment abdicating its right as fiction to be selective,
subjective or unrealistic. Those of as who teach *Things Fall Apart* as
literature in the hope of reaffirming traditional values may do well to
bear in mind that the values we discover in the text will be most likely
our own. Achebe's novel is a brilliant resolution of the conflict experienced by his generation between traditional and Western notions of
manhood, courage and the construction of communal values. Such
resolution is seldom if ever about choosing between two clearly
defined alternatives and inevitably involves a process of selection.
When our students accuse Achebe of sexism or Emecheta of historical inaccuracy, what their statements really attest is the creation for
better or worse of an African literary canon, based on a highly selective system of values shared by Achebe and his cohort of African intellectuals that has come to be used as a way of reading history: a
touchstone for the literature as well as for the society of the post-
colonial age. Time, perhaps, to rename *Things Fall Apart*—

Things Are Consolidated?

EMMANUEL OBIECHINA

Following the Author in *Things Fall Apart*†

My advice to the teacher of *Things Fall Apart* is simple, just three
words: follow the author. Because the novel takes place in the past
and in an African community, students may find aspects of its world
and its cultural values unfamiliar. Teachers may also be handicapped
by unfamiliarity; indeed, many critical works about the novel address
this need by providing background information. But even without
such studies, notes, and commentaries, or in spite of them, perceptive teachers who follow the verbal signposts established by the
author within the narrative should find the novel accessible. Unlike
many other novels, *Things Fall Apart* provides its own notes and commentaries and does not even seem to need its glossary.

In this novel, Chinua Achebe is quintessentially a teacher. George
Eliot sees the novelist as a "teacher or influencer of the public mind."[1]
(Allott 94), but Achebe's role as teacher goes beyond influencing the

---

† From *Approaches to Teaching Achebe's* Things Fall Apart. Ed. Bernth Lindfors (New York:
   The Modern Language Association of America, 1991), 31–39. Reprinted by permission of
   the Modern Language Association of America.
1. Miriam Allott, *Novelists on the Novel* (London: Routledge, 1956) 131–32.

public mind—or the public's moral taste or the action of the intelligence. For Achebe, literature is a form of communication requiring the transference of experience from the author to the reader. In *Things Fall Apart*, Achebe is preoccupied not only with the experience itself but also with the best manner of conveying it. He anticipates likely difficulties for the reader and attempts to resolve them by using well-chosen strategies of technique and language. Teachers who follow the author's lead can navigate the world and experience contained in the novel without too much strain.

Achebe is, of course, aware that he uses his works to educate the reader. In an essay titled "The Novelist as Teacher," he defines his role graphically:

> Here then is an adequate revolution for me to espouse—to help my society regain belief in itself and put away the complexes of the years of denigration and self-abasement. And it is essentially a question of education, in the best sense of that word. . . . I would be quite satisfied if my novels (especially the ones I set in the past) did no more than teach my readers that their past— with all its imperfections—was not one long night of savagery from which the first Europeans acting on God's behalf delivered them. (*Morning* 44–45)

Teachers of *Things Fall Apart* should know this essay because it throws light on Achebe's intentions in the novel. He sets out to remove misunderstandings and to restore the truth of a way of life that has been misrepresented over the centuries. Achebe scrupulously pursues the truth of the characters' humanity, and he is wholly sensitive to the historical, cultural, and psychological impulses operating on the characters and their society. The fundamental role he has set for himself as an African novelist readily explains his choice of title, themes, and creative stances.

As explainer and teacher, Achebe positions himself strategically, at a vantage point from which he sees everything, in order to explain everything. He is the controlling consciousness of the narrative, "the Watcher," as Henry James would describe him (Allott 131–32). His guiding hand directs the action, deploys emphases, defines relevances, and assesses the ethical qualities of individual and group conduct throughout the novel. He also corrects misrepresentations and distorted views of the characters and their society.

So important is the task of education to the author that he presses one of his characters, Obierika, into service as a secondary center of consciousness. Obierika, the friend of Okonkwo, is close to the center of the action. Yet he differs so much from the hero that he almost serves as a foil. As a philosophical, moral man whose views and comments always deserve respect, he provides the voice of reason and sobriety.

Deeply exposed to the traditional life of Umuofia, Obierika understands it in great detail, in its triumphant and tragic aspects, in its strengths and weaknesses. Apart from the author, Obierika is the most reliable guide in *Things Fall Apart*, a role Achebe deliberately assigns him. Teachers should recognize and exploit the novel's two sources of authoritative guidance, and both teacher and students should test their interpretations of the novel against the insights provided by these sources.

First and foremost, the teacher of *Things Fall Apart* should determine through close textual study the verbal signposts the author uses to convey his insights. The most important signposts are the key statements that develop a large part of the novel's action and character exploration. Often the author edges in such statements as if they were not important, when instead they constitute the pivots on which much else depends. Readers unattentive to Achebe's organizational strategies may overlook these signposts because they are intrusive rather than obtrusive. For example, in the book's first paragraph, which describes the famous wrestling match between young Okonkwo and Amalinze the Cat, Achebe comments that Okonkwo's "fame rested on solid personal achievements" (3). This sentence could easily be lost as the novel moves on to describe the life of Okonkwo's father, and yet the statement is central to unraveling the hero's character. The author includes several similar statements: "And he did pounce on people quite often," "[h]e had no patience with unsuccessful men," "[h]e had had no patience with his father," "his whole life was dominated by fear, the fear of failure and of weakness" (3, 9). These kernels around which the author builds the hero's character represent what I call the intrusive mode of Achebe's verbal signposts. Achebe subsequently fleshes out and dramatizes these keynote statements in different contexts. Indeed, like the controlling tones in a musical symphony, these statements are played and replayed in a variety of pitches, harmonies, melodies, and rhythms because of their strategic importance in the total scheme of character and social explorations.

Thus, Achebe elaborates the statement that Okonkwo's fame is based on solid personal achievements in a number of contexts on subsequent pages. So firmly established is this aspect of the hero's identity that when another character, displeased with Okonkwo's lack of humility, suggests that his success is a matter of luck, the author intervenes to correct the misrepresentation: "If ever a man deserved his success, that man was Okonkwo" (19), asserts the authorial voice, and it proceeds to enumerate his accomplishments. Okonkwo is a flawed hero, but Achebe does not want him blamed for the wrong reasons.

The statement that Okonkwo "did pounce on people quite often" provides another example of Achebe's technique (3). Several incidents bear out this comment: Okonkwo breaks the sacred Week of Peace by beating his youngest wife (21), he beats and takes a shot at his second wife (27–28), he cuts down Ikemefuna in the fatal bush (43), he murderously beats his son Nwoye for going to Christian services (107), and he impulsively beheads the court messenger before hanging himself (144). Impulsive violence is an aspect of his character. If we add to this trait the fact that anger is the only emotion the hero is capable of experiencing, we have the picture of an impetuous and violent man doomed to fall, in spite of his great personal achievements.

The author establishes his signposts so clearly that he leaves no ambiguities or ethical fluidities in matters requiring definite and precise judgment. In Ikemefuna's death, for example, several ethical conditions are at issue. Ikemefuna's life at Umuofia is full of pathos, but the author makes it clear that readers need to separate the pity they feel for a young child caught in the complexities of adult politics from their evaluation of that politics. Another consideration is the morality of Okonkwo's participation in the murder of a child who regards him as a father.

References to Ikemefuna occur many times in connection with the hero's personal achievements:

> As the elders said, if a child washed his hands he could eat with kings. Okonkwo had clearly washed his hands and so he ate with kings and elders. And that was how he came to look after the doomed lad who was sacrificed to the village of Umuofia by their neighbours to avoid war and bloodshed. The ill-fated lad was called Ikemefuna. (6)

Elsewhere, we learn that the war threatening the peaceful relations between Mbaino and Umuofia is a just war, ratified by the communal assembly and sanctioned by the oracle. Okonkwo is the emissary who carries the ultimatum to the enemy:

> And so when Okonkwo of Umuofia arrived at Mbaino as the proud and imperious emissary of war, he was treated with great honour and respect, and two days later he returned home with a lad of fifteen and a young virgin. The lad's name was Ikemefuna, whose sad story is still told in Umuofia unto this day. (9)

Ikemefuna is also linked to Okonkwo's standing in the community:

> At the most one could say that [Okonkwo's] *chi* or personal god was good. But the Ibo people have a proverb that when a man says yes his *chi* says yes also. Okonkwo said yes very strongly; so his *chi* agreed. And not only his *chi* but his clan too, because it judged a man by the work of his hands. That was why Okonkwo had been chosen by the nine villages to carry a message of war to their enemies unless they agreed to give up a young man and a virgin to atone for the murder of Udo's wife. And such was the

> deep fear that their enemies had for Umuofia that they treated
> Okonkwo like a king and brought him a virgin who was given to
> Udo as wife, and the lad Ikemefuna. (19–20)

Even though these passages appear repetitious, they are not. Each
differs contextually and has additional layers of information that clarify one aspect or another of the narrative. The first quotation broadly
states Ikemefuna's status. The boy is not a war hostage but a sacrificial victim given by his people to atone for his father's murder of the
Umuofia woman. The author's choice of words provides the insight.
Achebe refers to Ikemefuna as "the doomed lad who was sacrificed
to the village of Umuofia by their neighbours to avoid war and bloodshed" and as "the ill-fated lad." In the third passage the phrase "to
atone for the murder of Udo's wife" underlines Ikemefuna's judicial-
sacrificial destiny. This idea is so important that Achebe repeats it in
the context of Okonkwo's report to the elders:

> The elders, or *ndichie*, met to hear a report of Okonkwo's mis-
> sion. At the end they decided, as everybody knew they would,
> that the girl should go to Ogbuefi Udo to replace his murdered
> wife. As for the boy, he belonged to the clan as a whole, and there
> was no hurry to decide his fate. Okonkwo was, therefore, asked
> on behalf of the clan to look after him in the interim. And so for
> three years Ikemefuna lived in Okonkwo's household. (9)

The author devotes ample attention to the issue of war and peace.
Laws and conventions exist for regulating conflicts among peoples. In
Umuofia, determining whether a war is just has such significance that
it is vested in the Oracle of the Hills and the Caves who, when necessary, forbids the people from going into "*a fight of blame*" (9). If the
war is to be just, people must follow the proper conventions and first
attempt to settle the issue amicably, such as by exacting a reparation.
If peaceful methods fail, the society makes a formal declaration of
war. In the quotation, the intruded clause "as everybody knew they
would" underscores the existence of the law of war between neighbors. Again, the fact that "there was no hurry to decide his fate" shows
that the matter does not involve personal feeling. Chapter 7 begins:

> For three years Ikemefuna lived in Okonkwo's household and
> the elders of Umuofia seemed to have forgotten about him. (37)

No one seems eager to terminate Ikemefuna's young life. But if the
elders have forgotten about him, the ever-vigilant oracle has not, and
so, at the appropriate time, it moves against him.

But while the author justifies the clan's action as following tradition,
he condemns Okonkwo's participation in Ikemefuna's murder. The
text provides abundant evidence of Achebe's position, emphasizing
Ikemefuna's integration into Okonkwo's household and the warm

relationship between the boy and Okonkwo that makes Okonkwo's action unnatural. Even though Okonkwo treats him "with a heavy hand," as he treats everyone else, the author informs us that

> there was no doubt that he liked the boy. Sometimes when he went to big village meetings or communal ancestral feasts he allowed Ikemefuna to accompany him, like a son, carrying his stool and his goatskin bag. And, indeed, Ikemefuna called him father. (20)

This bond is not lost on the thoughtful elders. When the time comes for Ikemefuna to be killed, the oldest man in Okonkwo's village visits Okonkwo to warn him against being involved: "That boy calls you father. Do mot bear a hand in his death" (40). Okonkwo ignores the warning and actually cuts the boy down when he runs to him for protection in the fatal bush, crying, "My father, they have killed me!" (43).

Obierika condemns Okonkwo's action:

> If I were you I would have stayed at home. What you have done will not please the Earth. It is the kind of action for which the goddess wipes out whole families. (46)

Okonkwo's excuse—that he only carried out the earth-mother goddess's command—is not convincing. Obierika offers the more convincing and morally sound view that, should the oracle demand the death of his son, Obierika would neither dispute the oracle's wish nor be the one to carry it out.

Obierika provides significant insights in the later part of the novel, particularly after Okonkwo goes into exile for unintentionally killing Ezeudu's son. Obierika sees the punishment as far too heavy for the offense, but as a good traditionalist he tries to accommodate it. It is easy to see why the author, who reports Obierika's perception with approval, uses him as a center of consciousness:

> Obierika was a man who thought about things. When the will of the goddess had been done, he sat down in his *obi* and mourned his friend's calamity. Why should a man suffer so grievously for an offence he had committed inadvertently? But although he thought for a long time he found no answer. He was merely led into greater complexities. He remembered his wife's twin children, whom he had thrown away. What crime had they committed? The Earth had decreed that they were an offence on the land and must be destroyed. And if the clan did not exact punishment for an offence against the great goddess, her wrath was loosed on all the land and not just on the offender. As the elders said, if one finger brought oil it soiled the others. (87)

When Okonkwo returns to Umuofia after his years of exile, so much has changed that the old society is hardly recognizable. Obierika offers an invaluable and completely reliable picture of the collapse of tradition in an effort to help Okonkwo see the futility of armed resistance to the new forces:

> It is already too late. . . . Our own men and our sons have joined the ranks of the stranger. . . . How do you think we can fight when our own brothers have turned against us? The white man is very clever. He came quietly and peaceably with his religion. We were amused at his foolishness and allowed him to stay. Now he has won our brothers, and our clan can no longer act like one. He has put a knife on the things that held us together and we have fallen apart. (124–25)

But Okonkwo's inner weaknesses and some external factors combine to neutralize the effect of such a sensible appeal, and the hero plunges deep into his disaster. Finally, Obierika provides the hero's epitaph:

> That man was one of the greatest men in Umuofia. You drove him to kill himself; and now he will be buried like a dog. (147)

Things Fall Apart reveals Achebe's integrity, knowledge, and historical and cultural visions, particularly in its handling of the central themes of cultural conflict and change. His understanding of the traditional agrarian culture works to build an impressive picture of its social, political, economic; and religious institutions and values; its arts and crafts; and its modes of perceiving reality. Achebe's representation of that society is so clearly and comprehensively drawn that, when the new forces begin to impinge on it and to undermine its stability, the reader can easily follow the drama.

In painting this picture of the traditional way of life, Achebe justly describes not only the positive aspects but also the negative ones. He sidesteps the temptation to idealize or romanticize that way of life. Teachers and students of *Things Fall Apart* should trust Achebe's perspective and adopt a close reading of his novel, paying particular attention to the verbal signposts through which the author clarifies his themes. Readers should also note Obierika's views and observations with care, because the author uses Obierika to convey some of the novel's finest insights. By testing their views and interpretations against those of the author and of Obierika, teachers and students enjoy the benefit of the author's excellent pedagogical design.

ROBERT M. WREN

Things Fall Apart in Its Time and Place[†]

Students may have difficulty approaching *Things Fall Apart* because they know little about African history and nothing at all about the history of southeastern Nigeria, the locale of the novel. The novel seems abstracted in time and place, a mythic Africa, even though Achebe roots the characters and action in a realistic, if fictional, world. Achebe's world is not mythic and should not be seen as such. Viewing Okonkwo's predicament as part of an ongoing historical process is important to the author's intention: Achebe wants to demonstrate that Europe did not bring "civilization" to "savages" (unless one accepts the older European senses of both words); he wants to show that civil order existed in a framework of tradition, political understanding, and faith. That framework falls apart under the rule of European strangers. A closely integrated society with a common will—a community in the truest, richest sense of that word—loses its integrity when the Europeans take over. The invaders cannot appreciate the society they have "infected with individualism."

The novel takes place at the beginning of the twentieth century, when British authorities, missions, and trade penetrated the Igbo hinterland east of the Niger River. The society described in part 1 is civil and ordered. To this society, in part 2, come the colonial officer and the missionary, invaders as incomprehensible as they are uncomprehending. With them come still other strangers, Africans from far and near, who do the colonial bidding as soldiers, messengers, agents, and teachers. These invaders render the traditional mechanisms of order ineffective, and, as a result, the novel's community, Umuofia, becomes confused and divided. Okonkwo, the central character, falls victim to the confusion and hangs himself, an abomination. The District Commissioner, after but a moment's thought, resolves to note the event in the book he is writing, *The Pacification of the Primitive Tribes of the Lower Niger*.

The words *pacification* and *primitive* are used with great irony at the end of the novel. My approach to *Things Fall Apart* uses these two concepts as keys to understanding both the novel and the culture that Achebe invites his readers to share.

Students and teachers need to look at two larger histories. One is the unfamiliar and unexpected reality of centuries of life and action

---

† From *Approaches to Teaching Achebe's* Things Fall Apart. Ed. Bernth Lindfors (New York: The Modern Language Association of America, 1991), 38–44. Reprinted by permission of the Modern Language Association of America.

among the people of the lands portrayed in the novel. This history needs less explication because the novel itself is its testimonial. The other history—more familiar, perhaps, yet little known—is the European "scramble for Africa" that took place in the nineteenth century. One of the many results of this movement was that Britain secured control of the great, populous, and varied territory that now constitutes the nation called Nigeria.

That territory has never had any integrity save one imposed by the colonial powers. Hundreds of different ethnic and linguistic communities are crushed into one "nation." The largest of these communities are those of the Hausa-speaking peoples (among whom are other, bilingual peoples) of the northern regions of Nigeria. The Yoruba of the southwest make up the second largest group, and third in numbers are the Igbo of the southeast. The Igbo are, collectively, Achebe's own people, but they are not homogeneous. "Igbo" villages only a few miles apart once spoke languages—all called "Igbo"—that were as different as German and Dutch are in northern Europe. (Education and other forces are blending out the differences, leading to what may in time become a unified Igbo language.) The dialects, cultures, and political systems of Igbo east of the great Niger River are unlike those of the Igbo on the western side. And, if we may leap over several other, smaller ethnicities, Igbo language and culture radically depart from those of the Yoruba in the southwest—as much as, say, German does from Italian. At the same time, Yoruba and Igbo cultures differ from northern Nigerian Hausa cultures even more greatly—as much, perhaps, as British culture differs from Russian. The conquerors crushed all this diversity into a single nation.

The "pacification," as it is ironically identified at the end of the novel, occurred between 1900 and 1920, a time span that roughly indicates the period from the start of the action of *Things Fall Apart* to the beginning of Achebe's third novel, *Arrow of God*. The first movement of conquest, a campaign against an Igbo people called the Aro in the far southeast of Igboland, began early in December 1901 and continued into January 1902. According to J. C. Anene, the British believed that the destruction of the Aro's great oracle would break a perceived Aro political hegemony and open all the hinterland to colonization. Anene shows that the British were wrong. True, many villages did accept the newcomers, but they were not villages ruled by the Aro. Many others did not know or did not care about British power or were unfriendly or were uncomprehending (231–37). The fictional Abame, site of a massacre reported early in part 2 of *Things Fall Apart*, provides an example of a village that did not understand British power. The Abame slaughter paved the way for a more peaceful invasion of Umuofia and neighboring villages by colonial officers and missionaries. The same process occurred at and around an actual town, Ahiara. Ahiara was one of many Igbo towns "punished" (in the colonial term) for resistance after the supposed success of the Aro expedition. (The last "collective punishment" took place long after Ahiara, in 1920.)

The facts of the Ahiara massacre closely conform to Obierika's account of the Abame incident. On 16 November 1905, J. F. Stewart, traveling by bicycle from Owerri, missed his way, fell into unfriendly hands, and was killed. A. E. Afigbo found that the Ahiara people "took him to their neighbours . . . to show *what* they had caught," because "they did not know he was a human being" (*Warrant Chiefs* 67). Nearly a month later, according to Colonial Office records, a Captain Fox leading two groups of black soldiers (each probably with a white officer) visited Ahiara briefly but found few people. Some days later, returning troops slaughtered many people in villages where Stewart was thought to have been held. Four hundred seventy-one locally made guns (like Okonkwo's inaccurate piece in the novel) were confiscated, and, probably, the towns themselves were burned ("Southern Nigeria"; "Southern Nigeria Dispatches"). The novel and history meet.

Achebe knew the story of Ahiara; it was famous because Stewart's death was the pretext for the Bende-Onitsha hinterland expedition, which destroyed an oracle at Awka, subdued the Ahiaras and other resistant groups, and opened the way for motor-road construction. This second British campaign, much more than the Aro expedition, made the land accessible to British government officials and missionaries. Abame symbolizes this conquest, and the true story, like Achebe's fiction, explains why relatively few towns risked government wrath. Surprisingly, a few towns and a few men did resist, defying the power of the British authorities to the end.

Subjection by indiscriminate slaughter and terror, with indifference to individual guilt or local law, was illegal and a contradiction of traditional British justice. However, no one knew how else to subdue these Igbo towns. Each was independent of every other town, and each was ruled by a consensus of leading citizens—as in Umuofia—and not by an autocratic chief. The long-term effect of rule by terror was to make the British settlers sacred (or at least sacrosanct); in *No Longer at Ease* Achebe comments, of a later period, "To throw a white man was like unmasking an ancestral spirit" (65). It was not only not done, it was not thought of.

African agents of the British were protected similarly, whether they were Igbo from distant places or local Christian converts, like the hothead Enoch in the novel. Of the colonial agents the worst were the court messengers, or *kotma*, true individualists without loyalty to any person or principle save self-interest—the perfect opposite of Igbo collective mores. Many of these *kotma*, Achebe says, were from Umuru, the name the novel gives to Onitsha, the great trading center on the high east bank of the Niger. The Church Missionary Society (Anglican) and the Holy Ghost Fathers (Roman Catholic) set up the first hinterland Igbo mission stations and schools there. The missionaries attracted Onitsha's alien commercial community: migrants lured by money, they became traders who adapted to the changes and created what would in time become the greatest market in western Africa. The more devout students of the missionaries became mission agents; many others became clerks to civil government or to European authorities; the less successful students (or the less scrupulous) might become court messengers, responsible for carrying messages from district officers to the local chiefs. They could not function as mere messengers, however, because the democratic Igbo villages did not recognize chiefs. As a result, *kotma* became colonial police to the disorderly democracies, those same democracies that had policed themselves successfully for as long as memory could reach. In the novel, *kotma* bring men for trial, guard the prison, beat the prisoners, demand bribes of them, and force men of honor to do degrading work. Although hated, they nevertheless share the almost sacred protection given the British, which is why the townspeople are astonished that Okonkwo would, at a critical moment, kill one.

The British understood obedience to orders; the Igbo people did not. The Igbo understood open discussion and collective rule; the British did not. The colonial officers did not know Igbo, and the elders of the towns did not know English. Both sides were forced to work through interpreters who—to make bad matters worse—were *kotma* or of the same individualistic kind as *kotma* and were prone to bribery, as Achebe says in chapter 20. (In Achebe's *Man of the People*, a former interpreter, Odili's father, is hated but rich by local standards.) The district commissioner in *Things Fall Apart* supports the ruthlessness of the *kotma*. Treacherously, the Commissioner invites the leading men of Umuofia to a "palaver." When they are unarmed and seated, the *kotma* arrest them. Again Achebe is true to history. Such deception of honorable citizens was a common practice, though some British colonial officers protested against it as early as 1900 (Afigbo, *Warrant Chiefs* 69).

The British brought injustice. That, however, was not their only disruptive contribution. They also brought trade, a major element in the imagined process of "civilization" that the British believed they were giving to savages. In Umuofia, Achebe says in chapter 21, "palm-oil and kernel became things of great price" (126). The palm, the abundant source of this wealth, was virtually a gift from nature; the technology of extracting the oil was, along with cultivation of the yam, a prime basis for life in the tropical forest region, where yam and palm oil were the staples of all diets, soap was made from oil and ashes, and oil was burned in lamps and worn as a cosmetic and as a dressing for the hair. In England, the oil's major use was to lubricate the machines of industry (it was also an ingredient in domestic products, like soap). In Africa, the villagers spent their new wealth on imports from Europe—cotton cloth, tobacco, beads, gin, porcelain plates, and iron pots.

Trade, government, and religion were the colonial trinity, and the greatest of these was the dominant European religion, Christianity. In the novel, Christianity is still at its first stage, that of winning converts. Investigating Achebe's account of the conversions, Afigbo reports that it may "with appropriate caution, be treated as containing reliable historical information" (*Warrant Chiefs* 66). The new faith, Achebe and Afigbo agree, attracted the alienated members of the community, the misfits, and the outcasts. Only slowly did persons of dignity and respect adopt the new faith.

Like Nwoye in the novel, Achebe's father was a convert. In the essay "Named for Victoria, Queen of England," Achebe writes that his father, Isaiah Achebe, was an orphan raised by his maternal grandfather, Udo Osinyi. Unlike Nwoye, who argued with Okonkwo, Isaiah Achebe did not leave his grandfather because of a quarrel. Isaiah Achebe was a true convert. His teacher and mentor was a missionary named G. T. Basden, whom Achebe has immortalized as Mr. Brown in the novel. Basden, like Brown, was a patient man, ready to discuss theology with non-Christians; like Brown, Basden was presented with an elephant tusk in appreciation of a quarter century of service in the Onitsha-Ogidi-Awka area, which is Achebe's home ground. Basden reported his discoveries in two books, the richer of which is titled *Niger Ibos*. Not surprisingly, descriptions of ceremonies in *Things Fall Apart* are often close to Basden's: both writers learned the traditions of Achebe's home, Ogidi—Basden as sympathetic visitor, Achebe as indigene.

The religion of Umuofia was, to Basden, superstition—primitive but interesting, like the "bad bush" (Evil Forest in the novel) into which twins and other abominations (like Okonkwo's father) were put to die (Basden 58). When missionaries lived in the "bad bush" and survived, they seemed to prove the power of the new religion. To Achebe, of course, the old religion is more than interesting; the Oracle of the Hills and the Caves, for example, plays a vital role in the novel. Basden's discussion of oracles goes beyond anthropological commentary, condemning them as frauds, as priestly deceptions designed to bilk the credulous of wealth, freedom, and life. The oracle in Achebe's novel does not match Basden's characterization, but it surely is related to two that Achebe knew, one at the adjacent town of Ogbunike and the other at his mother's home in Awka. K. Onwuka Dike follows Sidney R. Smith (a missionary who, with Basden, worked in the Ogidi area) in identifying Ogbunike not as a source of help, as in the novel, but merely as a source of slaves (40). Not long ago, while visiting the oracle Ogba, a cave in the Nkisi stream, I was told by a small boy how, in the old days, the guilty met two fates in the cave, one apparent, one real. The apparent fate was death, for blood would appear in the stream to deceive anxious waiting relatives. The blood, the boy told me, was chicken blood, for the priests did not kill their victims but instead took them captive and sold them to Aro traders. My guide scurried among labyrinthine entrances and exits to show how the priests might perplex supplicants before betraying them. This story matches the one Basden tells about the oracles. The only exception was the oracle he knew best, from long service in the Awka area. At Awka's oracle, he says, the guilty were in fact killed. Further, he says that the oracle was consulted for blessings and charms. The Awka oracle was called Agbala (82), the same name Achebe gives to the Oracle of the Hills and the Caves— Agbala, to whom people "came when misfortune dogged their steps . . . or to discover what the future held for them or to consult the spirits of their departed fathers" (12). Fiction is surely the better testimony.

Discussion of oracles opens the way to the other great history, that of the falsely labeled "primitive" world of the Igbo past, before the coming of the British. I briefly describe only two aspects of that history here: the system of titles that dominates masculine life in Umuofia and the dedication of people to gods, or *osu*.

The *ozo* titles are associated with an ancient society that was probably a thousand or more years old in 1900. In Umuofia, as in all the communities in a large region encompassing most of today's Anambra State, the *ozo* titles are held in the highest respect. Okonkwo grows up disgraced by his father, who never took a title and was therefore less than a man. Okonkwo's ambition is to take the highest titles in the land, and his failure to do so accounts in part for the anger that takes him to his death and shame. The origin of the *ozo* titles is lost in the past, available only by conjecture. The evidence hints that, long ago, the region was led by the king-priests of Nri, who were arbitrators of great disputes, loci of the highest priestly powers, and exclusive creators and owners of the *ozo* title. Whatever *ozo* titles a community might devise, the elementary ceremony by which a citizen became a full man could be sanctified only by the priests of Nri. The *ozo* title was no mere honor. It united a man with his ancestors; with an *ozo* title a man became immortal, a living god. He could achieve this position by accumulating wealth and honor (rarely, honor alone was enough, and sometimes wealth might do); the wealth was necessary because the initiate had to reward every person in the community who held the *ozo* title.

In the sacred city of Nri, which lies east of Achebe's home in Ogidi and south of Awka, certain treasures identified with Igbo-Ukwu have been excavated (Shaw, *Igbo-Ukwu* 268–70). Artifacts discovered there demonstrate the existence of a high culture and extensive trade, probably by the ninth century (Christian calendar) and extending for several hundred years. Conflict with the Aro may have brought the Nri hegemony to its end (Wren, *Achebe's World* 87–89). Nri provided the leadership that created the village societies of which Achebe writes. Their stability was ensured by Nri's spiritual (not military) enforcement of the rites of Ani, the earth goddess, and the granting of *ozo* titles. Each higher grade of *ozo* title required the distribution of greater wealth, so that no man became too rich or too powerful to control—no man could become a king, and every capable man with an *ozo* title was a god.

Against the high role of the *ozo* titles Achebe sets the painful reality of *osu*. Below both the free citizens and their slaves (the latter only alluded to in chapter 6) were the outcasts, the *osu*, people dedicated to a god as a kind of living sacrifice. From the moment of their sacrifice, the *osu* and their descendants became all but untouchable. The *osu* in the novel are among the first converts to the new church, a church that teaches the unity of all people and offers hope to victims of society's rigid forms. Like the antagonism that Okonkwo feels toward his father, and that Nwoye feels even more strongly toward Okonkwo, the *osu* represent a weakness, a subtle flaw in the structure of the Igbo world—a flaw that makes it possible for things to fall apart.

Understanding the historical context can help students see that the society of *Things Fall Apart*, which at first appears to be a seamless community that might have existed unchanged for an eternity, is something quite different. Its fragility, covertly shown in part 1, slowly becomes obvious when Umuofia is subjected to the rack of colonial injustice and when the traditional society's fragmented power is tested by the new religion that dares to live in the Evil Forest and survives. Behind the community and facing it is history. Achebe captures history in a few crucial years, the years that shaped the present most decisively for the people of southeastern Nigeria.

ATO QUAYSON

Realism, Criticism, and the Disguises of Both: A Reading of Chinua Achebe's *Things Fall Apart* with an Evaluation of the Criticism Relating to It[†]

> It is only when we go to the riverside that we can gauge the size of
> the water pot.   Ewe Proverb

> No matter how well the hen dances, it can not please the hawk.
>   Akan Proverb

The proverbial epigraphs to this essay seek to integrate the enterprise of criticism into a traditional African cultural context. The first points to the relativity at the heart of all critical pursuits: it is mainly in relation to the literary enterprise that the critical one is validated. Furthermore, no criticism can hope to completely encompass the total significance of the literary artifact, just as no water pot can hope to take in all the river's water. On the other hand, all critical enterprises harbour a certain predatoriness which the relationship between the dancing hen and the hawk can be taken to figure. The critical enterprise is never completely satisfied with the work of its predecessors, and thus, continually seeks to tear open previous critical discourses to make space for its own activity.

These two proverbs are recalled to contextualize my own critical exercise. In offering a critique of the general evaluation of *Things Fall Apart*, I am conscious of the perceptive work that has been undertaken on the novel since its publication some three decades ago. Much of the criticism relating to the novel, however, shares implicit assumptions with the nature of the "realism" that the work itself offers. These assumptions subtly valorize the hermeneutical and exegetical approaches to the work without paying attention to the fact that its "realism" is a construct whose basic premises cannot be taken unproblematically. To help problematize the nature of the novel's realism, I shall, in the second part of this essay, focus on its construction of women and the feminine. This specific reading is offered as a model open to further modification and an alternative to the dominant tendencies in the area of the criticism of African literature. Ultimately, I intend to suggest that the representationalist readings that relate to [Achebe's] work are, though valid, grossly inadequate and that it is preferable to adopt a multi-tiered approach

† From *Research in African Literatures* 25.4 (Winter 1994): 117–36. Reprinted by permission of Indiana University Press.

to his work and to African literature in general that will not take them as merely mimetic of an African reality but will pay attention to them as *restructurations* of various cultural subtexts. This will hopefully liberate more exciting modes of literary analyses that would pay attention to the problematic relationships that African literary texts establish with their cultural backgrounds. This will also pave the way for a proper examination of other works that do not rely on realist modes of discourse for their re/presentations of Africa. I bear in mind that if I now "hawk" other critiques, mine will soon be "hen" for subsequent ones; that is exactly as it should be, for it is impossible to say a last word on a writer as fine as Achebe.

I

Achebe's work, particularly *Things Fall Apart*, has inspired a great amount of criticism. In surveying this criticism, it is useful to bear in mind that the nature of that criticism is symptomatic of the evaluation of African literature in general.[1] The issues posed in relation to Achebe often pervade the critical practice relating to African lirerature. But, perhaps, it is only Biodun Jeyifo and Chidi Amuta who have attempted to define a typology of the criticism in the field. Jeyifo's two-tier typology holds greater potential for elaboration, and it is to his that I turn to contextualize criticism of Achebe's work. Jeyifo defines the purview of post-coloniality as the dismantling "of bounded enclaves and subjectivities" (Jeyifo 52). He shares in this definition the tendency evident in *The Empire Writes Back* to perceive post-colonial practice as a discourse concerned with a self-definition that foregrounds the tensions with the imperial power and emphasizes the differences from the assumptions of the imperial center (Ashcroft 2). The implicit assumption that post-colonial literatures are in a perpetual umbilical dance with the metropolitan center, counter-productive though it is, will not be taken on here. Jeyifo divides post-colonial writing and criticism into two distinct fields which he names the post-coloniality of "normativity and proleptic designation" and the "interstitial or liminal" post-coloniality. The post-coloniality of normativity and proleptic designation is one in which the writer or critic speaks to, or for, or in the name of the post-independence nation-state, the regional or continental community, the panethnic, racial or cultural agglomeration of homelands and diasporas (Jeyifo 53).

---

1. I focus attention mainly on the criticism of Achebe's novels set in the past, though the attitudes relating to them are pertinent to those relating to novels set in the post-Independence era. Indeed, James Olney and also Eustace Palmer see Achebe's novelistic career as paradigmatic of the development of the African novel in general.

The normativity in this conception of post-coloniality often entails a return to cultural sources, the projection of a futurist agenda, and the celebration of cultural authenticity. Indeed, Achebe himself espouses such an agenda in relation to his work. In his famous words:

> I would be quite satisfied if my novels (especially the ones I set in the past) did no more than teach my readers that their past— with all its imperfections—was not one long night of savagery from which the first Europeans acting on God's behalf delivered them. (*Novelist as Teacher* 45)

Ignoring for the time being the implications of these remarks for constructing the social role of the writer,[2] I note the implicit confidence expressed about the role of realism in the project of recovering cultural authenticity. Realism is so powerful as a conduit for social criticism, that it is taken to pass on the verities available to other empiricist social discourses. Perhaps it is David Lodge, in *The Modes of Modern Writing*, who offers a definition of realism closest to that implied in Achebe's confident assertions on the role of his work:

> [Realism is] the representation of experience in a manner which approximates closely to descriptions of similar experience in non-literary texts of the same culture. (25)

The assumption that realism shares a community of values with other non-literary discourses was particularly important in the general conceptions of the role of literature in the newly emergent African nations. And especially in the period just before and after Independence in West Africa when a burgeoning newspaper culture and the Onitsha Market Literature[3] emphasized an empiricism and rationalism embodied in a recourse to "facts" and factual reporting, the perceived affinities between the economy of realism and those of other non-literary discourses were taken for granted in the espousals of cultural authenticity. A remark by an early reviewer of Achebe's *A Man of the People* to the effect that the novel was "worth a ton of documentary journalism" (*Time* 19 Aug 1966: 84, ctd. in Larson 16) encapsulates the expressed confidence in the shared "factuality" of the protocols of both novelistic realism and newspaper reportage in general.

2. In varying degrees this was the informing sentiment behind the general accounts of African critics in the sixties and seventies such as those of Obiechina, Gakwandi, Ogungbesan, and Palmer.
3. It is significant that romance seems to have dominated the discourse of Onitsha Market Literature. But romance is in fact rationalism of a different order because modern romance generally depicts victory over the tribulations of the "real" world. Indeed, the market literature was an expression of a "Mills and Boon" reading culture that has become very powerful.

The confidence Achebe expresses in the realism of his early novels was shared by his critics and led to several critical formations which sought to elucidate the representationalist aspects of his work. The critical tendency that seemed to take the novels most evidently as in a one-to-one relationship to reality was that which sought to recover anthropological data about the Igbos from the novels. Charles Larson elicits such an anthropological reading from *Things Fall Apart*, though he introduces his work by deprecating that same tendency in Achebe's earliest reviewers. "What is clearly needed," writes Larson, "is the reviewer equipped to examine African fiction both from a cultural (anthropological) and an aesthetic (literary) point of view, though I am not trying to suggest that the two are ever totally separated" (Larson 16). He goes on to affirm that the first part of the novel is "heavily anthropological, but contains the seeds of germination for the latter half of the book" (Larson 30). Proceeding from such a premise, it is not difficult for him then to conclude that there is very little scenic description related to the building of mood and atmosphere in the Western sense, and that Achebe's descriptions are used directly for functional rather than for aesthetic purposes. In discussing the passage in which Ikemefuna is led into the forest to be murdered, Larson asserts that the description of the forest is given just to let the reader know where he is; the boy could not have been killed in the village anyway, so the forest scene is an inescapable necessity imposed on Achebe. In other words, the novel is intent on giving only factual information. Because of his anthropological biases, Larson fails to see that the whole scene is rich with meanings and can be read as an important symbolic expression of the darkness at both the centre and margins of all cultures.

Obiechina duplicates this tendency from an insider's perspective. In his *Culture, Tradition, and Society in the West African Novel*, he sees the novel as reflective or mimetic of traditional beliefs and practices in an almost unmediated way, being interested, as he is, in showing how the cultural and social background "gave rise to the novel there, and in far-reaching and crucial ways conditioned the West African novel's content, themes and texture" (Obiechina 3). Within Obiechina's formulation, "culture," "tradition," and "society" become paradigmatic of the real West African world reflected in the novels he studies. In this way the novels become amenable to an "anthropological harvest" in which details are read from cultural background to fictional world and back again.

These readings of Achebe are better understood in the context of a general rhetoric that sought to define an authentic African worldview opposed to the Western one. Criticism, in this context, tried to demonstrate the extent to which the narrative had "naturalized" the borrowed form of the novel by its specifically African discursive strategies. Several critics devoted themselves to arguing the "Africanness" of the text such as was evident in proverb use (Egudu; Lindfors; Shelton), in the oral rhythms concealed in the text (McCarthy), or in the patterns of temporality that are arguably relatable to African cultural sources (JanMohamed).

A more subtle version of the Africanness rhetoric seems to be offered by criticism that sees Achebe's work as setting itself against the construction of the African available within Western fiction. In her recent book on Chinua Achebe, C. L. Innes undertakes a contrastive pairing of Achebe with Joyce Cary, in which she establishes a typology of the "preferred." She draws inspiration for this from Achebe's own remarks about the factors that led him to write novels as a corrective to some of the jaundiced images about the African that were purveyed in writings by Westerners. Achebe's fictionalization of African reality is to be preferred to Cary's because Achebe is closer to the reality of Africa:

> In challenging Cary's 'superficial picture', a representation to be observed on the surface without critical intervention, Achebe challenged not only the vision depicted but also the manner of the depiction, not only the story, but the mode of story-telling, and the consequent relationship between reader and writer. (Innes 18)

Innes explores the novel's Africanness in relational terms, and this suggests that it is the construction of different representations of the same world that is at stake. It is necessary to be alerted to the modes of perception of the African encrusted in reactionary discourses such as those of Cary. Representation is a subtle process imbricated within the textual strategies deployed by realist discourse. But it is important to note how such an approach privileges the realism of the preferred version and ignores the potential exclusions of such a version. In Achebe's specific evocation of the Igbo world, it is possible to further contrast him with other Igbo writers, such as Buchi Emecheta, to show that his version of African reality requires as much interrogation and qualification as those proffered by the Carys.

Side by side with this type of criticism was another which sought to identify Africanness as a first step towards coralling the rural novels into a more radical political agenda. Indeed, the position of Chinweizu et al. in *Towards the Decolonization of African Literature* can be taken to represent the most radical expression of this agenda. They attacked many of the leading African writers and critics for obscurantism and a divorce from African oral sources and advocated a return to a traditional afrocentrist literary and critical practice. The reactionary essentialism concealed in this position was quickly discovered and attacked by both writers and critics. It is now fashionable

to address the *bolekaja*[4] formation in surveys of African literature in
derogatory terms, but it seems to me that the nature of the *bolekaja*
radicalism derives precisely from an unquestioning confidence in
the capacity of realism for reflecting the real. Their fear was that,
if the wrong "reality" was reflected, it would have a corrupting influence on readers, and ultimately militate against the larger processes
of political decolonization which were at the centre of their concerns. In this sense they share the same attitudes that inform all
criticism accepting realism at face value and ignoring its construct-
edness as an "ism."

All these critical formations in relation to Achebe's work can he
perceived as united in subtle maneuvers that take the culture of the
realist novel as most truthfully inscribing the space and time of history. Palmer can be taken to be representative of this notion:

> Broadly speaking, the African novel is a response to and a record
> of the traumatic consequences of the impact of western capital-
> ist colonialism on the traditional values and institutions of the
> African peoples. (Palmer 63).

It is interesting how such a formulation, and the critical practice
informed by it, defines a novelistic agenda that emphasizes "record,"
grounding it in rationalism and empiricism. Furthermore this type of
formulation permits the exclusion or underprivileging of the counter-
realist and non-rationalist. In Palmer's own practice, when he
engages with Tutuola, he is at pains to show that Tutuola is merely a
teller of tales and not a novelist. His work thus requires a different
level of seriousness:

> Tutuola is not strikingly original, but we can then go on to assert
> that whereas *realism* and *originality* are expected of the formal
> novel, the teller of folk tales is expected to take his subject mat-
> ter and the framework of his tales from the corpus of his people's
> traditional lore. (Palmer 12; emphasis added).

Since Palmer has already suggested that the African novel is
supremely concerned with "record," it is easy to see how his conception of Tutuola's work underprivileges the type of mythological
discourse that his writing engages in. But more importantly, it serves
to institute a subtle dichotomy between realism and non-realism,
with the added suggestion that the non-realist is not properly the staple of the novel form. All the debates around Tutuola seem to me to
adumbrate what Karin Barber ("African-language Literatures and

---

4. *Bolekaja*, which literally means "come down and fight," was borrowed from a phrase used
   by the conductors of Nigerian passenger lorries in their fiercely competitive touting for pas-
   sengers and was adopted as a description of the Chinweizu et al. type of critical stance.

Post-colonial Criticism") detects at the center of post-colonial and Commonwealth literary criticism: the desire to bracket out certain forms of discourse, and to underplay or dismiss the viral activity of oral literature. Much of the criticism of African literature, she says, seeks to give oral tradition only an originary role in the construction of typologies of the Europhone African literatures. The oral tradition is seen mainly as a reservoir of materials to be exploited by the modem writer. This maneuver forecloses the possibility of seeing oral literature as vitalizing its own traditions of writing as expressed in indigenous language literatures. It seems to me that, additionally, the elements of oral literature employed by writers and elucidated by critics are seen mainly in the role of subserving an essentially rationalist and empiricist realist discourse. The African novel is made to yield reflections of Africa, and there is often an unconscious urge to read them as recording an "African" reality that comes without mediation. Thus, when a Tutuola gives full vent to the transgressive potential inherent in oral literary traditions, his work can only be seen in terms of the problematic. His work disturbs the process of establishing mimetic adequacy in the representation of the African world view.

It is perhaps fruitful at this stage to note Hayden White's general scepticism about the definitions of realism to make room for a contextualization of the relationship between realist and non-realist discourses in the representations of Africa:

> In my view, the whole discussion of the nature of "realism" in literature flounders in the failure to assess critically what a generally "historical" conception of reality consists of. The usual tactic is to set the "historical" over against the "mythical," as if the former were genuinely *empirical* and the latter were nothing but *conceptual,* and then to locate the realm of the "fictive" between the two poles. Literature is then viewed as being more or less *realistic,* depending upon the ratio of empirical to conceptual elements contained in it. (3n)

Realism is ultimately a construction that is privileged because it is seen as reflecting History and Truth in its engagement with empirical data. But it is a construction that needs to be interrogated. In the context of African literature, the myths and legends are important sources for the construction of an African world view. It is in fact significant that from the very inception of African literature, a tradition that draws dominantly from oral literature and its modes of perception has grown alongside the more realist tendency. We can number writers like Soyinka, Awoonor, Armah, and lately Laing, Okri, and Bandele-Thomas in the ranks of those who draw mainly on a mythic consciousness, but it is still disturbing that no full-length study has

yet been made in which these writers are seen as together exempli-
fying a specific mode of literary consciousness.[5] The crucial thing
though, is to regard their works as drawing from the wealth of cultural materials to produce *re/structurations* of the culture within a
general mythopoeic practice. But it is a type of *re/structuration* that
realism itself participates in so that any representationalist reading of
realism is a manoeuvre that, consciously or unconsciously, ignores
the problematic status of the "realist" text.

In order that African novels, be they realist or counter-realist, are
not rapidly incorporated into an anthropological-representationalist
reading of African reality, it is important to regard them all as symbolic discourses that continually restructure a variety of subtexts: cultural, political, historical and at times even biographical.[6] And it is
useful to bear in mind that a palpable gap is forever instituted
between the narrative text and the subtexts it appropriates. It is then
fruitful to regard the African novel as only partially reflecting a "reality" beyond itself; one reflected in a highly problematic way, forever
struggling to be self-sufficient within itself, but always involved in
various relationships with its informing matrix. It then becomes possible to endorse Homi Bhabha's desire to see a shift in the criticism
of post-colonial literatures from the perception of the text as representationalist to seeing it as a *production* (see Bhabha). But it seems
to me also important not to privilege the textual as solely generative
of meanings. The text is meaning/ful partly in relation to the culture
from which it borrows its materials and with which it establishes
varying relationships. This view of the text permits the recovery of a
cultural matrix for the text, and at the same time opens up a space
for an interrogation of the assumptions upon which it is grounded.

Perhaps this strategy would satisfy someone like Chidi Amuta, who
is radically opposed to what he sees as a hegemonic traditionalist aesthetic that governs the criticism of African literature. In relation to
Things Fall Apart and *Arrow of God*, he makes the assertion that they
have become axiomatic reference points for diverse interests and
opinions intent on rediscovering and commenting on "traditional
African society" and "the culture conflict" inaugurated by the advent

5. Soyinka perceived this tendency towards the mythopoeic in African literature as early as
   in 1963 and tried to account for it in "From a Common Backcloth." Richard Priebe also
   assessed the general attitudes towards this mythopoeic tendency and argued for the perception of a specific literary tradition deriving from Amos Tutuola and growing around the
   mythopoeic (Priebe 1973), but the insights these two suggested do not seem to have been
   taken up in later critical assessments of African literature. The mythopoeic tendency in
   writers like Awoonor and Armah were recognised but the critical assessments of their work
   were not integrated within an analysis of what relationships their efforts had with the discursive universes of Tutuola and even of Soyinka.
6. The terms in which Frederic Jameson defines narrative as a socially symbolic act are very
   usseful in this context, except that I do not think it is necessary to always grasp the narrative
   text as an essentially strategic confrontation between classes. See *The Political Unconscious.*

of colonialism, stock concepts which have since been adumbrated into a "mini-catechism" (Amuta 130). The "traditionalist aesthetic" can be incorporated into a multi-tiered activity of recovering significance for the text without necessarily lapsing either into a febrile essentialism or a constrictive formalism.

We can return finally to address Jeyifo's second formulation of post-coloniality. For him, interstitial or liminal post-coloniality "defines an ambivalent mode of self-fashioning of the writer or critic which is neither First World nor Third World, neither securely and smugly metropolitan, nor assertively and combatively Third World-ist. The very terms which express the orientation of *this* school of post-colonial self-representation are revealing: diasporic, exilic, hybrid, in-between, cosmopolitan" (Jeyifo 53). In short, acutely aware of the antinomies that riddle existence. It is interesting that Jeyifo *names* those he thinks are the dominant figures of this formation of the post-colonial (Gabriel García Márquez, Salman Rushdie, Edward Said, Homi Bhabha), suggesting that the consciousness of the antinomic began with them. This, I think, is mistaken. "The African writer's very decision to use English," writes JanMohamed, "is engulfed by ironies, paradoxes, and contradictions" (JanMo-hamed 20). I agree with him and add that the very choice of the metropolitan language for the writing of post-colonial literatures secretes liminality into the inaugural act of post-colonialist representation itself. Furthermore, in the most sensitive of post-colonial writers, the representation is done with an uneasy awareness of the subtle contradictions inscribed in an emergent syncretic culture: on the one hand, the loss of a pristine traditional culture is regretted, but this is mingled with an awareness of its more reprehensible potential. And on the other, the ruthless economic competition of urbanization and Westernization is deprecated while an awareness of the greater possibilities for vertical mobility, self fulfilment, and freedom is registered. In that sense, the condition of interstitiality or liminality is of the very essence of post-colonial writing, though each text establishes a different relationship to this conundrum. Jeyifo's typology breaks down and is particularly subverted by his own reading of Achebe's *Things Fall Apart* in which he emphasizes the novel's productive ambivalences and liminality in its continual relativization of *doxa* (represented by Okonkwo) as against paradoxa or irony (represented by Obierika and those at the margins of the text, such as *osus* and women).

What emerges, then, from the discourses of post-colonial criticism, is that it is new reading strategies that have come into being and are at issue, focusing on aspects of post-colonial texts that had hitherto been silenced. It is, to borrow an apt formulation of Irigaray's in another context, the "spaces that organize the scene, the blanks that sub-tend the scene's structuration and yet will not be read as such" (Irigaray 137–38) that have come into account in the readings of post-colonial literatures. And in the particular context of the criticism of African literature, the requirement that it move away from the dominant representationalist rhetoric to more nuanced approaches that will take account of the hitherto "silent spaces" and the subtle and often problematic relationships between text and context becomes patently imperative.

II

This reading of *Things Fall Apart*, then, is offered as a means of exposing the gap that exists between the realist African text and the reality that it is seen to represent. The novel is particularly useful for this enterprise because of its highly acclaimed (and well deserved) literary status and the fact that it has been taken unproblematically since its publication thirty years ago.

It seems fruitful to conceive of the realism of *Things Fall Apart* as constructed on two levels simultaneously. At one level, the novel concerns itself with a description of Umuofian culture and its subversion by the contact with Western imperialism. This level of the novel can be perceived as metonymic of an Igbo or African reality. In Jakobsonian terms, the narrative progresses metonymically, with narrative elements selected for attention because they exist in discernible contiguous relation to one another. Significantly, however, the text frequently departs from the overarching narrative of the fall of Okonkwo and the division of the clan to pursue numerous anecdotes and digressions that are demonstrably not related to the main narrative but embody subtle qualifications of it. Furthermore, within the context of the unfolding events, the narrative generates a secondary level of conceptualization that can be seen as symbolic/metaphorical. This level subtends the metonymic text but gathers around itself all the antinomies associated with metaphor: ambiguity, contradiction, irony, and paradox.

The symbolic/metaphorical level of conceptualization reveals two closely related strata both at the level of content, the culture of Umuofia, and *also* at the level of the narrative's discursive strategies in general. On the one hand, Umuofia, as a culture, has institutions governed by a viable symbolic order. Though the narrative text itself reflects some of the central concerns of the culture, both in relation to the cultural institutions and more generally in relation to the culture's governing symbolic system, it employs certain discursive strategies that articulate a symbolic/metaphorical system not relatable solely to the symbolic order reflected by the actual culture. The narrative's own order is derivable from the various configurations of significances, and in its structuration of the narrated events. And it is at this strategic level of symbolic structuration that the novel's hieratchization of gender and the subtle subversion of its proferred hierarchy are played out, showing that the novel's realism, in the characteristic manner of a *writing* continually produces excessive meanings. Taking it at face value then becomes inadequate and problematic.

Several critics have rightly pointed out that Okonkwo's downfall is mainly due to a neurotic concern with "manliness." Okonkwo pursues distinction, in the words of Abiola Irele, with an "obsessive single-mindedness that soon degenerates into egocentricity, until he comes to map out for himself very narrow limits of action or reflection" (Irele 11). Almost every critic of the novel pays attention to the nature of Okonkwo's tragic character, relating it to the narrow limits of action defined by his society as "manly" and showing how his character precludes the exercise of the more "feminine" virtues of tolerance, tenderness and patience. Innes argues that it is a flaw encoded in the very symbolic order of Umuofian society and purveyed by its linguistic codes. Okonkwo's attitudes are framed by the culture's language and its implications, and it is this that makes him "unable to acknowledge the mythic implications of femininity and its values" (Innes 117). What seems to have been ignored, however, is the fact that in totally focalizing the narrative through Okonkwo and the male-dominated institutions of Umuofia, the novel itself implies a patriarchal discourse within which women, and much of what they can be taken to represent in the novel, are restricted to the perceptual fringes. In spite of this demonstrable patriarchy, however, Okonkwo is at various times ironized by the text suggesting the inadequacy of the values he represents and ultimately those of the hierarchy that ensures his social status. It is important to stress that it is not just Okonkwo's values that are shown as inadequate, but those of a patriarchal society in general, he representing an extreme manifestation of the patriarchy that pervades the society as a whole.

Part of the structuration of the male-female hierarchy in the novel derives from what Chantal Zabus, in talking about the use of proverbs in *Things Fall Apart*, refers to as the "ethno-text." She defines the term in relation to "the discursive segments that belong to the vast corpus of African traditional oral material" (Zabus 20). Her focus is mainly on the implications for the demise of orality that the transposition of traditional discursive elements into the Europhone novel implies, but it is useful to expand the term ethno-text to embrace all the traditional cultural practices that are depicted in a novel, be they linguistically based or not. It is the structuration derivable from Igbo culture itself that arguably offers the raw materials for the construction of the fictional world of Umuofia.[7] It is noticeable, for instance, that the female principle has a very important part to play in Umuofia's governing cosmogony. Ani, goddess of the earth, "played a greater part in the life of the people than any other deity" (26). The Week of Peace set aside for her before the celebration of the New Yam Festival is a time of tolerance, relaxation, and peaceful co-existence. And so important is Ani that all the society's activities are judged in terms of what is or is not acceptable to her; indeed, she is "the ultimate judge of morality and conduct" (26). G. D. Killam has been led to suggest, from an examination of the role of Ani in the lives of the people, that "a powerful 'female principle' pervades the whole society of Umuofia" (20). It is important to note, however, that this powerful female principle is most potent at a symbolic/metaphorical level. It finds its most powerful expression at the level of the clan's governing cosmogony. And, at all times, the female principle always attracts some masculine essentiality in its definition. Ani has constant communion with the "fathers of the clan" because they are buried within her. She has a male priest, while Agbala, god of the Hills and Caves, has a priestess as spokesperson. And in the arena of the traditionally most masculine centred activity, war, the governing principle of Umuofian war medicine is believed to be an old woman with one leg, *agadi-nwayi* (9). The clan's cultural values institute the feminine in a very powerful position within the governing symbolic system, taking care to suggest a subtle interfusion of the two principles of male and female. In that sense, Umuofia's governing symbolic system suggests a necessary balancing of the two principles, so that the notion of a pervasive single essence "female principle" requires qualification.

At the level of the metonymic realist description of the institutional practices of Umuofia, however, the ethno-text yields a completely different reality. Umuofia is a male dominated society, and the narrative reflects this aspect of the culture. The continuing emphasis in the text is on depicting male dominated activities—the oratory of men before the gathered clan, the acquisition and cultivation of farmlands, courage and resourcefulness in sport and war and the giving and taking of brides. The text's focus on the patriarchy inscribed in the ethno-text is particularly evident in the portrayal of the political institution of justice. Since the Umuofians are acephalous, their central political power is invested in the *ndichie*, council of elders, and in the *egwu-gwu*, masked spirits of the ancestors who come to sit in judgement over civil and criminal disputes.

It is in the attitude of women to the *egwu-gwu* that the hierarchy of power is unmasked. The *egwu-gwu* emerge to sit in judgement

7. Several studies have been devoted to uncovering the Igbo background behind Achebe's novel but perhaps the most wide-ranging and systematic is Wren's *Achebe's World*.

with "guttural and awesome" voices. And the sounds of their voices are no less mystifying than the sounds that herald their entry:

> *Aru oyim de de de dei!* flew around the dark closed hut like tongues of fire. The ancestral spirits of the clan were abroad. The metal gong beat continuously now and the flute, shrill and powerful, floated on the chaos.
>
> And then the *egwu-gwu* appeared. The women and children sent up a great shout and took to their heels. It was instinctive. A woman fled as soon as an *egwu-gwu* came in sight. And when, as on that day, nine of the greatest masked spirits in the clan came out together it was a terrifying spectacle. Even Mghafo took to her heels and had to be restrained by her brothers. (63)

It is interesting that in its presentation of the scene the narrative betrays its attitude to the relationship between women and power. Significantly, the *egwu-gwu* are described in an idiom of grandeur, the "tongues of fire" recalling the dramatic events of Pentecost recorded in the Acts of the Apostles 2.1–4. And the women's "instinctive" flight at their emergence can be read as the awestruck response to these masked ancestral spirits. A few lines later, however, the women reveal they have more knowledge of the reality behind the masked spirits than they care to express: "Okonkwo's wives, and perhaps other women as well, might have noticed that the second *egwu-gwu* had the springly walk of Okonkwo. . . . But if they thought these things they kept them within themselves" (64–65). The narrative paints the scene with so much detail, objective distancing and humour, that it is impossible not to regard it as of the clearest "realistic" vintage. But the "thoughtful silence" of the women before this all-important masculine institution is ironic. The narrative works both to reveal the "natural" and "instinctive" female attitude to Power and also to ironize the pretensions of the masculine social instiutions. But it is important to note that the irony does not work to radically undermine the hierarchy at the centre of the power structure because the women constrain themselves to "thinking" their knowledge, but leave it unexpressed.

Some aspects of the narrative can be construed wholly as fictional constructions and not as trajectories of the ethno-text. Here it is the narrative, in terms of its own discursive strategies, that is responsible for any impression of patriarchy that comes across. In the relationships in Okonkwo's household, for instance, we find a subtle definition of his masculinity that depends on a particular view of the women in his domestic set-up. Twice we are told Okonkwo beats his wives. The first time, it is Ojiugo, his last wife. The narrator's preface to the incident must be noted:

> Okonkwo was provoked to justifiable anger by his youngest wife, who went to plait her hair at her friend's house and did not return early enough to prepare the afternoon meal. (21)

If Okonkwo's anger is "justifiable" then the narrative has passed judgement on Ojiugo's "irrationality" and "thoughtlessness" from her husband's perspective. And it is significant that the text does not bother to let Ojiugo explain herself on her return. It is just reported that "when she returned he beat her very heavily" (21). In Okonkwo's anger he forgets that it is the Week of Peace, and even when he is reminded, he does not stop because, as we are told, he "was not the man to stop beating somebody half way through, not even for fear of a goddess" (21). In earning a severe reprimand from Ani's priest for flouting the rules governing the observance of the Week of Peace, his "manly" values are clearly shown as inadequate, but his character as derivable from this scene is as significant in terms of his attitudes to his wives as it is in his attitudes to the cultural mores he violates. In this segment of the narrative, however, there is a tacit but emphatic foregrounding of the social as against the private, because the beating occurs during a period of heightened cultural consciousness due to the Week of Peace.

At another time it is Ekwefi who is to suffer the brunt of her husband's violent temper. In this instance it is only to satisfy his suppressed anger at the enforced laxity that precedes the New Yam Festival (27–28). Both these instances are explications of what the text has already told us earlier on but only now depicts:

> Okonkwo ruled his household with a heavy hand. His wives, especially the youngest, lived in perpetual fear of his fiery temper, and so did his little children. (9)

The importance of this method of characterization for the patriarchal discourse inscribed in the text is that it depends on a binary opposition being established between Okonkwo and the other characters. And it is a binarism that frequently takes him as the primary value. When the binarism works to undermine Okonkwo and his relative values, it regularly foregrounds other men-folk around whom alternative values in the text can be seen as being organized. Obierika and Nwoye are important nuclei of alternative values in this sense. In relation to his wives, however, the binarism implies a secondary role for them. Whatever significance is recovered for them must be gleaned from their silence, for they are not portrayed by the narrative as contributing to the *action* and its outcome.

The essential discursive operation of containing the significance of the women is most evident in relation to the handling of Ekwefi and Ezinma. The text builds them up till they seem to be alternative centres of significations, but it frustrates the completion of these significations by banishing them out of the narrative at some point. Ezinma and her mother Ekwefi are the only female characters developed by the narrative. We are told that Ekwefi ran away from her first husband to marry Okonkwo (28). By focusing on the relationship between her and her daughter, the narrative reveals the joys of motherhood and the closeness that mother and daughter enjoyed:

> Ezinma did not call her mother *Nne* like all children. She called her by her name, Ekwefi, as her father and other grown-up people did. The relationship between them was not only that of mother and child. There was something in it like the companionship of equals, which was strengthened by such little conspiracies as eating eggs in the bedroom. (54)

The warmth depicted in the relationship between mother and daughter aids in eliciting the reader's empathy with them, and thereby opens up a space for possible significations around these two. The significations, however, seem to be limited to a definition of maternal and filial instincts only. The episodes around Ekwefi's pursuit of Chielo when her daughter is taken on a nocturnal round of the villages by the priestess are significant in that respect (72–76). And when she stands with tears in her eyes at the mouth of the cave into which Chielo has entered with her daughter and swears within herself that if she heard Ezinma cry she would rush into the cave to defend her against all the gods in the world, we know we are seeing terribly courageous maternal, and indeed human, instincts at play. Indeed, the scene even gains wider significance if perceived in contrast to Okonkwo's handling of Ikemefuna who called him "father." In both instances where parental instincts are put to the test, the central characters are, significantly, taken outside the village into the forest. In Ekwefi's case as in Okonkwo's, an element of eeriness governs the atmosphere, with Ekwefi's situation being the more frightening of the two. And both episodes involve the enigmatic injunction of deities, but whereas Ekwefi is prepared to defy the gods in defence of her daughter, Okonkwo submits to cowardice and participates in Ikemefuna's ritual murder. Ekwefi has been given admirable but limited stature by the text, and this is partly because it refuses to lend her a more crucial role in the action.

In Ezinma, we see a tough-minded and questioning personality. When her mother tells her the tale of the Tortoise and the Birds, she is quick to point out that the tale does not have a song (70). She joins the ranks of other male characters who *pose* questions of varying interest in the narrative: Obierika, Nwoye, Rev. Brown, Okonkwo, the strict commissioner. Interestingly, her questions are posed in relation to what is not of great consequence in the narrative, the tales of women told in their huts at night to children, a context which Okonkwo thinks his sons should be excluded from, the better to ensure the growth of their "manliness." At another time, Ezinma ventures to carry her father's stool to the village *ilo*, a move she is reminded is the male preserve of a son (32). And when she sits, she often fails to adopt the proper sitting posture prescribed for her sex and has to be forcefully reminded by her father in his characteristic bellowing command (32). When, in the quest for her *iyi-uwa*, she calmly takes her impatient father, a renowned medicine-man, and indeed much of the village on a circular "treasure-hunt," we see she enjoys the momentary leadership position that the situation permits her (56–60).

It is also significant that Ezinma comes to take the place of a boy and someone that can be trusted in her father's eyes.[8] At periods when he is in the greatest emotional crises, Okonkwo instinctively turns to his daughter. Such is the case for instance after his participation in the murder of Ikemefuna. After the boy's sacrifice "he does not taste food for two days" and drinks palm-wine "from morning till night." His eyes were "red and fierce like the eyes of a rat when it was caught by the tail and dashed against the floor" (44). On the third day, he asks Ekwefi to prepare him roast plantains, and these are brought by Ezinma. We notice the filial attachment that passes between the two:

> 'You have not eaten for two days,' said his daughter Ezinma when she brought the food to hint. 'So you must finish this.' She sat down and stretched her legs in front of her. Okonkwo are the food absent-mindedly. 'She should have been a boy,' he thought as he looked at his ten-year-old daughter. He passed her a piece of fish. (44)

The narrative further registers a crucial position for Ezinma in our eyes when it tells us that during his enforced exile Okonkwo "never stopped regretting that Ezinma was a girl" and that of all his children "she alone understood his every mood. A bond of sympathy had grown between them" (122). It is to her that her father gives the task of convincing her other sisters not to marry any eligible man from Mbanta, but to wait till they return to Umuofia to make a better social impact on arrival. Thus, the space for registering significations around Ezinma, and for exploring a viable notion of femaleness that would offer a possible contrast with Okonkwo's notions of manliness are clearly built by the narrative. It is then highly problematic that Ezinma vanishes from the story after the return from exile, and is

8. It is significant that in seeing her as a "son" Okonkwo attempts to erase his daughter's femininity. This then becomes a manifestation of his neurotic concern with "manliness" and his attitude towards his daughter opens up a further space for a criticism of his values.

never referred to again. It is as if to suggest that in the crucial exercise of delineating the climactic consequences of the meeting of the two cultures at the end of the novel, there is no space for women.

How, we might speculate, would the novel have been if it were to have focused on Ezinma's reaction to the changes in Umuofia from the specific standpoint of the institution of marriage? Or how would the society's value systems have been perceived if their interrogation had been focalized through Ezinma instead of Nwoye and Ohierika? And what would our attitudes to Okonkwo's death have been if Ezinma's reaction to the event had been registered alongside Obierika's? In fact, is it not valid to ponder what the reaction of the womenfolk in general was to the mores of the society and the radical changes that unfold in the course of the narrative? There seems to be an unconscious recognition of the potential inherent in Ezinma and Ekwefi's characterization for subverting the patriarchal discourse of the text. The significations around them go to join the various meanings around those "othered" by Umuofia and the narrative, such as twins, *osus* and those who die of abominable ailments. These come briefly into the perceptual horizon, and though marginalized, remain potentially disruptive, partly because the mere fact of their presence constitutes a qualification of what has been centralized by the narrative. Though it has foregrounded the masculine in the male-female hierarchy inscribed at the level of the description of events, the narrative has also opened the hierarchy to a subtle interrogation of its values, even if ultimately leaving it intact. Considering the ways in which women are handled in the novel, it is possible to perceive *Things Fall Apart* as operating a mode of realism that does not just "name" an African reality; it also seeks to fix certain concepts such as those around "woman" within a carefully hierarchized system of values that underprivileges them. In this light, *Things Fall Apart* would almost answer to the charges levelled by Hélène Cixous at the language of philosophical systems in general: they are all phallocentric and seek to privilege the masculine in the patterns of male-female binary pairs often proffered as "natural." Cixous's charge would require some qualification in the context of *Things Fall Apart*, however, particularly because its hierarchization of the masculine-feminine undergoes a continual subversion revealing a more profound contradiction at the heart of its construction of the "natural" relations between "masculine" and "feminine."

If, on the one hand, patriarchy is privileged by both the ethno-text and the narrative itself, then this same patriarchy is alternatively shown as sitting uneasily within the general discourse of symbolization that the text constructs. And it is in the area of the political themes of the novel that this is most evident. The contact between the colonizing and the traditional cultures is attended by a subtle construction of the male-female polarities which this time are not hierarchical but rather intermingle and change places in restless slippage.

When the whiteman first appears on the perceptual horizon of Umuofia, he is naturalized by being linked to the marginal. The white man is first referred to as an albino (52). And later, when their violent intrusion into the perceptual horizon through the riot of Abame has to be confronted, Obierika reflects other previous self-satisfied attitudes to these whitemen in his reporting of the rout:

> I am greatly afraid. We have heard stories about the white men who made the powerful guns and the strong drinks and took slaves away across the seas, but no one thought the stories were true. (99)

In other words, they were harmless because they inhabited what was thought to be the realm of the fictive. When whitemen make their first physical appearance in the shape of Christian missionaries, they are first confined to the Evil Forest in which were buried "all those who died of the really evil diseases, like leprosy and smallpox" (105). They were not wanted in the clan and so were given land that was thought to be only marginally useful to the clan. But the early Christianity is depicted by the narrative as embodying and stressing qualities considered womanish—love, tolerance, affection and mercy[9]; Okonkwo characteristically evaluates the missionaries as a "lot of effeminate men clucking like old hens" (108). A feminine "valence" attaches to the Christians. In this sense, the early relationship between Umuofia and Christianity describes a male-female hierarchy in which Umuofia is masculine and privileged. In effect the narrative suggests that the white missionary vanguard of the colonizing enterprise possessed an initial effeminacy which was amusing and, in effect, tolerable.

The effeminacy turns out to be highly contradictory and sinister, however. The church succeeds in attracting to itself all those marginalized by the society, *efulefus, osus*, and the men of no title, *agbala*. In doing this, it emasculates the society, making it incapable of standing as one. And as Obierika observes with uncanny perspicacity, "the whiteman has put a knife on the things that held us together" (124). In figuring the whiteman's intrusion firstly in terms of "effeminate clucking," and now in terms of an invading knife, the narrative prepares the way for an inversion of the implied male-female hierarchization that it suggested in describing the first contact between the

---

9. Weinstock and Ramadan make the same point in relation to the symbolic structure of masculine and feminine patterns inscribed at the level of folktales and proverbs in the novel, suggesting that Christianity represents an apotheosis of the feminine values.

missionaries and the culture of Umuofia. Indeed, it is significant that at the crucial point when Okonkwo seeks to assert the possibilities of a violent rebellion, his own clan breaks into a catatonic "effeminate" confusion. At that point the text transfers the feminine valence with which it first constructed the whiteman onto the Umuofians. The shift of the feminine valence from the invaders to the invaded helps to define an important contradiction at the heart of the text's attitudes to the colonial encounter. Colonialism is perceived at one and the same time as feminine (in the missionaries) and masculine (at the level of the British administration and their ruthless exercise of power). And for colonialism to be able to succeed, Umuofia has to be transformed from the essential masculinity which has governed the textual construction of the society, to an enervated femininity at the crucial point when rebellion was an option. In that sense, the narrative depicts Umuofia's "castration," with Okonkwo's suicide representing the ultimate overthrow of its masculinity.[1]

It is arguable, then, that the textual strategies have ascribed different values to the male-female hierarchy at two different levels of the text. At the level of metonymic realistic description, a certain ironized patriarchy governs the construction of the fictional Umuofia that derives its impulse partly from the ethno-text. But at the level of symbolic conceptualization, the narrative has hinted at its own patriarchal discourse which it has proceeded to undermine most powerfully when describing the colonial encounter. Then, the male-female hierarchy that has governed the text completely collapses, and its place is taken over by an exchange of the "masculine" and "feminine" among the two poles of the contending cultures. *Things Fall Apart* thus explores a loving image of Umuofia at the same time as it reveals a dissatisfaction with the values of the society it describes in such detail. And this is undertaken at a more subtle level than the mere explication of content can reveal. In a very important sense, the "naming" of a pre-colonial culture and the depiction of its subversion by a marauding imperialism has involved the necessary construction of philosophical categories both *within* the pre-colonial culture and *between* it and the invading one which fail to stand still, involving a doubling back of the categories such as to problematize the very assumptions on which the enterprise of "naming" was undertaken in the first place. The novel thus reveals that its own realism is a construction traversed by both sensitivity and ambivalence so that it cannot be addressed unproblematically.

1. Other critics interpret the ambivalence in the novel's description of the colonial encounter as a function of the improper "targetting" of readership.

What is important, in the context of criticism relating to *Things Fall Apart* and the African novel in general, is that critics often take novelistic realism at face value. They thus fail to perceive the more subtle workings of the texts they engage with and fail to interrogate the assumptions on which they are based. And even more crucially, they fail to see that "realism" is an "ism" and a careful *restructuration* of various subtexts, so that its relationship to the Real can not be taken for granted. In focusing on the novel's handling of patriarchy, women and the feminine, I have tried to suggest that reading "culture" out of a novel is valuable but inadequate, and that this needs to be supplemented with an awareness that *Things Fall Apart*, like African novels in general, possesses a richly ambivalent attitude to its culture that can only be discovered by paying attention both to the reality processed and to the larger discursive strategies employed. Every "ism," to echo Soyinka in *Kongi's Harvest*, is an "absolutism," and that is true of realism as well as criticism in all its disguises.

Style and Language

BERNTH LINDFORS

The Palm-oil with Which Achebe's Words Are Eaten[†]

> Among the Ibo the art of conversation is regarded very highly, and
> proverbs are the palm-oil with which words are eaten.
>
> Chinua Achebe

Chinua Achebe is a writer well known throughout Africa and even
beyond. His fame rests on solid personal achievements. As a young
man of twenty-eight he brought honor to his native Nigeria by writing *Things Fall Apart*, the first novel of unquestioned literary merit
from English-speaking West Africa. Critics tend to agree that no
African novelist writing in English has yet surpassed Achebe's achievement in *Things Fall Apart*, except perhaps Achebe himself. It was
published in 1958 and Achebe has written three novels and won several literary prizes since. During this time his reputation has grown
like a bush-fire in the harmattan. Today he is regarded by many as
Africa's finest novelist.

If ever a man of letters deserved his success, that man is Achebe.
He is a careful and fastidious artist in full control of his art, a serious
craftsman who disciplines himself not only to write regularly but to
write well. He has that sense of decorum, proportion and design
lacked by too many contemporary novelists, African and non-African
alike. He is also a committed writer, one who believes that it is his
duty to serve his society. He feels that the fundamental theme with
which African writers should concern themselves is

> that African peoples did not hear of culture for the first time
> from Europeans; that their societies were not mindless but fre-
> quently had a philosophy of great depth and value and beauty,
> that they had poetry and, above all, they had dignity.[1]

† From *Critical Perspectives on Chinua Achebe*. Ed. C. L. Innes and Bernth Lindfors (Washington: Three Continents, 1978), 47–66. Reprinted by permission.
1. Chinua Achebe, "The Role of the Writer in a New Nation," *Nigeria Magazine*, No. 81 (June
1964), p. 157.

Each of Achebe's novels[2] sheds light on a different era in the recent history of Nigeria. *Things Fall Apart* (1958) is set in a traditional Ibo village community at the turn of the century when the first European missionaries and administrative officials were beginning to penetrate inland. In *Arrow of God* (1964) the action takes place in a similar environment about twenty-five years later, the major difference being that the missionaries and district officers have by this time become quite firmly entrenched. Achebe switches to an urban scene in *No Longer at Ease* (1960) in order to present a picture of the life of an educated Nigerian in the late nineteen-fifties. He brings the historical record right up to contemporary times in *A Man of the People* (1966), a devastating political satire that ends with a military coup. Achebe's novels read like chapters in a biography of his people and his nation since the coming of the white man.

What gives each of Achebe's novels an air of historical authenticity is his use of the English language. He has developed not one prose style but several, and in each novel he is careful to select the style or styles that will best suit his subject. In dialogue, for example, a Westernized African character will never speak exactly like a European character nor will he speak like an illiterate village elder. Achebe, a gifted ventriloquist, is able to individualize his characters by differentiating their speech. Of course, any sensitive novelist will try to do this, but most novelists do not face the problem of having to represent in English the utterances of a character who is speaking another language. To resolve this problem, Achebe has devised an African vernacular style[3] which simulates the idiom of Ibo, his native tongue. One example of this style will suffice. In *Arrow of God* a chief priest tells one of his sons why it is necessary to send him to a mission school:

> "I want one of my sons to join these people and be my eye there. If there is nothing in it you will come back. But if there is something there you will bring home my share. The world is like a Mask dancing. If you want to see it well you do not stand in one place. My spirit tells me that those who do not befriend the white man today will be saying *had we known* tomorrow." (p. 55)

In an article on "English and the African Writer," Achebe demonstrates that he could have written this passage in a different style:

---

2. Chinua Achebe, *Things Fall Apart* (London, 1958); *No Longer at Ease* (London, 1960); *Arrow of God* (London, 1964); *A Man of the People* (London, 1966). All quotations are from these editions.
3. I discuss this at more length in "African Vernacular Styles in Nigerian Fiction," *CLA Journal*, 9 (1966), 265–73. See also Gerald Moore, "English Words, African Lives," *Présence Africaine*, No. 54 (1965), pp. 90–101; Ezekiel Mphahlele, "The Language of African Literature," *Harvard Educational Review*, 34 (Spring 1964), 298–305; and Eldred Jones, "Language and Theme in *Things Fall Apart*," *Review of English Literature*, 5, No. 4 (October 1964), 39–43.

I am sending you as my representative among those people—just
to be on the safe side in case the new religion develops. One has
to move with the times or else one is left behind. I have a hunch
that those who fail to come to terms with the white man may
well regret their lack of foresight.[4]

Achebe comments, "The material is the same. But the form of the
one is *in character* and the other is not. It is largely a matter of
instinct, but judgement comes into it too."[5]

Achebe's use of an African vernacular style is not limited to dialogue. In *Things Fall Apart* and *Arrow of God*, novels set in tribal society, the narrative itself is studded with proverbs and similes which help
to evoke the cultural milieu in which the action takes place. In *No
Longer at Ease* and *A Man of the People*, on the other hand, one finds
the language of the narrative more cosmopolitan, more Westernized,
more suited to life in the city. Here are some similes drawn from narrative portions of *Things Fall Apart* (TFA) and *Arrow of God* (AOG):

> . . . like a bush-fire in the harmattan. (TFA, p. 1)
> . . . like pouring grains of corn into a bag full of holes. (TFA, p. 19)
> . . . as if water had been poured on the tightened skin of a drum.
> (TFA, p. 42)
> . . . like a yam tendril in the rainy season. (TFA, p. 45)
> . . . like the snapping of a tightened bow. (TFA, p. 53)
> . . . as busy as an ant-hill. (TFA, p. 100)
> . . . like the walk of an Ijele Mask lifting and lowering each foot
> with weighty ceremony. (AOG, p. 84)
> . . . like a grain of maize in an empty goatskin bag. (AOG, p. 100)
> . . . as one might pull out a snail from its shell. (AOG, p. 118)
> . . . like a bad cowry. (AOG, p. 146)
> . . . like a lizard fallen from an iroko tree. (AOG, p. 242)
> . . . like the blue, quiet, razor-edge flame of burning palm-nut
> shells. (AOG, p. 274)

Now here are some similes drawn from narrative portions of *No
Longer at Ease* (NLAE) and *A Man of the People* (AMOP):

> . . . as a collector fixes his insect with formalin. (NLAE, p. 1)
> . . . swivelling their hips as effortlessly as oiled ball-bearings.
> (NLAE, p. 18)
> . . . like a giant tarmac from which God's aeroplane might take
> off. (NLAE, p. 24)
> . . . like an enchanted isle. (NLAE, p. 28)
> . . . like the jerk in the leg of a dead frog when a current is applied
> to it. (NLAE, p. 137)

4. *Transition*, No. 18 (1965), p. 30. The same article appears in *Moderna Sprak*, 58 (1964),
438–46.
5. *Ibid.*

. . . like a panicky fly trapped behind the windscreen. (NLAE,
    p. 149)

. . . as a dentist extracts a stinking tooth. (AMOP, p. 4)

. . . like that radio jingle advertising an intestinal worm expeller.
    (AMOP, p. 29)

. . . as I had been one day, watching for the first time the unveiling
    of the white dome of Kilimanjaro at sunset. (AMOP, p. 45)

. . . as those winged termites driven out of the earth by late rain
    dance furiously around street lamps and then drop panting
    to the ground. (AMOP, p. 51)

. . . like a slowed up action film. (AMOP, p. 145)

. . . like a dust particle in the high atmosphere around which the
    water vapour of my thinking formed its globule of rain.
    (AMOP, p. 146)

In the urban novels one also finds similes drawn from village life, but
in the novels set entirely in tribal society one finds no similes drawn
from urban experience. This is altogether fitting, for Achebe's urban
characters have lived in villages, but most of the characters of his village novels have had little or no exposure to cities. Here again we see
Achebe using judgment and instinct to select the type of imagery that
is appropriate to the time, place and people he is trying to picture. It
is Achebe's sensitive use of appropriate language that lends an air of
historicity to his novels.

I have taken time to comment on Achebe's artistry because the
argument I intend to pursue is based on the premise that Achebe is
an exceptional literary artist. I believe that he is both a conscious and
an unconscious artist, that he has an instinct for knowing where
things belong and a talent for putting them there, and that he possesses a shrewd sense of what is *in character* and what is not. All
these qualities are displayed in his deliberate search for an appropriate language for each novel, a style that will not only suit his subject
and evoke the right cultural milieu but will also help to define the
moral issues with which the novel is concerned.

It is my contention that Achebe, a skillful artist, achieves an appropriate language for each of his novels largely through the use of
proverbs. Indeed, Achebe's proverbs can serve as keys to an understanding of his novels because he uses them not merely to add
touches of local color but to sound and reiterate themes, to sharpen
characterization, to clarify conflict, and to focus on the values of the
society he is portraying. Proverbs thus provide a "grammar of values"[6]

---

6. I have borrowed this phrase from M. J. Herskovits, who once said, ". . . the total corpus of
the proverbs of Africans, as with proverb-users in other societies, is in a very real sense their
grammar of values." *Dahomean Narrative* (Evanston, 1958), p. 56. For another discussion
of Achebe's proverbs, see Austin J. Shelton, "The 'Palm-Oil' of Language: Proverbs in
Chinua Achebe's Novels," *Modern Language Quarterly*, 30, No. 1 (1969), 86–111.

by which the deeds of a hero can be measured and evaluated. By studying Achebe's proverbs we are better able to interpret his novels.

Things Fall Apart is the story of Okonkwo, a famous warrior and expert farmer who has risen from humble origins to become a wealthy and respected leader of his clan. His entire life has been a struggle to achieve status, and he has almost attained a position of preeminence when he accidentally kills a kinsman. For this crime he must leave his clan and live in exile for seven years. When he returns at the end of the seventh year, he finds that things have changed in his home village. White missionaries have established a church and have made a number of converts. White men have also set up a court where the district commissioner comes to judge cases according to a foreign code of law. Okonkwo tries to rouse his clan to take action against these foreigners and their, institutions. In a rage he kills one of the district commissioner's messengers. When his clan does not support his action, he commits suicide.

Okonkwo is pictured throughout the novel as a wrestler. It is an appropriate image not just because he is a powerful brute of a man and a renowned wrestler, not just because his life has been a ceaseless struggle for status, but because in the eyes of his people he brings about his own downfall by challenging too powerful an adversary. This adversary is not the white man, but rather Okonkwo's *chi*, his personal god or guardian spirit.[7] Okonkwo is crushed because he tries to wrestle with his *chi*. The Ibo have a folktale about just such a wrestler.

> Once there was a great wrestler whose back had never known the ground. He wrestled from village to village until he had thrown every man in the world. Then he decided that he must go and wrestle in the land of spirits, and become champion there as well. He went, and beat every spirit that came forward. Some had seven heads, some ten; but he beat them all. His companion who sang his praise on the flute begged him to come away, but he would not. He pleaded with him but his ear was nailed up. Rather than go home he gave a challenge to the spirits to bring out their best and strongest wrestler. So they sent him his personal god, a little, wiry spirit who seized him with one hand and smashed him on the stony earth.[8]

7. There has been some controversy about the meaning of "chi." See Austin J. Shelton, "The Offended *chi* in Achebe's Novels," *Transition*, No. 13 (1964), pp. 36–37, and Donatus Nwoga, "The *chi* Offended," *Transition*, No. 15 (1964), p. 5. Shelton prefers to translate it as "God within," but Nwoga, an Ibo, supports Achebe's translation of it as "personal god." Victor Uchendu, an Ibo anthropologist, describes *chi* as "the Igbo form of guardian spirit" (*The Igbo of Southeast Nigeria*, New York, 1966, p. 16). I have followed Achebe and Uchendu here.

8. Quoted from Achebe's *Arrow of God*, pp. 31–32. A variant of this tale can be found in Cyprian Ekwensi, *Ikolo the Wrestler and Other Ibo Tales* (London, 1947), pp. 34–37. Another variant appears in F. Chidozie Ogbalu, *Niger Tales* (Aba, n.d.), pp. 9–11.

Although this tale does not appear in *Things Fall Apart*, there is sufficient evidence in the novel to suggest that Okonkwo is being likened to one who dares to wrestle with a spirit. A hint is contained in the first paragraph of the opening chapter which tells how Okonkwo gained fame as a young man of eighteen by throwing an unbeaten wrestler "in a fight which the old men agreed was one of the fiercest since the founder of their town engaged a spirit of the wild for seven days and seven nights." (p. 1) And later, when Okonkwo commits the sin of beating one of his wives during the sacred Week of Peace, ". . . people said he had no respect for the gods of his clan. His enemies said his good fortune had gone to his head. They called him the little bird *nza* who so far forgot himself after a heavy meal that he challenged his *chi*." (p. 26)

Achebe uses proverbs to reinforce the image of Okonkwo as a man who struggles with his *chi*. Notice in the following passage how skillfully this is done:

> Everybody at the kindred meeting took sides with Osugo when Okonkwo called him a woman. The oldest man present said sternly that those whose palm-kernels were cracked for them by a benevolent spirit should not forget to be humble. Okonkwo said he was sorry for what he had said, and the meeting continued.
>
> But it was really not true that Okonkwo's palm-kernels had been cracked for him by a benevolent spirit. He had cracked them himself. Anyone who knew his grim struggle against poverty and misfortune could not say he had been lucky. If ever a man deserved his success, that man was Okonkwo. At an early age he had achieved fame as the greatest wrestler in all the land. That was not luck. At the most one could say that his *chi* or personal god was good. But the Ibo people have a proverb that when a man says yes his *chi* also says yes. Okonkwo said yes very strongly; so his *chi* agreed. And not only his *chi* but his clan too, because it judged a man by the work of his hands. (pp. 22–23)

When Okonkwo returns from exile, he makes the mistake of believing that if he says yes strongly enough, his *chi* and his clan will agree. No doubt he should have known better. He should have accepted his years in exile as a warning from his *chi*. In his first months of exile he had come close to understanding the truth:

> Clearly his personal god or *chi* was not made for great things. A man could not rise beyond the destiny of his *chi*. The saying of the elders was not true—that if a man said yea his *chi* also affirmed. Here was a man whose *chi* said nay despite his own affirmation. (p. 117)

However, as the years of exile pass, Okonkwo's fortunes improve and he begins to feel "that his *chi* might now be making amends for the past disaster." (p. 154) He returns to his clan rich, confident, and eager to resume his former position of leadership. When he finds his village changed, he tries to transform it into the village it had once been. But although he says yes very strongly, his *chi* and his clan say nay. Okonkwo the wrestler is at last defeated.

Quite a few of the proverbs that Achebe uses in *Things Fall Apart* are concerned with status and achievement:

> . . . the sun will shine on those who stand before it shines on those who kneel under them. (p. 5)
> . . . if a child washed his hands he could eat with kings. (p. 6)
> . . . a man who pays respect to the great paves the way for his own greatness. (p. 16)
> The lizard that jumped from the high iroko tree to the ground said he would praise himself if no one else did. (p. 18)
> . . . you can tell a ripe corn by its look. (p. 18)
> I cannot live on the bank of a river and wash my hands with spittle. (p. 148)
> . . . as a man danced so the drums were beaten for him. (p. 165)

Such proverbs tell us much about the values of Ibo society, values by which Okonkwo lives and dies. Such proverbs also serve as thematic statements reminding us of some of the major motifs in the novel— e.g., the importance of status, the value of achievement, the idea of man as shaper of his own destiny.

Sometimes in Achebe's novels one finds proverbs expressing different views on the same subject. Examined closely, these proverbs can provide clues to significant differences in outlook or opinion which set one man apart from others. For example, there are a number of proverbs in *Things Fall Apart* comparing parents and their children. Most Ibos believe that a child will take after his parents, or as one character puts it, "When mother cow is chewing grass its young ones watch its mouth." (p. 62) However, Okonkwo's father had been a failure, and Okonkwo, not wanting to be likened to him, had striven to make his own life a success. So impressive were his achievements and so rapid his rise that an old man was prompted to remark, "Looking at a king's mouth, one would think he never sucked at his mother's breast." (p. 22) Okonkwo believed that one's ancestry was not as important as one's initiative and will power, qualities which could be discerned in a child at a very early age. "A chick that will grow into a cock," he said, "can be spotted the very day it hatches." (p. 58) He had good reason for thinking so. He himself had achieved much as a young man, but his own son Nwoye had achieved nothing at all.

> How could he have begotten a woman for a son? At Nwoye's age, Okonkwo had already become famous throughout Umuofia for his wrestling and his fearlessness.

> He sighed heavily, and as if in sympathy the smouldering log
> also sighed. And immediately Okonkwo's eyes were opened and
> he saw the whole matter clearly. Living fire begets cold, impotent
> ash. He sighed again, deeply. (p. 138)

It is worth noting that in complaining about Nwoye's unmanliness,
Okonkwo says, "A bowl of pounded yams can throw him in a
wrestling match." (p. 57) All the proverbs cited here are working to
characterize Okonkwo and to set him apart from other men, especially from his father and his son. The proverbs reveal that no one,
least of all Okonkwo himself, considers him an ordinary mortal;
rather, he is the sort of man who would dare to wrestle with his *chi*.

Obi Okonkwo, who is Okonkwo's grandson and the hero of
Achebe's second novel, *No Longer at Ease*, is a very different kind of
person. When he returns from studies in England, he is an honest,
idealistic young man. He takes a high paying job in the civil service
but soon finds that his salary is not sufficient to meet the financial
demands made upon him. He also gets involved with a woman his
parents and clan despise. In the end he is caught taking bribes and is
sent to prison.

Obi is an unheroic figure, a good man who slides rather than falls
into evil ways. His actions are ignoble and unworthy. When he
begins taking bribes, he tries to satisfy his conscience by refusing to
take them from people he knows he cannot help. Kinsmen who
attend his trial cannot understand why he took such risks for so little
profit; one says, "I am against people reaping where they have not
sown. But we have a saying that if you want to eat a toad you should
look for a fat and juicy one." (p. 6) But Obi lives by half measures,
by resolute decisions mollified by irresolute actions. He falls in love
with Clara, a woman whose unusual ancestry Obi's parents look
upon with horror, and he wants to marry her. A friend warns him not
to pollute his lineage: "What you are going to do concerns not only
yourself but your whole family and future generations. If one finger
brings oil it soils the others." (p. 75) Obi, feeling he must free himself from the shackles of tradition, becomes engaged to Clara but
later yields to parental pressure and breaks off with her. When she
reveals she is pregnant, he arranges for her to get an abortion. More
shameful, at least in the eyes of his clan, is Obi's refusal to return
home for his mother's funeral, an action that leads one dismayed
clansman to suggest that Obi is rotten at the core: "A man may go
to England, become a lawyer or doctor, but it does not change his
blood. It is like a bird that flies off the earth and lands on an ant-hill.
It is still on the ground." (p. 160) Obi never gets off the ground,
never reaches heroic heights, never stops swallowing undernour-
ished toads.

Helping to set the tone of the story are a great number of proverbs which comment on or warn against foolish and unworthy actions. Besides those already mentioned, one finds:

> He that fights for a ne'er-do-well has nothing to show for it except a head covered in earth and grime. (p. 5)
>
> The fox must be chased away first; after that the hen might be warned against wandering into the bush. (p. 5)
>
> . . . he replied that a man who lived on the banks of the Niger should not wash his hands with spittle. (pp. 10, 135)
>
> . . . like the young antelope who danced herself lame when the main dance was yet to come. (p. 11)
>
> When a new saying gets to the land of empty men they lose their heads over it. (p. 48)
>
> A person who has not secured a place on the floor should not begin to look for a mat. (p. 60)
>
> Shall we kill a snake and carry it in our hand when we have a bag for putting long things in? (p. 80)
>
> . . . digging a new pit to fill up an old one. (p. 108)
>
> . . . a man should not, out of pride and etiquette, swallow his phlegm. (p. 156)
>
> . . . The little bird *nza* who after a big meal so far forgot himself as to challenge his *chi* to single combat. (p. 163)
>
> A man does not challenge his *chi* to a wrestling match. (p. 40)

The last two proverbs cited here may remind us of Okonkwo, but no one could mistake Obi for his grandfather. Okonkwo erred by daring to attempt something he did not have the power to achieve; this makes him a tragic hero. Obi erred by stooping to take bribes; this makes him a crook. To put it in proverbial terms: Okonkwo wrestles his *chi*, Obi swallows a toad. It is not only the stupidity but the contemptibility of Obi's ways that many of the proverbs in the novel help to underscore.

An important theme in *No Longer at Ease* is the conflict between old and new values. Obi's people tax themselves mercilessly to raise funds to send him to England for university training. The "scholarship" they award him is to be repaid both in cash and in services when he finishes his studies. They want him to read law so that when he returns he will be able to handle all their land cases against their neighbors. They expect a good return on their investment because Obi is their kinsman; they have a saying that ". . . he who has people is richer than he who has money." (p. 79) Obi, however, immediately asserts his self-will by choosing to read English instead of law. When he returns he starts to pay back the loan but refuses to allow his kinsmen to interfere in his personal life. He especially resents their efforts to dissuade him from marrying Clara. Having adopted Western values, Obi believes that an individual has the right to choose his own wife. It is this that brings him into conflict with his parents and kinsmen. Obi's Western education has made him an individualist, but his people still adhere to communal values.[9]

Obi's people attach great importance to kinship ties, and their beliefs regarding the obligations and rewards of kinship are often revealed in their proverbs. Even when a prodigal son like Obi gets into trouble, they feel it is necessary to try to help him: ". . . a kinsman in trouble had to be saved, not blamed; anger against a brother was felt in the flesh, not in the bone." (p. 5) They also have a song which cautions:

> He that has a brother must hold him to his heart,
> For a kinsman cannot be bought in the market,
> Neither is a brother bought with money. (p. 129)

Certainly it would be very wrong to harm an in-law for ". . . a man's in-law was his *chi*." (p. 46) And conflict within the clan should be avoided, for in unity lies strength: "If all snakes lived together in one place, who would approach them?" (p. 81) Those who prosper are expected to help those who are less fortunate: ". . . when there is a big tree small ones climb on its back to reach the sun." (p. 96) But all the burdens should not fall on one man: ". . . it is not right to ask a man with elephantiasis of the scrotum to take on small pox as well, when thousands of other people have not had even their share of small diseases." (p. 99) Obi accepts some of the values expressed in these proverbs, but his own individualistic attitude is probably best summed up in the saying "Ours is ours but mine is mine." (p. 32) Obi's problem lies in having to make choices between the old values and the new, between "ours" and "mine."

Ezeulu, hero of Achebe's third novel, *Arrow of God*, is faced with a similar problem. As chief priest of a snake cult Ezeulu is committed to traditional ways, but just to be on the safe side he sends one of his sons to a mission school to "be [his] eye there" and to learn the white man's ways. This action draws criticism from some of the leaders of the clan, criticism which rapidly mounts into angry protest when the Christianized son is caught trying to kill a sacred python. Ezeulu also falls afoul of the district officer by declining to accept an official appointment as paramount chief of his village. For this he is thrown into prison for two months. When he returns to his village he envisions himself as an avenging arrow in the bow of his god, an instrument by which his god intends to punish his people. Ezeulu therefore refuses to perform certain rituals which must be performed before new yams can be harvested. This precipitates a crisis which results in the destruction of Ezeulu, his priesthood and his religion.

---

9. This theme is discussed by Obiajunwa Wali in "The Individual and the Novel in Africa," *Transition*, No. 18 (1965), pp. 31–33.

To understand Ezeulu one must comprehend his deep concern over the way his world is changing. This concern is expressed both in his decision to send one of his sons to a mission school and in the proverbs he uses to justify his decision. He tells his son that a man must move with the times: ". . . I am like the bird Eneke-nti-oba. When his friends asked him why he was always on the wing he replied: 'Men of today have learnt to shoot without missing and so I have learnt to fly without perching.' . . . The world is like a Mask dancing. If you want to see it well you do not stand in one place." (p. 55) Months later Ezeulu reminds his son that he must learn the white man's magic because "a man must dance the dance prevalent in his time." (p. 234) Ezeulu explains his decision to the village elders by comparing the white man to a new disease: "A disease that has never been seen before cannot be cured with everyday herbs. When we want to make a charm we look for the animal whose blood can match its power; if a chicken cannot do it we look for a goat or a ram; if that is not sufficient we send for a bull. But sometimes even a bull does not suffice, then we must look for a human." (p. 165) Ezeulu's son is to be the human sacrifice which will enable the clan to make medicine of sufficient strength to hold the new disease in check. In other words, Ezeulu decides to sacrifice his son in order to gain power to cope with the changing times.

The question is whether Ezeulu's action is an appropriate response to the problem. Some elders think it is not and blame Ezeulu for bringing new trouble to the village by taking so improper a step. The importance that Ezeulu's people attach to appropriate action is reflected in many of the proverbs in the novel. For example:

> If the lizard of the homestead neglects to do the things for which its kind is known, it will be mistaken for the lizard of the farmland. (pp. 20–21)
> . . . let us first chase away the wild cat, afterwards we blame the hen. (p. 122)
> We do not by-pass a man and enter his compound. (p. 138)
> We do not apply an ear-pick to the eye. (p. 138)
> . . . bale that water before it rises above the ankle. (pp. 156, 197)
> When a masked spirit visits you you have to appease its foot prints with presents. (p. 190)
> . . . a traveller to distant places should make no enemies. (p. 208)
> . . . a man of sense does not go on hunting little bush rodents when his age mates are after big game. (p. 209)
> He who sees an old hag squatting should leave her alone; who knows how she breathes? (p. 282)

Sending a son to a mission school is regarded by some elders as a highly inappropriate action for a chief priest to take, no matter what his motivation.

Ezeulu's enemies interpret his deed as a gesture of friendship toward the white man. Thus, when the district commissioner rather curtly commands Ezeulu to appear in his office within twenty-four hours and Ezeulu calls the elders together to ask if they think he should heed the summons, one unfriendly elder replies in no uncertain proverbs that Ezeulu must either suffer the consequences of friendship with the white man or do something to end the friendship:

> ". . . does Ezeulu think that their friendship should stop short of entering each other's houses? Does he want the white man to be his friend only by word of mouth? Did not our elders tell us that as soon as we shake hands with a leper he will want an embrace? . . . What I say is this . . . a man who brings ant-ridden faggots into his hut should expect the visit of lizards. But if Ezeulu is now telling us that he is tired of the white man's friendship our advice to him should be: You tied the knot, you should also know how to undo it. You passed the shit that is smelling; you should carry it away. Fortunately the evil charm brought in at the end of a pole is not too difficult to take outside again." (pp. 177–78)

It is worth noting that the proverb about bringing ant-ridden faggots home is quoted twice by Ezeulu himself. He uses it to reproach himself when his mission-educated son is found trying to kill a sacred python. (p. 72) Here, momentarily at least, Ezeulu seems willing to accept responsibility for the abomination. Ezeulu uses the proverb a second time when a friend accuses him of betraying his people by sending his son to the white man's school. Ezeulu counters by pointing out that he did not bring the white man to his people; rather, his people brought the white man upon themselves by failing to oppose him when he first arrived. If they wish to blame someone, they should blame themselves for meekly submitting to the white man's presence and power. "The man who brings ant-ridden faggots into his hut should not grumble when lizards begin to pay him a visit." (p. 163) This is a key proverb in *Arrow of God* for it enunciates a major theme: that a man is responsible for his actions and must bear their consequences.

But in addition to being responsible for his actions, a man is also expected to act responsibly. This idea is conveyed in another key proverb which is used four times in the novel: ". . . an adult does not sit and watch while the she-goat suffers the pain of childbirth tied to a post." (p. 258, cf. pp. 21, 31, 189) Ezeulu uses this proverb twice to reprimand elders for encouraging the village to fight a "war of blame" against a neighboring village. He reminds them that elders must not neglect their duty to their people by acting irresponsibly. It is quite significant that this same proverb is used later by the elders to rebuke Ezeulu for failing to perform the ritual that will permit new yams to be harvested. (p. 258) The elders suggest that Ezeulu is doing nothing to prevent or relieve the suffering of his people. They urge him to do his duty by performing the necessary ritual. They urge him, in other words, to act responsibly.

Ezeulu answers that he has a higher responsibility, for his god, Ulu, has forbidden him to perform the ritual. The elders then say that if Ezeulu will perform the ritual, they themselves will take the blame for it: ". . . if Ulu says we have committed an abomination let it be on the heads of the ten of us here. You will be free because we have set you to it, and the person who sets a child to catch a shrew should also find him water to wash the odour from his hand. We shall find you the water." (p. 260) Ezeulu answers, ". . . you cannot say: do what is not done and we shall take the blame. I am the Chief Priest of Ulu and what I have told you is his will not mine." (pp. 260–61) Ezeulu sincerely believes that he is the instrument of a divine power, "an arrow in the bow of his god." (p. 241) When his actions bring disaster upon himself and his people, he does not feel responsible but rather feels betrayed by his god.

> Why, he asked himself again and again, why had Ulu chosen to deal thus with him, to strike him down and cover him with mud? What was his offence? Had he not divined the god's will and obeyed it? When was it ever heard that a child was scalded by the piece of yam its own mother put in its palm? What man would send his son with a potsherd to bring fire from a neighbour's hut and then unleash rain on him? Who ever sent his son up the palm to gather nuts and then took an axe and felled the tree? (p. 286)

Tortured by these questions, Ezeulu finally goes mad.

The elders come to regard Ezeulu as a man who brought tragedy upon himself by failing to recognize his own limitations. In order to act appropriately and responsibly, a man must know his limitations. This idea finds expression in many of the proverbs in the novel:

> . . . like the little bird, *nza*, who ate and drank and challenged his personal god to a single combat. (p. 17)
> . . . no matter how strong or great a man was he should never challenge his *chi*. (p. 32)
> The man who carries a deity is not a king. (p. 33)
> A man who knows that his anus is small does not swallow an udala seed. (pp. 87, 282)
> . . . only a foolish man can go after a leopard with his bare hands. (p. 105)
> The fly that struts around on a mound of excrement wastes his time; the mound will always be greater than the fly. (p. 282)

To sum up, Ezeulu, in trying to adjust to the changing times, takes certain inappropriate actions which later lead him to neglect his duties and responsibilities. Not knowing his limitations, he goes too far and plunges himself and his people into disaster.

Achebe's most recent novel, A Man of the People, is set in contemporary Nigeria and takes as its hero a young schoolteacher, Odili Samalu. Odili, who tells his own story, is moved to enter politics when his mistress is seduced by Chief the Honourable M. A. Nanga, M.P. and Minister of Culture. Odili joins a newly-formed political party and prepares to contest Nanga's seat in the next election. He also tries to win the affections of Nanga's fiancée, a young girl Nanga is grooming as his "parlour wife." In the end Odili loses the political battle but manages to win the girl. Nanga loses everything because the election is so rough and dirty and creates such chaos in the country that the Army stages a coup and imprisons every member of the Government.

In Nanga, Achebe has created one of the finest rogues in Nigerian fiction. Claiming to be a "man of the people," Nanga is actually a self-seeking, grossly corrupt politician who lives in flamboyant opulence on his ill-gotten gains. He is fond of pious platitudes—"Not what I have but what I do is my kingdom" (p. 3); "Do the right and shame the Devil" (p. 12)—but his ruthless drive for money and power is far from pious. When criticized, he accuses his critics of "character assassination" and answers that ". . . no one is perfect except God." (p. 75) He frequently complains of the troubles and burdens that Government Ministers have to bear and readily agrees when someone remarks, "Uneasy lies the head that wears the crown." (p. 68) Nanga has enormous power which he is willing to use to help others provided that they in turn help him. In a country in which "it didn't matter *what* you knew but *who* you knew," (p. 19) Nanga was obviously a man to know.

The maxims quoted here help to characterize Nanga and his world. They are sayings borrowed from a foreign culture and are as often misapplied and abused as are the manners and institutions which have also been borrowed from Europe and transplanted in contemporary Africa. Nanga quotes these maxims but does not live by them; similarly, he gives lip service to democratic elections but does everything in his power to subvert and manipulate them. Detribalized but imperfectly Westernized, adhering to no systematic code of values, Nanga battles to stay on top in a confused world. He is one of the most monstrous offspring produced by the tawdry union of Europe and Africa, and his misuse of non-African mottoes and maxims exposes not only his own insincerity and irresponsibility but the moral chaos in the world in which he lives.

Odili, a more thoroughly Westernized African, is a man of far greater virtue and integrity. His narrative is sprinkled with imported metaphors and proverbial expressions—e.g., "kicked the bucket," (p. 28) "pass through the eye of a needle," (p. 63) "one stone to kill two birds with," (p. 152) "attack . . . is the best defence," (p. 162) "a bird in the hand" (p. 165)—but he always uses them appropriately. Whatever he says can be trusted to be accurate and honest. Somehow Odili has managed to remain untainted amidst all the surrounding corruption and his clear vision provides an undistorted view of a warped society.

Contemporary Nigeria is, after all, the real subject of the novel. What sort of society is it that allows men like Nanga to thrive while men like Odili suffer? Some important clues are provided in the proverbs in the novel. In contemporary Nigeria one must, for example, be circumspect:

> . . . the proverbial traveller-to-distant-places who must not cultivate enmity on his route. (p. 1)
> . . . when one slave sees another cast into a shallow grave he should know that when the time comes he will go the same way. (p. 40)
> . . . if you respect today's king, others will respect you when your turn comes. (p. 70)
> . . . if you look only in one direction your neck will become stiff. (p. 90)

But one must not be unduly inquisitive:

> . . . naked curiosity—the kind that they say earned Monkey a bullet in the forehead: (p. 153)
> The inquisitive eye will only blind its own sight. (p. 164)
> A man who insists on peeping into his neighbour's bedroom knowing a woman to be there is only punishing himself. (p. 164)

One should take advantage of opportunities (". . . if you fail to take away a strong man's sword when he is on the ground, will you do it when he gets up . . . ?" p. 103); capitalize on good fortune ("[would] a sensible man . . . spit out the juicy morsel that good fortune placed in his mouth?" p. 2); and avoid wasting time on trivialities (". . . like the man in the proverb who was carrying the carcass of an elephant on his head and searching with his toes for a grasshopper" p. 80). Most important of all, one must be sure to get one's share. Like the world of Obi Okonkwo in *No Longer at Ease*, this is a world in which "ours is ours but mine is mine." (p. 140)

One must not only get one's share, one must also consume it. Eating is an important image in the novel. Politicians like Nanga tell their tribesmen, "Our people must press for their fair share of the national cake." (p. 13) Those who stand in the way of such hungry politicians are branded as "the hybrid class of Western-educated and snobbish intellectuals who will not hesitate to sell their mothers for a mess of pottage." (p. 6) These intellectuals, Nanga says, "have bitten the finger with which their mother fed them." (p. 6) Although some people believe that God will provide for everyone according to His will ("He holds the knife and He holds the yam," p. 102), the politicians know that the fattest slices of the national cake together with the richest icing will go to the politicians who hold the most power. This is the reason elections are so hotly contested. In these elections people are quite willing to support a corrupt politician like Nanga in the belief that if he remains well fed, he may let a few crumbs fall to his constituents. When someone like Odili protests that such politicians are using their positions to enrich themselves, the people answer cynically, "Let them eat, . . . after all when white men used to do all the eating did we commit suicide?" (p. 161) Besides, who can tell what the future may bring? ". . . who knows? It may be your turn to eat tomorrow. Your son may bring home your share." (p. 162) It is not surprising that Odili sums up this era as a "fat-dripping, gummy, eat-and-let-eat regime . . . a regime which inspired the common saying that a man could only be sure of what he had put away safely in his gut or, in language ever more suited to the times: 'you chop, me self I chop, palaver finish.'" (p. 167)

The reason such an era comes to an end is that the politicians make the mistake of overeating, of taking more than their share. In proverbial terms, they take more than the owner can ignore. This key proverb is used four times in the novel. Twice it is applied to a miserly trader who steals a blind man's stick: "Josiah has taken away enough for the owner to notice," people say in disgust. "Josiah has now removed enough for the owner to see him." (p. 97) Odili later reflects on the situation and the proverb:

> I thought much afterwards about that proverb, about the man taking things away until the owner at last notices. In the mouth of our people there was no greater condemnation. It was not just a simple question of a man's cup being full. A man's cup might be full and none the wiser. But here the owner knew, and the owner, I discovered, is the will of the whole people. (p. 97)

In the middle of his campaign against Nanga, Odili wishes that "someone would get up and say: 'No, Nanga has taken more than the owner could ignore!'" (p. 122) But it is only after much post-election violence and an army takeover that Odili's wish comes true. Only after such upheavals result in the establishment of a new order do people openly admit that Nanga and his cohorts "had taken enough for the owner to see." (p. 166)

Thus, in *A Man of the People*, as in Achebe's other novels, proverbs are used to sound and reiterate major themes, to sharpen characterization, to clarify conflict, and to focus on the values of the society

Achebe is portraying. By studying the proverbs in a novel, we gain insight into the moral issues with which that novel deals. Because they provide a *grammar of values* by which the actions of characters can be measured and evaluated, proverbs help us to understand and interpret Achebe's novels.

Achebe's literary talents are clearly revealed in his use of proverbs. One can observe his mastery of the English language, his skill in choosing the right words to convey his ideas, his keen sense of what is *in character* and what is not, his instinct for appropriate metaphor and symbol, and his ability to present a thoroughly African world in thoroughly African terms. It is this last talent that enables him to convince his readers "that African peoples did, not hear of culture for the first time from Europeans; that their societies were not mindless but frequently had a philosophy of great depth and value and beauty, that they had poetry and, above all, they had dignity."[1]

ABDUL JANMOHAMED

Sophisticated Primitivism: The Syncretism of Oral and Literate Modes in Achebe's *Things Fall Apart*[†]

I

The use of the English language and literary forms by African (and other Third World) writers must be understood in the context of a larger social, political, and ideological dialogue between British, and particularly colonialist, literature on the one hand and the ex-colonized writers of the Third World on the other. Faced by the colonialist denigration of his past and present culture and consequently motivated by a desire to negate the prior European negation of indigenous society, the African writer embarks on a program of regaining the dignity of self and society by representing them, in the best instances, in a manner that he considers unidealized but more authentic. This negative dialogue transcends the literary polemic about authentic "images" of Africans and manifests itself in an opposition of forms as well: thus, for instance, Chinua Achebe is drawn to realism partly in order to counter the "racial romances" of Joyce Cary.

However, some critics have argued that the African end of this dialogue is unable to negate colonialist literature totally precisely because it relies on the English language to do so. The question that underlies this criticism is indeed an important one: can African

1. See footnote 1, above.
† From *Ariel* 15.4 (October 1984). By permission of *Ariel: A Review of International English Literature.*

experience be adequately represented through the alien media (ones that were fashioned to codify an entirely different encounter with reality) of the colonizers' language and literary forms or will these media inevitably alter the nature of African experience in significant ways? But the question cannot be answered very easily. While the ideological sentiment behind this criticism is perfectly understandable and laudable, the critics who want Third World writers to abandon European languages and forms have not concretely examined the results of the contemporary syncretic literatures of the Third World. Whatever answers are ultimately given to the underlying question, the concrete evidence must be scrutinized first. Thus I would like to bracket temporarily the controversy about English in order to examine, in this essay, an issue that, one can argue, has causal priority: how is the encounter between the predominantly *oral* cultures of Africa and the *literate* cultures of the colonizer represented and mediated by anglophone African fiction? Is such fiction, which, to stress the obvious, is *literate* and written in *English*, able to do justice to the phenomenology of oral/mythic cultures, which is radically different from that of chirographic cultures? From an ideological viewpoint we must also inquire whether or not the adoption of the alien language makes a significant contribution to the negative dialogic relation between African and English literatures.

The African writer's very decision to use English as his medium is engulfed by ironies, paradoxes, and contradictions. He writes in English because he was born in a British colony and can receive formal education only in English. More significantly, however, he is compelled to master and use English because of the prevailing ideological pressures within the colonial system. At the surface level these manifest themselves through the ethnocentric narcissism of the European colonialists who will only recognize the other as a "civilized" human being if he recreates himself in their image by adopting the appropriate European language as well as literary forms. This applies to all aspects of culture and politics: for instance, the granting of "independence" itself is contingent upon the adoption of some version of Western parliamentary democracy. At a deeper level the insistence that the colonies accept European forms, values, and beliefs represents a deliberate, if subconscious, strategy to ensure an unproblematic change from dominant to hegemonic colonialism. "Independence" marks the transition from the dominant phase, where "consent" of the dominated is obtained by direct coersion, to the hegemonic phase, where "consent" is procured through the ideological formation of the dominated subject. Thus the adoption of European languages, and subsequently European values, beliefs, etc., by the native remains crucial to the hegemonic transfer, which generates, as by-products, anglophone, francophone, etc., Third World writers who may or may not be involved in a negative dialogue with European literature. (Some writers, such as V. S. Naipaul, who has clearly adopted the "author function" of the colonizer, are more inclined to represent a version of the colonialist viewpoint.) Finally, a potential writer from a British colony is induced to use English because it is an intimate part of a powerful society that will control all technological and cultural development in the foreseeable future.

Yet the decision to use English produces a contradiction between, on the one hand, the unconscious and subconscious phychic formations of most Third World writers, determined by the indigenous languages, and, on the other hand, the more superficial, conscious formation, determined by the formal, public function of English in most colonies. The problem is compounded by the fact that, unlike English, most African languages were non-literate and that the noetic structures of these oral cultures are significantly different from those of chirographic ones. The African writer who uses English, then, is faced at some level with the paradox of representing the experience of oral cultures through literate language and forms. Chinua Achebe, on whose first novel I shall concentrate, is subconsciously aware of this problem and has depicted in his fiction not only the material, political, and social destruction of indigenous societies caused by colonization but also the subtle annihilation of the conservative, homeostatic oral culture by the colonialists' introduction of literacy. Thus his novels not only depict the materiality of the destroyed and destroying worlds, but as chirographic representations of oral cultures they also become simultaneous agents of the preservation and destruction of the oral world. The style and structure of *Things Fall Apart*, I shall argue, do encode the phenomenology of oral cultures and thereby create a new syncretic form and contribute to the negative dialectics by deterritorializing, to some extent, the English language and the novelistic form.

II

The differences between oral and chirographic cultures have been articulated most thoroughly and systematically by Jack Goody and Walter J. Ong, and the following, somewhat schematic summary of these differences is based on their modulated analyses. Goody correctly emphasizes the fact that traditional anthropological formulations of the differences between these kinds of cultures through the binary and ethnocentric categories such as civilized/savage, rational/irrational, scientific/mythic, hot/cold, etc., are essentially manichean, that is, they tend to valorize morally one term at the expense of the other and to characterize the differences as being qualitative, categorical, and ontological rather than quantitative, material, and technological. Both Goody and Ong insist that the essential differences between these cultures can be explained through a scrutiny of literacy and its effects. The point, as Goody puts it, is that the "relationship between modes of thought and the modes for the production and reproduction of thought . . . [lies] at the heart of the unexplained but not inexplicable differences that so many writers have noted," that changes in the modes of production and reproduction of thought, i.e., (alphabetic) literacy and later printing, are bound to affect the very content and modes of thought.

Literacy, by isolating thought on a written surface, tends to alienate language, knowledge, and world in positive and productive ways. When an utterance "is put in writing it can be inspected in much greater detail, in its parts as well as in its whole, backwards as well as forwards, out of context as well as in its setting; in other words, it can be subjected to a quite different type of scrutiny and critique than is possible with purely verbal communication. Speech is no longer tied to an 'occasion'; it becomes timeless. Nor is it attached to a person; on paper, it becomes more abstract, more depersonalized." This kind of scrutiny eventually leads to the development of syllogistic and other forms of analysis. By allowing one to record events as they occur, to store them for long periods of time, and to recall them in their original forms, literacy eventually builds up a dense representation of the past and thus leads to the development of historical consciousness and secular teleology. The availability of a dense past and more sophisticated analytic tools in turn encourages greater reflexivity and self-scrutiny. One must emphasize again that oral cultures are unable to develop these characteristics not because of some genetic racial or cultural inferiority but simply because they lack the proper tool, namely literacy. Yet in the absence of these essential features of chirographic societies, the phenomenology of oral cultures tends to be characterized by the following traits: it defines meaning and value contextually rather than abstractly; it is conservative and homeostatic; its universe is defined by mythic rather than historical consciousness; it valorizes collectivity rather than individuality; and it is dominated by a totalizing imperative.

Oral cultures tend to define concepts through situational, operational frames of reference that are minimally abstract. Ideas are comprehended either through their concrete manifestations or through their context, but rarely in terms of other abstract ideas; lexis is controlled through direct semantic ratification, through experience rather than logical definition. Writing, on the other hand, creates a context-free or "autonomous" discourse. Written words are no longer directly bound up with reality; they become separate "things," abstracted from the flow of speech, shedding their close entailment with action and context.

Since the conservation of conceptualized knowledge in oral cultures depends on memory, that which is not memorized through repetition soon disappears. This mnemonic need establishes a highly traditionalist or conservative set of mind that tends to inhibit experimentation and innovation. On the other hand, the mind in chirographic cultures, freed from this mnemonic constraint, is not only able to experiment but, perhaps more significantly, to record and build on innovations and changes. Consequently, oral societies tend to adopt a protective attitude towards their epistemological and phenomenological categories and established theories and practices, whereas literate societies, particularly after they have embarked on a program of "scientific" inquiry, are more sceptical, critical, and analytic. The former tend to systematize and valorize belief, the latter, doubt. A corollary of the conserving function of the oral community is its homeostatic imperative, that is, its decision to maintain the equilibrium of the present by sloughing off memories which no longer have present relevance. The present needs of oral societies constantly impose their economy on past remembrances, and past events that are released from memory can never be recuperated in non-literate cultures.

The inability of oral cultures to document this past in a systematic and detailed manner, of course, means that they are dominated not by a historical but a mythic consciousness. As an account of origins, myth differs from history in that its claims cannot be verified with anything like the kind of accuracy available to literate societies. Based on this fundamental difference, Ernst Cassirer makes further distinctions between oral/mythic and scientific/historical consciousness that seem to be accurate but that are unfortunately formulated in fundamentally ethnocentric, manichean terms. However, at the very least, one can say that because the noetic economy of oral/mythic consciousness is not burdened by the needs of ratification it is able to develop a more fluid symbolic exchange system. This fluidity not only facilitates the enactment of the central teleological imperative of oral cultures, i.e., to maintain a constant homeostatic balance, but also permits the development of a specific relation between collectivity and individuality (weighted towards the former) and the economy and configuration of its totalizing imperative.

Communication in oral societies necessarily takes place in "primary group" relationships, that is, through intimate face-to-face contact. The result of this "intimate association, psychologically, is a certain fusion of individualities in a common whole, so that one's very self, for many purposes at least, is the common life and purpose of the group." Thus oral cultures tend to valorize collectivity over individuality and to create "individual" personality structures that are in fact communal and externalized, not inclined towards introspection. The externalized individual, then, is easily managed through the symbolic exchanges involved in communal ritual and practices. Writing and reading, on the other hand, are solitary achievements that tend at least momentarily, to throw the psyche back on itself, and the knowledge that one's thoughts, when they are committed to writing, can endure in time encourages the emergence and recognition of individuality.

According to Ong, sight (and hence writing) isolates, while sound (and hence speech) incorporates. Whereas sight situates the observer outside what he views, at a distance, sound pours into the hearer; while sight is unidirectional, sound is enveloping. The centring action of sound affects man's sense of the cosmos. For oral cultures, the cosmos is an ongoing event with man at its centre. Man is the *umbilicus mundi*. In such societies, where the word has its existence only in sound, the phenomenology of sound enters deeply into a human being's feel for existence. All the characteristics of oral cultures discussed above relate intimately to the unifying and centralizing effect of sound. If we add to this tendency the fact that, in the absence of the analytic categories that are predicated on writing, oral cultures must conceptualize and verbalize all their knowledge with more or less close reference to the human lifeworld, assimilating the alien, objective world to the more immediate, familiar interaction of human beings, then we begin to glimpse the totalizing imperative of oral cultures. In such societies words, ideas, and reality are intrinsically bound; they are part of the same continuum. There is little distinction made between the pragmatic and non-pragmatic, the phenomenal and the numenal. All mundane reality is impregnated with spiritual significance, and the entire cosmos inheres in the most insignificant object; metonymy and metaphor, as essential phenomenological and epistemological structures, are more deeply integral to the oral consciousness than they are to the chirographic mind. If man is the centre of the fluid symbolic economy of such a society and if such a universe is conceptualized through its humanization, then potentially man has total control of it if he only knows the correct formulas and practices. In such a culture an "individual" can easily become the emblem of the desires and conflicts of the entire society, and this characteristic is, of course, important for the production of heroic, epic narratives.

Narrative is more functional in oral cultures than in others for two reasons. Since oral cultures cannot generate abstract or scientific categories for coding experience, they use stories of human (or anthropomorphized animal) action to organize, store, and communicate knowledge and experience. Second, such societies use narratives to bind a great deal of cultural signification that exists in less durable verbal forms. Thus, for example, oral narratives will often incorporate folktales, orations, genealogies, proverbs, etc. Unlike the linear or pyramidal plots of chirographic narratives, which are predicated on careful written revision, the plots of oral narratives are episodic and non-sequential: the narrator will report a situation and only much later explain, often in great detail, how it came to be. Yet, as Ong insists, this is not due to the narrator's desire to hasten into the midst of action. Such an interpretation is a product of literate cultures which assume that a linear plot has been deliberately scrambled. The episodic oral "plot" is really a product of the narrator *remembering* the story in a curious public way—remembering not a memorized "text" or a verbatim succession of words but themes, episodes, and formulae, which, along with the entire story, are *already known* by the audience as part of the culture's myths.

The narrative thus simultaneously exists as a public and private event: "as a traditional and external fact, the oral tale is foreseeable; as a literary fact (poetic, individual experience, etc.), the produced oral text has an internal finality that finds support in the foreseeable." The relation between the public (already known) and private (a specific retelling) version of a narrative is dialectical. The narrative is a potentiality that exists prior to the productive act of the narrator, while a specific performance of the story is a variation and an innovation that refers to the potentiality just as *parole* refers to *langue*. Thus creativity as well as aesthetic appositeness lie in choosing a formal element (proverb, folktale, etc.) and in (re)arranging of episodes in a plot sequence in ways that are appropriate to the specific narrative context. The oral narrative, then, is "situational" in a double sense: it proceeds episodically, that is, it reports a situation that is modified or explained much later and apparently at random; and the specific performance is partly determined by the narrative situation, that is, by the interaction between audience and narrator. The "scrambled" sequence of an oral narrative, with its necessary recapitulations and postponed amplifications and explanations, results in repetition or copia as one of its characteristic features. Yet repetition must not be mistaken for redundancy (a term that Ong uses as a synonym). As Harold Scheub has shown, it has an aesthetic function; oral narratives deliberately cultivate and intensify repetitions in order to realize their cumulative effects. We may add to this the possibility that the neotic function of repetition may be to reinforce the homeostatic imperative of oral cultures because well-modulated repetition would have the effect of recreating the balance of an already known, ordered, controlled, and rhythmically harmonious universe. A specific aesthetic corollary of copia that also characterizes oral narrative is the predominance of parataxis, both at the level of syntax and that of larger narrative units—formulas, episodes, etc.

The noetic economy of oral narratives also tends to generate heroic figures, not for romantic or deliberately didactic reasons but for more basic ones. In the first place, outsized characters are more memorable than the "ordinary" individuals of literate texts, and this is, of course, an important consideration for cultures without texts. In addition to encouraging triumphalism this economy also prefers heroic "flat characters" because around them can be organized the most significant elements of the culture: in fact these characters serve as the emblems of the culture and can be used to manage all kinds of non-narrative elements embedded in the story. Psychic and social interiority, the "roundedness" of well-developed chirographic characters, is rarely a significant concern of these narratives. Since such narratives emblemize, through the heroic figure, the totality of the culture and since the formal features of such stories evoke the noetic structures of an oral universe, the very performance of an oral narrative is itself a profoundly totalizing act. As Ngal insists, such narratives incorporate and commune with the core of the culture and evoke a "sense of belonging to a common history." I think it might be more accurate to say that such narratives allow the narrator and the audience to (re)integrate themselves with the totality and the totalizing imperative of their culture. As Goody points out and as Ruth Finnegan's study illustrates, while the content of these narratives can vary widely, the formal characteristics invariably remain constant.

III

Chinua Achebe's style in *Things Fall Apart* is consonant with the oral culture that he represents. In fact, the congruence between the style, elements of the narrative structure, and characterization, on the one hand, and the nature of the culture represented, on the other, account for the success of the novel: because Achebe is able to capture the flavour of an oral society in his style and narrative organization, *Things Fall Apart* is able to represent successfully the specificity of a culture alien to most Western readers.

His sentence structure is on the whole paratactic; it achieves its effect largely through juxtaposition, addition, and aggregation. Consider the opening paragraph of the novel:

> Okonkwo was well known throughout the nine villages and even beyond. His fame rested on solid personal achievements. As a young man of eighteen he had brought honor to his village by throwing Amalinze the Cat. Amalinze was the great wrestler who for seven years was unbeaten, from Umuofia to Mbaino. He was called the Cat because his back would never touch the earth. It was this man that Okonkwo threw in a fight . . .

In spite of the glaring opportunities for consolidating the short, simple sentences and subordinating some of them as modifying clauses, thereby emphasizing the more important elements, Achebe refuses to do so precisely because syntactic subordination is more characteristic of chirographic representation than it is of oral speech. The desired effect of this parataxis, which, as we will see, is echoed in the narrative organization of the novel, is the creation of a flat surface: since one fact is not subordinated to another more important one, everything exists on the same plane and is equally important. Of course, as one proceeds through the novel one begins to see that all the details coalesce around the heroic figure of Okonkwo, but while reading any one paragraph or chapter the initial effect is one of equivalence. This style and its effects, it must be emphasized, are deliberate. As Achebe himself has shown by comparing a more abstract and hypotactic version of a paragraph from *Arrow of God* with the concrete and paratactic original, the former is inappropriate for the protagonist of the novel and his context. The deliberateness of this style is also emphasized by its contrast with passages of oratory at political gatherings, funerals, and other formal occasions when the language, though still paratactic, is characterized by greater rhetorical formality. For instance, Uchendu's avuncular advice to Okonkwo is not only very dramatic and punctuated effectively with rhetorical questions but is also tightly structured according to the demands of the logic of his argument.

The effect of parataxis, however, is modulated by the repetition of various kinds of details. Significant facts keep resurfacing like a leimotif: for example, Okonkwo's achievement of fame through wrestling is introduced in the first paragraph on page seven, then repeated again on pages eleven and twenty-nine, and finally the narrator devotes an entire chapter to the importance of this sport in Igbo culture. At times virtually identical statements are repeated. Chapter three begins with the following statement: "Okonkwo did not have the start in life which many young men usually had. He did not inherit a barn from his father. There was no barn to inherit." This is followed by a two-page depiction of his father's laziness, which ends with "With a father like Unoka, Okonkwo did not have the start in life which many young men had. He neither inherited a barn nor a tile, nor even a young wife." Playing against the flat surface of the paratactic prose, such repetitions create a sense of rhythm and valorize some facts above others. This does produce a kind of subordination, but the fact that these repetitions are embedded in a flat narrative surface implies that they must be understood in terms of the overall situation; without the context these facts lose their value. In this novel significance is a function of recurrence, not of logical analytic valorization. The importance of context is illustrated by the fact that meaning of complex concepts is defined by reference to concrete situations rather than abstract elaboration. Thus, for example, *efulefu,* a worthless individual, is defined as follows: "The imagery of an *efulefu* in the language of the clan was a man who sold his machete and wore the sheath to battle." Or the apparent contradiction between the two definitions of *chi* as they appear on pages twenty-nine and thirty-three is explained by the context, which makes it clear that the *chi* is in agreement with the self when one is in harmony with one-self and the entire culture but that it becomes antagonistic when one is alienated from self and society. Though repetition and contextual definition modify the flat surface of the narrative, they do not, as we shall see later, create a distinction between background and fore-ground. Rather their function is to create a series of patterns on that surface.

Elements of the narrative structure and organization repeat and amplify, on a different register, the same effects. Yet the narrative, like the style, is a product of a double consciousness, of a syncretic com-bination of chirographic and oral techniques. Just as the style repre-sents in writing the syntax and thought patterns of oral cultures, so the narrative operates on two levels: in its novelistic form the story of Okonkwo is unique and historical, yet it is told as if it were a well-known myth. The narrative acknowledges the latter fact in its open-ing sentence: "Okonkwo was well known throughout the nine villages and even beyond." The story of his poverty "was told in Umuofia," and that of Ikemefuna's sacrifice "is still told to this day." Similarly other aspects of this narrative manifest themselves as circulating oral tales, and the white colonizers first appear to the hero in the form of stories. The reader is left with an impression that these tales are loosely connected but that the narrator of *Things Fall Apart* will (re)stitch them in his own unique order. However, even though the "myth" about Okonkwo and his family is common knowledge it has to be told (and heard) as if for the first time. Thus, for example, after introducing the fact of Nwoye's apostasy and after depicting for sev-eral pages the first encounter between the Christian missionaries and the Igbos, Achebe returns to Nwoye's conversion with the following sentences: "But there was a young lad who had been captivated [by Christianity]. His name was Nwoye, Okonkwo's first son." This pre-sentation of the apostasy, the name of the character, and his parent-age as if for the first time is not due, we must assume, to narrative amnesia. Rather it is a part of the process of remembering in a pub-lic way, a product of returning, after a "digression" and in the absence of a text, to the facts. This technique of public remembrance, which seems to annoy many "literate" readers, accounts for the pervasive pattern wherein Achebe introduces a topic and then repeatedly returns to it in order to explain it piecemeal (see, for example, the series of reversions to the story of Ikemefuna until he is finally exe-cuted in chapter seven). Aspects of this pattern can be accounted for by the need to foreshadow, which is common to both chirographic and oral narratives. The overall effect of this pattern of postponements and reversions, of the juxtapositions of central themes and "digressions" is to create an interlocking mosaic of episodes out of which the significance of the story gradually emerges.

By proceeding through public remembrance the narrative makes ample use of periphrasis, which, according to Achebe, is a highly prized technique of Igbo conversation: "Among the Igbo the art of conversation is regarded very highly, and proverbs are the palm-oil with which words are eaten. Okoye was a great talker and he spoke for a long time, skirting round the subject and then hitting it finally." Like Okoye, the narrator skirts around his subject but carefully maintains certain ambiguities (which we shall examine later). The first chapter provides a good example of this narrative circularity. It covers the following subjects in that order: Okonkwo's fame, wrestling ability, personality, his father's character and indebtedness, Okonkwo's shame, his struggle for recognition and wealth, and his consequent custody of Ikemefuna, and the latter's destiny. In this spiral the chapter encapsulates the entire plot of part one of *Things Fall Apart*. The other twelve chapters of part one explore all of these issues in much greater detail, but not in the same order. In fact, the topics are thoroughly scrambled and a great deal of space is devoted to the depiction of the central events in the life of an agrarian community—planting, harvesting, etc., and the various festivals that accompany them—as well as rituals such as marriages, funerals, convening of the legal-spiritual court of the *egwugwu*, etc. Out of the one-hundred-and-eighteen pages that comprise part one of the novel only about eight are devoted, strictly speaking, to the development of the plot. The narrator is therefore anxious to represent the cultural "background" as much as the heroic figure, and in doing so he is able to depict the core of his culture and show that Okonkwo is one of its heroic representatives. Having thus depicted the interconnected totality of the culture and having established Okonkwo as its emblem in part one of the novel, the narrator, who in keeping with the already known narrative, is sensitively aware of the arrival of the destructive colonialists and their chirographic culture, changes the organization and the pace of the second and third parts of the novel: the plot now follows a more rigorous and increasingly urgent chronological and causal pattern until it ends suddenly with Okonkwo fixed as a minor detail in a minor book of a vast chirographic culture. The elaborate oral narrative that has been sustained throughout the novel is startlingly displaced by a causal, "objective" paragraph about Okonkwo in the District Officer's book.

However, the narrative principle that leads to this dramatic end is not causality but contiguity. As the outline of the first chapter illustrates, most often the narrative proceeds through association of subject matter. At times, however, the association focuses explicitly on a word, such as "household" which provides the link between the three parts of the second chapter. Achebe's studied avoidance of causality as an organizational principle is consonant with the epistemology of oral cultures, which have not developed their analytic capacities because they do not have access to literacy. The subsequent dependence of the plot on contiguity results in parataxis at the narrative level, which in turn reinforces the flat surface of the novel.

Nowhere is the decision to preserve this flatness, the refusal to emphasize the divisions between foreground and background, between the phenomenal and the numenal more apparent than in the narrator's management of the border between the secular and the sacred. In pure oral cultures such a distinction does not exist, but Achebe and his novel both exist in the margins of chirographic and oral cultures. The author is thus challenged with the unenviable task of ensuring that his characters do not seem foolish because they believe in the absence of that border while he is obliged to acknowledge it for the same reason. Achebe meets this challenge by endowing his characters and narrator with a double consciousness. At the beginning of the legal-spiritual court where *egwugwus* first appear, the narrator tells us that "Okonkwo's wives, and perhaps other women as well, might have noticed that the second *egwugwu* had the springy walk of Okonkwo. And they might also have noticed that Okonkwo was not among the titled men and elders who sat behind the row of *egwugwu*. But if they thought these things they kept them within themselves. The *egwugwu* with the springy walk was one of the dead fathers of the clan. He looked terrible. . . ." Thus the narrator demonstrates for us the double consciousness—the awareness of the border and its deep repression—of the characters, while admitting to the reader that Okonkwo is "dressed up" as an *egwugwu* and then proceeding to deny that admission (i.e., Okonkwo "*was* one of the dead fathers . . .", italics added). By maintaining a deliberate ambiguity, a double consciousness in keeping with the syncretism of a written narrative about an oral culture, the narrator refuses to emphasize either the chirographic/scientific or the oral/mythic viewpoint, thereby once again reinforcing the flat surface.

The same effect is obtained through the monotony of the narrative voice and the timeless aura of the story. The voice remains unchanged even when it is retelling a folktale recounted by one of the characters. The chronology is extremely vague; temporal locations are designated only by phases such as "many years ago," "years ago," "as old as the clan itself," "the worst year in living memory," and so on. The only specific periods in the novel are associated with ritual punishment: Ikemefuna's three years in Okonkwo's custody and

Okonkwo's seven years in exile. Otherwise the novel is as timeless as one with a historical setting (indicated most obviously by the arrival of English colonialists to this area, around 1905) can be: the narrative, as an aggregation of an already known, circulating stories, exist in seamless mythic time rather than segmented historical time.

Characterization too is a product of the oral aesthetic economy; it is, however, more clearly modified by the historicizing demands of the (chirographic) novelistic imperatives. As Bakhtin points out, in the historicizing move from the epic to the novel, it is "precisely the zone of contact with an inconclusive present (and consequently with the future) that creates the necessity of [the] incongruity of man with himself. There always remains in him unrealized potential and unrealized demands." Unlike the tragic or epic hero, who can be incarnated quite satisfactorily within the existing sociohistorical categories, the "individual" in the novel invariably raises the issue of his inadequacy to his fate and situation, and thereby calls into question the efficacy of the existing sociohistorical categories. The movement from the monochronic and totalized world of the epic to the historicized and dialogic world of the novel also leads to the disintegration of the individual in other ways: "A crucial tension develops between the external and the internal man, and as a result the subjectivity of the individual becomes an object of experimentation and representation. . . ." *Things Fall Apart* is delicately poised at the transition from the epic (oral) to the novel (chirographic). In keeping with its oral origins, Achebe's novel entirely lacks the tension between internal and external man. Although Okonkwo's repression of the "feminine" emotions and Nwoyo's revulsion towards the discarding of twins and the execution of Ikemefuna are so crucial to the plot and the meaning of the novel, Achebe never explores them as dense interiorities (as a contemporary western writer would have). Rather he stays on the flat surface and represents the emotions through concrete metaphors. Consider, for example, Okonkwo's "meditation" of his son's apostasy. As he contemplates the incredulity of his son's action, Okonkwo, whose nickname is "Roaring Flame," gazes into the fire in his hut. The narrator finally presents the results of the ruminations as follows: "[Okonkwo] sighed heavily, and as if in sympathy the smoldering log also sighed. And immediately Okonkwo's eyes were opened and he saw the whole matter clearly. Living fire begets cold, impotent ash. He sighed again, deeply." From our viewpoint, the crucial aspect of this procedure is that Achebe chooses to represent interiority only through its concrete, material manifestation or reflection. Similarly, Nwoye's revulsion is represented through metaphors of physical sensation: when confronted with Ikemefuna's death "something seemed to give way inside him, like the snapping of a tightened bow." Thus, unlike Wole Soyinka's

The Interpreters, Things Fall Apart refuses to "experiment" with the representation of subjectivity in a way that is familiar to contemporary Western readers.

However, the externality of representation does not mean that Okonkwo lacks subjectivity. The reader is made fully aware of the pride and anger with which the hero attempts to mask his shame and fear. In fact, the narrative focuses on the binary relationship of these emotions to the point where other aspects of the hero's psyche are ignored. Thus in keeping with the tradition of oral narrative Okonkwo remains a relatively flat character, whose efficacy must be judged not according to the criteria of some vague realistic notion of "rounded-ness" but rather in terms of his twofold narrative function. First, he is an emblem of his culture. Through his mundane preoccupations and tribulations—his involvement in harvesting, planting, building houses, weddings, funerals, legal and spiritual rituals, etc.—we are allowed to penetrate the interiority of the Igbo culture before the arrival of British colonizers. Consequently when he commits suicide—which not only cuts him off from his ancestors but which is also the product of a complicated alienation from the principle of the conti-nuity of ancestral lineage (he rejects his father, kills his foster son, and drives away his real son)—his death leaves us with the feeling of massive cultural destruction, of an end of traditional Igbo culture. His second, ideological function is tied to the first; his shame and pride are also emblematic: the former represents the shame produced among the colonized by the colonizers' rhetoric about savagery and the latter reflects the resurgence in the African's pride in the moral efficacy of his culture as he understands it. For if Achebe introduces us to traditional Igbo culture through Okonkwo, he is doing so in order to show that it was civilized and, by extension, that the colo-nized individual need not be ashamed of his past. Yet in the process of using Okonkwo as an emblem Achebe also accedes to novelistic pressures. The transformation of Okonkwo from a heroic figure to an insignificant detail in a paragraph about savage custom is clearly a deflationary movement that raises questions about his potentiality and his adequacy to his situation. The novel is content neither with leaving Okonkwo as a completely stylized heroic figure nor with the impulse to idealize traditional Igbo culture. The reflexivity of the novel manifests itself through the dialogic relation between Okonkwo and his friend Obierika. While the former, driven by his fear, voices a simplified version of his culture's values, the latter voices its doubts. Obierika briefly but significantly questions general practices such as the discarding of twins and Okonkwo's participation in the execution of Ikemefuna, and at the end of the novel he is left contemplating the transition of Okonkwo from hero to pariah. Similarly, Nwoye's apos-tasy opens up another horizon: by espousing the new chirographic culture he creates the potential for one of his descendents to write a novel like *Things Fall Apart*.

Achebe's first novel, then, can be seen as a unique totalizing and syncretic achievement. Its totalizing ability is most clearly visible in its syncretism. While rescuing oral cultures from their inevitable transitoriness, writing also alienates the objects as well as the unreflexive (or rather less reflexive) subject of that world by allowing one to examine them at a distance. In turn the fixity, distance, and scrutiny permitted by writing facilitate greater familiarity with and understanding of self and the world. This dialectic of distance and proximity, of alienation and understanding is inevitably involved in the configuration of Achebe's novel. *Things Fall Apart* documents, among other things, the destruction of oral culture by a chirographic one. However, Achebe uses that very process of chirographic documentation in order to recreate and preserve a symbolic version of the destroyed culture; in recording the oral culture's preoccupation with the present, Achebe historicizes its evanescence. The novel incorporates its own condition and occasion into itself. However, the most fascinating aspect of this totalization is that while *Things Fall Apart* depicts the mutual misunderstanding and antagonism of the colonizing and colonized worlds, the very process of this depiction, in its capacity as a *written oral* narrative, transcends the manichean relations by a brilliant synthesis of oral and chirographic cultures. By deliberately adhering to a flat surface Achebe obtains a result curiously similar to the effect obtained by one of Picasso's paintings: the illusion of depth and perspective, of the third dimension in symbolic representation, is deliberately wrenched and displaced in order to create a two-dimensional representation that includes within it an abstract reminder about the third dimension. While Picasso drew his inspiration from West African art, Achebe draws his from West European fiction. Like Picasso's paintings, Achebe's novel presents us with sophisticated primitivism, with a deliberate return to an innocence re-presented.

IV

The syncretism of Achebe's fiction, most clearly evident in *Things Fall Apart* and *Arrow of God*, has two important ideological consequences. As we saw at the beginning of this essay, the Third World writer uses European languages because of certain ideological and technological pressures. In Achebe's case there is an additional compulsion to write about his culture in English because not to do so would leave the definition and representation of his society at the mercy of (usually) racist colonial writers. However, under these constraints he uses English in a way that deterritorializes it. By deliberately simplifying and willing a certain kind of poverty he pushes the English language to its limits: the rhythm of the endless paratactic sentences negates the diversity and complexity of which the language is capable. The deliberate simplicity is combined with a dryness and sobriety of voice to create a new register. Achebe develops a mythic voice that can evoke sympathy and concern while remaining entirely neutral. This neutral, mythic voice, which is entirely new in modern English literature, is able to recuperate a vanishing cultural experience without lapsing into sentimentality or spitefulness. In addition to this innovative deterritorialization, Achebe is able to expand the English language through the transfusion of Igbo material. For example, the transliterated proverbs reintroduce into the language a kind of figurative, analogical element that has gradually been displaced by the scientific-empiric consciousness that favours precision based on literalness. Finally, as we have seen, Achebe also expands the form of the novel through his sophisticated primitivism. Thus we must conclude that *Things Fall Apart* is able to do justice to the phenomenology of oral cultures and that by deterritorializing the English language and the novelistic form, Achebe's novel also contributes to the negative dialogic relations between African and English literatures. Achebe takes the English language and the novelistic form and creates a unique African form with them. Of course, this does not mean that African fiction cannot be written in African languages, but it also does not mean that English can be excluded as a language of African fiction on purely ideological grounds.

The second ideological implication of the syncretism is a less happy one. Both the synthesis of oral and chirographic cultures enacted by the form of *Things Fall Apart* and its deterritorialization of English contradict the substance of the novel and thereby reveal the major ideological implication embedded in the contradiction. The content creates a longing for a vanished heroic culture, but the linguistic and cultural syntheses within the form of the novel point to future syncretic possibilities. While the content laments a loss and points an accusing finger at colonialist destruction, the form glories in the pleasures of a new formal synthesis and transcends the manichean antagonisms of the colonizer and the colonized. Thus while the initial layer of the emotive intentionality coincides with the traditional ideology of colonized resentment and bitterness and reveals the ideological bondage of the colonized man who is caught between historical catalepsy and cultural petrification, the deeper layer of emotive intentionality which finds pleasure in linguistic and formal syncretism implies a freedom from that ideological double-bind. Achebe's long silence in the field of fiction is probably due to his preoccupation with catalepsy and petrification and perhaps to the ideological pressure to discard the use of English as creative medium.

Chinua Achebe: A Chronology

1914	Amalgamation by Lord Lugard of northern and southern territories to form the colonial state of Nigeria
1914–18	First World War
1929	Aba Women's Revolt and beginning of resistance to British Administration in eastern Nigeria.
1930	Birth of Chinualumogu at Ogidi to Isiah and Janet Achebe; baptized as Albert.
1935–44	Attends the local elementary school.
1944–48	Attends Government College, Umuahia, a prestigious high school modeled on the British public (private) school system.
1948–53	Educated at University College, Ibadan, affiliated with London University; later to become the University of Ibadan. Enrolls in Medicine but switches to Arts after the first year; subjects include English, Latin, and History. Graduates 1953.
1954	Joins the Nigerian Broadcasting Corporation as producer, Talks Department.
1956	Sent on training program with BBC in London; first of several visits to the United Kingdom and Europe.
1958	*Things Fall Apart* published by Heinemann; the novel wins the Margaret Wrong Prize the following year.
1960	Nigerian independence on October 1. Tafawa Balewa installed as prime minister. Publication of *No Longer at Ease*. Achebe awarded the Nigerian National Trophy for Literature.
1961	Marriage to Christie Chinwe Okoli, former fellow student at Ibadan.
1962	Publication of *The Sacrificial Egg and Other Stories* at Enugu. Achebe becomes the founding editor of the Heinemann African Writers Series.
1963	Nigeria is declared a republic, with veteran nationalist Nnamdi Azikiwe as ceremonial president.
1964	Publication of *Arrow of God*. Wins the Jock Campbell *New Statesman* Award. Achebe appointed director, External Service, of the NBC (Radio Nigeria).

1966   Publication of *A Man of the People*, which appears a week before a military coup led by Major Nzeogwu. Major General Johnson T. U. Aguyi-Ironsi takes over as head of the government in January. General unrest in the country, marked by massacres of Igbos in northern Nigeria. In July, assassination of Ironsi in a counter coup by Hausa officers; Lieutenant Colonel Yakubu Gowon emerges as military leader. Massacres of Igbo in the North continues, and amid a state of insecurity in the country, Achebe is obliged to leave Lagos for eastern Nigeria.

1967   Secession of eastern region and declaration of Biafra as an independent state on May 30. Beginning of the Nigerian civil war. Poet Christopher Okigbo is killed in first few months of the war. Achebe serves in the Ministry of Information of the dissident republic.

1970   Rendition of Biafra on January 15 marks formal end of the civil war. Achebe appointed Senior Research Fellow in Literature at the University of Nigeria, Nsukka.

1971   Founds *Okike: An African Journal of New Writing*. Publication of poetry collection, *Beware, Soul Brother*.

1972   *Girls at War and Other Stories* published. Achebe receives the Commonwealth Prize for *Beware, Soul Brother*.

1972   Visiting Professor of Literature at the University of Massachusetts, Amherst, where he delivers the lecture "An Image of Africa," later published in *The Massachusetts Review*.

1975   *Morning Yet on Creation Day* (essays) published. In Nigeria, Gowon is toppled in a coup led by General Murtala Muhammed and goes into exile in Britain.

1975–76   Visiting Professor of Literature at the University of Connecticut, Storrs.

1976   General Muhammed assassinated and is succeeded by General Olusegun Obasanjo as head of the military government. Achebe appointed Professor of Literature at the University of Nigeria, Nsukka.

1979   Return to civilian rule in Nigeria under a new constitution. Alhaji Shehu Shagari elected executive president. Achebe receives the Nigerian National Merit Award and the Order of the Federal Republic. Becomes first chairman of the Association of Nigerian Authors. In April, meets James Baldwin at the annual conference of the African Literature Association in Gainesville, Florida.

1982   *Aka Weta* (a volume of Igbo-language verse), edited by Achebe and Obiora Udechukwu.

1983   Elected deputy president, People's Redemption Party; publishes the pamphlet *The Trouble with Nigeria*. Shagari re-elected but deposed by a military coup a few months later. Death of Mallam Aminu Kano, leader of the People's Redemption Party. Military coup on December 31: General Buhari and General Idiagbon appointed joint heads of new military government.

1985   Buhari and Idiagbon deposed in a coup led by Major-General Ibrahim Babangida.

1986   Achebe elected pro-vice-chancellor of the State University of Anambra in Enugu.

1987   Publication of *Anthills of the Savannah*. Visiting fellow, University of Massachusetts, Amherst.

1988   Publication of *Hopes and Impediments* (essays).

1989   Distinguished Visiting Professor at the City College of New York.

1990   Celebration of Achebe's sixtieth birthday at Nsukka. On his journey back to Lagos, Achebe badly hurt in car accident. Achebe accepts a position as Charles P. Stevenson Professor of Literature at Bard College in upstate New York.

1993   In Nigeria, presidential elections in preparation for return to civilian rule. Moshood Abiola declared winner, but results cancelled by Babangida. A joint civilian-military government is formed, but is overthrown six months later by Sanni Abacha.

1995   Ken Saro-Wiwa executed amid growing domestic tensions in Nigeria.

1998   Death of Abacha and return to civilian rule with Obasanjo as president.

1999   Returns to Nigeria after nine years in the United States, at Bard College. Delivers Odenigbo Lecture in Owerri, Imo State. Visit turns into a local and international media event.

2000   Publishes *Home and Exile*, based on the MacMillan-Stewart lectures delivered at Harvard University in 1999. Seventieth birthday marked by conference at Bard College, attended by an international roster of scholars and writers, including Toni Morrison, Wole Soyinka, Ali Mazrui, Nurrudin Farah, Ngugi Wa Thiong'o, Sonia Sanchez, John Ashbery, Don Burness, and a live video feed from Nelson Mandela. Jimmy Carter, Kofi Annan, and Nadine Gordimer send letters of felicitations.

2001   Receives honorary degree from Haverford College, Pennsylvania.

2002   Travels to South Africa for the first time at the invitation of Steve Biko Foundation to deliver the twenty-fifth anniversary Lecture of Steve Bantu Biko. In attendance are University of Cape Town officials, South African government dignitaries, and Nelson Mandela, former president of South Africa, with his wife, Gracia Machel. Receives Honorary Degree from University of Cape Town.

Receives the prestigious *Friedenspreis des Deutschen Buchhandels*. (The Peace Prize of the German Book trade).

2004   Publishes *Collected Poems* (Anchor Books).

2005   Visits United Kingdom for Africa '05. Holds conversation with Caryl Phillips at the South Bank Centre, London. BBC chooses *Things Fall Apart* as part of the Africa Lives reading series.

2006   Receives honorary degree from Usman Dan Fodio University, Sokoto, Nigeria.

Receives honorary degree from the University of Toronto. This is Achebe's fortieth honorary degree.

2007   Receives the ManBooker International Prize for lifetime achievement. Delivers keynote address at a conference in memory of Christopher Okigbo at the University of Massachusetts, Boston.

2008   Fiftieth Anniversary of the publication of *Things Fall Apart*. Thirty-eight conferences and events planned in countries all over the world.

Announced: A collection of seventeen autobiographical essays called *Reflections of a British Protected Child*, to be published before the end of the year.

Selected Bibliography

• indicates a work included or excerpted in this Norton Critical Edition

WORKS BY CHINUA ACHEBE

Novels

Things Fall Apart. 1956. New York: Anchor Books, 1994.
No Longer at Ease. 1960. New York: Anchor-Doubleday, 1994.
Arrow of God. 1964. New York: Anchor-Doubleday, 1989.
A Man of the People. 1966. New York: Anchor-Doubleday, 1990.
Anthills of the Savannah. 1987. New York: Doubleday, 1988.
The African Trilogy: Things Fall Apart, No Longer At Ease, Arrow of God. London: Pan Books, 1988.

Short Stories

The Sacrificial Egg and Other Stories. Onitsha, Nigeria: Etudo, 1953.
Girls at War and Other Stories. New York: Anchor/Doubleday, 1973.

Poetry

Christmas in Biafra and Other Poems. Enugu: Nwankwo, 1971.
Collected Poems: New and Other Poems. New York: Anchor, 2004.

Children's Fiction

How the Leopard Got His Claws. Cambridge: Cambridge University Press, 1966.
The Flute. New York: Third Press, 1973.
The Drum: A Children's Story. Enugu: Fourth Dimension, 1977.

Essays And Nonfiction

• *Morning Yet on Creation Day: Essays.* London: Heinemann, 1975.
The Trouble with Nigeria. Enugu: Fourth Dimension, 1983.
The World of the Ogbanje. Enugu: Fourth Dimension, 1986.
• *Hopes and Impediments: Selected Essays, 1965–1987.* London: Heinemann, 1988.
The University and the Leadership Factor in Nigerian Politics: Strategies for Nigerian Development. Enugu: Abic, 1988.
Beyond Hunger in Africa: Conventional Wisdom and an African Vision. London: Heinemann, 1990.
"African Literature as Restoration of Celebration." *Chinua Achebe: A Celebration.* Ed. Kirsten Holst Petersen and Anna Rutherford. Oxford; Portsmouth, NH: Heinemann, 1991. 1–10.
• With Robert Lyons. *Another Africa.* New York: Anchor, 1998.
Home and Exile. New York: Oxford University Press, 2000.

591

Journal Articles (Selected)

"English and the African Writer." *Transition* 4.18 (1965): 27–30.
"The Black Writer's Burden." *Présence Africaine* 59 (1966): 135–40.
"Culture and International Understanding." *Daily Times* (Lagos) 22 May 1971: 7.
"This Earth, My Brother." *Transition* 41 (1972): 69–70.
"The Bane of Union: An Appraisal of the Consequences of Union Igbo for Igbo Language and Literature." *Anu Magazine* 1 (1979): 33–41.
"Metaphor of the Rain and the Clock." *Daily Times* (Lagos) 10 Nov. 1979: 7.
"The Uses of African Literature." *Okike* 15 (1979): 8–17.
"Why Writers Need an Association." *West Africa* 3339 (27 July 1981): 1692–194.
"The Okike Story." *Okike* 21 (July 1982): 1–5.
"Africa Is People." *Massachusetts Review* 40.3 (1999): 313–21.
"The Day I Finally Met Baldwin." *Callaloo* 25.2 (Spring 2002): 502–4.

Edited Collections

The Insider: Stories of War and Peace from Nigeria. Enugu: Nwankwo-Ifejika, 1971.
With Dubem Okafor. *Don't Let Him Die: An Anthology of Memorial Poems for Christopher Okigbo.* Enugu: Fourth Dimension, 1978.
With C. L. Innes. *African Short Stories.* Portsmouth, NH: Heinemann, 1985.
With C. L. Innes. *The Heinemann Book of Contemporary African Short Stories.* Portsmouth, NH: Heinemann, 1992.

Interviews

Achebe, Chinua, and Nuruddin, Farah. "Chinua Achebe with Nuruddin Farah: Writers in Conversation." *Guardian Conversations.* London: ICA, 1986.
Baker, Rob, and Ellen Draper. "'If One Thing Stands, Another Will Stand Beside It': An Interview with Chinua Achebe." *Parabola* 17.3 (Fall 1992): 19–28.
Brooks, Jerome. "The Art of Fiction." The *Paris Review* 133 (Winter 1994): 142–67.
• Lindfors, Bernth, ed. *Conversations with Chinua Achebe.* Jackson: University Press of Mississippi, 1997.
Samway, Patrick H. "An Interview with Chinua Achebe." *America* 22 June 1991: 684–87.
• Serumaga, Robert. "Interview [with Chinua Achebe]." *African Writers Talking: A Collection of Interviews* Ed. Dennis Duerden and Cosmo Pieterse. London: Heinemann, 1972.

CRITICISM AND SECONDARY SOURCES

On Things Fall Apart

Aji, Aron. "Ezinma: The Ogbanje Child in Achebe's *Things Fall Apart.*" *College Literature* 19.3–20.1 (1992): 170–75.
Appiah, Kwame Anthony. Introduction to *Things Fall Apart.* Everyman Edition. New York: Everyman's Library, Alfred A. Knopf, 1992. Ix–xvii.
Azodo, Ada Uzoamaka. "Masculinity, Power and Language in Chinua Achebe's *Things Fall Apart.*" *Emerging Perspectives on Chinua Achebe.* Vol. 1. Ed. Ernest N. Emenyonu. Trenton, NJ; Asmara, Eritrea: African World Press, 2004. 49–65.
Begam, Richard. "Achebe's Sense of an Ending: History and Tragedy in *Things Fall Apart.*" *Studies in the Novel* 29.3 (Fall 1997): 396–411.
• Cobham, Rhonda. "Problems of Gender and History in the Teaching of *Things Fall Apart.*" *Chinua Achebe's* Things Fall Apart: *Modern Critical Interpretations.* Ed. Harold Bloom. Philadelphia: Chelsea House, 2001.

Criswell, Stephen. "Okonkwo as Yeatsian Hero: The Influence of W. B. Yeats on Chinua Achebe's *Things Fall Apart.*" *Literary Criteria* II 30.4 (1995): 1–14.

Gikandi, Simon. "Chinua Achebe and the Invention of African Culture." *Research in African Literatures* 32.3 (2001): 3–9.

Heywood, Christopher. "Surface and Symbol in *Things Fall Apart.*" *Journal of the Nigerian English Studies Association* 2 (November 1967): 41–47.

Hoegberg, David. "Principle and Practice: The Logic of Cultural Violence in Achebe's *Things Fall Apart.*" *College Literature* 26.1 (1999): 69–80.

• Irele, F. Abiola. "The Crisis of Cultural Memory in Chinua Achebe's *Things Fall Apart.*" Chap. 7. *The African Imagination.* New York: Oxford University Press, 2001. 115–53.

• Iyasere, Solomon O. *Understanding Things Fall Apart: Selected Essays and Criticism.* New York: Whitston, 1998.

• JanMohamed, Abdul. "Sophisticated Primitivism: The Syncretism of Oral and Literate Modes in Achebe's *Things Fall Apart.*" *Ariel* 15.4 (1984): 19–39.

Jeyifo, Biodun. "Okonkwo and His Mother: *Things Fall Apart* and Issues of Gender in the Constitution of African Postcolonial Discourse." *Callaloo* 16.4 (1993): 847–58.

• ———. "For Chinua Achebe: The Resilience and the Predicament of Obierika." *Chinua Achebe: A Celebration.* Ed. Kristen Holst Peterson and Anna Rutherford. Oxford; Portsmouth, NH: Heinemann, 1990. 51–70.

Kortenaar, Neil ten. "Becoming African and the Death of Ikemefuna." *University of Toronto Quarterly* 73.2 (2004): 773–94.

• ———. "Chinua Achebe and the Question of Modern African Tragedy." *Philosophia Africana* 9.2 (2006): 83–100.

———. "How the Centre is Made to Hold in *Things Fall Apart.*" *Postcolonial Literatures: Achebe, Ngugi, Desai, Walcott.* Ed. Michael Parker and Roger Starkey. Basingstoke: Macmillan, 1995. 319–36.

Lindfors, Bernth. "Achebe at Home and Abroad: Situating *Things Fall Apart.*" *Literary Griot* 10.2 (1998): 10–16.

———. ed. *Approaches to Teaching Achebe's* Things Fall Apart. New York: The Modern Language Association, 1991.

MacKenzie, Clayton G. "The Metamorphosis of Piety in Chinua Achebe's *Things Fall Apart.*" *Research in African Literatures* 27.2 (1996): 128–39.

• McCarthy, Eugene B. "Rhythm and Narrative Method in Achebe's *Things Fall Apart.*" *Novel* 18.3 (1985): 243–56.

McLaren, Joseph. "Missionaries and Converts: Religion and Colonial Intrusion in *Things Fall Apart.*" *Literary Griot* 10.2 (1998): 48–60.

• Obiechina, Emmanuel. "Following the Author in *Things Fall Apart.*" *Approaches to Teaching Achebe's* Things Fall Apart. Ed. Bernth Lindfors. New York: Modern Language Association, 1991. 31–39.

Ogbaa, Kalu. *Understanding* Things Fall Apart: *A Student Casebook to Issues, Sources, and Historical Documents.* Westport, CT: Greenwood, 1999.

Ogede, Ode. *Achebe's* Things Fall Apart. *A Reader's Guide.* London: Continuum, 2007.

Okpewho, Isidore. *Chinua Achebe's* Things Fall Apart. *A Casebook.* New York; Oxford: Oxford University Press, 2003.

Osei-Nyame, Kwadwo. "Chinua Achebe Writing Culture: Representations of Gender and Tradition in *Things Fall Apart.*" *Research in African Literatures* 30.2 (1999): 148–64.

• Quayson, Ato. "Realism, Criticism and the Disguises of Both: A Reading of Chinua Achebe's *Things Fall Apart.*" *Research in African Literatures* 25.4 (Winter 1994): 117–36.

Robertson, P. M. "*Things Fall Apart* and *Heart of Darkness:* A Creative Dialogue." *International Fiction Review* 7.2 (1980): 106–12.

• Snead, James. "European Pedigrees/African Contagions: Nationality, Narrative and Community in Tutuola, Achebe and Reed." *Nation and Narration.* Ed. Homi K. Bhabha. London: Routledge, 1990. 231–49.

Stock, A. G. "Yeats and Achebe." *Journal of Commonwealth Literature* 5 (1968): 105–11.

Traore, Ousseynou B. ed. *Discourse on Iroko: 40th Anniversary Symposium on Things Fall Apart. Literary Griot* (Special Issue) 10.2 (1998).

Turkington, Kate. *Chinua Achebe: Things Fall Apart.* London: Arnold, 1977.

General

Alabi, Victoria A. "Mother is Supreme": A Semiotic Reading of Motherhood and Womanhood in Three Novels of Achebe." *Emerging Perspectives on Chinua Achebe.* Vol. 2. Ed. Ernest N. Emenyonu and Iniobong I. Uko. Trenton, NJ; Asmara, Eritrea: African World Press, 2004. 385–93.

Anozie, Sunday. *Sociologie du roman africain.* Paris: Aubier-Momtaigne, 1970.

Booker, Keith. *The African Novel in English. An Introduction.* Portsmouth, NH: Heinemann, 1998.

Ulli Beier, ed. *An Introduction to African Literature.* London: Longman, 1967.

Booth, James. *Writers and Politics in Nigeria.* New York: Africana Publishing, 1981.

• Carroll, David. *Chinua Achebe: Novelist, Poet, Critic.* Basingstoke: Macmillan, 1990.

Cobham, Rhonda. "Making Men and History: Achebe and the Politics of Revisionism." *Approaches to Teaching Achebe's* Things Fall Apart. Ed. Bernth Lindfors. New York: The Modern Language Association of America, 1991. 91–100.

Douthwaite, John. "The Art of the Word in Achebe." *Emerging Perspectives on Chinua Achebe.* Vol. 2. Ed. Ernest N. Emenyonu and Iniobong I. Uko. Trenton: Africa World Press, 2004. 3–32.

Egudu, R. N. "Achebe and the Igbo Narrative Tradition." *Research in African Literatures.* 12.1 (1981): 43–54.

Ekwe-Ekwe, Herbert. *African Literature in Defence of History: An Essay on Chinua Achebe.* Dakar: African Renaissance, 2001.

Emenyonu, Ernest N., ed. *Emerging Perspectives on Chinua Achebe.* Vol. 1. *Omenka. The Master Artist.* Trenton, NJ: Africa World Press, 2004.

Emenyonu, Ernest N., and Iniobong I. Uko, eds. *Emerging Perspectives on Chinua Achebe.* Vol. 2. *Isinka. The Artistic Purpose. Chinua Achebe and the Theory of African Literature.* Trenton, NJ: Africa World Press, 2004.

Ezenwa-Ohaeto. *Chinua Achebe: A Biography.* Oxford: James Currey, 1997.

Gakwandi, Arthur. *The Novel and Contemporary Experience in Africa.* London: Heinemann, 1977.

Gates, Henry L., and Appiah, K. A., eds. *Chinua Achebe: Critical Perspectives Past and Present.* New York: Amistad, 1997.

Gikandi, Simon. "Chinua Achebe and the Invention of African Literature." *Research in African Literatures* 32.3 (2001): 3–9.

———. *Reading Chinua Achebe: Language and Ideology in Fiction.* Oxford: James Currey, 1991.

• Graff, Gerald. "The Vanishing Classics and Other Myths." *Beyond the Culture Wars: How Teaching the Conflicts Can Revitalize American Education.* New York: Norton, 1992.

Griffiths, Gareth. "Language and Action in the Novels of Chinua Achebe." *African Literature Today* 5 (1971): 88–105.

Griswold, Wendy. *Bearing Witness: Readers, Writers and the Novel in Nigeria.* Princeton, NJ: Princeton University Press, 2000.

Ihekweazu, Edith, ed. *Eagle on Iroko: Selected Papers from the Chinua Achebe International Symposium 1990.* Ibadan: Heinemann Educational Books, 1996.

• Innes, C. L. *Chinua Achebe.* Cambridge: Cambridge University Press, 1990.

Innes, C. L., and Bernth Lindfors, eds. *Critical Perspectives on Chinua Achebe.* Washington: Three Continents, 1978.

Irele, F. Abiola. "The Tragic Conflict in the Novels of Chinua Achebe." *Black Orpheus* (Ibadan) 1.17 (1965) Repr. in Beier, 167–78; and Innes and Lindfors, 10–21.
• JanMohamed, Abdul. "Sophisticated Primitivism: Syncretism of Oral and Literate Modes in Achebe's *Things Fall Apart*." *Ariel* 15.4 (1984): 19–39.
Izevbaye, Dan S. "West African literature in English: beginnings to the midseventies." *The Cambridge History of African and Caribbean Literature.* Vol. 2 Ed. F. Abiola Irele and Simon Gikandi. New York: Cambridge University Press, 2004. 472–503.
Jeyifo, Biodun. "An African Cultural Modernity: Achebe, Fanon, Cabral and the Philosophy of Decolonization." *Democracy and Socialism.* 21.3 (November 2007): 125–41.
Khayyoom, S. A. *Chinua Achebe: A Study of His Novels.* London: Sangam, 1999.
Kalu, Anthonia C. "Achebe and Duality in Igbo Thought." *Chinua Achebe's Things Fall Apart: Modern Critical Interpretations* Ed. Harold Bloom. Philadelphia: Chelsea House, 2001. 57–70.
Killam, G. D. *The Writings of Chinua Achebe.* London: Heinemann, 1977.
• Kortenaar, Neil ten. "Chinua Achebe and the Question of Modern African Tragedy." *Philosophia Africana* 9.2 (August 2006): 83–100.
Larson, Charles. *The Emergence of African Fiction.* London: Macmillan, 1978.
• Lindfors, Bernth. "The Palm-Oil With Which Achebe's Words are Eaten." *Critical Perspectives on Chinua Achebe*, Ed. C. L. Innes and Bernth Lindfors. Washington: Three Continents, 1978. 47–66.
Livingston, Robert Eric. "Discourses of Empire." *African and Caribbean Literature.* Vol. 1. Ed. F. Abiola Irele and Simon Gikandi. New York: Cambridge University Press, 2004. 255–88.
• McCarthy, Eugene B. "Rhythm and Narrative Method in Achebe's *Things Fall Apart.*" *Novel* 18.3 (1985): 243–356.
Morrison, Jago. *The Fiction of Chinua Achebe: A Reader's Guide to Essential Criticism.* New York: Palgrave Macmillan, 2007.
Moses, Michael Valdez. *The Novel and the Globalization of Culture.* New York: Oxford University Press, 1995.
Muoneke, Romanus Okey. *Art, Rebellion and Redemption: A Reading of the Novels of Chinua Achebe.* New York: Peter Lang, 1994.
Newell, Stephanie. *West African Literatures.* Oxford: Oxford University Press, 2006.
Njoku, Benedict Chiaka. *The Four Novels of Chinua Achebe: A Critical Study.* New York: Peter Lang, 1984.
Nnolim, Charles E. "The Form and Function of the Folk Tradition in Achebe's Novels." *Ariel* 14.1 (1983): 35–47.
Obiechina, Emmanuel. *Culture, Tradition and Society in the West African Novel.* Cambridge: Cambridge University Press, 1975.
———. "Narrative Proverbs in the African Novel." *Research in African Literatures.* 24.4 (1993): 123–40.
Obumselu, Ben. "African Eden: Cultural Nationalism in the African Novel." *Ibadan Studies in English* 1 (June 1970): 1–35.
Ogbaa, Kalu. *Gods, Oracles and Divination: Folkways in Chinua Achebe's Novels.* Trenton, NJ: Africa World Press, 1992.
Ogede, Ode. *Achebe and the Politics of Representation.* Trenton, NJ: Africa World Press, 2001.
Ogu, Julius N. "The Concept of Madness in Chinua Achebe's Writings." *Journal of Commonwealth Literature* 18 (1983): 48–54.
• Ohadike, Don C. "Igbo Culture and History." *Chinua Achebe: Things Fall Apart: Classics in Context.* Portsmouth, NH: Heinemann, 1996. xix–xlix.
Ojinmah, Umelo. *Chinua Achebe: New Perspectives.* Ibadan: Spectrum, 1991.
Okechukwu, Chinwe. *Achebe the Orator: The Art of Persuasion in Chinua Achebe's Novels.* Westport, CT: Greenwood, 2004.

- Okere, Augustine C. "Achebe and Christianity." *Emerging Perspectives on Chinua Achebe.* Vol. 2. Ed. Ernest N. Emenyonu and Iniobong I. Uko. Trenton: Africa World Press, 2004. 115–33.
- Olney, James. "The African Novel in Transition: Chinua Achebe." *South Atlantic Quarterly* 70 (1970): 299–316.

  Omotoso, Kole. *Achebe or Soyinka? A Study in Contrasts.* London: Hans Zell, 1996.

  Owusu, Kofi. "The Politics of Interpretation: The Novels of Chinua Achebe." *Modern Fiction Studies* 37.3 (1991): 459–71.
- Palmer, Eustace. *An Introduction to the African Novel.* London: Heinemann, 1972.
- Pandurang, Mala. "Chinua Achebe and the 'African Experience': A Socio-Literary Perspective." *Chinua Achebe: An Anthology of Recent Criticism.* Ed. Mala Pandurang. Delhi: Pencraft International, 2006. 13–25.
- Phillips, Caryl. "Was Joseph Conrad Really a Racist?" *Philosophia Africana* 10.1 (2007): 59–66.

  Ravenscroft, Arthur. *Chinua Achebe.* Harlow: Longman, 1977.

  Reddy, K. Indrasena. *The Novels of Achebe and Ngugi: A Study in the Dialectics of Commitment.* New Delhi: Prestige, 1994.

  Rutherford, A., and K. H. Peterson, eds. *Chinua Achebe: A Celebration.* London: Heinemann, 1991.

  Scafe, Suzanne. "Wherever Something Stands, Something Else Will Stand Beside It": Ambivalence in Achebe's *Things Fall Apart* and *Arrow of God." Changing English: Studies in Reading & Culture* 9.2 (2002): 119–32.

  Simola, Raisa. *World Views in Chinua Achebe's Works.* Frankfurt am Main: Peter Lang, 1995.
- Snead, James. "European Pedigrees/African Contagians: Nationality, Narrative, and Communality in Tutuola, Achebe, and Reed." *Nation and Narration.* Ed. Homi K. Bhabha. New York: Routledge, 1990. 231–49.
- Stock, A. G. "Yeats and Achebe." *Journal of Commonwealth Literature* 5 (1968): 105–11.

  Stratton, Florence. *Contemporary African Literature and the Politics of Gender.* London: Routledge, 1994.
- Taiwo, Oladele. *Culture and the Nigerian Novel.* New York: St. Martin's Press, 1976.

  Turner, Margaret E. "Achebe, Hegel and the New Colonialism." *Chinua Achebe: A Celebration* Ed. Kristen Holst Petersen and Anna Rutherford. Portsmouth, NH: Heinemann, 1991. 31–40.

  Ugah, Ada. *In the Beginning: Chinua Achebe at Work.* Ibadan: Heinemann, 1990.

  Wren, Robert M. *"Things Fall Apart* in Its Time and Place." *Approaches to Teaching Achebe's Things Fall Apart* Ed. Bernth Lindfors. New York: The Modern Language Association, 1991. 38–44.

  Yousaf, Nahem. *Chinua Achebe.* Tavistock: Northcote House, 2003.

  Zabus, Chantal. "The Logos Eaters: The Igbo Ethno-Text." *Chinua Achebe: A Celebration.* Ed. 19–30.

  Zachernuk, Philip. *Colonial Subjects: An African Intelligentsia and Atlantic Ideas.* Charlottesville, VA: University Press of Virginia, 2000.

Background

Afigbo, Adiele. *Ropes of Sand: Studies in Igbo History and Culture.* Ibadan: Oxford University Press, 1981.

Ajayi, J. F. Ade. *Christian Missions in Nigeria.* London: Longman, 1965.

Anene, J. C. *Southern Nigeria in Transition, 1885–1906.* Cambridge: Cambridge University Press, 1966.

Basden. G. T. *Among the Ibos of Nigeria.* 1921. London: Frank Cass, 1966.

Crowther, Samuel Ajayi. *Journal of an Expedition up the Niger and Tshadda Rivers*. London: Church Missionary House, 1855.

Diké, K. Onwuka. *Trade and Politics in the Niger Delta, 1830–1885*. Oxford: Clarendon Press, 1956.

Isichei, Elizabeth. *A History of the Igbo People*. London: Macmillan, 1976.

Mockler-Ferryman, A. F. *Up the Niger*. London: George Philip and Son, 1892.

Nwankwo, Nkem. *Danda*. London: Heinemann, 1964.

Nwoga, Donatus Ibe. "The Igbo World of Achebe's *Arrow of God*." *RAL* 12.1 (1981): 14–42.

———. *The Supreme God as Stranger in Igbo Religious Thought*. Ahiazu Mbaise: Hawk Press, 1984.

Ubahakwe, Ebo. *Igbo Names: Their Structure and their Meaning*. Ibadan: Daystar Press, 1981.

• Uchendu, Victor. *The Igbo of Southeast Nigeria*. International Thomson Publishing, 1965.

Onwuejeogwu, M. A. *An Igbo Civilization: Nri Kingdom and Hegemony*. London: Ethnographica, 1981.

Wren, Robert M. *Achebe's World: The Historical and Cultural Context of the Novels of Chinua Achebe*. Washington, DC: Three Continents Press, 1980.

Reference

Booker, M. Keith, ed. *The Chinua Achebe Encyclopedia*. Westport, CT: Greenwood Press, 2003.

Gikandi, Simon, ed. *Encyclopedia of African Literature*. New York: Routledge, 2003.

Zell, Hans, and Helen Silver. *A Reader's Guide to African Literature*. London: Heinemann, 1972.